ISBN 978-1-5280-7319-6
PIBN 10096929

THE

ONTARIO REPORTS,

VOLUME XXV.

CONTAINING

REPORTS OF CASES DECIDED IN THE QUEEN'S
BENCH, CHANCERY, AND COMMON
PLEAS DIVISIONS

OF THE

HIGH COURT OF JUSTICE FOR ONTARIO.

WITH A TABLE OF THE NAMES OF CASES ARGUED,
A TABLE OF THE NAMES OF CASES CITED,
AND A DIGEST OF THE PRINCIPAL MATTERS.

―――――

JAMES F. SMITH, Q. C.

REPORTERS :

QUEEN'S BENCH DIVISION..........E. B. BROWN.
CHANCERY DIVISION .... { A. H. F. LEFROY,
                               { GEORGE A. BOOMER,
COMMON PLEAS DIVISION ....GEORGE F. HARMAN,
                                           BARRISTERS-AT-LAW.

―――――

TORONTO:
ROWSELL & HUTCHISON,
KING STREET EAST.
―――
1895.

Rec. July 13, 1795.

ROWSELL AND HUTCHISON, LAW PRINTERS, TORONTO.

JUDGES

OF THE

HIGH COURT OF JUSTICE

DURING THE PERIOD OF THESE REPORTS.

QUEEN'S BENCH DIVISION :

Hon. John Douglas Armour, C. J.
  "   William Glenholme Falconbridge, J.
  "   William Purvis Rochfort Street J.

CHANCERY DIVISION :

Hon. John Alexander Boyd, C.
  "   Thomas Ferguson, J.
  "   Thomas Robertson, J.
  "   Richard Martin Meredith, J.

COMMON PLEAS DIVISION :

Hon. Sir Thomas Galt, Knt., C. J.
  "   John Edward Rose, J.
  "   Hugh MacMahon, J.

Attorney-General :

Hon. Oliver Mowat.

A TABLE

OF THE

CASES REPORTED IN THIS VOLUME.

TABLE

OF THE

NAMES OF CASES CITED IN THIS VOLUME.

A.

B.

B—VOL. XXV. O.R.

L.

M.

Mc.

Y.

MEMORANDA.

On the 1st of September, 1894, the HONOURABLE SIR THOMAS GALT, Knight, Chief Justice of the Common Pleas, resigned his office.

. On the 5th of October, 1894, WILLIAM RALPH MEREDITH, one of Her Majesty's Counsel, was appointed a Judge of the Supreme Court of Judicature for Ontario; a Justice of the High Court of Justice for Ontario, a member of and President of the Common Pleas Division of the High Court of Justice for Ontario, with the title of Chief Justice of the Common Pleas, in the place of the HONOURABLE SIR THOMAS GALT, resigned.

ERRATA.

Page 196, line 5 from bottom, for " *Shaw* v. *Keler* " read " *Shaw* v. *Kaler.* "

" 255, lines 9 and 12 from top, for " Whelam " read " Whelan."

" " line 16 from top, for " *Cooper* " read " *Township of Notta-wasaga.* "

" 272, line 1, for " Chancery Division " read " Common Pleas Division."

" 361, marginal note, for " Boyd, C. " read " Meredith, J."

" 467, line 16 from top, for " defendants " read " plaintiffs."

REPORTS OF CASES

DECIDED IN THE

QUEEN'S BENCH, CHANCERY, AND COMMON PLEAS DIVISIONS

OF THE

HIGH COURT OF JUSTICE FOR ONTARIO.

[COMMON PLEAS DIVISION.]

FRASER v. BUCHANNAN.

District Court—Order of Master for Trial of Action Therein—Subsequent Judgment of High Court Judge—Jurisdiction of Master—Appeal.

In an action brought for damages to the plaintiff's house situated in a provisional judicial district, an order was made by the Master in Chambers, assuming to act under the Unorganized Territory Act, R. S. O. ch. 91, directing that the issues of fact be referred to the District Judge, reserving further directions and questions of law arising at the trial for the disposal of a Judge in single Court. Notice of trial was given for the District Court, and the case was heard by the District Judge, who made certain findings of fact, assessed the damages, and directed judgment to be entered for the plaintiff. The plaintiff moved for judgment on such findings before a Judge in single Court, the defendant at the same time appealing from the judgment or report, whereupon the Judge disposed of both motions, directing judgment to be entered for the plaintiff for the amount found by the District Judge.

On appeal to the Divisional Court :—

Held, that, apart from the question of the jurisdiction of the Master to make the order, as the parties had treated it as valid, and the subsequent order of the Judge in single Court remained unreversed and not appealed from the Court would not interfere ; that if the question of the jurisdiction of the Master were involved the appeal should have been to the Court of Appeal.

IN an action brought against the defendant for damages ^{Statement.} sustained by the plaintiff by reason of his house and furniture, situated in the Provisional Judicial District of

1—VOL. XXV. O.R.

Statement. Thunder Bay, being damaged through certain blasting operations carried on by the defendants, the Master in Chambers, on the 25th of January, 1893, made the following order :

"It is ordered that the issues of fact in this action be and the same are hereby referred to the presiding Judge of the District Court of the Provisional Judicial District of Thunder Bay, sitting at Rat Portage, commencing on the 6th day of June next, for the purpose of trial :

"And it is further ordered that further directions and the question of law, if any, arising on the trial of this action, in the District Court, be disposed of by a Judge of the Supreme Court of Judicature sitting in single Court in Toronto, to be brought up for argument before the said Judge in single Court upon a seven days' notice of motion :

"And it is further ordered that the costs of and incidental to this motion be costs in the cause."

Acting on this order the plaintiff's solicitor gave notice of trial of the action for the sittings of the District Court of the Provisional District of Thunder Bay, for the District of Rainy River, at Rat Portage on the 6th of June, 1893.

The learned Judge of the District Court made the following findings of fact; and directed that judgment be entered as therein stated :

"In accordance with amended order I tried this cause at the last sittings of the District Court of the District of Thunder Bay, holden at Rat Portage on the 5th day of June, instant, without a jury, reserving judgment ; and find as follows:

1. "That plaintiff was in peaceable possession and occupation of the premises in question at the time of the blasting operations complained of, and for some years previous thereto.

2. "That the house in which he and his wife and family were living was damaged by reason of its close proximity to the blasting operations complained of, to the extent of $134.63, and chattels therein were damaged to the extent of $25.00.

3. "That the work of blasting out the new track of the   Canadian Pacific Railway Company (the operations complained of) was conducted in a workmanlike manner, and without recklessness or gross negligence, and with as much regard to safety as was consistent with the due prosecution of such dangerous and hazardous work.

4. "That the plaintiff is entitled to recover in this action from the defendant the sum of $159.63, being the cost of the actual damage done to his house and to the chattels therein contained, for which sum and costs the plaintiff is at liberty to enter judgment on and after the 7th day of September next (1893).

"JOHN M. HAMILTON,

"June 29th, 1893."   "*J. D. C. T. B.*"

The plaintiff treating the proceedings before the district Judge as being an examination of witnesses and findings of fact thereon, moved in Court before GALT, C. J., for judgment on such findings.

The defendant at the same time appealed from the report and findings.

The learned Chief Justice directed that judgment be entered for the plaintiff for the amount of damages found by the district Judge.

In Michaelmas Sittings, 1893, the defendant moved to set aside the findings or judgment of the district Judge, and also the subsequent judgment directed to be entered by GALT, C. J., and to enter a non-suit or judgment for the defendant; or to reduce the damages; or for a new trial, upon different grounds set out in the motion.

In Hilary Sittings, February 12th, 1894, before a Divisional Court composed of ROSE and MACMAHON, JJ. *Aylesworth*, Q. C., supported the motion.

English, contra.

The arguments and cases cited, sufficiently appear in the judgments.

Judgment.   March 3rd, 1894.   MACMAHON, J.:—

MacMahon,
J.

The contention of the defendant is that there was no
authority in the Master in Chambers to make the order;
and that consequently all the proceedings before the district
Judge were *coram non judice.*

By " The Unorganized Territory Act," R. S. O. ch. 91, sec.
76 : " The High Court or a Judge thereof may direct that
any action for the recovery of lands lying in the provisional
judicial district * * in which any sittings of a County
or District Court are to be held, or any other action pending in the High Court, shall be tried at such sittings; or may
order that the witnesses shall be examined and the facts
ascertained at such sittings and the questions of law arising
thereon reserved for the opinion of the Court; or may
make such like order for the purpose of facilitating the
determination of the matters in dispute in the action as he
may think fit."

The argument was that one of the exceptions to the
authority conferred on the Master in Chambers by Rule
30, was " the referring of causes."

I do not regard the order as directing a reference. It is
of an alternative character, and might perhaps in one view
be regarded as an order for the trial of the action; or it
might be regarded as an order for the examination of the
witnesses and the ascertainment of the facts, with a reservation of the questions of law arising for the opinion of the
Court. I regard it as being an order of the latter character.

If the Master in Chambers had power to make the order
(as to which I at present express no opinion), then the
Divisional Court would have no jurisdiction to entertain
this motion, as the appeal should have been to the Court
of Appeal. Then if the Master in Chambers was without
jurisdiction in making the order, has the defendant's acts
and conduct deprived him of the right to apply to the
Divisional Court ?

The defendant did not object to the learned Master's jurisdiction, at least there was no appeal from his order, and it was treated as being valid by the defendant—he appearing with his witnesses without raising any question as to the jurisdiction—before the district Judge where a large number of witnesses were examined on either side. Then, as appears when the plaintiff moved for judgment on the findings of fact, the defendant moved by way of appeal from the report or findings, both motions being heard in Court by Sir Thomas Galt, and it may be the defendant by his conduct and acquiescence has waived any right he might have had to say that the proceedings were *coram non judice*. However, the respective parties had the judgment of the High Court on their respective motions, and there can, therefore, be no appeal to the Divisional Court.

In reference to the orders made in this case, and the conduct of the parties subsequent thereto, I would refer to the remarks of Brett, L. J., in *Mellin* v. *Monico*, 3 C. P. D. 142, at p. 158, and to the judgment of Draper, J., in *Smith* v. *Rooney*, 12 U. C. R. 661, at p. 662.

The motion must be dismissed with costs.

ROSE, J. :—

I agree that it is unnecessary to determine whether the Master in Chambers acted without jurisdiction in making the order he did. Possibly he did ; but, if he had jurisdiction, it was contrary to the practice of the Court for him to make an order of reference to a judicial officer of equal or superior rank. If he had jurisdiction, it is of course clear that no appeal could be had to this Court from the order of the learned Chief Justice ; but that the appeal must be to the Court of Appeal.

And having regard to the facts as stated by my learned brother, shewing that both parties treated the order as valid, and acted thereon, taking their chances of a favourable judgment from the local Judge, and from the learned

Judgment.

Rose, J.
Chief Justice and the orders of the learned Chief Justice standing unreversed and unappealed from, I do not think it a seemly or convenient practice to enter upon an enquiry into the regularity of the proceedings, as such question, if it involves the question of jurisdiction, can be raised upon an appeal to the Court of Appeal, if the party appealing has not by acquiescence lost his right to now object.

And I the more readily come to this conclusion as on the material before us we cannot say that the defendant has shewn that the title to the land occupied by the house was in the railway company. Before we could so determine additional evidence would be required.

As far as we can see there is not much to lead us to doubt the justice of the decision.

Appeal dismissed with costs.

G. F. H.

[COMMON PLEAS DIVISION.]

GRANT V. ARMOUR ET AL.

Hire of Goods—Agreement to Return—Contract—Damage Occasioned by Unforeseen Accident—Liability.

Where there is a positive contract to do a thing not in itself unlawful, the contractor must perform it or pay damages for non-performance, although in consequence of unforeseen causes the performance has become unexpectedly burdensome or even impossible.

The defendants hired the plaintiff's scow and pile driver, at a named price per day, they to be responsible for damage thereto, except to the engine, and ordinary wear and tear, until returned to the plaintiff. While in the defendants' custody, by reason of a storm of unusual force, the scow and pile driver were driven from their moorings and damaged :—

Held, that the defendants were liable for the damages thus sustained, and for the rent during the period of repair.

Taylor v. *Caldwell*, 3 B. & S. 826 followed.
Harvey v. *Murray*, 136 Mass. 377 approved.

THIS was an action tried by FALCONBRIDGE, J., without Statement. a jury, at the Toronto Assizes, in December, 1893.

The action was brought to recover the price agreed to be paid by the defendants for the hire from the plaintiff of a steam pile driver and scow on the terms of the contract set out in the judgment of MACMAHON, J., and also for damages to the hired articles.

During the period covered by the contract the pile driver and scow were blown away by a storm and were sunk. The defendants raised and repaired them, and besides denying liability for rent during the period of repair sought by way of counter-claim to recover from the plaintiff the amount paid by them for repair.

The other facts are stated in the judgment.

The learned Judge reserved his decision, and subsequently on the 14th December, 1893, found as follows:

"As I read the agreement, the defendants are responsible for the whole time, from Tuesday, 11th April (the engineer having been paid apparently by both parties), to 26th June, being the sum of $1,105.

I find that plaintiff did not take possession of the wreck, nor do more than assist the defendants in the difficulty in which they found themselves after the storm of 20th April; and I find that plaintiff did not enter into any binding agreement not to claim anything for the time during which the scow should be rebuilt.

I disallow plaintiff's claim for injury to tools, etc., as being too vaguely put forward in evidence.

I disallow plaintiff's claim for damages to the pile driver and scow. The evidence shews that, except as a matter of reputation of the articles, they are as good as ever.

And, following my first two findings, the counter-claim is also dismissed.

There will be judgment for plaintiff for $355, in addition to the $750 paid into Court, with full costs, and the counter-claim will be dismissed with costs."

The defendants moved on notice to set aside the judgment entered for the plaintiff and to have the judgment entered in their favor.

The plaintiff also moved to increase the amount of the judgment by allowing to the plaintiff the damages sustained by him for injury to the tools, etc., and also to the pile driver and scow.

In Hilary Sittings, February 14th, 1894, before a Divisional Court, composed of GALT, C. J., and MACMAHON, J., *R. M. Macdonald* supported the defendants' motion and shewed cause to the plaintiff's.

D. Macdonald, contra.

The arguments and cases cited sufficiently appear from the judgment.

March 3, 1894. MACMAHON, J.:—

The contract between the plaintiff and the defendants is under seal, and is dated the 5th of April, 1893, and is in the following words: "I, Robert Grant, of the city of

Toronto, contractor, agree to furnish the following, for sheet Judgment. piling, at the breakwater in Toronto harbour, viz.: a pile MacMahon, driver, with machinery, scow, oil, fuel and engineer, for J. the sum of $17 per day, payment to be made by an order given at once on the Toronto Harbour Commissioners. The said Armour and Hynes to be responsible to me for any damage to any of the above plant or machinery, with the exception of the engine and ordinary wear and tear. The driver to be ready by Monday next, the 10th instant. Time to be dated from Monday, the 10th, or Tuesday, the 11th instant, providing engineer is paid for Monday up to the time the scow is returned to her moorings. Watchman to be employed."

The scow with pile driver and other plant on board was being used by the defendants in building a breakwater from opposite the Queen's wharf in Toronto harbour to the Island. The scow was tied up on the night of the 19th of April, on the east side of the piles driven to form a part of the breakwater. A storm of unusual force (reaching almost a hurricane force) on the morning of the 20th April, tore the scow from her moorings, and she was driven westward about two miles where she sank.

The scow was raised by the defendants and taken to a dry dock owned by Alexander Coghill, who was directed by the defendants to repair her and the pile driver, which he did, and was paid therefor by the defendants.

A question frequently arising out of contracts for the hire of chattels as to whether the bailee of a chattel is liable to the bailor for the value when the article has been destroyed without the negligence of the bailee, does not arise here.

The law in such cases has been settled by *Taylor* v. *Caldwell*, 3 B. & S. 826. Mr. Justice Blackburn, in delivering the judgment of the Court said, at p. 833 : " There seems no doubt that where there is a positive contract to do a thing, not in itself unlawful, the contractor must perform it or pay damages for not doing it, although in consequence of unforeseen accidents the performance of his

contract has become unexpectedly burdensome or even impossible. The law is so laid down in 1 Roll. Abr. 450, Condition (G.), and in the note (2) to *Walton* v. *Waterhouse*, 2
Wms. Saund. (6th ed.), 421 and is recognized as the general
rule by all the Judges in the much discussed case of *Hall* v.
Wright, E. B. & E. 746. But this rule is only applicable
when the contract is positive and absolute, and not subject to any condition, express or implied; and there are
authorities which, as we think, establish the principle, that
where, from the nature of the contract, it appears that the
parties must from the beginning have known that it
could not be fulfilled unless when the time for the fulfil-
ment of the contract arrived some particular specified
thing continued to exist, so that, when entering into the
contract, they must have contemplated such continuing
existence as the foundation of what was to be done ; there,
in the absence of any express or implied warranty that the
thing shall exist, the contract is not to be construed as a
positive contract, but as subject to an implied condition
that the parties shall be excused in case, before breach, performance becomes impossible from the perishing of the
thing without default of the contractor. There seems
little doubt that this implication tends to further the
great object of making the legal construction such as to
fulfil the intention of those who entered into the contract. For in the course of affairs, men in making
such contracts in general would, if it were brought to their
minds, say that there should be such a condition."

And in Edwards on Bailments, 3rd ed., sec. 380, the law
is stated to the like effect in very concise terms, thus :
"The bailee may bind himself by an express contract for
the absolute return of the property in as good a condition
as it was when he received it. He may assume a greater
obligation than the law would impose upon him under the
circumstances ; that is to say, the law will enforce against
him the very terms of his contract, in their fair meaning."
See also Story on Bailments, 9th ed., sec. 36.

The defendants agree by the contract (1) " to be responsible for any damage to any of the plant or machinery with the exception of the engine and ordinary wear and tear ; and (2) to pay for such plant at the rate agreed upon up to the time the scow is returned to her moorings."

The only damages for which the defendants were not liable by the terms of the contract was the ordinary wear and tear. They were, therefore, simply carrying out the terms of the contract when they employed and paid Coghill to repair damages which were not the result of ordinary wear and tear. Upon principle one would say that the defendants were in so doing properly interpreting the contract into which they had entered. But the point is covered by authority by the case of *Harvey* v. *Murray*, 136 Mass. 377, where the defendant hired the plaintiff's piano, and agreed to pay a certain sum per quarter, and "to return it in as good order as when received (customary wear and tear excepted). The piano was taken to the defendant's house when, by inevitable accident, the house was blown over and the piano was injured. In giving judgment in that case, the Court said : " The mention in the contract now before us that customary wear and tear are excepted from the defendant's agreement furnishes an additional reason for holding that injury from inevitable accident is not excepted."

This case is on all fours with the above authority, and is conclusive of it.

[The learned Judge then considered the findings of the trial Judge in which he agreed, and concluded] :

The result is that the judgment of Mr. Justice Falconbridge is confirmed, and the defendants' motion dismissed with costs, and the plaintiff's motion dismissed without costs.

GALT, C. J., concurred.

[COMMON PLEAS DIVISION.]

O'CONNOR v. THE HAMILTON BRIDGE COMPANY.

*Master and Servant—Negligence — Dangerous Machinery—Absence of
Guard—Common Law Liability— Workmen's Compensation for Injuries Act—Factories Act.*

A drilling machine manufactured by a well-known maker and similar
to those generally in use was put up for the defendants in their factory.
The plaintiff a workman acting under the orders of the defendants'
foreman for the purpose of oiling the shafting on the arm in which the
drill worked tried to push a portion of it up and down the arm, and in
order to do so, knowing that the machine was in motion, pressed his
body against the revolving drill, which was not in motion when the order
was given to him, and his clothes catching in an unguarded set-screw
on the spindle, he was seriously injured. No other accident had occurred
on the machine, which was quite new and in good order, and which
according to the evidence was sometimes made with the set-screw sunk
in the spindle.

In an action for damages the jury found that the accident was caused
by the defendants' negligence, and without any negligence on the part
of the plaintiff.

On appeal the Divisional Court was equally divided.

Per GALT, C. J.   There was no evidence of negligence to submit to the
jury either at common law or under the Workmen's Compensation for
Injuries Act, nor any liability under the Factories Act.

Per ROSE, J.   There was evidence of negligence both at common law and
under the Workmen's Compensation for Injuries Act; the want of a
guard to the set-screw as required by the Factories Act constituted
such negligence at common law; and the absence of such guard being
also a defect in the condition or arrangement of the machinery within
the Workmen's Compensation for Injuries Act.

Statement.   THIS was an action tried before ARMOUR, C. J., with a
jury, at Hamilton, on the 7th September, 1893.

The action was brought to recover damages for a
serious injury suffered by the plaintiff a workman while
in the service of the defendants, manufacturers of iron
bridges.

The facts may be briefly stated as follows : There was
a machine in the defendants' factory known as a "radial
drill" used for drilling holes in iron plates, which consisted of an iron horizontal arm moving laterally on a post
on which the shafting to drive the drill was fixed. On
the arm was placed what was called a buggy, which
moved as required from one end of the arm to the other.
In the buggy was fixed a revolving spindle, and in a

hole in the spindle the drill was fastened by means of a
set-screw projecting about an inch and a-half from the
side. The horizontal arm was some five or six feet
from the ground, the spindle and drill projecting down-
wards from it two or three feet. The machine, which
was quite new, had been in the factory for a few days
before the accident, and had been manufactured and placed
there by a well-known maker.

On the morning of the accident, the plaintiff was told
off by the foreman of the machine shop, one Kempster, to
assist one Gearing, the man in charge of the drill, in
working it. Before starting the machine, they oiled it,
and the plaintiff alleged that he told Kempster the shaft
was all ice and that the oil ran off as fast as it could be
put on, and that Kempster then told him to run the buggy
up and down the arm a few times to thaw the ice off.
This was denied by Kempster, who stated that he said
nothing to plaintiff after directing him to assist in working
the machine.

Before oiling, the plaintiff had pulled out the buggy
from the post to about half way on the shaft by means of a
lever attached to the buggy. Finding the buggy stiff, he
tried to move it in different ways, but could not, and
coming round to the front, he put his two hands upon the
jacket round the spindle and placing the weight of his body
against it and shoving started the buggy on the shaft, and
in doing so, got his clothes entangled in the set-screw in
the spindle and drill, which had been put in motion by
Gearing, and being twisted about and thrown against
some iron horses, received the injuries complained of.

There was no evidence that Kempster was aware that
the machine was in motion when he was said to have
ordered the plaintiff to move the buggy up and down. An
expert witness called for the plaintiff stated that these
machines were made sometimes with the set-screw projecting and sometimes with the head of the screw sunk,
the latter being the safer. The plaintiff had been working
in the shop off and on for two years, principally about

rivetting machines, and had not worked at the machine in question before the day he was injured.

In answer to questions put to the jury, they found that the plaintiff was acting under orders : that the defendants' company was guilty of negligence in not having the set-screw guarded: that the accident was caused by the set-screw catching in the clothes of the plaintiff; and that the plaintiff was not guilty of contributory negligence; and they assessed the damages at $2,000.

The defendants moved on notice to set aside the judgment and to have judgment entered in their favour.

In Hilary Sittings, February 6th, 1894, before a Divisional Court composed of GALT, C. J., and ROSE, J., *Osler*, Q. C., and *Walker*, Q. C., supported the motion. No negligence on the defendants' part was proved. The plaintiff was told to oil the shaft at the time the machine was not in motion. The machine was afterwards put in motion, not by the defendants' foreman, but by Gearing, a fellow workman, and the plaintiff knowing the machine was in motion, of his own accord, runs the risk of then oiling it. It was the plaintiff's own negligence that caused the accident. The machine was a new one put up by competent persons employed by the defendants. They had no reason to suspect that it was not properly erected, and that any injury would be sustained by any defect in the arrangement of the machinery or plant. There was, therefore, no negligence on the defendants' part for which they could be held responsible. The case does not come within the Workmen's Compensation for Injuries Act, R. S. O. ch. 141 : *Callender* v. *Carlton Iron Co., Limited*, 9 Times L. R. 646 ; *Race* v. *Harrison*, 9 Times L. R. 567 ; *Kiddle* v. *Lovett*, 16 Q. B. D. 605. Neither does the case come within the Factories Act, R. S. O. ch. 208, as this was not a part of the machinery which required to be guarded. The Act only applies to moving machinery ; and the spindle was not moving machinery, it was merely a

Argument.

handle of a tool. Moreover, under the Factories Act, the breach of the Act subjects the defendant to a penalty only, and not to a civil action: *Atkinson* v. *Newcastle and Gateshead Waterworks Co.*, 2 Ex. D. 441; *Finlay* v. *Miscampbell*, 20 O. R. 29; *Rodgers* v. *Hamilton Cotton Co.*, 23 O. R. 425.

G. Lynch-Staunton, contra. The action is maintainable at common law. At common law the master must take reasonable precautions to protect his workmen, and must guard dangerous machinery. This was moving machinery within the meaning of the Act: *Hamilton* v. *Groesbeck*, 19 O. R. 76, 19 A. R. 437; and under section 15 of the Factories Act it should have been guarded. The breach of the Factories Act is evidence of negligence, and this gives an action at common law: *Rodgers* v. *Hamilton Cotton Co.*, 23 O. R. 425; *McCloherty* v. *Gale Manufacturing Co.*, 19 A. R. 117; *Finlay* v. *Miscampbell*, 20 O. R. 29; *Thompson* v. *Wright*, 22 O. R. 127; *Dean* v. *Ontario Cotton Mills Co.*, 14 O. R. 119; *Smith* v. *Baker*, [1891] A. C. 325. The want of a guard was also a defect in the condition or arrangement of the machinery within the meaning of the Workmen's Compensation for Injuries Act, R. S. O. ch. 141. It is no answer that the machine was a new one. It was the defendants' duty to see it was properly guarded: *Stanton* v. *Scrutton*, 9 Times L. R. 236; *Morgan* v. *Hutchings*, 6 Times L. R. 219; *McCloherty* v. *Gale Manufacturing Co.*, 19 A. R. 117.

March 3, 1894. GALT, C. J. :—

At the time when the plaintiff was told to oil the shaft in company with a man named Gearing the spindle was not in motion. Gearing had gone to oil the machine at the same time the plaintiff went to oil the shaft. As soon as Gearing had done oiling he started the machine to distribute the oil. The spindle was spinning when the plaintiff endeavoured to move the buggy.

Kempster denied he had given instructions to the plain-

tiff to run the buggy along the shaft, stating it required
two men to do so; but the jury have found he did; but, if
so, it is manifest from the evidence that he was not aware
that Gearing had put on the power; and it is plain that
when the plaintiff attempted to move the buggy and put
his hands on the jacket he must have been aware the
spindle was working at great speed.

I am now considering the question as if the action were
at common law; and, in my opinion, the plaintiff cannot
succeed. He was aware of the danger, for he saw the
spindle revolving, and must have known it was dangerous
to handle it; he did so of his own accord, for it is manifest
Kempster knew nothing about it, Gearing having set the
instrument in motion without any instructions from him.

The law as laid down by Bramwell, B., in *Ogden* v.
Rummens, 3 F. & F. at p. 755, is: "If a master knew of a
danger which his servant did not, and set him to it, why he
would be liable; but otherwise, if he did not know of it,
or if his servant did; if a man chose to run a risk it was
his own look out."

In the present case the machine had been in the shop
for only a few days, the set-screw extended only an inch
and a half from the spindle, and there is no evidence that
any of the workmen was aware of any danger arising from
it; and moreover, the plaintiff was aware that the spindle
was in motion when he endeavoured to move the buggy by
placing his hands on the jacket and throwing his weight
against it, owing to which the accident happened.

Then as to the Workmen's Compensation for Injuries
Act. By sub-sec. 1 of sec. 3 of the Act, as amended by 52
Vic., ch. 23 (O.), "Where personal injury is caused to a
workman—1. By reason of any defect in the condition or
arrangement of the ways, works, machinery, plant, buildings or premises connected with, intended for, or used in
the business of the employer," the workman shall have
the same right of compensation as if the workman
had not been a workman employed in the service of the
employer.

Judgment.

Galt, C.J.

By sec. 5 of the original Act, R. S. O. ch. 141, a workman shall not be entitled to compensation under sub-sec. 1 of sec. 3, " unless the defect therein mentioned arose from or had not been discovered or remedied owing to the negligence of the employer or of some person in the service of the employer, and entrusted by him with the duty of seeing that the ways, works, machinery or plant, was in proper condition."

According to the evidence the machinery in question had been furnished by a well-known firm, and was the same as had been in general use for many years; there was no evidence that any similar accident had happened; moreover it had been in the factory for only a few days; consequently there was nothing to shew that any employee of the defendants had been guilty of negligence in not seeing the machine was in proper condition.

In the case of *Kiddle* v. *Lovett*, 16 Q. B. D. 605, which was tried without a jury before Denman, J., his lordship, at p. 610, says, after referring to the English statute which is similar to our own : " I cannot find in the present case as a fact that there was any negligence of the kind required by sub-sec. 1 of sec. 2. Nor, if this had been a case tried by a jury, do I think that it ought ever to have been left to a jury."

At the conclusion of the evidence, his lordship, the Chief Justice stated in reply to the learned counsel for the defendants, "I do not think it comes under the Workmen's Compensation for Injuries Act, myself"; but, as stated by him in his opening address to the jury, he would submit certain questions to them in order to avoid further litigation in case the Court should be of opinion that the plaintiff was entitled to recover under the common law, the Workmen's Compensation for Injuries Act, or the Factories Act.

I confess I am unable to see any evidence which would entitle the plaintiff to recover under the common law or the Workmen's Compensation for Injuries Act.

Then, as to the Factories Act. I concur in the opinion expressed by the Court of Chancery in *Finlay* v. *Miscampbell*, 20 O. R. 29, that it is a penal Act, that is to say, that if a manufacturer is guilty of any breach of the provisions, he is liable to a penalty; but it by no means follows that, if a person is injured by reason of such neglect, he is absolutely entitled to succeed in a civil action.

As said by Channell, B., in *Britton* v. *Great Western Cotton Co.*, L. R. 7 Ex. 130, referred to by Boyd, C.: "I agree with what has been said by my brother Bramwell on the construction of the statute, and with the distinction between a statutory and common law liability, not by any means questioning the proposition, however, that in either case contributory negligence on the part of the person injured would afford a defence."

By the third paragraph of the statement of claim the plaintiff alleges, "On the morning of the 22nd of December, 1892, the plaintiff was directed by William Kempster * * to help in running a large drill used for drilling rivet holes in large iron plates; and said Kempster set plaintiff to oil the gearing and shaft of said drill while the same was in motion."

There is nothing whatever in the evidence to sustain this allegation. The plaintiff was directed by Kempster to oil the shaft, and at that time the gearing was not in motion, and it was not until after the oiling had been done, he was told to run the buggy up and down, nor was Kempster aware, at the time he so directed the plaintiff, that the gearing was in motion.

One of the questions submitted to the jury was: Was the plaintiff taking proper care in the means he took to run it up and down? Answer. Yes, according to his own judgment.

This answer appears to me conclusive against the plaintiff. He acted entirely on his own judgment, and it was from this action he sustained the unfortunate injury.

There should be judgment for the defendants.

ROSE, J. :—

In answer to questions, the jury found that the plaintiff was acting under orders: that the defendant company was guilty of negligence in not having the set-screw guarded: that the accident was caused by the set-screw catching in the clothes of the plaintiff; and that the plaintiff was not guilty of contributory negligence; and assessed the damages at $2,000.

I have come to the conclusion that there was evidence to go to a jury, both at common law and under the Workmen's Compensation for Injuries Act. At common law, because there was evidence upon which the jury might find that there was a breach by the defendants of the provisions of the Factories Act, which breach, under the decisions of *Finlay* v. *Miscampbell*, 20 O. R. 29, and *Thompson* v. *Wright*, 22 O. R. 127, afforded evidence of negligence.

The drill was set in what is called a jacket, which was part of a perpendicular shaft made to revolve by force applied from the engine through other shafting, etc.; so that if the decision in *Hamilton* v. *Groesbeck*, 19 O. R. 76, as to the meaning of the word "moving," is adopted, I think this was a moving part of the machinery within the meaning of that case. This, therefore, being a moving part of the machinery, it was the duty of the defendant company to have the same securely guarded, under the provisions of section 15 of the Factories Act. It might have been securely guarded according to the evidence of the witnesses; it was not guarded; and the jury have found that the accident was the result of the want of a guard. There was, therefore, evidence to go to the jury of negligence on the part of the defendants. And contributory negligence being negatived, unless we are prepared to say that there was not evidence to go to the jury, and say there should have been a nonsuit, I think we should not interfere. The defendant has no reason to complain of the manner in which the case went to the jury, the observations of the learned Judge from time to time being prejudicial rather than helpful to the plaintiff's cause.

On the question of common law liability reference may be had to the cases of *Holmes* v. *Clark*, 6 H. & N. p. 348, and *Senior* v. *Ward*, 1 E. & E. 385, therein referred to.

I think the fair result of the decisions in *Morgan* v. *Hutchings*, 6 Times L. R. 219; *Stanton* v. *Scrutton*, 9 Times L. R. 236 ; *McCloherty* v. *Gale Manufacturing Co.*, 19 A. R. 117, is that this want of guard was a defect in the condition or arrangement of the machinery within the meaning of the third section of the Workmen's Compensation for Injuries Act as amended by section 3 of the Act of 1889.

As said by Lord Esher in *Morgan* v. *Hutchings*, "The object of the Act was protection of workmen. * * If the machine was in such a condition that it could not be safely used by the workman without whose assistance it could not be worked, then it was defective. This was assumed by all the Judges in the case cited, who only doubted as to whether a defect had arisen from the negligence of the employer. Any other view would render the Act quite useless and valueless to the workmen to be protected."

This case is referred to in a foot note to *Hamilton* v. *Groesbeck*, 19 O. R. 76, at p. 82, added under the direction of the learned Chief Justice of that Court, who was the trial Judge herein, in the following words : "*Sed vide Morgan* v. *Hutchings*, 6 Times L. R. 219, decided since this decision."

I do not see how the learned Chief Justice could have nonsuited or withdrawn the case from the jury ; and I see no object in sending the case back for a new trial as certainly the damages were not excessive. If the Factories Act requires an employer to guard any part of machinery which he introduces into his factory, I think it is no answer for him to say that the machine had been in the factory for a few days only, as in this case, and that he was ignorant of the cause of damage against which it was necessary to guard; for, it seems to me, that it was the

intention of the Act that before any machinery shall be put in operation so as to be a source of danger to workmen, the employer should examine it and every part so that such parts as are required to be guarded shall be guarded before the danger of accidents can arise.

As I have come to the conclusion that the plaintiff is entitled to succeed at common law, it follows that he is entitled to retain his verdict for the full amount of damages awarded, and is not restricted to the $1500 limited by the Workmen's Compensation for Injuries Act.

I think the motion must be dismissed with costs.

G. F. H.

[QUEEN'S BENCH DIVISION.]

COFFEY v. SCANE.

*Arrest—Order for—Discharge from Custody under—Order not Set Aside—
Action for Malicious Arrest—Reasonable and Probable Cause—Departure from Ontario—Inference of Intent to Defraud—Action for Imposing
on Judge by False Affidavit—Material Facts—Burden of Proof—" Absconded," Meaning of—Misdirection.*

In an action for damages for arrest under an order made in a former action
the plaintiff recovered a verdict for $1,000. Upon motion to set it aside,
made before a Divisional Court composed of ARMOUR, C.J., and
FALCONBRIDGE, J. :—

Held, per ARMOUR, C.J., that so long as the order for arrest stood, an
action for maliciously and without reasonable and probable cause arresting the plaintiff could not be maintained.

Erickson v. *Brand*, 14 A. R. 614, distinguished.

2. Where a creditor, by affidavit, satisfies the Judge that there is good
and probable cause for believing that his debtor, unless he be forthwith
apprehended, is about to quit Ontario, the inference is raised that he is
about to do so with intent to defraud ; for he is removing his body,
which is subject to the jurisdiction of the Courts of Ontario, and liable
to be taken in execution, beyond the jurisdiction of such Courts.

Toothe v. *Frederick*, 14 P. R. 287, commented on and not followed.

Robertson v. *Coulton*, 9 P. R. 16, approved and followed.

3. The fact that the plaintiff, being a resident of Ontario, and having
numerous creditors therein, including the defendant, left the Province
without paying them, and went to reside permanently in the United
States, whether he left openly or secretly, and whether he announced
his departure and intentions beforehand or concealed them, and that
he came back to Ontario for a temporary purpose, intending to return
to the United States, afforded reasonable and probable cause for and
justified his arrest.

4. Considering the action as one for imposing upon the Judge by some
false statement in the affidavit to hold to bail, and thereby inducing him
to grant the order for arrest, the fact falsely suggested or suppressed
must be a material one for the Judge to consider in granting the order,
and the burden is upon the plaintiff of shewing that the Judge was
imposed upon.

5. The word " absconded " truly described the going away of the plaintiff,
whether he went away secretly or openly, and he was properly described
as an absconding debtor.

FALCONBRIDGE, J., adhering to the views expressed in *Scane* v. *Coffey*, 15
P. R. 112, was of opinion that the plaintiff had a cause of action, but
thought there should be a new trial on the grounds of excessive damages and misdirection ; and concurred *pro formâ* in the decision of
ARMOUR, C.J.

Statement.

THIS was an action for damages for the arrest and imprisonment of the plaintiff, under an order made in the
action of *Scane* v. *Coffey*, the facts of which are stated in
the report of a motion made in that action to discharge
the defendant therein from custody : 15 P. R. 112.

The statement of claim in the present action alleged :

2. That on or about the 16th March, 1892, the defendant falsely and maliciously and without reasonable or
probable cause, made an affidavit in an action then depending in the County Court of the county of Kent (wherein
the present plaintiff was defendant) to the effect that the
plaintiff was indebted to the defendant in the sum of
$114.87, upon a certain indenture of lease, and upon a pro-
missory note made by the plaintiff and one John Watson,
bearing date the 29th May, 1879, for $3,900, in favour of
one James Scane, from whom the defendant purchased the
said promissory note during the spring of 1891, for valuable consideration, and that the plaintiff had paid on account
of said note on the 16th May, 1885, the sum of $5, and on
the 5th June, 1886, the sum of $5 ; and that the plaintiff
in or about the spring of 1891, absconded from this Province and went to the United States of America, with the
intent to defraud his creditors generally and the defendant
in particular, and for the purpose of defeating his creditors
in the collection of their claims against him, and of pre-
venting the defendant in particular from recovering the
amount due to him from the plaintiff, and that he, the defendant, verily believed that unless the plaintiff, who had
returned to Ontario to conduct a sale at the town of Ridgetown, were forthwith apprehended, he would again quit
this Province with a view to defeating and defrauding his
creditors and the defendant in recovering the claims owing
by the plaintiff, and upon such false affidavit the defendant
procured from the junior Judge of the County Court an
order for the arrest and imprisonment of the plaintiff until
he should have given bail.

3. That in the making of the affidavit and in the application for the order for arrest the defendant imposed upon
the Judge and deceived him by false statements and sup-
ression of the truth, and concealed from the Judge facts
and circumstances well known to the defendant, and the
defendant neglected to make and abstained from making
reasonable inquiries in regard to and from procuring a

Statement.

knowledge of many facts and circumstances which he could have readily made, procured, and ascertained, and which would shew that the plaintiff was not guilty of the matters charged against him by the defendant, and the defendant so acted fraudulently and maliciously, with the object of wrongfully obtaining the order for arrest and procuring the arrest and imprisonment of the plaintiff, and he did thereby and by such false statements wrongfully obtain the order for arrest and procure the arrest and imprisonment without any reasonable or probable cause for so doing.

4. That the plaintiff was arrested under the order by a sheriff's officer and constable, acting under the directions of the defendant, on or about the 16th March, 1892, at the town of Ridgetown, and was taken as a prisoner in custody by the said officer in the day time through various public streets of the town on foot, and was conveyed by railway to the town of Chatham, in the county of Kent, and there imprisoned in the common gaol until he gave bail. The junior Judge of the County Court afterwards made an order, confirmed on appeal by the Queen's Bench Divisional Court, directing his unconditional release.

5. That, in consequence of such false affidavit and of the acts and conduct of the defendant and of such arrest and imprisonment, the plaintiff had suffered great pain of body and mind, as well as annoyance and disgrace and loss of time and loss of credit and reputation.

6. That, in further consequence of such acts, conduct, arrest, and imprisonment, the plaintiff was put to great trouble, expense, and costs in and about defending himself and bringing to the knowledge of the Judge and Courts the true facts and circumstances and procuring his discharge from custody and in travelling to and from Ridgetown and to and from his family in Chicago and in loss of time and employment and in being discharged by his employer on account of his detention and the publicity of the false charges and the arrest and imprisonment made and the injury to the plaintiff's standing and repu-

tation in consequence thereof and in seeking other employment.

And the plaintiff claimed $5,000 damages.

The defendant by his statement of defence (1) denied
the allegations contained in the second and third paragraphs of the plaintiff's statement of claim; (2) and he
did not admit the allegations contained in the fourth,
fifth, and sixth paragraphs of the said statement of claim;
(3) and he said that he had reasonable and probable cause
for believing and did believe that the plaintiff absconded
from this Province in or about the month of March, 1891,
with intent to defeat and defraud his creditors in general,
and the defendant, who was a creditor of the plaintiff, in
particular; (4) and that in the proceedings complained of
he pursued what he verily believed to be his remedy under
the statute in that behalf, and was not in any way actuated
by malice or other improper motive.

Issue.

The action was tried at the Sittings of this Court held at
Sandwich in the spring of 1892, before STREET, J., and a
jury.

It appeared that the plaintiff had previous to the year
1891 lived for about twenty years in the vicinity of
Ridgetown; that he was an auctioneer, and had been a
constable; that he had become much in debt, owing the
defendant and others; that he left Ridgetown for Chicago
on the 4th January, 1891, to attend a competition of
auctioneers, the prize being a position as auctioneer with a
salary; that he won the prize; that he returned to Ridgetown to make arrangements with his wife as to whether she
would stay there temporarily or go to Chicago; that while
at Ridgetown, and at the end of January, 1891, some
twenty-five or thirty of his friends gave him a dinner;
that he then returned to Chicago and remained there till
the 4th March, 1891; that on the 12th March, 1891, he
moved his family to Chicago, taking with him bedding
and pictures, and selling his household furniture on the

market at Ridgetown; that he saw the defendant at an hotel at Ridgetown between the 5th and 12th March, 1891, and had a conversation with him.

The plaintiff in his evidence said that on that occasion the defendant asked him if he could pay the balance of the rent, $50, to which he replied that he was short of funds and could not pay him, but would as soon as possible; that he had made arrangements with a Mr. Teetzel, to whom he would send money to pay his creditors as fast as he could make it; that he had let Teetzel have his house and lots, and Teetzel was to collect rents and apply them, with what he (the plaintiff) could send on, to pay creditors. Defendant seemed to be satisfied, and said that would be all right. The plaintiff also told the defendant that he need not be afraid of his not coming back to Ontario, for he had sheep out on shares, and he would have to come back to attend to them when they came due. He had not then sold his furniture; but he told the defendant he was going to sell it on the market and move to Chicago.

On cross-examination the plaintiff said that he did not tell defendant how many sheep he had; he admitted that the sheep were not his, but were in his hands as executor or trustee; and that he did not tell defendant that. The plaintiff also said that he told defendant he was going to send money to Mr. Teetzel, not for defendant, but to pay off his debts, which would include defendant's; that he did send money to Teetzel, not for defendant, but for defendant's brother; that he did not tell defendant he had conveyed his house to Teetzel, but that Teetzel had the house; he did not say Teetzel had it for creditors, but looked after it and collected the rent to pay the creditors, as far as it went, with what money he (the plaintiff) could send. The plaintiff also said that he supposed it would appear from what he said to defendant that he had put his property in the hands of Teetzel for the benefit of creditors; and that was the way it went, too; that that property was mortgaged for $400, and it sold for $500; that Teetzel got the purchase money and paid off the mortgage, and kept the balance for his own debt, which, with the rent he had collected, paid off his debt; and there was nothing in the house for any of the creditors except Teetzel; that Teetzel had the house before he (the plaintiff) ever owed defendant anything.

The cross-examining counsel then said to the plaintiff: "There was nothing in the sheep, there was nothing in the house, and nothing came of your promise to remit to Teetzel? That is so, is it not, apparently? It looks like it, does it not? It is all in the future, and the man in Chicago?" And the plaintiff answered, "Yes, and the World's Fair." Counsel then said, "There are two or three points in your examination put more clearly than you put them now. Speaking of what you said to the defendant as to Teetzel's house, would this be the proper way of putting it, 'I told him that I left my house and lot with Mr. Teetzel, he would collect the rent and $7 a month and pay it as far as it went to my creditors, and I would send him money to pay my creditors, and I would send money as fast as I could, and I thought we parted good friends, and I have not paid him'; would that be true?" And the plaintiff answered, "Yes, I guess that is about right." Counsel then read the following from the plaintiff's deposition:—"I told Mr. Scane I left sheep; I left I do not know how many. They belonged to my first wife. I told him I had sheep. How we came to speak about the sheep, I said he need not be scared about my running away, as I had about a thousand sheep, and I would have to come back to look after them. I said I had a lot of sheep, and I would have to come back to look after them."

It appeared that from the time the plaintiff went to Chicago until he was arrested, he had earned about $3,700, and had only paid to his creditors in Ontario about $300, and that he had paid the defendant nothing and had never communicated with him.

In March, 1892, the plaintiff came back to Ridgetown to conduct a sale there on the 15th and 16th days of March, 1892, and on the latter day he was arrested under an order for arrest obtained by the defendant upon an affidavit made by him that the plaintiff was justly and truly indebted to him in the sum of $114.87, the whole amount of which was due and owing by the plaintiff to him ; that in or about the spring of the year 1891 the plaintiff, being indebted to him in respect of the foregoing matters, and being, as he was then informed by various parties whose names he did not then recollect, otherwise considerably indebted, absconded from this Province and went to the United States of America, with the intent to defraud his creditors generally, and him, the defendant, in particular, and for the purpose of defeating his creditors in the collection of their claims against him, and of preventing him, the defendant, from recovering the amount so justly due to him as aforesaid by the said plaintiff ; that the said plaintiff left no property exigible in execution, or out of which he had been able to realize the amount of this said claim against him ; that he was yesterday advised over the telephone by one Wilbury Scane, of the town of Ridgetown, that the said plaintiff was in Ridgetown, and that he intended to conduct a sale there to-day, and then return to the said United States of America ; that he was not aware that the said plaintiff had, since the time he so absconded, to the time set out in the preceding paragraph, been in this Province, although he had been on the lookout for him ; that the said plaintiff, prior to his absconding as aforesaid, conveyed his property to one William Teetzel, as he was informed by the said Teetzel, but the said property was insufficient to satisfy the claim of the said Teetzel against the plaintiff, and the said Teetzel further informed him that there were other unsatisfied creditors of the said plaintiff ; that he verily believed that, unless the said plaintiff should be forthwith apprehended, he would again quit this Province with a view to defeating and defrauding his creditors, and him, the defendant, in recovering the claims justly owing by him ; and that he, the defendant, would be thereby deprived of the money justly due to him, and be defeated in the recovery of the same from the plaintiff.

It appeared by the deposition of the defendant, parts of which were put in, that the defendant learned shortly after his conversation with the plaintiff between the 5th and 12th days of March at the hotel at Ridgetown, that some of the plaintiff's admirers had given him a dinner. The order for the plaintiff's arrest was not set aside, but he was discharged out of custody under the order.

The jury found a verdict for the plaintiff and $1,000 damages, and judgment was ordered by the learned Judge to be entered for this amount with full costs of suit.

On the 18th May, 1893, the defendant moved to set aside the verdict and judgment, and for a judgment of nonsuit or for the defendant, or for a reduction of the damages, or for a new trial, or for such judgment as to the Court might seem just, upon the following grounds, among others :—

1. That the learned Judge was wrong in holding and directing the jury that the defendant had not reasonable and probable cause for making the affidavit and the arrest complained of.

2. That the learned Judge erred in directing the jury that the defendant in his affidavit withheld facts from the Judge, and from this they could infer malice.

. 3. That the learned Judge erred in directing the jury that as the plaintiff, when he left Canada in the year 1891, left openly, he could not be said to have absconded, as the term "abscond" meant going away secretly.

4. That the learned Judge erred in directing the jury that, as what the plaintiff said to the defendant at the conversation in the Queen's hotel, just before the plaintiff quitted Canada in 1891, about the house and lot and the sheep, had not been mentioned in the defendant's affidavit, they could not take into consideration that deceit was practised upon the defendant thereby, or that the defendant relied upon or was influenced by those representations in making the arrest.

5. That the learned Judge should have told the jury

that if what the plaintiff so told the defendant operated on the mind of the defendant, and made him think that the plaintiff had quitted the country with intent to defraud his creditors generally, or him, the defendant, the defendant was justified in causing the arrest.

6. That the learned Judge should have told the jury, if they found that the defendant believed the plaintiff had quitted the country with intent to defraud as aforesaid, there was no malice, although as a fact the defendant might be mistaken.

7. That the damages awarded the plaintiff were excessive and were not warranted by the evidence or circumstances.

8. That the verdict was contrary to law and evidence and the weight of evidence.

The motion was argued before ARMOUR, C. J., and FALCONBRIDGE, J., on the 18th May, 1893.

Osler, Q. C., (*M. Houston* with him), for the defendant. According to the plaintiff's own evidence, he deceived the defendant about the assets which he said he had. There was no assignment to Teetzel for the benefit of creditors, and the sheep were not the plaintiff's own. There was reasonable and probable cause for making the affidavit to hold to bail: *Robertson* v. *Coulton*, 9 P. R. 18. The case was presented improperly to the jury as to the meaning of the word " abscond." An absconding debtor in this country is one who goes away, whether secretly or openly, without paying his creditors. See Wharton's Law Lexicon, 9th ed., p. 5, and Lawson's Concordance, *sub verb.* " Abscond," citing *Fitch* v. *Waite*, 5 Conn. at p. 121. The damages are excessive.

Matthew Wilson, Q. C., (with him *Edwin Bell*), for the plaintiff. *Robertson* v. *Coulton*, 9 P. R. 18, is referred to by Mr. Justice Osler, who decided it, in *Erickson* v. *Brand*, 14 A. R. at p. 653. In *Toothe* v. *Frederick*, 14 P. R. at p. 289, the Chancellor also refers to *Robertson* v. *Coulton*, and holds that if a debtor has no assets, his quitting the coun-

try cannot be an injury to his creditors. See also *Rogers*
v. *Knowles*, 14 P. R. 290, n. *Kersterman* v. *McLellan*, 10
P. R. 122, is the only case of a previous departure which is
to be found. The defendant nowhere says he was deceived
by the statement of the plaintiff. The defendant stated
what was untrue, or failed to disclose material facts:
Riddell v. *Brown*, 24 U. C. R. 90.

Osler, in reply. It should have been left to the jury to
say whether the conclusion of the defendant that the
plaintiff was about to leave the jurisdiction was a reasonable one. That conclusion was justified by the untruth of
the plaintiff's remarks about the house and the sheep.

March 3, 1894. ARMOUR, C. J. :—

In the view I take of this case, it is unnecessary for me
to deal with the objections raised to the Judge's charge
and to the amount of damages assessed by the jury.

If the maintenance of the action depended upon the question whether the plaintiff shewed a want of reasonable
and probable cause for the arrest, I should hold that the
action failed, for the undisputed facts shewed beyond a
doubt that the defendant had reasonable and probable
cause for the arrest.

The fact that the plaintiff, having numerous creditors,
including the defendant, in Ontario, and being a resident
of Ontario, left Ontario in the month of March, 1891,
without paying his creditors, and went to reside permanently in the United States, whether he left Ontario
openly or secretly, or whether he announced his departure
and intentions beforehand or concealed them, and that he
came back to Ontario for a temporary purpose in March,
1892, intending to return to the United States, afforded
not only reasonable and probable cause for his arrest, but
fully justified it.

Where a creditor for $100 or upwards shews by affida-
vit such facts and circumstances as satisfy the Judge
that there is good and probable cause for believing that

Judgment.
Armour, C.J.
his debtor, unless he be forthwith apprehended, is about to
quit Ontario, the inference is raised that he is about to do
so with intent to defraud his creditors generally or such
creditor in particular.

And the reason that such inference is raised is that he
is removing his body, which is subject to the jurisdiction
of the Courts of Ontario, and liable to be taken in execution, beyond the jurisdiction of such Courts and beyond
the reach of their process.

And this is plainly shewn by the terms of the bail-bond
required by the statute to be entered into by the party
whose arrest is effected under the provisions of the
statute.

The inference so raised and the reason for it were lost
sight of in *Toothe* v. *Frederick*, 14 P. R. 287, where *Robertson* v. *Coulton*, 9 P. R. 16, is criticized, and where it is
said : " Take the case of a person indebted, without substance, who contemplates removing from Ontario to better his condition ; it seems to be in the teeth of the statute
to hold that such a one is leaving with intent to defraud
creditors."

The same reasoning would apply to a person indebted
with substance, who contemplated removing from Ontario
to better his condition, leaving his whole substance behind
him ; and so the statute would only be applicable to a
person indebted with substance who contemplated removing from Ontario, taking his substance with him, which
is certainly not a construction which has ever been put
upon the statute.

In *Robertson* v. *Coulton*, 9 P. R. 16, my brother Osler
laid down the law as it has always obtained in this Province, with his usual accuracy, where he says : " But the
defendant admits that he was about to leave Ontario. He
says that his intention was well known, and that he never
attempted to conceal it, as he was going away with intent
to better his condition, being unable to pay his debts in
Canada. Therefore, he says, he was not going away with
intent to defraud. I think the plaintiff has nothing to do

with the defendant's reasons. The facts are enough for
him. The defendant is indebted to him, and he is about
to withdraw from the jurisdiction. That has always been
considered sufficient to warrant an arrest."

The action for maliciously and without reasonable and
probable cause arresting the plaintiff could not, I think I
may say without at all trenching upon the decision in
Erickson v. *Brand*, 14 A. R. 614, be maintained here, for
the order for arrest stands, and as long as it stands it is a
judicial determination that the facts stated in the defendant's affidavit upon which it was made, established reasonable and probable cause.

The plaintiff is, therefore, driven to the form of action
suggested in *Daniels* v. *Fielding*, 16 M. & W. 200, that
the defendant by his affidavit imposed upon the Judge by
some false statement, some *suggestio falsi* or *suppressio
veri*, and thereby induced the Judge to grant the order for
arrest.

It is said in that case, at p. 206: "The foundation on which
such an action must now rest is that the party obtaining the
capias has imposed on the Judge by some false statement,
some *suggestio falsi* or *suppressio veri*, and has thereby
satisfied him, not only of the existence of the debt to the
requisite amount, but also that there is reasonable ground
for supposing the debtor is about to quit the country. But
how will it be if, without any such fraud or falsehood, a
plaintiff, upon an affidavit fairly stating the facts, succeeds
in satisfying a Judge that the defendant is about to quit
the country, and so obtains an order for a *capias* to arrest
the defendant, even though he may not himself believe
that the defendant does intend to leave the country ? If,
indeed, the party arrested had not such intention, he has
the power, under section 6, of making a substantive application to a Judge or to the Court, praying to be discharged
out of custody ; and this will be done as a matter of course,
if the party arrested succeeds in satisfying the Judge or
Court that he has not nor ever had the intention imputed to him. But such discharge affords no ground of

Judgment.
Armour, C.J. action against the party at whose instance the party discharged has been held to bail, provided only that the
original order of the Judge has been fairly obtained."

The fact falsely suggested or suppressed must obviously
be a material one for the Judge to consider in granting the
order for arrest; and I fail to find in the affidavit made
by the defendant, and upon which the order for arrest was
made, any false statement of any material fact which, if
truly stated, or any suppression of any material fact which,
if stated, ought to have operated with the Judge to induce
him to withhold his order for arrest.

The burden lay upon the plaintiff of shewing that the
Judge was imposed upon; and, in the absence of the
Judge's evidence, we could only hold that he was imposed
upon, upon its being shewn that there was some false
statement in the affidavit of a material fact which, if
truly stated, or some suppression of a material fact which,
if stated, would undoubtedly have prevented his granting
the order for arrest.

It would never do for us to hold that he was imposed
upon, upon a supposition that he took one meaning rather
than another from some word used in the affidavit.

Nor could we hold that he was imposed upon by the
defendant's omitting to state in his affidavit that the plaintiff had told him before he went away in March, 1891, that
he intended to go away, nor that he then told him that
he had a thousand sheep which he was leaving behind him,
which was untrue, nor that he had put his property in the
hands of Mr. Teetzel for the benefit of his creditors, which
was also untrue, nor that he, the defendant, had learned
that some of the plaintiff's admirers had given him a dinner
before he left in March, 1891, for these were all immaterial
facts and should not have operated with the Judge to
induce him to withhold his order for arrest.

Mr. Teetzel was not called to shew that he had not given
the information to the defendant which the defendant
alleged in his affidavit had been given to him by Mr.
Teetzel.

But it was said that when the defendant stated in his Judgment. affidavit that the plaintiff "absconded from the Province," Armour, C.J. this was a false statement, because the word "abscond" means to go away secretly, whereas the plaintiff went away openly.

But how are we to say that the Judge understood from the use of the word "absconded" that the plaintiff had gone away secretly, and was thereby imposed upon? It was for the plaintiff to shew that he was imposed upon, and he did not shew it.

But whether the plaintiff went away secretly or openly was immaterial, for he left the country without paying his debts, that owing to the defendant among the rest.

I think, moreover, that the word "absconded" truly described the going away of the plaintiff, whether he went away secretly or openly, and that he would be properly described as an absconding debtor.

The definition of the verb to "abscond" given in Sweet's Law Dictionary is "to leave one's ordinary residence or country to avoid legal proceedings;" and the definition given in Wharton's Law Lexicon is "to go out of the jurisdiction of the Courts, or to lie concealed in order to avoid any of their processes."

The Imperial Act 14 & 15 Vic. ch. 52, providing for the arrest of debtors about to quit England with intent to avoid or delay creditors, is entitled "An Act to facilitate the more speedy arrest of absconding debtors."

The Imperial Act 33 & 34 Vic. ch. 76, providing for the arrest of persons going abroad with a view of avoiding payment of the debt for which a summons has been granted, or of avoiding service of a petition of bankruptcy, or of avoiding appearing to such petition, or of avoiding examination in respect of his affairs, or otherwise avoiding, delaying, or embarrassing proceedings in bankruptcy, is entitled "An Act to facilitate the arrest of absconding debtors."

The Act of this Province respecting absconding debtors provides that if a person resident in Ontario, indebted to

any other person, departs from Ontario with intent to
defraud his creditors, and at the time of his so departing
is possessed to his own use and benefit, of any real or personal property, credits, or effects therein not exempt by
law from seizure, he shall be deemed an absconding debtor.

I think, therefore, that it is impossible for us to hold that
the Judge was imposed upon by the defendant in his affidavit by any false statement therein, by any *suggestio
falsi* or *suppressio veri*, which induced the Judge to make
the order for arrest, and that the action must be dismissed with costs.

· I refer to *Erickson* v. *Brand*, 14 A. R. 614; *Re Crispin*,
L. R. 8 Ch. 374; *Fitch* v. *Waite*, 5 Conn. 117 ;*Scott* v. *Mit-
chell*, 8 P. R. 518 ; *Damer* v. *Busby*, 5 P. R. 356; *Smith* v. *Mc-
Kay*, 10 U. C. R. 412 and 613; *Wanless* v. *Matheson*, 15
U. C. R. 278 ; *Riddell* v. *Brown*, 24 U. C. R. 90 ; *Baker* v.
Jones, 19 C. P. 365.

FALCONBRIDGE, J. :—

After the fullest consideration, and having had the
advantage of a perusal of my Lord's judgment, I find
myself unable to recede from the view of the case taken
by my brother Street and myself in *Scane* v. *Coffey*, 15
P. R. 112, although it is true we did not there say, in so
many words, that the present ·plaintiff has a cause of
action, but only removed the term imposed by the learned
local Judge that he should bring no action.

I cannot agree, therefore, that he had no cause of action,
nor that his action ought to be dismissed.

But I think the damages awarded to the plaintiff were
excessive and not warranted by the facts and circumstances.

And I think that the learned trial Judge's definition of
the word "absconding" in his charge to the jury laid
more stress on the *secret* departure than is warranted by
the preponderance of authority, although he was not without authority, *e. g.,* Abbott's Law Dictionary, *sub verb.*

"Abscond": "To depart clandestinely out of the jurisdic- Judgment.
tion of Courts, or conceal oneself within it, for the purpose Falconbridge,
of avoiding process." J.

I am of opinion that there ought to be a new trial without costs.

But, as we both agree that the verdict and judgment
should be set aside, I agree with the decision of the Chief
Justice *pro formâ* in order that there may be no difficulty
in the way of an appeal from our decision.

R. B. B.

[QUEEN'S BENCH DIVISION.]

ARTHUR v. GRAND TRUNK RAILWAY COMPANY.

*Water and Watercourses—Diversion of Watercourse by Railway Company
—Remedy—Compensation—Arbitration Clauses of Railway Act, 51
Vic. ch. 29 (D.)—Plan—Riparian Proprietors—Infringement of
Rights—Cause of Action—Damages—Permanent Injury—Definition
of Watercourse—Permanent Source—Surface Water—Misdirection—
New Trial.*

By sec. 90 (*h*) of the Railway Act of Canada, 51 Vic. ch. 29, a railway
company have power to divert any watercourse, subject to the provisions of the Act ; but in order to entitle themselves to insist upon
the arbitration clauses of the Act, they must, having regard to secs.
123, 144, 145, 146, and 147, shew upon their registered plans their intention to divert.

The defendants built an embankment which entirely cut off the plaintiff's
access to the water of a stream by diverting it from his farm :—

Held, that the diversion, not the damage sustained therefrom, gave him
his cause of action ; and the proper mode of estimating the damages
was to treat the diversion as permanent and to consider its effect upon
the value of the farm.

McGillivray v. *Great Western R. W. Co.,* 25 U. C. R. 69, distinguished.

The alleged watercourse was a gully or depression created by the action
of the water. The defendants disputed that any water ran along it,
except melted snow and rain water flowing over the surface merely.
The plaintiff contended that there was a constant stream of water, only,
if ever, ceasing in the very dry summer weather :—

Held, per STREET, J., that without a permanent source, which, however,
need not necessarily be absolutely never failing, there cannot be a
watercourse ; and that, as the attention of the jury was not expressly
called to the difference in effect between the occasional flow of surface
water and the steady flow from a source, and as a passage read to the

jury from the judgment in *Beer* v. *Stroud*, 19 O. R. 10, divorced from its
context, might have misled the jury, there should be a new trial.
Per ARMOUR, C. J., that what the Judge told the jury could not be held
to be misdirection without reversing the decision in *Beer* v. *Stroud ;*
and the objection to the charge was too vague and indefinite.

Statement.   THIS was an action brought by the plaintiff against the
defendants to recover damages owing to their having
diverted a watercourse running through his farm in the
township of Cramahe, and was tried before FALCONBRIDGE,
J., at Cobourg, on 25th and 26th October, 1893, with a
jury. The defendants denied the existence of a watercourse and pleaded not guilty by statute : R. S. C. ch. 66,
sec. 83 ; also the Railway Act, 51 Vic. ch. 29, sec. 287 (D.)
public Acts.

The evidence shewed that the plaintiff was the owner of
and in occupation of a farm through which the alleged
watercourse ran ; that about the year 1890 the defendants
had altered their line of railway and built an embankment to the north of the plaintiff's land, and that in so
doing they had obstructed the flow of the water, which,
the plaintiff claimed, had formerly run from thence through
his land. The defendants insisted that there were no regular or defined banks to the alleged watercourse, and that
the water which ran through it was derived merely from
melting snow and heavy falls of rain, and was therefore of
so intermittent a character as not to constitute a watercourse.

Under an order made by Sir THOMAS GALT, C. J., in
Chambers, the jury were taken to view the *locus in quo.*

Being asked by the learned trial Judge to assess the
damages for the six months next before the bringing of
the action, and to assess also the whole damage to the
plaintiff's farm by the cutting off of the watercourse, they
assessed the first mentioned damages at $12 and the second
at $350. Thereupon the learned Judge ordered judgment
to be entered for the plaintiff for $350 and costs.

During the Michaelmas Sittings, 1893, the defendants
moved by way of appeal from this judgment, upon the
ground that a nonsuit should have been entered, because

Statement.

the plaintiff, if entitled to compensation, should have proceeded under the arbitration clauses of the Railway Acts,
and not by action ; and upon the ground that no watercourse was proved, and that if proved no diversion of it
to the injury of the plaintiff was proved ; or to reduce
the damages to $12, on the ground that the plaintiff was
entitled to succeed only for the damages found for the six
months preceding the bringing of the action ; or for a new
trial upon the ground of misdirection and non-direction.

That portion of the charge of the trial Judge objected
to and the nature of the objection appear in the judgment
of STREET, J.

The motion was argued before the Divisional Court
(ARMOUR, C. J., and STREET, J.) on 24th November, 1893.

Osler, Q. C., for the defendants.   The question is whether
there was a living stream passing to the north of the
Kingston road through the old track of the defendants to
the plaintiff's land, and, if so, whether the construction
of the defendants' new line has interfered with the flow
to the plaintiff's land.   We contend that the alleged stream
has no defined channel, and that the Judge's charge was
wrong.   The plaintiff's claim is not really to a right of
watercourse, but to a right of ravine or gulch.   Even if
Beer v. *Stroud*, 19 O. R. 10, is good law, it is not applicable to this case.   In *Williams* v. *Richards*, 23 O. R. 651.
it is said that *Beer* v. *Stroud* does not enlarge the law.
The Judge's charge was too broad.   I refer to *Crewson* v.
Grand Trunk R. W. Co., 27 U. C. R. 68 ; *McGillivray* v.
Millin, ib. 62; *Darby* v. *Crowland*, 38 U. C. R. 338.
Damages can be recovered only for six months before
action : *McGillivray* v. *Great Western R. W. Co.*, 25 U. C.
R. at p. 76.   At all events the action does not lie ; the
plaintiff's remedy, if any, is arbitration for compensation,

Wallace Nesbitt, on the same side.   There was here no
vital life in the source of supply.   It is enough if the
flow arises periodically from natural causes, and the learned
Judge should have told the jury that it must so arise.   The

Argument. defendants are not liable for interrupting the flow of mere soakage. There must be a living stream, as distinguished from water from the clouds, though there may not be a perennial flow. As to the six months' limit, I refer to *McArthur* v. *Northern and Pacific Junction R. W. Co.*, 15 O. R. 733; 17 A. R. 86. As regards these defendants, the clause has never been repealed.

Clute, Q. C. (with him *J. W. Gordon*), for the plaintiff, referred to 51 Vic. (D.) ch. 29, sec. 90 (h); *Re Shade and Galt and Guelph R. W. Co.*, 13 U. C. R. 577 ; *Ross* v. *Grand Trunk R. W. Co.*, 10 O. R. 447 ; *Scanlon* v. *London and Port Stanley R. W. Co.*, 23 Gr. 559; *Beer* v. *Stroud*, 19 O. R. 10; *Williams* v. *Richards*, 23 O. R. 651; *Dudden* v. *Guardians of Clutton Union*, 1 H. & N. 627; *Chamberlain* v. *Baltimore and Ohio R. W. Co.*, 29 Am. & Eng. R. R. Cas. 533.

March 3, 1894. STREET, J.:—

By sub-sec. (h) of sec. 90 of the Railway Act, 51 Vic. ch. 29, (D.), the defendants have power to divert the course of any watercourse, subject to the provisions of the Act, but we are of opinion that in order to entitle themselves to insist upon the arbitration clauses of the Act, they must shew upon their registered plans their intention to do so. See sections 123, 144, 145, 146, and 147 of the Act. See also *Ware* v. *Regent's Canal Co.*, 3 DeG. & J. 212; *Parkdale* v. *West*, 12 App. Cas. 602. No evidence was given at the trial of the filing of any such plan, and we think that the objection that compensation should have been sought under the Act, and not by way of action, cannot be sustained.

The learned Judge has ordered judgment to be entered for the whole injury to the value of the land caused by the diversion of the watercourse, treating the injury as a permanent one, and assessing the damages for all time to come. The defendants object that such a judgment will be no bar to a future action, and that the damages can

Judgment.

Street, J.

properly only be assessed from time to time as they are
sustained. The rule itself is clear enough, that a judgment recovered upon any cause of action is a bar to any
further claim upon the same cause of action. It is in the
application of the rule to particular cases, and the ascertaining in each case what is the precise cause of action,
that the difficulty arises. In the present case, was it the
fact of the defendants having diverted the watercourse or
the fact of the plaintiff having sustained damage from their
doing so, that gave the plaintiff a cause of action? If it
was the former, then a recovery now will be a bar to any
future action; if the latter, the damages only can now be
assessed which the plaintiff has sustained, and he may
bring a new action for any future damage which he may
sustain; because each fresh happening of damage will be
a new cause of action: *Darley Main Colliery Co.* v.
Mitchell, 11 App. Cas. 127; *Clegg* v. *Dearden*, 12 Q. B.
576.

I am of opinion that in the present case the defendants,
when they diverted the watercourse, did an act which
was wrongful, and that it was this act, and not the damages flowing from it, which gave the plaintiff his cause of
action.

Every proprietor on the banks of a natural stream has
a right to use the water, provided he so uses it as not to
work any material injury to the rights of other riparian
proprietors, but so soon as he uses it in such a way as to
diminish the quantity or quality of the water going on to
the lower proprietors, or to retard or stop its flow, he exceeds his own rights and infringes upon theirs, and for
every such infringement an action lies: *Sampson* v. *Hod-
dinott*, 1 C. B. N. S. 590; *Kensit* v. *Great Eastern R. W.
Co.*, 27 Ch. D. 122.

The defendants here have done an act which has entirely
cut off the plaintiff's access to the water of the stream by
diverting it away from his farm. That is an infringement
of the natural right which he possessed to the flow of the
water; the diversion is not temporary in its character,

and we are not at liberty to treat it as other than permanent. The proper mode of estimating the damages is to
treat it as permanent, and to consider the effect upon the
value of the farm that the permanent abstraction of the
water will have. This the jury have done, and I see no
reason for reducing the amount.

The case of *McGillivray* v. *Great Western R. W. Co.*, 25
U. C. R. 69, cited to us by the defendants' counsel, is
plainly distinguishable, the damages being there given for
the negligent construction of a culvert which the Court
thought the defendants had agreed to make.

The objection to the charge is that the definition given
by the learned trial Judge to the jury of a watercourse
was likely to mislead them. The learned Judge told them
that a watercourse was "a stream of water ordinarily
flowing in a certain direction through a well defined channel with bed and banks; that the law has always been
considered in Ontario to be that a channel made by mere
surface water and snow is not a watercourse, unless there
is ordinarily and most frequently a moving body of water
flowing to it;" then he read to them an extract from the
judgment of the Chancellor in *Beer* v. *Stroud*, 19 O. R.
10, telling them that that case seemed to .carry the law
further in favour of the plaintiff than any former judgment of our Courts. The extract he read was as follows:
"It is not essential that the supply of water should be
continuous, and from a perennial living source. It is
enough if the flow arises periodically from natural causes
and reaches a plainly defined channel of a permanent character. Thus a recognized 'course' is obtained, which is
originated and ascertained and perpetuated by the action
of the water itself." He had already told the jury that
" the principles which are applicable to streams of running
water do not extend to the flow of mere surface water
spreading over the land." The objection to the charge is
evidently not correctly reported, but I think it may be
gathered from the report to have been that the jury might
understand from the charge that mere surface water com-

ing two or three times a year during wet seasons and making a channel for itself during those seasons, would in
law create a watercourse.

In order to consider the view which the jury may have
taken of the charge, it is necessary to look at the evidence
to see what questions were in dispute with regard to the
alleged watercourse. Both parties appear to have agreed
that there was a gully or depression through the plaintiff's
farm, which had been created by the action of the water—
at all events, upon this part of the case the jury are not
likely to have been misled by any ambiguous language in
the charge, because they had themselves been over the
ground and had a view of it. What was disputed by the
defendants was that any water ran along this gully excepting mere surface water, that is to say, melted snow in the
spring and during the winter thaws, coming from an accu-
mulation of snow and ice upon the higher land to the
north, and rain water after heavy rains at other seasons of
the year flowing over the surface merely, and ceasing with
the rain which produced it. The plaintiff, on the other
hand, contended that there was a constant stream of water
having its source in the high grounds to the north, and
only, if ever, ceasing in the very dry summer weather. It
is plain, I think, that mere surface water flowing during
short intermittent periods as the result of the melting of
snow and ice, or of a sudden shower or succession of
showers, and ceasing to flow at all other times of the year,
even though the flow be through a channel cut by the
water itself, cannot convert the channel into a watercourse.
Without a permanent source, which, however, need not
necessarily be absolutely never failing, there cannot be a
watercourse. Such a source may be under ground or above
ground; it may be a spring, or a swamp, or a lake, or a
glacier; the flow from it may vary in volume with the
seasons, and may entirely cease from temporary causes;
but it must be sufficient to act as a reserve, to prevent the
flowing of the water from depending upon the happening
of a thaw or a storm, and to create a stream which shall
be reasonably constant in its flow.

It appears to me that the attention of the jury was not expressly called to the difference in effect between the occasional flow of surface water and the steady flow from a source; the language quoted from the judgment in *Beer* v. *Stroud* is to be taken in connection with the facts of that case and with other language used in the same judgment and modifying the quotation. Taken without the context, it may have misled the jury here, and I am of opinion that there should on this account be a new trial. The costs of the last trial and of the motion to be taxed to the successful party.

ARMOUR, C. J. :—

I agree with the judgment of my learned brother except in respect of the alleged misdirection of the learned Judge.

The learned Judge read to the jury the law as laid down in *Beer* v. *Stroud*, 19 O. R. 10, from the report of that case, and I think, therefore, that we cannot hold what he thus told them to have been a misdirection without reversing the decision of the Court in that case, which it is not our province to do, but that of an appellate Court.

Besides, I think that the objection, if such it can be called, as taken, was too vague and indefinite to form a ground for setting aside the verdict.

The motion should, in my opinion, be dismissed with costs, but no proceedings are to be taken to enforce the judgment, unless and until the plaintiff delivers to the defendant a release by himself and the mortgagees of his land of any further claim in respect of the cause of action herein sued for, and for damages in respect of such cause of action, and if the parties differ as to the form of the release, it will be settled by the registrar of this Division.

E. B. B.

[QUEEN'S BENCH DIVISION.]

McDONALD v. DICKENSON ET AL.

*Municipal Corporations—Rebuilding of Culvert—Obstructions in Highway
—Negligence—Accident—Liability of Servants of Corporation—Muni-
cipal Councillors—Officers fulfilling Public Duty—R. S. O. ch. 73—
Notice of Action—Pathmaster.*

Two of the defendants, members of a township council, were appointed by resolution of the council a committee to rebuild a culvert,
and they personally superintended the work, and were paid for doing
it, but there was no by-law authorizing their appointment or payment.
The other defendants were employed by them, and did the work. The
plaintiff met with an accident on the highway near the culvert, owing,
as she alleged, to the negligence of the defendants in obstructing the
road with their building materials, and brought this action for damages
for her injuries :—

Held, that the defendants were not fulfilling a public duty, and were not
entitled to notice of action under R. S. O. ch. 73 :—

Held, also, that that statute is applicable only to officers and persons fulfilling a public duty for anything done by them in the performance of
it, when it may be properly averred that the act was done maliciously
and without reasonable and probable cause, and therefore not to actions
for negligence in the doing of the act :—

Held, lastly, that one of the defendants, who was pathmaster for the
beat in which the culvert was situated, did not come within the protection of the statute as pathmaster, because he was not employed as such
in doing this work, but as a day labourer.

THE cause of action, as stated in the claim, was that on Statement.
or about the 18th June, 1892, the plaintiff was lawfully
driving along Talbot road in the township of Yarmouth,
and when about four miles west of Aylmer, and while
driving westward to St. Thomas, owing to obstructions
placed and excavations made in that road unlawfully by
the defendants, the plaintiff's horse became frightened
and ran away, the conveyance in which the plaintiff was
driving was upset, she was thrown out and seriously injured, and the vehicle and other property were damaged.

The action was tried before STREET, J., with a jury at the
Sittings of this Court at St. Thomas held in the Spring
of 1893.

On the Talbot road between Aylmer and St. Thomas
there was a fill between the hills of a depth variously
estimated at from fourteen to seventeen feet, and a railing

extended along each side of the fill, and in this fill there was a culvert which required renewing, and on the 4th April, 1892, a resolution was passed by the council of the township of Yarmouth that the reeve and Mr. Luton be a committee to rebuild this culvert.

The defendant Brower was the reeve and the defendant Luton was the first deputy reeve of the township, and they superintended the work, and appeared to have been paid by the township for such superintendence. The defendant Luton bought tiles for the culvert and had them shipped to New Sarum, and employed the defendants the Tisdales to draw the tiles to the culvert. The defendant Dickenson was employed to work by the day at putting in the culvert, and he happened to be at the same time the pathmaster for the beat in which the culvert was situated. The tiles were large, two and one-half feet long and forty inches outside, and thirty-one inches inside diameter, and some of them were placed on the north side of the fill at the end of the railing, and as the plaintiff was driving along the road to St. Thomas her horse shied at these tiles and upset the conveyance and she was injured.

The defendants raised the objection that they were fulfilling a public duty, and the placing of the tiles on the side of the road was done by them in the performance of such public duty, and that they were, therefore, entitled to the protection of the Act R. S. O. ch. 73, and were entitled to notice of action, and the learned Judge, being of this opinion, dismissed the action.

At the Easter Sittings, 1893, of the Divisional Court the plaintiff moved to set aside this judgment and for a new trial.

The motion was argued before ARMOUR, C. J., and FALCONBRIDGE, J., on the 25th May, 1893.

J. A. Robinson, for the plaintiff. R. S. O. ch. 73, sec. 1, provides that in case an action is brought against any officer or person fulfilling any public duty, for anything by him done in the performance of such public duty, it shall be expressly alleged in the statement of claim that the act was done maliciously and without reasonable and probable cause. This enactment cannot apply to an action of this kind. We could not shew that the acts complained of were done maliciously and without reasonable and probable cause. These defendants in doing the acts complained of were not officers or persons fulfilling any public duty. They were not appointed by by-law and were not public officers, except Dickenson, who was a pathmaster, but was not acting in that capacity. The defendants Brower and Luton were probably appointed under the powers given by 55 Vic. (O.) ch. 42, sec. 479 (2), and if so, they had no right to appoint deputies, and even if they themselves were public officers, the other defendants were not. *Davis* v. *Carling*, 8 Q. B. 286, is not applicable; it was decided under the Imperial Statute 5 & 6 Will. IV. ch. 50.

Tremeear, on the same side. The acts of the defendants in obstructing the road were not necessary for the performance of the work they were doing.

J. M. Glenn and *J. A. McLean*, for the defendants Dickenson, Brower, and Luton, referred to *Spry* v. *Mumby*, 11 C. P. 285; *Sage* v. *Duffy*, 11 U. C. R. 30; Robinson & Joseph's Dig. p. 30 *et seq.*; *Howarth* v. *McGugan*, 23 O. R. 396.

C. F. Maxwell, for the defendants the Tisdales.

Robinson, in reply, cited *Wilkins* v. *Day*, 12 Q. B. D. 110; *Harrison* v. *Brega*, 20 U. C. R. 324; *Ross* v. *McLay*, 26 C. P. 190; 40 U. C. R. 83.

March 3, 1894. The judgment of the Court was delivered by

ARMOUR, C. J. :—

The learned Judge rightly held that the defendant Dickenson did not come within the protection of the Act as a pathmaster, because, although he happened to be the pathmaster of that particular beat in which the culvert was situated, he was not employed in doing the work as a pathmaster, but was employed by Luton to do the work under Brower and him as a day labourer.

The learned Judge, however, held that the defendants Brower and Luton were entitled to the protection of the Act as persons fulfilling a public duty, and that the other defendants were working under them and were entitled to the like protection.

It is difficult to see how the defendants Brower and Luton could be said to be, in rebuilding this culvert, fulfilling a public duty arising out of the common law or imposed by any Act, either of the Imperial or Dominion Parliament or of the Legislature of this Province.

I do not see that the position of the defendants differed in any respect from that of any other person or stranger to the council, that the council might have employed to see to the doing of this work, or from that of any contractor for the work, so far as entitling them to the protection of the Act.

The law, no doubt, imposed the duty upon the municipal corporation of keeping the road in repair, but it did not impose any such duty upon the individual members of the corporation.

The defendants Brower and Luton were not appointed by by-law, as they might have been, commissioners, superintendents, or overseers over this road under section 479 of the Consolidated Municipal Act, 1892.

But section 231 of the said Municipal Act having provided that the council of every township and county may pass by-laws for paying the members of the council for their attendance in council, or any member while attending on committee of the council, at a rate not exceeding three dollars per diem, and five cents per mile necessarily travelled (to and from) for such attendance, this provision is made use of by township and county councillors by getting themselves appointed as a committee to see to the doing of various jobs required to be done upon the roads and bridges within their respective townships and counties Judgment. to add to their emoluments and increase the value of their Armour, C.J. office.

No by-law was produced authorizing the payment of the defendants Brower and Luton, but they were paid under the name of a committee to do this work ; they were doing the work because they were paid for it, and not because of any duty imposed upon them by law to do it : *Corporation of Chatham* v. *Houston*, 27 U. C. R. 550.

I am of the opinion, moreover, that the Act R. S. O. ch. 73 is not applicable to the subject-matter of this suit, and this is made more apparent by looking into the history of the Act and examining the preamble of the Act 14 & 15 Vic. ch. 54, and sec. 16 of the Act 16 Vic. ch. 180 : *White* v. *Clark*, 11 U. C. R. 137.

This Act is, in my opinion, only applicable to officers and persons fulfilling a public duty for anything done by them in the performance of such public duty when it may be properly averred of the act when done that it was done maliciously and without reasonable and probable cause, and is not, therefore, applicable to actions for negligence in the doing of the act. And the notice of action required to be given by the Act is only so required where the action is for the doing of the act maliciously and without reasonable and probable cause : *Harrison* v. *Brega*, 20 U. C. R. 324 ; *Harrold* v. *Corporation of Simcoe*, 16 C. P. 43 ; *Ontario Industrial L. & I. Co.* v. *Lindsey*, 3 O. R. 66 ; *Walton* v. *Apjohn*, 5 O. R. 65 ; *County of Bruce* v. *McLay*, 11 A. R. 477.

The motion will, therefore, be absolute for a new trial ; the costs of the former trial and of this motion to be costs in the cause to the plaintiff in any event of the suit.

E. B. B.

[QUEEN'S BENCH DIVISION.]

BALL ET AL. V. TENNANT.

Assignments and Preferences—R. S. O. ch. 124, sec. 4—Assignment for Benefit of Creditors—Several Property of Partners—Covenant of Indemnity—Creditors—Execution of Assignment by.

An assignment under R. S. O. ch. 124, for the general benefit of creditors, made by the members of a trading partnership, in the words mentioned in sec. 4, vests in the assignee all the properties of each of the partners, several as well as joint, including a covenant to indemnify one of the partners against a mortgage, which covenant vests under the term "property."

Where such an assignment has been acted upon by the creditors, it is not open to the objection, even if made by an execution creditor, that no creditor executed it.

Cooper v. *Dixon*, 10 A. R. 50, distinguished.

Judgment of ROBERTSON, J., varied.

THIS was an action brought to enforce a mortgage of lands made by one Kenneth Cross to the plaintiffs on the 1st October, 1891.

The plaintiffs claimed possession of the mortgaged lands, payment of the mortgage money, and, in default of payment, foreclosure.

It was alleged in the statement of claim that the defendant became the owner of the equity of redemption by a deed of conveyance to him from Cross, dated the 8th January, 1892, subject to the plaintiffs' mortgage and a prior one; and that in and by the deed the defendant covenanted with Cross to pay the mortgages and indemnify and save him harmless against them. It was also alleged that on the 31st October, 1892, Cross had assigned to the plaintiffs all the benefit of the defendant's covenant contained in the deed of 8th January, 1892; and by virtue of this covenant and assignment the plaintiffs claimed payment of the mortgage money from the defendant.

By his statement of defence the defendant denied the allegations of the statement of claim, and, amongst other things, alleged:

(16). That Kenneth Cross was not at the time of the alleged assignment possessed of any right, claim, or de-

mand, or cause of action, which could be legally assigned Statement.
to the plaintiffs, and the alleged assignment was, as against
the defendant, invalid, and passed no right, title, or interest to the plaintiffs, as against the defendant, which the
plaintiffs did not theretofore possess.

(17). That there was no privity of contract existing
between the defendant and the plaintiffs, and that the
plaintiffs were not entitled in law to maintain this action
as against the defendant; and the defendant craved the
benefit of this objection as if he had formally demurred
to the statement of claim.

(18). That previous to the date of the alleged assignment to the plaintiffs, and on or about the 6th October,
1892, Kenneth Cross, together with one Douglas Scott,
assigned all his assets, real and personal, and all his property, rights, claims, and demands of any and every nature
whatsoever, including the cause of action herein, if the
same existed, which the defendant denied, to William
Alexander Campbell and George H. May, by virtue of an
assignment alleged to be for the benefit of creditors.

Issue.

The cause was tried at the sittings of this Court in the
Chancery Division for the city of Toronto held in the
spring of 1892, by ROBERTSON, J.

The following facts were shewn.

Indenture of mortgage, dated 1st October, 1891, from
Kenneth Cross to the plaintiffs, of certain lands therein
described, securing $750 with interest at eight per cent.
payable as therein set forth, with a covenant for the payment thereof by the said Kenneth Cross to the plaintiffs.

Indenture of bargain and sale, dated 8th January, 1892,
of the said lands with other lands, from Kenneth Cross to
the defendant, containing a covenant on the part of the defendant, his heirs, administrators, and assigns, with the said
Kenneth Cross, that he would assume and pay off as they
matured the said mortgage to the plaintiffs and a mortgage on the same lands to a Mrs. McCraney, and would save
harmless the said Kenneth Cross from the payment thereof

or any interest thereon as mentioned, and from all costs, damages, or expenses arising thereon or any way incidental thereto.

Indenture, made the 30th September, 1892, in pursuance of R.S.O. ch. 124, being an Act respecting Assignments and Preferences by Insolvent Persons, between Douglas Scott, of the city of Toronto, and Kenneth Cross, of the same place, trading under the name of Scott & Cross, contractors, the debtors of the first part, William Alexander Campbell and George Henry May, of the city of Toronto, accountants, the assignees, of the second part, and the several firms, persons, and corporations who were creditors of the said debtor, thereinafter called the creditors, of the third part, by which, after setting out the inability of Scott & Cross to pay their debts in full, the debtors assigned to Campbell & May "all their personal property which may be seized and sold under execution, and all their real estate, credits, and effects," upon trust to sell and convert into money, and out of the proceeds to pay the liabilities of the debtors ratably, and without preference or priority ; which said indenture was executed by the said debtors and by the assignees, but was not executed by any party of the third part.

Indenture made the 31st October, 1892, between the said Kenneth Cross, of the first part, and the plaintiffs, of the second part, whereby, for the consideration therein mentioned, the said Kenneth Cross granted and assigned to the plaintiffs the covenant contained in the said indenture of the 8th January, 1892, made by the defendant, and all benefit, right of action, and advantage which he then had or might thereafter have against the defendant, or any other person or persons whomsoever, by virtue of the said covenant.

It appeared that the defendant had made one payment of interest upon the mortgage of Janet McCraney, and one payment of interest on the mortgage to the plaintiffs, some time in the spring of 1892.

It was also shewn that Douglas Scott and Kenneth Cross were in partnership under the name of Scott &

Cross at the time the plaintiffs' mortgage was made, and
that they continued in partnership under the same name
until they made the assignment to Campbell and May;
and that the lands mortgaged to the plaintiffs were the
property of Kenneth Cross and not of the partnership.

The learned Judge gave judgment on the 4th September,
1893, in favour of the plaintiffs for the amount claimed,
and, in default, foreclosure and possession.

At the Michaelmas Sittings of the Divisional Court,
1893, the defendant moved to set aside this judgment and
to enter judgment for him, on the grounds, among others :
(1) That the judgment was contrary to law and evidence,
and the weight of evidence, and judgment should have
been entered for the defendant; (2) That no privity of
contract was shewn between the plaintiffs and the defendant, either directly or through the assignment by Cross
to the plaintiffs; (10) That the assignment from Cross to
the plaintiffs was invalid and ineffectual, and no right of
action passed thereunder, because the right of action
under the said covenant had been previously assigned
by Cross to another person, and because nothing was intended to pass to the plaintiffs by the assignment to them.

The motion was argued before ARMOUR, C. J., and
FALCONBRIDGE, J., on the 22nd November, 1893.

R. U. Macpherson, for the defendant. This covenant before being assigned to the plaintiffs was assigned to the
assignees for creditors, and nothing passed to the plaintiffs.
R. S. O. ch. 124, sec. 4, shews what passed by the assignment for creditors. The covenant or right of action therein
was "property" or "rights," and therefore passed. But it
is said the assignment was by the firm of which Cross was
a member. I contend the assignment covered the individual property of each partner. The assignment is executed
by each of the partners. The intention of the Act is that
all property shall pass: *Blain* v. *Peaker*, 18 O. R. 109 ;
Re Unitt and Prott, 23 O. R. 78. A covenant for or right
of indemnity passes as personal property : *Irving* v. *Boyd*,
15 Gr. 157, 162. In *Heward* v. *Mitchell*, 10 U. C. R. 535, the

words "all their" were held to include individual property. See also Burrill on Assignments, 5th ed., pp. 480, 481 ; *Von Wettberg* v. *Carson*, 44 Conn. 287 ; *Williams* v. *Hadley*, 21 Kans. 350 ; *Butler* v. *Butler*, 54 L. J. Ch. 197 ; *Jones* v. *Skinner*, 5 L. J. N. S. Ch. at p. 90 ; Stroud's Judicial Dictionary, *sub verb.* "property ;" *Sayer* v. *Dufaur*, 17 L. J. Q. B. 50. There is no privity between the plaintiff and the defendant : *Frontenac L. & I. Co.* v. *Hysop*, 21 O. R. 577, and cases there cited. Under the wording of the covenant in this case, it would not by itself give any cause of action. You have to look at the deed in which it is contained, to see what it means.

N. F. Davidson, for the plaintiffs. In the deed of assignment the words used are "all their" property, etc. The words "and of each of them" should have been added if the intention was that individual property should pass. Even if the assignment includes individual property, this particular right would not pass, the mortgage not being at the time in arrear. It is not a chose in action which would go to benefit creditors. But at any rate only partnership property passed : *McKitrick* v. *Haley*, 46 U. C. R. 246 ; *Nelles* v. *Maltby*, 5 O. R. 263. No creditor executes the deed of assignment, and so it is void : *Cooper* v. *Dixon*, 10 A. R. 50.

[Certain other points were argued by counsel, but as the judgment does not deal with them, they are not set out here.]

March 3, 1894. The judgment of the Court was delivered by

ARMOUR, C. J. :—

The assignment from Scott and Cross to Campbell and May, being of "all their personal property which may be seized and sold under execution, and all their real estate, credits, and effects," by force of the statute R. S. O. ch. 124, sec. 4, vested in Campbell and May all the real and personal estate, rights, property, credits, and effects, whether vested or contingent, belonging at the time of the assignment to the assignors, except such as were by law exempt from seizure or sale under execution.

And this assignment vested in the assignees, in my opinion, all the property of each of the partners, several as well as joint, under the words made use of therein : *Heward* v. *Mitchell,* 10 U. C. R. 535 ; *Mills* v. *Kerr,* 7 A. R. 769 ; *Hanson* v. *Paige,* 3 Gray 239 ; *Judd* v. *Gibbs, ib.* 539 ; *Coggill* v. *Botsford,* 29 Conn. 439 ; *Von Wettbery* v. *Carson,* 44 Conn. 287. And the statute R. S. O. ch. 124, sec. 5, provided ;for the mode of distribution of the property, several as well as joint.

This assignment was made under the provisions of the statute, and the evidence shewed that it had been acted upon by the creditors, and the objection raised in *Cooper* v. *Dixon,* 10 A. R. 50, could not, therefore, avail against it, even on behalf of an execution creditor.

I am of the opinion that under the words used in this assignment, and the force given to the assignment by the statute R. S. O. ch. 124, sec. 4, the covenant contained in the indenture of the 8th January, 1892, by which the defendant bound himself to indemnify Cross against the plaintiff's mortgage, became vested in the assignees.

I think that it vested in the assignees under the term "property," and that it was a property beneficial to the assignees, for if the plaintiffs had proved their claim against the estate of Cross, the assignees could have enforced the covenant against the defendant, and have thus 'exonerated the estate of Cross from the plaintiffs' claim to rank thereon : *Irving* v. *Boyd,* 15 Gr. 157 ; *British Canadian Loan Co.* v. *Tear,* 23 O. R. 664.

This covenant having, therefore, become vested in the assignees, nothing passed by the assignment thereof by Cross to the plaintiffs by the indenture of the 31st October, 1892.

The judgment of the learned Judge must, therefore, be varied by confining it to a judgment for foreclosure and possession, with costs, and there will be no costs to either party of this motion.

E. B. B.

[CHANCERY DIVISION.]

TENNANT & COMPANY v. GALLOW.

Fraudulent Preference—Voluntary Transfer—Subsequent Sale to Innocent Purchaser—Following Proceeds Thereof.

An insolvent debtor, for the purpose of defeating the plaintiffs' claim against him, by voluntary deed conveyed the equity of redemption in certain lands to another creditor who, as previously arranged with the grantor, sold the property to an innocent purchaser and applied the proceeds in payment of all encumbrances on the property and all his own debts and those of certain other creditors of the grantor, and of a commission to himself in respect to the sale, and paid over the final balance to the grantor :—
Held, that the plaintiffs had no right of action against the fraudulent grantee to recover any part of the purchase money.
Masuret v. Stewart, 22 O. R. 290, and *Cornish v. Clark,* L. [R., 14 Eq. 184, distinguished.

Statement. THIS was an action brought by Tennant & Company, suing on behalf of themselves and all other creditors of the defendant Anderson, against Edward Gallow and Adam Anderson, in which the plaintiffs set up in the statement of claim that they were lumber merchants, the defendant Gallow a money broker, and the defendant Anderson a builder, all residing in Toronto : that on April 27th, 1893, the defendant Anderson was in insolvent circumstances, his only estate consisting of an equity of redemption in a certain building lot in Toronto : that on April 19th, 1893, the plaintiffs issued a writ against Anderson to recover the balance due on certain promissory notes, which writ was served upon him on the same day, and judgment recovered, and writs of *fieri facias* against goods and lands issued thereon on May 6th, 1893 : that on April 27th, 1893, Anderson in collusion with Gallow, in order to defeat, hinder, and delay the plaintiffs from recovering their claim, transferred the said lots to Gallow, who took the said transfer with full knowledge of Anderson's insolvent circumstances and of the plaintiffs' writ of summons having been served upon him : that on May 19th, 1893, Gallow transferred the land to one Esther Carter for

Statement. $8,300, of which he received $1,099.19, the balance being applied in payment of encumbrances on the property, which sum of $1,099.19 the plaintiffs claimed should be applied towards payment of their judgment and the claims of other creditors of Anderson, and that, at all events, Gallow was a trustee for Anderson's creditors in respect of the said sum, and asked for an order for payment of the said sum into Court by Gallow accordingly.

The remaining facts of the case, as established by the evidence, are set out in the judgment.

The action was tried at the Chancery Sittings at Toronto, on February 15th, 1894, before MEREDITH, J., without a jury.

W. R. Riddell, for the plaintiffs.
Miller, Q. C., for the defendant Gallow.

March 13th, 1894. MEREDITH, J. :—

The impeached conveyance was made on the 27th day of April, 1893.

At that time the grantor was indebted to the plaintiffs upon certain promissory notes, and was indebted to divers other persons, and was in insolvent circumstances, as both he and the grantee knew.

The grantor had on the 19th day of that month been sued by the plaintiffs upon the notes, and served with the writ of summons in that action, and judgment was recovered against him in it, on the 6th day of May following, for the amount of the notes and interest and costs, and writs of *fi. fa.* goods and lands were thereupon sued out, and were placed in the sheriffs' hands for execution on the 13th day of that month.

The lands conveyed were at the time of the conveyance heavily mortgaged and charged. The grantee was the second mortgagee in order of priority, and he had been pressing for payment of his mortgage by means of a sale of the lands—the only means of satisfying it and any other claims against it, owing to the mortgagor's insolvent circumstances.

No new consideration was given for the making of the impeached conveyance, which was in effect the transfer of the grantor's equity of redemption; it was a voluntary conveyance, and was made by and between the parties with the intention and for the purpose—either expressly stated or tacitly agreed to between them—of defeating the plaintiffs in the recovery of the debt, in respect of which the action was then pending, out of the property conveyed, and to prefer other creditors, as well as to enable the grantee to sell the lands and satisfy all his just claims, against it and the grantor, out of the proceeds; and the grantee was to account to the grantor for the proceeds of the sale, and to pay to him, or his order, the surplus if any.

The lands were subsequently, on the 19th day of May, sold to a *bonâ fide* purchaser for value without notice of any of the facts upon which the conveyance in question is now impeached. The sale was a better one than the parties expected, and there was a larger surplus, after payment of all charges and encumbrances against the lands, than had been looked for. This surplus was in part paid out by the grantee, upon the directions in writing of the grantor, to certain of the latter's simple creditors, including the grantee, and in satisfaction of a commission of $200 for the grantee's services in this sale, and another commission of $125, which, on the 14th day of March, the grantor had agreed to pay the grantee for other services in connection with the same property, and which was to be paid when some other lands in the grantor's name should be disposed of, an event which has not yet happened; and the balance of this surplus—$314—was paid over by the grantee to the grantor; the last of all these payments was made, and the accounts between the parties stated and settled and a general release given by each to the other, on the 26th day of May; the expressed consideration for the release by the grantor of the grantee being the sum of $314, the balance of the surplus proceeds of the sale.

The writ in this action was issued on the 13th day of July following.

The action was brought, and endeavoured to be sup-.ported at the trial, on the authority of *Masuret* v. *Stewart*, 22 O. R. 290 ; but Mr. Riddell was obliged to admit that in at least one of its features it is not like that case, namely, that in this case the whole of the proceeds of the sale to the *bond fide* purchaser had been appropriated and paid over before the writ of summons in this action was issued ; and that the fact that the proceeds were yet in the hands of the transferee of the debtor in the *Masuret case*, when action brought, was considered an essential ingredient by the Divisional Court in its judgment in that case ; and that, therefore, it might not be considered as binding authority in the plaintiff's favour.

That Court certainly did deal with that case as an exceptional one, and expressly endeavoured to avoid a conflict with the line of cases holding that the proceeds, in the shape of money, of a *bond fide* subsequent sale, cannot be reached by an action of this kind : see *Davis* v. *Wickson*, 1 O. R. 369 ; *Stuart* v. *Tremain*, 3 O. R. 190; and *Robertson* v. *Holland*, 16 O. R. 532. It was said that it was admitted in argument that the facts took it outside of any of the cases.

In this case it was the intention that the property should pass, and the subsequent sale was actually made by the grantee ; but so it must have been in the *Masuret case* ; the very object of the parties was to pass the title out of the debtor and so to prevent the property being reached by execution ; the property does pass, and under such transmission the *bond fide* purchaser takes and holds ; it is only as against creditors that the transaction is declared void : that is, it is voidable at their instance if attacked before the property has so passed to a *bond fide* purchaser ; hence the constantly recurring applications for an injunction to restrain any such transfer.

There can be no doubt that, had the debtor done just what his grantee did, the plaintiffs would have no cause of action such as this ; they could not follow the proceeds of

the sale or any part of them; nor could they have prevented
the debtor from so disposing of the property and so applying the proceeds : *Abell* v. *Morrison*, 23 Gr. 109 ; *Hepburn*
v. *Patton*, 26 Gr. 597, and *Campbell* v. *Campbell*, 29 Gr.
252.

This case is not brought within the authority of the
Masuret case, and, therefore, the plaintiffs cannot recover
because of the binding authority of that case only.

Then it was contended that it is brought within the
authority of *Cornish* v. *Clark*, L. R. 14 Eq. 184, referred
to with approval in the *Masuret case*; that that case
shews that the proceeds of a *bond fide* sale may be followed and reached by creditors.

But that was not a case of following the proceeds of such
a sale; it was the case of a father in effect settling all
his property upon his children in fraud of creditors. Part
of it consisted of money which was given equally to his
daughters ; part of it thrashing machines, one of which
was given to each of his sons ; and the rest a mortgage
which was given to a trustee to be divided between his
daughters and the children of a deceased daughter. As
between the beneficiaries, the judgment provided for payment of funeral and administration expenses of the father—
who had meanwhile died—and of his debts, and the plaintiffs' costs, by the beneficiaries, ratably in proportion to
the amount and value received and to be received ; but
this was only as between them, and it does not appear that
any of them objected to such a provision ; the plaintiffs'
rights were expressly left unprejudiced by this provision.
But the money received by the daughters was directed to
be paid into Court.

There was nothing new in a decree reaching moneys so
settled or paid in fraud of creditors ; as long ago as the case
of *Partridge* v. *Gopp*, Amb. 596, it was expressly held that
they could be. But that is not the question involved here
or in *Masuret* v. *Stewart*, or *Davis* v. *Wickson*, and cases of
that class. If it were in any of them it would be surely
in all ; and the money might, one would think, be reached

by garnishee proceedings upon this ground:—as against
creditors the property was theirs not the grantees, the
money is theirs as the proceeds of what was theirs : though
the grantee might have an absolute defence against any
action by the grantor he could not, as against the creditors, set it up because as against them his title is void. But
such is not the law : see *Vyse* v. *Brown*, 13 Q, B. D. 199.

In both *Partridge* v. *Gopp*, and *Cornish* v. *Clark*, the
father had died before the action was brought; and it is
said that even in respect of property not exigible before the
debtor's death, his creditors could after his death sue persons
claiming it under a fraudulent deed, as executors *de son
tort*, the property settled being assets in their hands :   May
on Fraudulent Conveyances, 2nd ed., p. 19 : *Whittington*
v. *Jennings*, 6 Sim. 493 ; *Norcutt* v. *Todd*, Cr. & Ph. 100 ;
Barrack v. *McCulloch*, 3 K. & J. 110.

It is said that the right of a person defrauded under
the Statutes of Elizabeth to elect to avoid a deed as
fraudulent, may be lost in either of the following ways :

1. It may be lost by the deed having become for value
by a consideration *ex post facto* before any steps are taken
by that person to impeach it.

2. The voluntary grantee may have divested himself of
the property by a *bonâ fide* transfer of it for value to a
bonâ fide purchaser for value without notice of fraud;
May on Fraudulent Conveyances, 2nd ed., p. 325.

The principle enunciated in the line of cases to which I
have referred, namely, that "the right of the plaintiff in
this class of cases is to have any impediment removed or
declared invalid which intercepts the action of his writs of
execution.   So long as the property of his execution
debtor remains distinguishable, and so long as no purchaser
for value without notice intervenes, so long may the
Court award relief against that property in the hands of
fraudulent or voluntary holders.   But where, as here, the
first holder sells the property obtained from the debtor
and receives the proceeds in a shape that cannot be ear-
marked, there is no jurisdiction to go beyond the further

remedy which the statute of Elizabeth prescribes, namely,
that all parties to fraudulent conveyances aliening or
assigning thereunder shall forfeit a year's value of the
lands, and the whole value of the goods, whereof half shall
go to the Crown and half to the party aggrieved, to be
recovered by action of debt as mentioned in section 2
of the Act": *Davis* v. *Wickson*, 1 O. R., at pp. 374-5 :
is quite intelligible and clearly defined and in accord with
the principle upon which such cases as *Hepburn* v. *Patton*,
was decided, and with the long prevailing view here of
the effect of the Statute of Elizabeth and the provincial
Acts against unjust preferences.

So too the principle upon which the Courts in the United
States of America act—the other extreme. There the
debtor is considered, in a sense, but a trustee of his property for his creditors, and his transferee in fraud of
creditors is likewise so treated and held liable to account
with greater strictness—even if one may not say with
great harshness in some cases—than an ordinary trustee
for the benefit of creditors.

But I am yet unable to perceive any middle ground, any
exception out of the first mentioned principle to which the
other principle can in effect be applied. If such a transferee is not accountable as a trustee, how can he be made
to account ? And if he be liable as for a debt due from him
to the debtor, why are not garnishee proceedings the proper remedy ? See Blair v. Smith, 15 N. E. R. 817.

In *Harvey* v. *M'Naughton*, 10 A. R. 616, Osler, J. A., in
delivering the judgment of the Court of Appeal, said of such
a claim as that made in this case, that " the plaintiffs would
have had a difficult task to maintain an action which has at
least the merit of novelty as regards the constitution of
the suit and the nature of the relief sought."

The entire absence of any English or Canadian cases, or
anything in the books, supporting the plaintiffs' claim, to
be entitled to follow the proceeds of the sale, is almost
conclusive against him. There could not but have been many
such cases if there were any such right. The cases in the

United States of America are very numerous and clear;
but the principle there adopted is nowhere, that I have
seen, said to be founded upon, or supported by, English
cases.

The result there is certainly highly satisfactory in
many cases; but would it not be legislation rather than
adjudication to adopt the principle here? Such legislation
as R. S. O. ch. 124, sec. 8, would seem to indicate that the
view of the legislature to be that it would. There express
provision is made for following the proceeds of such a sale;
but only in cases where the debtor has assigned under the
provisions of the Act for the benefit of creditors: see
Robertson v. *Holland*, 16 O. R. 532.

The plaintiffs' action, therefore, entirely fails, and must
be dismissed; but it will be dismissed without costs, for the
defendant Gallow has also entirely failed upon the facts
pleaded by him and supported by his own testimony at the
trial; as stated at that time, I find those facts against him,
but he succeeded upon a point of law which might have
been raised and determined without a trial.

Action dismissed without costs.

A. H. F. L.

[QUEEN'S BENCH DIVISION.]

JOHNSON v. GRAND TRUNK RAILWAY COMPANY.

Railways—Accident at Crossing—Negligence—Findings of Jury—Release of Cause of Action—Settlement Pending Action—Validity of—Trial of Issue as to.

In an action to recover damages for the death of the plaintiff's husband, who was killed at a railway crossing by a train of the defendants, the jury found that the engine bell was not rung on approaching the high-way nor kept ringing until the engine crossed it ; that the deceased did not see the train approaching in time to avoid it ; and that he had no warning of its approach ; and assessed damages at $1,000 :—

Held, that the plaintiff was entitled to judgment upon these findings, notwithstanding that the jury, to a question whether the deceased, if he saw the train approaching, used proper care to avoid it, answered "we don't know."

After the action was at issue an agreement was made between the defen-dants and the plaintiff, the latter an ignorant person and without the advice of her solicitor or other competent advice, and misled by state-ments made on behalf of the defendants, whereunder she received $500 from the defendants and executed a release under seal of the cause of action. She afterwards repudiated the agreement and paid back the $500. At the trial the defendants set up the release :—

Held, upon the evidence, that the release was ineffectual :—

Held, also, that it was not necessary that a separate action should be brought to try the validity of the release.

Emeris v. *Woodward*, 43 Ch. D. 185, distinguished.

Statement.   THIS was an action brought by the plaintiff, Mary E. Johnson, as administratrix of her husband, Jeremiah Johnson, deceased, against the defendants, to recover dam-ages for his death, which she alleged was caused by negli-gence on their part. The deceased was driving along a street in Hamilton on 18th February, 1893, and was killed at a crossing of the defendants by one of their trains. The defendants denied that the accident was caused by any negligence on their part ; they also set up at the trial a release under seal executed by the plaintiff of the cause of action, after the action was at issue. The plaintiff replied that the release was obtained by misrepresen-tation.

The action was tried before ARMOUR, C. J., at the Assizes at Hamilton, on 6th September, 1893. The issues raised by the pleading of the release were tried by the learned Chief Justice without a jury, after the other issues had been disposed of by the jury.

The following questions were submitted to the jury :—

1. Was the bell rung at the distance of eighty rods from the highway, and kept ringing until the engine crossed the highway ? To which they answered " No."

2. Did the collision take place when the team was on the railway track or before it got upon the track ? To which they answered, " Horses on track."

3. Did the deceased see the train approaching before the collision, or did he not see it ? A. " Not in time to avoid it."

4. If he saw the train approaching before the collision, did he use proper care to avoid it ? A. " We don't know."

5. If he did not see the train approaching before the collision, ought he to have done so if he had used proper care ? A. " No, he had no warning."

6. What damages has the plaintiff sustained ? A. " One thousand dollars."

The learned Chief Justice then proceeded to try without a jury the issue as to the release after action. It was shewn that one Stroud, who had known the deceased in his lifetime, and who carried on the business of a hide buyer and cattle shipper, in which capacity he had large dealings with the defendants, went to the plaintiff's house on Saturday 19th August, with Mr. Pope, an agent for the defendants, and proposed and advised that she should settle the action, which she finally agreed to do for $500 and her costs. Her solicitor was away from Hamilton at the time, and was not aware of the settlement until his return several days later, when upon his advice the plaintiff repudiated it, and returned the money, or tendered it back to the defendants by a marked cheque, which they held. The evidence as to what took place between the plaintiff and Stroud and Pope was conflicting. The learned Justice, after hearing the evidence and argument, delivered the following judgment :—

Judgment.
Armour, C.J. November 6, 1893. ARMOUR, C. J. :—

I do not think that the release relied upon by the defendants ought to be allowed to stand in the way of the plaintiff's recovery.

The plaintiff was a coloured woman, and, although literate in the sense of being able to read and write, was ignorant and illiterate and of a low order of intelligence.

The release was obtained behind the back of the solicitor for the plaintiff, and the action was one in the settlement of which such a person as the plaintiff ought to have had for her protection the advice and assistance of her solicitor.

In such a case the circumstances under which a release has been so obtained must be closely examined to see that no unfair advantage has been taken of the person from whom it has been obtained, and it has been held that "no release obtained from the plaintiff after an action has been commenced and counsel employed, in the absence of the plaintiff's counsel, and without his consent or knowledge, should bind the party unless the utmost good faith is shewn on the part of the defendant in obtaining the same ": *Bussian* v. *The Milwaukee, Lake Shore, and Western R. W. Co.*, 56 Wis. 325, 335.

Stroud was, I find, in obtaining the release, acting solely in the interest of the defendants and on their behalf, and was representing to the plaintiff, in obtaining the release, that he had been a friend of her husband and was acting as her friend in procuring the settlement of the case for her.

And the arguments, representations, and persuasions which she swears he made use of to induce her to agree to the settlement, and which I find he did make use of, were thus more effective in inducing her to agree to the settlement, than they would have been had he not represented that he was acting as her friend in procuring the settlement for her.

It was also, as I find, represented to her and she was led

to believe, in order to induce her to agree to the settlement,
that her solicitor had been seen and that he was a consent-
ing party to it.

By the finding of the jury the sum paid for the release
turns out to have been inadequate, but if the release had
been assailed on the ground of inadequacy of consideration alone, I should not have found that, paid when it was
paid, the consideration was inadequate.

Looking at the circumstances under which and the representations upon which the release was obtained, and
having regard to the principles which equity applies to
such transactions so had, I have come to the conclusion
that the release cannot be upheld. Judgment will, therefore, be for the plaintiff for one thousand dollars damages
with full costs of suit.

The defendants moved against this judgment at the
Michaelmas Sittings of the Divisional Court, 1893, and
asked for an order setting aside the findings of the jury
and directing judgment to be entered for the defendants,
upon the ground that there was no evidence to sustain the
findings of the jury; or for a new trial, upon the ground
that the findings were insufficient and were contrary to
the evidence; and for a declaration that, upon the evidence relating to the release, judgment should have been
entered for the defendants, and for judgment accordingly;
or for a new trial on the ground that the issue as to the
release should have been first disposed of, or should have
been the subject of a separate action.

The motion was argued before the Divisional Court
(FALCONBRIDGE and STREET, JJ.,) on 7th December, 1893.

Osler, Q. C., for the defendants, referred, upon the question as to the release, to *Emeris* v. *Woodward*, 43 Ch. D.
185; *Gilbert* v. *Endean*, 9 Ch. D. 259; *Pryer* v. *Gribble*,
L. R. 10 Ch. 534; *Lee* v. *Lancashire, etc., R. W. Co.*, L. R.
6 Ch. 527; *Bellamy* v. *Connolly*, 15 P. R. 87.

Stuart Livingston, for the plaintiff, cited *McAlpine* v. *Carling,* 8 P. R. 171 ; *Bussian* v. *Milwaukee, etc., R. W. Co.,* 56 Wis. 325 ; *Wallace* v. *Small,* Moo. & M. 446 ; *Nicholson* v. *Smith,* 3 Stark. 128.

March 3, 1894. The judgment of the Court was delivered by

STREET, J. :—

I am of opinion that upon the findings of the jury, notwithstanding the indefinite answer to the fourth question, the plaintiff was entitled to have judgment entered in her favour. Negligence has been found on the part of the defendants, and the fact has also been found that the deceased had no warning of the approach of the train, and did not see it in time to avoid it. Upon these findings the plaintiff is entitled to a verdict, unless the deceased was guilty of contributory negligence, and the jury have been unable to find that he was.

As to the foundation in the evidence for the findings themselves, I do not see how we can say that it is insufficient to support them. There was the usual contradictory evidence on the question of the ringing of the engine bell, and the jury, as usual, decided against the railway company. The evidence of the train hands to the effect that the deceased drove into the train and was not run into by it, was met by the fact that the body was found in the cattle guard, where it could hardly have been found had he not been struck by the engine. The answer to the third question is almost self-evident, and is supplemented by the answer to the fifth question, that proper care would not have enabled him to see the train before the collision. The last of these answers is the one most open to the attack made by the defendants. We cannot, however, say that the trial Judge could reasonably have withdrawn the case from the jury upon the point raised by this question, nor can we say that there was not evidence upon which the

jury might come to the conclusion set forth in their
answer.

The same remarks are applicable to the findings of the
learned Chief Justice upon the validity of the release. It
is quite true that a client is not under any absolute inca-
pacity to make a valid settlement of pending litigation
without the aid of his solicitor. But it is undoubtedly the
case that a settlement so made is open to many objections,
and is much more easily set aside, than one made with the
concurrence and knowledge of the solicitor. The parties
were not on equal terms here, for the plaintiff was an
ignorant coloured woman, and the defendants were represented by clever men of business; the plaintiff had no advice
which can be treated as equivalent to that of her own solicitor; her advisers were members or connections of her own
family, with no more knowledge of her chances of success
than she herself possessed. She was, therefore, without
sufficient advice for her protection. In addition to this,
the learned Chief Justice has found upon the evidence
that the candour and openness which should have been
shewn towards her under the circumstances, in order that
the release should be effectual, was wanting, and that statements were made to her by which she was misled. We
are quite unable to say that the view taken by him of the
evidence was wrong; and, adopting that view as the correct one, it is plain the release cannot stand.

I cannot agree in the contention that a separate action
was necessary to try the question of the validity of the
release. *Emeris* v. *Woodward*, 43 Ch. D. 185, was cited in
support of this view. That case certainly decides that it
is not proper to try such a question in a summary way
upon affidavits, and that it should be tried at the hearing
of an action, and it is said that it ought to be a "fresh
action." That is clearly the case where something has been
done under the settlement which renders it impossible to
proceed with the pending action without first getting rid
of the settlement, as, for instance, where it has taken the
shape of an order terminating the pending action. The

Judgment. form of the application to the Court in *Emeris* v. *Wood-*
Street, J. *ward* seems to indicate that such was the case there, or it
may have been that the plaintiff had allowed the time for
taking the next proceeding in the pending action to elapse,
and the Court must have tried the validity of the release
in order to dispose of the question of allowing him to proceed. I can see no reason under our present system for
requiring a new action to be brought to try a question
which the rules of pleading allow of our trying in the
pending action, and I, therefore, hold that this issue might
properly be tried as it here was.

I think that the motion should be dismissed with costs.

E. B. B.

[QUEEN'S BENCH DIVISION.]

FOWELL v. CHOWN.

Patent for Invention—R. S. C. ch. 61, sec. 46—Rights of Prior Manu-
facturer.

Section 46 of the Patent Act, R. S. C. ch. 61, does not authorize one who
has, with the full consent of the patentee, manufactured and sold a
patented article for less than a year before the issue of the patent, to
continue the manufacture after the issue thereof, but merely permits him to use and sell the articles manufactured by him prior
thereto.

THIS was an action tried before FALCONBRIDGE, J., without   Statement.
a jury, at Belleville on the 21st and 22nd November, 1892.

The plaintiff alleged himself to be the patentee of an invention called "Improvements in Milk Coolers and
Aerators" by letters patent of the Dominion of Canada,
dated 3rd March, 1892; alleged an infringement by the
defendant; and claimed an injunction and damages.

The defendant denied the plaintiff's statements; asserted
that he and the plaintiff were in partnership from 9th
July, 1890, to 29th January, 1892; that during that time
the alleged invention was the work of a foreman in the
employ of the firm; that the defendant during the existence of the partnership requested the plaintiff to join
him in an application for a patent, but that he refused, as
he did not consider that either of them was the inventor
or entitled to a patent for it; that the firm had been manufacturing the articles which were the subject of the patent
prior to the dissolution; and that the defendant sold his
entire interest in the business to the plaintiff, who continued the business, including the manufacture of the said
article; he denied any infringement, and said the patent was
illegal, invalid, and void; that the invention was not new
or unknown, but was in common use in Canada at the time
of the granting of the alleged patent; that it was in such
common use in Canada for more than one year before the
granting of the patent; that more than one year before the

granting of the patent other patents had been granted in
Canada and the United States covering the alleged invention.

Joinder of issue.

The facts are stated in the judgment.

After hearing the evidence, the learned Judge on the 4th
May, 1893, delivered judgment in favour of the plaintiff.

The defendant moved during the Easter Sittings of the
Divisional Court in May, 1893, to set aside this judgment
and to enter judgment for the defendant upon the following
amongst other grounds :—

1. That the alleged invention could not form the subject
of a patent, and that no patent could properly issue for it.

2. That the manufacture of articles covered by the said
patent formed a part of the business of the firm of the
plaintiff and defendant, and any interest which the plaintiff had therein was transferred to the defendant upon the
dissolution.

3. That the alleged invention was not new, and was only
a colourable modification of a principle long in use in aera-
ting milk.

4. If patentable, the defendant was entitled to a half
interest in the patent, inasmuch as it was invented (if at
all) by the defendant's foreman.

5. Even if the patent was valid, the defendant was entitled to use it, he having commenced to use it prior to
the issue of the patent with the consent of the plaintiff.

Or for a new trial upon the discovery of further evidence.

The motion was argued before the Divisional Court.
(ARMOUR, C. J., and STREET, J.) on 31st May, 1893, an d
after reserving judgment the Court ordered that the motion
should be adjourned in order that further evidence of certain prior patents and designs might be taken.

This having been done, the motion was again argued before the same Divisional Court during Michaelmas Sittings,
on 6th December, 1893.

Osler, Q. C., and *Clute*, Q. C., for the defendant.

E. G. Porter, for the plaintiff.

March 3, 1894. The judgment of the Court was Judgment.
delivered by Street, J.

STREET, J.:—

The statement of the plaintiff with regard to his alleged
invention is that while he was at the Toronto Exhibition
in the interest of the firm of which he and the defendant
were the only members, in September, 1891, he saw some
aerators there, and the idea occurred to him of getting up
an aerator to be founded upon and to include the cover of
the Empire State Milk Can.   That milk can was the subject of a patent which the defendant owned and which the
firm of Fowell & Chown was selling. That he thereupon
worked out a plan of the present aerator and returned to
Belleville, where he and the defendant lived, on Saturday
19th September, 1891, and mentioned the matter to the
defendant the same evening; that on Monday morning he
laid his design before Hill, the foreman in the firm's work-
shop, and by Monday evening the aerator had been constructed. It further appears that the defendant had gone
on Monday to Montreal to attend a fair there in the interest of the firm, and to exhibit and sell their wares. The
aerator constructed by Hill was sent to the defendant at
Montreal on Monday evening the 21st September, and I
think it is clear that it was sent him with the plaintiff's
consent. It was constructed in part out of the cover used
by the firm for the Empire State Milk Can, the cover being
reversed when used for this purpose. At the Montreal
fair the defendant sold the aerator which had been sent
to him to one Joel Gerrard, a man who kept a stove and
tin store in Waterloo.   The defendant says that with the
aerator he received a letter from the plaintiff, and that
upon his return he charged the sale on the firm's books,
which were produced, and which shewed the following
entry under date 26th September, 1891 : "Joel Gerrard,
Waterloo—terms 3 months. One 20 gallon Empire State
Can, $3.75, and one aerator, 75c."

Then the plaintiff attended a fair at Napanee on 1st October, 1891, on behalf of the firm, and while there on behalf of the firm sold to M. S. Madden, Napanee, one 40 gallon can for $6.50, and one aerator for $1.25, the aerator so sold being precisely the same article as that for which the plaintiff afterwards obtained his patent. Upon the plaintiff's return from Napanee he made the charge to Mr. Madden in the books of the firm. The plaintiff than proposed to the defendant that they should obtain a patent for the aerator, but the defendant refused, upon the ground, he says, that it was unneccessary to do so, as they already controlled the patent for the milk can, of which the cover formed a part of the alleged invention. On 3rd October the firm sold a third milk can and aerator to one John Lucas. The firm then proceeded to manufacture and sell the aerators to a number of persons with the plaintiff's knowledge and consent, and to manufacture them in considerable quantities. The dissolution took place on 25th January, 1892. At that time 21 of the aerators had been sold, and 105 remained in stock for sale, and material had been ordered for the manufacture of some 400 more. The plaintiff had sent in his application for a patent, dated 8th October, 1891 ; this had been withdrawn, and a second application had been sent in on 17th November, 1891. The drawings upon these applications were found to be incorrect, and new drawings were made and sent in with a new application on 29th January, 1892. It was upon this last application that the patent was issued in March, 1892. The agreement for the dissolution of partnership is dated 25th January, 1892 ; it provides, amongst other things that the defendant agrees to purchase all the share and interest of the plaintiff in the mercantile business of Chown, Fowell, & Co., now carried on by the said parties in partnership, for $8,600, and that a bill of sale should be executed by the plaintiff to the defendant, to carry the transfer into effect, and that the plaintiff should not enter into or carry on the stove or tin business at Belleville so long as the defendant is in such business. A bill of sale, dated 29th January, 1892, was executed by the plaintiff transferring to the defendant all his interest in the business theretofore carried on by the parties, together with the plant, book debts, etc., so as to comprise the whole interest of the plaintiff in the said business, stock-in-trade, plant, book debts, etc.; and the defendant agreed to pay all the firm debts. The matter of the right to the aerator appears to have been mentioned at the time of the execution of the agreement on 25th January, 1892, the plaintiff saying he intended to keep it, and that he said so immediately before the execution of the agreement; and the defendant saying that this took place after the execution of the agreement. Under these circumstances, I think the only proper plan will be to interpret the instrument itself, if necessary, as if no conversation at all had taken place with regard to what passed by it.

After the dissolution the defendant sold the 105 aerators on hand at the time, and then proceeded to manufacture others, and at the time of the trial he had sold about 370, which were manufactured after the dissolution.

The defendant relies upon the 46th section of the Patent Act, R. S. C. ch. 61, which should be read in connection with the 7th section of the same Act. The material parts of these sections are as follows:—

Section 7—" Any person who has invented any new and useful * * improvement in any * * machine, manufacture or composition of matter, which was not known or used by any other person before his invention thereof, and which has not been in public use or on sale with the consent or allowance of the inventor thereof, for more than one year previously to his application for patent therefor in Canada, may, on a petition * * obtain a patent," etc., etc.

Section 46—" Every person who, before the issuing of a patent, has purchased, constructed or acquired any invention for which a patent is afterwards obtained under this Act, shall have the right of using and vending to others the specific article, machine, manufacture or composition of matter patented and so purchased, constructed or acquired before the issue of the patent therefor, without being liable to the patentee or his legal representatives for so doing : but the patent shall not, as regards other persons, be held invalid by reason of such purchase, construction or acquisition or use of the invention, by the person first aforesaid or by those to whom he has sold the same, unless the same was purchased, constructed, acquired or used, with the consent or allowance of the inventor thereof, for a longer period than one year before the application for a patent therefor— making the invention one which had become public and in public use."

This section is founded upon section 12 of ch. 24, 12 Vic. (Canada), which is taken with very slight and apparently only verbal alterations from section 7 of the American Patent Act of 1839, being chapter 88 of the 3rd Session of the 25th Congress, to be found in the 5th volume of the U. S. Statutes at large, p. 354.

That section was interpreted in *McClurg* v. *Kingsland*, 1 How. S. C. U. S. 202, as putting the person having the prior use of the patented article upon the same footing as if he had a special license from the patentee to use his invention. The subject matter there in question was a process for smelting iron by altering the direction of the gates through which the molten metal was poured into the moulds. The process had been used by the defendants, with the consent of the inventor, for some months before the issue of the patent, and it was held that the statute authorized the continuance of the user by the defendants, notwithstanding the patent. This decision has been commented on in *Pierson* v. *The Eagle Screw Co.*, 3 Story Rep. 402, and in *Brickill* v. *Mayor of New York*, 18 Blatch. 273, as well as by the American text writers : see Walker on Patents, 2nd ed., par. 159 : and it appears to have been considered by Judge Story as a case which should be confined in its authority to the class of cases within which the facts of it bring it.

I have very carefully considered the various sections to
which I have referred in the light thrown upon them by
these American cases, and I find myself unable to bring
myself to the conclusion that the fact of the manufacture
and sale of these aerators by the firm of which the plaintiff and defendant were members, though with the full
consent of the plaintiff, conferred upon the defendant any
further right than that of using and selling to others the aerators which he had made prior to the issue of the patent.   I
think that it did not give him the right to continue the
manufacture of the aerators after the issue of the patent,
because the rights given by this section are rights which
are saved to the prior manufacturer out of the general prohibition contained in the remaining sections of the Act
against any dealing with the subject of a patent, and only
those rights should be taken to be saved which are expressed.   I do not find in the section any saving of a right
to continue the construction of a patented article ; but only
a right to continue to use and vend articles which have
been constructed ; and I do find the right to "use and
vend" after the issue of the patent brought out in sharp
contrast with the fact that the article which is to be used
and sold has been "constructed" before the issue of the
patent.

There are, no doubt, difficulties in the way of this construction, but, in my opinion, they are much more easily
overcome than those which beset the larger one.   I think
the construction to which I have inclined is perhaps helped
by a comparison of the language of the section now in
question with that used in section 8 of the same Act, by
virtue of which a person who has commenced in Canada
the manufacture of an article patented in another country,
after such patent and before the issue of a patent for it in
Canada, is expressly authorized to continue to *manufacture and sell* the article, notwithstanding the issue of the
patent in Canada.   The defendant's claim to a right to
continue the manufacture of these aerators after the
patent, has, therefore, in my opinion, no foundation under
section 46.

Judgment.
Street, J.

[The remainder of the judgment, dealing with the merits of the invention, is not reported, as it is not of importance except to the parties. The Court held that the plaintiff's aerator was a mere aggregation, as distinguished from a patentable combination, of old elements, and that the action could not be sustained.]

E. B. B.

[QUEEN'S BENCH DIVISION.]

SANGSTER ET AL. v. THE T. EATON CO. (LIMITED).

Negligence—Injury to Buyer in Shop—Invitation—Child of Tender Years —Accident—Active Interference—Contributory Negligence.

A woman went with her child two and a-half years old to the defendants' shop to buy clothing for both. While there a mirror fixed to the wall, and in front of which the child was, fell and injured him :—

Held, that it was a question for the jury whether the mirror fell without any active interference on the child's part; if so, that in itself was evidence of negligence ; but if not, the question for the jury would be whether the defendants were negligent in having the mirror so insecurely placed that it could be overturned by a child ; and if that question were answered in the affirmative, the child, having come upon the defendants' premises by their invitation and for their benefit, would not be debarred from recovering by reason of his having directly brought the injury upon himself.

Hughes v. *Macfie,* 2 H. & C. 744; *Mangan* v. *Atherton,* 4 H. & C. 388; and *Bailey* v. *Neal,* 5 Times L. R. 20, commented on and distinguished.

Semble, that the doctrine of contributory negligence is not applicable to a child of tender years.

Gardner v. *Grace,* 1 F. & F. 359, approved of.

Semble, also, that if the mother was not taking reasonably proper care of the child at the time of the accident, her negligence in this respect would not prevent the recovery by the child.

Statement.

THE plaintiff Arthur Sangster, an infant, by Frances Sangster, his mother and next friend, alleged that the defendants were an incorporated company carrying on business in the city of Toronto as general storekeepers, and held themselves out to do business as such with the public, and invited public patronage in the purchasing and sale of their goods. That the plaintiff Arthur Sangster

on or about the 18th March, 1892, in company with his
mother, attended at the place of business of the defendants to make some purchases, and while lawfully
there and during the time his mother was purchasing
or fitting on a jacket, a large plate glass mirror, which was
wrongfully, negligently, and carelessly placed and left by
the defendants in a dangerous and insecure position, fell
on the plaintiff Arthur Sangster, crushing him to the
floor and pinning him there with the corner or edge of the
said mirror across his hand.   That by reason of the
wrongful and negligent acts aforesaid of the defendants,
and in consequence of the said mirror falling on the said
plaintiff, his hand was greatly crushed and injured, from
which phlebitis ensued, and the plaintiff suffered constant
and intense pain and had been permanently injured, to
his great loss. That by reason of the negligence of the
defendants and of the happening of the injury to the said
Arthur Sangster, the plaintiff Frances Sangster had been
put to much trouble, loss, and expense in and about the
care of the said child and had incurred large doctors' bills
for medical attendance. And the plaintiffs claimed $2,000.

The defendants denied all charges of negligence made in
the statement of claim, and alleged that the accident,
if any, of which the plaintiffs complained, was due to the
carelessness or negligence of the plaintiffs, or one of them,
or carelessness or negligence imputable to them, or one of
them.   They further alleged that the negligence of the
plaintiffs, or one of them, so contributed to the happening
of the said accident, if any, that but for such negligence
the accident would not have happened.   And. the defendants submitted, as to the claim of the female plaintiff,
that the statement of claim disclosed no cause of action
against the defendants, and they claimed the same benefit
from this objection as if they had demurred to the statement of claim.

Issue.

The action was tried before STREET, J., and a jury, at
the Autumn Sittings, 1893, of this Court in Toronto.

It appeared from the evidence of the plaintiff, the mother of the injured child, who was about two and a-half years old, that she, taking him with her, went into the place of business of the defendants on the day mentioned for the purpose of purchasing clothing for herself and the child. She was fitting on a coat in front of a swinging mirror standing on the floor about four feet from the wall in the coat department, where there were also another mirror standing against the wall about three feet from her. She had been about twenty minutes in the place and had kept the child close to her. She saw him looking in the mirror against the wall about a foot from it and laughing. Turning to come towards her and taking a step or two forward the mirror fell on him. She did not see him touch or interfere with the mirror in any way.

The trial Judge held that no negligence was shewn and that there was no evidence of it to go to the jury, and dismissed the action with costs.

At the Michaelmas Sittings of the Divisional Court, 1893, the plaintiffs moved to set aside the judgment and for a new trial, upon the following grounds: (1) That the trial Judge erred in his decision; (2) That the judgment was premature and not sustained by facts and contrary to law, and the Judge improperly non-suited the plaintiffs; (3) That there was evidence to go to the jury.

The motion was argued before ARMOUR, C. J., and FALCONBRIDGE, J., on the 7th December, 1893.

Pedley, for the plaintiffs, referred to *Hasson* v. *Wood,* 22 O. R. 66; *Crawford* v. *Upper,* 16 A. R. 440; *Byrne* v. *Boadle,* 2 H. & C. 722; *Hughes* v. *Macfie, ib.* 744; *Lynch* v. *Nurdin,* 1 Q. B. 29.

Shepley, Q. C., for the defendants, cited Beven on Negligence, p. 41 *et seq.*; *Mangan* v. *Atterton,* L. R. 1 Ex. 239; *Waite* v. *North-Eastern R. W. Co.,* E. B. & E. 719; *Burchell* v. *Hickisson,* 50 L. J. Q. B. 101; *Carroll* v. *Freeman,* 23 O. R. 283; *Briggs* v. *Oliver,* 4 H. & C. 403; *Scott* v. *London and St. Katherine Docks Co.,* 3 H. & C. 596; *Smith* v. *Great Eastern R. W. Co.,* L. R. 2 C. P. 4.

March 3, 1894. The judgment of the Court was
delivered by

ARMOUR, C. J. :—

This case ought not, in my opinion, to have been withdrawn from the jury, for there were questions arising upon the evidence which must have been submitted to them.

The mother and child were both in the defendants' store, by the invitation of the defendants, for the purpose of purchasing garments suitable for each, and were so there for the benefit of the defendants.

"The class to which the customer belongs includes persons who go not as mere volunteers, or licensees, or guests, or servants, or persons whose employment is such that danger may be considered as bargained for, but who go upon business which concerns the occupier, and upon his invitation, express or implied. And, with respect to such a visitor at least, we consider it settled law, that he, using reasonable care on his part for his own safety, is entitled to expect that the occupier shall on his part use reasonable care to prevent damage from unusual danger, which he knows or ought to know; and that, where there is evidence of neglect, the question whether such reasonable care has been taken, by notice, lighting, guarding, or otherwise, and whether there was contributory negligence in the sufferer, must be determined by a jury as matter of fact:" *Indermaur* v. *Dames*, L. R. 1 C. P. 274; L. R. 2 C. P. 311.

It became, therefore, a question to be determined by the jury whether the mirror fell without any active interference with it on the child's part or not.

If it fell without any active interference on the child's part, that would afford evidence to go to the jury of negligence on the part of the defendants in having it so placed that it would so fall, for its so falling is more consistent with there being negligence than not, and, being entirely under the control of the defendants and their servants,

Judgment. if there was negligence, it was their negligence : *Scott* v.
Armour, C.J. *London and St. Katherine Docks Co.*, 3 H. & C. 596 ;
Briggs v. *Oliver*, 4 H. & C. 403 ; *Crisp* v. *Thomas*, 62 L.
T. N. S. 810 ; 63 L. T. N. S. 576 ; Smith on Negligence,
p. 246 and notes.

If it fell by reason of any active interference with it by
the child, the question for the jury would be whether the
child having been brought into proximity with the mirror
by the invitation of the defendants, and the mirror being
an object likely to attract the attention of a child and to
cause it to indulge its childish instinct by meddling with
it, the defendants were guilty of negligence in having the
mirror so insecurely placed that it could be overturned by
a child of such tender years.

If such a question was answered in the affirmative, I do
not think the child would be debarred from recovering by
reason of its having by its active interference with the
mirror brought the injury upon itself : *Lynch* v. *Nurdin*,
1 Q. B. 29 ; *Jewson* v. *Gatti*, 2 Times L. R. 381 and 441 ;
Birge v. *Gardner*, 19 Conn. 506 ; *Keffe* v. *Milwaukee
and St. Paul R. W. Co.*, 21 Minn. 207 ; *Schmidt* v. *Kansas
Distilling Co.*, 90 Mo. 284 ; *Lay* v. *Midland R. W. Co.*,
34 L. T. N. S. 30.

The cases of *Hughes* v. *Macfie*, 2 H. & C. 744 ; *Mangan*
v. *Atterton*, 4 H. & C. 388 ; and *Bailey* v. *Neal*, 5 Times L.
R. 20, are quite distinguishable from the case in judgment,
for in them there was no invitation, and the last one was
decided on the ground that the defendant was guilty of
no negligence.

The two former cases were commented on in *Clark* v.
Chambers, 3 Q. B. D. 327, and are said by some text
writers to be of doubtful authority : Pollock on
Torts, 3rd ed., p. 419, note *h* ; Beven on Negligence, p. 146 ; Shearman & Redfield on Negligence,
sec. 73 ; where it is said : " It was held in some English
cases, that if a child's own act directly brings the injury
upon him, while the negligence of the defendant is only
such as exposes the child to the possibility of injury, the

latter cannot recover damages. But these decisions have
been condemned in England, and are directly opposed to
the current of American cases."

The doctrine of contributory negligence is said not to
be applicable to a child of tender years: *Gardner* v. *Grace*,
1 F. & F. 359.

It may be prudent, however, in the present case, to avoid
further difficulty, to submit the question to the jury,
whether the mother was taking reasonably proper care of
the child at the time the accident occurred, although in
my view the negligence of the mother in this respect
would not, under the circumstances of this case, prevent
the recovery by the child: *Mills* v. *Armstrong*, 13 App.
Cas. 1 ; *Martin* v. *Ward*, 14 Ct. of Sess. Cas., 4th series, 814 ;
Cosgrove v. *Ogden*, 10 Am. Rep. 361; Pollock on Torts,
3rd ed., p. 418.

In my opinion, therefore, there must be a new trial, and
the costs of the last trial and of this motion will be costs
in the cause on the High Court scale to the plaintiffs in
any event of the suit.

E. B. B.

[QUEEN'S BENCH DIVISION.]

ROGERS ET AL. V. DEVITT.

Sale of Goods—Contract—Payment of Price—Property—Possession—
Trespass—Trover—Amendment—Account.

The defendant agreed to get out wood for the mortgagors of the plaintiffs,
whose mortgage covered certain wood then piled, as also future acquired
wood brought on the premises, and to place it upon the premises at a
specified price, and the mortgagors agreed to pay part of the price as
the wood was got out, and the balance in cash upon and according to
a measurement to be made by them. Subsequent to the date of the
mortgage, wood was got out, placed on the premises, and measured in
the presence of all parties, and the quantity agreed upon, and marked
with plaintiffs' mark :—

Held, that the property in the wood became at once vested in the mortgagors, and through them in the plaintiffs ; but such vesting did not
transfer the right of possession without payment of the price ; and, therefore, the plaintiffs could not maintain trespass or trover for wood taken
away by the defendant after appropriation and before payment of the
full price ; but were entitled, upon amendment of the pleadings, to a
declaration of their right to the property, and to possession upon payment of the amount due, and to an account of the wood not received by
them.

Statement.

THE plaintiffs by their statement of claim alleged that
in the month of May, 1893, they were mortgagees in possession of a large quantity of hard wood piled along
Orr Lake tramway and Medonte tramway of the Grand
Trunk Railway, in the county of Simcoe, under a mortgage made and executed in their favour by A. & R.
Fleming, who were the owners of the wood. That in the
months of June and July in that year the defendant
wrongfully seized and took possession of 455 cords of
the said wood, and wrongfully converted the same to
his own use. And the plaintiffs claimed to recover
from the defendant the sum of $1,305, the value of the
wood, and their costs of suit.

The defendant denied the plaintiffs' allegations, and
alleged that if, in fact, the plaintiffs held a chattel mortgage
on any wood since sold by the defendant, the said mortgage
was not made by or with the consent or authority of the
defendant, and that the wood belonged to the defendant
and not to A. & R. Fleming.

Issue.

The action was tried at the Autumn Sittings of this Court, 1893, in Toronto, by STREET, J., without a jury.

It appeared from the evidence that on the 11th August, 1892, A. & R. Fleming made a mortgage to the plaintiffs of the goods and chattels in the schedule A thereunto annexed described (which schedule described wood piled " on tramway between Orr Lake and Grand Trunk Railway," and wood piled "on the Medonte tramway on the Midland Division of the Grand Trunk Railway, near Coldwater") and also of all other hard wood, cord wood, and slabs which should or might thereafter be brought upon the said premises by the said mortgagors or either of them in lieu of, in addition to, or in substitution for the cord wood, hard wood, and slabs described in the said schedule.

On the 5th December, 1892, the defendant agreed in writing to take out and deliver to A. & R. Fleming one thousand cords, or as much more as he might cut or get cut that season, of beech and hard maple, all body wood, at the price of two dollars per cord * * to be delivered on the Medonte tramway * * the wood was to be piled close to railroad and convenient to load on cars. Fifty per cent. was to be paid over every month on all wood that he might get cut during each month, and the final measurement was to be made not later than the 15th day of April, 1893, by A. & R. Fleming, or their agent, and then settled for in cash according to their measurement, and it was agreed and understood that he was to have the loading of the wood on cars at twenty cents per cord, and he was to load the wood as requested by A. & R. Fleming, and as they directed it.

There was a similar agreement in writing made by the defendant for the delivery of five hundred cords at the Orr Lake tramway upon the same terms.

The defendant, in pursuance of these agreements, took out and delivered at the respective places mentioned in the contract, and piled it as required by the said agreements, a quantity of wood of the quality therein mentioned, and on the 14th day of April, 1893, the agent of the plaintiffs,

the agent of A. & R. Fleming, and the defendant went to
the Medonte tramway, and the wood there was measured
and found to be 798 cords, and was then marked with the
letter R, the plaintiffs' mark ; they then went to the Orr
Lake tramway, and the wood there was measured and
found to be 375 cords, and was also marked with the
letter R, the plaintiffs' mark.

On that occasion the agent of A. & R. Fleming and the
defendant agreed that they should call the wood at the
Medonte tramway 800 cords, and the wood at the Orr
Lake tramway 370 cords.

On the following day, the 15th day of April, 1893, the
defendant wrote the following letter to A. & R. Fleming:
" We have measured up on the Midland yesterday 800
cords, and 370 at Orr Lake, 1170 cords of hard wood in all.
I had about 300 cords of soft wood and 50 of hard wood
at Orr Lake, but had not time to go and measure it ; it was
dark ; and I will have 700 cords of hard wood swampt out
in another two weeks ; so you see how bad I need
money ; so please remit the balance as soon as possible ;
if you can't send it all at once, send me a cheque for $200,
that I will get it by Tuesday, and I can do ten days for the
balance, and I will leave it to yourself about the price.   I
have been offered $2.30 for all my hard wood that I have to
track on both roads, or $2.45 loaded by the Toronto Wood
Company ; so I think you can give me $2.30 loaded, and
that is giving you the best of it ; but perhaps you will do
better, so I will leave it to you, hoping I will get your
cheque on Tuesday, and oblige."

A. & R. Fleming assigned on the 9th May, 1893, and
on the 7th or 8th May, just before the assignment, the
following instrument ante-dated the 22nd day of April,
1893, was drawn up and signed by them and given to the
defendant :

" Received from T. Devitt, to the amount of twenty-
three hundred and ninety-five dollars in wood, and a
balance of seventy-five dollars on old account ; this
leaves a balance due T. Devitt of ten hundred and ten

dollars, which it is agreed and understood that he is to hold the wood measured by us for, until it is paid for."

Subsequently the plaintiffs, finding that the defendant had taken away portions of the wood measured and marked as above mentioned, brought this action.

The trial Judge was of the opinion that the property in the wood so measured and marked never became vested in the plaintiffs, and he dismissed the action with costs.

At the Michaelmas Sittings of the Divisional Court, 1893, the plaintiffs moved to set aside this judgment and to enter judgment for them for the value of the wood in question as disclosed by the evidence, or, in the alternative, for such value after deducting therefrom any moneys due the defendant in respect of the price thereof, with a reference to ascertain the amount so due, and for costs, including the costs of this motion, on the following among other grounds : (1) the judgment was against law and evidence ; (2) upon the evidence it was established that the property in the wood in question, prior to or contemporaneously with the delivery thereof to the plaintiffs by A. & R. Fleming, passed from the defendant to A. & R. Fleming under the contract between them ; (3) the evidence shewed that, with the knowledge and consent and in the presence of the defendant, delivery of the wood was made by A. & R. Fleming to the plaintiffs without any objection or claim by the defendant, and the defendant could not now, as against the plaintiffs, assert any claim to the property in the wood ; (4) in any case the defendant was not in a position to claim any higher rights against the plaintiffs in respect of the wood than an unpaid vendor, and ought to have been ordered to account for the value of the wood, less what was due him thereon.

The motion was argued on the 29th November, 1893, before ARMOUR, C. J., and FALCONBRIDGE, J.

Shepley, Q. C., for the plaintiffs. The trial Judge, I submit, was wrong in holding that the property did not pass. The property passed, even though the defendant had a lien on the wood for the price. The plaintiffs are at least entitled to the surplus after satisfying the lien, and to a reference to ascertain the amount due, and to their costs. I refer to Blackburn on Sales, 2nd ed., pp. 128, 141, 142; *Sweeting* v. *Turner*, L. R. 7 Q. B. 310; *Simmons* v. *Swift*, 5 B. & C. 857; *Cooper* v. *Willomatt*, 1 C. B. 672; *Wilmshurst* v. *Bowker*, 5 Bing. N. C. 541; 2 M. & G. 792; 7 M. & G. 882; *Key* v. *Cotesworth*, 7 Ex. 595; *Godts* v. *Rose*, 17 C. B. 229; *Mirabita* v. *Imperial Ottoman Bank*, 3 Ex. D. 164; *Shepherd* v. *Harrison*, L. R. 4 Q. B. 196; L. R. 5 H. L. 116; *Mersey Co.* v. *Naylor*, 9 Q. B. D. 648; 9 App. Cas. 434; *Kelsey* v. *Rogers*, 32 C. P. 624; *Corby* v. *Williams*, 7 S. C. R. 470; *Smith* v. *Hamilton*, 29 U. C. R. 394; *Bank of Montreal* v. *Mc-Whirter*, 17 C. P. 506.

J. T. Sproul, for the defendant. The property in the wood did not pass to A. & R. Fleming nor to the plaintiffs, though what was done may have put them in possession of the wood. I refer to Benjamin on Sales, 4th Eng. ed., pp. 282-304, 679. The plaintiffs have no *locus standi* at all.

March 3, 1894. The judgment of the Court was delivered by

ARMOUR, C. J. :—

I think it quite clear upon the evidence that the measuring and marking of the wood and what took place thereat, and the letter of the defendant written the next day, shewed an appropriation, by the assent of both the defendant and of A. & R. Fleming, of the wood so measured and marked to the contracts; and that the property in the wood so measured and marked thereupon became vested in A. & R. Fleming, and, through them, in the plaintiffs by virtue of their chattel mortgage.

But such vesting of the property in the wood so measured and marked did not vest the right of possession in A. & R. Fleming or the plaintiffs without payment of the price, for by the terms of the contract the wood was to be settled for in cash upon and according to the measurement.

"The buyer's right in respect of the price is not a mere lien which he will forfeit if he parts with the possession, but grows out of his original ownership and dominion, and payment or a tender of the price is a condition precedent on the buyer's part, and until he makes such payment or tender he has no right to the possession": *Bloxam* v. *Sanders*, 4 B. &. C. 941, 948.

There was nothing done by the defendant in respect of the measuring and marking of the wood or thereat which could be held to prevent his asserting his right to the possession of the wood until he was paid for it.

The action brought, which is plainly an action of trespass, clearly does not lie against the defendant for taking away the wood, for the plaintiffs had not possession of it, and it is equally clear that trover would not lie, for the plaintiffs had not both the right of property and the right of possession, both of which are necessary to the maintenance of an action of trover.

"The buyer, or those who stand in his place, may still obtain the right of possession if they will pay or tender the price, or they may still act upon their right of property if anything unwarrantable is done to that right. If, for instance, the original vendor sell when he ought not, they may bring a special action against him for the injury they sustain by such wrongful sale, and recover damages to the extent of that injury ; but they can maintain no action in which right of property and right of possession are both requisite, unless they have both those rights : *Gordon* v. *Harper*, 7 T. R. 9. Trover is an action of that description, it requires right of property and right of possession to support it": *Bloxam* v. *Sanders*, 4 B. & C. 941, 949; *Milgate* v. *Kebble*, 3 M. & G. 100;

Judgment.
Armour, C.J. *Donald* v. *Suckling*, L. R. 1 Q. B. 585; *Ex p. Chalmers*, L. R. 8 Ch. 289; *Grice* v. *Richardson*, 3 App. Cas. 319.

In the case of *Wilmshurst* v. *Bowker*, 7 M. & G. 882, referred to on the argument, the property and the possession had both passed to the buyer, and that case is therefore distinguishable from this.

The plaintiffs are therefore not entitled to recover in this action; but the facts are all before us and would warrant the granting of relief to the plaintiffs upon an amendment of their pleadings, and we proceed to treat the case as if the amendment had been made, and grant a decree declaring that on the 14th April, 1893, the plaintiffs became entitled to the property in the wood so measured and marked and to the possession thereof upon the payment of the amount due to the defendant in respect thereof, and directing an inquiry as to such amount, and declaring that the defendant is bound to account to the plaintiffs for so much of the said wood as has not been received by them, and directing an inquiry as to this.

The plaintiffs must pay the costs of the action up to the present time, but further directions and costs will be reserved until after the registrar of this Court, to whom the matter is to be referred, shall have made his report.

E. B. B.

[QUEEN'S BENCH DIVISION.]

ANDERSON v. WILSON.

*Arrest—Trespass to Person—Malicious Prosecution—Information—Utter-
ing Forged Note—Disclosing Offence—Warrant—Jurisdiction of Justice
of the Peace.*

The defendant laid an information charging that the plaintiff " came to
my house and sold me a promissory note for the amount of ninety dollars, purporting to be made against J. M. in favour of T. A., and I find
out the said note to be a forgery." Upon this a warrant was issued
reciting the offence in the same words, and the plaintiff was under it
apprehended and brought before the justice of the peace who issued it,
and by him committed for trial by a warrant reciting the offence in like
terms. The plaintiff was tried for forging and uttering the note, and
was acquitted :—

Held, that the information sufficiently imported that the plaintiff had
uttered the forged note, knowing it to be forged, to give the magistrate
jurisdiction, and therefore the warrant was not void, and an action of
trespass was not maintainable against the defendant, even upon evidence of his interference with the arrest.

Semble, that if the offence were not sufficiently laid in the information to
give the magistrate jurisdiction, and the warrant were void, an action
for malicious prosecution would nevertheless lie.

THIS was an action for malicious prosecution and for Statement.
trespass to the person, tried before MACMAHON, J., with a
jury, at the Autumn Sittings, 1893, of this Court at
Goderich.

It appeared that the plaintiff, whose name was George
Anderson, was the son of a Thomas Anderson who lived
some ten miles from the defendant's residence ; that the
defendant did not know the plaintiff nor his father.

Another Thomas Anderson, who also had a son whose
name was George Anderson, lived some four miles from
the defendant's residence, and with this Thomas Anderson
the defendant was well acquainted, and he also knew two
of this Thomas Anderson's sons, Gordon Anderson and
Ross Anderson, but he did not know his son George
Anderson.

Some time in March, 1891, a man came to the defendant's residence and stated that his name was George
Anderson, and that he was a son of Thomas Anderson, and
that his father wanted to get a note cashed which he held

against one James Mallough.   He produced the note, which was dated 20th January, 1891, and purported to be made by James Mallough, payable six months after date, to Thomas Anderson or bearer, for the sum of ninety dollars with interest at eight per centum per annum, and purporting to be indorsed by Thomas Anderson ; and the defendant, believing him to be George Anderson, the son of the Thomas Anderson with whom he was acquainted, gave him ninety-one dollars for the note.

Some time afterwards the defendant went to see George Anderson, the son of the Thomas Anderson with whom he was acquainted, and found that he was not the man who sold him the note ; he then went to see James Mallough, and found that the note was a forgery.

He next met the plaintiff in company with James Mallough, and, according to James Mallough's evidence, he said, in answer to James Mallough, who asked him if that was the man, that if he was George Anderson he was the man.   It was then arranged that the plaintiff and James Mallough should go the next day to the defendant's house in order that the plaintiff might be seen by a girl named Robertson, who was present, the defendant said, when he cashed the note, and who, the defendant said, would know the man.

They accordingly went the next day to the defendant's house and saw the girl Robertson, who at first said that the plaintiff was the man, but afterwards, being pressed by Mallough and told of the serious nature of the charge, said that she thought that the plaintiff's voice was different, and that he was a taller and a thinner faced man than the man that got the money.

After this, according to the defendant's evidence, he and the girl Robertson went one day to Dungannon, and being in a store there, they saw the plaintiff on the street, and the girl Robertson then said that the plaintiff was the man.

The defendant swore that at and from the time he saw the plaintiff in company with James Mallough and thenceforth he always believed him to be the man that sold him the note.

After the girl Robertson said at Dungannon that the plaintiff was the man, the defendant laid an information before one William Mallough, a justice of the peace, which information was as follows :—

"The information and complaint of William Wilson, of the township of West Wawanosh, in the county of Huron, and Province of Ontario, taken this sixteenth day of May, in the year of our Lord one thousand eight hundred and ninety-one, before the undersigned, one of Her Majesty's justices of the peace in and for the said county of Huron, who saith that some time between the twentieth and the last of March last past, George Anderson, of the village of Dungannon, came to my house and sold me a promissory note for the amount of ninety dollars, purporting to be made against James Mallough, in favour of Thomas Anderson, and I find out the said note to be a forgery."

Upon this information a warrant was issued by the said justice, reciting the offence in the same words as in the information, and was given to one Sproule, a constable, who apprehended the plaintiff thereunder, and brought him before the said justice, and the said justice thereafter issued his warrant of commitment of the plaintiff to the county gaol of the county of Huron, in which warrant was contained the following recital: "Whereas George Anderson was this day charged before me, William Mallough, a justice of the peace in and for the said county of Huron, on the oath of William Wilson, of the township of West Wawanosh, and in said county of Huron, that the said George Anderson sold to the said William Wilson a note, and it turned out to be a forgery."

Upon the plaintiff being committed to the county gaol he was brought before the Judge of the County Court, and, electing to be tried summarily, was tried for forging the said note, and for uttering it knowing it to be forged, and was acquitted, the girl Robertson swearing that he was not the man who sold the note to the defendant.

The Attorney-General refused to grant a fiat for the production of the record, and so the action for malicious prosecution had to be abandoned at the trial; but the plaintiff's counsel took the ground that no offence was charged in the information, and that the warrant was void, and evidence of what took place between the defendant and the constable Sproule, shewing a certain amount of interference on the part of the defendant, was given, which it was contended made the defendant liable as a trespasser for the apprehension of the plaintiff under the void warrant.

The trial Judge left the following questions to the jury, which they answered as follows:—

1. Did Wilson believe when he laid the information that the plaintiff was the man who sold him the note?

No.

2. Had Wilson reasonable grounds for such belief?

No.

4. What did Wilson say or what instructions did he give to Sproule, the constable?

I want him arrested.

5. Was Wilson actuated by any indirect motive in giving the direction he did give to Sproule?

Yes, to get the money for his note.

6. What damages do you say the plaintiff is entitled to?

One hundred dollars.

The learned Judge thereupon entered judgment for the plaintiff upon the causes of action founded upon the trespass to the person, for $100, with County Court costs, with right of set-off to the defendant, and for the defendant on the causes of action founded on malicious prosecution without costs.

At the Michaelmas Sittings of the Divisional Court, 1893, the defendant moved to set aside the findings of the jury and the judgment, and for judgment of non-suit, or for a new trial, upon the following grounds:—(1) There was no evidence proper to be submitted to the jury upon the charge of trespass, and the action should have been dismissed. (2) There was misdirection in that the trial

Judge instructed the jury that the defendant must shew
that he had reasonable and probable cause for setting on
foot the prosecution. (3) The findings of the jury were
contrary to the evidence and the weight of evidence.
(4) There was no evidence of an absence of reasonable
and probable cause, and no evidence of malice or indirect
motive. (5) The damages were grossly excessive and un-
supported by any evidence. (6) The defendant was improperly deprived of his costs of the issues on which he
succeeded without good or any cause.

The motion was argued before ARMOUR, C. J., and
FALCONBRIDGE, J., on the 5th December, 1893.

Garrow, Q. C., for the defendant, referred to *Dixon* v.
Wells, 25 Q. B. D. 249; *Smith* v. *Evans*, 13 C. P. 60;
Regina v. *Hughes*, 4 Q. B. D. 614; *Howard* v. *Gosset*, 10
Q. B. at pp. 387-390; *Grinham* v. *Willey*, 4 H. & N. 496;
Gosden v. *Elphick*, 4 Ex. 445; *Barber* v. *Rollinson*, 1 Cr.
& M. 330; *West* v. *Smallwood*, 3 M. & W. 418; *Stonehouse*
v. *Elliott*, 6 T. R. 315; *Morgan* v. *Hughes*, 2 T. R. 225;
Brown v. *Chapman*, 6 C. B. 365; *Hunt* v. *McArthur*,
24 U. C. R. 254; *Stephens* v. *Stephens*, 24 C. P. 424;
Munroe v. *Abbott*, 39 U. C. R. at p. 86; *Crawford* v.
Beattie, ib. 13.

M. G. Cameron, for the plaintiff. The action as it
went down for trial was for trespass only. The question
of reasonable and probable cause was, therefore, not plead-
able and not in issue. The defendant was clearly guilty
on the evidence of interfering in the arrest of the plaintiff
under the void warrant.

March 3, 1894. The judgment of the Court was delivered by

ARMOUR, C. J. :—

If the defendant had merely laid the information before
the magistrate, and had not interfered with the arrest, it
is quite clear that he would not have been liable to an ac-

Judgment.
Armour, C.J. tion of trespass, although the proceedings might be erroneous or without jurisdiction : *Carratt* v. *Morley*, 1 Q. B. 18.

If an offence was sufficiently laid in the information to
give the magistrate jurisdiction, and the warrant was not
a void warrant, such interference as was here shewn would
not make the defendant liable to an action of trespass, but
the plaintiff's only remedy would be by an action for
malicious prosecution.

If, however, the offence was not sufficiently laid in the
information to give the magistrate jurisdiction, and the
warrant was a void warrant, such interference as was here
shewn might make the defendant liable to an action of
trespass, and in such case the better opinion seems to be
that he might also be liable to an action for malicious prosecution.

In *Hunt* v. *McArthur*, 24 U. C. R. 254, it was held that
an action for malicious prosecution would not lie where
the defendant had laid the information before a justice of
the peace who was not a justice of the peace in the
place where the information was laid, but was a justice of
the peace for the place where the offence was committed.

In *Smith* v. *Evans*, 13 C. P. 60, the charge in the information was that the plaintiff did "abstract from the
table in the house of John Evans a paper, being a valuable
security," and it was ruled at the trial that malicious prosecution would not lie because no offence was charged.

In *Stephens* v. *Stephens*, 24 C. P. 424, the charge in the
information was that the defendant "had good reason to
believe that the death of Frederick Smith Stephens" (the
plaintiff's husband) " was caused by the administration of
some poisonous drug by Jane Stephens, his wife, on or
before the 15th of March last," and it was held that no
offence was charged in the information, and nothing · to
found the magistrate's jurisdiction, and that malicious prosecution would not lie.

The case of *Leigh* v. *Webb*, 3 Esp. 165, seems to have
been taken as a decision to the same effect, but that case
was determined simply upon the ground of variance between the declaration and the proof.

In *Jones* v. *Gwynn*, 10 Mod. 214, the action was for malicious prosecution in causing the plaintiff to be indicted for exercising the trade of a badger without a license, and it was objected that exercising the trade of a badger was not an offence indictable, and if so the action was not maintainable. Parker, Chief Justice, delivering the judgment of the Court, said : " I own my opinion to have been, at first, that where the indictment was neither scandalous, nor sufficient, this action would not lie, but upon further consideration I have changed my mind ; for the imprisonment, the vexation, and the expense, are the same upon a groundless and insufficient indictment as upon a good one * * And as the plaintiff is equally damnified by an insufficient as sufficient indictment, so the malice of the defendant is not at all less because the matter was not indictable ; nay, it is rather an aggravation.'

This case was followed in *Chambers* v. *Robinson*, 2 Str. 691 ; *Wicks* v. *Fentham*, 4 T. R. 247 ; and *Pippet* v. *Hearn*, 5 B. & Ald. 634.

See also, as to such want of jurisdiction as existed in *Hunt* v. *McArthur, Goslin* v. *Wilcock*, 2 Wils. 302.

In *Elsee* v. *Smith*, 2 Chit. 304, Bayley, J., said : " He makes the charge, and he prevails upon the justice to issue his warrant ; and upon that warrant being issued, he has no right to say, ' I am not liable for the consequences, because, true it is that I caused and procured the justice to issue his warrant, but the charge was not sufficient to authorize the justice to do what I required him.' I think that affords him no ground of defence."

See also *Rayson* v. *South London Tramways Co.*, [1893] 2 Q. B. 304, per Lord Esher.

I am of opinion, therefore, that malicious prosecution would lie against the defendant, although the offence was not sufficiently laid in the information to give the magistrate jurisdiction, and the warrant was a void warrant.

I think, however, that an offence was sufficiently laid in the information in this case to give the magistrate juris-

diction, and that the warrant was not a void warrant, and
that therefore the action of trespass is not maintainable.

In *Rex* v. *Ford*, Russell & Ryan C. C. R. 329, a prisoner
had produced a forged bank note; and from his conduct at
the time, which justified a suspicion that he knew it to be
forged, he was apprehended and taken to a constable, and
delivered with the note to the constable; and the charge
to the constable was " because he had a forged note in his
possession." After he had been in custody at the constable's
some hours, the constable was handcuffing him to another
man, when he pulled out a pistol and shot the constable.
The constable was not killed, but the prisoner was indicted
upon the 43 Geo. III. ch. 58, and it was urged on his
behalf that the charge imported no legal offence, for unless
he knew the note to be forged he was no felon, and if the
charge was insufficient the arrest was illegal, and killing
the officer (if that had taken place) would have been only
manslaughter. But the Judges were all of opinion that
this defect in the charge was immaterial; that it was not
necessary for such a charge to contain the same accurate
description of the offence as would be required in an indictment; and that the charge in question must have been
considered as imputing to the prisoner a guilty possession.

This decision was in 1817, and before the passing of the
Act 11 & 12 Vic. ch. 42, which contains the same provision as is contained in our R. S. C. ch. 174, sec. 58, that
" No objection shall be taken or allowed to any information, complaint, summons, or warrant for any defect
therein in substance or in form."

In *Crawford* v. *Beattie*, 39 U. C. R. 13, the charge
against the plaintiff was that he " did obtain by false pretences from complainant the sum of five dollars contrary
to law," and it was held that this " might, without contra-
vening any of the decided cases, by intendment be read
as importing the statutable offence of obtaining money by
false pretences with intent to defraud."

If an information charged a person with being in posses-

sion of goods recently stolen from the complainant, I think
that such an information would sufficiently import that
the person in possession of the goods had stolen·them to
give the magistrate jurisdiction.

In the present case the information charged that the
plaintiff came to the house of the defendant and sold him a
promissory note for the amount of ninety dollars, purporting to be made against James Mallough in favour of
Thomas Anderson, and that he had found out the said
note to be a forgery, and I think that this information
sufficiently imported that the plaintiff had uttered the
forged note knowing it to be forged, to give the magistrate jurisdiction.

The facts stated in the information shewed that a crime
had been committed which the magistrate had jurisdiction
to take cognizance of, and it was, in my opinion, the duty
of the magistrate upon receiving this information to take
action upon it, and I do not think that because the plaintiff was not directly but only inferentially charged with
uttering the forged note knowing it to be forged, that
there was no foundation for the jurisdiction of the magistrate, or that his warrant issued thereon was void.

See *Elsee* v. *Smith*, 2 Chit. 304, per Abbott, C. J.

In my opinion the action should be dismissed with costs.

[QUEEN'S BENCH DIVISION.]

BARNES v. DOMINION GRANGE MUTUAL FIRE INSURANCE ASSOCIATION.

Fire Insurance—Interim Contract—Termination of—Notice—R. S. O. ch. 167, sec. 114, Condition 19.

The plaintiff's testator applied to the defendants in writing for an insurance against loss by fire, and undertook in writing to hold himself liable to pay to the defendants such amounts as might be required, not to exceed $46.50, and signed a promissory note, in favour of the defendants, for $15.25. The defendants' agent gave him a written provisional receipt for his undertaking for $46.50, "being the premium for an insurance," etc.

The receipt contained a condition to the effect that unless the insured received a policy within fifty days, with or without a written notice of cancellation, the insurance and all liability of the defendants should absolutely be determined. No policy was sent within the time limited, nor was any notice of cancellation given within that time, nor until, by letter, two days before a fire occurred on the insured premises :—

Held, that the application, undertaking, note, and receipt constituted a contract of fire insurance within the provisions of R. S. O. ch. 167, which could be terminated only in the manner prescribed by the 19th of the conditions set forth in sec. 114, that is, when by post, by giving seven days' notice, and thus the contract was still subsisting at the time of the fire.

Statement. THIS was an action brought by Benjamin Barnes to recover the amount of loss sustained by the testator by reason of the burning of a building which, as he alleged, was insured by the defendants against fire.   The original plaintiff died *pendente lite*, and the action was revived in the name of his executrix as plaintiff.

Benjamin Barnes applied to an agent of the defendant association to insure his property, and signed an application, the material part whereof was as follows :—

"Application of B. Barnes, of the township of W. Williams, to the Dominion Grange Mutual Fire Insurance Association for insurance against loss or damage by fire or lightning to the amount of $1,500, for four years from the 13th day of January, 1891, on the following property. "

Indorsed on the application, under the heading, " Agents are particularly requested to answer the following ques-

tions," were the following among other questions and the
answers thereto :—

"28. What is the general estimation of the character of
the party to be insured? General estimation none too
good." "31. Are there any other circumstances connected
with danger of fire to the property proposed for insurance?
No other circumstances of danger." "32. Do you recom-
mend this as an unexceptionable risk? I do."

The agent of the defendants thereupon gave to Barnes
the following receipt :

"Provisional receipt No. 16. January 13th, 1891.

Received from B. Barnes, post-office Parkhill, an undertaking for the sum of $46.50, being the premium for an
insurance to the extent of $1,500 dollars on the property
described in his application of this date, numbered 16,
subject, however, to the approval of the board of directors,
who shall have power to cancel this contract at any time
within fifty days from this date by causing a notice to that
effect to be mailed to the applicant at the above post-
office. And it is hereby mutually agreed that unless this
receipt be followed by a policy within the said fifty days
from this date, the contract of insurance shall wholly
cease and determine, and all liability on the part of the
association shall be at an end. The non-receipt by the
applicant of a policy within the time specified is to be
taken, with or without notice, as absolute and incontro-
vertible evidence of the rejection of this contract of
insurance by the said board of directors. In either event
the premium will be returned on application to the local
agent issuing this receipt, less the proportion chargeable
for the time during which the said property was insured."
In the margin of the receipt were written the following words : "Paid per note on above $14.25 ; agent's fee,
$1. January 13th, 1891."

The "undertaking" referred to in the receipt was as
follows :

"Undertaking.

$46.50.   January 13th, 1891,
Policy No. 19960.

I, B. Barnes, being desirous of becoming a member of
the Dominion Grange Mutual Fire Insurance Association for
four years from the date hereof, agree to hold myself liable to
pay to the said association, at such times and in such manner
as the directors thereof may determine, such amounts as
may be required from time to time, not to exceed in any
case forty-six dollars and fifty cents.

B. BARNES."

And in the margin was the following: "Received on
this undertaking by note $15.25.

ANGUS McLEISH, Agent."

And the note was as follows :—

"January 13th, 1891.   No. 19960.

On the first day of May next I promise to pay to the
Dominion Grange Mutual Fire Insurance Association
$15.25 at the head office of the company, Owen Sound,
value received, being for premium on the application for
insurance to the amount of $1,500 this day made.   And
in case this note is not paid at maturity the policy to be
issued to me will become void, although the holder of the
note may proceed to collect the same.   B. BARNES."

And on the margin of the note was the following :—

Premium	$13 95
Policy fees........................	1 30
	$15 25

The fifty days referred to in the receipt expired on the
4th March, 1891, and the receipt was not followed by a
policy within the fifty days, nor was the contract of
insurance cancelled by the board of directors within the
fifty days, nor was any notice of cancellation mailed to
the applicant.

Barnes received a post card, posted at Owen Sound, on
the 17th day of April, 1891, addressed to B. Barnes, Esq.,
Parkhill, Ont., as follows :—

"The Dominion Grange Mutual Fire ⎱ To B. BARNES,
        Insurance Association.   ⎰   Parkhill P.O.

Owen Sound, April 17th, 1891.

DEAR SIR,—Your note given for policy No. 19960, amounting to $15.25, falls due on the first day of May next. Please remit promptly, returning this card with cash or post-office order.

Yours fraternally,

R. J. DOYLE, Manager."

On the 20th April, 1891, Barnes mailed at Parkhill a registered letter, addressed to the secretary of the defendants at Owen Sound, containing $15.25, the sum referred to in the above post card; and as a postscript to the letter he wrote: "I have not received any policy yet. I lost or mislaid your envelope or I should have sent the money before; if not right write back to me. Send this back with policy."

This money was received by the defendants and was carried into their cash book on the 23rd day of April, 1891, as having been received from Barnes.

The following letter was written by R. J. Doyle, the defendants' manager, per S. H., to Barnes, and, although dated on the 18th April, 1891, bore the Owen Sound post mark of the 20th April, 1891, and bore the Parkhill post mark of the 22nd April, 1891: "We return herewith undertaking No. 19960 and your short date note. The board have decided not to receive application. Thanking you for the offer of the risk."

On the 24th April, 1891, the insured property was burned, and on the 27th April Barnes notified the defendants' manager thereof by telegraph.

On the 29th April, 1891, R. J. Doyle, the defendants' manager, per S. H., wrote and posted the following letter to Barnes: "We received your application for insurance, dated the 13th of January last, on the 21st of January, and we wrote on the 3rd of February to our agent, Mr. McLeish, on the subject. The deposit should have been $18 instead of $13.95, and the undertaking should have been $60 instead of $46.50. On the 18th of April this application came before the board and was declined. We mailed you your undertaking and short date note on the 18th inst. We received your money here ou the 23rd inst., and we now return it herewith, viz., $15.25, as we cannot enter it in our books."

On the 9th May, 1891, Barnes returned the money to the defendants in the following letter : " I return you your insurance money, $15.25 (fifteen dollars twenty-five cents), which you dunned me for."

And on the 13th May, 1891, the defendants' manager wrote the following letter to Barnes : " We received to-day $15.25 from you for a note which was returned to you on the 18th of April last. We have no note against you for this amount. We have no insurance in this company in your favour in force since the expiry of your provisional receipt on the 3rd of March last. Your application for insurance was declined by the board, of which you were duly notified. There was no use in your sending this money here, as we have no claim against you."

On the application, which was produced from the defendants' custody, there appeared the following indorsement in pencil writing : " 4-2-'91. Unless agent give satisfactory explanation respecting question 28."

(Signed)   " A.E."

(Signed)   " J.F."

And the following indorsement in pen writing : " Declined 18-4-'91."

" Cancelled and notes returned 18-4-'91."

The action was tried at the Autumn Sittings, 1893, of this Court at London, by FALCONBRIDGE, J., with a jury. The Judge dismissed the action with costs.

At the Hilary Sittings of the Divisional Court, 1894, the plaintiff moved to set aside the judgment upon the grounds : (1) That a case was made out on the part of the plaintiff which should have been submitted to and not withdrawn from the jury. (2) That upon the evidence there was at the time of the fire in question an existing contract of insurance, and that the same had not been de- termined or put an end to. (3) That the statutory conditions applied to the insurance contract in question, and that the trial Judge erred in ruling that the condition provided for the determination of an insurance contract by notice was not applicable to the insurance contract in question. (4) That there was evidence which ought to have been submitted to the jury sufficient to support the plaintiff's reply of an estoppel by reason of the demand of payment of the first payment of the premium and the payment thereof pursuant to such demand, and the retention of the money paid by the testator until after the fire occurred, and that taken in connection with the alleged settlement there was evidence to go to the jury to support the plaintiff's claim, on the ground that the defendants were estopped by their acts and conduct from setting up the rejection of the application for insurance or the putting an end to the contract of insurance.

The motion was argued on the 12th February, 1894, before ARMOUR, C. J., and STREET, J.

W. R. Meredith, Q. C., for the plaintiff. The defendants set up that the effect of the transaction was that at the end of fifty days the insurance terminated. But there was a waiver by the application for the money and the receipt thereof. The defendants are estopped by their letter of the 17th April from setting up that there was then no existing contract. The provision in the interim receipt given by the defendants was in violation of the provisions of the Insurance Act, and the contract could not be terminated except in the manner pointed out by that statute: R. S. O. ch. 167, sec. 2, sub-sec. (6) ; sec. 114, sub-sec. 19. Where the statute deals with the matter, any variation is not binding on the insured. The application and receipt constitute a sufficient contract: *Cockburn* v. *British America Assurance Co.*, 19 O. R. 245. The contract having been entered into, it could not come to an end unless by giving notice and returning a part of the premium, as required by

Argument. the statute. The questions of waiver and estoppel should have been submitted to the jury. I rely on *Hawks* v. *Niagara District Mutual Fire Ins. Co.*, 23 Gr. 139; *Patterson* v. *Royal Ins. Co.*, 14 Gr. 169; *McIntyre* v. *East Williams Mutual Fire Ins. Co.*, 18 O. R. 79. The demand and payment of the premium made a fixed contract for four years, or at the worst, a contract only terminable under the statute.

Aylesworth, Q. C., for the defendants. There was an insurance contract for fifty days only. There was an un-accepted proposal for an insurance for four years. When the fifty-day contract had run its course, there was an end of it. The defendants did not take a premium for the whole term. They took only an undertaking to pay assessments during the term, not to exceed $46.50, and a promissory note for $15, which, for anything that appears, is the premium for the fifty days. The post card was not from the defendants; it was not proved to come from them. But, assuming that it came from them, what does it amount to? It is just a reminder from a clerk that a note is coming due. Even if it were the most formal act of the board of directors, it could amount to no more than if the cash had been paid on the 13th January, and it would still be open to the defendants not to accept the proposal. It is not the case of cancelling a contract; it is determining not to make a contract. They declined the proposal a week before the loss. The distinction between this case and the cases cited by my learned friend is to be found in the terms of the contract. There could be no waiver here. There was nothing to waive; the contract had ended, and could not be rehabilitated by the post card demanding payment of the note. I refer to *Harris* v. *Waterloo Mutual Fire Ins. Co.*, 10 O. R. 718.

Meredith, in reply, referred to Porter on Insurance, 2nd ed., p. 30.

March 3, 1894. The judgment of the Court was de-livered by

ARMOUR, C. J. :—

The application, undertaking, note, and receipt clearly constituted a contract of fire insurance within the provisions of the Ontario Insurance Act, R. S. O. ch. 167.

Looking at the terms of the receipt alone, it might well be argued that in order to put an end to the contract so constituted, there must have been an actual cancellation of the contract by the board of directors within fifty days from the date of the contract; that the omission to send a policy to the insured within fifty days was only an alternative method of giving notice to the insured that an actual cancellation of the contract had been made by the board of directors within the fifty days; that the omission to send the policy to the insured within the fifty days had no effect upon the contract ; and that, notwithstanding such omission, it continued to be in force.

There was, moreover, some evidence that a policy had in fact been issued within the fifty days, although it had not been sent to the insured.

But it is unnecessary to pursue the suggested argument further, for I think it plain that the contract so constituted could only have been terminated in the manner prescribed by condition 19 of the conditions set forth in section 114 of the Ontario Insurance Act, which provides that " the conditions set forth in this section shall, as against the insurers, be deemed to be part of every contract, whether sealed, written or oral, of fire insurance hereafter entered into or renewed or otherwise in force in Ontario."

Condition 19 provides that "the insurance may be terminated by the company by giving notice to that effect, and, if on the cash plan, by tendering therewith a ratable proportion of the premium for the unexpired term, calculated from the termination of the notice : in the case of personal service of the notice five days' notice, excluding Sunday, shall be given. Notice may be given by any company having an agency in Ontario by registered letter

Judgment. addressed to the assured at his last post-office address
Armour, C.J. notified to the company, and where no address notified
then to the post-office of the agency from which application
was received, and when such notice is by letter, then seven
days from the arrival at any post-office in Ontario shall
be deemed good notice. And the policy shall cease after
such tender and notice aforesaid, and the expiration of
five or seven days as the case may be."

The contract was actually cancelled by the defendants
on the 18th day of April, 1891, and the letter of that date
was mailed to Barnes at Owen Sound on the 20th day of
April, 1891, was not registered, but arrived at the Parkhill
post-office, which was Barnes' post-office, on the 22nd day of
April, 1891, and the fire occurred on the 24th day of April,
1891.

So that, if the letter of the 18th day of April, 1891, can
be treated as a notice terminating the contract, seven days
from its arrival at the Parkhill post-office had not elapsed
when the fire occurred, nor had seven days elapsed from
the time it was mailed ; and so the contract of insurance was still subsisting at the time of the fire.

In this, view it is unnecessary to deal with the fact that
the defendants sent to Barnes the post card of the 17th
day of April, 1891, that he mailed the money to pay his
note on the 20th day of April, 1891, that they received it
on the 23rd day of April, 1891, and carried it into their
cash book, and did not return it till the 29th day of
April, 1891, after the fire occurred.

*　　　*　　　*　　　*　　　*

There must be a new trial, and, as the defendants insisted upon having the learned Judge's ruling at the close
of the plaintiff's case, and said that they were certainly
prepared to take all responsibility in connection with it if
he ruled in their favour, they must pay the costs of the
last trial and of this motion immediately after the taxation
thereof.

[A portion of the judgment, dealing with some other
questions, is omitted.]

E. B. B.

[QUEEN'S BENCH DIVISION.]

TRIMBLE v. LANKTREE.

*Statute of Frauds—" Giving of Sheep to Double"—Contract not to be Per-
formed within a Year— Executed Contract.*

The Statute of Frauds does not apply to a contract which has been entirely
 executed on one side within the year from the making so as to prevent
 an action being brought for the non-performance on the other side.
And, therefore, where the plaintiff delivered sheep to the defendant within a year from the making of a verbal contract with the defendant
 under which the latter was to deliver double the number to the
 plaintiff at the expiration of three years :—
Held, that the contract was not within the statute.

THE plaintiff by her statement of claim alleged (2) that *Statement.*
in the year 1888 she delivered to the defendant forty-eight
sheep then owned by her, which he took from her upon a
contract that he would in three years deliver to her
ninety-six sheep, and he was to care for the sheep
delivered by her, and to have the enjoyment and profits
derived from the use thereof for the term; (3) that in
November, 1891, he delivered to her nine sheep on account
of the ninety-six then due, but neglected and refused to
deliver the remaining eighty-seven, which at that date were
worth $5 each ; and she claimed $435.

The defendant denied the delivery of the sheep to him,
and set up that the contract alleged was not in writing,
and was not to be performed within one year, and pleaded
the Statute of Frauds.

Issue.

The action was tried before STREET, J., without a jury,
at Orangeville, in the Autumn of 1893.

At the commencement of the trial the plaintiff applied
to amend the second paragraph of her statement of claim
so as to charge that in the year 1888 the defendant promised and agreed with the plaintiff that, in consideration
of the plaintiff not insisting upon the delivery by him to

Statement. her then of forty-eight sheep, which he was bound under
an agreement made between them in 1885 to deliver
to her in 1888, and extending the time for the performance of the agreement and the delivery of the sheep
for three years from that date, he would in 1891 deliver
to her ninety-six sheep, instead of forty-eight sheep, and
the plaintiff, in consideration of such agreement of the
defendant, did not then insist upon the performance by
the defendant of the former agreement, and extended the
time for the performance thereof by him for three years.

At the close of the evidence, the trial Judge allowed the
amendment.

The evidence was conflicting as to the time when the
first delivery was made.

The trial Judge came to the conclusion that 1881 was the
proper starting point, and that in that year she delivered to
the defendant six sheep, the bargain being that she should
get double the number every three years, and that in 1887
there ought to have been twenty-four sheep, and the defendant admitted that there were eighteen. The learned
Judge was of opinion, upon the authorities, that the agreement, being a verbal one, could not be enforced. But, proceeding upon the defendant's admission that there were
eighteen sheep on his place belonging to the plaintiff, and
deducting the nine which she admitted having received,
and taking the sheep at $5 a piece, he gave judgment for
the plaintiff for $45 and Division Court costs, with a set-
off to the defendant of the difference between Division
Court and High Court costs.

At the Michaelmas Sittings of the Divisional Court,
1893, the plaintiff moved to increase the amount of the
judgment to $435, or such amount as the Court might be of
opinion the plaintiff was entitled to, and giving to the
plaintiff her costs appropriate to the amount of such
increased judgment, and costs of this application, upon the
ground that on the law and the evidence the plaintiff was
entitled to recover from the defendant such increased
amount.

On the 30th November, 1893, the motion was argued Argument. before ARMOUR, C. J., and FALCONBRIDGE, J.

W. L. Walsh, for the plaintiff. The evidence of the plaintiff and her husband established the number of sheep and the time they were delivered to the defendant. The Statute of Frauds does not apply, the plaintiff's part of the agreement having been performed within the year: *Scouler* v. *Haley*, 8 U. C. R. 255; *Christie* v. *Clark*, 27 U. C. R. 21; 16 C. P. 544; *Christie* v. *Dowker*, 10 Gr. 199; *Halleran* v. *Moon*, 28 Gr. 319.

A. A. Hughson, for the defendant. The case is clearly within the statute. We are not dealing with an executed consideration. According to the amendment made at the trial, the time for the performance of the agreement made in 1885 was extended for three years. I refer to Edwards on Bailments, secs. 121, 415; *South Australian Ins. Co.* v. *Rundell*, 6 Moo. P. C. (N. S.) 341; Bullen and Leake's Precedents of Pleadings, 4th ed., part 2, p. 88.

Walsh, in reply, referred to *Clark* v. *McClellan*, 23 O. R. 465.

March 3, 1894. The judgment of the Court was delivered by

ARMOUR, C. J. :—

The " giving of sheep to double," is a very common transaction in this country, the giver getting back in three years double the number of sheep given, and the receiver being entitled to the increase and the wool.

It was strongly insisted upon before us that such a contract was within the Statute of Frauds, as a contract not to be performed within a year, and that no action could be maintained thereon, unless the agreement upon which such action should be brought, or some memorandum or note thereof, should be in writing and signed by the party to be charged therewith, or some other person thereunto by him lawfully authorized.

Judgment.

Armour, C.J.

But the Statute of Frauds does not apply to a contract which has, as in this case, been entirely executed on one side within the year from the making of the contract to prevent an action being brought for the non-performance of the contract on the other side: *Donellan* v. *Read,* 3 B. & Ad. 899; *Souch* v. *Strawbridge,* 2 C. B. 808; *Cherry* v. *Heming,* 4 Ex. 631; *Miles* v. *New Zealand Alford Estate Co.,* 32 Ch. D. 266; *Scouler* v. *Haley,* 8 U. C. R. 255; *Christie* v. *Clark,* 27 U. C. R. 21; 16 C. P. 544; *Christie* v. *Dowker,* 10 Gr. 199; *Halleran* v. *Moon,* 28 Gr. 319.

This is the rule in England, and it has been generally followed in the United States, although not in the State of New York: Browne on Statute of Frauds, sec. 289; *Bartlett* v. *Wheeler,* 44 Barb. 162.

[The remainder of the judgment, dealing with the evidence, is not reported, being of interest only to the parties. The Court took the year 1881 (as found by the trial Judge), as the date of delivery of six sheep to the defendant, and computed that the defendant in 1890 should have had forty-eight sheep, to which the plaintiff was entitled, and deducting the nine delivered, found that there were thirty-nine to be accounted for, which at $5 a piece would be $195, and gave judgment for the plaintiff for that sum with costs on the County Court scale and without set-off.]

E. B. B.

[CHANCERY DIVISION.]

GREENE & SONS COMPANY (LIMITED) V. CASTLEMAN ET AL.

Bills of Sale and Chattel Mortgages—Affidavit of Bona Fides—Incorporated Company—Officer of—Agent—Authority—R. S. O. ch. 125, sec 1.

Where the affidavit of *bona fides* of a chattel mortgage to an incorporated trading company was made by the secretary-treasurer, who was also a shareholder in the company and had an important share in the management of its affairs, there being however a president and vice-president :—
Held, that the affiant was to be regarded not as one of the mortgagees, but as an agent, and, as no written authority to him was registered, as required by R. S. O. ch. 125, sec. 1, the mortgage was invalid as against creditors.
Bank of Toronto v. *McDougall,* 15 C. P. 475, distinguished.
Freehold Loan Co v. *Bank of Commerce,* 44 U. C. R. 284, followed.

THIS was an action brought to restrain the defendant Castleman, the assignee of the defendant McManus for the benefit of creditors, from interfering with certain goods mortgaged to the plaintiffs by a chattel mortgage registered in the proper office in that behalf.   *Statement.*

The sole question in the action was the validity of the chattel mortgage, which was attacked by the defendant Castleman on the ground that it did not comply with section 1 of the Act respecting Mortgages and Sales of Personal Property, R. S. O. ch. 125.

The affidavit of *bona fides* was made by a Mr. Law, who was the secretary and treasurer of the plaintiffs, an incorporated trading company, and who was also a shareholder in the company. No authority in writing from the plaintiffs to Mr. Law was registered or in existence.

The section in question provides that " Every mortgage or conveyance intended to operate as a mortgage of goods and chattels, made in Ontario, which is not accompanied by an immediate delivery, and an actual and continued change of possession of the things mortgaged, or a true copy thereof, shall within five days from the execution thereof be registered as hereinafter provided, together with the affidavit of a witness thereto, of the due execution of such mortgage or conveyance,   * * *   and also with the

Statement. affidavit of the mortgagee or one of several mortgagees, or
of the agent of the mortgagee or mortgagees, if such
agent is aware of all the circumstances connected therewith and is properly authorized in writing to take such
mortgage (in which case a copy of such authority shall be
registered therewith.)"

The plaintiff made a motion for an *interim* injunction,
and, by consent, this was turned into a motion for judgment, and was argued before FERGUSON, J., in Court,
on the 29th March, 1894.

George Kerr, for the plaintiffs.

W. H. P. Clement, for the defendant Castleman.

The arguments of counsel and the cases cited are mentioned in the judgment.

April 28, 1894. FERGUSON, J. :—

This was a motion for an injunction, but, by consent of
counsel, it was changed into a motion for judgment. The
action is in respect of the validity of a chattel mortgage
made by the defendant Samantha McManus in favour of
the plaintiffs ; the objection raised against the validity
of the mortgage as against creditors, etc., being that the
affidavit attached or appended to it, commonly known as
the affidavit of *bona fides*, was made by Mr. Robert Law,
of the city of Montreal, who, it was contended, was only
an agent of the mortgagees ; there having been, as was
admitted, no written authority from the plaintiffs to him
registered with the mortgage, as required by the statute
commonly known as the Chattel Mortgage Act.

It was agreed between counsel that the only point or
question for determination in the case is as to whether or
not Mr. Robert Law, who made the affidavit, was in a
position to make it, within the meaning of the statute,
without having had and registered the written authority.

The Act providing for the registration of such a mortgage requires that there should be the affidavit of the

mortgagee or one of the mortgagees, or of the agent of
the mortgagee or mortgagees, if such agent is aware of all
the circumstances connected therewith, and is properly
authorized in writing to take such mortgage (in which case
such authority shall be registered therewith). There can,
I think, be no doubt that if Mr. Law was an agent only
of the plaintiffs, it was necessary to have and to register
the written authority referred to in the statute. This was
not really disputed. The contention, however, was that
Mr. Law was not a mere agent, but was and is one of the
plaintiffs, one of the mortgagees, and that no such authority was, nor was the registration of it, necessary.

The evidence shews that the plaintiffs, the mortgagees,
are a body corporate, carrying on business in Montreal as
wholesale dealers in furs, etc., and that Mr. Law was at
the time of the taking of this mortgage, and still is, the
secretary and treasurer of the company so incorporated;
that he was and is a member of the corporation, and one
of the original corporators; that, as such secretary and
treasurer, he had and has the personal superintendence
and management of the office affairs of the plaintiffs, and
acts for them in all matters connected with the financial
part of their business. It is shewn that he had a personal
knowledge of the plaintiffs' claim against the defendant
in respect of which the mortgage was taken. It is shewn
that there is a president and a vice-president of the company, neither of whom is Mr. Law, who is only secretary and treasurer, holding, however, 250 shares of the
stock.

The contention is that, in these circumstances, Mr. Law
is sufficiently one of the mortgagees to enable him to
make the affidavit as such, under the provisions of the
statute; that he was not an agent, but one of the principals; and that the registration of or having such an authority as above mentioned was not necessary to the validity
of the mortgage as against creditors, etc.

Many extracts from text books relating to the constitution of a corporation aggregate, and the position and

relative attitude of the members thereof in regard to
transacting business of the corporation, were referred to
by counsel, all of which I have taken occasion to peruse,
without, as it appears to me, having practically gained
much light in respect of that which I have to decide.

In the case *Bank of Toronto* v. *McDougall*, 15 C. P.
475, it was held (the Chief Justice doubting) that the
president'or other principal officer of a corporation, taking
a chattel mortgage for and in the name of the corporation,
does not act as its agent, but as principal in the exercise of
the corporate powers of the institution ; and that, therefore, the affidavit of *bona fides* was sufficiently made by
such officer without the authority in writing necessary
under the Act in the case of an agent. But, as it seems to
me, there is a clear difference between that case and the
present case.

In the case *Freehold Loan Co.* v. *Bank of Commerce*, 44
U. C. R. 284, the one who made the affidavit was the manager of the loan company, and it was held insufficient.
There Chief Justice Hagarty, in referring to *Bank of
Toronto* v. *McDougall*, said : " I do not see how we can
extend the doctrine there laid down to the case before us.
The manager of this company appears to us to stand in a
very different position from its president. The latter is
one of the corporation, the chief partner, and in a sense its
organ and representative."

The case *Baldwin* v. *Benjamin*, 16 U. C. R. 52, does not,
so far as I can perceive, cast any direct light upon what I
have here to determine. Nor does the case *Hobbs Hard-
ware Co.* v. *Kitchen*, 17 O. R. 363. Nor, so far as I can see
the case *Carlisle* v. *Tait*, 7 A. R. 10. Nor the case *Ross*
v. *Dunn*, 16 A. R. 552.

After a perusal of all the authorities referred to, I have
not changed the view that I entertained at the time of the
argument. I do not see how the doctrine laid down in
Bank of Toronto v. *McDougall* can be extended so as to
reach the present case without saying that in every case
in which a trading corporation takes from any person a

chattel mortgage, the affidavit of *bona fides* may be made
by any holder of stock in the corporation who happens to
be in the employment of the corporation, and is aware of
all the circumstances connected with the transaction, without the written authority or registration of the same ; and
this, I think, I cannot say.

I am quite aware that, as shewn by the evidence, Mr.
Law was largely interested in the plaintiff corporation,
and held an important position in the management of
their affairs and business; but I do not see where to make
the distinction, or where to draw the line, between his
position and that of such a person as the one I allude to
above.

I am of the opinion that the affidavit in question is not
such an affidavit as is required by the statute ; that there
should have been the written authority and a registration
of the same with the mortgage. I must, I think, hold
against the validity of the mortgage as against creditors,
etc., those protected by the statute.

Then, according to the agreement of counsel, the action
will be dismissed; and as to the costs, the usual result.

Action dismissed with costs.

E. B. B.

McLEOD v. WADLAND.

Mortgage—Payment and Discharge of first Mortgage—Ignorance of Subsequent Incumbrance—Right to Priority—Acquiescence.

The plaintiff paid off a first mortgage on certain lands, and procured its discharge, taking a new mortgage to himself for the amount of the advance in ignorance of the fact of the existence of a second mortgage. Shortly afterwards on ascertaining this fact he notified the defendant, the holder, that he would pay it off, and defendant relying thereon, took no steps to enforce his security. Subsequently, on the property becoming depreciated and the mortgagor insolvent, the plaintiff brought an action to have it declared that he was entitled to stand in the position of first mortgagee :—

Held, that the plaintiff by his acts and conduct had precluded himself from asserting such right.

Brown v. *McLean*, 18 O. R. 533, and *Abell* v. *Morrison*, 19 O. R. 669, distinguished.

Statement.   THIS was an action tried at the Spring Assizes, 1893, at Woodstock before ROSE, J., without a jury.

J. S. McKay, for the plaintiff.
Bicknell and George M. McKay for the defendant.

The evidence shewed that one George A. Murray, in November, 1886, gave to Mary Ann Murray, a mortgage on the north-east quarter of lot eight, in the ninth concession in the township of East Zorra, in the county of Oxford, containing fifty acres, to secure the payment of $2,270, payable on the 26th of October, 1891.

On the 12th March, 1887, George A. Murray gave to the defendant Henry Wadland a second mortgage on the same land to secure the repayment of $828, in seven months. Murray also gave to Wadland a chattel mortgage for the same amount on his live stock and implements on his farm as collateral security.

George A. Murray, in order to pay off and discharge the mortgage given by him to Mary Ann Murray, on the 13th of April, 1888, mortgaged said land to the plaintiff, to secure the payment of $2,516 in five years.

The plaintiff paid off and procured a discharge of the mortgage to Mary Ann Murray, which he registered. He made no search in the registry office, and was not at that time aware of the existence of the defendant's mortgage.

This action was commenced on the 6th of May, 1892; and the plaintiff claimed, as against the defendant, to stand in the position and to be entitled to all the rights and priorities of the mortgagee, whose mortgage he had paid off.

The other facts are stated in the judgment of the trial Judge.

April 26th, 1893.   Rose, J. :—

I find as a fact that when the plaintiff paid off the first mortgage, had it discharged and took a fresh mortgage he had no knowledge of the existence of a second mortgage, and had no intention of giving the defendant any priority or advantage. I will assume that the plaintiff could have obtained relief if he had come to the Court as soon as he discovered his mistake which was within about two months after paying off the first mortgage: *Brown* v. *McLean*, 18 O. R. 533; *Abell* v. *Morrison*, 19 O. R. 669.

But I also find that when the plaintiff discovered the existence of the defendant's mortgage he stated that he would pay the defendant the money due to him thereunder and take an assignment of his mortgage, and that the defendant believed that the plaintiff would so act, and relying on such statement took no steps to collect his security until the mortgagor had become insolvent and the land depreciated in value.

I further find that the plaintiff never notified the defendant that he intended to claim priority over the defendant until after such change in the condition of affairs.

The plaintiff had an equity to be relieved from the position in which he had been placed by want of knowledge, but when he slept on such right to come to the Court until the defendant's position was changed, I think an equal equity arose in the defendant's favour, and the equities being equal the defendant was entitled to the benefit of his legal position. It was urged that the defendant must be assumed to have known that the plaintiff had the right to come to the Court for relief and so should not have rested on any assumption that such right would not be acted upon. If so, I must also assume that the plaintiff knew of the existence of such right, and that it might be lost by delay, and further, that if he chose not to assert it the defendant's legal priority would prevail.

The plaintiff seems to me on such assumption to have acquiesced in the defendant retaining the position of priority thus acquired, and by his own delay and laches to have lost any right he had to assert his equity to be subrogated to the first mortgagee's position: " *Vigilantibus non dormientibus equitas subvenit.*"

The defendant must have judgment dismissing the plaintiff's action with costs..

The plaintiff moved a notice to set aside the judgment for the defendant and to enter it for the plaintiff.

In Hilary Sittings, February 12th, 1894, before a Divisional Court composed of GALT, C. J., and MACMAHON, J., *Aylesworth*, Q. C., supported the motion. The intention was to give the plaintiff a first mortgage and nothing has happened to take away his right. The plaintiff comes within the cases *Brown* v. *McLean*, 18 O. R. 533 and *Abell* v. *Morrison*, 19 O. R. 669, unless he is precluded from setting up the equity in his favor by laches. The defendant knew when he took his mortgage that he would be a second mortgagee. He has not been prejudiced by the delay. Nothing has happened which would constitute an election ; and, even if he did elect, there is nothing to prevent him under the circumstances from changing his mind and asserting his rights. There was no such acquiescence here as would bar the plaintiff : *Willmott* v. *Barber*, 15 Ch. D. 96 ; *Hanchett* v. *Briscoe*. 22 Beav. 496 ; *Farrant* v. *Blanchford*, 1 DeG. J. & S. 107.

Kappele, contra. The defendant was in the position of first mortgagee. The legal estate was in him. It was not incumbent on him to do anything. It rested with the plaintiff to take the proper steps and have the position of the parties changed. The plaintiff, instead of doing this, says he is satisfied with his position and intended to pay off the defendant's mortgage, as he considered the property ample to cover both mortgages. Had the plaintiff asserted his right to be first mortgagee, the defendant would have realized on his security when the mortgagor was in a position to have paid him off. It was not until after the position of the parties was changed, namely, when the mortgagor had become insolvent and the property depreciated in value, that the plaintiff attempted to set up his equitable right. There was an election on the plaintiff's part, and having elected he is bound by it. In any event there was such laches on his part as would prevent his now maintaining the action. The cases of *Brown* v. *McLean*, 18 O. R. 533 ; and *Abell* v. *Morrison*, 19 O. R. 669, are distinguishable. There the plaintiffs had the legal estate ; they also employed a professional man to search the title and did everything that a man could do to see that their interests were protected. The plaintiff also could not have compelled an assignment of the prior mortgages; to decide in the plaintiff's favour would have the effect of nullifying the Registry Act. He referred to the articles in the Canadian Law Times, 12 C. L. T. 1 ; *Rogers* v. *Wilson*, 12 P. R. 322 ; *Teevan* v. *Smith*, 20 Ch. D. 724.

Aylesworth, Q. C., in reply. The defendant may be right in his contention that the plaintiff could not have enforced an assignment of the prior mortgage, which he paid off, but the mortgagor could, and the plaintiff could have insisted before he paid over his money that the mortgagor should procure such assignment. The learned Judge has found against the plaintiff's contention based on the Registry Act, and the point has also been disposed of in the cases already referred to of *Brown* v. *McLean* and *Abell* v. *Morrison*. Those cases also were not dependent on the fact of the plaintiff's being the owner of the legal

16—VOL. XXV. O.R.

estate, but were based on the ground that the intention of the plaintiff in paying off the prior mortgage should be carried out, and he be declared first mortgagee.

March 3, 1894. MACMAHON, J.:—

According to the plaintiff's evidence, two months after he had taken the mortgage from Murray, he was informed by John Wadland (defendant's son) of the existence of the Wadland mortgage which John Wadland then wanted him (McLeod) to pay off.

The learned trial Judge found that when the plaintiff discovered the execution of the defendant's mortgage he stated that he would pay defendant the amount due and take an assignment of the mortgage; and that the defendant relying on such statements took no steps to collect his security until the mortgagor had become insolvent and the land depreciated in value. He also finds that the plaintiff never notified the defendant that he intended to claim priority until after such change in the condition of affairs.

The plaintiff said in his evidence that after he found out that the Wadland mortgage was registered prior to his, he was quite satisfied with his security. And John Wadland states that on one occasion, when speaking to the plaintiff as to the value of the mortgaged property, he stated, " my son says there is money enough for both." This farm was valued at that time at $3,500. And George A. Murray who was examined as a witness under commission stated that a year and a-half after he mortgaged to McLeod the farm was worth the amount due on both mortgages.

From John Wadland's evidence it is clear he was led to believe by the plaintiff that he would pay off the Wadland mortgage; and Murray's evidence is to the like effect. Murray said that two and a-half years after giving McLeod the mortgage he (McLeod) could have made the money out of him. Murray left Canada for the United States in September, 1891.

The land was subsequently sold under the Wadland mortgage for $2,100, the plaintiff's son becoming the purchaser; and it was agreed that the amount due to Wadland on his mortgage should be deposited in a bank to abide the result of this action.

There is ample evidence to support the findings of Mr. Justice Rose.

Upon the findings it were needless to discuss the effect of the decisions in *Brown* v. *McLean*, 18 O. R. 533, and *Abell* v. *Morrison*, 19 O. R. 669, upon which counsel for plaintiff relied, as the facts here prevent their having any application to this case. It must be admitted that in one way the case of the plaintiff is much stronger against the defendant than was that of either of the plaintiffs in *Brown* v. *McLean*, or *Abell* v. *Morrison*, as the defendant Wadland when he took his mortgage knew he was to occupy, and intended to occupy the position of second mortgagee. And had the plaintiff immediately on acquiring knowledge of the existence of the defendant's mortgage brought his action asking to be subrogated to the rights of the original mortgagee, Mary Ann Murray, it would have been necessary to consider the cases in 18 and 19 O. R. But the plaintiff was, up to the time that real estate had commenced to decline materially in value, quite satisfied with his position in the registry office as a subsequent incumbrancer to the defendant—he regarding the land as being ample for the satisfaction of his own and the defendant's mortgage; and he was in fact negotiating for payment of the defendant's mortgage as if the defendant were the prior incumbrancer. After such acquiescence the plaintiff is too late in coming to the Court for relief. His acquiescence is such that it would now be a fraud upon the defendant to deprive him of his legal rights acquired under the Registry Act: *Willmott* v. *Barber*, 15 Ch. D., at p. 105, *per* Fry, J. Even where a transaction might have been impeached on the ground of fraud, in order to render it unimpeachable, it is not necessary "that any positive act of confirmation or

Judgment.
___
MacMahon,
J.

release should take place. It is enough if proof can be given of a fixed and unbiassed determination not to impeach the transaction. This may be proved by acts evidencing acquiescence, or by mere lapse of time during which the transaction has been allowed to stand." Kerr on Fraud, 2nd ed., 332.

The motion must be dismissed with costs.

GALT, C. J., concurred.

G. F. H.

[CHANCERY DIVISION.]

COOK v. SHAW ET AL.

Restraint of Trade—Partial Covenant—Limited Time—Reasonableness—Public Policy.

On the purchase of a manufacturing business by the plaintiff from the defendants, the latter entered into a covenant with the plaintiff which was part of the terms of sale, that they would not engage directly or indirectly in the manufacture or sale of "bamboo ware and fancy furniture, either as principal, agent or employee at any place in the Dominion of Canada for the term of ten years from the date hereof. This clause does not prevent" (defendants) "from engaging in the retail business of furniture and bamboo ware selling. It covers wholesale or jobbing business" :—

Held, that as the restraint of trade was partial only, being confined to manufacturing certain articles and to selling them by wholesale or by jobbing and for a limited time, and as there was no evidence on which it could be held to be unreasonable, and the interests of the public were not interfered with, the agreement was not contrary to public policy.

Statement

THIS was an action brought by Thomas G. Cook for an injunction to restrain the defendants, Peter Shaw and S. A. Shaw, from violating the terms of an agreement entered into by them not to manufacture or sell bamboo ware or fancy furniture, and for damages.

The material facts and the covenant of the defendants are set out in the judgment.

The action was tried at the Brockville Assizes on March 12th, 1894, before ROSE, J., and a jury.

Hutchison and *Fisher* for the plaintiff.
W. J. Code, for the defendant.

The following cases were cited : *Wicher* v. *Darling,* 9 O. R. 311 ; *Maxim Nordenfelt, etc., Co.* v. *Nordenfelt,* [1893] 1 Ch. 630 ; *Mills* v. *Dunham,* [1891] 1 Ch. 576 ; *Badische Anilin Und Soda Fabrik* v. *Schott Segner & Co.,* [1892] 3 Ch. 447 ; *Rogers* v. *Maddocks,* [1892] 3 Ch. 346.

March 14, 1894. ROSE, J. :—

The examination of the defendant S. A. Shaw shews that the covenant has been broken, its terms wilfully violated : and an agreement entered into in good faith, as far as the plaintiff was concerned, all parties being of full age and competent understanding, and for a valuable consideration, has been disregarded by the defendants and without any excuse.

To this action claiming damages for such breach and an injunction to restrain further violation of the terms of the agreement, the sole answer set up is that the covenant was invalid as being too wide in its terms, and therefore against public policy.

I approach the construction of the covenant with the opinion that if possible it is the duty of the Court to enforce the contract which the parties have made, and not make a different one for them. See *McLean* v. *Brown,* 15 O. R. at pp. 317, 318, and cases there cited. And also remembering that in addition to the public policy here invoked there is another named by Sir George Jessel as " paramount," viz., that " men of full age and competent understanding shall have the utmost liberty of contracting, and that their contracts when entered into freely and voluntarily shall be held sacred, and shall be enforced by the Courts " : *Printing, etc., Co.* v. *Sampson,* L. R. 19 Eq.

Judgment.
———
Rose, J. 462, at p. 465, and quoted by A. L. Smith, L. J. in *Maxim
Nordenfelt, etc., Co.* v. *Nordenfelt,* [1893] 1 Ch. at p. 674.

The meaning of the covenant was not at first glance
very clear, owing to the manuscript addition made at the
defendants' request. As originally drafted it read as follows: " The said parties of the second part in consideration of the premises, for themselves and each of them, do
hereby covenant and agree with the said T. G. Cook that
the said S. A. Shaw and Peter Shaw, or either of them, will
not engage directly or indirectly in the manufacture or
sale of said bamboo ware and fancy furniture, either as
principal, agent, or employee at any place in the Dominion
of Canada for the term of ten years from the date hereof."
The manuscript addition was as follows: This clause does
not prevent the said parties of the second part from engaging in the retail business of furniture or bamboo ware
selling. It covers wholesale or jobbing business."

At the trial I thought that a fair rendering of the covenant would be that it restrained the defendants from manufacturing for sale by wholesale, or by jobbing, which
latter term was not defined, but which possibly means
something more than selling by retail and less than selling
by wholesale, but left them free to manufacture for themselves, to sell by retail. I, however, on reflection have not
been able to adhere to such view, and think the defendants
covenanted not to manufacture bamboo ware or fancy
furniture at all in Canada for a period of ten years, and
also not to sell by wholesale or do a jobbing business
within the same limits of time and space, leaving them
free to sell such wares or furniture by retail, and to engage
in any other business they thought proper.

Fortunately the whole law on the subject of agreements
in restraint of trade has been reviewed in the case of
Maxim Nordenfelt, etc., Co. v. *Nordenfelt,* above referred
to.

The rule deducible from the cases, and applicable to
that case, is stated by Bowen, L. J., at p. 667: "The
rule as to general restraint of trade ought not, in my

judgment, to apply where a trader or manufacturer finds it necessary, for the advantageous transfer of the good will of a business in which he is so interested, and for the adequate protection of those who buy it, to covenant that he will retire altogether from the trade which is being disposed of, provided always that the covenant is ~~one, the tendency of which is not injurious to the~~ public."

At page 662 the same learned Judge gives a resume of the common law doctrine up to this day, as follows: "General restraints, or in other words, restraints wholly unlimited in area, are not, as a rule permitted by the law, although the rule admits of exceptions. Partial restraints, or in other words, restraints which involve only a limit of places at which, of persons with whom, or of modes in which, the trade is to be carried on, are valid when made for a good consideration, and where they do not extend further than is necessary for the reasonable protection of the covenantee. A limit in time does not, by itself, convert a general restraint into a partial one. 'That which the law does not allow is not to be tolerated because it is to last but a short time only.' In considering, however, the reasonableness of a partial restraint, the time for which it is to be imposed may be a material element to consider." See also Lord Justice Smith's observations as to restriction being unlimited as to space, at p. 672.

In *Gravely* v. *Barnard*, L. R. 18 Eq. 518, it was decided that a legal consideration of any value is sufficient to support a contract in partial restraint of trade, and the Courts will not inquire as to its adequacy. This case was acted upon in *Rousillon* v. *Rousillon*, 14 Ch. D. at p. 359, and followed in *Wicher* v. *Darling*, 9 O. R. at p. 313.

The facts in the present case shew that the defendant S. A. Shaw, was carrying on a manufacturing and wholesale business, making sales to retail dealers in the Provinces of Ontario and Quebec, the Maritime Provinces and British Columbia. And it was this business she sold to the plaintiff. The restraining covenant was as stated by her in her examination for discovery "part of the terms agreed on in the sale."

I must, therefore, assume that the parties contemplated the possibilities of the business being extended to all parts of the Dominion, and the plaintiff did not desire the defendants to compete with him within such area for a limited time, and no doubt the defendant S. A. Shaw, obtained a larger sum of money by reason of the agreement not to compete. The parties thought such limitation as to time and space reasonable, and I have no knowledge that enables me to say it was unreasonable. I cannot say that it was larger and wider than the protection of the plaintiff can possibly require. See cases cited as to this rule in *Wicher* v. *Darling*, 9 O. R. at p. 313. The public cannot possibly suffer. As in the *Nordenfelt case* and some of the cases therein referred to, the manufactory was not to be closed, the public were still to be supplied from it by, as far as I know, just as good or it may be better workmen. Moreover, there were other manufactories in the Dominion from which similar articles might be obtained. Then the defendants are not prevented from working as artisans in the manufacture of furniture generally, but only of bamboo ware and fancy furniture.

One reason why I am not able to construe the covenant as permitting the manufacture of such articles for the purpose of sale by the defendants by retail is that it seems to me that would place the defendants in direct competition with the plaintiff; for if the defendants should carry on a large retail business in any place, selling articles manufactured by themselves, other retail dealers in such place might be less likely to purchase goods from the plaintiff. The defendants, of course, may compete with the plaintiff by setting up a retail store and procuring articles from some other factory; but of this the plaintiff has chosen to run the risk, possibly thinking that he could well compete with any other manufacturer.

If the defendants had agreed not to manufacture but to purchase from the plaintiff all the articles of the kind

named required by them, for the purpose of stocking a
retail store, thus securing for the plaintiff a customer for
the business sold to him, would such a contract be deemed
unreasonable or contrary to public policy ?

The restraint here is partial only, being confined to
manufacturing certain articles and to selling them by
wholesale or by jobbing, and to a limited time, ten years.
It does not deprive the public of any benefit, for the
market will not have its supply limited, and it does not
appear that competition will be in any wise lessened.

As to the defendants being prevented working at their
trade and thus becoming destitute: it was not made to
appear that either of the defendants was an artisan or
a worker at the trade. The defendant S. A. Shaw, was
the wife of her co-defendant, and was merely described as
a manufacturer carrying on business. Her husband was
referred to as the manager of her business. If they are
artisans there is nothing in the covenant to prevent them
obtaining employment with the plaintiff, nor is there anything to prevent them employing their skill in the manufacture of other goods. Certainly there is absolutely no
evidence to enable me to say, that by enforcing the
observance of this agreement, the defendants, or either of
them, will be prevented from working at their trade or be
in danger of becoming destitute. For all that appears, they
may be artisans skilled to carry on some other business,
and employing such skill in hiring and superintending
handy craftsmen or mechanics in the manufacture of the
ware and furniture named in the agreement. To sum up:—

The restraint is in my opinion partial. There is no
evidence on which I can hold it to be unreasonable, nor
can I find that the interests of the public are interfered
with, or that the defendants will be prevented from
working at their trade, and will be in danger of becoming
destitute. Therefore, the agreement is not in my opinion
contrary to public policy. See the *Nordenfelt case*, p.
674.

To adopt the language of Bowen, L. J., at p. 668, I hold

17—VOL. XXV. O R.

that as good faith demands that the defendants should be
bound by their solemn agreement ; and as the public can in
no way be injured by their being held to it, the injunction
must be granted.

If, as a matter of fact, either of the defendants is skilled
in the trade of making such ware or furniture, and has
no other trade, the restriction upon engaging in the service of any manufacturer as an employer is a severe restriction, and if the plaintiff consents the order may except
such service from its restraining effect.   If the plaintiff
desire such restraint to be enforced he may send a statement of his reasons and reference to authorities to the
Registrar after having served a copy on the defendant's
solicitor, who will, of course, be at liberty also to send a
statement in answer.

The plaintiff's counsel said at the trial that the plaintiff
did not wish to interfere with the defendants or either of
them, manufacturing in a small way, for the purpose of
selling by retail in their own shop.   Perhaps the solicitors
may agree upon terms in the order giving the defendants such license.   If the parties cannot agree upon the
terms of the order embodying the result of this, my opinion, they may send to the Registrar the minutes with a
statement of their differences, and I will endeavour to settle
them.

It was agreed that I was to assess the damages.   The
defendant S. A. Shaw, admitted making a profit of ten
per cent. on the sales, amounting in gross to about $500.
It was not stated whether the profit was gross or net.
Taking everything into account I assess the damages at
$30.   The plaintiff must have his costs.

G. A. B.

[CHANCERY DIVISION.]

CHURCH v. LINTON.

*Copyright—Circulars—Forms—" Books and Literary Compositions "—
R. S. C. ch. 62, and Amendment.*

The purely commercial or business character of a composition or compilation does not oust the right to protection of copyright, if time, labour, and experience have been devoted to its production.

The plaintiff, the proprietor of a school for the cure of stammering had obtained copyright for publications consisting of : (1) "Applicant's Blank," a series of questions to be answered by entrants to the school ; (2) "Information for Stammerers," an advertisement circular ; (3) " Entrance Memorandum," an agreement to be signed by entrants, and (4) " Entrance Agreement," similar to No. 3, but more formal :—

Held, that the plaintiff had copyright in the publications and was entitled to an injunction restraining infringement thereof.

Griffin v. *Kingston and Pembroke R. W. Co.*, 17 O. R. at p. 665, dissented from.

THIS was an action brought by Samuel T. Church, Statement. against George W. Linton, for an injunction to restrain the defendant from infringing certain copyright publications and for damages.

It appeared that the plaintiff was the principal and proprietor of a school for the cure of stammering, called " Church's Auto-Voce School," and had obtained copyright for four publications (1) called "Applicant's Blank," " Church's Auto-Voce Method," being a series of printed questions to be answered by the applicant as to the physical condition, particulars of his stammering and articulation, physical peculiarities, inclinations and habits ; (2) "Information for Stammerers," "Church's Auto-Voce Method," being a printed circular for distribution to the public as an advertisement for his school, giving particulars of the object of the training and the system on which applicants were admitted, treated and charged ; (3) " Entrance Memorandum," " Church's Auto Voce-School for the cure of Stammering," being a printed undertaking signed by the applicant to submit to the course, pay the fee, and perform other required conditions during the course, which was also to be signed by two sureties that he would do so; and (4) "Entrance agreement," "Church's Auto-Voce School, for the Cure of Stammering," being a more formal and particular agreement to the same effect as No. 3, also to be signed by the applicant and two sureties.

The defendant had been a pupil of the plaintiff, and after he had completed his course, he started another school with the same object, called Linton's Institute, for the Cure of Stammering, and issued two publications, called (1) "Applicant's Question Sheet; Linton's Institute for the Cure of Stammering; Information for Stammerers," and (2) "Entrance Condition of G. W. Linton's School for the Cure of Stammering," which the plaintiff alleged were infringements of his copyright publications in the following among other particulars:—

PLAINTIFF'S.

(2) The Auto-Voce method is strictly educational in its character, excluding all artifice, trickery, magnetism, hypnotism, faith cures, drugs or surgical operations or appliances, restoring the voice to a natural normal state, and strengthening the physical mental and moral organisms.

This method is not understood by any other than its author, Mr. S. T. Church, Toronto, Canada.

Under the Auto-Voce method, there has been no marked difference with regard to age as to results.

QUESTIONS.

1. Age? 7. Condition of health? 8. Is there any deformity of tongue, jaw or facial muscles? 9. Memory? 10. Occupation? 11. Does applicant use artificial teeth? 13. How far advanced in school studies? 20. Does the jaw drop and become rigid? 30. Is the applicant inclined to avoid society?

DEFENDANT'S.

(1) My method is strictly of an educational character, and excludes all trickery, hypnotism, faith cures, drugs or surgical operations, restores the voice to a natural normal state, and strengthens the mental, physical and moral organisms.

This method is known only by its author, Mr. G. W. Linton, Toronto, Canada.

Under my method, the age of the person does not signify as to the result.

QUESTIONS.

1. Age? 4. Health? 7. Has applicant any deformity of the tongue or jaw? 2. Memory? 5. Occupation? 8. Has applicant any artificial teeth? 21. How far is applicant advanced in education? 19. Does the jaw become rigid? 12. Is the applicant inclined to avoid society?

(3) I,————, agree of my own free will and accord to the following conditions and have subscribed my name thereto.

I bind myself to remain a regular daily student of Church's Auto-Voce school till I have successfully passed the requirements of the *fourth* and *highest grade* in the Auto-Voce course of training.

I promise not to converse with any person or persons, neither in the Auto-Voce school or out of it, regarding the method of training as a whole or any individual case. Neither to communicate the same to any person or persons by writing or otherwise.

(2) I,————, do hereby agree of my own free will and accord to the following conditions and have subscribed my name thereto.

I bind myself to remain a regular student of G. W. Linton's school for the cure of stammering until I have successfully passed the fifth and graduating grade in the course of said school.

I promise that I will at no time, either in the school or out of it, impart or attempt to explain to any person or persons, either by word of mouth, writing or in any other manner whatsoever the method by which I shall be cured, or the methods of instruction of said school.

The defendant, among other defences, denied that he was using the plaintiff's so-called method or system and alleged that he was using one of his own ; denied that the plaintiff was the author of the books and circulars, and that they were such literary or scientific or artistic works as to make them the subject of copyright, and that the plaintiff had any such copyright therefor which was valid.

The action was tried at Toronto on April 16th, 1894, before BOYD, C., without a jury.

Watson, Q. C., and *Bentley*, for the defendant. The papers in question are not within the Copyright Act : R. S. C. ch. 62, sec. 4. They are are not " literary, scientific or artistic works ": *Griffin* v. *Kingston and Pembroke R. W. Co.*, 17 O. R. 660.

George Bell, for the plaintiff. These papers come within the meaning of the word " book," as used in section 4 of the Act, and within the words " Literary * * works or compositions," in section 3. An advertisement with pictures has been held of copyright competence : *Maple & Co.* v. *Junior Army and Navy Stores*, 21 Ch. D. 369, at p. 376.

April 18th, 1894. BOYD, C. :—

The plaintiff has obtained copyright in respect of four productions called (1) " Applicant's Blank," giving a series of questions to be filled up with answers by the applicant for admission to the plaintiff's school ; (2) " Information for Stammerers," intended for circulation as an advertisement ; (3) " Entrance Memorandum," in the form of an agreement to be signed by the entrant ; and (4) " Entrance Agreement," which is like No. 3, but of a more extended character.

Objection is made as to the inherent invalidity of the copyright because the documents are not within the scope of the statute, ch. 62 R. S. C. Sec. 4, as amended by 52 Vic. ch. 29, sec. 1 (D.), applies to the author of any " book " * * considered as " a literary composition."

These sheets of printed matter are, of course, sufficient in form to be protected by the Act : *Griffin* v. *Kingston and Pembroke R. W. Co.*, 17 O. R. at p. 664.

Though these circulars as to their substance would fall within Charles Lamb's catalogue of " books which are no books—*a-biblia*," nevertheless under copyright law comprehensiveness they may be reckoned as books and literary compositions. The circulars distributed by railway companies are now called " literature." It has been held, moreover, that publications which are in the nature of business notices or usable as advertising mediums for distribution gratis or otherwise, may be the subject of copyright : *Grace* v. *Newman*, L. R. 19 Eq. 623, and *Maple & Co.* v. *Junior Army and Navy Stores*, 21 Ch. D. 369.

So one may copyright a book of forms or a series of papers to be filled in by applicants for liquor licenses : *Brightley* v. *Littleton*, 37 Fed. R. 103. In this the Judge said : " The matter must be original and possess some possible utility. The originality, however, may be of the lowest order, and the utility barely perceptible."

I do not go with the limitation suggested in 17 O. R. at p. 665, that the legislation is to be applied, having regard to

literary merit as an ingredient. The purely commercial
or business character of the composition or compilation
does not oust the right to protection if time, labour, and
experience have been devoted to its production. That
this is so in the present case the plaintiff testifies, and that
the papers must be of some merit and utility would seem
to be proved by the defendant's willingness to abstract or
convey various passages in them so as to form parts of his
rival advertisements. The invasion of the plaintiff's rights
as to this part of the case is well proved.

I gave judgment as to the other part of the action against
the plaintiff at the close of the hearing, and as the success
is thus divided, I give no costs.

The injury from the invasion of copyright is too insignificant to ground a reference for damages.

G. A. B.

[CHANCERY DIVISION.]

RE BAIN AND LESLIE.

Will—Devise—Falsa Demonstratio—Deed of Release—Recital—Estoppel— Title to Land—Statute of Limitations.

A testator by 'his will devised to his son G. "the property I may die possessed of in the village of M., also lot 28 in the 10th concession of B." In the early part of the will he had used the words "wishing to dispose of my worldly property." The testator did not own lot 28, and the only land he did own in the 10th concession of B. was a part of lot 29. The will contained no residuary devise.

Upon a petition under the Vendor and Purchaser Act :—

Held, that the part of lot 29 owned by the testator did not pass by the will to the son.

After the death of the testator, all his children executed a deed of release to the executors of his will, containing a recital that the part of lot 29 owned by the testator was devised to the son G., and that he was then in possession :—

Held, that there was no estoppel as among the members of the family, who together constituted one party to the deed :—

Held, however, upon the evidence, that G. had acquired a good title to the lands in question by virtue of the Statute of Limitations.

Statement.   PETITION under the Vendor and Purchaser Act presented to the Court by Helen Bain, the vendor.

Three questions were raised by the petition : (1) Whether the lands in question passed to George Tennant under the will of his father ; (2) Whether a certain recital in a deed of release enabled George Tennant to make title ; (3) If not, whether the petitioner could make title under the Statute of Limitations.

The facts are stated in the judgment.

The petition was argued before FERGUSON, J., in Court, on the 28th March, 1894.

Begue, for the petitioner, referred on the first point to *Summers* v. *Summers,* 5 O. R. 110 ; *Hickey* v. *Stover,* 11 O. R. 106 ; *Doe Lowry* v. *Grant,* 7 U. C. R. 125 ; *Wright* v. *Collings,* 16 O. R. 182.

G. W. Field, for the purchaser, cited, on the same point, *Re Shaver,* 6 O. R. 312 ; *Hickey* v. *Hickey,* 20 O. R. 371.

April 27, 1894. FERGUSON, J. :—

The petition is presented on behalf of Helen Bain, the vendor. She seems to be the assignee of two mortgages, each being upon 86 acres of lot 29 in the 10th concession of the township of Beverley, one bearing date the 9th day of September, 1888, and the other the 23rd day of June, 1889. These mortgages were made by George Tennant, he no doubt supposing that he was devisee of the lands under the provisions of the last will of his father, the late George Tennant, who died on or about the 14th day of March, 1877. In one of these mortgages his younger brother, Robert Tennant, joined as mortgagor. George and Robert were both young men at that time, and the will contains a provision that in case George should die unmarried, the gift to George should go to Robert. The matter was not discussed at the bar, but one may suppose that this was the reason of Robert's executing the mortgage, or one of the reasons. These mortgages were in favour of one John Wier, and appear to have been on the 10th day of January, 1885, assigned by Thomas Bain and John Wier, executors of the estate of the then late John Wier, to the petitioner, who from the documents and the petition appears to be the wife of the said Thomas Bain. There is before me nothing to shew the authority to these executors to assign these mortgages, except the statement that they were the executors of the estate. No discussion took place in regard to this, and I may, as I think, assume that there is no question as to such authority. The petitioner brought an action upon these mortgages, in which the lands were exposed for sale by public auction, but there was no bid equal to the amount fixed by the Master of the Court as a reserved bid. In the same action the lands were subjected to a sale by tender. There was no tender and no sale. But lately William Leslie, in this proceeding called the purchaser, has signed an agreement to purchase the land for the price $1,275, but not being satisfied with the title shewn him, the matter has been brought up on this petition under the Act. I do not at present see why the matter of the title was not dealt with in the action, if the offer made by Leslie had any relation to the proceedings that seem to have been pending. The parties have, however, seen fit to bring the matter up in this way, and I suppose they are entitled to a decision.

It was not disputed that the petitioner has the right to sell the lands if there exists a good title which came to the mortgagor George Tennant.

It was assumed throughout that the testator, the father of the mortgagor, had a good title. This I am not to investigate at all. But there is what is called a mistake in his last will which seems to have given rise to this discussion and trouble.

On the 28th day of July, 1878, and about fifteen months after the death of the testator, the then late George Tennant, all the children—nine in number—and the husband of one of them, executed a deed of release in favour of the executors of the will of the testator, containing a recital which states, amongst many other things, that the lands now in question were devised to George Tennant, the mortgagor, and that he was then in possession of the same. This statement in the recital does not mention the number of the lot, but it does say that the mortgagor was then in possession of the land devised or supposed to have been devised to him.

The questions submitted by the petition are three in number :—

1. Did the mortgaged premises pass by the will of the late George Tennant under the devise to the mortgagor, George Tennant ?

2. Could the mortgagor make title thereunder or by virtue of the same and the recital contained in the deed of release aforesaid, or had he any right thereby to convey the lands to the mortgagee ?

3. If not, can the petitioner, Helen Bain, make a good title under the Statute of Limitations to the purchaser, Leslie ?

The purchaser here seems not to be an unwilling one, and, as I understand, is quite prepared to perform his contract if a good title can be given him.

First, as to the will.   The devise to the mortgagor, George Tennant, is in these words : " *To my son George I give and bequeath the property I may die possessed of in the village of Morriston, township of Puslinch, also lot twenty-eight in the tenth concession of the township of Beverley.*"

In the early part of the will the testator used the words, " *being of sound mind, memory, and understanding, wishing to dispose of my worldly property.*"

The land in question here is 86 acres of lot 29 in the 10th concession of Beverley, land the testator did own ; and he did not, as is shewn, own, nor had he any interest in, lot 28 ; and in the argument it was sought to connect these words in the earlier part of the will with the words of this devise, and, by striking out the words " twenty-eight " as *falsa demonstratio*, make the devise read as a devise of all the lands the testator owned in the 10th concession of Beverley, and then, by shewing by the evidence that this part of lot 29 was all the land that the testator owned in the 10th concession, make it a good devise of the land in question.   No authority was referred to shewing, or, as I think, going to shew, that this could be done, and I am of opinion that it cannot be done.   The words in the early part of the will that I have referred to were manifestly used by the testator not as a description or any part of the description of anything.   They are in no way connected with any description.   They are, or are the equivalent of, words found in very many wills, expressing the intention of the testator to dispose of his property by his will, and, whether these or such words appear in the early part of a will or not, it is beyond question the intention of every or almost every testator to dispose of his worldly property.   I cannot bring myself to think that this expression stands at all in the position of the expression in the will in the case *Doe Lowry* v. *Grant*, 7 U. C. R. 125,

referred to by the Chancellor in *Hickey* v. *Stover*, 11 O. R.
at p. 113, and I am clearly of the opinion that this expression in this will cannot, in the effort to ascertain what the
testator meant by the words he employed in his will, be
pressed into doing the duty that is required of them by
this argument.

It is to be observed that the testator in this expression
did not use the word "all" or any word the equivalent of
it. He simply in the outset said, "*wishing to dispose of
my worldly property.*"

Again, this devise, taking it as not connected with what
immediately precedes it, is plain and unambiguous. As
said by the Chancellor in *Hickey* v. *Stover*, p. 112, the
devise is in its terms free from all ambiguity ; it is not
inherently absurd or insensible, and is not inconsistent
with any context. It would read: "*To my son George I
give also lot twenty-eight in the tenth concession of the
township of Beverley.*" So far the case seems to me in no
better plight than was the case *Summers* v. *Summers*, 5
O. R. 110. The testator apparently owned one lot or a
part of it, and he devised another lot.

It was also contended that one should read with this
devise what immediately precedes it in the will, which is:
"To my son George I give and bequeath the property I
may die possessed of in the village of Morriston, township
of Puslinch, also lot twenty-eight in the tenth concession
of the township of Beverley ;" so as to make the devise in
question in effect read: "To my son George I give and
bequeath the property I may die possessed of in the tenth
concession of Beverley ;" after striking out "lot twenty-
eight" as *falsa demonstratio.* This I cannot at all see my
way to doing. The two gifts are side by side, it is true,
but they are, so far as I can see, separate and distinct from
one another as any two gifts can be. Neither contains
any uncertainty of meaning or ambiguity. The words
sought to be, in effect, introduced into the devise in question have no grammatical relation to it, and cannot, in my
view, be held to have been intended to perform any office

whatever in relation to this gift. I think grammatical
construction forbids it; and if "lot twenty-eight" were
struck out, there would be no sufficient description left to
identify the land for the purposes of the will. Much that
I said as to the other and former argument seems applicable to this contention also; and I am of the opinion that
the lands in question, the part of lot twenty-nine, did not
pass by the will to George Tennant, the mortgagor; and I
do not see that the fact that the will contained no residuary
devise makes the matter anything different.

I have taken occasion to examine the authorities that
were referred to by counsel, and after the best consideration I have been able to bestow on the subject, such is my
conclusion respecting this devise.

Then as to the effect of the recital contained in the deed
of release to the executors. Recitals in deeds bind the
parties thereto and also parties claiming under such deeds:
Elphinstone, p. 140, American note, and cases there cited.
An estoppel is binding upon parties and privies, and it is
now settled that a recital may operate by way of estoppel:
2 Smith's L. C., 8th ed., p. 872 *et seq.* An estoppel is always
in some action or proceeding based upon the deed in which
the fact in question is recited. In a collateral action there
can be no estoppel: see Elphinstone, p. 141, the author
referring to *Carter* v. *Carter*, 3 K. & J. 645 (Wood, V.-C.).
Here no one is claiming under the executors or bringing
any action or proceeding on the deed containing the recital.
All the members of the family who executed this deed may
well be estopped as against the executors or anyone claiming under or through them, and so may all persons claiming through any member or members of the family be so
estopped, that is, so far as the executors or any one claiming through them has concern; but I do not see that there
is an estoppel as between or amongst the members of the
family who together constituted one party to the deed.
I am of the opinion that I expressed at the argument, that
there is not the estoppel contended for by reason of the
recital in the deed of release to the executors. There would

be, I think, stronger ground for contending that there was an estoppel by conduct on the doctrine of *Pickard* v. *Sears*, 6 A. & E. 469, and cases following that one ; but I think that the contention, if it had been made, would have also failed, even if the statement in the recital had been one of certainty to every intent, as a statement must be to afford an estoppel.

Then as to the claim by virtue of the Statute of Limitations. I am of the opinion that the evidence shews that the mortgagor, George Tennant, was in actual, undisturbed, continuous possession and· occupation of the land in question from the month of April, 1878, until the month of December, 1890 ; that his brother, Robert Tennant, became of full age about the commencement of the year 1879 ; that from the time Robert attained majority there was no disability of any one of the eight brothers and sisters of the mortgagor, the disability of Constance having ceased on the.first day of July, 1876, by statute ; that the mortgagor went into and remained in such occupation believing that the 86 acres of land in question had been devised to him by his father's will, and this being so, he must be considered as having been in possession of the whole of the 86 acres, though only a part of it may have been cleared and cultivated. I find upon the evidence that the mortgagor clearly had and enjoyed, adversely to every person and of his own right or supposed right, possession and actual occupation for a period of more than ten years before he gave up the possession and a tenant came in, there being no disability at any time during that period of any of his brothers or sisters ; and I find that the evidence sufficiently repels the idea of any claim having been made or any entry by the brothers or sisters of the mortgagor during that period. Robert may have had his five years after coming of full age to bring his action or make his entry, but he did not do either, and the statutory title thus gained by the mortgagor enured to the benefit of the mortgagee's title and gave him and those claiming under him a good title.

1. The answer to the first question submitted by the Judgment. petition is in the negative. Ferguson, J.

2. The answer to the second question so submitted is also in the negative.

3. The answer to the third question submitted by the petition is in the affirmative.

I do not say anything in regard to the periods of time of possession and occupation shewn after George Tennant ceased to occupy; for, after a good title by possession was acquired by him, such subsequent possession could not make it any better; and, besides, the evidence is not clear as to the taking of possession by the tenant referred to immediately upon George Tennant quitting possession, and so of the next succeeding tenants.

I am of the opinion that a good title by length of possession has been shewn, and that the vendor can convey a good title to the vendee, notwithstanding anything urged against the title.

As to the ability of George Tennant to acquire a title under the operation of the statute, see *Smith* v. *Smith*, 5 O. R. 690, and cases there referred to; see also *Hayes* v. *Coleman*, Cassels' S. C. Digest, p. 833-4, and cases there referred to.

Whatever, if anything, appears in the registry office will have to be looked after. With this I profess to do nothing.

There was only the ten years from the death of the testator to sue for dower.

The order may go to the effect above stated. The parties have made their own agreement as to costs. It has been assumed that George Tennant was not married when he made the mortgages.

Order in favour of the petitioner, the vendor.

E. B. B.

[CHANCERY DIVISION.]

MILLSON ET AL. V. SMALE.

*Infant—Action in Name of, without Next Friend—Motion to Set Aside
Proceedings after Coming of Age—Laches.*

An infant was a part owner of a patent right and engaged in business transactions with respect to it. Along with other part owners he signed a
retainer to solicitors to take proceedings to stop the infringement of
the patent, and the solicitors, not knowing that he was an infant,
brought an action for that purpose, using his name as a plaintiff, without a next friend. The action was prosecuted for a time with the
result that the infringement ceased, but it was subsequently dismissed
with costs against the plaintiffs for want of prosecution. More than a
year after he came of age, he moved to set aside all proceedings in
the action :—

Held, that, under the circumstances mentioned, he was not entitled to
relief on the ground of infancy.

Statement.

MOTION by Frank Wright, one of the plaintiffs, to set
aside the writ of summons and all subsequent proceedings
in the action. The facts are stated in the judgment.

The motion was argued before FERGUSON, J., in Court,
on the 28th March, 1894.

Rowell, for the applicant.

Hoyles, Q. C., for Daniel McAlpine, assignee of the
judgment against the plaintiffs.

Tremeear, for the solicitors on the record for the plaintiffs.

Acres v. *Little,* 7 Sim. 138 ; *Cooke* v. *Fryer,* 4 Beav. 13 ;
Guy v. *Guy,* 2 Beav. 460; Daniell's Ch. Pr., 6th ed., pp.
105, 106 ; Simpson on Infants, 2nd ed., pp. 468, 469, 471,
482 ; *Ex p. Brocklebank,* 6 Ch. D. 358 ; *Lipsett* v. *Perdue,*
18 O. R. 575; *Edwards* v. *Carter,* [1893] A. C. 360 ; *Beames*
v. *Farley,* 5 C. B. 178 ; *Wright* v. *Hunter,* 1 L. J. K. B.
248 ; Cordery on Solicitors, 2nd ed., pp. 57, 58, 107 ; *Macaulay* v. *Neville,* 5 P. R. 235 ; and R. S. O. ch. 123, sec
6, were referred to.

April 26, 1894. FERGUSON, J.:—

This motion, which is made on behalf of a plaintiff, Frank Wright, is for an order that the writ of summons and all proceedings "taken thereunder" be set aside, so far as the plaintiff Frank Wright is concerned; that the order of the Master in Chambers in this action dated the 5th day of December, 1890, be discharged or varied, so far as the same plaintiff is concerned; and that the order of this Court dated the first day of February, 1892, so far as the same affects the plaintiff Frank Wright, or directs that Messrs. Farley & McDonald, or the defendant, shall be entitled to any redress over against the plaintiff Frank Wright, be discharged or varied. The motion also asks that certain writs of execution issued herein, directed to the sheriff of the county of Middlesex, and the seizure and all proceedings had and taken thereunder, be set aside, so far as the same plaintiff is concerned, on certain grounds of irregularity stated in the motion.

As to the writs of execution no argument whatever was held before me, and I see by some of the evidence that certain writs were withdrawn and others issued or were being issued in their stead, from which I arrive at the conclusion that I need not give myself any trouble as to the irregularities stated in respect of those writs, although the fate of the writs is involved in the other part of the motion.

The writs of execution mentioned seem to be for the levying of the amounts of the costs of the defendant given by an order dismissing the action for want of prosecution. The ground taken by this plaintiff, Frank Wright, is that he gave no instructions for the bringing or prosecution of the action, and was not aware that the same was brought or was being prosecuted; and that he was an infant within the age of twenty-one years and was not competent to commence, institute, or prosecute the action.

The motion also asks that the amount for which the writs of execution are indorsed may be reduced, on the ground that the plaintiff Frank Wright, if liable to the present holder of the judgment or order, is liable only for a contribution as one of the co-plaintiffs against whom the order or judgment is—stating, in addition, that such holder is proceeding on behalf of Neil McAlpine, one of the plaintiffs in the action.   In regard to this, I do not see how, upon only the evidence before me, I can order the amount indorsed on the writs to be reduced, and I may add that as to this there was not any argument.

On the evidence it seems very plain that the plaintiff Frank Wright did give instructions for bringing and prosecution of the action and was well aware that the action was brought and prosecuted.

The ground really taken on behalf of this plaintiff, Frank Wright, was that he was an infant when the action was brought, and should not, for this reason, be bound by or held liable under the proceedings. This was the only matter argued before me.

The order of this Court referred to on the motion was made at the instance and on behalf of one Alexander Forbes, who was made a plaintiff without his knowledge or consent. It was an order directing the name of Forbes to be struck out of the proceedings, and indirectly declaring that the judgment or order should stand as a judgment against the plaintiffs other than the said Alexander Forbes. At the time that order was made, it was not known to the Court that this plaintiff was an infant at the commencement of the action.

After a perusal of all that was brought before me on this motion, I am of the opinion, that all that I have really to determine is, what is the position of this plaintiff, Frank Wright, as to liability, and what, if any, relief he is entitled to by reason of his having been an infant under the age of twenty-one years at the commencement of the action.

It is to be remarked that before this action this plaintiff, Frank Wright, was part owner of a patent right respecting some sort of patent fence; that he was in partner-

ship with one of his brothers in respect of this; that
after the commencement of the action, and while he was,
as he says, still an infant, he was making transactions, if
not in respect to other property, in respect of shares in
this patent; and from all that appears, I am not at all con-
vinced that he was, at the commencement of the action
or during the proceedings, that innocent being that he and
some of those who make affidavits on his behalf now
propose to paint or represent him as having been.

There appear to have been several part owners of this
patent, some of whom had the right in respect of certain
limited territories, the particulars of which rights are not
fully disclosed, nor does it seem material that they should
be.

It seems undisputed that the defendant commenced
to infringe this patent, and so invade the territories
respectively belonging to those who assumed to be the
rightful owners of the patent.

It was desirable that such infringement should be
stopped, and it appears that several of such owners combined for the purpose of so doing, and went to the office of
Messrs. Farley and McDonald, in St. Thomas, and there
signed a retainer whereby that legal firm was retained to
take such proceedings as they might deem advisable to
establish the validity of the patent and to stay or stop the
infringement. This retainer is signed by six of such
owners, and this plaintiff, Frank Wright, is one of the
six.

Such proceedings were commenced by the bringing of
this action, which was prosecuted for a time, the effect of
which seems to have been that the infringement ceased.
Counsel did not agree as to whether or not the defendant
who had been infringing left this country. It was, however, an undisputed fact that the infringement ceased. For
this, and perhaps other causes, the action was, as it
appears, not diligently prosecuted, and was dismissed for
want of prosecution, with costs. These costs are the
moneys which, with interest thereon, are claimed under

the above mentioned writs of execution, and as to which
the plaintiff Frank Wright seeks to be relieved, on the
ground of his infancy, although he has been of full age
since the 12th day of December, 1892.

Mr. McDonald, a member or a then member of the law
firm Farley & McDonald, was the one of that firm who
took the retainer and who chiefly managed and attended
to the matters of the action, and in his affidavit he
says that he did not know that this plaintiff was under
age; that he did not suppose nor did appearances indicate
that such was the fact; and he and Mr. Farley both say
that this plaintiff, Frank Wright, was several times in
their office in regard to the matters of the action and the
proceedings therein, and that it was never suspected or
supposed by them, or either of them, that he was not of
full age. Some of the affidavits, however, made in support of this motion afford indications that the youthful
appearance of this plaintiff, even at the present time, is
such that it should have at least been suspected that he
was then under age. It is a subject on which opinions
may differ widely; but one may presume that if either
Mr. Farley or Mr. McDonald had suspected or supposed
that this plaintiff was under the full age, they would
not have treated him as an adult, as they did. The
affidavits in support of the motion are, of course,
made after the deponents had been informed on the
subject and for the purpose of proving a case (I do not
mean dishonestly at all, but only that the deponents speak
from a more enlightened standpoint than do the others).

I have perused the cross-examination of the plaintiff
Frank Wright, and I do not consider it a document
making much in his favour. It seems to me to be to
some extent characterized by comparative want of candour.

The action and the proceedings in it were, as I think,
clearly for the benefit of the plaintiff Frank Wright,
who was an infant. I think it sufficiently appears that
he obtained a benefit from them, although, owing to the

nature of the subject, it may be difficult to state the
amount of that benefit in dollars and cents.   He says,
himself, that he did, pecunarily, fairly well with the
patent, and he finally sold out his interest. Such seems
an outline of the circumstances in which this plaintiff,
Frank Wright, asks to be relieved from liability, on
the ground that he was under age at the time of the
proceedings.

In the case *Ex p. Brocklebank*, 6 Ch. D. at p. 360, Lord
Justice James says : " In the Court of Chancery a suit on
behalf of an infant was brought in his name by a next
friend, in order to give security for the costs to the defendant, but if the suit had been commenced without the
intervention of a next friend, and the defendant chose to
appear, I know of no reason why it should not have
been prosecuted without a next friend."

In the case *Edwards v. Carter*, [1893] A.C. at p. 365, Lord
Herschell, L. C., in considering whether or not a reasonable
time had elapsed after the infant had attained full age for
him to repudiate or adopt the contract, says : " He knew
that he had executed a deed—he must be taken to have
known that that deed, though binding upon him, could be
repudiated when he came of age. And it seems to me
that in measuring a reasonable time, whether in point of
fact he had or had not acquainted himself with the
nature of the obligations he had undertaken is wholly
immaterial. The time must be measured in precisely the
same way whether he had so made himself acquainted or
not."

This would seem to answer much that is said in the
affidavits and evidence in support of the motion having
relation to the ignorance of the subject by this plaintiff,
even down to the present time, but I am not at all con-
vinced by the evidence that such ignorance of this plaintiff has an existence. On the contrary of this, I am led to
believe that he understood the matter with tolerable
clearness from the beginning.

If an action is commenced on behalf of an infant, without a next friend, the defendant may move to have it dismissed with costs to be paid by the solicitor : Daniell's Ch. Pr., 6th ed., p. 106.

If an infant is co-plaintiff with others, and on attaining twenty-one he wishes to repudiate the action, he should move on notice to have his name struck out as plaintiff, and I cannot think that in such a case the law would allow him *years* to consider whether he will do this or not. The interest of other persons concerned would seem to me to forbid this.

This plaintiff, Frank Wright, has, as shewn, been of full age since early in December, 1892. He had learned of the order made on the application of Alexander Forbes. He had spoken of this. He had been advised to the effect that he was not liable, because he was, or rather had been, an infant. As early, at least, as August, 1893, he carried to a solicitor a bill of costs that had before then been served upon him in this action, and was advised by the solicitor, and I must take the certificate of the Master and the affidavit of McLaws (the opposing solicitor), in preference to the evidence to the contrary, as shewing that that solici- tor attended the taxation of that bill and acted at such taxation as the solicitor of this plaintiff, Frank Wright.

The applicant here, Frank Wright, seems to have done nothing since he attained twenty-one in the way of repudiating liability. Whatever he has done in respect of the matter seems to me to point in the contrary direction.

Upon the whole case, and on all the evidence, after having considered it and endeavoured to understand it and its apparent contradictions, I am of the opinion that this plaintiff, Frank Wright, ought not to obtain the relief he asks on the ground of infancy. I think this motion should be refused, and it is refused, but there will be no costs.

Motion refused without costs.

E. B. B.

[CHANCERY DIVISION.]

REGINA

v.

CONNOLLY AND MCGREEVY.

*Criminal Law—Conspiracy—Agreement—Overt Acts—Acts of Co-conspira-
tors—Acts before Date Alleged in Indictment—Engineer's Report—
Entries in Books—Secondary Evidence—Examination in Civil Action—
Present to Official—Fictitious Tenders—Deceit—" Unlawful "—Right
of Reply.*

L. C. & Co., a firm of contractors in Quebec, tendered to harbour commissioners for certain work to be done with the approval of the Government,
sending in three tenders, one in their own name, and two in the names
of others, with a common mistake as to price of a portion of the work
in all three. The defendant McG., whose brother had been admitted
to the firm as a partner without the payment of any capital, was both a
member of Parliament and of the harbour commission. The three tenders with others were received and opened by the commissioners, the
defendant McG. being present, and were then forwarded to the Government at Ottawa, Ontario. The defendant McG. went to Ottawa and
succeeded in obtaining from the government engineer particulars of the
calculations and results of all the tenders sent in, of which he advised
his brother by letters. When the mistake in the price was notified by
the government engineer to the three tenderers, one tender was withdrawn, one was varied, so as to make it higher than others, and the
firm's was allowed to remain as it was with the manifest error, and so
became the lowest tender, and was thus accepted. One government
engineer was given a situation on the harbour commission, and the
chief engineer of the Public Works Department received a valuable present from the firm. As soon as the contract was executed, promissory
notes to an amount of many thousand dollars were signed by the firm and
given to the defendant McG., and he also received money from his
brother, whose only means of paying were his profits as a partner. On
an indictment for conspiracy against McG. and C., a member of the
firm :—

Held, that there is no unvarying rule that the agreement to conspire must
first be established before the particular acts of the individuals implicated are admissible in evidence, and that the letters written by the
defendant McG. at Ottawa were overt acts there in furtherance of the
common design, and admissible in evidence against all privy to the
conspiracy for which they might be prosecuted in this Province, and as
the defendant C. was, by his own admission, privy to the large payment after it was made, it was a matter for the jury to say whether he
was not throughout a participator in the proceedings : *Mulcahy* v. *The
Queen,* I. R. 1 C. L. 12, followed :—

2. The transactions, conversations, and written communications between
R. H. McG. (the partner), and his brother, the defendant McG., and the
other members of the firm, were receivable in evidence in the circumstances of this case. If at first not available against both defendants
they became so when the proof had so far advanced and cumulated as
to indicate the existence of a common design :—

3. Evidence as to the manner in which other contracts were obtained by

the firm previous to the date mentioned in the indictment was properly
received as introductory to the transaction in question :—

4. Letters written by a member of the firm in the name of an employee,
and purporting to be signed by him, were also properly in evidence :—

5. The report of the government engineer recommending the acceptance
of the firm's tender, was also properly in evidence as the object of all
that was done was to obtain a report in favour of the firm :—

6. Entries in the books of the firm were evidence against the defendant
C., and statements prepared therefrom by an accountant were good
secondary evidence in the absence of the books withheld by the
defendants :—

Query.—How far they were evidence against the defendant McG. who
was not a member of the firm.

7. The examination of the defendant C. in a civil action arising out of
these matters, he not having claimed privilege therein, could be used
against him on this trial :—

8. The evidence of an expert in calculating results on *data* supplied and
proper for an engineer to work upon, was admissible :—

9. Evidence of a present being made to an engineer in charge of the work
with the knowledge of one of the defendants was proper to be considered by the jury as casting light on the relations between the firm and
that officer :—

10. The use of fictitious tenders was a *deceit*, and if done to evade the
results of fair competition for the contracts it was "unlawful":—

11. Although evidence was called by only one of the defendants it might
have enured to the benefit of both, so the right to a general reply was
with the counsel for the Crown.

Statement. THIS was a case reserved for the opinion of the Chancery
Division of the High Court of Justice, pursuant to the
provisions of "The Criminal Code, 1892," by ROSE, J.

The two defendants, Nicholas K. Connolly and Thomas
McGreevy, were tried for conspiracy, and the indictment
was found by the grand jury of the county of Carleton,
at the Ottawa Winter Assizes for 1892. It contained
twenty counts in conspiracy and preliminary paragraphs
setting forth matters of inducement.

The matters of inducement were:

That the defendant Thomas McGreevy was a member
of the House of Commons for the Dominion of Canada;
that he was also a member of the Quebec harbour commission; that the Quebec harbour commissioners were
engaged in the construction of the Quebec harbour improvements, expending large sums of money therein, the works
being undertaken by contractors from time to time under
contract with the commissioners; that the Parliament of
Canada granted large sums of money by way of loan to
the commissioners to enable them to prosecute and com-

plete their works; that as to one of the works for which
aid was granted by Parliament, viz., that of "cross wall,"
the plans were subject to the approval of, and the contract
was awarded by the Governor in Council; that there existed a trading firm known as Larkin, Connolly & Co.,
having a place of business in Quebec, of which firm Nicholas K. Connolly and Owen E. Murphy were members and
partners; that the said firm were engaged in certain of the
works of the said Quebec harbour under contract, and both
the said defendants and said Murphy well knew that other
works were to be executed and large sums of money were
to be expended in and about the said harbour improvements, which were to include the works known as the
cross wall.

Of the twenty counts—the first set out that on the first
day of May, A. D. 1883, at the city of Quebec, in the
Province of Quebec, to wit: at Ottawa, in the said county
of Carleton, the said Nicholas K. Connolly and the said
Thomas McGreevy, unlawfully did conspire, * * together, by divers subtle means and devices, that in consideration of large sums of money to be paid by the said
Larkin, Connolly & Co., to the said Thomas McGreevy and
one Robert H. McGreevy, that the said Thomas McGreevy
should, during the time that he was a member of the
harbour commission, and during the time he was a member
of the said House of Commons of the said Parliament of
Canada, and contrary to his duty in those capacities,
secretly furnish information to Larkin, Connolly & Co., to
be procured by him in said capacities, * * and improperly use his influence as such in breach of trust * * in
procuring contracts, including that for the cross wall, from
said harbour commission, for said Larkin, Connolly & Co.,
and large gains, profits, and undue benefits.

The second count charged the same conspiracy between
the said Connolly, Thomas McGreevy and Robert H. Mc-
Greevy.

The third count charged the same conspiracy between

Statement. the said Connolly, both the McGreevys and one Owen E. Murphy.

The fourth count charged the same conspiracy between the same persons and Michael Connolly and Patrick Larkin.

The fifth count charged the same conspiracy between the defendants, together with divers others unknown.

The next five counts were the same repeated without any local venue being alleged.

The eleventh count charged a conspiracy with a venue, as in count one, between the said Nicholas Connolly and Thomas McGreevy, by false pretences to unlawfully obtain for said Larkin, Connolly & Co., in whose profits the said Thomas McGreevy and Robert H. McGreevy were interested large sums [of money of and from the said harbour commission, with intent to cheat and defraud the said commission.

The next four counts made the same charge against the defendants and the others named as co-conspirators as in counts two, three, four and five, and the next five counts repeated the same charge of conspiracy without any local venue.

The defendants were tried at the Assizes at Ottawa, in the county of Carleton, on November 14th, 15th, 16th, 17th, 18th, 20th, 21st, and 22nd, 1893, before ROSE, J., with a jury, and a verdict of " guilty " was rendered.

Osler, Q. C., *Kerr*, Q. C., and *Hogg*, Q. C., for the Crown.
S. H. Blake, Q. C., and *Lash*, Q. C., for the defendant Connolly.
Aylesworth, Q. C., and *J. A. Gemmill*, for the defendant McGreevy.

It appeared that Larkin, Connolly & Co., were a firm of contractors in the Province of Quebec, composed of Patrick Larkin, the defendant Nicholas K. Connolly, Michael Connolly and Owen E. Murphy, and that during the year 1883, one Robert McGreevy (brother of the defendant) was

secretly admitted as a partner in the profits without supplying any capital. The Quebec harbour was controlled and
managed by a board called the Quebec harbour commission, which was engaged in expending large sums of money
in harbour improvements. These improvements were
made with the sanction and approval of the Minister of
Public Works for the Dominion of Canada, which latter
furnished by way of loan under the various statutes in
that behalf the greater part of the funds to pay for the
works.

During all the periods in question the defendant Mc-
Greevy was a member of the House of Commons for
Canada, as well as a member of the Quebec harbour commission. Tenders were advertized for from time to time
by the commission for certain works, among which was
what was called the "cross wall."

A meeting of the members of the firm of Larkin, Connolly & Co., was held at their office in Quebec, at which
Robert McGreevy, as a prospective partner, was present,
and who became a partner within a month, and it was
decided to tender for the works, and three separate tenders were then prepared and subsequently sent in, one in
the name of the firm; one in the name of John Gallagher
(an employee of the firm), and one in the name of George
Beaucage. Gallagher's tender was prepared and sent in
by Michael Connolly, and Beaucage was a person who was
controlled by Robert McGreevy in the interests of the firm.

All the tenders sent in (five in number) were opened on
May 2nd, 1883, by the commissioners, the defendant Mc-
Greevy being present, and were then forwarded to the
Department of Public Works in Ottawa, to be "moneyed
out," as to quantities, prices, etc., by an engineer of that
department, with a view to ascertaining which tender was
the lowest.

The defendant McGreevy left Quebec on May 3rd, and
arrived in Ottawa on the 4th, from which place he wrote
the letters, making certain suggestions in the interest
of the firm, mentioned in the judgments of the Chancellor

Statement. and Ferguson, J., and obtained certain information from the engineer as to the figures of the different tenders and furnished the same to his brother for the use of Larkin, Connolly & Co.

In the three tenders made in the interest of Larkin, Connolly & Co., a mistake had seemingly been made in giving a price for piling at so much per foot of the length of the pile, instead of so much per foot of the pile work when finished.

The chief engineer of the government wrote all three tenderers, pointing this out, and asked if it was a mistake. Michael Connolly wrote a letter in Gallagher's name withdrawing his tender. Robert McGreevy, who had in the meantime procured an assignment of Beaucage's tender, put such a price on the pile work as would raise that tender higher than any of the others sent in, and Larkin, Connolly & Co., refused to amend their's although they had tendered at 25 cents per lineal foot of pile, amounting to $500, while the other two independent tenders at $8 and $10.50 per foot of pile work amounted to $20,000 and $26,000 respectively. This had the effect of making Larkin, Connolly & Co.'s tender, which amounted in all to $634,340, the lowest by $8,731.

The chief engineer of the government who was also consulting engineer for the harbour commission, reported in favour of Larkin, Connolly & Co.'s tender, and pursuant to an order in Council, the chairman of the commission authorized a contract with that firm.

Immediately after the contract for the cross wall was executed, promissory notes of the individual members of the firm of Larkin, Connolly & Co. to the extent of $25,000 were signed and given to the defendant McGreevy, and he subsequently obtained in the same manner notes of the firm to the extent of $22,000 and $25,000, or $72,000 in all, for which he gave no value except his said efforts and services in aid of the firm. He also received a large amount of the profits, which came to his brother as a partner in the firm. The evidence also shewed that, although Larkin, Connolly

& Co.'s tender was apparently the lowest, yet they received $70,000 more for the work than it would have cost, if the tender of another firm (Peters & Moore), one of the independent tenderers, had been accepted.

The defendant Connolly endorsed one or more of the notes given to the defendant McGreevy, and signed the yearly audit of the firm's books, in which they appeared under expense or suspense account, and for which, admittedly, no commercial value was secured by the firm.

It also appeared that a present was made to the chief government engineer, and payments were made to the inspectors of the work from time to time.

Other facts sustaining the charges set forth in the several counts and in the particulars furnished by the Crown appear in the judgments herein.

Objections were taken at the trial to the admission of the evidence set out in the first nine paragraphs following, which were overruled, and the evidence admitted, and the case reserved the questions whether the evidence was proper to be submitted to the jury in support of the indictment. The case also reserved the objections taken to the Judge's charge to the jury set out in paragraphs 10 and 11, and to the right of reply being allowed to the Crown under the circumstances mentioned in paragraph 12.

1. Objection was taken that there was no evidence to be submitted to the jury in support of the indictment, and that no overt act in Ontario, in pursuance of the conspiracy, had been shewn: the objection was overruled, and the defendant Connolly was then called and examined as a witness on his own behalf.

2. The evidence of R. H. McGreevy as to transactions, conversations, and written communications between himself and other persons including Thomas McGreevy, Owen E. Murphy, Michael Connolly and Patrick Larkin, mentioned in the indictment, and as to the acts of himself and the said Murphy and Michael Connolly, as well as certain written communications between him and the said other persons, were received as evidence against both defendants.

3. Evidence of the tenders for, and how a contract for
dredging the Quebec Harbour Works was obtained in 1882
by Larkin,Connolly & Co., from the harbour commissioners, was received and submitted to the jury as evidence
against both defendants.

4. Two letters from John Gallagher, one to the Public
Works Department, and the other to H. F. Perley, the
government engineer, were received in evidence and read,
on the undertaking of counsel to subsequently prove them.

5. A report from the government engineer to the Minister of Public Works, recommending Larkin, Connolly &
Co.'s tender as the lowest, was also received in evidence.

6. Entries in the books of Larkin, Connolly & Co. (not
made personally by the defendant Connolly), and statements in writing made by the witness W. H. Cross (an
accountant) from the accounts in said books, were also
received.

7. The depositions of the defendant Connolly taken for
discovery in an action in the Exchequer Court, were
received in evidence against him, and he was called as a
witness on his own behalf, he was cross-examined and said
he did not desire to make any changes in them.

8. The evidence of the witness W. T. Jennings (an
engineer), and his calculations respecting the tenders, and
the work executed, from figures furnished to him, was
received.

9. The evidence of the witness Robert H. McGreevy as
to an agreement between the members of the firm of Larkin, Connolly & Co. to give a present to the government
engineer, and to make payments to inspectors of the works,
was received.

10. The Judge's charge was objected to on the ground
that the jury should have been told the communications between R. H. McGreevy and others were not evidence
against the defendant Connolly until a conspiracy was
proved.

11. That the Judge should not have told the jury it was
" unlawful " for one person to put in several tenders.

12. That as the defendant McGreevy did not call any witnesses, his counsel should have had the right to address the jury last.

The case reserved was argued on January 8th, 9th, 10th, and 20th, before BOYD, C., and FERGUSON and MEREDITH, JJ.

Aylesworth, Q. C., for the defendant McGreevy.   The whole and only evidence against the defendants, except the documentary evidence, is that of the defendant, McGreevy's brother, who was largely indebted to him, and a co-conspirator, although not prosecuted.   He did not owe his position as a partner in the firm to his brother's influence, as he had been previously a partner with Larkin, Connolly & Co. in other contracts : and so far from there being any scheme on the part of the defendant, Thomas McGreevy, to have his brother admitted into partnership in the harbour improvements contract, it is shewn that the defendant was not aware that he was or was to be a partner until weeks after the information as to tenders was obtained.   Beaucage's interest was assigned to Robert McGreevy for value, viz., $5,000, weeks before the contract was awarded.   Any possible conspiracy affecting Thomas McGreevy, could only be through the medium of Robert McGreevy, and he testifies there was no arrangement between him and his brother.   Even the memorandum of information said to have been given to Robert by Thomas was not signed or dated or shewn to have been in existence until after all details of the tenders had been published.   The error in the sheet piling price, was a genuine mistake ; the great difference in the prices shew this.   Gallagher's tender was withdrawn with the approval of the proper authority, as was usual.   The letters from Thomas to Robert should not have been received in evidence, and they prejudiced Thomas on his trial.   There was no evidence of any conspiracy in Carleton county or in Ontario ; no overt acts were proved there.   The evidence

Argument. of any contracts previous to May 1st, 1883, should not have been received, as that is the date laid and fixed in the indictment in this case. There was no evidence that the defendant Connolly was ever in Ontario. The entries from the firm's books should not have been received in evidence; the books were not evidence against the defendant McGreevy at all, as he was not concerned in them, nor against the defendant Connolly who had never made any entries in them. The examination of the defendant Connolly in the civil suit in the Exchequer Court, should not have been received; there was no cross-examination or explanation. Connolly's evidence in this case " that it was true," was not given until after the case against McGreevy had been closed, so it could not be received against him, and not being evidence against the one, could not be against the other on this indictment. The trial Judge erred in allowing the Crown to address the jury last: *Regina* v. *LeBlanc*, 13 C. L. T. 441.

S. H. Blake, Q. C., and *Lash*, Q. C., for the defendant Connolly. The jury should have been told not to regard any evidence of any acts of the alleged individual conspirators, until they were satisfied that an agreement between them had been proved. There should have been an elimination of all that took place in the Province of Quebec in respect to the harbour commission; and the trial Judge erred in giving the acts and conduct of each of the two defendants together to the jury before any agreement was proved. The act of one cannot bind the other until an agreement is proved. The evidence that Robert paid Thomas large sums, proves nothing but that he was paying his own debts, as he was largely indebted to Thomas at the time. The books of the firm shew that the sums paid were all retained in a suspense account. That controverts any idea of a conspiracy. Connolly's examination in the Exchequer Court should not have been received, as there was no opportunity for cross-examination. Gallagher's letters were not proved, and should not have been received. The books of the firm were not evidence, much less the ex-

tracts and statements made from them by the witness,
Cross, the accountant. No mere calculations or estimates,
based on figures supplied, such as those made by the witness, Jennings, even if he was an expert, should have been
received, they were too uncertain. The jury should have
been told first to endeavour to ascertain if a conspiracy or
agreement had been proved, and if not, that the acts of
parties, the letters, etc., could not be considered. We refer
to *Hardy's Trial Case,* 24 *Howard's State Trial,* 199, at p.
451; *John Horne Took's Case,* 25 St. Tr. 1, 302, 311; *The
Queen's Case,* 2 B. & B. 302, 311; *Regina v. Murphy,*
8 C. & P. 297; *McKenna's Case* (1842), Ir. Cir. Rep.
(Six Circuit Cases) 461; *Regina v. Duffield,* 5 Cox C. C.
404; *Regina v. Esdaile,* 1 F. & F. ruling at p. 231; *Williamson v. Commonwealth,* 4 Grattan (Va.) 547; *Clawson v.
The State of Ohio,* 14 Ohio S. R. 234; *The People v. William
G. Saunders,* 25 Mich. 119; *Shields v. McKee,* 11 Bradwell
(Ill.) 188; *Logan v. United States,* 144 U. S. R. 263, at p.
308-9; *Luttrell v. State,* 21 S. W. R. 248; *Jones v. North,*
L. R. 19 Eq. 426; *The Mogul Steamship Co. v. McGregor,*
23 Q. B. D. 598, [1892] A. C. 25; *In re Carew Estate,* 26
Beav. 187; *Heffer v. Martyn,* 36 L. J. N. S. Chy. 372;
Metcalf v. Bouck, 25 L. T. N. S. 539; Roscoe's Criminal
Evidence, 11th ed., 180; Wright on Criminal Conspiracies,
Bl. ed. 219, 220; *State v. Hadley,* 54 N. H. 224; *The State
v. Walker,* 32 Me. 195; *Regina v. Owen,* 9 C. & P. 238;
Regina v. Colmer, 9 Cox C. C. 506; *Rex v. Davis,* 6 C. &
P. 177; Wheater's Ca., 1 Lewin's Crown Cases, 157; *The
Queen v. Coote,* 9 Moo. P. C. 463.

Osler, Q. C., and *Hogg,* Q. C. The evidence shews Larkin, Connolly & Co. made a profit of over $954,000 or 43½
per cent. on the amount they expended, while a fair and
proper profit would have been from 15 to 25 per cent., and
out of that profit $350,000 was paid away and disposed of
without receiving any return of commercial value. That
represents the shares of the two McGreevys, $117,000 of
which went direct to the defendant, the harbour commissioner and Member of Parliament. The defendants are in

contempt for the non-production of the firm's books which
their counsel undertook to produce, and the evidence of
the accountant, Cross, as to the contents of the books may
be treated as good secondary evidence of the contents of
the audits, signed by the defendant Connolly. Even if this
was a proper case for a new trial, no new trial should be
granted except upon the condition that the contempt be
purged by the production of the books. The evidence shews
a corrupt agreement between the defendant McGreevy and
the firm, and a conspiracy to defraud the Quebec harbour
commission, which the jury has believed, and on which they
have found their verdict, which should not be disturbed.
The acts of the parties and the contracts are all to be added
together, and the reasonable inference is, that there was an
agreement, and that is the way the conspiracy is proved.
The notes given to Thomas McGreevy were signed after
the contract was awarded, but they were ante-dated, and
the amount, although charged in a suspense account, was
paid or borne by the partners of the firm out of the profits. No value was received for them, except his influence
and questionable services. The yearly audit of the books
shewing how these notes were charged, was signed by the
defendant Connolly. The letters written by Thomas Mc-
Greevy at Ottawa, were overt acts in this Province, in furtherance of the common design. The ostensible mistake in the
three tenders being the same, and the disposal of two of them
in the interest of the firm, shew the scheme. The Crown can
give evidence of anything in the indictment or particulars,
and the evidence respecting the contracts in 1882, was
properly received, as particulars of it were given before
the trial. The evidence of Jennings was that of an expert,
founded on figures supplied, was properly received, and
shewed that Larkin, Connolly & Co.'s tender was not the
lowest, although it so appeared. It was the obtaining of
the secret information by Thomas McGreevy, that enabled
the firm to manipulate the tenders. The evidence of Connolly in the Exchequer Court, was properly received:
Regina v. *Goldshede*, 1 Car. & Kir. 657 ; *Rex* v. *Mer-*

ceron, 2 Stark. R. 366 ; *Regina* v. *Chidley,* 8 Cox C. C. 365 ;
Regina v. *Scott,* 7 Cox C. C. 164 ; *The Queen* v. *Widdop,*
L. R. 2 C. C. R. at p. 8 ; *Ex p. Schofield, In re Firth,* 6
Ch. D. 230 ; *Rex v. William Haworth,* 4 C. & P. 254 ; Roscoe's Criminal Evidence, 11th ed., 139 ; *Ex p. Reynolds, In
re Reynolds,* 20 Ch. D. 294 ; *The Queen* v. *Coote,* L. R. 4
P. C. 599 ; *Smith* v. *Beadnell,* 1 Camp. at p. 33 ; Taylor on
Evidence, Bl. ed., secs. 888, 889, 890. The acts and declarations of any one conspirator are evidence against them
all : *Regina* v. *Shellard,* 9 C. & P. 277 ; *The Queen* v. *Blake,*
6 Q. B. 126. Where they are in the nature of an act in
furtherance of the common design, the jury may infer the
conspiracy : Archbold's Criminal Pleading and Evidence,
21st ed., 1105 ; *Ford* v. *Elliot,* 4 Ex. 78.

We refer also to *Regina* v. *Duffield,* 5 Cox C. C. 404 ;
Rex v. *Roberts,* 1 Camp. 399 ; *Blake* v. *The Albion Life
Association Society,* 4 C. P. D. at p. 97 ; *Rex* v. *Cope,* 1
Str. 144 ; Wright on Criminal Conspiracies, 212, 216 ;
The King v. *Hunt,* 3 B. & Ald. 566 ; *The Waterloo
Mutual Ins. Co.* v. *Robinson,* 4 A. R. at p. 301 ; *The
King* v. *Brisac,* 4 East. 164 ; *The King* v. *Bowes,* cited
in 4 East. at p. 171 ; *The Queen's Case,* 2 Brod. & Bing.
at p. 310 ; *Regina* v. *Gallagher,* 13 Cox C. C. 61 ; *Regina*
v. *Murphy,* 8 C. & P. 297 ; *The King* v. *Whitehead,* 1 Dow
& Ry. N. P. 61.

Blake, Q. C., in reply. The government accounts only
shew a profit of 30 per cent. which is moderate. The
firm's books were taken away by process of law. The
indictment cannot be enlarged by particulars. The charging of the notes against the firm was disputed when
discovered ; that negatives any previous agreement to pay
them. There was nothing wrong in Thomas McGreevy
hastening the engineers in Ottawa, and if possible indicating the terms. If any extra profits were made it was
because there were expensive alterations made in the contract after the work commenced. I refer to Hilliard on
New Trials, 2nd od., 411, 413 ; *Campbell* v. *Prince,* 5
A. R. at p. 335 ; *Pirie* v. *Wyld,* at p. 430 ; *The Con-*

federation Life Ass. of Canada v. *O'Donnell,* 13 S. C. R.
218, at pp. 224, 226 ; *Bank of Hamilton* v. *Isaacs,* 16
O. R. at p. 454; *The Queen* v. *Gibson,* 18 Q. B. D. 537, at
p. 542; Rapelge on Criminal Procedure, sec. 349, pp. 479,
480.

February 15, 1894. BOYD, C. :—

A study of the evidence satisfies me that this is a case
which could not properly be withdrawn from the jury.
There is abundant circumstantial evidence to warrant the
verdict of guilty, and no sufficient reason exists to warrant
the interference of this Court of Appeal, either upon the
case reserved or upon the application for a new trial.

As to the evidence received and the manner in which it
was received, it is enough to say that the discretion of the
trial Judge was rightly exercised. There is no unvarying
rule that the agreement to conspire must first be established before particular acts of the individuals implicated
are admissible.

The charge of Coleridge, J., in *Regina* v. *Murphy,* 8 C.
& P., at p. 310, conveniently summarizes the usual method
of proving a charge of conspiracy : " Although the common
design is the root of the charge, it is not necessary to prove
that the parties came together and actually agreed in terms
to have this common design, and to pursue it by common
means, and so to carry it into execution. This is not necessary, because in many cases of the most clearly established
conspiracies there are no means of proving any such thing,
and neither law nor common sense requires that it should
be proved. If you find that these two persons pursued by
their acts the same object, often by the same means, one
performing one part of an act, and the other another part
of the same act, so as to complete it, with a view to the
attainment of the object which they were pursuing, you
will be at liberty to draw the conclusion that they have
been engaged in a conspiracy to effect that object. The
question you have to ask yourselves is, ' Had they this

common design, and did they pursue it by these common
means—the design being unlawful ?'"

That course, which was also approved of by our own
Court of Queen's Bench in *Regina* v. *Fellowes*, 19 U. C. R.,
48, was the one adopted in this case under the direction of
the Judge. It was competent for the jury to group the de-
tached acts and view them as indicating a well-understood
or concerted purpose on the part of all the actors and privies. Their conclusion I am not disposed to quarrel with,
for I think the whole body of facts is inconsistent with any
other conclusion than that of concerted action between the
defendants. A consideration of the matters in evidence, as
to the first transaction respecting the cross wall contract
shews results that support the indictment and supplies
evidence of overt acts in Ontario, sufficient to find jurisdiction.

In the preparation of tenders there was a meeting of the
members of the firm of Larkin, Connolly & Co., at Quebec.
Robert McGreevy was there and assisted—it being then
understood that he was to be a partner, though the precise
terms were not fixed till the writing of the 6th June, 1883—
Tenders (three) were then prepared in the names of Gallagher (an employee of the firm) of Beaucage, who was controlled by Robert McGreevy in the interest of the firm,
and of Larkin, Connolly & Co. In all of these appeared
(what is said to be) a common mistake—in the rate charged
per foot for sheet-piling.

On the 2nd May these and other tenders for the cross
wall were opened at Quebec by the harbour commissioners, the defendant Thomas McGreevy, one of the commissioners, being then present.

These tenders were not disposed of by the commissioners, but were to be passed upon at Ottawa by the
Public Works' Department. In this way the tenders
reached the hands of Mr. Boyd, engineer in that Department at Ottawa, in order to be moneyed out or extended,
upon estimates of quantities fixed by him.

Thomas McGreevy (defendant), who was also a Member

of Parliament, appears to have left Quebec on the night of the 3rd May, and arrived at Ottawa on the 4th. To that effect he writes his brother Robert on the 5th May, 1883, in a letter containing this passage: "The tenders for cross wall only arrived here yesterday and are locked up until Monday, when he will commence his calculation. I will write you on Tuesday and let you know the result. Larkin was here yesterday. I told him that it would be useless to get Peters (another tenderer) out of the way, as it would be tantamount to giving the contract to the highest tender, that you would have to stick to Beaucage's tender, as it was fair."

On 7th May, Monday, the defendant again writes from the House of Commons to his brother Robert: "I hope to let you know to-morrow about the result of the cross wall tenders. Have your arrangements right with Beaucage before result is known. I will give you timely notice." Robert had anticipated the receipt of this letter by procuring a transfer of interest from Beaucage on the 4th May for the benefit of Larkin, Connolly & Co.

On Tuesday, 8th May, the Member of Parliament again writes his brother that he had seen Boyd that morning, and the letter continues: "I will meet him this afternoon about it and know the result."

Thomas McGreevy thereafter obtained from Mr. Boyd a view of figures shewing the comparative extension of the sheet-piling totals, as tendered for by Peters, Samson and Larkin, Connolly & Co., and this was sent or given to his brother Robert. I think it is evident from Robert McGreevy's evidence that he had access also to information as to the other tenderers' prices and the estimates of quantities on which the government engineer figured, and *that* pending the final acceptance of the successful tender. But apart from this, the memorandum as to sheet-piling afforded a clue, by means of which Larkin, Connolly & Co. were able to obtain the footing of lowest tenderers.

On May 16th, Gallagher sent in a letter of withdrawal, said to be prepared after conference with the defendant

Nicholas Connolly. On the next day, 17th May, was written the letter of the chief engineer, Perley, to Beaucage and Gallagher, calling attention to the evident mistake in their prices for sheet-piling, and answers from them (inspired or written by the firm) were sent on 19th May as to Gallagher and on the 21st as to Beaucage.

On 17th May, Thomas McGreevy, from the House of Commons at Ottawa, writes his brother : " As I told you yesterday to try and get a good plan and as quick as possible, in answer to the letter that Gallagher & Beaucage will receive about their tenders to bring them over L. & C. so as their tender will be the lowest. The contract will be awarded from Ottawa direct."

The plan suggested by Thomas McGreevy was carried out by such amended prices being put upon the sheet-piling as would when extended for Beaucage and Gallagher put their tenders higher than Larkin, Connolly & Co.'s, whereas Larkin, Connolly & Co. declined to correct the error in their sheet-piling prices, and thereby kept themselves lower than Peters.

The memorandum in Thomas McGreevy's writing, taken from Boyd's calculations, shewed in moneyed out tenders :

" Sheet-piling totals.

" Peters, $20,000, or $8 per running foot.

" Samson, $26,000, or $10.50 per running foot.

" Larkin, Connolly & Co., $500, or 25 cents per running foot."

As between Larkin, Connolly & Co.'s total tender and that of Peters, as extended, the difference was :

Peters............................	$643,071
Larkin, Connolly & Co..............	634,340
The difference was	$8,731

in favour of Larkin, Connolly & Co. Had a reasonable figure been placed on the sheet-piling in response to Perley's letter by Larkin, Connolly & Co., that would have sent up their tender some thousands of dollars above the Peters' tender.

Mr. Perley's official communication of the result on 23rd May, 1883, was in favour of Larkin, Connolly & Co.'s tender, and on the 4th June, pursuant to order in Council, the chairman of the harbour commission authorized the contract to be signed with that firm.

On the same day Kinnipple & Morris, engineers of the commission, were dismissed, and the vacancy was filled soon after by the appointment of Mr. Boyd, who had assisted the defendant Thomas McGreevy to the private information already detailed.

When the contract was secured to the firm of Larkin, Connolly & Co., $25,000 worth of notes of the firm, representing no consideration other than the services hereinbefore set forth (ante-dated to the 1st May, 1883), were handed to Robert McGreevy to be given to his brother, and of this sum $17,000 appears to have gone to satisfy a judgment of *McCammon* v. *Thomas McGreevy*. One or more of these notes was signed by the defendant Nicholas Connolly: his share was charged against him in the books of the firm, and was (as he himself admits) passed in the yearly audit of the books of the firm, sooner than break up the concern.

As to the outcome of the transaction (omitting details): Though Larkin, Connolly & Co. were apparently the lowest tenderers on the cross wall contract, yet the calculations of Mr. Jennings shew that taking the quantities as executed, if the contract had been awarded on the Peters & Moore tender, their total price, according to the scale of values given, would have been some $70,000 less than what was paid to Larkin, Connolly & Co. on the ostensible lowest tender.

I may quote a pertinent passage at this point from the judgment of Whiteside, C. J., in *Mulcahy* v. *The Queen*, I. R., 1 C. L. at p. 36, which was approved of by the House of Lords, S. C., L. R., 3 H. L. at p. 328, as to overt acts : "The bare consulting of those who merely deliberate, though they may not agree on a plan of action, is of itself an overt act, because it is a step towards the prosecution of the

Judgment.
Boyd, C.

design. The adoption of a plan is a further step and all who assent to it are in the same position as if they had met and planned it." So the letters I have extracted are acts admissible against all privy to the conspiracy, as said by Grose, J., in *Hardy's Trial* by Gurney, "in many circumstances of this sort, it has been determined that *Scribere est agere*": McNally's Rules of Evidence, p. 623. See also the charge of Bayley, B., in *Watson's Case*, 32 State Trials p. 7.

As to the defendant Connolly, the general evidence and his own admissions shew that he was the managing and resident partner of the firm, had been a contractor in a large way for over twenty years, and took part in signing cheques and in the financial matters of the firm, and was, by his own admissions, privy to this large payment after it was made. But it was eminently a matter for the jury to say whether he was not throughout a participator in the proceedings of this one transaction which worked so harmoniously to a result favourable to the partnership in which he was chief member: *Rex* v. *Cope*, 1 Str. 144.

I do not propose to dwell upon the series of transactions which follow this and reflect a like result. Taking this as a sample, it justifies the verdict, and it shews overt acts in Ottawa in furtherance of the common design.

I take it that the propositions laid down in Starkie's Criminal Pleadings pp. 30, 31 and repeated in later authors, are too well understood to be canvassed by the defendants. They are thus expressed: "An indictment for a conspiracy may be tried in any county, in which an overt act has been committed in pursuance of the original illegal combination and design * *.

So several defendants were holden to have been properly convicted upon an indictment for a conspiracy, though no joint conspiracy had been proved in the county where they were tried, but only overt acts done in consequence of a general conspiracy, evidenced by various acts in other counties." (Edition of 1824.)

This suffices to answer the first matter reserved.

As to the 2nd and 10th, they may be taken together. The transactions, conversations and written communications between Robert McGreevy (the secret partner in the firm) and Thomas, his brother, and the other members of the firm, were properly receivable in the circumstances of this case. If at first not available against both defendants, they became so, if and when, the proof had so far advanced and cumulated as to indicate the existence of a common design on the part of the two defendants, jointly or with others. I am satisfied that such a scheme was well proved on the whole, and that being so, what was said or done by either defendant or other conspirator in pursuance of the one end is evidence against both or all.

The third point is as to the reception of evidence concerning the dredging contract of 1882. That seems to me to be not irrelevant and admissible as introductory to the later transaction, inviting as it did the secret partnership of Robert McGreevy with the Larkin firm and the manipulation of unreal tenders. Besides, it is specified in the particulars furnished to the defendants before the trial; and then as matters of procedure are subject to the provisions of "The Criminal Code, 1892" (see 56 Vict., ch. 32, sched. sec. 981).

Section 617 says that the particular is to be entered on the record, and the trial shall proceed as if the indictment had been amended in conformity with such particular. The evidence was in this view relevant to the pleadings, and thus not subject to the objection urged.

There was some argument as to the time mentioned in the indictment as the date of the conspiracy, " to wit, 1st May, 1883," precluding evidence of an earlier date. The same objection was overruled by Holt, C. J., in *Rex* v. *Charnock*, 12 Howard's State Trials, at p. 1397, who said : " The day is not material, but only a circumstance, but in form some day before the indictment preferred must be laid * * . Nor are the witnesses * * tied up to the particular time or place mentioned in the indictment." It matters not how far back the conspiracy reaches or did

begin, if it was afterwards pursued, proof may be given of
it, at p. 1399.

Fourth. The letters purporting to be signed by John Gallagher were properly in evidence, as they were written in his name by Michael Connolly, brother and partner of the defendant, and in connection with the tenders in question.

Fifth. Perley's report was also properly in evidence on the ground, stated at the trial, that the object of all was to procure a report in their favour.

Sixth. The entries in the books of the firm were of use in fixing a knowledge on the defendant Connolly of the suspicious disbursements of his firm. The results of the payments were in the audits, signed by Connolly, and these books and papers came to the custody of Connolly, and by the undertaking of the counsel of the defendants to produce them, were admitted to be in the joint custody of the defendants. The statements of Cross, prepared therefrom, were good secondary evidence in the absence of the originals, withheld by the defendants.

Strictly speaking, the entries in the books of the firm may not have been evidence against the defendant Thomas McGreevy, unless the view be taken that he is connected with the firm through his brother, the secret partner.

But apart from this and from what appears in the books it is well proved that $117,000 of the money of the firm went direct to Thomas McGreevy or for his benefit.

As against Connolly, who said he managed the finances and who signed the yearly audits, the evidence was well received; if a wider use of it was made against McGreevy, it does not seem to me a material circumstance which did affect or should affect the result. There was no mistrial, in consequence, which calls for the interposition of an Appellant Court. See Section 746 of the Criminal Code.

Seventh. The depositions of Connolly in the Court of Exchequer could be used against him on this trial. It was open for him to have claimed protection in the civil proceedings and then what he said would have been privileged

—but failing this, what he then said is evidence generally against him. See *Regina* v. *Garbett*, Den. C. C. 236; *Regina* v. *Scott*, 1 Dears & B. C. C. 47; *Regina* v. *Fee*, 13 O. R. at p. 596; and *The Queen* v. *Coote*, 9 Moo. P. C. N. S. 463.

Eighth. The evidence of Jennings was that of an expert and was admissible, as calculating results on *data* supplied by the officers (*e. g.*, Boyd), of the Government, who moneyed out the tenders. Some of his calculations were hypothetical, but others, which he gives, rest upon an absolute basis, proper for an engineer to work upon.

Ninth. The evidence of a present to Perley, who was chief engineer of the government at Ottawa, and afterwards consulting engineer for the harbour commissioners, was a matter proper to be considered by the jury. The present was made with the privity of the defendant Nicholas Connolly, and cast light upon the nature of the relations between the firm and this influential officer. Proverbially, a "gift perverteth the judgment," and this manner of dealing by the firm of Larkin, Connolly & Co., appears to have been part of a system that extended to other public officers connected with the works under contract.

Eleventh. The judge commented adversely on the practice of putting in various apparently competing tenders, and yet all under the control of one person—speaking of it as "unlawful." It is apparent that these tenders could be used to the disadvantage and prejudice of public interests, and that the government disapproved of the practice.

This is evident from letters put in by the defendants themselves. Sir H. Langevin, on 31st July, 1882, writes to the secretary-treasurer of the Quebec harbour commission: "I desire to know whether the commissioners have reason to believe that the tenders received, which are lower than the one they prefer, have been made in good faith, and that there has not been collusion with respect to the withdrawal of these tenders." Whereunto replies the officer on the 8th August: "I am instructed respectfully to declare that the commissioners consider that it

Judgment.

Boyd, C.

is not necessary that they should defend themselves against a suspicion of knowledge on their part of collusion between the tenderers for the harbour works."

The Judge commented on the epithet, explaining, if deceit were practised upon the Department in order to obtain an undue advantage, then such a course was not permitted, and therefore, *unlawful*. This exposition appears unobjectionable ; " unlawful " is of elastic meaning ; the use of these fictitious tenders was a " deceit " in itself, and if employed to further the ends of those in combination so as to evade the results of fair competition for the contracts, then it was " unlawful " in the sense of being a thing of public mischief. See now the Code incriminating this practice, sec. 133.

Twelfth. As to the order for addresses at the close of the evidence ; if that is a matter proper for reservation (which I doubt), it cannot be said that there was any violation of proper procedure. If the provisions of the Code apply, then, according to section 661, as evidence for the defence was given, the right of reply was with the prosecution— *a fortiori* if the counsel was acting on behalf of the Attorney-General. But if the Code does not apply, then the old rule was that on a joint indictment for one offence when the evidence for the one would enure to the benefit of the other, the right to a general reply was with the prosecution, though evidence was given by only one defendant : *Regina* v. *Hayes*, 2 M. & R. 155 ; *Regina* v. *Jordan*, 9 C. & P. 118.

It is not needful to say more than that all the points reserved should be ruled in favour of the Crown, and that the motion for a new trial should be refused.

FERGUSON, J. :—

The defendants were indicted for an alleged conspiracy. The trial took place in the city of Ottawa, in the county of Carleton. This is a case reserved by the learned Judge, pursuant to provisions contained in the Code of 1892.

The first paragraph of the case seems to be the most important one, and is in these words: "At the conclusion of the case for the Crown, objection was taken on behalf of the defendants, that there was no evidence to be submitted to the jury in support of the indictment, and that no overt act in Ontario in pursuance of the conspiracy had been shewn. I overruled the objection, and the defendant Connolly was then called and examined as a witness on his own behalf. I reserve, for the opinion of the Chancery Division of the High Court of Justice, pursuant to the provisions of the Criminal Code, 1892, the question whether there was evidence proper to be submitted to the jury in support of the indictment."

The Crown did not profess to be able to prove the conspiracy alleged by any direct evidence as to the making in fact of an agreement constituting a conspiracy. What was relied on was that this should be presumed or inferred by the jury from facts to be given in evidence against the defendants.

At the bar before us, there was some discussion on the subject as to whether or not acts of an alleged co-conspirator could or should be given in evidence against others of the conspirators before the existence of the conspiracy had been established by other independent evidence.

It is now, as I think, entirely beyond question that a conspiracy can be established without any proof of the making of the agreement in fact, between or amongst the alleged co-conspirators.

In the case *Regina* v. *Fellowes*, 19 U. C. R. 48, at pp. 57 and 58, the Chief Justice, in delivering the judgment of the Court, said: "It was clearly unnecessary to prove that these four defendants, or any two of them, actually met together and concerted such a proceeding as appears to have been carried out. That they did combine and conspire to effect by fraud the return of Mr. Fellowes may be inferred from all the circumstances; and if the jury were satisfied from their conduct either together or severally, that they were acting in concert, then they were right in looking upon the conspiracy as proved."

Upon this proposition alone it seems scarcely necessary Judgment.
to refer to authorities. Yet, as there are questions im- Ferguson, J.
mediately connected with it which were subjects of discussion, more or less, I will, at the risk of being considered tedious, refer shortly to a few of the cases and
statements found in the books.

A conspiracy is generally a matter of inference deduced
from certain criminal acts of the parties accused, done in
pursuance of an apparent criminal purpose in common
between them: Archbold's Criminal Pleading and Evidence, 21st ed., 1105, citing *Rex.* v. *Brisac,* 4 East 171; and
Mulcahy v. *Regina,* L. R. 3 H. L. 306, 317; and it is further
said that the prosecutor may go into general evidence of
the matter of the conspiracy, before he gives evidence to
connect the defendants with it: *Rex.* v. *Hammond,* 2
Esp. 718.

The acts and declarations of any of the co-conspirators,
in furtherance of the common design, may be given in evidence against all: Archbold 1105, *Regina* v. *Shellard,* 9
C. & P. 277, and *The Queen* v. *Blake,* 6 Q. B. 126. And
if one overt act be proved in the county where the venue
is laid, other overt acts either of the same or others of the
conspirators may be given in evidence, although in other
counties: *King* v. *Bowes,* referred to in 4 East at p. 171.

A passage occurs in Archbold, at p. 1106, which is this:
" But before you give in evidence the acts of one conspirator
against another, you must prove the existence of the conspiracy, that the parties were members of the same conspiracy, and that the act in question was done in furtherance of the common design." This seems entirely logical
to me, but no decided case seems to be cited by the author
precisely supporting it.

In *King* v. *Bowes,* cited in 4 East 171, the learned
Judge said: "The trial proceeded upon this principle;
where no proof of actual conspiracy embracing all the
several conspirators was attempted to be given in *Middlesex,* where the trial took place, and where the individual
actings of some of the conspirators were wholly confined

to other counties than *Middlesex*; but still the conspiracy as against all having been proved from the community of criminal purpose, and by their joint co-operation in forwarding the objects of it, in different places and counties, the locality required for the purpose of trial was holden to be satisfied by overt acts done by some of them in prosecution of the conspiracy in the county where the trial was had."

That case seems to indicate very plainly that where there is no direct evidence of the fact of conspiracy the acts of each and every of the alleged conspirators can be given in evidence for the purpose of proving that there was a conspiracy, if such acts were done apparently in furtherance of the common design.

In the case, *Ford* v. *Elliott*, 4 Exch. at p. 81 (where, however, the real question was one of fraud), Alderson, B., said : " It is a mistake to say that a conspiracy must be proved before the acts of the alleged conspirators can be given in evidence. It is competent to prove insulated acts as steps by which the conspiracy itself may be established." I also refer to the language of Williams J., in *The Queen* v. *Blake*, 6 Q. B., at p. 139, which is to the same effect.

The subject is treated of in Wright on Criminal Conspiracies, Bl. ed., commencing at p. 212. Very clear and forcible language on the subject is used by Judge King in *Commonwealth* v. *McClean*, 2 Parsons (Pa.) 368.

After having examined the authorities on this subject that were referred to at the bar, I am of the opinion that a statement made by one of the counsel for the Crown, so far as it goes, correctly expresses the meaning of the law on the subject. It was this: " Wherever the writings or words of any of the parties charged with or implicated in a conspiracy can be considered in the nature of an act done in furtherance of the common design, they are admissible in evidence, not only as against the party himself, but as proof of an act from which *inter alia* the jury may infer the conspiracy itself."

It is, of course, different where the writings or words
amount to an admission merely of the person's own guilt,
and cannot be deemed an act in furtherance of the common
design.

The mode adopted in the present case to prove the
alleged conspiracy, was by proving acts from which it
could be inferred or deduced by the jury.

The defendant Nicholas K. Connolly was the managing
member of the firm Larkin, Connolly & Co. Robert
McGreevy was a member of that firm, and so far as one
sees, he was, at all events in some sense, the medium of communication between that firm and his brother, the defendant Thomas McGreevy, who was a member of the Quebec
harbour commission, and also a member of the House of
Commons of Canada.

Large contracts were to be given by the harbour commission, through the government, for the improvement of
the harbour in various ways, the harbour commission,
as to part at least, giving debentures and the government
furnishing or paying the money.

The defendant Thomas McGreevy was necessarily a considerable portion of his time in Ottawa, and there were
interviews there between him and his brother Robert.

I have perused with as much care as I have been able
the evidence and the correspondence respecting the contracts that are shewn to have been awarded to the firm,
Larkin, Connolly & Co., the tenders that were made for
or in respect of the same, what was done in regard to
these tenders, and what was done with a large amount of
the moneys received by that firm as payment to them for
work done upon the contracts.

I do not, however, intend going through this evidence
here, for it is so long that it may be said to be almost endless.
I deem it necessary to refer to only one of the contracts,
the tenders for the same, etc., and this, in a brief manner.
As shewn by the evidence, there were four tenders for this
contract, which is called the "cross wall contract": one by
Gallagher, one by Beaucage, one by Peters & Co., and one

by Larkin, Connolly & Co. There was another tender, that of Samson & Samson, but it seems to have been so much higher than the others that little is said about it. Robert McGreevy's evidence shews that he, on behalf of Larkin, Connolly & Co., was the real owner of the tender put in by or in the name of Beaucage, and that Gallagher's tender was in the interest of Larkin, Connolly & Co.

He says there was a meeting (of the members of the firm, or most of them, I presume), in the office of Larkin, Connolly & Co., at the preparation of those three tenders. In each of those tenders, there occurred an error, in respect of the sheet-piling. The error in each was the same error. The errors were the same according to the evidence of Robert McGreevy, except a little variation in price, and they (the errors) were in tendering for this part of the work at a price per lineal foot, measuring length-wise of the piles to be planted or driven, instead of lengthwise of the piling (which was to be eight feet thick) when the work was complete. The tenders as to this part were about twenty-six cents per lineal foot, and the wit-ness says that the proper price per foot measured along the line of the work when done would be about ten dollars per lineal foot.

These tenders had to be worked out upon the quantities in the office of the department at Ottawa, "moneyed out" as it was called, and in doing this, there would manifestly be a very wide difference between the result when the price is applied to the lineal foot of piling and when it is applied to the lineal foot of the work when completed; and by obtaining the correction of such an error, a large difference would be made in the price of the work. It is also manifest that in "moneying out" tenders put in with such an error, they would appear to be lower than really intended, and might, for this reason alone, be considered lower than tenders of other people.

A photograph of a memorandum proved to be in the handwriting of the defendant, Thomas McGreevy, in re-spect of these tenders is put in evidence.

It is : " Sheet-pilings totals.
" Peters, $20,000, or $8 per running foot. ,
" Sampson, $26,000, or $10.50 per running foot.
" Larkin & Co., $500, or 25 cents per running foot."

Robert McGreevy is asked if he had any correspondence
with his brother Thomas McGreevy, in reference to this
matter, and he answers, " I think so."

A letter is then put in. It is dated Ottawa, 5th May,
1883, and is from Thomas McGreevy to Robert McGreevy,
Amongst other things it contains this " The tenders for
cross wall only arrived yesterday and are locked up till
Monday, when he will commence his calculation. I will
write you Tuesday and let you know the result. Larkin
was here yesterday. I told him it would be useless to get
Peters out of the way as it would be tantamount to giving
the contract to the highest tender, that you would have to
stick to Beaucage's tender, as it was fair."

Another letter of the 7th May, 1883, " House of Commons, Canada," from Thomas to Robert McGreevy, says :
" I hope to let you know to-morrow about the result of
cross wall tenders. Have your arrangements with Beaucage before the result is known. I will give you timely
notice."

In a letter written from the House of Commons on the
8th May, 1883, Thomas McGreevy says to Robert, " I seen
Boyd " (the engineer) " this morning. He has not finished
cross wall yet. I will meet him this afternoon about it
and know the result."

And in a letter of the 17th May, 1883, written from the
House of Commons, Thomas McGreevy, amongst other
things, says to Robert McGreevy : "As I told you yesterday to try and get a good plan as quick as possible, in answer to letters that Gallagher and Beaucage will receive
about their tenders, to bring them over L. & C., so as their
tender will be the lowest. The contract will be awarded
from Ottawa, direct. * * I think you were wrong in
tendering without a cheque, accepted by such a pair of
cut-throats."

On the same day, the 17th of May, 1883, a letter was or had been sent by Perley, the chief engineer, to the tenderers, calling attention to the mistake or supposed mistake in the tenders, and asking, amongst other things, if an error had really been made, and if so, requesting them to state a price per lineal foot in the line of the work.

There can, I think, be no doubt that this is the letter referred to in the one of Thomas McGreevy of the same date, where he refers to the letters that Gallagher and Beaucage will receive about their tenders.

On the 21st of May, 1883, Beaucage or Robert McGreevy for him, answered Perley's letter, acknowledging the error in the tender, and referring to it as a very serious one, and stating prices per lineal foot, varying according to the thickness of the sheeting from $15 to $19 per foot.

There is a letter without date written from the St. Louis Hotel by Robert McGreevy to Murphy, asking him to send Connolly over " to-morrow morning," to send a letter to Perley for Gallagher in answer to one sent him on the 17th by Perley, asking an explanation on piles.

There is a letter to the secretary of the Public Works, apparently from Gallagher, and bearing date the 16th of May, 1883, withdrawing Gallagher's tender, on condition of the deposit cheque being returned.

Robert McGreevy says that the defendant, Nicholas Connolly, was a party to the withdrawal of this tender. He also says that the interview referred to in the letter from his brother Thomas of the 17th May took place in Ottawa.

On the 4th of May, 1883, Beaucage signed a document by which he agreed to transfer all his rights in his tender (which was dated the 2nd of May, 1883) to Larkin, Connolly & Co., for the expressed consideration of $5,000. This was the position of Beaucage, and it appears from Gallagher's evidence and otherwise that he knew nothing whatever of the tenders, that his name was simply used by Larkin, Connolly & Co.

The evidence on this immediate subject need not, I
think, be further pursued. It seems entirely plain
that all this manipulation of and in respect to these
tenders was for the purpose of bringing out Larkin,
Connolly & Co.'s the lowest, and lower than that
of Peters & Co., which would be done by their not
seeking to make any correction respecting the price of the
sheeting, and that much that was done after the interview
between Robert and Thomas McGreevy in Ottawa on the
16th of May and after Thomas' letter of the 17th May,
was in pursuance of the instructions in that letter, to try
and get a good plan as quickly as possible in answer to
letters that Gallagher & Beaucage were to receive about
their tenders to bring them out over Larkin, Connolly &
Co.'s tender so that Larkin, Connolly & Co.'s tender would
be the lowest.

The plans that were adopted succeeded, and the contract
was awarded to Larkin, Connolly & Co. The outcome, in
a financial point of view, is shewn by the evidence of
Jennings, and referred to in the judgment of the Chancellor.

It appears that a "large sum in excess" of what Peters &
Co. tendered to do the work for was paid Larkin, Connolly
& Co.

As soon as the contract was executed, or very soon thereafter, promissory notes amounting to no less a sum than $25,-
000 were made by the firm, Larkin, Connolly & Co., and given
to Robert McGreevy, to be given by him to the defendant
Thomas McGreevy, and Robert says to the best of his
recollection he gave these notes over accordingly to the
defendant, Thomas McGreevy ; and he says he does not
know of the firm getting anything in the way of commercial value for this sum. He says that part of this
sum went to pay a judgment debt of the defendant
Thomas McGreevy of $17,000, and that he, as a partner
of Larkin, Connolly & Co., was made to contribute his
share of this sum of $25,000.

There was also a sum of $22,000 and another sum of
$25,000 that went from Larkin, Connolly & Co. to the

defendant Thomas McGreevy, and when Robert McGreevy
is asked if he had any idea of what the defendant Thomas
McGreevy did for the sum of $72,000, he said he had
an idea that he did all he could for the firm, and
further on, being asked what did he, Thomas, do for
the firm, he answers : " Well, he did a good deal by way of
advancing their interests in Ottawa."

There is a large volume of evidence respecting this and
other matters, but I do not think it needful to pursue it
further, except to point out that it is shewn that Robert
McGreevy put into the firm a very unimportant sum
towards the necessary capital, and did little or no work,
and yet received a very large sum as his share of the
profits arising whilst he was a member of the firm, out of
which he paid or gave to the defendant Thomas McGreevy
no less a sum than $58,000, and that the defendant Thomas
McGreevy received directly from the firm Larkin, Connolly & Co. the sum of about $117,000, and that, accord-
ing to the evidence of Robert McGreevy, so far as he
knows, no commercial value was given for either of these
sums.   From all that appears, one would say that it is fair
to suppose that if such commercial value had been given,
Robert McGreevy would have been aware of it, and it
nowhere appears that any such value was given.

There is, as I have said, much more evidence, and there
are many more subjects upon which evidence was given.
But if it were assumed that there were only the facts and
the evidence I have alluded to, could it be said that there
was not evidence to go to the jury, from which they might
reasonably infer the existence of the conspiracy ?   I am
unable to perceive (saying nothing at present as to the
venue for trial) how the case could have been properly
withdrawn from the jury for want of evidence to support it.

This first paragraph of the case goes on and says " that
no overt act in Ontario,   *   *   had been shewn."   This
seems to me to presuppose that the agreement, combination
or conspiracy charged, took place, if at all, outside of the

county of Carleton, and outside of Ontario, presumably,
I apprehend, in Quebec, and to presuppose further and indirectly admit that in such case, if there had occurred an
overt act in the county of Carleton, that would be a proper
place of trial.

The case seemed to proceed, at least, so far as the argument before us had concern, upon this view, and looking at
it in this way I am of opinion that each of the four letters
written and sent from Ottawa, by the defendant Thomas
McGreevy, one on the 5th May, 1883, one on the 7th
May, 1883, one on the 8th May, 1883, and one on the 17th
May, 1883, three of which indicate that they were written
in the House of Commons, was an *overt act*, which took
place in the county of Carleton; that each of these letters
being in the nature of an act done in furtherance of the
common design, was properly admitted in the first place as
an act, from which, with other acts, the jury might infer
the conspiracy itself; that each of them is evidence, not
only against the writer of them, but against the co-conspirator or co-conspirators, and that each of them is an
overt act, as above, done in the county of Carleton, and
in this view and this being so, the county of Carleton was
a proper place for the trial.

But I do not perceive why it should be assumed that
the conspiracy took place outside of the county of Carleton.
For its very existence it is left to be inferred by the jury
from other facts. No evidence is given to shew where it
took place, and the jury have not found that it occurred
at any particular place. It is neither found nor proved
that it occurred outside of that county, and it might well
have occurred in the city of Ottawa, within that county.
The pleading of the Crown does not, as I read it, shew or
charge that the act of conspiracy alleged took place outside of that county, any more than it does that it took
place within that county, and the Crown brings the proceedings, and goes to trial in that county.

If it were assumed that the fact of the combination
or conspiracy occurred in the county of Carleton, there

would be no room for discussion as to venue or overt acts in relation to it. Besides, if it be considered that the indictment in this respect should have been different, it is a pleading that was amendable.

2 and 9. The second and the ninth paragraphs of the case have reference to certain evidence of Robert McGreevy, and for purposes here they may, to an extent, be taken together. For some reasons, no doubt good ones, the trial proceeded upon the whole of the twenty counts in the indictment, and the finding is in respect of all these counts. In some of these counts Robert McGreevy, and the others named in these paragraphs, are charged as conspirators. It is not necessary that all the alleged conspirators should be prosecuted at the same time. What is done or said by those that are not prosecuted, if it appears to be in furtherance of the common design—the conspiracy—is evidence admissible, not only against themselves, if they were prosecuted, but against any of the conspirators who are prosecuted. For these reasons the evidence of Robert McGreevy, so far as it disclosed anything in furtherance of the common design was, I think, admissible; and I think one searches in vain through the evidence alluded to in these paragraphs for evidence .not so admissible, for items of such evidence which can be said to have occasioned substantial wrong or miscarriage.

3. As to the third paragraph of the case, I think this falls under the principle of the case of *Blake* v. *The Albion Life Assurance Society*, 4 C. P. D. 94, and that the evidence was properly enough admitted.

4. As to the fourth paragraph of the case, it seems to be quite correct that the letters were received in evidence and that the undertaking of counsel regarding them was not redeemed. But one cannot fail to see by the evidence that the true position, authorship and character of these letters were fully disclosed and that in that light they were good evidence. Counsel seems merely to have been disappointed by the evidence of Gallagher. The letters became during the trial, evidence, proper to be received as I think.

5. When one sees the position occupied by Mr. Perley, the chief engineer, the report alluded to appears, as I think, to be one of those things that the alleged conspirators desired to be sent in as a step towards the accomplishment of the ultimate object or purpose, and for this reason if there were none other, I cannot see that it was improperly admitted.

6. The entries in the books referred to in the sixth paragraph were not, it is true, made by the defendant Connolly, but, as it appears he signed the yearly audit of these books, such audits shewing the alleged improper and spurious disbursements made by his firm.

The statements of the witness Cross, taken from the books, appear to have been received as secondary evidence on account of the books not having been produced pursuant to the undertaking of counsel for the defendant Connolly, as well as the other defendant. It is said that the books were after going into the custody of the defendant Connolly and others, withheld. I do not desire to make any remarks as to this. I do not, however, think that the defendant Connolly has any real ground of complaint in respect of the reception of this evidence.

The books would not, in the usual course, be evidence against the defendant, McGreevy. They shew, as it appears, payments of large moneys which it was suggested went to the defendant McGreevy in part. But apart altogether from these books, it was proved, one may say, almost indisputably, that no less a sum than $117,000 went directly from this firm to him, the defendant McGreevy, and assuming that the books were not as against this defendant strictly admissible, one cannot, as I think, see that their reception was productive of substantial wrong.

7. The depositions referred to in the seventh paragraph were put in as against the defendant Connolly. This course seems to be justified by the decision in *The Queen v. Coote*, L. R. 4 P. C. 599. He did not, in the Exchequer Court, object when the questions were asked him, so as

Judgment.

Ferguson, J.

to bring himself within the exception, which, in *The Queen* v. *Coote*, is said to be the only exception. Then as to the defendant McGreevy, the contents of the depositions became evidence, when on his cross-examination, the defendant Connolly virtually said that the depositions were true in all respects.

8. As to the eighth paragraph, I do not see any fatal objection to the evidence of the witness W. T. Jennings, looking at it as evidence of an expert. True he made many calculations, some of which appear to have been of a tentative character, but some of them, so far as I can see, were otherwise, and based on solid foundation.

9. As to the ninth paragraph, in addition to that I have before said respecting this paragraph, I may say that I am of the opinion that the agreements, understandings and payments referred to, were matters not improper to be placed by evidence before the jury as casting further light upon the subject under consideration, if it is conceded that they were of any importance for or against the defendant.

10. As to the tenth paragraph, I am of the opinion that the course pursued by the learned Judge was the correct one.

11. As to the eleventh paragraph, the word "unlawful" has various significations. The putting in of several tenders as appears to have been done in this case, seems to me to be insincere, untruthful and fraudulent, and most certainly intended to deceive the parties to whom the tenders are given, and very possibly a person would not be permitted to retain and hold a pecuniary advantage gained by such means. The learned Judge did not tell the jury that the act was an indictable offence, or in so many words that it was a criminal act. I am not prepared to say that the learned Judge was in error or so far in error as to constitute a sufficient reason for giving effect to the defendants' contentions.

12. This paragraph is as to the order of the addresses of counsel. The case was in this way peculiar. The defen-

dants were tried together. At the close of the case for Judgment.
the Crown, the defendant McGreevy announced his inten- Ferguson, J.
tion not to call any witnesses, but the other defendant
did call witnesses or a witness. What the learned Judge
said in ruling, was this : " As Mr. Justice Taschereau puts
it, the statute has not been substantially changed. I think
we will follow the old practice as a convenient one." I
do not see that we should interfere on this ground : section 661 Code.

MEREDITH, J. :—

Upon the bold, plain, and undenied main features of this
case, any twelve men might very reasonably find that the
defendants had expressly or tacitly conspired with other
persons to obtain by improper and deceitful means large
sums of the public funds ; and that the conspirators very
successfully carried out their scheme and effected their
purpose ; though this would be only an aggravation of the
crime, which was the conspiracy alone : and they might
also have reasonably found that the conspiracy was in
fact entered into at Ottawa.

And, that being so, there seems to me to be no difficulty
in upholding the verdict : but nothing would be gained by
my dealing in detail with the many minor points reserved :
that has already been twice done : I can usefully add
nothing more to all that has been said, in the judgments
just delivered, respecting them.

I desire, however, to guard against seeming to assent to
the proposition ' that where a conspiracy is entirely formed
in one Province it may be properly tried in any other
Province in which a mere overt act is alleged to have been
committed by any one of the conspirators. The question
is one of jurisdiction as well as of venue ; but even if it
affected only the place of trial, it is, in my opinion, a question at least worthy of careful consideration, notwithstanding the statements upon the subject contained in the text
books, and the judgments in some cases in the Courts

of the United States of America, all of which seem to be based upon the case of *The King* v. *Brisac*, 4 East, 164, in which, however, it was not necessary to determine the point, and it was not determined: it is more worthy of such consideration, where, as here, the question is one of jurisdiction as well, and having regard especially to the provisions of the Criminal Code, section 640, and the different constitutions of the Courts of the several Provinces, the different laws respecting property and civil rights in them (a conspiracy to do a civil wrong being in most cases a crime), the great extent of this Dominion, and the provisions for the trial of criminal cases by mixed juries in some of the Provinces only.

It may fairly be asked whether the case of treason, so much relied upon, is an analogous case; for in treason there is, generally, no crime without an overt act; while in conspiracy the crime is complete without any overt act beyond the act of conspiring, which alone is the crime.

And it may be suggested that perhaps the crime of conspiracy is sometimes confused with the crime conspired to be committed, or the wrong conspired to be done: an entirely different offence.

The consequences of holding everything everywhere done in furtherance of the objects of the conspirators is a new conspiracy or a renewal of the old one seems to me somewhat farfetched; the result might work grave injustice, and must be unsatisfactory upon the question of jurisdiction.

It would surely be a thing to be regretted, if there could be several trials and acquittals and convictions, under different jurisdictions, for in reality, in common sense, the one crime; also, if, for one instance, persons, all, and always, residents in the Province of British Columbia could be in the Province of Prince Edward Island charged with, and brought to trial upon a charge of, conspiracy, alleged to have been committed in the former Province, to do an alleged civil wrong there, solely because someone alleged to have been authorized to do so is alleged to have

written, in the latter Province, a letter alleged to have
been in furtherance of the alleged object of the alleged
conspirators.

The law is certainly not so clear that the question,
when it arises, may not be thoroughly dealt with upon its
merits.

But this case does not call for a consideration of the
question ; it was not reserved ; nor intended to be ; nor
would be, as the learned trial Judge has stated ; and, as I
have already mentioned, there was evidence upon which
the jury might have found, if the question had been
submitted to them, that the conspiracy, in part at all
events, was formed within the jurisdiction of this Court,
and within the county in which the case was tried, and
that was sufficient to found jurisdiction there.

Judgment supplementary to that of MEREDITH, J. :—

BOYD, C. :—

In view of what my brother Meredith has said I think
it advisable to read a supplementary judgment.

The question of locality of the conspiracy for the purpose of Provincial jurisdiction is not, in truth, before us.
It was not raised in pleadings nor broached in the Court
below at the trial or before the learned trial Judge.   Consequently it does not appear upon the points reserved,
though they were not stinted in number, nor was it advanced in the elaborate and minute argumentation of the
case before this Court of Appeal.   I must assume, not that
the point was overlooked, but considered and passed over
in silence, because not relied upon.

The only way in which it could possibly be now
entertained would be in respect of a new trial in
order that the question of jurisdiction might be raised.
Non constat upon the present evidence that the *locus* of
the conspiring was not within Ontario, *e. g.*, at Ottawa,
for the evidence while establishing the agreement by
reason of the overt acts does not localize the initial agree-

ment or common understanding. There is enough in the case to justify a finding that the common purpose was entered into at Ottawa, through Robert McGreevy as the intermediary with his brother Thomas, for Robert says he represented the claims of the firm to Thomas in writing and in speaking to him, *i. e.,* at Ottawa. Apart from this, a new trial is not sought on this ground.

But had the point been before us or were it properly open for consideration, I should say it ought not to prevail. The matter was apparently suggested by the proviso in section 640 of the Code : " That nothing in this Act authorizes any Court in one Province of Canada to try any person for any offence committed entirely in another Province, except in," etc. (providing for the case of defamatory libel). That is to say, the Code does not authorize an offence committed entirely in one Province to be tried in another.

But there is nothing in the Code to prohibit the trial of conspiracies as they had been under the former law, and the place was defined as in the quotations already given from Starkie. That is, the venue may be where the agreement was entered into, or where any overt act was done in the pursuance of the common design.

Such acts were proved to have taken place in Ottawa by the letters written, and the information procured and transmitted as already detailed. Now the *rationale* of this alternative venue is, that such an act is viewed as a renewal or a continuation of the original agreement by all conspirators. In opposition to what is laid down in the doubtful ruling, in *Regina* v. *Best*, 1 Salk. 179, the practice is otherwise stated (as found in Starkie and the later text writers), by Grose, J., in 1803, in *The King* v. *Brisac*, 4 East 164, mentioning with approval *The King* v. *Bowes*, a decision of 1787 (p. 171).

Of course the crime of conspiracy is complete when the agreement to do the wrong thing or to employ the wrong means is made, though there be no act in the execution of the design and then the place of trial is single and must be where the offence is complete. But if the matter goes

beyond intention and agreement and passes into execution
in other localities, then the conspiring mind manifests
itself wherever any overt act is done, and the offence is
thereby extended and continued elsewhere. This offence
was not "committed entirely" in the Province of Quebec,
even if the original concerted purpose was formed in the
city of Quebec, when that purpose was carried forward
into overt acts in the city of Ottawa and Province of
Ontario. Provincial jurisdiction in Ontario then attached,
and the case does not fall within the words or meaning of
the Code.

The counsel who argued *The King* v. *Burdett*, 3 B. & Ald.
at p. 737, said : " Conspirators may undoubtedly be tried for
a conspiracy, either in the county where the conspiracy originated, or in the county where the conspiracy is proved to
have been continued and carried into execution." And
again at p. 738: "The overt acts done by some of the
party in one county, while the rest may have been absent
in another county, prove the continuance of the conspiracy
in the county where the overt acts were committed."

Mr. Justice Holroyd, in his judgment in this case, as contained in 4 B. & Ald., at p. 138, adverts to the matter and
says : As to nuisances and conspiracies : "juries do
not confine their verdicts of guilty to such criminal acts or
consequences as occur in the county where the conspiracy
or the erection of the ' nuisance is laid and proved, but
extend them to such further acts and consequences of conspiracy and nuisance, as may occur or arise in another
county ; and judgment and punishment are in such cases
given and awarded to the full extent of the aggregate
offence."

That is a noteworthy expression, the overt acts were
not, as expressed by some American Judges, matters
merely of *aggravation*—they were matters of *aggregation*,—forming in the bulk one aggregate offence ; and
as to which, of course, there might be different localities.

In the same case (decided 1820), Abbott, C. J., com-
ments upon and approves of *The King* v. *Brisac*, and
Regina v. *Bowes*, at p. 178, and points out that treason

Judgment.

Boyd, C.

and misdemeanour are alike distinguishable from felony, at p. 179 on the ground that each act is an offence of the same species with every other, and with the whole, and then proceeds, "if any such part of the entire misdemeanour be proved to have been done, in the county in which the indictment is preferred, there is enough to satisfy the locality of trial," p. 180.

An author, Woolrych, whose works are examples of accurate research, writing in 1842 on "Misdemeanours," though referring frequently to *Regina* v. *Best* (as reported in Salkeld and Lord Raymond), does not rely on it as governing questions of venue, but says: "With regard to the county where the offence is to be tried, any one may be selected where an overt act of conspiracy has been attempted," p. 155. For this he cites the cases in 4 East, and refers to the citation of these by the counsel who argued, *Rex.* v. *Johnson*, 6 East 590.

The King v. *Brisac* appears in the seventh volume of Revised Reports, p. 551, and is there at p. 557 noted as being quoted from by the Judge in *Mulcahy* v. *The Queen*, L. R. 3 H. L. 306, 317. That case, therefore, I take to be of well recognized and unimpeachable authority, whereas the other case, as found in 1 Salkeld, is not, I think, correctly reported, having regard to the following con-considerations: The case was decided in 1704-5, and was reported in the folio of 1713, now known as sixth Modern, at p. 185, in very great detail, whereas in Salkeld the report is short, irregularly condensed, and the volume containing it was first published after his death in 1717 under the care of Lord Hardwicke, it is supposed.

The statement or *dictum* which appears, in *Regina* v. *Best*, 1 Salk. 174, that the "venue must be where the conspiracy was, not where the result of the conspiracy is put into execution," is not found in any of the contemporaneous or concurrent reports of the case: see 2 Lord Raym. 1167; Holt 151: and 6 Mod. case 186. This last contains the most detailed report of the case, and from it it appears that the passage given as judgment in 1 Salk. was the argument of counsel, citing from the Year Book (42 Edw. III. pt. 15).

Judgment.

Boyd, C.

These are the words of plaintiff's counsel: "In the Year Book, a conspiracy laid in one place to charge with a fact in another county and the venue came from the county where the conspiracy was laid." Reports of *The Queen* v. *Best* are also given in 6 Mod., pp. 137,;138.

In point of general accuracy the 6th Modern ranks high among the better class of old reports : see Wallace on Reporters, 227 ; but the Court did not think very highly of 1 Salk. in 5 Taunt, at p. 190.

Taking, however, the cue supplied by reference to the Year Book of 42 Edw. III. (found both in Salkeld and 6th Mod.), it can be demonstrated the law referred to assists the position I now take.   That Year Book is *inter alia* cited in *Bulwer's Ca.*, 7 Rep. 1 b, to sustain the following text : "If two conspire to indict a man in one county, and they by their malicious prosecution make the execution of their conspiracy in another county, and there cause the party to be indicted, the plaintiff may have his action of conspiracy in which county he will, for they put their conspiracy in one county in execution in the other * * . But if they conspire in one county, by force of which conspiracy without any other act by them, he is indicted in another county, then the writ ought to be brought in the county where the conspiracy was, for the defendants have done nothing in the county where the indictment was, nor were parties nor privies to the finding of the indictment, but only by the conspiracy in the other county."

The conspiracy in this case was a crime against the common law of the Dominion of Canada, and might, in my opinion, be prosecuted in any Province where an overt act was committed, so that no question of jurisdiction can upon the facts or law arise.

For these reasons (which are given without the advantage of hearing counsel) I would not entertain any possible objection that the proper place of trial has not been selected.

FERGUSON, J.   I agree in the conclusions of the Chancellor.

G. A. B.

ROBERTS v. BANK OF TORONTO ET AL.

Lien—Artisan's Lien—Manufacture of Bricks on Property of Another Person—Possession.

The plaintiff was employed to manufacture bricks for another in a brick-yard belonging to the latter, of which, however, the plaintiff held possession for the purpose of his contract, and remained and was in possession of the bricks at the time of their seizure by the sheriff under an execution against the owner of the brickyard, who, immediately after such seizure, made an assignment for the benefit of creditors :—

Held, that the plaintiff was entitled to a lien upon the bricks in priority to the execution and assignment for the benefit of creditors, and also in priority to the claim of a chattel mortgagee, though his mortgage covered brick in course of manufacture during its continuance.

Statement.   THIS was a trial of an interpleader issue in which the the plaintiff, John Roberts, affirmed, and the defendants, who were the Bank of Toronto, Henry W. Barber and G. M. Gardner, the assignee for the benefit of creditors of Thomas Robertson, denied that at the date of the assignment by Robertson to Gardner for the benefit of creditors, and at the time of the seizure of a quantity of brick by the sheriff of the county of York under an execution against Robertson in the suit of *Kieran* v. *Robertson*, and at the time of a certain distress made by the Bank of Toronto under a mortgage held by them the bricks in question were subject to the lien of the plaintiff as against the defendants.

The bricks were manufactured by the plaintiff during the season of 1893, for Robertson upon premises owned by the latter. On May 19th, 1893, Robertson made a chattel mortgage to the Toronto Wood & Shingle Company, to secure an indebtedness of upwards of $3,000, which mortgage covered brick then in the kilns, substitutions therefor or additions thereto, and all brick in course of manufacture from time to time during the continuance of the mortgage or of any renewals thereof. This mortgage was assigned for value to the defendant Henry W. Barber, as trustee for the Bank of Toronto, which bank also held an assignment of a judgment obtained by William Patrick Kieran against Robertson, and issued execution thereon under which the sheriff seized the bricks on December 6th, 1893. On December 8th, 1893, Robertson made an assignment for the benefit of creditors to Gardner. Besides which the Bank of Toronto had distrained upon the bricks upon a third mortgage upon the real estate held by them, as to which, however, the defendant Gardner, as assignee for the creditors, before the trial, admitted the validity of its claim to the extent of one year's arrears as provided by the Mortgage Act, R. S. O. c. 102,[sec. 17, which the bank accepted in full of its claim to this respect.

Roberts claimed a lien as a workman by virtue of his having spent his labour in the manufacture of the brick. He did not claim any registered lien under the Mechanics' Lien Act.

The action was tried at the non-jury sittings at Toronto before BOYD, C., upon April 16th, 1894.

Elgin Myers, Q. C., for the plaintiff. There was no surrender of possession. The plaintiff's lien attached, as the bricks were made, and prior to the mortgage in question. Section 3 of the Mortgage Act has not been complied with. I refer to *Moore* v. *Hitchcock*, 4 Wend. 293; *Chase* v. *Westmore*, Tudor's L. C. on Mercantile Law, 3rd ed., at p. 382; Jones on Liens, 2nd ed., secs. 731-2.

Blackstock, Q. C., and *R. McKay*, for the defendants Barber, and the Bank of Toronto. No lien exists as claimed. The plaintiff had no interest in the property. He worked for wages merely. Robertson had a right to deal with the brick as he pleased, irrespective of Roberts : Phillips on Mechanics' Liens, 13th ed., p. 802-3, secs. 479, 481; *King* v. *The Indian Orchard Canal Co.*, 11 Cush. 231; *McNeil* v. *Keleher*, 15 C. P. 470; *Forth* v. *Simpson*, 13 Q. B. 680. Roberts had no right to possession.

Bristol, for the defendant Gardner.

Myers, in reply. The brick-yard was separate from the farm, and the possession was in Roberts.

April 18th, 1894. BOYD, C. :—

The facts in *King* v. *The Indian Orchard Co.*, 11 Cush. 231, distinguish it from *Moore* v. *Hitchcock*, 4 Wend. 293, and from this case. In the former case the land belonged to the defendant, who leased it for a limited term to one Stearns for a brick yard. Stearns agreed with King as to the making of the bricks on which the lien was claimed. But the evidence showed that the possession of the yard was with Stearns, whose men occupied it during the whole period of manufacture, and it also appears that the plaintiff withdrew from the possession of the bricks a week before they were sold by Stearns to the defendants. In the latter case, *Moore* v. *Hitchcock*, the owner of the land supplied all material and hired the plaintiff to make the brick and deliver them on board a vessel at $1.75 per thousand. The Court held on the meaning of the contract. that the employer had no legal right to the possession till the brick were delivered, and that the plaintiff was in possession in fact at the time of the sale under execution. I find as a conclusion of facts in this case that the possession of the brickyard was in the plaintiff for the purpose of his contract with Robertson, the owner, and that the plaintiff remained and was in possession of the brick at the date of the seizure by the sheriff, and of the execution of the assignment for creditors. Though there was no written contract with the plaintiff yet the manner of dealing and the conduct of the business indicate that Robertson had in effect surrendered the possession of the yard to the plaintiff and his men, who alone worked there in the manufacture of the brick. That this would be sufficient possession for the attachment of an artisan's lien appears to be recognized by Bigelow J., in 11 Cush., p. 234. As pointed out in *Shaw* v. *Keler*, 106 Miss., 448, 450, the plaintiff in 11th Cush., wholly failed to make out his actual possession, but that cardinal fact is abundantly proved in the case in hand. The judgment will be for the plaintiff with costs.

A. H. F. L.

[QUEEN'S BENCH DIVISION.]

CONFEDERATION LIFE ASSOCIATION v. TOWNSHIP OF HOWARD.

Municipal Corporations — Drainage — Void By-law — Debenture Issued under — Action on — Estoppel — Money Had and Received.

Action to recover the amount of a debenture, one of a series issued by the defendants pursuant to their by-law passed for the levying of a special rate upon a particular locality for the purpose of cleaning out and repairing a drain :—

Held, following *Alexander* v. *Township of Howard*, 14 O. R. 22, and *Re Clark and Township of Howard*, 16 A. R. 72, that the by-law was void, the defendants having no power to pass it for such a purpose.

The debenture was silent as to the purposes for which it was issued, but referred to the by-law, which disclosed such purposes. There was no representation by the defendants that it was good :—

Held, that, although the plaintiffs were innocent holders and had paid the full value of the debenture, they could not recover upon it, because the defendants had no power to make the contract professedly made by it.

Webb v. *Commissioners of Herne Bay*, L. R. 5 Q. B. 642, distinguished.

Marsh v. *Fulton County*, 10 Wallace U. S. R. 676, specially referred to.

Held, however, that as the defendants were bound to keep the drain in repair and to pay for repairs out of their general funds, and as they had received the price of the debenture directly from the plaintiffs and had the full benefit of it, without giving any consideration, the plaintiffs were entitled to recover for money received by the defendants.

THIS was an action tried before FERGUSON, J., at Chatham Statement. and Toronto. The facts are fully stated in the judgment.

The case was argued at Toronto on 5th January, 1894.

J. C. Hamilton and *Snow*, for the plaintiffs.

M. Wilson, Q. C., and *E. Bell*, for the defendants.

March 27, 1894.   FERGUSON, J. :—

The defendants by their four several debentures dated the 1st day of January, 1884, promised to pay one John A. Elliott or bearer the sum of $500 on the 1st day of January, 1885, the sum of $500 on the 1st day of January, 1886, the sum of $500 on the 1st day of January, 1887, and the sum of $500 on the 1st day of January, 1888, and also the amount of the annual coupons for interest attached to the said debentures respectively.

The plaintiffs purchased these debentures and coupons
and became the holders of the same for value. The respective debentures that fell due on the 1st day of January in
the years 1885, 1886, and 1887, and the coupons attached
to the same, were duly paid by the defendants to the plaintiffs, but the defendants refused to pay the debenture that
fell due on the 1st day of January, 1888, although they
had year after year paid the amounts of coupons attached
to it, and the action is brought to recover the amount of
this debenture and the amount of the coupon still attached
to it, as well as interest since the 1st day of January,
1888, when, as the plaintiffs say, the same should have
been paid. The plaintiffs, as I understand their pleading,
also seek to recover the amount of this last debenture as
money lent by them to the defendants or money received
by the defendants to the use of the plaintiffs, saying that
they advanced the whole sum of $2,000 to the defendants
on the defendants' promise to pay the same, with interest,
in four equal instalments, on the 1st days of January in
the years 1885, 1886, 1887, and 1888, but that the defendants have not paid the last of such instalments.

The plaintiffs ask judgment against the defendants for
the amount of such last of the four debentures, $500, the
amount of the coupons still attached to the same, $35, and
interest on both sums from the 1st day of January, 1888,
at seven per cent. per annum. They ask, as I suppose in
the alternative, to recover from the defendants the sum of
$500 as money had and received by the defendants from
the plaintiffs.

The defendants by their statement of defence say that
these debentures were issued and sold in good faith to
John A. Elliott for a valuable money consideration paid by
Elliott to the council of the defendants, and applied by
said council, not for the ordinary or general purposes or
benefit of the defendant corporation, but in the doing of
certain local improvements, being drainage works to be
paid for, as the defendants supposed and intended, not out
of the general funds of the defendants, but by a local assess-

ment and rate upon the property benefited or to be _{Judgment.}
benefited thereby.   And before the issue of the said alleged _{Ferguson, J.}
debentures the council of the defendants in good faith
passed what purported to be a by-law of the defendants,
being by-law No. 16 of 1883, providing for the creation of
the debt represented by said debentures on the security of
the rate settled in such supposed by-law and for the issue
of the said alleged debentures and the raising of the said
money thereby, and applying the same to the doing of the
local drainage works aforesaid; and further providing for
the payment of such debentures by a local assessment and
special rate upon the lands benefited as aforesaid, which
said lands are particularly described and set out in the
said supposed by-law.

The defendants also say that after the passing of by-law
16 these debentures were issued, and that upon the face of
each of the debentures it is stated that it is issued pursuant
to this by-law No. 16.   They allege also that Elliott and
the plaintiffs were aware of the by-law and the contents
thereof and accepted the debentures and took the risk of
the by-law, and that the council of the defendants have
never declared that the debt represented by the said debentures and created on the security of the said special rate
was or is guaranteed by the municipality at large.

The defendants "admit" (they use the word "admit")
that on the 22nd January, 1884, the plaintiffs purchased
the debentures from Elliott for valuable consideration and
became the bearer thereof.   The plaintiffs, however, seek
to shew that their purchase of the debentures was from
the defendants themselves.

The defendants also say that the by-law No. 16 was
based upon and its validity depended upon the validity of
their by-law No. 6 of 1868 for the doing of certain drainage
works in the townships of Howard and Harwich, and they
allege that both Elliott and the plaintiffs had notice of
these by-laws.

The defendants then say that this by-law No. 16 was
not preceded by or based upon any proper or sufficient

petition or report of any engineer or provincial land surveyor, nor was the assessment or special rate thereby purported to be made or levied preceded by or based upon
any proper or sufficient assessment or charge by or through
any such engineer or surveyor, nor was any Court of
Revision held thereon, nor was any opportunity given
to the persons whose lands were assessed to appeal from or
with regard to the assessment or charge, nor was the by-
law advertised or otherwise published, nor were any lands
in Harwich assessed or charged thereunder, nor was the
assessment placed upon or extended to all the lands and
roads to be benefited by or assessable for the works in the
by-law provided for, nor were the persons whose property
was supposed to be assessed or charged thereby notified of
the said by-law or of the intention of the council to pass
the same, and in consequence thereof, and for other reasons,
the by-law is wholly illegal and void, and that by reason
of the invalidity of the by-law they are unable to raise the
moneys thereunder to pay the plaintiffs' claim.

The defendants also say that their reeve and treasurer
had not, nor had the defendants, any power or authority
(other than the said by-law) to make, issue, sell, or dispose
of the debentures, or to promise to pay the moneys claimed,
and that they had not power to pay the amount of the
debenture and coupon sued on otherwise than with moneys
raised and levied under the by-law, and they deny that
they promised to pay the said amount to the plaintiffs.

The defendants deny that they received any benefit from
the moneys advanced by the plaintiffs, or that such moneys
became part of the general fund of the defendants, or that
the moneys were applied for their use or benefit. They
say that the by-law, the assessment, and the debentures
and coupons were wholly void and beyond the powers of
the defendants and their council, and that no debt of the
defendants to the plaintiffs was incurred thereby or thereunder.

In the case *Alexander* v. *Township of Howard*, 14 O. R.
22, I expressed the opinion that the by-law in question here

was void, for the reasons there stated (as against the plaintiffs in that action).

In the case *Re Clark and the Township of Howard*, 16
A. R. 72, which was an appeal from the order made on a
motion to quash another by-law passed for the same purpose, namely, the maintenance and repair of the drain
known as the McGregor Creek drain, the Court held that,
as that drain had been constructed under the provisions of
the Municipal Act of 1866, the council had no power to
pass a by-law for the levying of a special rate upon a
particular locality for the purpose of keeping it in repair
or repairing it, and that it was to be kept in repair by the
municipality at large. That by-law was, as appears by the
report of the case, for the " repairing and cleaning out" of
the McGregor Creek drain. The present by-law was for
the purposes, as expressed in the recitals, of " cleaning out
and repairing " the same drain, so that it appears that each
of the by-laws was for the same purposes.

In the argument before me it was contended that the
McGregor Creek drain had never been fully completed, and
that I had so found in the *Alexander* case, and reference
was made to sub-sec. 16 of sec. 570. In the *Clark* case
aforesaid the subject is discussed and disposed of. It was
there held that the by-law could not be supported as a by-
law for the re-execution or completion of a work partly or
insufficiently executed under a former Act, and that this
sub-section did not apply. In his judgment Mr. Justice
Osler, in referring to the McGregor Creek drain, said
(p. 85) : " Such a drain may be said to have been constructed
under a contract between the municipality and the parties
petitioning for it, and *quá* repairs, no liability was assumed
by the latter or has been authorized by the legislature, or
can be imposed by the council." The learned Judge then
said : " This, I think, was a fatal objection to the by-law of
1883 in question in the case of *Alexander* v. *These Defendants*, 14 O. R. 22," which I may repeat is the by-law in
question now. In the same case Mr. Justice Burton said
(p. 80) : " I have not considered the other objections urged

to the sufficiency of the by-law because I think there was no
authority in the council to make a special assessment for
the maintenance and repair of this drain, to which the
whole township is bound to contribute."

The learned Judges of the Court of Appeal seem to have
thoroughly considered and dealt with the various statutes
on the subject, and, whether or not this were so, it would
not be for me to question, for a moment, the conclusions at
which they arrived and stated in their judgments.

The debenture sued on states on its face that it was
issued pursuant to by-law No. 16 of 1883, the by-law in
question in the *Alexander* case, 14 O. R. 22, and, for present
purposes, I must, with these authorities before me, hold that
that by-law was and is void, not only because it was passed
irregularly and without the performance of prerequisites,
but also because passed upon a subject and for a purpose or for purposes in respect of which there was no
power to pass a by-law such as this one is at all. It seems
that the by-law was from the beginning utterly void, and
would have been so even if all the formalities and all the
requirements in passing a by-law for the maintenance
and repairs of drains had been strictly attended to and
performed, because there was no power to pass such a by-
law on the subject, or for the purposes for which it was
passed.

The plaintiffs are, as I think, on the evidence, innocent
holders, in fact, of the debenture on which they have sued,
having paid the full value of it as also of the coupon; and
the question arises here as to whether or not they are as
such innocent holders for value protected, or whether or
not the defendants are estopped from saying that the debenture and coupon are not good and valid in the plaintiffs'
hands.

The plaintiffs referred on this question to the case,
amongst many others, *Webb* v. *The Commissioners of Herne
Bay*, L. R. 5 Q. B. 642. The case, however, is clearly distinguishable from the present one, for there there was
power to issue debentures on the subject. They had power

to issue debentures for money borrowed, and the debentures on their face purported to be debentures given for
money advanced to them, and, as said by Cockburn, C. J.,
were in the form prescribed by the Act 'under which the
commissioners carried on their 'operations. The infirmity
in the debentures was that they had really been given to
one of their own members for goods, and contrary to an
express provision in the Act. Yet there was power to issue
the debentures for the purposes stated on their face ; and
the Court held that the commissioners were estopped from
saying that the debentures were not good and valid in the
hands of an innocent holder.

In the present case the debenture does not on its face
say for what purpose it was issued, but does say that it
was issued pursuant to this by-law, No. 16 of 1883. The
by-law states on its face the purposes for which it was
passed, and these purposes, according to the decision to
which I have referred, were purposes for which the council
had no power to pass such a by-law. There is no representation by the defendants here that the by-law was passed
or the debenture issued for a purpose for which they had
power to pass the by-law and issue the debenture, as there
was in the case above, L. R. 5 Q. B. 642, and in that case
it is to be observed that the estoppel is placed on the common ground as in *Pickard* v. *Sears*, 6 A. & E. 469 ; *Freeman* v. *Cooke*, 2 Ex. 654 ; and *Re Bahia and San Francisco*
R. W. Co., L. R. 3 Q. B. 584.

With the best consideration I have been able to bestow
upon that case and the elements of the present case, in
respect of which it was put forth as an authority, I am of
the opinion that the cases are materially different, and that
it is not an authority. Take the debenture in the present
case, silent as to the purposes for which it was issued, but
referring to the by-law under which it was issued, which
disclosed the purposes. If one read both, it cannot be said
that there was a representation that the debenture was
good (though no doubt at the time it was thought by the
defendants it was good) and it turns out, according to the
authority I have referred to, that it was not good.

The cases *Pendleton County* v. *Amy*, 13 Wallace U.
S. R. 297; *Supervisors* v. *Schenck*, 5 Wallace U. S. R.
772; *Board of County of Knox* v. *Aspinwall*, 21 Howard
U. S. R. 539; and *Gelpcke* v. *City of Dubuque*, 1 Wallace
U. S. R. 175, are all cases in which there was power to
issue the bonds. The objection was that those things
required by the legislature to be done before the power
to issue the bonds should be exercised had not been done.
See the language of Mr. Justice Strong delivering the
opinion of the Court, 13 Wallace at p. 305, that of Mr.
Justice Clifford, 5 Wallace at p. 784, and that of Mr. Justice
Nelson, 21 Howard at p. 544.

Mr. Justice Strong said: "A purchaser is not always
bound to look farther than to discover that the power has
been conferred, even though it be coupled with conditions
precedent."

Mr. Justice Clifford said: "When a corporation has
power, under any circumstances, to issue negotiable
securities, the decision of this Court is that the *bond fide*
holder has a right to presume they were issued under the
circumstances which gave the requisite authority," referring
to 1 Wallace 203.

The language of Mr. Justice Nelson in delivering the
opinion of the Court, 21 Howard at p. 544, is to the same
effect.

These, as I have said, were all cases in which there was
the power to issue the bonds, if that power had been
exercised after performance of the prerequisites provided
for by the legislature.

The case *Marsh* v. *Fulton County*, 10 Wallace U. S. R.
676, seems to me much more like the present case so far
as this question has concern. There the railway company
was authorized to construct a railway from Warsaw, on
the M. river, to the east line of the State. An Act was
subsequently passed dividing the line into three divisions,
the western, central, and eastern, and each division was
created a new company. It was held that a subscription
of stock and issue of county bonds, authorized upon a vote

of the people of the county to the original corporation, could
not be legally made to one of the three new corporations,
and that the authority to contract must exist before any
protection as an innocent purchaser can be claimed by the
holder, and that that was a case in which the power to
contract never existed.

In the case *Sceally* v. *McCallum*, 9 Gr. at pp. 438 and 439,
the late Chief Justice Spragge, then Vice-Chancellor, in delivering judgment referred to the case *Athenæum Life Ins.
Co.* v. *Pooley*, 28 L. J. Ch. 119, saying that it was there
intimated by all the Judges who decided the case, that it
lies upon the party buying debentures to ascertain all facts
essential to their validity. The case *Sceally* v. *McCallum*
was much different in its facts from the present case. See
also Daniel on Negotiable Instruments, secs. 1520 and 1530.

After having examined many other cases bearing more
or less on the subject, I have arrived at the conclusion and
I am of the opinion that the plaintiffs cannot recover upon
this debenture and coupon, for the reason that the defendants had no power or authority to make the contract
professedly made by the debenture.

The question then presents itself: can the plaintiffs recover on the other case they present, namely, for money
lent, or for money received, to their use ?

At the trial and upon the argument there was a difference as to the manner in which the plaintiffs obtained the
debentures ; the defendants contending that they sold the
four debentures, one of which is the one sued on, to Elliott,
and that afterwards Elliott sold them to the plaintiffs ;
the contention for the plaintiffs being that they purchased
the debentures from the defendants directly.

Elliott was called as a witness. He said that he was a
banker and broker at Ridgetown ; that the township came
to him and asked him to sell these debentures for them,
and that he sold the debentures to the plaintiffs for the
defendants; that the defendants got the money, and that
it was the money of the plaintiffs the defendants got.
Elliott says that the defendants paid him for his services

in selling the debentures for them, and there is other
evidence of this (an account containing a receipt for such
payment).

Elliott says he is the plaintiffs' agent at Ridgetown in
life insurance only, and that he cannot say why his name
was used as payee in the debentures. He says that in the
sale of the debentures he acted as agent for both parties
and was paid a commission by each.

Mr. Mitton, the treasurer of the township, was called.
He was unable to contradict the statements of Elliott.
His evidence was to the general effect that the price of
the debentures had been received by the defendants, but
that from the books of the defendants it could not be traced
so as to see with accuracy what had become of it. He
said that only $754.02 had been paid for repairing the
drain pursuant to the provisions of the by-law. But it
was suggested, and not denied by the defendants' counsel,
that as large a sum as $1,000 was employed to retire notes
that had been given by the defendants to raise money to
be used in repairing the drain (in anticipation of the sale
of the debentures), and, according to his (Mitton's) evidence,
the sum of about $1,815 was assessed and collected under
the by-law—a somewhat larger sum having been assessed.

I am of the opinion that I must find, and I do find upon
the evidence, that the transaction of the sale of the debentures, including the one in question here, was a transaction
between the plaintiffs and the defendants made through
the instrumentality of an agent common to both, and that
the essence of the transaction was a sale by the defendants
of their own debentures to the plaintiffs, they receiving
the plaintiffs' money for them.

As before stated, the defendants were, according to the
decision of the *Clark* case, bound to keep this drain, that
is, their portion of it, in repair, and to pay for such repairs
out of the general funds of the township, or with moneys
levied upon the whole township, and not any particular
part of it; and it is difficult—it is to me impossible—to see
that the defendants' statement in their pleading that they

did not get the benefit of these moneys can be true. I
must find and conclude that the defendants did receive the
money from the plaintiffs and had the full benefit of it.
The most the defendants can say contrary to this seems to
me only that they allowed the money to become confused in
their books.

Then the defendants have had and have the plaintiffs'
money on a transaction between them and the plaintiffs,
the money having been received by them from the plaintiffs, without having given any consideration whatever for
it. True, it is, this was upon the sale of what was absolutely worthless, but the fact is nevertheless so.

If the plaintiffs had purchased the debenture sued on
from a third party, and there was no privity between
them and the defendants other than that supposed to have
been created through the worthless debenture, that, as it
seems to me, would have been a different case.

Here the plaintiffs' money went, as I think, wrongly,
but directly, from the hand of the plaintiffs, into the hand
of the defendants, that is, the money did not go through
the hand of any intermediate owner of the debenture.

In Pollock on Contracts, 5th ed., p. 154, the author says :
" It is settled that in general a cause of action on a ' contract
implied in law,' as it is conveniently called in our books, is
as good against a corporation as against a natural person.
Thus a corporation may be sued in an action for money
received on the ground of strict necessity ; it cannot be
expected that a corporation should put their seal to a promise to return moneys which they are wrongly receiving."

The case referred to is *Hall* v. *Mayor of Swansea*, 5
Q. B. 526, in which it was held that the corporation, defendants, having wrongly taken and withheld tolls which
of right belonged to the plaintiff, were liable to the plaintiff in assumpsit for " money had and received."

In *Jefferys* v. *Gurr*, 2 B. & Ad. 833, the guardians were
said to be, for the purpose of suing and being sued, in the
nature of a corporation, and it was held that the plaintiff

could recover against their treasurer for money paid to the use of the guardians.

Money paid by the plaintiff without consideration, or for a consideration that has failed, may be recovered back : *Straton* v. *Rastall*, 2 T. R. 366. So money given for worthless foreign bonds: *Young* v. *Cole*, 3 Bing. N. C. 724 ; or for a worthless cheque : *Turner* v. *Stones*, 1 D. & L. 122.

The failure of the consideration must be complete in order to entitle the plaintiff to recover the money, but where the consideration is severable (as I think it is here) complete failure of part may form a ground for recovering a proportionate part of the money paid for it : *Hirst* v. *Tolson*, 19 L. 'J. Ch. 441. I think the present case differs materially from the case *Lamert* v. *Heath*, 15 M. & W. 486, where it was held that the plaintiff could not recover as upon a failure of consideration where he has obtained that which he bargained for, although it turns out not genuine and valueless. There the defendant had purchased Kentish Coast Railway scrip, and Baron Alderson said : " The question is simply this—was what the parties bought in the market Kentish Coast Railway scrip ?" Here the plaintiffs purchased from the defendants their own debentures, which were bad. It was not a purchase from a third person in the market.

The case I have found to be a troublesome one. I am, however, of the opinion that the plaintiffs are entitled to recover their money as money received by the defendants. No question as to the Statute of Limitations is raised.

The evidence of Mitton shews, though I fancy he was speaking only from the defendants' books, that the sum of $2000 was received for the four debentures. They were for equal sums, $500 each. The money paid in respect of this last one is what is claimed here. Although the defendants have had this sum and have used and employed it as before stated, yet I do not see that it is a case for interest before action brought, (under the provisions of the statute.) The plaintiffs are, I think, entitled to recover, and there will be judgment for them for $500, with interest from the commencement of the action, and their costs of the action.   I do not see that the plaintiffs were bound to make the other township a party.

Judgment for the plaintiff for $500, interest as above, and costs.

The demurrer was not argued as a demurrer, and there will be no costs in respect of it to either party.

Order accordingly.

E. B. B.

[QUEEN'S BENCH DIVISION.]

HURDMAN V. CANADA ATLANTIC RAILWAY COMPANY.

Negligence—Railways—Licensee—Volenti non Fit Injuria—Loan of Engine and Crew—Evidence of.

In an action under Lord Campbell's Act for damages arising from the death of a servant of a lumber company, who was engaged in counting lumber in a car of the defendants in the lumber company's yard, caused by his being squeezed between two piles of lumber, owing, as the jury found, to the negligence of the defendants' servants in charge of an engine in giving the car too strong a push :—

Held, that, assuming knowledge on the part of the crew of the engine of the position of the deceased in the car, it would be a negligent act to propel the car so rapidly against another as to be likely to injure him ; and, there being a conflict of evidence as to the rate of speed, the case could not have been withdrawn from the jury.

2. That the knowledge of the crew that the deceased was in the car and of the probable consequences to him of the work in which they were engaged, if done without due care, imposed upon them a duty, whether he was there as a mere licensee or otherwise, to use the care necessary to avoid causing that injury.

Batchelor v. *Fortescue*, 11 Q. B. D. 474, distinguished.

3. The finding of the jury that the deceased voluntarily accepted the risks of shunting did not entitle the defendants to judgment ; he voluntarily accepted the risks of shunting, but did not give the defendants leave to run the risk of killing him by doing their shunting negligently.

Smith v. *Baker*, [1891] A. C. 325, applied and followed.

4. Upon the evidence, there was no loan to the lumber company by the defendants of the engine and its crew ; and the fact that the latter were acting under the direction of the servants of the lumber company in moving such cars as they were told to move did not make them the servants of the lumber company.

Cameron v. *Nystrom*, [1893] A. C. 308, followed.

THIS was an action tried before ROSE, J., and a jury, at Ottawa on the 27th September, 1893.

It was brought by the plaintiff, as administrator of the estate of Thomas F. Hurdman, deceased, to recover damages arising from his death, which took place under the following circumstances :—

The deceased was employed by the Sheppard & Morse Lumber Company at their lumber yard, situated about two miles east of the Ottawa station of the defendants, and close to the line of the defendants' railway. The railway company had lent rails to the lumber company, who had, at their own expense, constructed switches and sidings upon their own property, separated from the right of way of the railway company by a fence and by a gate controlled by the lumber company. The switches and sidings in the lumber company's yard were connected with the defendants' line by a switch. The lumber company shipped quantities of lumber over the defendants' railway, for which they paid freight from Ottawa station to the points of destination. The defendants were in the habit, when advised by the lumber company that loaded cars were awaiting removal, of sending an engine with its crew to the lumber yard, there collecting the loaded cars and making them up into a train, and then moving them to their own line, and thence to their several destinations. They were also in the habit of drawing to the defendants' yard such empty cars as were needed, and placing them in such parts of the yard as the lumber company should indicate For the services so rendered no charge was made to the lumber company. Originally the lumber company had done in their own yard by means of horses the work thus done by the defendants' engines, but this having been found inconvenient, the defendants had sent their engines. Upon the 30th December, 1892, the deceased was engaged with a boy named Asher in counting and tallying lumber which had been loaded in a box car of the defendants. There was a pile of lumber at each end of the car with a narrow space of some fourteen inches in width across the centre of the car between the piles. In this space the deceased was standing doing his work. He had been warned more than once on former occasions by his employers that he ran a risk of being squeezed between the piles of lumber in a moving car, but had disregarded the warning. Upon the day in question he continued his work after the engine sent by the defendants to make up a train, including the car in which he was working, had begun to draw it about the yard for the purpose of attaching it to the other loaded cars upon other sidings. The conductor in charge of the defendants' men had seen him in the car a few minutes before the accident and waited for him to finish his work and get out of the car, but the deceased told him not to wait, saying that it was all right, that they would soon finish counting and would look out for themselves. The defendants' men then drew it away, and shortly afterwards, intending to attach it to some loaded cars upon another siding, gave it a push by means of the engine and sent it down a slight grade towards these other cars. The force with which it struck the other cars was sufficient to cause the lumber in the car in question to shift, and the deceased was squeezed between the piles and instantly killed. The plaintiff charged that the accident was caused by negligence on the part of the conductor and men in charge of the engine in sending the car in question with unnecessary violence against the other cars, insisting that there was no danger to the deceased if this operation had been performed with reasonable care. The learned trial Judge submitted to the jury the following questions, to which their answers are added :—

1. Was there negligence in the management of the car in question?   Answer. There was negligence in the management of the car in question.

2. If so, state in what such negligence consisted? Answer. In giving the car too strong a push.

3. If there was negligence in the management of the car, was the accident the result of such negligence?

Answer. We believe the accident was the result of the negligence aforesaid.

4. Did the deceased, knowing the danger, voluntarily accept the risks of shunting? Answer. The deceased voluntarily accepted the risks of shunting.

The damages were assessed by consent at $750.

McCarthy, Q. C., and *Kidd*, for the plaintiff.
Chrysler, Q. C., and *W. Nesbitt*, for the defendants.

December 16, 1893. ROSE, J. :—

The facts of this case are fairly set out in a very carefully prepared memorandum handed in to me since the trial of the case by the counsel for the defendant company.

At the trial I thought there was evidence to go to the jury of negligence on the part of those in control of the engine. I am still of that opinion, and think I could not have properly withdrawn the case from the jury as to such question. The jury found negligence in the management of the engine, and therefore in the consideration of this case we start with negligence proven against the driver and the yard-master, Clark, who had control of the engine when the accident happened. The engine was the property of the defendant company. The driver and the yard-master were the servants of such company, and paid by it. The employment in which the men were engaged was apparently in the line of business which the company was carrying on, and apparently, therefore, the negligence was the negligence of the defendant company. But it is urged that on the occasion in question the driver and yard-master were not the servants of such company, but were the servants of the Sheppard & Morse Lumber Company, to which company the defendant company had lent the engine and the servants, and that therefore the servants were the servants of the lumber company, and the engine under the control of the lumber company.

There is no question about the law ; the difficulty is as

to the application of the law to the facts of this case.
Notwithstanding the fact that the engine belonged to the
defendant company, and that the driver and yard-master
were the paid servants of such company, if, at the
time of the accident, the work being performed was the
work of the lumber company, and if performed for the
lumber company by the-driver and yard-master under the
direction of the lumber company, and solely for the convenience of the lumber company, and if the defendant
company had solely for the convenience of the lumber
company lent to such company the engine and men, and
the work done was not the work of the defendant company, or being performed by such company, there is no
question that the negligence would not have been the
negligence of the defendant company.

It was shewn that by the original agreement between
the two companies, the tracks which were in the defendant
company's yard were laid down at the joint expense of the
two companies, the rails and ties being the property of the
defendant company, the land belonging to the lumber
company, which paid the expense of laying the tracks, and
it was also shewn that at first the lumber company would
not permit the engines of the defendant company to go
into the lumber yard, fearing accidents by fire, but shunted
their cars by horses, and drew the cars to the track of the
defendant company also by horses. Apparently, this practice changed and it became the custom for the defendant
company to send an engine down to and into the lumber
company's yard for the purpose of drawing the cars on to
the track and placing them in transit. On the occasion in
question the lumber company had notified the defendant
company that certain cars were prepared for shipment,
and an engine and two men went to the lumber company's
yard and were engaged in shunting the cars for the purpose
of getting them out upon the main line and placing them
in transit. The car in question had been loaded, but the
counting had not been completed, and the deceased and a
companion were in the car counting the lumber. But the

lumber company desired this car also to be taken away by the defendant company, although it had not been billed, which was to be done after it had left the yard. While shunting this last mentioned car, it was run violently against another car, causing the lumber to come together and causing the death of the lad Hurdman. If this shunting was merely the moving of the cars in the yard, simply and solely for the convenience of the lumber company, and not in anywise in performance of the contract or agreement between the two companies, if it was something done simply for the accommodation of the lumber company, and did not advance the work of the defendant company for which it was paid, and which it was under contract to perform, it probably would be difficult to say that the engine and the men in charge were, at the time of the accident, in the service of the defendant company. No doubt they were under the direction of the yard foreman as to what cars to take, and in that sense under his direction as to the shunting. But it seems to me upon this evidence—if I am to find the fact which the defendant's counsel have asked me to do—that the work being performed was in pursuance of the contract between the parties. It seems to me that if the engine in question had been run into the yard of the lumber company, simply and solely for the purpose of drawing therefrom laden cars which were ready for shipment, and if, after the engine had coupled on to such cars, by some negligence in the management of the train an accident had happened, it would be beyond question that the negligence would have been the negligence of the servants of the defendant company. And it seems to me to follow that if the shunting that was being done was for the purpose of placing the cars so that the engine might draw them from the yard and place them in transit under a contract between the companies, such work was the work of the defendant company, and being performed by it just as much as if the engine had been coupled on to the cars and the cars were already in motion for the purpose of leaving the yard.

In order to make myself clear, if possible, and at the risk of repetition, I say that had the engine in question been sent by the defendant company to the yard of the lumber company, simply and solely for the convenience of the lumber company, to transfer the cars by shunting from one part of the yard to another, either to give more room or for convenience in loading, or for any purpose not directly intended for the placing of the cars in transit, and had this been done by the defendant company at the request of the lumber company as a favour, so that such engine and the men managing it were under the control and direction solely and entirely of the lumber company, I do not think any liability would exist on the part of the defendant company. But if, as I think the evidence disclosed in this case, the work done was being done in the course of taking the cars out of the yard for the purpose of placing them in transit, then it seems to me that the evidence disclosed that the work done was being done by the defendant company, and the negligence found was the negligence of the servants of such company.

It would, perhaps, be sufficient for the disposition of the matter I am now considering to say that the defendant company has not shewn that the engine and the servants operating it were, at the time of the accident in question, the engine and the servants of the lumber company.

The following cases may be referred to:—*Jones* v. *Corporation of Liverpool*, 14 Q. B. D. 890 ; *Warburton* v. *Great Western R. W. Co.*, L. R. 2 Ex. 30 ; *Callender* v. *Carlton Iron Co.*, 9 Times L. R. 646 ; *Murray* v. *Currie*, L. R. 6 C. P. 24 ; *Murphey* v. *Caralli*, 3 H. & C. 462 ; *Rourke* v. *White Moss Colliery Co.*, 2 C. P. D. 205 ; and other cases cited in the memorandum to which I have referred.

It was further urged that the deceased voluntarily incurred the risk of the accident which resulted in his death. I think this argument is founded on a misapprehension of the difference between a result attributable to pure accident, not caused by negligence, in which case no action would lie, and a result caused by negligence. The finding

Judgment.

Rose, J.

of the jury that the deceased voluntarily accepted the risks of shunting, taken in connection with my charge, may, as argued by the counsel for the defendant company, be fairly read as a finding that the deceased knew that the car was to be put in motion, that he knew there was danger, that he was in a position of peril from the liability of the car being put in too rapid motion, and that the result of such rapid motion would be in the concussion to cause the lumber to go together and so to injure him and destroy his life, and that, knowing the danger and having it before his mind, and knowing the conditions which existed, he did, in that sense, voluntarily place himself in a position of danger, did run the chances of the car being run too rapidly, of there being a concussion, of the lumber coming together, and of the result which happened. But, assuming that all these facts were found as I have stated them, in the language which I have extracted from my charge, I do not think it assists the defendant company. I think Mr. McCarthy's illustration offered in argument was very apposite, viz., that when one went on board of a railway train, which he knew would proceed at a very high rate of speed, he knew that there was a risk of accident from negligence, and that if an accident occurred from negligence on a train moving at such a high rate of speed, it would probably be serious and result in death, and in that sense, going upon such a train, he voluntarily incurred such risk. But that would not excuse the railway company having control of such train from negligence of their servants causing the accident. So here, if, as found, the engine was managed with such negligence as to cause the accident, the servants of the defendant company in charge of its engine, knowing that the deceased was upon the car, cannot be excused from the result of such negligence simply because the deceased placed himself voluntarily in the car, knowing that if there was negligence, it would probably result in an accident which would cause his death. He certainly did not invite the negligence; he was justified in believing that there would be no negligence, that those in management of the engine, knowing that he was in the car, or having reason *Judgment.* to believe that he was in the car, would so manage the *Rose, J.* engine as not to cause trouble; and so I think that negligence having been found, the defendant company may not excuse itself from the result of such negligence by any argument founded upon the finding of the jury to which I have referred.

The result is that there must be judgment entered for the plaintiff for the sum of $750 and costs; the entry of judgment to be stayed until the first day of the next Sittings of the Divisional Court.

Against this judgment the defendants moved during the Hilary Sittings of the Divisional Court, 1894, upon the grounds following amongst others:—

That there was no evidence of negligence to be submitted to the jury; that the persons in charge of the engine were at the time acting under the control of the lumber company and not of the defendants; and that the defendants were therefore not liable for their acts; that upon the answer to the fourth question judgment in any event should have been entered for the defendants; and that the verdict was contrary to the evidence.

The motion was argued on the 9th and 10th February, 1894, before FALCONBRIDGE and STREET, JJ.

Wallace Nesbitt, for the defendants. The deceased had no business in the car at the time of the accident; he was there merely for his own convenience. If greater force was used in shunting than was proper, it was a mere error in judgment. The jury were not asked to find at what rate of speed the engine was moving. The crew of the engine were in fact not at the time the servants of the defendants, but of the lumber company, whose work they were performing. Upon the uncontradicted evidence the deceased was at the highest a licensee, and the defendants owed him no duty: *Harrison* v. *North Eastern R. W. Co.*, 29 L. T. N. S. 844; *Jones* v. *Grand Trunk R. W. Co.*, 18

S. C. R. 696. The deceased was *volens;* he took the risks of shunting; and the maxim *"volenti non fit injuria"* applies.

McCarthy, Q. C., (*Kidd* with him), for the plaintiff. The defendants are responsible for the acts of their servants, notwithstanding the fact that they were at the time performing the work of the lumber company. I refer to *Laugher* v. *Pointer,* 5 B. & C. 547; *Quarman* v. *Burnett,* 6 M. & W. 499; *Johnson* v. *Lindsay,* [1891] A. C. 371, 382; *Murray* v. *Currie,* L. R. 6 C. P. 24; *Rourke* v. *White Moss Colliery Co.,* 2 C. P. D. 205; *Donovan* v. *Laing,* [1893] 1 Q. B. 629; *Jones* v. *Corporation of Liverpool,* 14 Q. B. D. 890. This is certainly not a case of contributory negligence : *Thomas* v. *Quartermaine,* 18 Q. B. D. 685. When *"volenti non fit"* is sought to be applied in cases other than those between master and servant, it simply amounts to "leave and license;" it can have nothing to do with contract. *Scienter* is not *volens. Woodley* v. *Metropolitan District R. W. Co.,* 2 Ex. D. 384, is not applicable to this case, and has been shaken by *Smith* v. *Baker,* [1891] A. C. 325. I refer also to *Osborne* v. *London and North-Western R. W. Co.,* 21 Q. B. D. 220; *Membery* v. *Great Western R. W. Co.,* 14 App. Cas. 179; *Thrussell* v. *Handyside,* 20 Q. B. D. 359.

Nesbitt, in reply, on the point that the accident was the result of a mere error in judgment, referred to *Hutchinson* v. *Canadian Pacific R. W. Co.,* 17 O. R. 347; 16 A. R. 429; *Follet* v. *Toronto Street R. W. Co.,* 15 A. R. 346.

May 21, 1894. The judgment of the Court was delivered by

STREET, J. :—

In my opinion the learned trial Judge could not have withdrawn this case from the jury on the ground that there was no evidence of negligence to be submitted to them. There was, as is usual where this question is in dispute, a conflict of evidence as to the rate at which the cars were propelled when loosed from the engine. Assuming knowledge on the part of the persons in charge of the engine of the position of the deceased in the car, it would clearly be a negligent act to propel the car so rapidly against another as to be likely to injure the deceased. It is contended that the rate at which it was necessary to propel the cars in order to drive them as far as the cars to which they were to be coupled, was a matter of judgment on the part of the engineer, and that it was a mere error of judgment which could not amount to negligence if they were propelled too fast. But negligence often consists in an error in judgment; and here it was furthermore open to the jury to consider whether the persons in charge of the engine had exercised their judgment or had acted from mere carelessness.

The deceased appears to have been upon the car in question in discharge of his duty to his employers, the lumber company, at the very time of the accident. The lad Asher, who was with· him in the car at the time of the accident, says that at the time it happened the deceased had finished counting the lumber, but had not finished his work "on the tallies." Asher says that, so far as he was concerned, he had no further business in the car and merely remained in it in order that he might be carried to another part of the yard where he had business or wished to go, but it does not appear clearly that the deceased was ready to leave the car. If, therefore, it is material to determine this point, I should say that it is clearly shewn that the deceased had gone into the car upon his employers' business, and that it is not shewn that he was there as a mere volunteer or licensee at the time of the accident.

I think, however, that it is unnecessary to consider whether he was still at work for his employers in the car, or whether he was merely there for the purpose of being carried back to the place where he had got on to do his work, having finished it, for it seems to be well established and to have been assumed on all hands that the persons in charge of the engine knew he was in the car, and that the car was loaded with timber, for otherwise there would have been no question of negligence.

The defendants' servants must be taken to have known that the work in which they were engaged was work which, unless done with proper care and precaution, would very probably cause injury to the deceased, and this knowledge imposed upon them a duty towards him, no matter whether he were in 'the car as a mere licensee or otherwise, to use the care necessary to avoid causing that injury : *Heaven* v. *Pender*, 11 Q. B. D. 503 ; *Membery* v. *Great Western R. W. Co.*, 14 App. Cas. 179, 192 ; *Woodley* v. *Metropolitan District R. W. Co.*, 2 Ex. D. 384 ; *Thomas* v. *Quartermaine*, 18 Q. B. D. 685 at p. 688.

The knowledge on the part of the defendants' servants in charge of the engine of the presence of the deceased in the car, and of the probable consequences to him of the act which they were about to do, if it were done without due care, is sufficient to distinguish this case from *Batchelor* v. *Fortescue*, 11 Q. B. D. 474, and cases of that class, even supposing the deceased to have had no business in the car at the time of the accident. The Master of the Rolls says in his judgment upon the appeal in that case : " There was no evidence to shew that the defendant's workmen had reason to expect the deceased to be at the spot where he met with his death."

It is further contended that at all events the finding of the jury that the deceased voluntarily accepted the risks of shunting, entitles the defendants to have judgment entered in their favour, and the judgment of Cockburn, C. J., in *Woodley* v. *Metropolitan District R. W. Co.*, 2 Ex. D. 384, appears to support this view. That judgment, however, does not seem to have been concurred in by any of the other members of the Court, although the result at which he arrived was that which was adopted. It is, I think, inconsistent with the later authorities, and especially with *Smith* v. *Baker*, [1891] A. C. 325, which seems practically to decide, so far as the maxim " *volenti non fit injuria* "

is concerned, that it is not applicable at all to cases of negligence.

To apply what I conceive to be the result of that decision to the finding of the jury in the present case: the
deceased voluntarily accepted the risks of shunting, but
he did not give the defendants leave to run the risk of
killing him by doing their shunting negligently.

The defendants dispute their liability also upon the
ground that the persons in charge of the engine at the
time of the accident were not, as is alleged, acting at the
time under the direction of the defendants, but of the
lumber merchants in whose yard they were working. The
learned trial Judge, however, has found upon the evidence,
and I entirely agree in his finding, that there was no loan
to the lumber merchants by the defendants of the engine
and its crew, but that the defendants, as a part of their
business, sent their servants with the engine to draw loaded
cars from the yard to their own track for the purpose of
transporting them upon their line to the points for
which they were destined. The engine was never out of
the defendants' hands during this occupation; the lumber
merchants simply indicated to the men in charge of it the
cars which were to be drawn away, and they did such
shunting as was necessary to get empty cars out of the
way and make up full ones into a train. Then when
empty cars were required for loading, the defendants
drew them to the lumber yard and placed them where
they were needed.

It appears that no special charge of any kind was made
by the defendants for these services; but the defendants
were anxious to get freight for their cars and to facilitate
the business of their customers, the lumber merchants; it
is, therefore, entirely unnecessary that we should adopt
the somewhat far fetched idea of a loan of an engine and
its crew to the customers, because we find them working
in the customers' yard and upon the customers' switches
without any special arrangement or remuneration. I can
find, therefore, nothing in the facts of this case to bring

it within the line of cases of which *Rourke* v. *White
Moss Colliery Co.*, 2 C. P. D. 205, and *Donovan* v. *Laing*,
[1893] 1 Q. B. 629, are instances. The fact that the conductor and engine driver were to some slight extent acting
at the time under the direction of the servants of the
lumber company in this, that they were moving such cars
as they were told by them to do, can certainly carry the
case no further than did the facts in the late case of *Cameron* v. *Nystrom*, [1893] A. C. 308. In that case the plaintiff, a sailor on a vessel whose cargo was being discharged
by a stevedore under contract with the shipowner, was
injured by the negligence of one of the stevedore's men,
and brought an action against the stevedore to recover
compensation for his injuries. The defence of common
employment was set up. The Lord Chancellor, who delivered the judgment of the Privy Council, says (p. 312) :
" The relation of stevedore to shipowner is a well known
relation, involving no doubt the right of the master
of the vessel to control the order in which the cargo
should be discharged, and various other incidents of the
discharge, but in no way putting the servants of the
stevedore so completely under the control and at the disposition of the master as to make them the servants of the
shipowner, who neither pays them, nor selects them, nor
could discharge them, nor stands in any other relation to
them than this, that they are the servants of a contractor
employed on behalf of the ship to do a particular work."
See also *Quarman* v. *Burnett*, 6 M. & W. 499.

In my opinion, the men in charge of the engine here
must be treated as having continued to be the defendants'
servants throughout the work, and the defendants are
responsible for their acts.

The motion should be dismissed with costs.

E. B. B.

[QUEEN'S BENCH DIVISION.]

REID V. BARNES.

Master and Servant—Workmen's Compensation Act—56 Vic. ch. 26 (O.)—
"Servant in Husbandry"—Knowledge of Danger—Questions for Jury
—General Verdict—Non-Direction—New Trial.

In an action under the Workmen's Compensation Act and at common law
for damages for injuries sustained by the plaintiff while engaged in
digging a drain upon the defendant's farm, it did not appear that the
plaintiff engaged with the defendant to do any particular work, but
that he was first put by the defendant at mason work and then at
digging the drain :—

Held, that it was a question for the jury whether the hiring of the plaintiff was as a servant in husbandry within the meaning of 56 Vic. ch. 26
(O.), and whether the work he was engaged in was in the usual course
of his employment as such, and also whether the danger was known to
the defendant and unknown to the plaintiff or the converse.

The jury were asked certain questions, one being whether the hiring was
as a servant in husbandry, but they were told that they might give a
general verdict, and they gave one for the plaintiff, answering none of
the questions. The trial Judge in his charge gave them no instruction
on this point and no direction as to what the law was :—

Held, that they were not competent to find a general verdict, and there
should be a new trial.

THIS was an action under the Workmen's Compensation   Statement.
for Injuries Act for damages for injuries sustained by the
plaintiff, and alleged to have been caused by the defendant's
negligence, by reason of a defect in the condition or arrangement of the defendant's works, in not properly sloping
back or supporting the sides of a certain drain, in which
the plaintiff was digging as a workman in the defendant's
employment, the plaintiff alleging negligence of a person
in the defendant's service who had superintendence, etc.

The plaintiff also claimed at common law, alleging knowledge of the defendant and want of knowledge of the
plaintiff of the dangerous nature of the drain, etc.

The defendant pleaded :—(1) a general denial; (2) a
denial of negligence on his part or of any one for whose
acts or omissions he was liable ; (3) contributory negligence ; (4) that the plaintiff was well aware of the dangerous
nature of the employment, and voluntarily incurred the

risk; (5) the plaintiff's own negligence after being warned of the dangerous manner in which he was digging; (6) that the plaintiff was not a workman within the meaning of the Act and amendments; (7) that if there was any negligence, it was that of a fellow-workman engaged in a common employment.

The action was tried before BOYD, C., and a jury, at the Hamilton Spring Assizes, 1894.

The evidence as to the hiring was that of the plaintiff, who said he hired with the defendant, who was a farmer, on the 7th, four days before the accident; that the defendant asked him what he could do, and he told the defendant that he could team, and had worked at brickmaking, and also at stone mason work. There was nothing else said. The defendant started the plaintiff to work at mason work at the stable on the farm up to Friday the 10th; then the defendant took the plaintiff out to the drain and told him to go to work and dig it out; he went to work, and while digging the earth caved in and injured him. The object of the drain was to take water off the defendant's farm.

The trial Judge gave the jury the following questions to answer:—

1. How did the cave-in happen? Was it from the piling up of earth on the side, or from undermining?

2. If the bank was not undermined, was there a want of reasonable care in not having it shored up?

3. Who had the better means of judging as to the danger of cave-in, having regard to the nature of the soil and re-opening of the old drain?

4. Was the plaintiff so inexperienced in earth-work and digging that he needed information in order to judge of the liability to cave in of this drain?

5. Did the defendant know, or should he have known, that the place as dug out was unsafe and needed protection before and at the time of the accident?

6. Did the plaintiff go to the place where he was hurt as his own act, without being directed so to do by the defendant or by any one for the defendant?

7. If the plaintiff is not to blame for the accident, and if he was hurt to the extent claimed by him, or if he was hurt to any extent, what amount of damages should be paid ?

8. Was the hiring as a servant in husbandry, or as a workman to dig a drain, and that not as a part of farming work ?

The Judge, however, told the jury that they might return a general verdict; and they returned one for the plaintiff for $250 damages, for which amount he directed judgment to be entered for the plaintiff with costs.

At the Easter Sittings of the Divisional Court, 1894, the defendant moved to set aside this verdict and judgment, and to dismiss the action, or for a new trial, on several grounds, those chiefly argued being : (1) that the plaintiff was not a workman, but a servant in husbandry ; (2) that there was no liability at common law ; and (3) that the learned trial Judge was not justified, upon the answer to the jury to the first only of the questions submitted to them, in giving judgment for the plaintiff; that he should have insisted on all the questions being answered, or so many thereof as the jury could agree on, and a general verdict for the plaintiff should not have been received ; and for misdirection and for non-direction in not submitting the questions proposed by the defendant's counsel.

The motion was argued before ARMOUR, C. J., and FALCONBRIDGE and STREET, JJ., on the 23rd May, 1894.

Carscallen, Q. C., for the defendant. The general verdict is wrong ; the questions should have been answered. The plaintiff was a servant in husbandry and within the exception in 56 Vic. ch. 26 (O.), amending the Workmen's Compensation Act. Every labourer on a farm is a servant in husbandry. See Stroud's Judicial Dictionary, *sub verb.; Davies* v. *Lord Berwick,* 3 E. & E. 549 ; *Ex p. Hughes,* 23 L. J. M. C. 138. No knowledge was brought

home to the defendant. There should at least be a new
trial to have these questions determined.

Stuart Livingston, for the plaintiff. A general verdict
may be returned: *Furlong* v. *Carroll,* 7 A. R. 145. The
plaintiff was not a servant in husbandry: *Lowther* v. *Earl of
Radnor,* 8 East 113; *Branwell* v. *Penneck,* 7 B. & C. 536;
Brannigan v. *Robinson,* 8 Times L. R. 244; *McColl* v.
Black, 18 Ct. Sess. Cas., 4th ser., 507; *Pollock* v. *Cassidy,*
8 Ct. Sess. Cas., 3rd ser., 615.

June 8, 1894. The judgment of the Court was delivered
by

FALCONBRIDGE, J. :—

The 56 Vic. ch. 26 (O.) enacts that " ' Workman ' does not
include a domestic or menial servant or servant in husbandry, gardening, or fruit growing, where the personal
injury caused to any such servant has been occasioned by
or has arisen from or in the usual course of his work or
employment as a domestic or menial servant, or as a servant
in husbandry, gardening, or fruit growing   *   *   ."

[The learned Judge then set out the evidence as to the
hiring, *ubi supra,* and proceeded:]

In Stroud's Judicial Dictionary, *sub verb.,* " servant in
husbandry " is defined to be " a person, whether male or
female, whose *chief* employment is in works of husbandry;
i. e., the culture or keeping of the ground, or the management or working of horses or cattle, or the gathering in of
crops, or any other work strictly pertaining to the manual
labour required by farmers."

A person whose contract was that he should keep the
general accounts belonging to the farm, should weigh out
food for cattle, and set the men to work, should lend a
hand to anything if wanted, and especially should in all
things carry out the orders of his employer, was held not
to be a servant in husbandry, but rather a bailiff or superintendent: *Davies* v. *Lord Berwick,* 3 E. & E. 549. And
the compiling of a herd-book was there held not to be
husbandry work.

In *Lilley* v. *Elwin*, 11 Q. B. 742, the plaintiff, though
he was engaged as a waggoner, during the harvest worked
in the field generally, and the Court thought it must be
taken as part of his contract that he should do so, and
dealt with him as an agricultural labourer.

A dairy-maid, who was also to assist in harvesting of hay
and corn if required, and who had also to keep house and
cook for the men-servants and labourers and to make their
beds, etc., was adjudged by the justices to be a servant in
husbandry, and the Court held that they might so adjudge:
Exp. Hughes, 23 L. J. M. C. 138.

I am of the opinion that on the above authorities this
Court cannot say as a matter of law that the hiring of the
plaintiff was or was not as a servant in husbandry, nor that
the work he was engaged in was or was not in the usual
course of his work or employment as a servant in husbandry, and that these were matters to be passed on by
the jury. Nor can I say that the knowledge of the master
and the ignorance of the servant as to the danger, or the
converse thereof, are facts which appear undisputed one
way or the other, so as to enable us to dispose of the common law branch of the case. They, too, are questions for
the jury.

This brings me to the consideration of the way in which
the case was left to the jury.

The learned Chancellor propounded eight questions, saying to the jury, "Now, I give you these questions; I do
not say you must answer them, because, if you think upon
the evidence you can give a general verdict for the plaintiff
or for the defendant, you need not trouble to answer
these questions; but, if you find no difficulty in answering
them, it will, perhaps, be better to give answers to them,
rather than return a general verdict."

· *Furlong* v. *Carroll*, 7 A. R. 145, establishes that the
Judge, after having put questions, may nevertheless, in his
discretion, receive a general verdict.

But the difficulty I feel in this case is that the learned
Chancellor's charge was delivered with a view to the

Judgment.   answering of specific questions, and was not sufficiently
Falconbridge, instructive for the purpose of getting a general verdict.
    J.

I point as one instance to the matter of consideration
involved in the 8th question, viz., " Was the hiring as a
servant in husbandry, or as a workman to dig a drain, and
that not as a part of farming work ?"

As to this there is no word of instruction in the charge.

And again, the learned Chancellor says : "I have not
troubled you with the law, because that will be discussed
afterwards; I am putting it to you to get at the facts, if
you can, upon which the law will be applied."

They were not competent to find a general verdict without being told what the law was.

The jury did not even announce that they answered the
questions or any of them in a sense favourable to the plaintiff.

What happened when they returned was as follows:—
            (Jury returned at 11.47 p.m.)

THE FOREMAN : We have agreed upon a verdict of $250
for the plaintiff.

HIS LORDSHIP.—Have you answered any of the questions?

THE FOREMAN.— Some of them. The first one we
thought we had answered ; we thought that this man was
the agent for the defendant.

HIS LORDSHIP.—So you give a general verdict? You
do not answer more than one question. Have you put
any answers on the paper ?

THE FOREMAN.—No sir, we have no answers.

HIS LORDSHIP.—I will put the verdict in that shape
then.

Verdict for the plaintiff; damages $250.

There was a formal objection taken by defendant's
counsel to the reception of a general verdict, and I think,
under these circumstances, it cannot stand.

There will be an order for a new trial ; costs of the last
trial and of this motion to be costs in the cause to the successful party.

                                        E. B. B.

[QUEEN'S BENCH DIVISION.]

CAMERON ET AL. V. ADAMS ET AL.

Equitable Execution—Receiver—Will—Devise—Right to "a Home"—
Interest in Land.

A testator devised land to one in trust, first, to permit his nephew and
his wife and children to use it for a home, and, second, to convey it to
such child of the nephew as the latter should nominate in his will.
The nephew and his family were living upon the land at the time of
the making of the will and at the death of the testator, when there
were two dwelling-houses thereon. Afterwards the trustee and the
nephew's father-in-law, at their expense, improved and altered the
property so that the number of houses was increased to seven. The
nephew lived with his family in one and received the rents of the others.
In an action by judgment creditors of the nephew and his wife seeking
the appointment of a receiver to receive the rents in satisfaction of the
judgment :—

Held, that the judgment debtors took no estate in the land under the
will, and nothing more than the right to call upon the trustee to permit
them to use the land for "a home," which expression, however, meant
more than simply a house to live in ; that they were entitled to the
advantage of the increased value of the land ; and that their right to
the use of the land for a home could not be reached through a receiver
so as to make it available for the satisfaction of the plaintiffs' claim.

Allen v. *Furness,* 20 A. R. 34, distinguished.

AN action by judgment creditors of the defendants E. Statement.
Douglas Adams and Estella M. Adams for the appointment
of a receiver to receive the rents and profits of certain
land, to be applied on the judgment. The infant children
of these defendants were also made defendants. The
facts appear in the judgment.

The action was tried before FERGUSON, J., without a
jury, at Cornwall, on the 8th March, 1894.

D. B. Maclennan, Q. C., and *C. H. Cline,* for the plaintiffs, relied on *Allen* v. *Furness,* 20 A. R. 34; *McLean* v.
Allen, 14 P. R. 84.

Leitch, Q. C., and *R. A. Pringle,* for the adult defendants, cited *Fisken* v. *Brooke,* 4 A. R. 8 ; *Re Coleman,* 39
Ch. D. 443 ; *Godden* v. *Crowhurst,* 10 Sim. 642 ; *Re Parker,* 16 Ch. D. 44.

Dingwall, for the infant defendants.

Judgment.
Ferguson, J. June 1, 1894. FERGUSON, J. :—

The plaintiffs recovered a judgment of the County
Court of the united counties of Stormont, Dundas, and
Glengarry, against the defendants E. Douglas Adams and
Estella M. Adams for debt and costs, $226.01. These two
defendants are husband and wife. The action in the
County Court was upon a promissory note made by them.
This judgment, by an amendment thereof as shewn by the
exemplification, contains an order or adjudication that, so
far as the defendant Estella M. Adams has concern, the
amount shall be payable out of her separate property.

Executions have been issued upon this judgment and
duly placed in the hands of the proper sheriff to be executed, but the sheriff has failed to levy and realize any
sum, and, if requested to return the executions, will return
" no goods" and " no lands," respectively.

This action is brought for the purpose of having a
receiver appointed, who, when appointed, may, it is urged,
be able to obtain and receive certain moneys to be applied
in satisfaction of the plaintiffs' demand upon their judgment. The plaintiffs also ask for other incidental relief,
and have the equivalent of the general prayer.

The property out of which, or rather out of the rents or
profits of which, the plaintiffs expect to obtain satisfaction
of their judgment, and in respect of which the appointment of a receiver is asked, is most peculiarly circum-
stanced. It is lot No. 20 on the south side of Fourth
street, in the town of Cornwall.

It is undisputed that the late Pierrepoint Edward Adams,
who died about the 15th day of December, 1882, was at
the time of his death the owner in fee of this lot.

By his last will he, the late Pierrepoint Edward Adams,
devised the lot, the words of the devise being: " I give
and devise lot No. 20 on the south side of Fourth street,
in the town of Cornwall, to my brother Charles P. Adams
upon trust, as follows : first, to permit my nephew Emmet
Adams and his wife and children to use the same for a

home ; second, to convey the same to whichever of the children of the said Emmet Adams whom the said Emmet Adams shall nominate therefor in his last will and testament in writing duly executed."

This Emmet Adams named in the will is the defendant E. Douglas Adams, and he and his family were living upon this lot at and before the death of the testator. The will bears date the 2nd April, 1882, and, as this defendant in his evidence says he lived on the lot in the lifetime of the testator, and continued to live upon it after the testator's death, it is fair to assume that he and his family were living upon the lot at the time of the making of the will.

There are four children ; the youngest is four years old, and the "next youngest" is eleven. At the time of the testator's death there were only two children, and these and their father and mother were (there is little, if any, doubt) living upon this lot.

In his evidence, the defendant E. Douglas Adams says (and what he says in this respect is not disputed or contradicted), that at the time of the death of the testator there were two houses upon the lot, one single tenement and one double tenement; that the single tenement has since been changed into a double tenement. He says that a new building was erected by Charles P. Adams, the trustee, after the death of the testator, and that one of the buildings that were there in the lifetime of the testator has been made or converted into three tenements, and that there are now in all seven tenements on the lot. He says that Charles P. Adams, the trustee, paid for all these improvements, except the labour which was done by his, E. Douglas Adams', wife's father, and that he himself worked "some" upon the buildings, but only a little. He says that the tenement that he lives in is worth about $6 per month, that the other tenements are occupied, and that he gets, or should get, about $30 a month from the other six tenements, out of which the taxes have to be deducted. The building erected by Charles P. Adams took about thirty feet by sixty feet from the garden. This witness says that neither he nor his wife has any authority, by which he means authority from the trustee, to collect the rents, but that the rents have been paid to him. It appears from his evidence that his wife has some household furniture that she got from her father, but it is not of great value and is mortgaged. Charles P. Adams, the trustee, died about two years ago. He never prevented this defendant E. Douglas Adams from collecting the rents. He knew that the family was living on the rents, as this defendant in his evidence says.

No trustee has been appointed in the room of Charles P. Adams. So far as shewn by the evidence, one of the children of Charles P. Adams is an infant and living in Pont du Lac, in the State of Wisconsin ; another, an adult, lives in the State of Nebraska ; and another, Mary Pusinger, is dead, having left several infant children in the State of Nebraska. It is said that the debt for which the judgment was recovered was incurred for necessaries for the family ; Cameron, one of the plaintiffs, in his evidence says that when giving the credit he made no inquiry as to the necessities of the children, nor as to whether or not the defendant Estella M. Adams had any separate property.

By reading the declarations of the two trusts together, one sees, I think, that the right in equity taken by these defendants was one the continuance of which was to be during the life of E. Douglas Adams. But I cannot see that these defendants took by the gift any estate in the land. I cannot see that they took anything more than the right to call upon the trustee to permit them to use the lot for a home, just as stated in the will, which seems to be only what may be considered a right to claim from the trustee a permission or license to use the lot for the purpose stated, a thing that I think falls short of being an estate in the land.

That the testator did not use the word "home" as signifying merely a house to live in, appears, I think, from the fact that at the time of his death there were two houses upon the lot, a single tenement and a double tenement, yet the permission was to be to use the whole lot for a home.

The improvements that were made upon the lot after the death of the testator were not put there to any appreciable extent by these judgment debtors, or either of them. These improvements (the additional house erected and the changes made in the other houses or tenements) were chiefly paid for, or the expense of them borne, by the trustee and the father of the female judgment debtor. The improvements became part of the freehold of the lot, and the right of these defendants remained as to the whole lot, a part of which was covered by the new building. This part had been before used by the defendants as a garden, and it was not contended that their use of it as a garden did not fall within the meaning of the expression used by the testator.

As it appears to me, the bounty of the trustee and of the father of the female judgment debtor simply made the lot a better and more valuable lot to be used by the defendants as a home, and to be conveyed away by the trustee when the time should arrive and the event happen upon which, according to the terms of the trust, he was to do this, and that the defendants are now entitled to be permitted to use the whole lot as it is for a home. It also appears to me that if it can be made out and shewn that these judgment debtors, or either of them, are or is using this lot or any part of it otherwise than for a home, according to the meaning of the language of the will, he or she is doing something outside or in excess of any right given or intended by the testator, and that this, if there were to be any interference, would be a subject for interference by the trustee. I do not see how in this way they could acquire any larger right in respect of the lot than that given by the will, but I am of the opinion that it has not been shewn that the lot has been used, or is being used, otherwise than for a home, within what I think the meaning in this regard of the language of the will. The defendants were to be permitted to use the lot as a home;

Judgment.
———
Ferguson, J.

and this they are doing, having the advantage of the increased value of it, arising by the generosity of friends, who by their outlay increased the value of the freehold. As I have before stated, I think the testator could not have meant by the words of the will that a " home" was to be simply a house to live in.

The object of the plaintiff is to have a receiver, and through him obtain satisfaction out of the part of the benefit or advantage in respect of this lot that is above alluded to. The plaintiffs relied chiefly on the authority of the case *Allen* v. *Furness*, 20 A. R. 34, and the judgment of the Chancellor in that case. The defendant relies chiefly upon the case *Fisken* v. *Brooke*, 4 A. R. 8.

I cannot see that *Allen* v. *Furness* is at all like the present case. There property was given to a man for life for the support of himself and his children. This property yielded an income, and the Court saw its way to taking for the satisfaction of a creditor the part of the income that was thought really to belong to the debtor, arriving at the amount of this by making a division of the income. Here the judgment debtors and their children have the right to be permitted to use a lot for a home, which I think an entirely different thing.

The authorities on which the late Chief Justice Moss based his judgment in *Fisken* v. *Brooke* seem to me to be entirely against the plaintiffs' contention in this case. See those referred to on p. 17.

The subject is one that it must be admitted is perplexing. I have read these two cases, and all the authorities referred to in them, as well as some other cases referred to at the bar; and I have also been guilty of some independent search amongst the books, without finding a case directly in point. I have, however, arrived at the conclusion that this joint right to be permitted to use this lot for a home is not a thing that can be or should be reached through a receiver to make it available for the satisfaction of the plaintiffs' claim, and I am of the opinion that this action should be dismissed.

The action will be dismissed. The plaintiffs will pay
the costs of the guardian of the infants, commonly called
the infants' costs. Otherwise there will be no costs to any
party.

Order accordingly.

E. B. B.

———

[QUEEN'S BENCH DIVISION.]

KENNEDY ET AL. V. PROTESTANT ORPHANS' HOME ET AL.

*Will—Executors and Administrators—Succession Duty—55 Vict. ch. 6 (O.)
—Residue—Pro Rata, Meaning of.*

A testator devised and bequeathed all his real and personal estate to his
executors and trustees for the purpose of paying a number of pecuniary
legacies, some to personal legatees, and others to charitable associations,
and provided that the residue of his estate should be divided *pro rata*
among the legatees :—

Held, that it was the duty of the executors to deduct the succession duty
payable in respect of the pecuniary legacies, before paying the amounts
over to the legatees, and they had no right to pay such succession
duty out of the residue left after paying the legacies in full.

Where the residue of an estate is directed to be divided *pro rata* among
prior legatees they take such residue in proportion to the amount of
their prior legacies.

THIS was a motion on behalf of the plaintiffs, as executors of the last will and codicil of Joseph Keterson, for the
advice and direction of the Court, in the matter of the
will, upon the points mentioned in the judgment, where
the facts are fully stated.

The motion was argued upon May 8th, 1894, before
MACMAHON, J.

E. D. Armour, Q. C., for the plaintiffs.
Cartwright, Q. C., for the Attorney-General of Ontario.
Huson Murray, Q. C., for the Protestant Orphans' Home,
cited Theobald on Wills, 3rd ed. at pp. 136, 8 ; Pott's Law

of Succession, p. 218 ; *In re Johnston, Cockerell* v. *Earl of Essex,* 26 Ch. D. 538, at p. 554; *In re Higgins, Day* v. *Turnell,* 29 Ch. D. 697; *In re Bridger,* 10 Times L. R. 153.

W. Mortimer Clark, Q. C., for the Home for Incurables, cited Williams on Executors, 9th ed., vol. 2, p. 1506.

Alfred Hoskin, Q. C., for the defendant the Rev. A. Williams.

J. Reeve, Q. C., for the defendant Thompson. " Residue " means residue after payment of all charges to which the estate is subject. The charities wish to claim the right to saddle the individual legatees with these charges, but the Court will never marshal in favour of a charity : *Trethewy* v. *Helyar,* 4 Ch. D. 53. If the general law is that these charges would come out of the general residue, then, before you can take them out of particular legacies, there must be clear and distinct words.

Vickers, for the defendant Violet Hall. The will was made before the Act as to succession duty, which we submit, therefore, does not apply to it : *Baldwin* v. *Kingstone,* 16 O. R. 341, 18 A. R. 63.

May 10th, 1894.   MacMahon, J. :—

Motion on behalf of the plaintiffs' the executors of the last will and codicil of Joseph Keterson, deceased, for a construction of the said will and codicil.

The testator, Joseph Keterson, by his last will bearing date the 26th day of October, A.D. 1891, devised and bequeathed all his real and personal estate to his executors and trustees for the following purposes, namely : after paying his debts and funeral expenses to pay to The Protestant Orphans' Home $10,000, to The Home for Incurables, $7,000, to The Irish Protestant Benevolent Society $7,000, to The Boys' Home $5,000, to The Girls' Home $5,000, to The Newsboys' Home $2,000, to The Infants' Home $2,000, and to Violet Hall $3,000, to Miss Halfpenny, his housekeeper, $1,500, to the Rev. Alexander Williams $500, for the purposes therein mentioned, and

appointed the plaintiffs executors and trustees of his said
will.

By a codicil to the said will bearing date the 16th day
July, A.D. 1892, the said Joseph Keterson did further give
and bequeath to the Hospital for Sick Children $5,000, to
The Home for Aged Men and Women on Larch street
$4,000, to St. John's Parish $3,000, to be used in the erection of a church, to the said Miss Halfpenny $1,500, to
his son William if he should return, the sum of $1.00, to
The Protestant Orphans' Home $3,000, "the residue of my
estate to be divided *pro rata* amongst the legatees, and I
direct that the legacies named in the codicil be paid exclusively out of such part of my personal estate as may be
lawfully appropriated to such a purpose."

The testator died on July 17th, 1892.

The plaintiffs have administered the estate and paid the
debts and funeral expenses, and have paid to the Crown
succession duty upon the personal legacies. The personal
legatees named in the will, namely, Violet Hall, Miss Halfpenny, now Eleanor Thompson, and the Rev. Alexander
Williams claim that the succession duties should be paid
out of the residue of the said estate and should not be
charged against their respective legacies; and on the other
hand the charitable institutions therein named claim that
as they share in the residue, and their legacies are not subject to the charge for succession duties, that the personal
legatees should bear the succession duties out of their own
legacies.

The plaintiffs are in doubt as to whether the residue of
the said estate, which by the said codicil, is to be divided
pro rata amongst the legatees is to be divided amongst the
said legatees in equal sums, or whether the said residue
should be paid to the legatees in the proportion in which
their legacies are to be paid.

The amount of the residue of the said estate is large,
amounting in all to about the sum of $48,000.

By the Act for the payment of succession duties, 55 Vict.
ch. 6, sec. 3 (O.), it is provided : " This Act shall not apply

(s.s. 2) "To property given, devised, or bequeathed for religious, charitable, or educational purposes." And the 14th section provides: "Any administrator, executor, or trustee having in charge or trust any estate, legacy or property subject to the said duty shall deduct the duty therefrom, or collect the duty thereon upon the appraised value thereof from the person entitled to such property, and he shall not deliver any property subject to duty to any person until he has collected the duty thereon."

The argument by counsel for the personal legatees is, that as by the will the bequests to the various charitable institutions therein named, are not to be paid until two years—or longer, if the trustees deem it necessary—after the testator's demise, but that in the meantime the trustees were to pay off the other legacies, and that in case of a deficiency the said institutions were to abate *pro rata*, this afforded evidence that the testator intended such personal legatees should be paid in full the sums bequeathed to them ; and it was also urged that this contention is strengthened by the language of the codicil which provides that the residue of the estate is to be divided *pro rata* amongst the legatees, and which it is claimed means the residue after payment of all claims against the testator's estate, which would include payment of succession duty by the executors before the " residue " could be ascertained.

When the testator executed his will there was no question as to succession duties, the Act not having been assented to until the 14th of April, 1892. But the Act was in existence when the testator executed the codicil.

Then what is the law where there are legacies to be paid, and the will is silent as to payment of the duty ? Potts on the Law of Succession lays it down, p. 218, that "the executor must, with some exceptions, pay a duty in respect of each legacy, or share of residue handed over by him ; such duty being deducted from the legacy, etc., in respect of which it is payable."

In Dos Passos on the Law of Collateral Inheritance, Legacy, and Succession Taxes, the author at p. 210, says:

"A testator possesses the general power to relieve the Judgment. legatees from the payment of the tax by throwing it on MacMahon, J. the residue of the estate, where it is sufficient to make payment, but an intention that a devise shall be "free" of the tax as between the estate and the devisee must clearly appear. A mere declaration that it is to be clear of all charges and incumbrances, or other legal demands is not sufficient."

A large number of cases in which directions in wills entitled the legatees to be paid their legacies free from duty, are referred to in a note to Jarman on Wills, 5th ed., vol. 1, p. 151.

Then as to the argument founded upon the wording of the codicil providing for the division of the "residue" of the estate amongst the legatees, that it must mean the "residue" after payment of all debts and claims, for which the estate is liable, including legacy duty. "A 'residue' of personal estate means the personal estate which remains after payment of the testator's debts, funeral and testamentary expenses. and the costs of administration of the estate including the costs of an administration suit:" Daniel's Ch. Pr., 6th ed., vol. 2, p. 1035 ; *Trethewy* v. *Helyar*, 4 Ch. D. 53 ; *Fenton* v. *Wills*, 7 Ch. D. 33 ; *Blann* v. *Bell, ib.* 382 ; *In re Jones, Jones* v. *Caless*, 10 Ch. D. 40.

By sec. 14 of the Act 55 Vict. ch. 6, the executor is to deduct the duty from the legacy to be paid, and unless the will provides for the payment of the legacies free of duty, the executors have no authority to deduct from the residue of the estate the amount so paid. Where there is no direction in the will that the legacy is to be paid free from duty, and the executor pays the duty on account of the legatee, he may recover the amount so paid by action against the legatee : *Hales* v. *Freeman*, 1 B. & B. 391, where it is said by Park, J., at p. 399, that under the Act 36 Geo. III., ch. 32, the executor is made liable for the payment of the legacy duty for the benefit of the Government, and that the executor is no more than surety for the legatee.

It in nowise affects the question that the will was executed prior to the Act, 55 Vict. ch. 6. The will and codicil speak from the death of the testator (*In re Bridger, The Brompton Hospital for Consumption* v. *Lewis*, 9 Times L. R. 25, and in Appeal 10 Times L. R. 153), and the Act (subject to the exceptions mentioned in section 3) makes the duty payable on property—which includes real and personal property of every description—owned by a deceased person at the time of his death and passing either by will or intestacy.

The testator might, by the codicil to his will (which was executed subsequent to the passing of the Succession Duties Act) have provided for the payment of the legacies to the personal legatees free from duty. This not being done, the legacies to such legatees, are payable subject to the duty payable to the Crown, which must be borne by and deducted from their respective legacies.

No other meaning can be attached to the words in the codicil, " the residue of my estate to be divided *pro rata* amongst the legatees " than that the residue is to be divided amongst them in proportion to the amount of the prior legacies bequeathed to them. *Pro rata* never had any other meaning than " in proportion."

The costs of all the parties will be paid out of the residue now in hand.

A. H. F. L.

[CHANCERY DIVISION.]

MULCAHY V. COLLINS.

*Husband and Wife—Married Woman—Separate Estate—Contract respect-
ing—R. S. O. ch. 132.*

A married woman having been informed by a relative that he had made
his will in her favour, signed a promissory note three days after his
death, before she had seen the will, and some weeks before it was proved.
The will gave her a vested interest in the property bequeathed. She
also owned a promissory note of her husband :—

Held, that she was possessed of separate estate and had contracted with
respect to it.

Decision of STREET, J., 24 O. R. 441, affirmed.

THIS was a motion by way of appeal before the Divi- Statement.
sional Court on behalf of the defendant Elizabeth Collins,
from the judgment of STREET, J., herein, reported 24 O. R.
441.

The motion was argued upon February 26th, 1894, before
FERGUSON, ROBERTSON and MEREDITH, JJ.

W. Cassels, Q. C., for the defendant E. Collins.   There
is nothing in *Moore* v. *Jackson*, 22 S. C. R. 210, 19 A. R.
383, which shews that if a woman enters into a contract
when she has no separate property, she is bound by the
contract.   We have two decisions as to the meaning of
" unless the contrary be shewn" in R. S. O. ch. 132, sec. 3,
sub-sec. 3 ; *Leak* v. *Driffield*, 24 Q. B. D. 98, and *Sweetland*
v. *Neville*, 21 O. R. 412.   If having no separate property at
the time of the contract, the contract is not binding, it
does not become binding afterwards by her getting separate property.   The property here is not separate estate
within the meaning of the Act : *Fisken* v. *Brooke*, 4 A. R.
8.   When the note was made the will was unknown to
this woman.   She had been told she had had the land left
to her, but the will was not known to her.   We do not
know what debts there were.   The statute only binds
" unless the contrary be shewn" : R. S. O. ch. 132, sec. 2,
sub-secs. 1, 2, 3.   The claim against the insolvent cannot be

31—VOL. XXV. O.R.

property to sustain this action. She took nothing under
the will, which is separate property under the Act.

W. Macdonald, for the plaintiff. The will deals with
the farm. We proved the will and the property that
passed under it. R. S. O. ch. 132, sec. 2, provides that
"property" shall include a thing in action. Some interest
must have passed under the devise, and not being in possession must have been in action : *Colonial Bank* v. *Whinney*, 30 Ch. D. at p. 285. If the only property the married
woman had when contracting is of such a kind that it
would be absurd to suppose she contracted with reference
to it, then the contrary would be shewn, within the meaning of the Act. The woman here has not parted with the
property she took under the will, nor the debt against her
husband.

Cassels, in reply. If no estate ever came to the woman
under the will, as we contend, then the devise surely could
not give her capacity to contract. As to the debt against
the husband, could she by any possibility be supposed to
contract with reference to her claim against her husband
who had become insolvent ?

June 1st, 1894. FERGUSON, J. :—

Action upon a promissory note made by the defendants
(husband and wife) in favour of the plaintiff. The note
bears date the 4th day of September, 1891, and is for the
sum of $900. The judgment of my brother Street was for
the plaintiff against both defendants for the sum of $900,
with interest from the date of the note (less the sum of
$40 that had been paid on account) with costs of the
action.

The motion is against this judgment on the grounds that
it is against law and evidence and the weight of evidence,
and upon the ground that at the date of the making of
the note sued on, the defendant Elizabeth Collins had no
separate estate, and that the contract was not entered into
on the faith of her separate estate, and upon other
grounds.

The chief, I may say, the sole matter, argued before us, was as to whether or not Elizabeth Collins had at the date of the note any separate estate.

This defendant was married in February, 1864, and between the 5th day of May, 1859, and 2nd day of March, 1872. The second sub-sec. of sec. 4 of R. S. O. ch. 132, therefore applies to the case.

Sub-section 3 of section 3 of the same chapter, provides that every contract entered into by a married woman shall be deemed to be a contract entered into by her with respect, and to bind her separate property, unless the contrary is shewn; and sub-section 4 of section 3, provides that the contract shall bind not only the separate property which she is possessed of or entitled to at the date of the contract, but also all separate property which she may thereafter acquire.

There was no marriage contract or settlement, and this defendant had at the time of her marriage no money from any source.

She says in her examination, that she afterwards got money from her son Patrick; that this money was loaned to her husband; that Patrick took a note from her husband and handed the note to her, so that she would be sure of getting the amount, which was on the 4th day of February, 1888, as proved before the sheriff, the sum of $306.75, and she says that she has never been paid anything in respect of this but $20, which she got by way of dividend. It rather appears that her husband was at that time an insolvent, or at least in embarrassed circumstances, but I do not find any evidence shewing that he has hitherto remained so. This chose in action seems to me to be personal property: See the judgment of Fry, L. J., in *Colonial Bank* v. *Whinney*, 30 Ch. D. at p. 285, *et seq.*

This defendant's father-in-law died on the 30th day of August, 1891, five days before the date of the note in question, and according to the schedule of his property filed in the Surrogate office, he left an estate of the value of $6,870, and this defendant is the residuary devisee in

Judgment.
Ferguson, J. the will that he left. It was contended that she did not
know of the contents of this will at the time of the
making of the note. She, however, says that she knew
of the making of the will before the death of the testator; that he had told her of it; and that he told her
that he was leaving her the property so that she would
be all right; and that she understood she was to get control of the property at his death; manifestly she expected
to get more by the will then she did get. She expected
to have the control of the whole of the property of the
testator. This was as a fair conclusion from her evidence
what was in her mind at the time of the making of the
note sued on. She thought she had separate property, but
it turned out to be property different from what she
thought it was, but coming from the same source. She
says she has never parted with her interest in her father-
in-law's estate; that she still has all the interest she ever
had under the will.

There was on the argument a contradiction as to whether
this residuary gift will eventually turn out to be of any
or much value, and I do not see that the evidence sets the
contention at rest, and until the matters of the estate are
wound up, a thing that does not appear to have taken place,
one does not see how the question could well be settled by
the evidence. There might, of course, be an instance where
the estate would be so large, and the demands upon it so
small that there could be no doubt on the subject; but
this is not, as it appears to me, shewn to be that clear
case. The gift is, however, in the will, and the estate
appears to be considerable.

It appears to me that the right of this defendant under
the will of her father-in-law, is at the lowest a chose in
action, a right to have the estate duly administered, and
the residue, after satisfying all proper demands against it,
handed over to her; and assuming this to be so, such chose
in action is personal property (*Colonial Bank* v. *Whinney*,
above) belonging to this defendant and is separate estate
within the meaning of that expression as used in the
statute.

I am unable to see how it can be fairly said that this defendant had not "separate property" at the time of the making of the note sued on; and assuming that she then had, it is plain that she still has "separate property."

Then as to what is meant by the words in sub-section 3 of section 3, "unless the contrary appear," I refer to the judgment of the Chancellor in the case of *Sweetland* v. *Neville*, 21 O. R. 412, and the authorities there referred to. It does not appear to me that this separate property was "of such a nature that the presumption could not arise," and I think the gift to her in the will of her father-in-law, though it may possibly turn out not to be of great value, was property such as she could and might reasonably have contracted credit upon, and I think there is no evidence going to negative the presumption. I am of the opinion that the contract in question must be deemed to be a contract entered into by this defendant, with respect to, and to bind her separate property, such separate property being at the time of entering into the contract, her rights and right of action in respect of the residuary gift contained in her father-in-law's will, and the promissory note aforesaid.

I do not see that this case is governed at all by the decisions in *Braunstein* v. *Lewis*, 65 L. T. 449; *Palliser* v. *Gurney*, 19 Q. B. D. 519; *Stogdon* v. *Lee*, [1891] 1 Q. B. 661, or any of them.

I am, therefore, of the opinion that the judgment of my brother Street is right, and should be affirmed, and that this motion should be dismissed with costs.

MEREDITH, J. :—

The defendant's contentions are :—

1. That she took no separate property, within the meaning of the Act, under the residuary bequest in question ; and,

2. That if she did, having regard to its nature, and to the value of the debt due to her by her husband, it is

sufficiently shewn that the contract in question was not
one entered into by her with respect to and to bind her
separate estate : see section 3, sub-section 3, and section
2 of the Act.

It is in respect of the residuary bequest and the husband's debt only that the plaintiff claims to have shewn
the defendant was and is possessed of separate property.

I can perceive no good reason why the residue of the
testator's estate bequeathed to the defendant is not such
separate property ; and, so far as the evidence at the
trial shews, one might say such property of very considerable value. The inventory was by consent accepted as
evidence in this respect.

It is property which would devolve upon her personal
representatives, in case of her death before payment of
debts and before ascertainment of the amount of the surplus, and such as, apart from this question, could be
recovered by creditors under equitable execution : see
Flower v. *Buller,* 15 Ch. D. 665 ; *Pike* v. *Fitzgibbon,* 17 Ch.
D. 454 ; *In re Parsons, Stockley* v. *Parsons,* 45 Ch. D. 51 ;
and *Stogdon* v. *Lee,* [1891] 1 Q. B. 661.

And why could she not reasonably be deemed to have
contracted in respect of and to bind such property and the
debt due to her on the promissory note of her husband—
both or either ? One cannot doubt that, had she taken
nothing under the will, and had she been told that it was
not competent for her to contract except with regard to
and to bind the other property, her answer would have
been, then I enter into this contract expressly with respect
to and to bind that property.

All the property is of what may be called a commercial
character ; not at all like a wedding ring, or the clothing of
a married woman and her children ; nor like property not
subject to alienation ; it is just such property as she could
and would convert into money if possible, trade in and
deal with as anyone else not under disability would : see
Hyde v. *Hyde,* 13 P. R. 167 ; *Harrison* v. *Harrison, ib.,*

180; *Leak* v. *Driffield*, 24 Q. B. D. 98, and *Sweetland* v. Judgment.
Neville, 21 O. R. 412. Meredith. J.

The motion entirely fails and should be dismissed with
costs.

ROBERTSON, J., concurred.

A. H. F. L.

[CHANCERY DIVISION.]

HARTE v. THE ONTARIO EXPRESS AND TRANSPORTATION
COMPANY.

MOLSON'S BANK CLAIM.

*Company—Winding-up Act—Master in Ordinary—Jurisdiction—Fraudu-
lent Transfer—R. S. C., ch. 129—52 Vict. ch. 32 (D.).*

The Master in Ordinary or other officer of the Court to whom its powers
may be delegated is not a competent tribunal to decide questions of
fraudulent transfer arising in the course of a reference in winding-up
proceedings, under the Dominion Winding-up Act and amending Acts.

THIS was an appeal from the interim certificate of the Statement.
Master in Ordinary in reference to a matter arising in the
course of the winding-up proceedings before him of the
Ontario Express and Transportation Company, under R.
S. C. ch. 129, and the amending Act, 52 Vict. ch. 32 (D.).

In the course of proving the claim of the Molson's Bank
against the estate, it appeared by the evidence that certain
promissory notes had been transferred to the bank by the
company, within thirty days next before the commencement of winding-up proceedings under the Act, and the
liquidator proposed to try the question before the Master
in Ordinary as to whether the said notes had been transferred in contemplation of insolvency within the meaning
of sec. 71 of R. S. C. ch. 129.

By his certificate dated May 29th, 1894, the learned
Master stated : " I ruled that as the said Molson's Bank
came in to prove its claim as a creditor against the above
named company, all rights of the said bank as such creditor
were submitted to this Court, and were governed by the
statutory rules prescribed by Act, and that this Court
thereupon became a Court of competent jurisdiction under
the 71st section of the said Winding-up Act, and that
under the order of reference I have jurisdiction to try
the said question."

This appeal was brought on behalf of the Molson's Bank,
upon grounds stated in the notice of appeal as follows :

" The Winding-up Act, R. S. C. ch. 129, and the Winding-
up Amendment Act, 52 Vict. ch. 32 (D.), are special Acts
conferring certain powers upon the Court for the purpose
of winding-up proceedings, and the powers of the Court in
such winding-up proceedings are limited to the powers conferred by such Acts. Jurisdiction is not conferred upon
the Court by the said Acts to try in winding-up proceedings the question set out in the certificate. * * Under
the order of reference herein, no larger powers were
delegated to the Master in Ordinary than were conferred
by the said Acts upon the Court, and, therefore, the
Master in Ordinary has no power to try the said question
in these winding-up proceedings. The said question can
be tried only in an independent action to be brought by
the liquidator under the 31st section of said Winding-up
Act."

The Winding-up Order, which was dated March 2nd,
1892, provided in the usual way that, " for the purpose of
dealing with the matters hereinbefore mentioned and in
relation to the winding-up of the said company, the said
Master do, subject to appeal as from a Master acting under
an order of reference made in an action, have as full and
ample power as under the said statute and amending Act
is conferred upon a Judge of the High Court."

The appeal was argued before FERGUSON, J., on June
6th, 1894.

H. D. Gamble, for the appellants. This is precisely the
same question which was raised and decided in *In re The
Sun Lithographing Co., Farquhar's Claim,* 22 O. R. 57.
The Winding-up Amendment Act does not affect it at all,
and was in operation before that case. The Master's forum
is a creature of the Act, and has powers only where powers
are given by the Act. The power to try such question as
that under section 71, was not only not given, but, by the
terms of section 71, is relegated to a " Court of competent
jurisdiction."

Hoyles, Q. C., for the liquidator. In *The Sun Litho-
graphing Company* case, 22 O. R. 57, the Judge's attention
was not drawn to cases as to administration nor apparently
to the effect of the amending Act, 52 Vict. ch. 32, sec. 20
(D.). It is a question of convenience in each case : *In re
The Essex Land and Timber Co.,* 21 O. R. 367. See also
Merchants' Bank v. *Monteith,* 10 P. R. 458 ; *In re General
Rolling Stock Co.,* L. R. 7 Ch. 646 ; *In re Mercantile
Trading Co., Stringer's Case,* L. R. 4 Ch. 475 ; also an
unreported decision of ROBERTSON, J., in *Re Charles Stark
Co.* (a), in which, after referring to the authorities, the
learned Judge decided that the proceedings under a
Winding-up Order under the Dominion Winding-up Act
were analogous to administration proceedings, and that,
therefore, the Master should dispose of everything, unless
some special ground of inconvenience to his being allowed
to do so existed in the particular case.

FERGUSON, J. :—

I am of the opinion, that in this winding-up matter, the
Master is not a " Court of competent jurisdiction," within
the meaning of that expression in the seventy-first section
of the Act, for the purpose of trying the question as to

(a) January 10th, 1893. The question in that case was as to the
damages arising out of a claim for breach, in consequence of the liquidation of the company, of an agreement for the future supply of goods for a
period extending over many years.—REP.

the propriety and validity of the transfer of this property
(said to be of the value of $18,000) by the company to the
Molson's bank, which is alleged to be in contravention of
the section, and to operate an unjust preference.

The appeal will be allowed with costs.

A. H. F. L.

[CHANCERY DIVISION.]

TORONTO GENERAL TRUSTS COMPANY v. QUIN.

*Dower—Release by Marriage Settlement—Devolution of Estates Act—
Right of Election.*

Section 4 of the Devolution of Estates Act, R. S. O. ch. 108, which gives
the widow a right of election between her dower and a distributive
share in her deceased husband's lands, does not apply where by marriage
settlement she has accepted an equivalent in lieu of dower. In such
case she has no right to any share in the lands.

THIS was a special case for the opinion of the Court.
The defendant Annie Quin was married to her husband
on the 17th March, 1880. On the 5th March an antenuptial settlement was drawn up whereby the intended wife
agreed to accept the sum of $250 in lieu of and in full
satisfaction of her dower and right to dower which she in
the event of her surviving her husband might or could
thereafter in anywise have or claim, whether at common
law or otherwise howsoever, to or out of the lands, tenements, hereditaments and premises which either at the
time of the said intended marriage or at any future time
or times should be owned by the intended husband or in
which he might be in anywise interested.

The husband died in 1893, intestate, owning certain real
estate, and leaving his widow, the defendant Annie Quin,
and her children the defendants Charles W. Quin and
Mary Morrison McBain. The plaintiffs were the administrators of the estate of the deceased.

The question for the opinion of the Court was, whether the defendant Annie Quin, was entitled to share in the distribution of the said real estate of her deceased husband ; and if so what her share therein was.

The case was argued May 11th, 1894.

E. T. Malone, for the plaintiffs.

W. M. Douglas, for the defendants Charles W. Quin and Mary Morrison McBain, children of the intestate.

T. R. Slaght, for the defendant Annie Quin, the widow.

June 1st, 1894.   BOYD, C. :—

The widow in this case has no right of dower in the lands of her intestate husband. By marriage settlement and for valuable consideration she agreed to accept an equivalent in full satisfaction of her dower and right of dower which in the event of surviving her husband she could or might thereafter in anywise have or claim whether at common law or otherwise, howsoever, out of the then or the future lands owned by her husband. The lands, now assets, were then owned by the husband, and the question arises whether the widow can claim the distributive share or any part thereof provided for by section 4 of the Devolution of Estates Act, R. S. O. ch. 108.

The second sub-section declares the scope of the Act to be in regard to cases where there is an existing right to dower outstanding at the death of the husband. In such case the widow is put to her election to take dower or the distributive statutory share from the hands of the legal personal representative. Here the widow cannot so elect, for she has already received the equivalent for her dower from, and during the lifetime of her husband. She ought not to have both the then appraised value of her future dower and also the benefit of the share under the Act.

The case appears to be taken out of the purview of the statute by the antenuptial contract made between the parties afterwards married. The intention of the Act is

Judgment.

Boyd, C. that if the widow elects to take the statutory share she shall yield her dower for the benefit of the estate, and conversely if she takes dower she foregoes any other claim upon the proceeds of the real estate. But having already had the value of her dower paid during her husband's life, she cannot be allowed further to diminish his estate in respect of this marital claim after his death.

As I think the case is not within the statute, I answer the questions submitted in the special case thus :

1 and 2. The widow is not entitled to any share or interest in the real estate of the intestate.

3. As the situation is new and proper for submission to the Court I would give costs to all out of the estate.

G. F. H.

[QUEEN'S BENCH DIVISION.]

RE CLARK v. BARBER.

Prohibition—Money Payable by Instalments with Interest—Splitting
Demand—Division Court Act, sec. 77.

Where, under an agreement for the sale of land, the balance of the purchase money was payable by instalments with interest at a named rate
half-yearly, and three of the instalments, amounting to $240, as well as
the interest, amounting to $70, and three years' taxes were overdue;
and an action was commenced in the Division Court for the arrears of
interest and two years' taxes, amounting to $95.30 :—

Held, that the action did not come within section 77 of the Division Court
Act, whereby the splitting of causes of action is forbidden, and prohibition was refused.

Re Gordon v. *O'Brien,* 11 P. R. 287, not followed.

THIS was a motion for a writ of prohibition to the Statement.
Tenth Division Court of the county of York.

By an agreement for the sale of land, dated the 7th of
September, 1889, for the sum of $612, the purchase money
was payable as follows:—$212 within one year, and the
balance of $400 in five yearly instalments of $80 each,
with interest half-yearly at the rate of 7 per cent. per
annum. The purchaser was also to pay the taxes. The
$212 was duly paid, but default was made in the payment
of the three succeeding instalments of principal and interest, and also of the taxes.

On the 7th of May, 1894, after three instalments
of principal and interest, amounting to $240, were due,
together with the interest thereon, as well as the taxes for
the years 1891, 1892, 1893, an action was commenced in
the said Division Court to recover the arrears of interest,
amounting to $70, and the taxes for the years 1891 and
1892, amounting to $25.30, making a total claim of $95.30,
no claim being made for the arrears of principal or for the
taxes of 1893.

The defendant contended that the arrears of principal,
interest and taxes constituted one entire account under the
contract, and that the claim here constituted a splitting

up of the cause of action, there being no abandonment of the arrears of principal due, or of the taxes for 1893.

June 1st, 1894. *R. B. Beaumont* supported the motion. *R. M. Macdonald*, contra.

The following cases were referred to: *Re McKenzie* v. *Ryan*, 6 P. R. 323, and the cases there referred to; *Re Gordon* v. *O'Brien*, 11 P. R. 287; *Public School Trustees of Nottawasaga* v. *Township of Nottawasaga*, 15 A. R. 310.

June 4, 1894. BOYD, C. :—

This is not a case of splitting the cause of action which is forbidden by the Division Court Act, sec. 77. The claim is founded on a contract to pay for land of which the principal money had been reduced to $400. This balance was to be paid in "five yearly instalments with interest at seven per cent., payable half-yearly." What does this mean?

Is the interest to be reckoned on the whole sum of $400, or only on the instalment?

It means, I think, a half-yearly payment on the whole principal unpaid, and it is, therefore, a thing distinct and severed from interest on the instalment merely. An action might have been brought for the interest due for the first half year upon default made: an action might also have been brought for the first instalment not paid at the time fixed; but it strikes me that these would be for different causes of action, though they might be combined, if all was overdue at the date of suit. In the case of pleading there would be separate counts, one for the principal and another for the interest, though both were agreed to be paid by the one contract. Had the interest been in respect of the instalment only, then I think that the whole would form one cause of action in which such limited interest might and should be regarded as incidental or accessary to the fraction of the principal.

In Copinger's County Court Practice (Ireland), p. 62, it is
said : " Any two demands which would require to be stated
in distinct counts, may be sued for separately ; separate
gales of rent may be recovered by separate processes, likewise sums of money lent at different times. So two
separate processes may be brought for use and occupation
for different years ; for though both actions may be combined in one it is not compulsory on the plaintiff so to
combine them : *Wallace* v. *Whelam*, Ir. C. C. 582." See
also *Kimpton* v. *Willey*, 1 L. M. & P. 280, 282; S. C., 19
L. J. C. P. 269.

The decision of Crampton, J., in *Wallace* v. *Whelam*, is
not conformable to the decision of O'Connor, J., in *Re
Gordon and O'Brien*, 11 P. R. 287, but the Irish case
appears to me the more reasonable. The case in appeal of
Public School Trustees of Nottawasaga v. *Cooper*, 15 A. R.
310, seems also opposed in principle to the case of *Gordon
and O'Brien*. No doubt in such a case as suing for three
gales of rent in the Superior Court in three separate
actions, the Court would consolidate or deal with the mul-
tiplication of actions in awarding costs—but that does not
go to shew that there is only *one* cause of action.

There appears to be nothing affecting jurisdiction in the
point that the contract still remains in writing, not carried
out by the execution of deed and mortgage. The agreement to pay remains, and can be enforced by action :
Yates v. *Aston*, 4 Q. B. 182.

I refuse the motion to prohibit with costs.

                                        G. F. H.

[CHANCERY DIVISION.]

MERRITT v. THE CITY OF TORONTO.

Municipal Corporations—Auctioneer—Right to Issue License therefor—Power to Prohibit—R. S. O. ch. 184, sec. 495, sub-sec. 2.

Section 495 sub-sec. 2 of the Municipal Act R. S. O. ch. 184, which empowers any city, etc., to pass by-laws for the "licensing, regulating and governing of auctioneers," etc., is only for the purpose of raising a revenue and does not confer any right of prohibition so long as the applicant is willing to pay the sum fixed for the license. Where, therefore, a city refused to license the plaintiff as an auctioneer on the ground that he was a person of a notoriously bad character and ill-repute, a mandamus was granted, compelling the issue of the license to him.

Statement. THIS was an action brought against the city of Toronto for a mandamus to compel the issue to the plaintiff of a license permitting him to carry on the business of an auctioneer in the city under the terms and conditions of the by-law of the city regarding licenses to auctioneers; and for damages by reason of the wrongful refusal to issue such license.

The defence set up by the defendants was that the plaintiff was a person of notoriously bad character and ill-repute, into whose custody the goods and moneys of the public should not be entrusted; and that they were therefore justified in refusing to issue a license to him.

This defence was demurred to.

March 8, 1894. *J. E. Jones,* for demurrer.
W. R. Meredith, Q. C., contra.

April 5th, 1894: ROSE, J. :—

No question arises as to the constitutional powers of the legislature. The only question is what powers were conferred upon municipal councils by sec. 495, ch. 184, R. S. O. 1887, which enacts that "the council of any county, city and town separated from the county for municipal purposes may pass by-laws for the following purposes" (amongst others) sub-sec. 2 : " For licensing, regulating and govern-

ing auctioneers and other persons selling or putting up for
sale goods,wares, merchandise or effects by public auction;
and for fixing the sum for every such license and the time
it shall be in force."

In the present case the council of the defendant corporation refused to license the plaintiff as an auctioneer upon
the ground that he was a person of notoriously bad
character, and of ill repute, justifying the refusal under
a by-law passed upon an assumption that power to pass
such a by-law was conferred upon the council by the
above section.

It is to be remembered that the right to carry on the
business of an auctioneer was the plaintiff's common law
right, and if the council had the power to prohibit him
from carrying it on, such power must have been conferred
by language clear and admitting of no doubt.

It will be observed that the power conferred by sec. 92,
sub-sec. 9 of the B. N. A. Act upon Provincial legislatures to
make laws relating to shop, saloon, tavern, auctioneer
and other licenses was for the sole purpose of raising a
revenue for provincial, local, or municipal purposes.

In *Russell* v. *The Queen*, 7 App. Cas. 829, at p. 837, it is
stated that the Act then under consideration could not have
been passed under sub-sec. 9, which provided for passing a
fiscal law, and see also *Hodge* v. *The Queen*, 9 App. Cas.
117.

Indeed the language used in sub-sec. 2 of sec. 495 shews
that the legislature had the scope of sub-sec. 9 plainly in
view.

It cannot then be intended that under powers conferred
to raise a revenue any power to prohibit was given save
such as might be necessary to compel those who might
wish to carry on the business of an auctioneer to take out
a license and pay the fee.

The power to pass by-laws regulating and governing
auctioneers must, I think, mean power to pass by-laws to
regulate and govern licensed auctioneers, and does not
imply any power to limit the granting of licenses to any

33—VOL. XXV. O.R.

particular class. If, having accepted a license, a licensee violate any reasonable rule or regulation laid down for regulating the manner of carrying on his business or governing him in carrying it on, he may, no doubt, be punished according to the provisions of the by-law passed for such purpose.

In *Bannan* v. *Corporation of Toronto*, 22 O. R. 274, the learned Chancellor held that the power to regulate did not include the power to forfeit. If there is no power to forfeit a license for breach of any rule or regulation it seems to me an *a fortiori* case that there is no power to prohibit for an anticipated breach of the law. If the plaintiff, although he has (if he has), in the past been a person of notoriously bad character and of ill repute, desires to carry on the business of an auctioneer in obedience to the law including any rules or regulations passed by the council he should have an opportunity of doing so. If he break the law he will be liable to the punishment enacted but not, under the section in question, to forfeiture of his common law rights. To such extent as the by-law in question purports to confer upon the council the right to refuse a license to the plaintiff on the ground taken, I think it is *ultra vires*, and to such extent the demurrer must be allowed.

I do not think the plaintiff could compel the city to transfer a license which is personal in its nature. Any one accepting a license must accept it subject to any provisions governing its transfer, and to such extent the demurrer must be overruled.

The plaintiff has substantially succeeded and must have the costs of the demurrer as costs in the cause in any event.

G. F. H.

[COMMON PLEAS DIVISION.]

PHELPS v. LORD ET AL.

Will—Devise—Charitable Bequest—Indefiniteness—Scheme.

A testator by his will devised to certain named persons who were appointed the executors and trustees thereof, the remainder of his estate to be used to further "the cause of our Lord Jesus Christ" :—
Held, that the legacy was not void for indefiniteness, and discretion having been given to the executors and trustees, it was not necessary that a scheme should be directed.

THIS was a motion for judgment for the plaintiff on the statement of claim, or for such order as on the pleadings the Court might deem proper. Statement.

The plaintiff alleged in the statement of claim that she was the only surviving heir-at-law of George William Hamilton, late of Niagara Falls, deceased, and that the defendants were the executors and trustees named in the last will and testament of said deceased.

The testator died on the 13th April, 1893; and by his will, among other things, devised as follows : "The remainder of my property, real and personal of every name and kind which I now have or may hereafter acquire, I leave in the hands jointly of Theodore L. Pitt, John R. Lord and Henry C. Allen, to be used to further the cause of "Our Lord Jesus Christ."

John R. Lord and Henry C. Allen, who were appointed executors of the will, took probate thereof.

The residue of the estate amounted to $10,000 and upwards.

The defendants alleged that they had no beneficial interest in the estate, and were only interested therein as trustees, and that they were desirous of executing the trusts of the said will in accordance with the express wishes of the testator, and they submitted the proper construction of the will and their rights thereunder to the judgment and direction of the Court.

It was admitted (for the purpose of the argument only) that the plaintiff was the only surviving heir-at-law of the testator.

German, for the motion.
Moss, Q. C., and *Fraser*, contra.

March 17th, 1894. MACMAHON, J. :—

In *Powerscourt* v. *Powerscourt*, 1 Molloy 616, decided in 1824 by Lord Manners, it was held that where there was a devise to trustees in trust to lay out in their discretion £2,000 per annum until the testator's son should come of age, " in the service of my Lord and Master, and, I trust, my Redeemer," that these words established a good charitable devise. So in *Whicker* v. *Hume*, 14 Beav. 509 (1851), a gift to trustees to apply in such manner as they in their uncontrolled authority should think proper, "for the benefit, advancement, and propagation of learning in every part of the world as far as circumstances will permit," was held a good charitable bequest.

In *Felan* v. *Russell*, 4 Ir. Eq. 701 (1842), where the testatrix bequeathed the residue of her personal property to William Russell, " to be by him applied for such pious purposes and uses as should appear to him to be most conducive to the honour and glory of God and the salvation of my soul," upon a bill to administer her assets, this bequest was deemed to be a good charitable bequest ; and it was, with the consent of William Russell, referred to the remembrancer to settle a scheme.

In *Lea* v. *Cooke*, 34 Ch. D. 528 (1887), where a testator bequeathed legacies to " General William Booth * * for the spread of the Gospel," and General William Booth was the general superintendent of a religious unincorporated society, and as such superintendent, it was under his absolute control, it was held that the legacies were good charitable bequests, and that the legacies should be paid to William Booth without a scheme. See also *Townsend* v. *Carus*, 3 Hare 257, and *Anderson* v. *Kilborn*, 22 Gr. 385. .

Upon the authorities the legacy is not void for indefiniteness.

The other question is as to whether there should be a reference directing that a scheme should be prepared.

The testator gave the trustees of his will a discretion as to how the fund was to be used for the advancement of the cause he had in view, and where that is the case the authorities shew it is a reason for not directing a scheme.

In *Powerscourt* v. *Powerscourt*, 1 Molloy 616, at p. 618, Lord Manners said: "It remains only to decide whether this trust shall be executed by referring it to the Master to settle a scheme, or by leaving it to the trustees to exercise their discretion as the will directs, under the control of this Court. I think the latter is the right course," etc. See also *Horde* v. *Earl of Suffolk*, 2 Myl. & K. 59, where there was a discretion in the legatee, no scheme was directed, and *Lea* v. *Cooke*, 34 Ch. D. 528.

It is not a case in which a discretion given to the trustees by the will should be interfered with so long as they carry out the intention of the testator.

The action must be dismissed; but I shall follow the rule laid down in *Whicker* v. *Hume*, 14 Beav. 509, at p. 527 (where the will was filed by the heir-at-law), and direct that the costs of all the parties be paid out of the estate.

G. F. H.

[CHANCERY DIVISION.]

IN RE KOCH AND WIDEMAN.

Executors and Administrators— Will—Power of Sale—Surviving Executors
—Devolution of Estates Act, R. S. O. ch. 108 and Amendments.

Where executors are given express power to sell lands, whether coupled
with an interest or not, such power can be exercised by a surviving
executor.

The Devolution of Estates Act and amendments do not interfere with an
express power of sale given by a will to executors extending beyond
the periods of vesting prescribed by those Acts.

Statement.

THIS was a petition under the provisions of the Vendors
and Purchasers' Act. The question to be determined was
whether the vendor John Koch, as surviving executor of
the will of Christian Heisey, could sell the lands in question under the provisions of the will, or under the Devolution of Estates Act, or under the Trustees and Executors
Act, and whether with or without the concurrence of the
official guardian.

The testator died 11th June, 1892, leaving his will,
dated 6th February, 1892, containing the following provisions :

"I direct my executors hereinafter named to convert
into cash such of my personal effects as are not otherwise-
herein disposed of ; and I direct all my just debts, funeral
and testamentary expenses to be paid and satisfied by my
executors hereinafter named as soon as conveniently may
be after my decease, including a tombstone to mark the
place of my burial, the same to be erected and paid for
from said proceeds.

"I give, devise and bequeath all my real and personal
estate of which I may die possessed of or interested in in
the manner following, that is to say :

"I give to my beloved wife Selina Heisey, all my household goods of every description, including beds and

bedding, to have and to hold to her, her heirs, executors
and assigns, for her and their sole and only use forever.

"I also give and devise to my said wife Selina, the use
and occupation of one and three-quarter acres of land
with the appurtenances thereon belonging, being situate
on the south-west corner of lot number nineteen, in the
eighth concession of the said township of Markham,
fronting on the eighth concession line, sixteen rods by
seventeen and one-half rods deep, said premises to be
occupied and owned by my said wife, so long as she
remains my widow only; my executors to see that the
line fence on the east side of said lot be placed on the
boundary line herein described. I further give and bequeath to my said wife $150 a year, in half-yearly pay-
ments of $75 each, to be paid to her out of the rent of my
farm where I now live, the first payment to be made on
the first day of the first October or April after my decease
until my farm shall be sold, and after the sale of my farm,
I give to my beloved wife the interest on $2,500 at six per
per cent., or the above $150, payable as above half-yearly,
so long only as she remains my widow. I also give my
said wife one cow and all the fowls. The provisions made
by me herein for my wife are accepted by her in lieu of
dower from my estate. The balance of my real estate
being composed of ninety-six and one-half acres (96½), more
or less (my homestead), being composed of part of lot number nineteen, in the eighth concession of the said township
of Markham, I order, instruct and hereby empower my
herein named executors to sell and convey by title-deed or
deeds, at any time within three years after my decease;
the purchaser to pay not less than $3,000 at the time of
the purchase, and the balance to be paid as my executors
may consider for the best interest of my legatees.

"I direct that my executors leave $2,500 in mortgage
on the land or invest that amount on real estate on first-
class mortgage at interest payable half-yearly, and pay the
same to my wife during her lifetime or remains my
widow."

The testator then set out a number of sums which he had paid to his children during his lifetime, except two of them, John and Albert, to whom he had not given anything, and proceeded : " I give and bequeath to my twelve beloved children above named, respectively, enough to make them $500 each, to include the amounts already received as above stated, said several sums of $500 each to be paid out of the money that shall be realized out of the sale of my real estate ; and I give and bequeath to my son Jacob Heisey, in addition to the five hundred dollars, my silver watch ; and I desire that my son Jacob shall have his $500, or a part of it, out of the first sums realized from the sale of the aforesaid real estate.

" I devise and bequeath to my granddaughter Lilly Serene Tefft, $200, in addition to her share in her deceased mother's share. The $338 or residue bequeathed to my deceased daughter Martha Tefft, I desire to have placed at interest and it divided equally between her surviving children proportionately as they arrive at the age of twenty-one years.

" If any of my children die before having received their full share and leaving issue, the deceased share shall be equally divided between his or her children, and should any of my said children die without issue, then his or her share shall be divided equally between the surviving brothers and sisters of the deceased.

" If there is no tombstone placed at the grave of my deceased daughter Tefft, I desire my executors to place a tombstone at the grave and deduct the price thereof from her legacy. After the decease or marriage of my wife Selina, I desire my executors to sell, and I hereby empower them to give a title-deed to that part of my real estate set apart for her occupation.

" If any one of my legatees shall make any law costs to test the validity of this my will, I order and direct that the share provided herein for such legatee shall be by him or her forfeited and such amount shall be applied in payment of such costs as between solicitor and client. I have

notes against some of my children, and I provide that all
notes which I now hold or may hereafter take from any
of my children with interest accumulated thereon shall
be a charge against their legacy and shall be deducted
from the share coming to the said legatee.

"All the residue of my estate not hereinbefore disposed of
I give, devise and bequeath unto my said children and
their issue, as aforesaid provided for, to be divided between
them my children share and share alike, from time to
time, as the money shall become available.

"And I nominate and appoint John Koch and John
Byer, of the said township of Markham, farmers, to be
executors and trustees of this my last will and testament."

Probate was granted to the two executors named in the
will. After the grant of probate, John Byer, one of the
executors, died.

The personal estate proved insufficient to pay the debts,
and the surviving executor John Koch, for the purpose of
raising money for the payment of the debts and legacies, and
of carrying into effect the provisions of the will, entered
into a contract in writing on 27th March, 1894, with the
respondent Daniel Wideman, for the sale to him at the
price of $5,500, of the land described in the will as the
homestead.

The children of the testator's deceased daughter, Martha
Tefft, referred to in the will, were infants.

The respondent objected to the title upon the ground
that the express power in the will was to the two executors, and could not be exercised by the survivor; and that
the power given by the Devolution of Estates Act had
expired before the date of the contract and could not be
exercised, at all events, without the concurrence of the
beneficiaries and the official guardian.

The questions arising were argued before STREET, J., in
Court on 1st May, 1894.

A. H. Marsh, Q. C., for the petitioner.
No one appeared for the respondent.

May 14, 1894. STREET, J. :—

The question here raised appears to me to be directly
within the authority of *Re Ford*, 7 P. R. 451, decided by
Proudfoot, V. C., in January, 1879, and in accordance with
the principle of that decision, I hold that the express
power of sale given by Christian Heisey to his executors,
was properly exercised by John Koch, the surviving executor, after the death of his co-executor.

It was considered by the learned Judge who decided that
case, that the presumption to be drawn from the terms of
the will| was that the proceeds of the sale of the land
were to be invested by the executors in their own names ;
and this being so, that the power of sale was not a bare
power which might not survive, but a power coupled with
an interest which certainly would survive.

In the will of Christian Heisey, we have an express
direction to the executors to leave part of the purchase
money on mortgage on the land and to pay the interest to
the widow.

Having in view the course of modern legislation, and
the strength of the opinions which have been expressed in
favour of the position that an express power of sale to
executors, even though unaccompanied by an interest, sur-
vives and follows the office, I should be prepared to hold
that the power of sale in this will was well executed
by the surviving executor, even though it should be held
to be a power without an interest : *Howell* v. *Barnes*, Cro.
Car. 382 ; Sugden on Powers, 8th ed., 128 ; *Re Stephenson*,
24 O. R. 395 ; R. S. O. ch. 110, sec. 28.

The Devolution of Estates Act does not appear to contain any provision interfering with an express power of
sale such as is contained in this will. The will gives the
executors three years from the testator's death in which to
dispose of the land.

The first section of the amending Act, 54 Vic. ch. 18 (O.),
enacts that real estate not disposed of by the executors or
administrators within twelve months after the testator's

death, shall go to the devisees or heirs beneficially entitled, unless the executors or administrators have registered a caution as therein provided. But the effect of this enactment, I think, is not to be extended beyond the revesting in the devisee or heir, as the case may be, of the estate which would, but for the 4th section of the Devolution of Estates Act, ch. 108, R. S. O., have vested in him upon the testator's death.

The Act in question is intended, as appears on its face, to aid executors and administrators to deal with the estates which are required for the payment of debts where such aid is necessary to enable them to do so; there is nothing in it to interfere with the provisions which testators may themselves have made as to the time and manner in which their estates are to be dealt with. Where such provisions have been made by a testator, the Act may supplement, but does not detract from them, and certainly does not destroy the express directions of a will as to the time and manner of conversion, for the purpose of vesting an absolute title in a beneficiary at an earlier period than the testator intended him to have it. The executor here has a power of sale under the will and can exercise it under the will without regard to the Act. If he had taken it under the Act that would have been a different thing, and he must have exercised it within the time limited by the Act or not at all. See *Re Booth's Trusts*, 16 O. R. 429.

I determine the question submitted to me as follows :— The express power of sale contained in the said will, did survive to the petitioner John Koch, and he can under the provisions of that power make a valid conveyance to the respondent by way of completing the contract for sale.

As agreed by the parties, there will be no costs to either party of the petition.

G. F. H.

[CHANCERY DIVISION.]

Re Chillman Infants.

Infant—Custody of—Religious Faith of Father—Testamentary Guardian.

Orphan children having been clandestinely taken from the custody of
their uncle, the testamentary guardian under the will of their father,
who had predeceased his wife, by their aunt, a Roman Catholic, claiming
guardianship under an invalid instrument in her favour, signed by the
mother of the children, and it appearing that their father, a Protestant,
had desired the children to be brought up in his own faith, an order
was made for their delivery to the custody of their uncle as testamentary guardian.

Statement.   THIS was an application by Thomas Jackson for a writ
of *habeas corpus* for the return to him of Gertrude Chillman, an infant, between twelve and thirteen years of age.

F. E. Hodgins, for the applicant.

N. Murphy, for the respondent.

The facts are stated in the judgment.

May 16th, 1894.   STREET, J. :—

James Chillman died on 2nd October, 1892, at Toronto,
leaving him surviving his widow, Anne Chillman, and five
infant children whose custody is in question upon this
application ; Gertrude, the eldest, being now between
twelve and thirteen years of age.

By his will he appointed Thomas Jackson of Toronto,
engineer, his wife's brother, to be the guardian of his
children, and probate of the will was granted to Thomas
Jackson, who was also the executor named in it, on 13th
October, 1892.

The children continued to live with their mother until
her death, which took place at Toronto, on 12th April,
1894.   A few days before her death, she executed a paper,
not under seal, by which she put her children and her property into the charge of her sister, Sadie Feldcamp.

After the death of Anne Chillman, Thomas Jackson
took charge of the children and had them in his custody

for a few days, at the end of which time they were clandestinely taken away by Sadie Feldcamp, who, however,
later on, returned all but the eldest child, Gertrude, who
still remains with her.

The present application is made by Thomas Jackson for
a *habeas corpus* commanding the return of Gertrude to
him, and for an order declaring him entitled to the custody
of all the children.

The application is opposed by Sadie Feldcamp, who
wishes the care of all the children to be entrusted to her,
claiming to be entitled as guardian appointed by the
alleged will of her sister, Anne Chillman, deceased, supporting her claim by the argument that it appears from
the affidavits and papers filed, to be in the interest of the
children that she should take them.

It further appears from the affidavits that the father of
the children was a member of the Church of England;
that Thomas Jackson is a Protestant, and that Sadie Feldcamp is a Roman Catholic. Thomas Jackson swears that
he was appointed guardian of the children by their father
in order that they might be brought up as Protestants, and
that he has made arrangements for their being placed in a
Protestant Orphans' Home in Toronto, where they will be
well cared for.

It further appears, I think, from the affidavits, that
Sadie Feldcamp is not possessed of any means to support
the children.

It is alleged that she has made application to the Surrogate Court for probate of the alleged will of her sister,
Mrs. Chillman, but at the time of the argument probate
had not been granted, and I have not since been informed
of any grant. I cannot assume that probate will ·be
granted of an instrument in the form of the one in question. It appears to be intended to take effect immediately
upon its execution, and, therefore, to be not testamentary
in its character : *Patch* v. *Shore*, 2 Dr. & Sm. 589 ; *Re Robinson*, L. R. 1 P. & D. 384.

Not being under seal it cannot take effect as an appointment of Miss Feldcamp by deed under R. S. O. ch. 137, sec. 14.

The matter, therefore, appears to stand thus: The father of the children has appointed Thomas Jackson to be their guardian by his will, and the mother has made no valid appointment. The testamentary guardian proposes to place the children in a proper home where they will be brought up in the religious faith of their father. On the other hand, Miss Feldcamp has only in her favour the informal expression of the wishes of their mother, that she should take charge of them; she is not possessed of means to do so properly, and if entrusted with their custody, she will naturally bring them up in her own, that is to say, the Roman Catholic faith. I say nothing as to the charges which have been made against her moral character; she has denied them all, and it is not necessary that I should consider them.

In the very late case in the English Court of Appeal, *Re McGrath Infants*, [1893] 1 Ch. 143, at p. 148, Lord Justice Lindley, upon a similar application, says: " As regards religious education it is settled law that the wishes of the father must be regarded by the Court and must be enforced unless there is some strong reason for disregarding them. The Guardianship of Infants' Act, 1886, which has so greatly enlarged the rights of mothers after their husbands' deaths, has not changed the law in this respect * * *. The wishes of the father if not clearly expressed by him must be inferred from his conduct. If the father is dead it will be naturally inferred that in the absence of evidence to the contrary his wish was that the children should be brought up in his own religion; that is, the religion which he professed. This inference is one which the Court in the absence of evidence to the contrary is bound to draw, and is practically not distinguishable from a rule of law to the effect that an infant child is to be brought up in its father's religion, unless it can be shewn to be for the welfare of the child that this rule should be

departed from, or the father has otherwise directed."
See also section 22 of R. S. O., ch. 137.

In the present case, I can find no good reason at all for interfering with the rights of the guardian appointed by the father, and I must grant the order asked for, for a writ of *habeas corpus* for the production and handing over by Sadie Feldcamp and Lizzie Toban to Thomas Jackson of Gertrude Chillman, and must declare him entitled as testamentary guardian to the custody of all the children of James Chillman, deceased.

Had the alleged appointment by Anne Chillman of Sadie Feldcamp as guardian of the children been valid under section 14 of R. S. O., ch. 137, so as to give her a joint guardianship with Thomas Jackson, I should have acted, I think, upon the powers in section 15 of the Act, and directed that, for the present, at all events, and until further order, the children should be placed in the home in question.

I think the costs of the application must be given against Sadie Feldcamp, whose action in removing the children without consulting their testamentary guardian cannot be justified.

G. F. H.

[CHANCERY DIVISION.]

REGINA v. BELL.

*Public Morals—By-law against Swearing in Street or Public Place—
Private Office in Custom House.*

A city by-law enacted that no person should make use of any profane
swearing, obscene, blasphemous or grossly insulting language, or be
guilty of any other immorality or indecency in any street or public
place:—

Held, that the object of the by-law was to prevent an injury to public
morals, and applied to a street or a public place *ejusdem generis* with a
street, and not to a private office in the custom house.

Statement.

IN Hilary Sittings, 1894, *Herbert Mowat* obtained an
order *nisi* to quash a conviction made by Hugh Miller, a
Justice of the Peace for the city of Toronto, acting for the
Police Magistrate in his absence and at his written request.

The defendant was convicted under a by-law of the city
of Toronto, intitled " A by-law relative to public morals,"
which made provision for the punishment of a number of
matters relating to public morals.   Clause four of the by-
law was as follows: "No person shall make use of any
profane swearing, obscene, blasphemous, or grossly insulting language, or be guilty of any other immorality or
indecency in any street or public place."

The conviction was "for that the defendant did on the
18th November, 1893, at the city of Toronto, in the county
of York, in a public place, to wit: in the custom house,
in said city, unlawfully make use of grossly insulting
language to Angelo Gianelli (the complainant), by calling
him, the said Angelo Gianelli, a 'damned scoundrel and
liar,' contrary to the form, of a certain by-law of the
municipality in the said city of Toronto, passed on the 13th
day of January, 1890, No. 2449, and entitled 'A by-law
relative to public morals,' in such case made and provided."

It appeared by the evidence that the words complained
of were used in the defendant's office in the custom house,
behind a counter in his room, where he carried on his

occupation as a gauger, which place was private. The defendant there made his analysis of wine, liquors, etc. There was a rule against admitting the public to such an office, and a partition and counter separated the private part of the office from the public part, which partition was too high for a man to see over. The words were spoken in the presence of one other person.

In Easter Sittings, 23rd May, 1894, *Langton*, Q. C., supported the order *nisi*. The place where the alleged offence was committed, was not a public place within the by-law. " Public place" in clause four of the by-law, must be read in connection with the preceding words "in any street," and must be a place *ejusdem generis* with "street": *Case* v. *Storey*, L. R. 4 Ex. at p. 323 ; *Langrish* v. *Archer*, 10 Q. B. D. 44 ; Maxwell on Statutes, p. 399. He was stopped by the Court.

F. W. Garvin, contra. The custom house was a public place within the by-law : *Parker* v. *The State*, 26 Texas 204, 207 (where a law office was held to be a public place within a statute respecting gaming in a public place), and *Regina* v. *Wellard*, 14 Q. B. D. 63.

May 25, 1894. Rose, J. ;—

The object of the by-law was to preserve public morals. To be within its provisions an offence must have been committed in a public place, such as a street, square, park or other open place, or where "the public may have" the right to be. This was not such a place. The conviction must, therefore, be quashed, and as the matter is a personal one between the informant and the defendant, the informant must pay the costs. The usual order for protection against an action will be made.

MacMahon, J., concurred.

G. F. H.

[CHANCERY DIVISION.]

RE SHEPHERD AND COOPER.

Prohibition—Division Court—Claim for $200 on Contract signed by Defendant—Evidence of Performance of Conditions on Plaintiff's Part.

A Division Court has no jurisdiction to entertain a claim for $200 on a contract signed by defendant where to entitle plaintiff to recover evidence *ultra* must be given to shew that conditions of the contract on the plaintiff's part have been complied with.

Statement.   THIS was a motion for a writ of prohibition to the Tenth Division Court of the county of York to restrain the plaintiff from proceeding further with the claim on the ground that it was beyond the jurisdiction of the Court; and also because a counter claim of the defendant had been disallowed.

The claim was on an agreement signed by the parties whereby the defendant agreed " to rent the Grand Opera House, heated, licensed, lighted, attachés on stage and in front, ushers and doorkeepers, and the use of the billboards, tickets, etc., for the sum of $250 for three nights and Wednesday matinee, January 29th, 30th, and 31st. Rules of theatre to be observed."

The defendant disputed the plaintiff's claim and also counter-claimed for $200 damages by reason of the plaintiff's refusal to perform the contract by allowing the defendant to use certain bill-boards, etc.

The case came for trial before the presiding Judge and a jury. At the commencement of the trial the plaintiff limited his claim to $200, abandoning the excess $50.

At the conclusion of the plaintiff's case, the defendant's counsel objected that the amount sued for was beyond the jurisdiction of the Court, and that there was no power to abandon the excess.

The learned Judge overruled the objection on the ground that it should have been taken at the commencement of the trial. In support of his counterclaim evidence was given shewing that the plaintiff had refused to allow the defendant to use certain bill-boards which were within

the contract. The learned Judge, however, held that the Statement.
plaintiff was not bound to post the bills himself, and therefore was not liable under the counter-claim, which he withdrew from the jury, who found for the plaintiff for the $200

June 1st, 1894. *H. M. East*, for the motion.
C. Millar, contra.

June 4, 1894. BOYD, C.:—

The claim of the plaintiff rests upon an agreement by
which he agrees to rent defendant a building heated, lighted,
with ushers, doorkeepers, etc., for $250 for three nights, ac-
cepted by the defendant. The signature of the defendant
authenticates the contract, but it does not relieve the plaintiff
from proving that all the appliances to serve the purpose
for which the building was rented were duly furnished.
He throws off $50 and sues for the $200, but in my opinion
the case is not within the Division Court Act. Sec. 70, sub-
sec. *c.* of R. S. O., ch. 51, has been much discussed, and is
followed with decisions not all in the same lines. But the
great weight of opinion is against entertaining jurisdiction even though the contract be signed by the defendant
if evidence *ultra* has to be given in the way of shewing
that everything was furnished according to contract in
order to entitle the plaintiff to recover. Evidence must be
given here of the consideration passing to the defendant—
that the building was used, and that it was furnished according to stipulation before payment can be called for.

The cases are all collected in Mr. Bicknell's useful book
on the Statutes, (a) p. 73, and the late case of *Re Wallace*
v. *Virtue*, 24 O. R. 558, does not change the great weight of
authority as being against the compelling of the Division
Court to try this case.

I give effect to the motion for prohibition, and the costs
will be to the defendant and be set off against the claim of
the plaintiff.

                                                      G. F. H.

(a) Bicknell & Seager on the Division Court Act and Amendments.

RE CHAMBERS AND THE CORPORATION OF THE TOWN-SHIP OF BURFORD.

Municipal Corporations—Way—Highway By-law—Description of Land—Clerical Error—Publication—Semi-monthly Newspaper.

A municipal by-law establishing a public highway is not void for uncertainty when the boundaries of the land so declared are described in the by-law with sufficient precision to enable them to be traced upon the ground, and if so properly described, it is not necessary when private ground has been taken to distinguish it as such.

The fact that one of two parallel courses in a description has by obvious clerical error been incorrectly given in the published notice is not a valid objection to such a by-law.

Where there is no paper published in the township weekly or oftener, it is not obligatory to publish the required statutory notice of the by-law in a paper issued therein semi-monthly.

Statement.   THIS was a motion to quash By-law No. 425 of the township of Burford, in the county of Brant, establishing a common and public highway in that township.

The by-law recited that certain lands in the by-law thereinafter described had been used as a public road and highway for thirty years and upwards, and public money had been expended thereon and for opening the same, and statute labour had usually been performed thereon, and that it was a continuation northward of the public road highway between the 10th and 11th concessions of the township already existing and established, and lying between the south halves of lots six and seven in the latter concession ; and that it was desirable in the interest of the public that the same should be clearly established by by-law.

The lands were described in the enacting part of the by-law as follows : " All and singular that certain parcel or part of land in the township of Burford, in the county of Brant, described as follows, that is to say : commencing at the north-east angle of lot number seven, in the eleventh concession of the township of Burford where a stone has

been planted, then south sixteen degrees and ten minutes
east thirty-four chains and four links to a stake, then
north seventy-eight degrees and thirty minutes east one
chain to a stake, then north sixteen degrees and ten
minutes west thirty-four chains and four links to the
north-west angle of lot number six in the said eleventh
concession, then westerly in a straight line one chain to
the place of beginning, containing three acres and two-
fifths of an acre."

The by-law then enacted that the said road was established as a common and public highway.

The objections to the by-law are set out in the judgment.

May 31st, 1894.   *S. Alfred Jones* supported the motion.
Harley, contra.

June 5th, 1894.   Boyd, C. :—

The by-law is attacked as void for want of certainty in
the description of land to be taken.   This is not apparent
to me ; the boundaries are given with precision so that no
one going over the ground could fail to see and know what
was being taken.   It is true this by-law does not speak
of it or deal with it as partly private property, but as
forming part of a highway used and travelled for thirty-
eight years on which public money has been expended ;
but I am not able to pass upon this matter of title as between
the adverse contentions.   Suffices it to say that the corporation were liable to make proper compensation to the private
owner if part of his land is really taken by this by-law.
There is no doubt upon the ground as to what is being
taken, though there may be a dispute as to the ownership
of part of what is so being taken.

Again objection is made because of an error in the notice
published as to one of the courses which by clerical error is
given as twenty-four chains and four links, instead of thirty-
four chains and four links; but the parallel course is correctly given and the error appears to be so obvious as not

Judgment.
Boyd, C. to be calculated to mislead. It is the fault of the proof-
reader and the municipality should not suffer on this
account.

It is further objected that the publication was not
according to the statute, because a paper called the " Scotland Sun," is published in the township, and this advertisement of the intended action of the council was not put in
that paper. It appears that this is a semi-monthly paper
and is not one that is contemplated by the statute which
applies to one published weekly (or oftener) in four successive issues of which the notice is to appear in four successive weeks.(a) There being no paper in the township
appearing once a week or during each week, the statute
does not make it obligatory to use a paper published as in
this case twice a month, and the objection fails.

No other grounds were argued and these failing the
application should be dismissed with costs.

G. F. H.

(a) 55 Vic. ch. 42, sec. 546 (2).

[CHANCERY DIVISION.]

HANDY V. CARRUTHERS ET AL.

*Timber—Standing Timber—Parol Sale of—License to Cut—Revocation of—
Statute of Frauds—Trespass—Justification.*

As a general rule a contract for the sale of standing timber which is not
to be severed immediately is a sale of an interest in land.

Upon a parol sale of timber for valuable consideration, with a parol
license to enter upon the land during such time as should be necessary
for the purpose of cutting and removing the timber, the defendant during the period allowed by the contract continued to cut and remove
notwithstanding he was notified not to do so :—

Held, in an action of trespass and for damages for timber cut after the
notice, that he was at liberty to shew the existence of the parol agreement in justification of what he had done, and under which no right of
revocation existed, and to shew the part performance as an answer to
the objection founded on the Statute of Frauds.

THIS was an action of trespass brought by one Alfred Statement.
Handy against Wallace Carruthers and another for cutting
timber on the plaintiff's land under the circumstances set
out in the judgment of the trial Judge.

The action was tried at the Sittings at Barrie, on April
25th, 1894, before STREET, J., without a jury.

Haughton Lennox and *G. W. Lount,* for the plaintiff.
W. A. Boys, for the defendants.

The facts appear in the judgment.

May 21, 1894. STREET, J. :—

The plaintiff sought to recover damages from the defendants for cutting timber upon a parcel of land owned by
him in the township of Vespra, under the following circumstances :—

In the fall of the year 1890, the plaintiff sold to the defendants by parol the timber upon the land in question,
the consideration being a horse then delivered by the defendants to the plaintiff of the value of about thirty dollars.

Judgment.

Street, J.

In the negotiations it was at first stipulated that the timber should be removed within three years, but upon the defendants stating that they might be prevented by other engagements from removing it within that time, it was agreed that they should have such further time as should be necessary for the purpose.

After the expiration of the three years the defendants continued to cut and remove the timber and the plaintiff notified them not to do so. His contention was that he had only sold them the right to cut during a period of three years which had expired. The dispute upon this point and the question of damages were the matters to which the evidence at the trial was directed. I found in favour of the defendants' contention at the conclusion of the evidence and reserved the questions of law and the amount of damages for further consideration.

Upon the question as to whether this sale is to be treated as a sale of an interest in land or a sale of chattels the authorities are in a most unsatisfactory condition. The current of the later cases seems to have set towards a return to the general rule, so far as possible, that a contract for the sale of growing timber which is not to be severed immediately is a contract for the sale of an interest in land: *Summers* v. *Cook*, 28 Gr. 179; *McNeill* v. *Haines*, 17 O. R. 479; *Lavery* v. *Pursell*, 39 Ch. D. 508.

It is extremely difficult to say upon what principle it can be said that a sale of trees to be severed in two years is a sale of chattels, while a sale of trees to be severed in ten years is a sale of an interest in land. Following the cases above cited from our own Courts I think that the parol sale here intended was a sale of an interest in land; that is to say, a parol sale of timber with a parol license to enter upon the land for the purpose of cutting and removing the trees.

The defendants have justified what would otherwise be a trespass by setting up the plaintiff's license to do what they did; but the license was revoked by notice and the defendants continued to enter upon the land and cut and remove timber from it.

Judgment.

Street, J.

The question to be determined is whether the license having been given for a valuable consideration and not having expired was revocable by the plaintiff.

At law this would be the case even though the license were for a valuable consideration, unless the license were coupled with an interest: *Wood* v. *Leadbitter*, 13 M. & W. 838 : but I think the making of the agreement for the sale of the timber with the license to enter and remove it, founded upon a valuable consideration, may be shewn as an answer to the plaintiff's claim, and that the objection founded upon the Statute of Frauds is met by shewing the part performance.

If the plaintiff here instead of suing for the timber cut after the attempted revocation of the license had sued for the value of all the timber cut during the whole period, the defendants would clearly, I think, have been entitled to shew, notwithstanding the Statute of Frauds, the existence of the parol agreement under which they had acted; and that agreement thus let in would have shewn a complete answer to the plaintiff's claim and not merely an answer to a part of it: in the same way being sued for what he has cut since the attempted revocation, I think he may shew the existence of an agreement for a valuable consideration under which he was entitled to do what is charged as a trespass, and under which no right of revocation existed. See *McManus* v. *Cooke*, 35 Ch. D. 681, 692.

I am of opinion, therefore, that the action should be dismissed with costs.

G. A. B.

[CHANCERY DIVISION.]

QUEEN'S COLLEGE v. CLAXTON.

*Mortgage—Payment off—Demand of Assignment to Nominee of Mortgagor
—Subsequent Encumbrancers—R. S. O. ch. 102, sec. 2.*

Where a mortgagor of land subsequently conveyed his equity of redemption to several grantees, one of whom agreed to pay off the mortgage,
and some of whom also executed further mortgages upon the land, and
the first mortgagee proceeding to foreclose and to sue the mortgagor
upon his covenant, the latter requested him to assign his mortgage to a
third party who had advanced the money and paid off the mortgage :—

Held, that the first mortgagee was bound under R. S. O. ch. 102, sec. 2,
to execute the assignment as asked, notwithstanding the subsequent
encumbrances.

Teevan v. *Smith*, 20 Ch. D. 724, distinguished ; *Kinnaird* v. *Trollope*,
39 Ch. D. 636, followed.

Decision of ARMOUR, C. J., affirmed.

Per BOYD, C.—Even if the redemption money had been that of the mortgagor himself, it would have made no difference.

Statement. THIS was a motion by way of appeal from an order of
ARMOUR, C. J., requiring the plaintiffs, who were mortgagees seeking foreclosure, to execute an assignment of
their mortgage to the nominee of the mortgagors under
circumstances which are fully set out in the judgment of
ROBERTSON, J.

The motion was argued on February 21st, 1894, before
BOYD, C., and FERGUSON and ROBERTSON, JJ.

Langton, Q. C., for the plaintiffs. The solicitor was never
informed that it was not the mortgagor's money. There
was a question to be considered by the mortgagees, and
they *bonâ fide* consulted their solicitor, and even if he was
wrong, did the mortgagees do anything unreasonable in
acting, as they did, and so writing to the solicitor of the
defendant? The Act not applying, there was no right to an
assignment : *Magnus* v. *Queensland National Bank*, 36
Ch. D. 25 ; *Teevan* v. *Smith*, 20 Ch. D. 724; *Alderson* v.
Elgey, 26 Ch. D. 567 ; *Gooderham* v. *The Trader's Bank*,
16 O. R. 438 ; *Rogers* v. *Wilson*, 7 C. L. T. 399, 12 P. R.
322. As to costs : *In re Watts, Smith* v. *Watts*, 22 Ch. D.

Statement.

at p. 12-14; *Little* v. *Brunker*, 28 Gr. 191; *National Pro-vincial Bank of England* v. *Games*, 31 Ch. D. at p. 593; *Cotterell* v. *Stratton*, L. R. 8 Ch. 295.

C. J. Holman, for the defendants. Hughson had no interest in the land, and we were entitled to the assignment: *Kinnaird* v. *Trollope*, 39 Ch. D. 636 ; *Palmer* v. *Hendrie*, 27 Beav. 349. Our statute is much wider than the English: R. S. O. ch. 102, sec. 2.

Langton, in reply. Our Act is in the same terms as the English Act, and *Teevan* v. *Smith*, and other cases on that Act must rule. When a mortgagee has notice of a prior right to that of the mortgagor, he may refuse to assign his mortgage to the nominee of the mortgagor without the consent of the holder of the prior right.

June 1st, 1894. ROBERTSON, J. :—

This is an appeal from an order dated February 6th, 1894, made by the Chief Justice of the Queen's Bench Division, sitting in Chambers, by which it is ordered that the plaintiffs forthwith execute an assignment of the mortgage sued on in this action to Eleanor S. Smith, such assignment to be settled by the local Master at Kingston, in case the parties differ as to same, and upon payment of the costs thereof, and of any reference to the said Master, do deliver the same to the said Eleanor S. Smith, and that the plaintiffs do pay to the defendants, J. H. Hughson and John Claxton, their costs of the motion. And the motion here is to reverse the said order in so far at any rate as it directs the plaintiffs to pay any costs, and for an order for payment to the plaintiffs of their proper costs of the said application, on the ground that no order was under the circumstances necessary or proper directing the execution of an assignment, and that no misconduct on the part of the plaintiffs appeared which justifies either their being deprived of their proper costs of the said application as mortgagees, or their being ordered to pay costs.

The facts appear to be as follows : The plaintiffs are first
mortgagees, and the defendants, John Claxton and John
Henry Hughson, are mortgagors ; the defendant Elizabeth
Ann Hughson is the wife of John H. Hughson, and joined
for the purpose of barring dower ; the mortgage is to secure
$1,600 and interest, the total amount of which endorsed on
the writ is $1,810.93; the mortgage bears date October 16th,
1883, and was in default, when this action was commenced
for foreclosure on December 14th, 1893. The lands embraced in the mortgage consist of lot No. 12 in the fourteenth concession of the township of Stonington, 100 acres ;
also part of lot No. 13 in the fourteenth concession of the
said township 100 acres ; also lot 13 in the fifteenth concession of the said township. Subsequently, the defendants,
Peter Cameron, Ann E. Warner, Charles W. Singleton,
Johanna Hughson, Sarah F. Hughson, and Wesley Hughson, became grantees, respectively, of different portions of
the mortgaged premises, with notice of the plaintiffs'
mortgage.

The affidavits shew that the original mortgagors are not
now interested in the mortgaged premises, but have an
undoubted right to redeem by reason of their covenant to
pay the mortgage money contained in the mortgage. The
mortgagor, John H. Hughson, had no title in any of the
lands at the time of the mortgage ; he, however, joined in
the personal covenant for payment only. Then after the
date of the plaintiffs' mortgage, Claxton the owner, conveyed
absolutely, lot No. 12 in the fourteenth concession to Peter
Cameron, who still owns the lot, subject to the plaintiffs'
mortgage, which he agreed to pay off, and was to apply part
of the purchase money in so doing. Claxton also conveyed
absolutely lot 13 in the fifteenth concession to Johanna
Hughson ; and lot 13 in the fourteenth concession to Ann E.
Warner ; so that Claxton has absolutely assigned his equity
of redemption in the mortgaged property. Johanna Hughson, however, has conveyed her equity of redemption to
Wesley Hughson, who has mortgaged to one Brown. And
Ann E. Warner has mortgaged her equity to one Strange,

and has since conveyed her equity of redemption in and
to about six acres of her lot to Charles W. Singleton,
Strange having released these six acres from the operation
of his mortgage.

This was the state of matters at the commencement of
this action, and also on January 6th, 1894, when Mr.
Mudie, solicitor for Eleanor S. Smith, informed the plaintiffs' solicitor, to whom he paid the mortgage money,
interest and costs, that she required an assignment, and
not a release, of the mortgage from the plaintiffs to her, she
having advanced the money, on the faith of getting such
assignment, at the request of Peter Cameron, and John H.
Hughson, with which to pay off the plaintiffs' claim.

There having been delay, caused by the unwillingness
of the plaintiffs' solicitor to advise that the plaintiffs should
assign, for the alleged reason that " there are subsequent
incumbrancers, whose rights intervene, and he (Mr. McD.)
represents one of them," Mr. Mudie, on January 15th,
wrote Mr. J. B. McIver, the treasurer of Queen's College,
in these words : " The mortgage from Claxton and Hughson
in question herein having been paid in full, principal,
interest and costs by me, on behalf of the original mortgagors, I now send you an assignment of the said mortgage in
duplicate in favour of Eleanor S. Smith, to whom the said
mortgagors require Queen's College to assign and convey
the mortgage debt and property instead of having a discharge executed. Kindly procure the due execution as
soon as may be," etc.

On January 16th, Mr. McIver wrote in reply as follows:—
" In reply to your application for an assignment of this
mortgage, our solicitor writes me as follows : ' I have
read and considered the application made on behalf of
these mortgagors for an assignment of this mortgage. The
mortgage has been paid off by the mortgagors' solicitor
presumably with their funds, and in such a case,
according to the authorities, it seems to me the first
mortgagee holds the estate in the lands for the next incumbrancer, if he has notice of another incumbrance. In

this case, as I know, there are several subsequent incumbrances, and I don't think the mortgage should be kept
alive by the mortgagors as against them. I have, therefore to return you the assignment sent me. As the matter
seems to be a legal one, any further correspondence had
better be made to the college solicitor.' "

On the same day, Mr. Mudie wrote to Mr. McIver, as
follows :—" I sent the assignment of mortgage to you
because, as I understand it, you apply the seal of the
college and forward the documents to Maclennan, J. A.,
chairman of the trustees for signature, and I now again
tender this assignment to you, because of your letter sent
me, on returning this assignment to me to-day. I have to
state, that not one dollar of the money paid by her, belongs
to the mortgagors or either of them. The entire sum was
advanced by Eleanor S. Smith, a client of mine, to whom
the mortgage should now be assigned, in pursuance of the
direction of the mortgagors, of which direction I now send
you a copy, and I will shew the original, if required. I
therefore again demand of you, that the enclosed assignment be duly executed."

The direction of the mortgagors is in these words :—

" KINGSTON, January 11th, 1894.

" Queen's College v. Claxton.

" We require you to assign and convey the mortgage
debt and premises secured and described in the mortgage
sued on in this action, to Eleanor S. Smith, of the city of
Kingston, married woman, whose money has been paid
to you in full of your claims.

" (Signed)   JOHN CLAXTON,

" J. H. HUGHSON,

" By JOHN MOODIE, his Attorney.

" To Queen's College, at Kingston."

It appears also, that on January 20th, a similar
document was signed by R. E. Kent and John Strange,
and on January 23rd, a similar request was signed by
Peter Cameron, and on January 24th, a similar request
was signed by Wm. A. Brown, and on January 26th,

a similar request was signed by Elizabeth A. Hughson,
Johanna Hughson, Wesley Hughson, Sarah Frances Hughson, Mrs. A. E. Warner and Peter Cameron, being every
subsequent owner or incumbrancer who are interested in
any portion of the lands described in the plaintiffs' mortgage, except the defendant Charles W. Singleton.

The statute under which the applicants claim that the
plaintiffs should assign to their nominee is R. S. O. 1887, ch.
102, sec. 2, which is in these words: " Where a mortgagor
is entitled to redeem, he shall, by virtue of this Act, have
power to require the mortgagee, instead of giving a certificate of payment or reconveying, and on the terms on
which he would be bound to reconvey, to assign the mortgage debt and convey the mortgaged property to any
third person, as the mortgagor directs ; and the mortgagee shall, by virtue of this Act, be bound to assign and
convey accordingly."

Now the action is brought by the plaintiffs, not only
against the original mortgagors, and the wife of one of them,
although she had no right to dower, and all the subsequent
persons who are interested in the equity of redemption, for
foreclosure, but against Claxton and Hughson on their
covenants to pay the principal money and interest. These
two, therefore, on the authority of *Kinnaird* v. *Trollope*,
39 Ch. D. 636, are entitled to redeem, notwithstanding
the fact, that Claxton, who was the only one entitled to
the lands at the time of the mortgage, has since then
absolutely assigned his equity of redemption, in the mortgaged property ; by reason of the covenant to pay the mortgage money he has a right to redeem and is entitled upon
paying the mortgage money, to require the mortgagees to
assign to his nominee.

Now how does the case stand? On Saturday, January 6th, the money was paid to the plaintiffs' solicitor, at
which time his managing clerk who received the cheque
was requested to send over the mortgage and title deeds
to Mr. Mudie's office, which he promised to do on the
following Monday, when the bank had paid the cheque.

This was not done, and matters stood in this way until
January 16th, when Mr. Mudie, the solicitor for the mortgagor and Mrs. Eleanor S. Smith, wrote the letter before
referred to, enclosing a copy of the written requirements
to assign, together with an assignment in duplicate for
the plaintiffs to execute, to Mr. McIver, the treasurer of the
plaintiffs, requesting him to have it duly sealed and
executed, etc. This assignment, on the advice of the
plaintiffs' solicitor, was returned unexecuted.

In my judgment the mortgagors and Mrs. Smith had
done everything that was necessary to entitle them to have
the assignment duly executed, but they did more than this,
they procured at much trouble and expense a request from
each of the other parties who might be considered in any
way interested in the lands as vendees, mortgagees, or
otherwise, before the original notice of motion was served.

Mr. Macdonnell, the plaintiffs' solicitor, admits that he
knew on January 15th that the mortgage had been paid
off by some one other than the mortgagors, although I
think it is strange that he was not made aware of the fact
on January 8th by his managing clerk Farrell, when
he handed him Mr. Mudie's cheque on that day. Mr.
Macdonnell says that he was aware that there were subsequent incumbrances, but he does not say that they were
created by either of the mortgagors, he could not have said
so, had he examined the title, for the reason that he would
have found that Claxton, the owner, had conveyed absolutely his equity to the other persons already pointed out
by me.

In this case it appears to me there were special reasons
why both Claxton and Hughson should require this mortgage to be assigned and not discharged. Peter Cameron
had agreed to pay it off; he purchased one of the mortgaged
lots, subject to the mortgage, and had it been discharged,
that lot would have been freed from the incumbrance, and
it appears by the affidavits that he, Cameron, had agreed
with Mrs. Smith to pay it off within a year, in consideration
of her advancing the amount.

The plaintiffs' solicitor and Mr. Langton, Q. C., before us Judgment.
relied on *Teevan* v. *Smith*, 20 Ch. D. 724, but the facts here, Robertson, J.
are not what they were in that case.   Here the first mortgagors had not created a subsequent mortgage, the equity
of redemption was conveyed absolutely ; so that as between
them and subsequent owners there was no equity.   There
was no mortgagee claiming through the original mortgagor
as mortgagor, in other words there was no one who could
compel the original mortgagors to pay the mortgage
money, except the first mortgagees, and they only because
of the covenant to pay.   And the plaintiffs here having
sued on the covenant to pay principal and interest contained in the mortgage, the mortgagor, although having
absolutely assigned his equity of redemption, acquired a
new right to redeem, and is entitled upon payment of the
mortgage money to a reconveyance to himself, subject to
the equity of redemption vested in Cameron, and the other
purchasers, and being thus entitled they became under
the statute "mortgagors entitled to redeem." This was held
in the late case of *Kinnaird* v. *Trollope*, 39 Ch. D. 636,
already referred to.   I do not think, therefore, that these
applicants should be made to pay costs, because of the
erroneous view taken by the plaintiffs' solicitor; but on
the contrary, I think, the plaintiffs should pay them the
costs occasioned by their refusal to do an act which the
statute declares they shall by virtue of the Act be bound
to do.

I think the appeal should be disallowed, the order of the
Chief Justice affirmed, and the plaintiffs should pay the
costs.

BOYD, C. :—

The mortgagees in this case refused to act upon the
request of the mortgagor, who procured the payment, to
have the security transferred to his nominee pursuant to
R. S. O. ch. 102, sec. 2. It was said that subsequent mortgagees had not assented, and *Teevan* v. *Smith*, 20 Ch. D.

724, was relied upon as justifying the refusal. That case is not an authority which applies where the subsequent mortgages are not created by the original mortgagor, as is pointed out in *Kinnaird* v. *Trollope*, 39 Ch. D. 636. Even had the money come from the mortgagor he was liable on the covenant to pay, and was being sued by the mortgagees. He had conveyed all the land to others who as between him and the mortgagees were primarily liable to pay the mortgage and relieve him. So that he became merely the surety for all claiming through and under him, and was entitled on payment to have the mortgage kept alive for his protection, and to enable him to recover from those who were liable to indemnify him.

The price of redemption being accepted with all interest and costs, I think the meaning of the whole transaction was that the mortgage was to be given over, and proper transfer made to the nominee of the mortgagor. The terms of the conveyance might be settled afterwards if this much had been conceded, but it was not. Blame rests on the mortgagees who did not respond as they should have done to the reasonable request of the mortgagor, and I cannot think that this Court should interfere with the order of the Chief Justice in order to reconsider or modify the imposition of costs. The order in this regard is justified by such cases as *Cliff* v. *Wadsworth*, 2 Y. & C. C. 598; *Charles* v. *Jones*, 33 Ch. D. 80.

The money supplied to satisfy the first mortgagee with a view to keep the mortgage on foot to secure the contributor of the money, necessarily subrogated this person as a purchaser to all the benefits of the first mortgagee and this would probably have been so even if a discharge had been executed : See 56 Vict. ch. 21, sec. 76, sub-sec. 2 (O.), which was in force at the date of this transaction.

I think the appeal fails, and costs should follow the result.

FERGUSON, J., concurred.

A. H. F. L.

[CHANCERY DIVISION].

MORRIS v. DINNICK ET AL.

Principal and Agent—Contract—Commission on Sales—Time—Absence of Express Contract to Manufacture.

In a written contract of agency the principal agreed to pay to the agent a fixed commission on all sales of goods manufactured by the former effected by or through the latter. The contract was made terminable at the end of a year on a month's notice by either party ; but it contained no express agreement by the principal to employ for any period or to manufacture any goods :—

Held, that these terms could not be imported into the contract by implication.

THIS was an appeal from the judgment of STREET, J., Statement. dismissing with costs an action brought by Edward D. Morris against C. R. S. Dinnick, Christopher C. Mitchell, and George Duthie trading under the name, style and firm of The Campbellville Terra Cotta Co.

The action was for damages for the wrongful dismissal of the plaintiff who had entered into the following contract in writing with the defendants :

"TORONTO, November 11th, 1893.

" MR. E. D. MORRIS,

    " Toronto, Ont.

" Dear Sir,—

" We hereby agree to pay you a commission of eight per cent. on all sales of goods manufactured by us, whether such sales are made by you personally or by us or any persons on our behalf, and in consideration, therefor, you are to use all diligence to make sales of such goods, and for that purpose you are to act as our agent, and whenever you think it advisable, you are to visit such localities outside of Toronto for the purpose of promoting and effecting the sales of our manufacture, you paying your own expenses in such cases. You also agreeing to assist generally in making and promoting sales of our goods both by correspondence, interviews, and otherwise. The above commission to be paid to you from time to time

Statement. as collections are made from sales of goods, and you have the liberty of inspecting the books of this company at any reasonable time, and from time to time as you desire.

In one year from this date, it shall be at the option either of yourself or ourselves to determine this agreement on giving to the other one month's notice in writing of intention of determining the same.

" Yours truly,
" (Signed)   CAMPBELLVILLE TERRA COTTA CO.
" C. R. S. DINNICK, Mng."
" MESSRS. THE CAMPBELLVILLE TERRA COTTA CO.
" Dear Sirs,—I hereby agree to the above agreement.
" Yours truly,
"(Signed)   E. D. MORRIS."

The action was tried at Toronto, on April 19th, 1894, before STREET, J., without a jury.

Allan McNab, for the plaintiff.
W. R. Riddell, for the defendants.

It appeared that the three defendants were carrying on business under the name of The Campbellville Terra Cotta Co., and that soon after the making of the agreement, the defendant Dinnick bought out the other two defendants' interests, and notified the plaintiff that the agreement was at an end, alleging that the company had ceased to exist. No evidence was given at the trial of any sales made by or on behalf of the company, and the action was dismissed on that ground.

From this judgment the plaintiff appealed to the Divisional Court, and the appeal was argued on June 22nd, 1894, before BOYD, C., and FERGUSON, J.

E. T. English, and *Allan McNab*, for the appeal. The agreement was one of hiring for at least a year, and the defendants had no power to cancel it within that time.

The evidence shews that to induce him to enter into the agreement representations were made by the defendants to the plaintiff of what the volume of the business was, and that he could earn a good income.　It was the conduct of the defendants which prevented him from earning that income, and although no sales were made, that was not his fault.　The true measure of his damage and what he is entitled to recover, is, what he could have earned but for the conduct of the defendants.　The trial Judge should have admitted evidence as to that.　The case was not tried out. We refer to *Pilkington* v. *Scott*, 15 M. & W. 657 ; *Whittle* v. *Frankland*, 31 L. J. M. C. at p. 85 ; *McIntyre* v. *Belcher*, 14 C. B. N. S. 654 ; *Turner* v. *Goldsmith*, [1891] 1 Q. B. 544.

Riddell, contra.　The cases cited differ from this.　They are cases of existing partnerships and of master and servant, without any complication.　Here the partnership was dissolved and the agreement was a hiring on commission.　A partnership is dissolved by the death of a partner, and the relationship of master and servant then ceases : *Burnet* v. *Hope*, 9 O. R. 10.　The defendants were not bound to continue the business : *Beswick* v. *Swindells*, 3 A. & E. at p. 882.　There is no implied contract to continue the partnership or the business : *Hamlyn & Co.* v. *Wood & Co.*, [1891] 2 Q. B. 488 ; *Rhodes* v. *Forwood*, 1 App. Cas. 256 ; *In re English and Scottish Marine Insurance Co.—Ex p. Maclure*, L. R. 5 Ch. 737 ; *Stirling* v. *Maitland*, 5 B. & S. 840.　In *Cowasjee Manabhoy* v. *Lallbhoy Vullubhoy*, L. R. 3 Ind. App. 200 at p. 206, the plaintiff was, as here, paid by commission and not by salary, and this distinction has often been recognized by the courts.

English, in reply.　In *Hamlyn & Co.* v. *Wood & Co.*, [1891] 2 Q. B. 488, the agreement only applied to the grains " if manufactured."　In *Beswick* v. *Swindells*, 3 A. & E. 868, the term was " if in business."　The dissolution of the partnership makes no difference : *Turner* v. *Goldsmith*, [1891] 1 Q. B. 544.

Judgment.

Boyd, C.

June 30th, 1894. BOYD, C. :—

There is no express contract of employment for any term on the face of the contract. The relation is not that of master and servant, but is expressly one of agency. The words are " we agree to pay a commission * * on all sales of goods manufactured by us, * * and in consideration, therefor, you are to use all diligence to make sales * * and for that purpose you are to act *as our agent.*"

There is no undertaking to manufacture any defined quantity of goods, or indeed to manufacture at all ; and according to the class of cases applicable, no such term should be implied.

The case is more in the lines of *Rhodes* v. *Forwood*, 1 App. Cas. 256, than of the later decision *Turner* v. *Goldsmith*, [1891] 1 Q. B. 544.

In the *Rhodes'* case it was an agreement of agency to sell coals on commission, and one in which there was no express contract to employ. In the *Turner* case there was an express contract to employ as traveller for five years, and as it was provided that he should sell goods manufactured *or sold* by the defendant, it could not be taken that the parties contracted in contemplation of the continuance of the defendant's manufactory as the foundation of what was to be done, as they might buy articles in the market to supply the traveller. The agreement was one as to service and not merely of agency. As said in the *Rhodes'* case, the stopping of the business was within the power of the principal, and it is not for the agent to complain unless there is some express term in the contract which binds the principal to carry on the concern at whatever disadvantage.

In brief, this plaintiff was to get commission on the sale of all goods manufactured by the defendants, but they did not say they would manufacture ; and the continuance of the concern was, therefore, left at large to be determined by the interests of the principal.

I may cite as pertinent, the comment of Lord Chelmsford in 1 App. Cas. at p. 268 : "But what is there in the agreement to prevent its coming positively to a premature end, either by the agents giving up business, or the owner giving up the colliery ? The mere agreement of seven years, or the provisions for the determination of it on either side, will not be sufficient, and if it had been intended that the relation of the parties should absolutely continue for seven years, it ought to have been provided for, and not being provided for it cannot, in my opinion, be taken to have been intended."

And further, I may cite Lord Penzance, at p. 272: "Upon such an agreement as that, surely, unless there is some special term in the contract that the principal shall continue to carry on business, it cannot for a moment be implied as a matter of obligation on his part, that, whether the business is a profitable one or not, and whether for his own sake he wishes to carry it on or not, he shall be bound to carry it on for the benefit of the agent, and the commission that he may receive."

In *Roche* v. *Walsh*, 27 C. P. 555, it was held that under agreement signed by both, by which the plaintiff was to act as book-keeper for five years, there was no obligation on the part of the defendant to continue his business or retain the plaintiff in his employment for that period. See also *Fox* v. *Smith*, 6 L. R. Ir. 319, (1879) and *Hamlyn & Co.* v. *Wood & Co.*, [1891] 2 Q. B. 488.

Altogether upon the admitted facts of the case, it seems to me needless to prolong this litigation, and I would, therefore, affirm the judgment of nonsuit with costs.

FERGUSON, J.:—

Prior to the making of the agreement between the plaintiff and the three defendants, Dinnick, Mitchell and Duthie, these defendants were manufacturing and intending to manufacture plain and ornamental terra cotta pressed and vitrified bricks, and on the 11th of November,

Judgment.

Ferguson, J. 1893, the agreement was entered into : the defendants then
professing to trade under the name of The Campbellville
Terra Cotta Company, the manager thereof, being the
defendant Dinnick.

By the agreement the defendants agreed to pay the
plaintiff a commission of eight per cent. on all sales of
goods manufactured by them, whether such sales were
made by the plaintiff personally, or by the defendants, or
any person or persons on their behalf, and in consideration
therefor the defendant was to use all diligence to make
sales of such goods, and for that purpose the plaintiff
was to act as the agent of the defendants, and whenever
the plaintiff should think it advisable to travel and visit
other places for the purpose of making sales and to assist
generally in promoting and making sales of the goods.
The commission was to be paid from time to time as
collections were made from sales of goods. The agreement provided that in one year from its date either party
to it might determine it by giving one month's notice in
writing.

The plaintiff alleges that about the 15th day of January,
1894, the defendants repudiated the contract, and notified
him that they would not carry out or perform the same,
and this does not seem to be denied by the defendants.
Whether or not the word " repudiated " is properly applied
may possibly be questioned ; but the motion was argued
on the footing that the contract was made as alleged by
the plaintiff, and that in January, 1894, about two months
after it was made, the defendants notified the plaintiff
that they would not go on under it. The plaintiff sues for
damages for alleged breach of the contract and refusal to
manufacture any kind of brick whatever.

At the trial the learned Judge found upon the evidence,
and I think correctly, that the defendants had not sold,
nor had the plaintiff for them sold any goods, and the
action was dismissed with costs.

It seems entirely clear on the evidence that no collections were made or money received for any goods sold,.

though an order may have been received for a small
quantity.

The agreement does not provide for the payment of any
salary to the plaintiff; nor does it provide that the defendants shall carry on the business for any stated period,
and the plaintiff's commission of eight per cent. was to be
paid from time to time as collections were made from sales
of goods. No such collections were ever made. It
appears that the defendants did not go on with the business. They sold their plant. It is said in the evidence
that the partnership was dissolved.

As no sales were made, or at all events no collections
from sales were made or got in by the defendants, it is
difficult to see how the plaintiff can recover unless he can
shew that the defendants were bound to carry on their
business for the year to enable him to make or earn a
commission by sales of their goods and collections from
such sales. It seems clear that the defendants did not by
express terms so bind themselves by their contract, and
the question arises as to whether there is such a stipulation by implication, that is, can or should a term to
this effect be added to the contract by implication? In
the case *Hamlyn & Co.* v. *Wood & Co.*, [1891] 2 Q. B. at
p. 491, Lord Esher said : " I have for a long time understood that rule to be that the Court has no right to imply
in a written contract any such stipulation, unless, on considering the terms of the contract in a reasonable and
business manner an implication necessarily arises that
the parties must have intended that the suggested stipulation should exist." The language of the other learned
Judges seems to be to the same effect.

In the case *Rhodes* v. *Forwood*, 1 App. Cas. 256, a part
of the headnote is : " Where two parties mutually agree,
for a fixed period, the one to employ the other as his sole
agent in a certain business, at a certain place, the other
that he will act in that business for no other principal
at that place, there is no implied condition that the business itself shall continue to be carried on during the period

named." And it was held that an action for damages for
breach of the alleged agreement could not be sustained.

From a perusal of these cases, and the case *In re
English and Scottish Marine Insurance Co.—Ex p.
Maclure*, L. R. 5 Ch. 737, and others, I have arrived at the
opinion, that no stipulation that the defendant should
carry on the business for any period can be imported into
this contract by necessary implication, and that as the
plaintiff was to be paid from time to time only as collections were made from sales, and no such collections were
made, the learned Judge was quite right in dismissing the
action.

The motion should be refused with costs.

G. A. B.

[CHANCERY DIVISION.]

CHURCH

v.

THE CORPORATION OF THE CITY OF OTTAWA.

Damages—Inadequacy of—Negligence—New Trial.

Although it is unusual to interfere with a verdict of a jury in an action of
tort on the ground of the inadequacy of the damages found, still such
verdicts are subject to the supervision of the Court, and if the amount
awarded be so small that it is evident the jury must have overlooked
some material element of damage in the plaintiff's case, a new trial will
be granted.

A practising physician having been badly if not permanently injured
through the negligence of the defendants, it appearing also that his
professional business had suffered to a considerable extent, was awarded
$700 by the jury:—

Held, that there must be a new trial on the ground of inadequacy of the
damages.

Statement.   THIS was a motion by the plaintiff to set aside the finding of the jury on the question of damages, and the judgment entered thereon, and for a new trial, on the ground
that the damages were insufficient upon the evidence.

The action was tried at the Spring Assizes for 1894, at Statement. Ottawa, before FALCONBRIDGE, J., and a jury.

McCarthy, Q.C., and *McLaurin* for the plaintiff.
Aylesworth, Q.C., and *McTavish*, Q.C., for the defendants.
Kidd, for the third party.

It appeared that the plaintiff who was a physician, having a large practice in the city of Ottawa, in getting into his carriage, after nightfall, on one of the streets of the defendant municipality had stepped into a hole and ruptured the *tendo Achillis* in such a manner that it was anticipated the injury would be permanent, and evidence was given to shew a falling off of his professional earnings during the half year following the accident of upwards of $3,000.

The following questions were submitted to and answered by the jury:

Q. Was the accident to the plaintiff caused by the negligence of the defendants, the city of Ottawa? A. Yes.

Q. Did the defendant corporation have notice of the defect in the highway; or ought they to have known that such existed? A. They ought to have known.

Q. At what sum do you assess the damages? A. $700.00.

Q. Was the hole or excavation in Albert street, placed, made, left or maintained by Dr. Hurdman.* A. No.

The plaintiff moved against this finding as to the amount of the damages to the Divisional Court, and asked for a new trial on the ground of their insufficiency, and the motion was argued on June 21, 1894, before BOYD, C., and FERGUSON, J.

W. R. Riddell, and *Charles Macdonald*, for the motion. The damages are utterly inadequate to compensate the plaintiff for the injury. The evidence shews a falling off of income of $3,000 for six months or $6,000 a year,

---

* The occupant of an adjoining house, brought in as a third party by the defendant corporation.—REP.

and that the injury may be permanent, to say nothing of the pain and inconvenience caused to him. *Phillips* v. *The London and South-Western R. W. Co.*, 4 Q. B. D. 406, and 5 Q. B. D. 78, is on all fours with this case, and there a new trial was ordered, because as here, the jury omitted to take into consideration some of the elements of damage properly involved in the plaintiff's claim. See also *McNamara* v. *The Village of Clintonville*, 62 Wis. 207; *Stewart* v. *The City of Ripon*, 38 Wis. 584; Mayne on Damages, 5th ed., 454, 515, 583.

Aylesworth, Q.C., contra. The evidence shews that the plaintiff did not consider the accident a serious one, and he did not take proper care of himself. He did not even take sufficient rest, and the jury are entitled to consider whether if sufficient rest had been taken the injury would have been as serious as it has turned out: *Rowley* v. *London and North-Western R. W. Co.*, L. R. 8 Ex. 221. The jury has the right to consider the plaintiff's conduct aggravating: Mayne on Damages, 5th ed., 582, and cases there cited; *Phillips* v. *South-Western R. W. Co.*, 4 Q. B. D. 406; 5 Q. B. D. 78. The quantum of damages cannot be attacked unless it was such an amount as no reasonable twelve men could arrive at: *Praed* v. *Graham*, 24 Q. B. D. 53. The smallness of a verdict is no ground for a new trial: *Mauricet* v. *Brecknock*, 2 Doug. 509.

Riddell, in reply, cited Hilliard on New Trials, 2nd ed., 574.

June 30, 1894. BOYD, C. :—

The leading case as to new trial for inadequate damages in the case of injuries is *Phillips* v. *London and South-Western R. W. Co.*, 4 Q. B. D. 406, and 5 Q. B. D. 78. It was argued that the rules there observed in testing the propriety of the amount are not applicable to this country.

But in a case decided in this country a little earlier, the same questions were discussed where the verdict was complained of as excessive. The jury in question gave $7,000 for injury to an architect by a railway accident, and in appeal to the Privy Council it was not disturbed. Sir R. P. Collier said that the law of Canada as expressed in the Quebec Code was not far different from the law of England upon the same subject. The Article of the Code provides: " If the amount awarded be so small or so exces- sive that it is evident the jury must have been influenced by improper motives or led into error, then a new trial must be granted ": *Lambkin* v. *South-Eastern R. W. Co.*, 5 App. Cas., at p. 361.

A somewhat serious injury was here inflicted upon the plaintiff, a physician of repute in the city of Ottawa, which has involved much pain and has probably crippled him permanently. His business also has to a greater or lesser extent suffered. It does seem that whatever view be taken of the evidence if he is entitled to recover at all, it should be for a much larger sum than $700, which is the present appraisement of his damages.

The opinion I entertained during the argument remains, that there should be a new trial. The costs will abide the result.

I do not mean to indicate by these citations that the measure of damages should be the same in a case of injury inflicted by a railway company, or by the negligent act of an individual, as in the case of liability placed upon a muni- cipal corporation for non-repair of roadway; but I regard the present as a case in which the damages should be measurably increased.

FERGUSON, J.:—

There is early authority going to shew that as a general rule the Court will not set aside a verdict in an action for a tort on account of the smallness of the damages: *Mauricet* v. *Brecknock*, 2 Doug. 509.

In Mayne on Damages, 582, *et seq.*, it is said that where the action is for unliquidated damages, the Court will not grant a new trial on account of their being too low, unless there has been some mistake in a point of law on the part of the Judge who presided, or in the calculation of figures by the jury; or unless it appears that the jury have omitted to take into consideration some of the elements of damage, and that the alleged reason is that new trials came only in the room of attaints, as being an easier and more expeditious remedy, and no attaint could lie for giving too small damages, referring in respect to this last statement to the above case in 2 Doug.

In 3 Graham and Waterman on New Trials, at p. 1166, it is said that even in personal torts, where the finding is grossly inadequate, and the compensation given entirely disproportioned to the injury, the Court will interfere and grant relief.

In the case *Phillips* v. *London and South-Western R. W. Co.*, 5 Q. B. D., at p. 78, James, L. J., in delivering the judgment said, at p. 85 : " We agree that Judges have no right to overrule the verdict of a jury as to the amount of damages, merely because they take a different view, and think that if they had been the jury they would have given more or would have given less, still the verdicts of juries as to the amount of damages are subject, and must, for the sake of justice, be subject, to the supervision of a Court of first instance, and if necessary of a Court of Appeal in this way, that is to say, if in the judgment of the Court the damages are unreasonably large or unreasonably small, then the Court is bound to send the matter for reconsideration by another jury."

The Court affirmed the decision of the Queen's Bench Division, that Division having granted a new trial on the ground that the damages, though being £7,000, were inadequate, and it appearing that the jury had omitted to take into consideration some of the elements properly involved in the plaintiff's claim. Chief Justice Cockburn, at the conclusion of his judgment which was the judgment of the Court, said : " There can be no doubt of the power of the Court to grant a new trial where in such an action " (one

for personal injury) " the damages are excessive. There
can be no reason why the same principle should not apply
where they are insufficient to meet the justice of the case."

The case *McNamara* v. *The Village of Clintonville*, 62
Wis. 207, is the case of a medical gentleman against a
municipal corporation for damages occasioned by negligence, and is instructive in regard to the manner of
measuring the damages in such cases. The same may be
said of the case *Stewart* v. *City of Ripon*, 38 Wis. 584. In
the former of these two American cases (the one in 62
Wisconsin) the Court referred to the same case, *Phillips* v.
The London and South-Western R.·W. Co., 5 C. P. D. 280,
where the case was before the Court of Appeal after the
new trial had been had, in which £16,000 had been
awarded, and a rule for a new trial refused. On p. 290,
Brett, L. J., explains what was meant by the expression in
the case *Rowley* v. *London and North Western R. W. Co.*,
L. R. 8 Ex. 221, that it would be a misdirection to tell the
jury that they ought to try to give a perfect compensation.
The learned Judge says that what was meant was a perfect arithmetical compensation; and that the reason is that
it would be impossible to bring before the jury all the circumstances that would entitle them to come to a conclusion of that kind.

In the case *Lambkin* v. *The South-Eastern R. W. Co.*, 5
App. Cas. 352, an appeal from Quebec, the Court in delivering judgment, after remarking that the law of Lower
Canada as expressed in the 11th sec. of Art. 426 of the
Code was not far different from the law of England, said,
at p. 261 : " If the amount awarded be so small or so
excessive that it is evident the jury must have been influenced by improper motives, or led into error, then a new
trial must be granted."

In the present case ingenious arguments were held for
the purpose of shewing that the plaintiff had not proved
by actual figures that he has sustained damages to an
amount greatly larger than the sum awarded him by the
jury, and that for this reason the verdict should stand.

Judgment

Ferguson, J.

I am of the opinion, however, that these arguments and contentions should not prevail. It seems to me impossible to peruse the evidence and arrive at any conclusion but the one, that the sum given by the jury is greatly inadequate to compensate the plaintiff for the injuries that he has sustained; and that in arriving at the small sum they gave by their verdict the jury must have overlooked some of the elements of the plaintiff's case entitling him to claim damages, otherwise they must have arrived at a larger sum as the amount of compensation. How much larger it would be improper to indicate or suggest. I think it a case in which the Court has the power to interfere. I think this is shewn by the authorities. And I think the plaintiff is entitled to have the verdict set aside and a new trial. I think the costs should abide the event.

G. A. B.

[CHANCERY DIVISION.]

SHEPPARD

v.

THE BONANZA NICKEL MINING COMPANY OF SUDBURY.

Company—Mining Company—Acquisition of Land—Mortgage to Secure Purchase Money—Execution of Contract—Presumption.

Where a company has power to acquire land for the purposes of its incorporation, it has the power to give a mortgage for and to bind itself by covenant to pay the purchase money.

Where the power to contract exists, a person contracting with the company need not enquire whether the proper formalities of execution by the company have been complied with in a contract under its corporate seal.

THIS was an appeal from a judgment for the plaintiff, in an action on a covenant in a mortgage made by the defendants. *Statement.*

The mortgage was given for part of the purchase money of some mining lands purchased by the defendants, a mining company, incorporated under R. S. O. ch. 157.

Among the defences set up was one that the company had no power to make the mortgage, (which was duly executed by the president and the secretary under the company's seal), as no by-law had been passed authorizing those officers to sign such a document.

The action was tried at Toronto on May 12th, 1894, before ROSE, J., without a jury.

Osler, Q.C., and *Raymond*, for the plaintiff.
J. K. Kerr, Q.C., and *Bitzer*, for the defendants.
Judgment was reserved and subsequently given.

May 17, 1894. ROSE, J. :—

The company acquired the land and has not paid for it. To purchase it was one of the objects of incorporation. The president and secretary were authorized by the by-laws to put the seal of the company to all deeds, etc. It

39—VOL. XXV. O.R.

Judgment.
___
Rose, J.

was admitted that the plaintiff had a vendor's lien for the unpaid purchase money, which could be enforced if the mortgage was invalid, but it was contended that the agreement to pay the purchase money could not be enforced as there was no express provision in the charter or by-laws to enable the company to buy land on credit.

There is express power to buy lands. This implies the power to promise to pay and to pay for them. Payment must be out of the assets of the company, and until the company applies its assets in payment of the purchase money the obligation to pay remains undischarged and subject, I should say, to be enforced by the Court. Once admit the power to purchase involving the obligation to pay, and I do not see room for further argument against the plaintiff's right to have judgment ordering the company to pay the balance remaining unpaid.

There is some, though slight evidence of adoption by the shareholders of the act of the president and secretary, if I should hold that the statement of audit reached all the shareholders, as it shewed the mortgage debt as one of the liabilities.

I do not think it should be assumed that the president and secretary executed this mortgage without the directors' sanction.

Having regard to such cases as the *The Ontario Co-operative Stonecutters' Association* v. *Clarke*, 31 C. P. 280; *The Corporation of the County of Wentworth* v. *The Corporation of the City of Hamilton*, 34 U. C. R. 585, and the numerous authorities there referred to, including *The South of Ireland Colliery Company* v. *Waddle*, L. R. 3, C. P. 463, 4 C. P. 167; *McDougall* v. *Lindsay Paper Company*, 10 P. R. 247; and *Greenstreet* v. *Paris*, 21 Gr. 229; I think the plaintiff must have judgment as prayed, with costs.

From this judgment, the defendants appealed to the Divisional Court, and the appeal was argued on June 16th, 1894, before BOYD, C., and FERGUSON, J.

J. K. Kerr, Q. C., for the appeal. The mortgage is invalid.
It is *ultra vires* of the company. There was no by-law
authorizing any of the officers to make one, and they had
no power to do so without a by-law : R. S. O. c. 157, sec.
38. The audit used to prove knowledge to the shareholders in which the mortgage was mentioned, merely
shewed that the property was subject to a mortgage, but
not that it was made by the company. The mortgage
is not the company's contract. I refer to Brice on
Ultra Vires, 2nd ed., 592, 604 ; *Riche* v. *The Ashbury
Carriage and Iron Co.*, L. R. 9 Ex. 224 ; *Irvine*
v. *The Union Bank of Australia*, 2 App. Cas. 380 ;
Ernest v. *Nicholls*, 6 H. L. C. 419 ; *The Royal British
Bank* v. *Turquand*, 6 E. & B., at p. 332 ; *In re Patent
File Co. Ex p. Birmingham Banking Co.*, L. R. 6 Ch.
83 ; Lindley's Law of Companies, 5th ed., 235 ; *Fountaine*
v. *Carmarthen R. W. Co.*, L. R. 5 Eq., at p. 321. In *Greenstreet* v. *Paris*, 21 Gr. 228, the mortgage was sanctioned
by the shareholders.

McCarthy, Q.C., and *Raymond*, contra. The mortgage
in question was not made for borrowed money. The
company had power to acquire lands for the purposes
mentioned in their charter. Land was so acquired, and
the mortgage was given as part payment of the purchase money. No by-law was necessary for that. In
this action, the plaintiffs are suing on the covenant.
That is a contract, and the company could contract, even
if it could not mortgage. This was an ordinary transaction of a trading corporation. They referred to *Bickford*
v. *The Grand Junction R. W. Co.*, 1 S. C. R. 696 ; *Long*
v. *Hancock*, 12 S. C. R. 532, at p. 545 ; *Shears* v. *Jacob*,
L. R. 1 C. P., at p. 517 ; Lindley's Law of Companies, 5th ed.
174, 191, 192, 203. A mortgage under the seal of the company is good unless displaced by evidence of fraud and the
onus of proving that is on the defendants : *The Royal
British Bank* v. *Turquand*, 6 E. & B. 327 ; *Agar* v. *The
Athenæum Life Assurance Society*, 3 C. B. N. S. 725,
at p. 756. The audit report used at the general meeting

shewed the mortgage, and thus it came to the knowledge
of the shareholders : *McDougall* v. *Lindsay Paper Mill
Co.*, 10 P. R., at p. 352.

Kerr, Q. C., in reply. Even if the company had the
power to make the mortgage, it must be exercised under
the statute, and there was no by-law : R. S. O. ch. 157,
sec. 38 ; Lindley's Law of Companies, 5th ed., 170. In
Shears v. *Jacob*, L. R. 1 C. P. 513, express power was given.

June 30th, 1894. BOYD, C. :—

The Bonanza company was chartered to " acquire, sell,
dispose of, and deal generally in mining claims and lands,
to work and operate mines, to smelt and refine minerals,
and to carry on a mining business in all branches." The
corporation was therefore of a trading character, and had
power to acquire and dispose of lands which would by
necessary implication involve the power to mortgage lands
for the purchase money, and to agree therein to pay such
money.

Under the Act of incorporation, R. S. O. ch. 157, general
corporate powers as to acquiring, alienating, and conveying
real estate, are given to the company. By section 36, the directors have power to make or cause to be made for the
company any description of contract which the company
may by law enter into. By section 59, in no case shall it be
necessary to have the seal of the company affixed to
certain contracts or to prove that the same were made in
pursuance of any by-law or special vote or order.

By the by-laws of the company, it is provided that
the duty of the president shall be to sign all bonds, deeds,
mortgages, stock and conveyances ; and the duty of the
secretary shall be to keep the seal of the corporation, and
that he shall, with the president, sign all conveyances,
obligations and contracts. (Ratified May 29th, 1891.)

On 26th December, 1891, the mortgage in question was
duly executed under the seal of the company by the president and secretary. It was in the form of a charge under
the Land Titles Act, and had expressed in it the covenant

that the mortgagors and their successors and assigns will Judgment.
pay the mortgage money. The instrument was given to Boyd, C.
secure the balance of purchase money on land acquired
for the operation of the company.

It was not needful to express this liability, because by
the terms of the Land Titles Act, ch. 116, sec. 29, such a
provision to pay the money secured is implied, unless there
be an entry in the register negativing the implication.

I do not feel pressed with the objection that this mortgage for part of the price was *ultra vires* by the company.
The general test is given thus by Cotton, L. J., in *The
Queen* v. *Sir Charles Reed*, 5 Q. B. D. at p. 488: "The power
of a corporation established for certain specified purposes
must depend on what those purposes are, and except so
far as it has express powers given to it, it will have such
powers only as are necessary for the purpose of enabling
it in a reasonable and proper way to discharge the duties
or fulfil the purposes for which it was constituted." Here
the company might buy the mining locations it needed,
in the same way as an individual, and might do so by
paying part of the price and giving a mortgage with usual
covenants for the balance.

Then, the power existing, the Court will not scrutinize
as to how it came to be formally carried out in the face of
a duly authenticated and properly drawn instrument under the corporate seal. The rule established by authority is, that where the proposed dealing is not inconsistent
with the constitution of the company, the party contracting need not enquire into the regularity of the internal
proceedings. It is to be assumed that all is being done in
due course, and the disclosure that such was not the case,
will not avail to displace or nullify a completed instrument
or transaction.

The Royal British Bank v. *Turquand*, 6 E. & B. 327;
Agar v. *The Athenæum Life Assurance Association*, 3
C. B. N. S. 725; *In re Barned's Banking Co.—Ex p. The
Contract Corporation*, L. R. 3 Ch. at p. 116. This ground
of defence fails.

*   *   *   *   *   *

Judgment. FERGUSON, J. :—

Ferguson, J.

The action is upon a covenant contained in a mortgage given by the defendants to secure the purchase money of a mining location, or part of it. Or it may be stated thus : The defendants purchased this mining location and gave their promise under their seal to pay the purchase money or part thereof.

The purposes for which the defendants were incorporated, as shewn by their charter, were to acquire, sell, dispose of and deal generally in mining claims and lands, to work and operate mines, to smelt and refine minerals and to carry on a mining business in all its branches.

The defendants did purchase this location. They took possession and have possession of it pursuant to their purchase, and they have worked upon the location. They gave the mortgage containing the covenant sued on, which document is sealed with their seal and signed by their president and secretary. The case is not to be confounded with a case of the defendants borrowing money upon a mortgage which would fall under the provisions of the thirty-eighth section of the Act, ch. 157 R. S. O.

The question here is whether or not the defendants had power to enter into a binding engagement to pay for property purchased by them; the purchase being clearly within the limits and scope of the powers given by the charter, a purchase falling and being within the expressed purposes for which the defendants were incorporated, and I cannot entertain any doubt that the defendants had such power.

Then where a party dealing with the company ascertains the existence on the part of the company to do the act, that is to make and give him the obligation, he may go on with the dealing without inquiring as to any formalities that may have been prescribed as preliminaries. He may presume without inquiry, that these have been properly attended to : *The Royal British Bank* v. *Turquand*, 6 E. & B. 327; *Agar* v. *The Athenæum Life Assurance*

Association, 3 C. B. N. S. 725 ; *Re Joint Stock Companies Winding-up Acts, Lane's* case, 1 DeG. J. & S. 504, per Lord Westbury, and there are many authorities to this effect. The provisions of section 59 of the Act do not, so far as I can see, stand in the plaintiff's way.

I do not see any sufficient reason for thinking that the defendants are not liable *primâ facie* upon the covenant on which they are sued in this action, and I am of the opinion that the effort of the defendants to get rid of this *primâ facie* liability by proving fraud, misrepresentation, etc., entirely fails.

*   *   *   *   *   *

I am of the opinion that the judgment should be affirmed with costs.

G. A. B.

[CHANCERY DIVISION.]

JOHNSTON v. THE CORPORATION OF THE CITY OF
TORONTO.

*Municipal Corporations—Construction of Sewer—General Plan—Subsequent
Erection of Houses—Insufficient Fall—Negligence.*

A municipal corporation having properly constructed a sewer in a street
in the municipality according to a general plan of drainage adopted by
them is not liable to the owner of houses subsequently erected on the
street because the sewer has not been constructed sufficiently deep to
allow a proper fall to the drains from the houses.
Decision of STREET, J., at the trial affirmed.

Statement.   THESE were two actions, which had been consolidated,
and were brought by the occupants of two adjoining
houses against the municipal corporation of Toronto for
damages alleged to have been occasioned by the negligence
and improper conduct of the defendants in respect to the
sewer constructed by them in the street upon which the
houses were.

The circumstances of the cases are fully stated in the
judgments.

The action was tried on January 26th, 1894, before
STREET, J., and a jury, who at the conclusion of the plaintiffs' evidence, delivered the following judgment dismissing the action.

STREET, J. :—

The way in which this matter stands is this. The complaint is that the sewer on King street is not low enough
to admit of any greater fall than was given to this drain.
Under these circumstances, I do not think the plaintiffs can
succeed, because the city is not bound to make a sewer of
any particular depth. If there had been any evidence here
that the sewage from the sewer ran back into any part of the
house occupied by the plaintiffs, I might then have thought
there was some evidence of negligence. But here the

evidence is not that at all; the evidence is that the house the plaintiffs occupied was flooded by sewage from the plaintiffs' own house; that there was a stoppage and a leak in his own premises, and it was by means of that leak and that stoppage that their own sewage backed up into the cellar and into the kitchen. The whole complaint is, that the city sewer ought to have been dug so much deeper so as to give a greater fall from the house to the sewer. That is not, in my opinion, a ground of action at all. There is also the evidence of the only expert called, Roy McCrimmon, that if the iron drain had been continued in a straight line out to the trap, there would have been no trouble with the sewage at all, that that would have given sufficient fall to carry it off into the sewer. But because the person who was building the houses wished to make a particular kind of drain for the two houses, he did not continue that iron pipe straight on, but turned it down, and thus prevented a portion of it from having the fall it would otherwise have had. So in every aspect of the case, however it is put, I think it is plain that the city is not responsible for the trouble the plaintiffs had, arising as it did from the fact that the main sewer was not deep enough, and that, it appears to me, is not an actionable thing. Under the circumstances of the case, I think the action must be dismissed with costs. It is one action tried in the Chancery Division.

The plaintiffs now moved by way of appeal from this judgment before the Divisional Court, and the motion was argued on March 2nd, 1894, before FERGUSON, ROBERTSON, and MEREDITH, JJ.

McCullough, for the plaintiffs. As to the depth of the drains, the city cannot say to the owner of a lot of land you must dig so deep and no deeper: 29–30 Vict. ch. 51, (C.), sec. 296, sub.-sec. 50-5.

It is not disputed that it is impossible to drain that property with the sewer at the present depth. The municipality in constructing sewers should do so with a reason-

Argument. able regard for the interests of property owners.   They should construct them in such a manner as though they were themselves to suffer the whole risk or the loss of the improper construction, as though it were their own property that was to be affected.

I refer to the *Rochester White Lead Co.* v. *The City of Rochester*, 3 N. Y. (Comstock), at p. 469 ; *Nims* v. *Troy,* 59 N. Y. 500; *Henley* v. *Mayor of Lyme Regis*, 5 Bing. 91 (a) ; Dillon on Municipal Corporations, 4th ed., p. 1331. It was negligence in the defendants not to remedy the evil which they could so easily have done after it had been complained of.   There was no reason why the sewer should not have been three feet deeper to commence with.   This was negligence at the beginning.

H. L. Drayton, for the defendants.   The evidence shews the drain was constructed about eighteen years ago, and there is no evidence that it was improperly constructed. When the owner built his cellar, he knew he could not drain into the street sewer.   The liability on the corporation is not a statutory liability : *Noble* v. *Corporation of the City of Toronto*, 46 U. C. R. 519, 542.   It must be a common law liability or a contractual liability.   There can be no recovery here at common law—that was on the maxim *sic utere tuo.*   Here the injury is caused by the plaintiffs, who must, therefore, shew a contract if they are to recover.   On the duty of the municipality I cite the authorities collected in American and English Encyclopedia of Law, vol. 6, at p. 26 ; Dillon on Municipal Corporations, 4th ed., p. 1334; *Johnston* v. *District of Columbia*, 6 Sup. Ct. Rep. (U. S.) 923.

McCullough, in reply.   The construction of sewers is not a duty imposed on municipal corporations, but a privilege which they exercise at their peril : *Winn* v. *Village of Rutland*, 52 Verm. 481.

(a) For same case in Appeal, see 2 Cl. & F. 331.—REP.

June 1st, 1894. FERGUSON, J. :—

There were, as we were told at the bar, two actions, one
by the husband and the other by the wife, he and she trading separately, each of the actions being to recover damages
alleged to have been occasioned by the alleged negligence or improper conduct of the defendants in respect of
the sewer on King street west, and the drainage of the
buildings numbers 799 and 801, which I understand to be
situate on the north side of the street (King street west),
number 799, having been occupied by the husband, and
number 801 by the wife. These actions, we were told,
were consolidated for the purposes of the trial and were
tried together. At the close of the trial the learned Judge
entered a nonsuit, giving his reasons for so doing. The
form employed was a dismissal of the actions.

This sewer at the place in question, was and is, as appears by the evidence, a portion of a system of drainage
adopted and carried into effect by the defendants according
to certain levels, and for a considerable district or area in
the city. This sewer was so in existence and in use long
before the building of the houses in the occupation of the
plaintiffs, respectively, or either of them. No complaint,
whatever, is made in respect of the construction or repair
of this sewer according to the general plan so adopted by
the defendants. After a perusal of the whole of the evidence, it is plain to me that what is really complained of
is, that the sewer is not sufficiently deep to properly drain
the cellars of these houses.

Much is said in the evidence regarding the connecting
drain, the inclination of it, its being too flat or having
insufficient inclination, the plumbing in the houses,
the traps and the manner of their construction, which
seems to me, especially in view of the other existing fact
above referred to, to be beside the real case, and immaterial
to what has really to be determined between the parties.
The evidence as to what was said and done on the occasion
of the deposit of the $15 to stand against the cost of an

examination of the connecting pipes, does not, as I think, shew anything really in the plaintiffs' favour in the actions; and I think it clear that the defendants were not bound, when constructing the Niagara street sewer or at any time thereafter, to connect the drainage of the plaintiffs' houses therewith, although in the circumstances this might and probably would have been a convenient and beneficial thing for the plaintiffs and the owners of the houses that they occupy.

It is, as I think, clear upon the evidence, that the defendants' sewer on King street at the place in question is not, in fact, sufficiently deep to properly drain the cellars of the houses in question; and I also think it clear that no method of laying the connecting drains and traps, and that no manner of plumbing within the houses, or all these combined could, or can by possibility overcome the one great difficulty, namely, the sewer not being sufficiently deep to drain the cellars, or in other words, the cellars being too deep to be properly drained by the sewer at its present level, which is, as I think, and have no doubt the real difficulty between the parties.

As already stated, this sewer is part of a system of drainage adopted by the defendants. The evidence of Roy McCrimmon, who is the son of the man who built the houses, shews clearly that this sewer was there and in use at and before the time the houses were built; that this was known to his father when he built them, and that the calculation and intention were that the cellars of the houses were to be drained by this sewer. The depth of the sewer, the depth of the cellars, and the inclination from the bottom of the one to the bottom of the other · (that is the difference of such depths or levels), is fully shewn in the evidence, and the wonder to me is why, in the circumstances, and with full knowledge on the subject, the cellars were made so deep as they are.

The evidence shews, as was remarked by the learned Judge, that the sewage, the presence of which is complained of, is all sewage from the plaintiffs' own houses.

There is not even the case of sewage or water being
"backed up" or coming from the defendants' sewer into
the cellars of the plaintiffs' houses or either of them.

We have then, the case of a sewer having been properly constructed and maintained by the defendants according to a plan of drainage adopted by them; and these houses having been afterwards erected with cellars too deep to be drained by that sewer, it being the sewer by which it was intended the houses should be drained, and the houses are situated in the proper and appropriate location for draining them thereby; and it seems to me that the only complaint the plaintiffs can really make is, that the plans and levels adopted by the defendants in this system of drainage, were erroneous and wrong, and such a complaint seems to be met by many authorities against it.

In the case of *Johnston* v. *City of Columbia*, 6 Sup. Ct. Rep. (U. S.) at p. 924, Mr. Justice Gray, in delivering the judgment of the Supreme Court said : "The duties of the municipal authorities in adopting a general plan of drainage and determining when and where sewers shall be built, at what size and at what level are of a *quasi* judicial nature, involving the exercise of deliberate judgment and large discretion, and depending upon considerations affecting the public health, and general convenience throughout an extensive territory, and the exercise of such judgment and discretion in the selection and adoption of the general plan or system of drainage is not subject to revision by a Court or jury in a private action for not sufficiently draining a particular lot of land. But the construction and repair of sewers according to the general plan so adopted, are simply ministerial duties; and for any negligence in so constructing a sewer, or keeping it in repair, the municipality which has constructed and owns the sewer, may be sued by a person whose property is thereby injured."

The judgment of Cooley, C. J., in *City of Detroit* v. *Beckman*, 34 Mich. 125, referred to in the American and English Encyclopedia of Law, vol. 6, at p. 26, is to the

Judgment. same effect, and the viciousness of a theory that would
Ferguson, J. submit such a question to the decisions of juries is there
pointed out by the learned Chief Justice.   See also Dillon
on Municipal Corporations, 4th ed., pp. 1334 and 1335.

Where, however, the duty as respects drains and sewers
ceases to be judicial or *quasi* judicial, and becomes ministerial, the municipal corporation is liable to the same
extent and on the same principles as a private person or
corporation would be in like circumstances: Dillon, *ib.*, p.
1331.

I have perused with care, as I think, all the authorities
referred to on the argument, and I think that none of
them are in conflict with the doctrine above stated, and I
am clearly of the opinion that it applies to the present
cases, and so I think the plaintiffs cannot recover against
the defendants.

I am, for these reasons, of the opinion that the learned
Judge was quite right in dismissing the actions, and that
this motion should be refused with costs.

MEREDITH, J. :—

The evidence discloses a very insanitary and highly
unsatisfactory state of affairs, quite enough, one would
think, to account for all the ill-health attributed to it, if
not more.

But the question is, who, in the eyes of the law, is answerable for all this ?

The real cause of it is plain ; indeed, there can practically be no two opinions respecting it.

The common sewer of the city is insufficient for the
drainage needs of the houses in question as they are constructed ; it is a sluggish sewer of insufficient depth.

But neither the owner, nor the tenant, was ever required
by the defendants to drain, or discharge sewage, into it ; if
either had been, the case might present a very different
question ; neither has anything ever been paid for the use
of it : see *Stretton Derby Brewing Co.* v. *Mayor of Derby*
(1894), 1 Ch. 431.

The owner, at the time of building the houses, sought
and obtained leave to drain and discharge sewage from
the houses into it, that was all; and sought and obtained
that permission with a full knowledge that his sewer pipes
were placed, or must be placed, too low to afford proper
drainage. In order to have a sufficient depth of cellar
without raising the ceiling above its present height, he
took these risks; and the inevitable consequences flowed.
He had the benefit of the cellar drainage at times, with
the certainty of a backing up into the cellar, through the
weeping tiles, of sewage from his own houses at other
times, whenever the common sewer was too full to carry
away all the sewage and surface water with which it
would sometimes be surcharged. It was not suggested that
the common sewer was out of repair, or that it was not properly built, that is, in accordance with the original plan of
construction; though, of course, it was said to be, and no
doubt was, insufficient in its plan for the present requirements of the largely increased community, though it may
have been quite sufficient for the then need of the community when constructed.

However, the owner chose to dig deeper rather than
build higher, and so had not sufficient fall; to dig so deep
that that common sewer, as it existed to his knowledge,
could not efficiently drain the cellars.

So that, upon the main question, unless it can be said,
as a matter of law, that the defendants were bound to furnish an efficient system of sewerage for all those who drain,
with their leave, into common sewers, the ruling of the
trial Judge in this respect was right.

I know of no positive law requiring that, nor any authority for it.

And that was the real question in controversy, as stated
by counsel at the close of, and throughout, the trial.

The placing of the weeping tiles was faintly urged, it is
true, but rather as a peg to hang the case upon when it
seemed to be falling from the main point. But it does not
hold, for:

1. There is no evidence to connect the defendants with the placing of them there.

2. They were evidently placed there with the assent of, or by, the owner. It was most important for him to drain the cellars; that was one of his main objects; that was why his drain was constructed with an insufficient fall. Without such drainage the effect of stagnant water there always would doubtless have been worse than an occasional flooding of sewage such as occurred. But for need of, and to get, such drainage the "soil" pipes could and would have been constructed with quite a sufficient fall.

3. But if the "weeping" tiles were a greater evil than benefit, it was the simplest of things to have removed them and to have plugged the ends of the double Y into which they entered.

It seems to me somewhat farcical to base upon the existence of these weeping tiles a serious claim to large damages.

In this view of the case, it is not necessary to consider whether the depositions of the defendants' officer were admissible as evidence upon the trial or not; nor whether the case should have been re-opened to admit the testimony of the proposed witness Wright. The result would have been the same had both been admitted.

The motion, therefore, fails, but not for lack of sympathy for the plaintiffs in their troubles, and must be dismissed with costs if asked; but one may fairly express the hope that, in view of all the circumstances of the case, costs will not be exacted.

ROBERTSON, J. :—

I concur in the judgment of my brothers Ferguson and Meredith, in dismissing the motion to set aside the nonsuit herein, with costs in both of these actions.

A. H. F. L.

[CHANCERY DIVISION.]

REDFERN ET AL. V. POLSON ET AL.

Company—Contract to Transfer all Shares—Winding-up Order before Completion—Specific Performance.

The shareholders of a company sold and transferred part of their property, and also contracted that they would, within a year, transfer their charter by assigning all their stock to the purchaser's nominee. Part of the purchase money was paid at once, but the purchaser did not nominate a person to whom the shares should be transferred. After an order for the winding-up of the company had been made, the liquidators brought this action for the balance of the purchase money :—

Held, that they were entitled to recover.

Decision of MacMahon, J., affirmed.

THIS was an action brought by the liquidators of the Statement. Owen Sound Dry Dock Ship Building and Navigation Company, Limited, to recover the balance of purchase money, due under a contract of sale, entered into between the company and the defendant F. B. Polson, under the circumstances which are set out in the judgment of MacMahon, J. The defendants were F. B. Polson and Duncan Morrison, mentioned in the judgment, the Polson Iron Works Company of Toronto, Limited, the Contractors and sole Shareholders of the Owen Sound Dry Dock Ship Building and Navigation Company, and certain individuals known collectively as "The Polson Lenders," who claimed the money under an assignment made to them by the defendants, the Polson Iron Works Company. On February 8th, 1893, an order was made for the winding-up of the Polson Iron Works Company, and on April 4th, 1893, E. R. C. Clarkson, liquidator of that company, was added as a party defendant.

The action was tried at the Owen Sound Autumn Assizes on September 11th, 1893, before MacMahon, J., without a jury, who, at the conclusion of the evidence, arrived at certain findings of fact, and afterwards gave judgment as follows :—

Judgment.

MacMahon,
J.

MacMAHON, J. :—

The sole shareholders of the Owen Sound Dry Dock, etc. Company, sold the dry dock buildings, etc., to the defendant Polson, for $16,000, and in addition agreed to transfer the charter of the company by assignment of their stock to the nominees of Polson within one year of the acceptance of the offer, which offer was made on the 22nd of November, 1888.

The conveyance of the Dry Dock Company's premises was made to Franklin B. Polson, on the 8th of February, 1889, when $15,500 was paid on account, and the balance of $500, was, by agreement of that date, between the Polson Iron Works and the Dry Dock Co., deposited in the Molsons Bank, to the credit of F. B. Polson and Duncan Morrison, to be paid over upon the charter of the Dry Dock Company, being transferred in accordance with the agreement in reference thereto.

On February 20th, 1889, F. B. Polson, in consideration of one dollar, conveyed the dry dock and appurtenances to " The Polson Iron Works Company, and also by the said deed he assigned and transferred to the latter company, all his right and interest, benefit, and powers, in all the covenants of the Dry Dock Company to him in the deed of 8th of February."

In the purchase, F. B. Polson admitted he was acting for the Polson Iron Works Company, of which he was managing director and secretary-treasurer.

The charter of the Dry Dock Company was to be transferred by the assignment of the stock to the nominees of F. B. Polson, within one year from the acceptance of the offer.

An order, under the Winding-up Act, was made on the 8th of November, 1890, for the winding-up of the Dry Dock Company.

A demand of the $500 deposited was made on F. B. Polson, on behalf of the liquidators of the Dry Dock Company, on the 18th of December, 1890.

It was contended for the defendants, F. B. Polson and the Polson Iron Works Company, that the stock could not be transferred in accordance with the agreement, because by the winding-up order the Dry Dock Company was in a moribund condition. Brice on Ultra Vires, 3rd ed., p. 787, was cited as authority for this. What that author does say is : " A company, when it is actually in winding-up, is in a moribund condition, so that it cannot exercise its powers and capacities, or rather, it cannot exercise them in any way which will be inconsistent with the winding-up, or which will give rise to rights or impose on it liabilities such as to interfere with the position of parties constituted by the actual existence of the winding-up."

By the R. S. C. ch. 129, sec. 15, sub.-sec. 2 : " All transfers of shares except transfers made to or with the sanction of the liquidator, and every alteration of the status of the members of the company after the commencement of such winding-up, shall be void."

The sole shareholders of the Dry Dock Company who had agreed to transfer their shares, had fully paid up their stock, so there could be no alteration in the status of the members of the company. The liquidators demanded the $500 and so are assenting to the transfer of the stock, that being a benefit to the creditors of the company.

A contract for the purchase of shares in a joint stock company entered into, but not completed by transfer before the presentation of a petition for winding-up the company under the Companies Act, 1862, (25–26 Vict. ch. 89), is not rendered void by the 153rd section of that Act. And a broker who has bought shares for a customer under such circumstances, and who has, in accordance with the rules and regulations of the Stock Exchange, been compelled to pay the price of them to the person from whom he bought, is entitled to recover back from his principal the money so paid : *Chapman* v. *Shepherd*, L. R. 2 C. P. 228. And see *Evans* v. *Wood*, L. R. 5 Eq. 9; *Tennant* v. *The City of Glasgow Bank*, 4 App. Cas. 615.

Judgment

MacMahon,
J.

The stock under the offer of November 22nd, 1888, and
agreement of February 13th, 1889, was to be assigned "to
the nominees of said Polson." Had Polson required the
stock to be assigned to himself or to any named person or
persons the owners of the stock would have been compelled
to assign. No demand was ever made by Polson, and no
nominee was ever appointed by him, and so long as the
holders of the stock were as alleged willing and ready to
assign it either to Polson or his nominee, they were not in
default.

The plaintiffs are entitled to judgment for the $500 in
the Molsons Bank, and any interest accrued thereon, and
to their costs of suit against the defendants other than
John Corbet, Robert Corbet, John Harrison and Robert
Simpson, but against the defendant Clarkson, only in his
official character as liquidator of the Polson Company;
the defendants, John Corbet, Robert Corbet, John Harrison, and John Simpson to assign the said stock to F. B.
Polson, leaving the same for him at the Molsons Bank,
Owen Sound, at the time the money is withdrawn.

The defendants moved by way of appeal before the Divisional Court on February 27th, 1894.

Hoyles, Q. C., for the defendants. We were ready to pay
over our money. *Doogood* v. *Rose*, 9 C. B. 139, shews that
the averment of readiness and willingness to perform the
plaintiffs' part is necessary: Story on Contracts, 5th ed.
p. 513; Addison on Contracts, 9th ed., p. 131; *Studholme*
v. *Mandell*, 1 Ld. Raym. 279. I refer also to Emden on
Winding-up Companies, 4th ed., p. 256; Parsons on Contracts, 8th ed., p. 479-80; *Howell* v. *Coupland*, 1 Q. B. D.
258; *Emerson's* case, L. R. 1 Ch. 433.

Marsh, Q. C., for the plaintiffs. It was no duty of ours
to make a tender of transfer. The defendants did not want
the transfer. The winding-up order did not affect the
rights of vendor and purchaser: Fry on Specific Performance, 3rd ed., secs. 914, 917, 1527-9.

Hoyles, in reply. They were bound to hand over the things we contracted for: Leake on Contracts, 3rd ed., pp. 86, 608; Brice on Ultra Vires, 3rd ed. pp. 774, 787, 790; *In re The Oriental Bank Corporation*, 54 L. J. Ch. 481, especially at p. 485; *Taylor v. Caldwell*, 3 B. & S. 826.

June 1st, 1894.   FERGUSON, J. :—

Having perused the whole case and the evidence, and examined the authorities referred to by counsel as well as those referred to in the judgment and some others, I am of the opinion that the findings and the conclusion arrived at by the learned trial Judge are correct, and I do not see that I am called upon to write out the case again by elaborating another judgment. The judgment of the trial Judge taken together with his findings * at the close of the trial seems to state all that is needful in the case, and I am of the opinion that it should be affirmed with costs, any assent by the Court to the

*The findings of fact were as follows :—

MACMAHON, J.—I propose dealing with questions of fact now, and I will have to regard the legal aspect of the case after I have an opportunity of examining the authorities.

I find that when the offer was made by the four, and only shareholders of the Dry Dock Company, of the 22nd of November, 1888, to Mr. Polson, on behalf of the Polson Iron Works Company, that they were offering to accept $16,000 in cash for the Dry Dock, the land, the buildings, and the machinery, and that possession was to be given on the 1st of January, 1889 ; that the Dry Dock Company, or those having the stock, also agreed to transfer the charter, which they proposed doing by assigning the stock of the company of which they were the owners to the nominees of Mr. Polson. The transfer was not to be made until one year after the acceptance of the offer ; and the reason why the transfer was not to be made for the year, is stated in the offer itself, which was to enable the Dry Dock Company to dispose of the other assets remaining on their hands. That offer was accepted, and was acted upon by the conveyance of the property, which bears date the 8th of February, 1889. The property mentioned in the offer was conveyed—that is, the dock, the land, and the buildings—and there is a receipt for the amount of $15,500, paid on the 8th of February, 1889. The sum of $500, being the balance of the purchase money, was to be deposited in the Molsons Bank, to the credit of Mr. F. B. Polson and the present Judge Morrison, which was to be paid over to the secretary-treasurer of the company upon the charter transfer that may be necessary may be obtained in the winding-up proceedings. I understand that the money has been paid into Court by the Molsons Bank, and, if so some variation in details may be necessary.

MEREDITH, J. :—

The one question is really whether the defendants are absolved from payment of the $500 because the company has been put into compulsory liquidation under the Winding-up Act.

What the defendants were to get and what the $500 were withheld to answer for, was really a transfer of the whole of the shares of the Dry Dock Company. It is so stated in the agreement, though also incorrectly referred to as a transfer of the charter, something which could not be done except in so far as a transfer of the whole of the shares to nominees of the purchasers might effect it by giving to them, if lawful shareholders, complete control of the company.

The transfer was to have been made in one year from the 22nd day of November, 1888, the then shareholders and persons interested in the company desiring the control

of the Dry Dock Company under the 47th Victoriæ, being transferred in accordance with the agreement in reference thereto. That money was placed in the hands of these stakeholders, or to their credit, for the purpose of ensuring the assignment to Polson of this stock, or to his nominee.

A memorandum on the back of the deed speaks of the charter of the Dry Dock Company being transferred; but it speaks of it as being transferred only in accordance with the agreement which, as I have already stated, was to be by the assignment of the stock, and that assignment was to be to Polson's nominee. I find, as a fact, that no nominee was named, and that the Dry Dock Company had no notification from Mr. Polson or from the Polson Company, that they desired that the stock should be transferred to anyone—to themselves or to anybody else.

The Dry Dock Company, at that time, I find, had assets, including the steamer Cambria, and also some debts which were owing to them, and no notification was ever given by the Dry Dock Company to Polson, or to the Polson Company, that they desired the $500 to be paid to them, or that they were prepared then to transfer the stock. No notification was ever given until after the Dry Dock Company went into liquidation; but on

of it meanwhile so that they might validly dispose of
and close its other assets and business: but the order for
the winding-up of the company was not made until nearly
two years after, and in the meantime nothing was done
towards finally closing the transaction between the parties
in this respect. It is important to ascertain why, and
the reason is, I think, obvious. There could be no transfer in accordance with the terms of the agreement until
the purchasers had named the persons to whom the shares
were to be transferred. But there was no nomination
made, nor any demand or request of any transfer, because,
I have no doubt, it had become apparent that the transfer
would be a thing of no value; nothing would be gained,
and something might possibly be lost, by it. The company
was in debt, it would not profit any new set of shareholders to pay the debts in order to retain the charter, as
it is termed. It hardly needs the purchaser's testimony
to confirm this view of the situation, but we have it in these
words:

" Q. Why did you object after the year to take the charter
or stock and pay the $500 if it is a valuable charter?

the 18th day of December, 1890, notice was given by the solicitors of the
liquidators to Duncan Morrison and Mr. F. B. Polson, that they were then
prepared to transfer the charter of the company; and demanding payment
of the $500.

The question that I have to consider is whether the liquidator was in
a position to make the transfer of the stock at that time; for without that
I do not see how the plaintiffs can succeed in this action to recover the
$500, that is, assuming that Mr. Polson, or the Polson Company, were
obliged to notify the Dry Dock Company of the appointment of any
nominee.

I think that these are all the findings, that it is necessary that I should
make until I have had an opportunity of looking at the authorities. The
evidence that has been put in by the plaintiffs of Mr. Polson is that during
a conversation, he stated that when they (meaning the Dry Dock Company) told us (Pollock & Co.) they were ready to transfer the charter,
we would hand them over the $500. That was evidence intended to
shew that as soon as the Dry Dock Company notified them of their
readiness and willingness to transfer the charter—which was to be done
by an assignment of the stock—that they were perfectly prepared to take
it and were willing that the $500 should pass into the hands of the Dry
Dock Company.

Judgment. A. Polson & Co. were not in a position to use it; they
Meredith, J. could have if they had given it inside the year.

Q. Why could'nt you use it now ? A. The firm has
gone into liquidation.

Q. You and Mr. Miller could still have taken the
charter ? A. We did not want it. We have made other
arrangements. We are running the boat business as private individuals."

Beside, this, as a matter of strict right, it was the purchaser's duty to prepare the transfer and tender it for
execution, as well as name the persons to whom the shares
were to be transferred: see *Humble* v. *Langston*, 7 M. &
W. 517; *Maxted* v. *Paine* (2), L. R. 6 Ex. 132; *Stephens*
v. *DeMedina*, 4 Q. B. 422; *Bowlby* v. *Bell*, 3 C. B. 284.

So there has been no default on the part of the vendors,
the whole default has been on the part of the purchasers;
they might have had the transfer of the shares, but they
did not want it.

There has been, and there need be, no failure of consideration: but because the shares purchased were really
worthless, and that has become apparent, the defendants
do not want them, but seek to retain the $500.

The winding-up order did not relieve them: it would
not, altogether apart from any question of default. It is
said that shares may be bought and sold after the making
of the winding-up order, and that a contract of that kind is
binding upon a party though he was ignorant of the fact
that the company was in liquidation: see *Rudge* v. *Bowman*,
L. R. 3 Q. B. 689; *Biederman* v. *Stone*, L. R. 2 C. P. 504;
and *Paine* v. *Hutchinson*, L. R. 3 Ch. 388.

All that the defendants can contend for as standing in
the way of their getting the shares which they bargained
for is the 15th section of the Act, which is in these words:

"15. The company, from the time of the making of the
winding-up order shall cease to carry on its business
except in so far as is, in the opinion of the liquidator,
required for the beneficial winding-up thereof.

2. All transfers of shares, except transfers made to or
with the sanction of the liquidators, under the authority

of the Court, and every alteration in the status of the
members of the company, after the commencement of such
winding-up, shall be void; but the corporate state and all
the corporate powers of the company, notwithstanding it
is otherwise provided by the Act, charter or instrument of
incorporation, shall continue until the affairs of the company are wound up."

The transfer is to be void unless made with the sanction
of the liquidator under the authority of the Court: the
liquidator has sanctioned the transfer which the defendants
are entitled to—it is he who seeks to recover the $500 in
this action—and he had first offered to do and procure all
things needful to a valid transfer of the shares: the judgment in question in effect gives the requisite authority, but
it can readily be put in a more formal and proper shape in
the winding-up proceeding. The required consent could
hardly have been refused in a case of this kind, the stock
being fully paid up, the main object of the provision of the
statute being the prevention of the escape of solvent shareholders, who should be contributories, from liability for
their shares. The sanction and authority could hardly have
been refused in a case where refusal would, without gaining
anything, have lost to the liquidator the $500 and interest.

The corporate state and all the corporate powers of the
company are continued: there seems nothing to prevent
the defendants, notwithstanding their default, yet having
all that they bargained for; but they do not want that
at the cost of paying the debts and the expenses incurred
since their default.

Their purchase proved worthless to them, and therefore
they did not and do not want the thing purchased; but
that is no excuse for non-payment of the price.

The motion, in my opinion, wholly fails, and should be
dismissed with costs.

ROBERTSON, J., concurred.

Judgment affirmed with costs.

A. H. F. L.

[CHANCERY DIVISION.]

McCausland

v.

Quebec Fire Insurance Company et al.

Insurance—Fire Insurance—Statutory Condition 9—Divided Risk—Proportion of Loss—Costs—Appeal to Divisional Court.

Statutory condition 9 of the Ontario Insurance Act, provides that in the event of there being other insurances on the property, the company shall only be liable for the payment of a ratable proportion of the loss or damage.

Plaintiff had insured his building against fire in two different companies in separate amounts for the front and rear portions, and the whole building, without division, in a third company. A fire took place damaging both front and rear, nearly all the injury being done to the rear :—

Held, by Rose, J., that the proper method of ascertaining the relative amounts payable by the different companies, was to add the amount of all the policies together without reference to the division of the risks, and that each company was liable for its relative proportion to the whole amount insured.

An appeal lies to a Divisional Court from the order of a trial Judge who has awarded costs on a wrong principle.

Statement. THIS was an action brought by Joseph McCausland against the Quebec Fire Insurance Company, the Alliance Assurance Company, and the Liverpool and London and Globe Insurance Company, for the amount of a loss by fire on buildings insured in three separate policies in the defendant companies.

There was no dispute as to the loss or its amount, but the companies could not agree as to the relative portions payable by each.

The action was tried at the non-jury sittings on March 16th, 1894, before Rose, J.

George Kerr, and *Rowell*, for the plaintiff.
Riddell and *Charles McDonald*, for the Quebec Company.
Armour, Q. C., for the Alliance Company.
A. Hoskin, Q. C., for the Liverpool Company.

It appeared that the premises insured were built at different times, the old part fronting on King street, and the
new part on Pearl street, in the city of Toronto.   One
policy was issued by the Liverpool and London and Globe
Company for $3,000, dividing the risk into two portions,
placing $2,000 on the part on King street, and $1,000
on the part on Pearl street ; another policy for $2,000
was issued by the Alliance Assurance Company, placing
$1,000 on each part ; and the Quebec Fire Insurance
Company issued a policy for $2,000 on the whole building,
making no division.

A fire occurred injuring the building, and the damage
was appraised at the sum of $2,819.81, of which $162.55
was in respect of the front or King street building, and
$2,657.26, in respect of the rear or Pearl street building.

The Quebec Fire Insurance Company, contended that
as the total amount of all the policies was $7,000, and as
their's was $2,000, they were liable to pay two-seventh's
of the whole loss, or $805.66.

The other two companies claimed as follows :

REAR BUILDING.

London and Liverpool and Globe Co. insure $1,000,		
loss is $2,657.26, and pays		$ 664.31
Alliance Co. insure	$1,000,	
loss is $2,657.26, and pays		664.32
Quebec Co. insure	2,000,	
loss is $2,657.26, and pays		1,328.63
	$4,000	$2,657.26

FRONT BUILDING.

London and Liverpool and Globe Co. insure $2,000.00,		
loss is $162.55, and pays		$ 88.55
Alliance Co. insure	1,000.00,	
loss is $162.55, and pays............		44.28
Quebec Co. insure	*671.37,	
loss is $162.55, and pays............		29.72
	$3,671.37	$162.55

*Balance of Quebec Company's policy after deducting loss payable on
front building.—REP.

March 16th, 1894.   ROSE, J. :—

Starting with the case *The Trustees of the First Uni-tarian Congregation of Toronto* v. *The Western Assur-ance Co.*, 26 U. C. R. 175, I am unable to appreciate any serious difficulty in determining the facts (or rather the application of the law to the facts) in this case. It may be that I have failed to appreciate the difficulties that have appeared to counsel, but to my mind the case seems now reasonably simple.

The statutory condition, which is in all the policies,—and I do not deal with the policy in the Quebec Company as containing any other than statutory conditions for the purpose of this my judgment—provides for the payment of a ratable proportion of the loss or damage. If we can determine what ratable proportion means, the difficulty is, of course, at an end.

And I think that may be determined very simply. Take the ordinary case of insurance policies by two companies upon one piece of property—say one policy for $2,000, and the other for $1,000, and a loss occurring of say $400.

The companies are to contribute to the payment of this loss in ratable proportions. How is the ratable propor-tion ascertained ?   You add together the policies and find the whole insurance is $3,000. One company pays one-third, and the other company two-thirds. Therefore it seems to me the language of this condition is not in effect different from the language in the *Unitarian Con-gregation* case.   The condition in that case was: " That in case of loss the assured should recover from them only such portion thereof as the amount assured by them should bear to the whole amount assured on the property." Those words " as the amount assured by them should bear to the whole amount assured on the property," are not found in the statutory conditions, nor do I think they were necessary.

Proportion must be established by relation to the assurance. There is nothing else to establish proportion

Rose, J.

by. Then we come to the decision in the *Unitarian Church* case which is on facts that I cannot distinguish from the facts of this case. It was there held that the amount insured is to be taken upon the whole property without regard to whether the risks were divided or not. Applying that rule I find there is due here the sum of $7,000—$3,000 in one company, $2,000 in another, and $2,000 in a third. If I wish to ascertain how much the Quebec Company has to bear, I take it as two to seven— two-sevenths. If I wish to know how much the London and Liverpool Company has to bear I take it as three-sevenths, and if I wish to ascertain how much the Alliance Company has to bear I again have two-sevenths, alto- gether making seven-sevenths, and it seems to me that that is exactly in accordance with what the *Unitarian Church* case decides.

I think, therefore, the plaintiff is entitled to recover against the London and Liverpool Company three-sevenths, against the Quebec Company two-sevenths, and against the Alliance Company two-sevenths.

And if we adopt the scheme of division suggested by Mr. Riddell for the Quebec Company, we arrive at the same result. If we apply or apportion the insurance, which I may call the blanket insurance to the values of the properties and take the front portion of the building as being sixty per cent. of the whole value, and the rear portion forty per cent. of the whole value, and apply the insurance according to the figures given, we reach the same result.

In each case the Quebec Company would bear two- sevenths of the loss. Reaching, therefore, the same result by two different modes of calculation, one upon authority, and the other, it seems to me, upon reason and justice, I am the more assured that the conclusion I have arrived at is not contrary to justice, and, therefore, may be right.

The Quebec Company must have its costs. The other companies must pay the costs of the plaintiff.

[After argument by the plaintiff's counsel against pay- ment of the Quebec Company's costs, in which he offered

to put in certain correspondence, before action, with the
solicitors of the Liverpool Company, which the trial Judge
refused to receive, the learned Judge continued]:

I think that where a plaintiff brings an action against
three defendants in which the issues are distinct, as between the plaintiff and each defendant, where one of the
defendants is shewn to have been in the right from the
beginning, and the other two defendants are shewn to have
been in the wrong, prior to the action; where there are no
cross claims, nor any relief sought as between the defendants, there is no reason why the defendant who did succeed should not receive his costs, and there being no issue
on the record between the defendants, there is no reason
why I should compel the other defendants to pay the costs
of the successful defendants.

From this judgment the plaintiff appealed on the ques-
tion of being ordered to pay the costs of the Quebec Fire
Insurance Company, and the appeal was argued in the
Divisional Court, on June 20th, 1894, before BOYD, C., and
FERGUSON, J.

George Kerr, for the appeal. The dispute in this
action was really between the defendant companies as to the
relative proportions they each should pay. The plaintiff
was indifferent, but had to proceed against all three to
recover what was due him. The plaintiff could have
shewn that, if the trial Judge had allowed the letter offered
to be put in. The Judge erred in refusing that. That
was not the exercise of a discretion as to costs. I refer to
Child v. *Stenning*, 5 Ch. D. 695; 7 Ch. D. 413, and 11
Ch. D. 82, 308.

A. Hoskin, Q. C. (called upon by the Court) contra. This
is a matter of discretion against which, having once been
exercised, there is no appeal. The plaintiff should have
decided which companies were liable, and brought his
action against them. He did not rely on *The Trustees of
the First Unitarian Congregation of Toronto* v. *The West-*

ern Assurance Co., 25 U. C. R. 175, but brought in the
Quebec Company as a defendant, and having failed as to
that company, should pay their costs and not compel the
other companies to pay them. I refer to *In re Beddoe—
Downes* v. *Cottam*, [1893] 1 Ch. at p. 554; *Harpham* v.
Shacklock, 19 Ch. D. at p. 215; *In re Gilbert* v. *Hudle-
stone*, 28 Ch. D. at p. 550; *Church* v. *Fuller*, 3 O. R. 417;
Mitchell v. *Vandusen*, 14 A. R. 517 at p. 520; *Russell* v.
Russell, [1892] Prob. at p. 156; *Hornby* v. *Cardwell*, 8
Q. B. D. at p. 335; *Williams* v. *Sir C. M. Burrell*, 1 C. B.
402; Con. Rule 1170.

Kerr, in reply.

June 30th, 1894.   BOYD, C. :—

The objection is raised that the costs were awarded in
the exercise of the Judge's discretion, and cannot, therefore, be considered as a subject of appeal.

The Judge states that he gave costs to the Quebec Insurance Co. to be paid by the plaintiff, because the plaintiff failed as to them, and there were no cross-claims between the defendants, and that separate actions might
have been brought against each company.

An appeal lies from the order awarding costs on a wrong
principle, though there is no appeal from the exercise of
an erroneous discretion on particular facts : Snow's Annual
Practice, 1894, p. 1081; *Child* v. *Stenning*, 11 Ch. D. at p.
86, and per Lindley, L. J., in *Young* v. *Thomas*, [1892] 2
Ch. D. pp. 136-7.

The Judge declined to receive or look at the correspondence prior to action, which is, however, admissible in
order to guide in the award of costs.   And although
technically there were not cross-claims between the defendants, yet the defendants who failed, desired the other
defendants to be sued with them on the same record, as
was, indeed, the most convenient and serviceable way of
dealing with these cases of combined insurances.

I think this is an appealable matter, specially having

Judgment.
Boyd, C.

regard to the correspondence which was excluded by the
trial Judge in disposing of the costs. There appears to be
miscarriage in putting upon the plaintiff the costs of the
defendant, the Quebec Insurance Company, for the dispute arose out of the differences of opinion and practice
as to the manner in which the three companies who had
insured the plaintiff's premises, should contribute to the
amount of loss sustained by him.

Two of the companies, the Alliance and the Liverpool,
asserted that the Quebec Company should pay a larger
proportion, and suggested or agreed that an action should
be brought against the three companies as defendants,
wherein all matters might be adjusted. In the pleadings
of these two companies, they set up the claim they made
against the third (the Quebec Company); spread upon the
record figures shewing the manner in which the one loss
should be apportioned, and set forth that the usage and
custom of insurance companies was according to the manner of distribution insisted on by them. The Quebec
Company set up that they had satisfied the plaintiff, and
pleaded ignorance of the relations existing between the
plaintiff and the other companies, while it was alleged the
said companies are seeking through the plaintiff to ease
themselves by compelling the defendant to pay.

The litigation was really and in essence attributable to
the refusal of the Alliance and Liverpool to pay their proper
share of the loss, and this was so found by the learned Judge.
It would be a proper consequence from this state of facts, to
direct that the costs of the Quebec Company who succeeded,
should be borne by the other companies who failed.

To this extent the judgment as to costs should be modi-
fied, and the appellants should have the costs of this
motion against the two companies.

FERGUSON, J. :—

The action is against three fire insurance companies for
the loss sustained by the plaintiff, the total amount of
which was undisputed.

The plaintiff had a policy of each company on the Judgment. property that was destroyed or injured by fire; and the Ferguson, J. difficulty was as to the manner of distributing the liability for the loss amongst the companies, defendants.

Each of the defendants had before action offered a certain sum as the amount for which it was liable.   These sums were accepted without prejudice to the rights of the plaintiff.   When, however, these were added together, their sum was not sufficient to satisfy the plaintiff, the admitted amount of the loss that he was entitled to be paid.   There was remaining a balance of between $500 and $600.

The defendants did not agree as to the theory or manner in which the distribution amongst them should be made. The Quebec Company proposed one method in this respect, and the other two companies another method, and from this fact alone, arose the difficulty.

At the trial the learned Judge held that the method of distribution proposed and adopted by the Quebec Company was the right one, and the contrary as to the method proposed and adhered to by the other two companies.

The judgment was in favour of the Quebec Company, with costs against the plaintiff and against the other two companies with costs in favour of the plaintiff.   The plaintiff asked that these two companies should be ordered to pay him the costs that he was ordered to pay the Quebec Company, and this was refused.

The plaintiff desired to read certain letters before action, which he contended had a bearing on the question.   The learned Judge declined to receive these letters on the ground, as it seems, that there was no issue on the record between the defendants.   Although, technically, there is not such an issue on the record, yet these two companies do state in their defence the mode of distribution of the loss, which they said and contended was the right mode; and this was different from the mode adopted and adhered to by the Quebec Company.

On the question of costs, I think the letters were receiv-

Judgment.

Ferguson, J. able in evidence, and if they had been read to the learned
Judge, we cannot say that his view might not have been
different from that which he finally expressed. These
two companies not only proposed, but urged as a way of
getting to the end of the difficulty, that an action should
be brought against the three companies, which is what the
plaintiff finally did.

It seems to me plain that the conduct and contention
before action of these two companies, was the cause, and
the sole cause of the litigation ; and I think it cannot be
said that during the litigation, there was not a strife
between them and the Quebec Company. I think the
learned Judge was in error in not reading or hearing read
the letters before action ; and I do not see that in varying
his order as to costs, we are interfering with the " discretion" as to costs.

I am of the opinion that there should be an order that
these two companies should pay the plaintiff the costs that
he has to pay the Quebec Company, or, as it may now be
done, I believe, an order that they pay the costs of the
Quebec Company.

The judgment should, I think, be varied accordingly.

G. A. B.

[CHANCERY DIVISION.]

WILSON v. TENNANT.

Malicious Prosecution—Charge of Stealing Several Articles—Reasonable and Probable Cause for Part of Charge—Damages.

In an action for malicious prosecution of a charge of theft of several articles, the trial Judge held that there was no reasonable and probable cause for charging the theft of some of the articles, and withdrew the case as to them from the jury, but held otherwise as to the other articles, and directed the jury that the fact that there was reasonable and probable cause to charge the theft of some of the articles only bore upon the question of damages, and the jury found a verdict for the plaintiff :—

Held, that there was no misdirection.

Per MEREDITH, J., dissenting : that if the ruling of the trial Judge were right, the damages were excessive, and apparently assessed under a misunderstanding of the effect of such ruling ; that the trial Judge could not in any case rightly have ruled as he did without first having findings of the jury upon certain material facts ; that there had been a mistrial, and that there ought to be a new trial.

Johnstone v. *Sutton,* 1 T. R. 547, considered and distinguished ; *Reed* v. *Taylor,* 4 Taunt. 616, followed.

THIS was a motion to set aside the verdict entered for the plaintiff in this action, which was brought against the defendant for maliciously issuing a warrant against the plaintiff, and having him arrested on a charge of stealing a number of articles, to wit :—a number of sticker knives, a piece of leather belting, one ripsaw, table, and a quantity of moulding. Statement.

The action was tried at Toronto, on January 19th, 1894, before STREET, J., who withdrew the action from the jury, so far as the charge of stealing the sticker knives was concerned, upon the ground that there was reasonable and probable cause for laying the information as to them, but he held that there was no reasonable and probable cause for the charge as concerned the other articles, and left the case to the jury, directing them as follows :

" Then you come to the question of damages. You may take into account in working out the question of damages the other circumstances of the case. If, for instance, you think Mr. Tennant was justified, under the direction I

have given you, in laying the information against Mr.
Wilson for stealing these other things, that may affect your
view of the damages that you should give upon the question of the moulding, because the whole of the damages
have not been improperly, in that case, incurred. That is
to say, if Mr. Tennant had left out of this information
altogether any reference to this moulding, still he might
have had the right, under the law, as I have laid it down
to you, to lay an information for stealing the other articles
that he charges to have been stolen. It is only a question,
then, which bears upon the damages."

The jury found a verdict for the plaintiff with $1,200
damages.

The present motion was argued on March 2nd, 1894,
before FERGUSON, ROBERTSON and MEREDITH, JJ.

Clute, Q. C., for the defendant. It is alleged that the plaintiff can recover damages because the Judge has not found
reasonable and probable cause for including some of the
articles. This is not so : Taschereau's Criminal Code, 3rd
ed., pp. 686, 696 ; Criminal Code, 55-56 Vict. ch. 29 (D.),
sec. 626, sub-sec. 4 ; R. S. C. 174, secs. 134 and 202. Here
were a number of articles taken ; but one charge preferred
before the magistrate. There was reasonable and probable
cause for laying the information: *Winfield* v. *Kean*, 1
O. R. 193, at p. 199. Where then was the additional damage : *Campbell* v. *McDonell*, 27 U. C. R. at p. 352. As to
the question of reasonable and probable cause : *Hicks* v.
Faulkner, 8 Q. B. D. 167.

Parkes for the plaintiff. The indictment cannot be said
to have charged only one felony. It says the stealing was
in April. The various articles might have been found to
have been stolen on different days, if so, this would not have
been one felony. The gravamen of malicious prosecution
is not the peril of conviction, but the scandal, and vexation,
and expense the plaintiff has been put to : *Macdonald* v.
Henwood and Preston, 32 C. P. at p. 440. Is not the

addition of charges of stealing other articles a source of
vexation, scandal and expense: Stephen on Malicious Prosecution, at p. 20.   The fact that there was reasonable and
probable cause for accusing the plaintiff of the theft of
one article should only affect the question of the amount
of damages.   It cannot deprive the plaintiff of his right of
action for having been accused without reasonable and
probable cause of stealing other articles.

June 1st, 1894.   FERGUSON, J.:—

The action is for malicious prosecution, and was tried
before my brother Street, with, of course, a jury.

The charge that had been made by the defendant was
a charge of stealing a number of articles which are called
sticker knives, a ripsaw, a table, ten feet of leather
belting and a quantity of moulding.   As to the part of the
charge that alleged the stealing by the plaintiff of the
sticker knives, the learned Judge, at the trial, ruled in
favour of the defendant, stating that upon the undisputed
facts, there was no evidence to lead to the belief that the
defendant did not think that these sticker knives had
been stolen from him, and that he could not say that
there was not reasonable and probable cause for his laying
the information before the magistrate, that these knives
had been stolen.   And the learned Judge withdrew this
part of the case from the consideration of the jury.

This ruling was confined to this one part of the charge
made by the defendant against the plaintiff before the
magistrate, which was afterwards embodied in a bill
brought before the grand jury who, however, ignored it.

The case, so far as it had relation to the remaining
parts of the charge made by the defendant against the
plaintiff, went to the jury, and they found a verdict for
the plaintiff against the defendant James Tennant, and
assessed the damage at the sum of $1200.

The learned Judge had dismissed the action as against
the defendant Amelia J. Tennant, with costs; there being
no evidence at all against her.

Judgment.

Ferguson, J.

The motion is against this verdict. The chief contentions on behalf of the defendant James Tennant were there having been probable cause for prosecuting in respect of some of the property alleged to have been stolen, this should be considered and held a justification as to the whole of the charge made, and so the verdict should have been for the defendant James Tennant, and also that the damages given by the jury are excessive.

As to the first of these contentions, in the case *Reed* v. *Taylor*, 4 Taunt. 616, the headnote is : " If a plaintiff declares that the defendant maliciously and without probable cause, preferred an indictment, setting it forth, the averment is proved if some charges in the indictment were maliciously and without probable cause preferred, although there was good ground for others of the charges preferred."

In delivering judgment, Mansfield, C. J., said : " The question is, whether, if a man prefers an indictment containing several charges, whereof for some there is, and for others there is not probable cause, this does not support a count for preferring that indictment without probable cause. I am of opinion that it does."

Mr. Justice Gibbs said : " To support this action, there must be a want of probable cause and malice. The charge here is not that the defendant imputed perjury without probable cause, but that he preferred that indictment without probable cause. There is no probable cause for some of the charges in the indictment, therefore, this indictment is preferred without probable cause."

In the case *Ellis* v. *Abraham*, 8 Q. B. 709, Lord Denman, delivering the judgment of the Court, said (p. 713) : " This was an action for malicious prosecution for perjury. The indictment for perjury contained two assignments of perjury. The plaintiff, as to one of these only gave evidence to shew that the charge was malicious and without reasonable or probable cause and left the case there, and the jury found a verdict for him. A new trial has been moved for, on the ground that the defendant was not per-

mitted to shew that there was reasonable and probable Judgment.
cause for the charge contained in the other assignment of Ferguson, J.
perjury. The Court, upon consideration, is of opinion
that such evidence was not admissible, and the rule must
be refused."

If these cases are taken as a guide to a proper conclusion, they seem to me to indicate that the course adopted
by the learned trial Judge was the right one. Some
expressions in the judgment in the case *Johnstone* v.
Sutton, 1 T. R. at p. 547, decided by Lord Mansfield and
Lord Loughborough, seem at first view to be looking in
the opposite direction. The case seems of a complicated
character, and has relation to a prosecution before a court
martial. The Court said: "Under all these circumstances, we have no difficulty to give our opinion, that in
law, the commodore had a probable cause to bring the
plaintiff to a fair and impartial trial," and further on,
"this probable cause goes to both parts of the charge;
the disobedience and obstructing the public service. But
if it went to the disobedience only, it would equally avail
the defendant in this cause."

On p. 546, where the Court discusses the nature of the
charges, it is said : "The charges against the plaintiff before
the court martial were formally two, but in reality and
effect one, to wit: The disobedience of the defendant's
verbal orders, public signals, etc. The second charge is a
consequence of the first." It so appears to me that the
authority of this case is not against what is decided in
either of the other two cases above referred to.

It seems to me that the language used by the learned
Judges in *Reed* v. *Taylor*, 4 Taunt. 615, is much in point in
the present case. It may be said here that there was no probable cause for some of the charges made in the information
and the indictment, and that therefore the information was
laid, and the indictment preferred without probable cause.
There may well have been probable cause for laying an
information against the plaintiff for theft without its necessarily following that there was probable cause for laying

Judgment. this particular information, or preferring this particular

Ferguson, J. indictment.

In the case *Winfield* v. *Kean,* 1 O. R. at p. 199, the late
Chief Justice Cameron quotes from the charge of the trial
Judge, the late Mr. Justice Patterson, where that learned
Judge said in charging the jury: " The question is whether
the plaintiff has shewn that there was an absence of reasonable and probable cause. It is generally a question for
the Court to say whether he has done so or not. In this
case I have not felt that it was my province to pronounce
upon that, for this reason—if a man is charged with fifty
things, and he is only properly charged with stealing one,
he cannot maintain an action."

I do not find in the judgments of the learned Judges in
banc, any reference made to this statement in the charge
further than its appearing in the liberal quotation from it
by Chief Justice Cameron, and I do not perceive that to
express this view was necessary for the purpose of determining any element of that case.

I have perused and considered as well as I have been
able all the cases and authorities that were referred to on
the argument, and I have arrived at the conclusion that
so far as this contention has concern, the view expressed
by my brother Street, and the course adopted by him were
correct, or at least not against the defendant. The learned
Judge might, I think, properly have said that there was
no probable cause for preferring this particular indictment,
or laying this information.

As to the other contention : the damages awarded seem
large. There was, as I think, however, no misdirection,
and I do not at present see how we can interfere on this
ground.

Motion refused with costs.

MEREDITH, J. :—

The learned trial Judge never ruled upon the question,
whether having regard to the whole charge made, there
was reasonable and probable cause, nor has that been
decided in the judgment just delivered.   He treated the

charge as separable, ruling that there was reasonable and probable cause as to the machine knives, and withdrew the case to that extent from the jury. If he were right, the damages are excessive, and must have been given under some misapprehension of that ruling; for if the laying of the information and all that was done by way of further prosecution of the charge were justified, as was held, by reasonable and probable cause for the prosecution for theft of the knives, it is hard to perceive what great damage, if any, arose from the addition of the other goods to the one charge.

I am not prepared to assent to the proposition, that in no case can the matter be separated, as it was by the trial Judge, and if it can be, it seems to me to follow that the plaintiff should have only such damages as he has sustained by reason of the addition of that for which there was not reasonable and probable cause.

The cases do not leave this question as plain as it might be : see *Reed* v. *Taylor*, 4 Taunt. 616 ; *Delisser* v. *Towne*, 1 Q. B. 333 ; *Ellis* v. *Abrahams*, 8 Q. B. 709 ; *Boaler* v. *Holder*, 3 Times L. R. 546 ; and *Delisser* v. *Towne*, 1 Q. B. 337, note (*a*), and 339, note (*b*); *Johnstone* v. *Sutton*, 1 T. R. 510 ; and *Winfield* v. *Kean*, 1 O. R. 193.

Reed v. *Taylor*, seems quite in point, and seems to decide that a plaintiff may recover damages for the whole prosecution, if there be want of reasonable and probable cause in respect of any of the acts charged. It seems difficult to me to understand that that must always be so ; that for instance, in this case, if the learned trial Judge's ruling were right, the plaintiff should have the same rights as if the charge had been wholly without reasonable and probable cause; for it is plain to me, that had the charge been limited to the knives, the like prosecution in all respects, and the same, or almost the same injury would have been sustained by the plaintiff; so I am not surprised to find early objection to the judgment in *Reed* v. *Taylor*: see *Delisser* v. *Towne*, 1 Q. B. at p. 340, note (*b*); or at the suggestion, that it is not accurately

reported; if it was intended to apply to all cases of
malicious prosecution.

Again, I am not satisfied that the ruling that there was
reasonable and probable cause in respect of the knives
could rightly have been made without the intervention of
the jury; they might, for instance, have found that the
defendant did not honestly believe the plaintiff guilty;
that, in view of the facts that the knives of the defendant's wife were mixed with a greater number of like
knives of the defendant, so that but one person, who was
absent, could tell the one from the other, that the plaintiff
had told the defendant that he had taken the knives, and
that such bad feeling had grown up and existed between
them that they came to blows, and parted with the defendant smarting under a sense of having had the worst of it,
he had out of spite, unfairly made the complaint and
stated the case to counsel. And even if the finding of the
jury upon these facts were favourable to the plaintiff, he
would yet have the admitted fact against him that he
made such a charge in the circumstances of this case without as much as making any demand for the knives after
the parties angry tempers had subsided : see *Huntley* v.
Simson, 27 L. J. Ex. 134.

It seems to me, therefore, that however looked at, the
case has not been rightly tried; and I am unable to see
how we can set off one error against another, and be satisfied justice has been done.

I would set aside the judgment and verdict, and direct
a new trial. The judgment seems to me in form obviously
wrong. The plaintiff has judgment upon the whole cause
of action alleged in the pleadings, though the trial Judge
held that he failed as to part, and said that he withdrew
that part from the consideration of the jury.

ROBERTSON, J. :—

I agree with my brother Ferguson, that the motion to
set aside the verdict, etc., should be dismissed with costs.

Motion refused with costs.

A. H. F. L.

[CHANCERY DIVISION.]

O'HARA v. DOUGHERTY.

Evidence—Action for Malicious Prosecution—Proof of Acquittal—Production of Original Records by Clerk—Certified Copy.

In an action for malicious prosecution, the plaintiff sought but was not permitted to prove his acquittal before the County Judge's Criminal Court of a charge of misdemeanour, by means of the production of the original record signed by the County Judge under the Speedy Trials Act, R. S. C. ch. 175, and produced and verified by the Clerk of the Peace in whose custody it was, or else by being allowed to put in a copy thereof, certified by that officer :—

Held, that the evidence should have been admitted in either of the above two forms, and judgment dismissing the action was set aside and a new trial ordered.

Decision of MACMAHON, J., at the trial reversed.

THIS was a motion to set aside the judgment of MAC- Statement. MAHON, J., dismissing the action, which was for malicious prosecution, upon the ground of wrongful rejection of evidence under the circumstances, which are fully set out in the judgment of Mr. Justice Robertson.

The motion was argued on March 1st, 1894, before BOYD, C., and ROBERTSON and MEREDITH, JJ.

Carscallen, Q. C., for the plaintiff. The record was the only one we could procure. There could be no better evidence of the termination of the criminal proceedings in our favour. The record is the final record, and is so directed by the statute, and is signed by the Judge. The necessity of an exemplification and the fiat of the Attorney-General does not apply to misdemeanour: *Morrison* v. *Kelly*, 1 W. Bl. 385; *Queen* v. *Ivy*, 24 C. P. 78; *Rex* v. *Smith*, 8 B. & C. 341.

The Court here called on the defendant.

Howard, for the defendant. In criminal proceedings the word record is used in two senses. That is how the difficulty arises. Wharton (*sub voce*) defines "record" as a "remembrance,"—a document made out after the proceedings—not for use in the proceedings : *Browne* v. *Cumming*, 10 B. & C. 70. The form of record in Schedule A. of the Speedy Trials Act, R. S. C. ch. 175, is only intended for the use of the Judge. [ROBERTSON, J., cites *McCann* v. *Preneveau*, 10 O. R. 573.]

[*Carscallen.*—But the record we produced here was the record of the whole proceedings.] I refer to Russell on Crimes, 5th ed., vol. 3, at p. 413. This was a case of a misdemeanour. The practice has always been to have a regular record drawn up after termination of a case—and the Courts have found it prudent to insist that that should be the document produced to them at any trial at which the proceedings have to be proved. If Schedule A. of R. S. C. ch. 175, is a record in the nature of a judgment roll, the other side might be right. But it was not a document intended to be used in any other Court.

Carscallen, in reply.—An exemplification or certificate of acquittal in case of misdemeanour cannot be refused by the officials. *Legatt* v. *Tollervey*, 14 East. 302, has never been overruled, and having the original record in Court, I was entitled to avail myself of it.

June 1st, 1894. ROBERTSON, J. :—

The plaintiff, in September 1891, was charged with malicious injury to property, by the defendant, before a justice of the peace, in and for the county of Haldimand, and was committed for trial, and was subsequently tried before the County Judge's Criminal Court for that county, under "The Speedy Trials Act," R. S. C. ch. 175, and acquitted. This action for malicious prosecution was then brought, and at the trial, which took place at Hamilton, in the county of Wentworth, the counsel for the plaintiff proposed to prove, by the Clerk of the Peace and Crown Attorney for Haldimand, the determination of the criminal proceedings, by the production of the original record, signed by the county Judge, which, having been objected to, was ruled against. The counsel then offered to pro-

duce an examined copy of the record, which was also rejected, the learned trial Judge (Mr. Justice MacMahon)
having expressed himself as follows :—

"I am quite clear on it. If I had the slightest doubt in
my own mind, I would not stop the case, I am quite
clear that you cannot, and I am quite clear that the Clerk
of the Peace has no right to bring the originals out of his
office, and I am quite clear that there is no right to make
up a roll and send an exemplification here without the
fiat of the Attorney-General."

And judgment was ordered to be entered for the defendant with costs.

The motion was to set aside the judgment ordered and
for a new trial, on the following grounds :—

1. That the learned Judge erred in refusing to receive
in evidence the record, indictment and papers produced
by the Clerk of the Peace in and for the county of Haldimand, as evidence of the acquittal of the plaintiff on the
charge preferred by the defendant against her in question
in this action.

2. The record produced by the said Clerk of the Peace
was made up under chapter 175, section 7, of the Revised
Statutes of Canada, 1886, and is evidence of the acquittal
and termination of proceedings in respect of said charge.

3. That the evidence produced and offered by the plaintiff of the termination of the criminal proceedings in
respect of said charge and of the acquittal on said charge
was sufficient.

The charge laid against this plaintiff was a misdemeanour, and so far back as the time of Lord Mansfield, in
a similar action, where the plaintiff had been indicted for
keeping a disorderly house, and acquitted, that eminent
Judge received the evidence, against objection by the
Solicitor-General, of the Clerk of the Peace for the West-
minster Sessions, who produced the original record of the
acquittal, holding that though a copy of the record, granted
by the Court, before which the acquittal is had, in order
to ground an action for malicious prosecution, where the

Judgment.

Robertson, J. party had been indicted for felony, is necessary, the practice is otherwise, in case of misdemeanour : *Morrison* v. *Kelly*, 1 W. Bl. 385.

Rex v. *Smith*, 8 B. & C. 341, was an indictment for conspiracy. The second count stated that at the General Quarter Sessions of the Peace, etc., a certain bill of indictment against Smith for a certain felony therein mentioned was duly preferred and found by the Grand Jury, and that it then became necessary to examine one W. B. as a witness in support of such indictment, and that the defendant conspired to prevent W. B. from attending and being examined. At the trial, the prosecution, in order to prove the allegation that a bill was found against Smith, called the Deputy Clerk of the Peace, who produced an indictment endorsed a " true bill," but there was no general heading or caption to it. For defendants, it was objected that this could not be admitted for want of a caption. The witness then stated that it was not the practice to make up the record until they were desired to do so, but that in his book minutes were made of the proceedings from which the records were afterwards made up. The book was produced, and the following minutes read : " Monmouthshire Sessions, July 10th, 1826. At the General Quarter Sessions of the Peace, held at Usk, in and for the said county, this 10th day of July, 1826, before A. B. C. D.," etc. Then followed a minute of the business done at these sessions. The learned Judge received this as evidence of the caption of the indictment against Smith, and two of the defendants were found guilty. In Michaelmas Term, Ludlow, Serg't., obtained a rule *nisi* for a new trial, etc., on the ground that the minute book ought not to have been received to prove the finding of the bill. Russell, Serg't., shewed cause, and after argument the Court gave judgment making the rule absolute. Lord Tenterden, C. J., in his judgment (at p. 343), said : " In order to prove the finding of an indictment, it has always been the practice to have the record regularly drawn up and to produce an examined copy,"

etc. And Bayley, J., said: " The caption is a necessary   Judgment.
part of the record, and the record itself, or an examined Robertson, J.
copy, is the only legitimate evidence to prove it."

Before 32 & 33 Vict. ch. 29 (The Criminal Procedure
Act), sec. 77, now R. S. C. ch. 174, sec. 244, the record commenced with a caption—which is a history of the proceedings, as extracted from the register, or minute book,
kept by the clerk of the Court before which the proceedings were had, and was entered immediately before the
indictment is set out; now, however, by reason of the
foregoing statute, this is not necessary, but section 244
states :—" The statement of the arraignments and the proceedings subsequent thereto, shall be entered of record,
in the same manner as before the passing of this Act, subject, etc., to rules, etc." So that a proper record is just as
necessary now as before the passing of the Act, in all
criminal cases tried before a jury on an indictment found
by a grand jury. So that an indictment by itself cannot
be called or treated as a record, although it is a necessary
part of such record.

In *McCann* v. *Preneveau*, 10 O. R. 573, the action was
for malicious prosecution and slander. The malicious prosecution arose out of a charge before a magistrate, and a
subsequent indictment preferred at the Quarter Sessions.
In proof of the termination of the criminal proceedings,
the plaintiff produced in evidence, which was admitted
subject to objection, the original indictment, endorsed " no
bill." The plaintiff had a verdict, but on motion to set
such aside, it was held that this was not sufficient, but a
record should have been regularly drawn up and an
examined copy produced, and the case of *Rex* v. *Smith*,
was referred to as being " exactly in point." With the
greatest respect for the learned Judges who constituted the
Court when that case was decided, I regret to say, I cannot
agree with the opinion therein expressed. In my humble
opinion the case referred to is not at all in point; at the
same time I think the conclusion come to in *McCann* v.
Preneveau, was the correct one, but not for the reasons

given. The only evidence of the termination of the legal proceedings was the production of the original indictment with "no bill" endorsed thereon. That certainly afforded insufficient evidence of itself. What was wanted to make the proof complete was the testimony of some member of the grand jury, who was present at the time the bill was ignored, the foreman who signed the endorsement would have been the most satisfactory witness of that, but any member of the grand jury present when the bill was ignored would have been qualified to give the testimony, could he have spoken to the fact. In *Freeman* v. *Arkell*, 1 Car. & P. 135, this was done, and Park, J., received the evidence, but afterwards, at the close of the case, nonsuited the plaintiff, because he thought the proceedings before the magistrate formed so leading a feature of the case that it could not be made without them. Afterward, in Michaelmas term, 1825, a rule *nisi* was granted, and was ultimately made absolute for a new trial. In a note to the reported case, on the question of calling the grand juror to prove who the prosecutor was, it is said this is generally proved by calling one of the grand jury. A grand juror may be called to prove any substantive fact within his knowledge, but not anything which he hears as a grand juror, or which comes within his oath of secrecy. In fact, on principle, I do not see what other evidence could be given—there could not be a record of acquittal—for the simple reason that there was nothing on which the party could be tried. There was, strictly speaking, no indictment ; a bill had been sent before the grand jury, but they ignored it, and consequently it never had become an indictment. An indictment is defined to be a written accusation of one or more persons of a crime presented upon oath, by a jury of twelve or more men, termed a grand jury : Chitty's Criminal Law, vol. 1, p. 168 ; or, as stated in Burn's Justice, 30th ed. vol. 3, p. 2, an indictment is said to be, "an accusation found by an inquest of twelve or more, upon their oath." So that the only possible way of proving that a bill was sent before the grand jury, and ignored, is by pro-

duction of the original bill, with the indorsement "no bill,"
signed by the foreman endorsed thereon, and by calling a
witness to prove that fact, and that the prosecutor was the
person against whom the action was brought, for maliciously prosecuting such charge before the grand jury.

In *Rex* v. *Smith* there had been a "true bill," therefore
an indictment, on which the party charged had either been
convicted or acquitted, in either of which cases the only
evidence of that fact would be the production of the original record of the conviction or the acquittal, which record
is enrolled, and thereby became a judgment of the Court of
Record. And that was why it was held in *Rex* v. *Smith*,
that the production of the indictment was not proper evidence of the fact which was necessary for the prosecution
to make out in that case. I submit, therefore, with great
deference, that *Rex* v. *Smith* was not at all in point with
the case of *McCann* v. *Preneveau.*

I might add that there was nothing by which a record
could be made up. The grand jury had not presented the
party as alleged in the bill; it therefore fell to the ground.
I think, therefore, that while *McCann* v. *Preneveau* was
properly decided, it happens only to be so because of the
want of the additional evidence mentioned. The production of the "no bill," as returned by the grand jury, was a
step in the right direction, and would have been sufficient
with the other evidence referred to, had it been offered.
There is no other way of proving such a fact. I do not
think, however, it is necessary to discuss the case further,
nor would I have done so, had not the counsel for the
defendant on this motion referred to it in support of his
contention.

In *Aston* v. *Wright*, 13 C. P. 14, the action was for
maliciously and without probable cause arresting the
plaintiff. At the trial, the plaintiff produced an exemplification of an indictment, not of the record of acquittal properly made up with a caption, etc., but instead,
the entry made in the book kept by the Clerk of the
Peace, in which the proceedings before the Court of

Judgment.

Robertson, J. General Quarter Sessions were entered, was extracted in these words: "In the matter of the *Queen* v. *John Wright*, false pretences, jury sworn, witness for the prosecution, John Aston, verdict of not guilty, directed on hearing the evidence of John Aston." And then followed these words: "All and singular which premises by the tenor of these presents we have commanded to be exemplified. Witness, the Hon. S. B. H., chairman of the said Court of Quarter Sessions of the Peace, signed by the Deputy Clerk of the Peace." That, of course, was not an exemplification of the record of acquittal, but merely of the indictment and of the entry in the sessions minute book. The verdict having been given for the plaintiff, it was moved against and subsequently came by way of appeal to the Court of Common Pleas, and was held not to be sufficient evidence to sustain the action. Draper, C. J., delivered the judgment of the Court, and at p. 19, says: "It appears to me impossible to hold that the document produced as an exemplification of a record of acquittal shews any record at all. It wants almost every thing to make it one. It may be an exemplification of a document in the Clerk of the Peace office, but it is no exemplification of a record that the plaintiff was indicted, tried and acquitted. I think, therefore, judgment of nonsuit should be entered."

In the *Queen* v. *The Inhabitants of Yeoveley*, 8 A. & E. 806, the original sessions book was produced to prove the existence of an order made by the sessions, in which book the orders and other proceedings of the Court were made up and recorded after each session by the Clerk of the Peace from minutes taken by him in Court, which book was the record itself, no other being kept. The minutes of each session were headed with an entry containing the style and date of the sessions, and the names of the justices in the usual form of a caption, and at the end of the proceedings of each session the book was signed "by the Court, John Charge, Clerk of the Peace." This was held proper evidence of the the order of sessions.

These and many other cases which might be cited, make Judgment.
it clear to my mind that the "record" itself, or an examined Robertson, J.
copy of it, or an exemplification of it, is receivable in
evidence to shew the determination of criminal proceedings. In cases tried otherwise than before the County
Judge's Criminal Court, under the Speedy Trials Act, I am
of opinion that it is only by such evidence that the fact
can be proved; for instance, the production of the original
indictment, or a copy, or an exemplification of it, does not
afford the necessary evidence.

The case before us is one which arose out of a charge
which was tried under the latter Act, under the Speedy
Trials Act, and the proceedings were conducted in this
way, as the statute points out. On a person being committed for trial on a charge of being guilty of an offence
triable at a Court of General Quarter Sessions of the Peace,
it is the duty of the sheriff within twenty-four hours after
such person has been committed, to notify the Judge in
writing of the fact, whereupon the Judge causes the prisoner to be brought before him; and the Judge having
obtained the depositions, states to the prisoner that he is
charged with the offence, describing it, and that he has the
option to be forthwith tried before him without a jury, etc.
If the prisoner elects to be tried by the Judge, then a day
is appointed for his trial, and it then for the first time
becomes necessary to make an entry of record, which the
Clerk of the Peace or Crown Attorney then makes, by noting
the fact in his Court book, and he also prepares what
the statute declares a "record," the form of which is given
in Schedule A. and B. to the Act. Now, this is the statutory
record; it contains all the necessary ingredients of the
ordinary record before referred to, except the venire, that
being of course unnecessary, for the obvious reason that
the sheriff is not required to cause to come the twelve good
men and true, to try the prisoner, etc., but the justice is
there, and the verdict of guilty or not guilty is stated,
and if the former, the sentence passed is also entered
thereon, and signed by the Judge. Now, that is a com-

plete record, not only in fact, but declared to be so by the statute itself; and it is required to be filed among the records of the Court of General Sessions, as a part of such records.

Then the case resolves itself into this small compass. On the trial of this action the Clerk of the Peace having the custody of the records of the Court before whom the plaintiff in the action was tried and acquitted, under *subpœna duces tecum* produced the original record; the learned Judge refused to receive it as evidence, nor would he receive an examined copy thereof, and the plaintiff's action was dismissed. With great respect, I think he was in error. I think he must have overlooked the prime fact that it was the record, and not an indictment that was in the custody of the witness. If it had been the latter I entirely agree that the production of an indictment, with an endorsement of " no bill " on it, or an endorsement of " not guilty," even in a case of misdemeanour, would not be receivable as evidence.

In the first case, a presentment, or what is usually called an indictment, is not such until a " true bill " is found ; until then, it is a mere statement of the form of complaint, made out by the Crown officer and sent before the grand jury, giving that body the information as to the nature of the charges which they are to enquire into; if upon the enquiry, they find the charge true, the foreman endorses on what up to that time is really only a bill, but which becomes an indictment the moment he signs, the finding of " true bill," which is endorsed on the back. If the jury do not agree that the charge is made out, then it never becomes an indictment, but is " no bill," and in the latter case, there is nothing to enter on the roll of record.

It appears also, that the learned trial Judge required an exemplification. I think he was in error in this also. Any one who had obtained a copy and could swear to it as such, is a capable witness, and the copy thus verified is good evidence of what the record contained. It is not

necessary to have it exemplified. An exemplification re-   <small>Judgment.</small>
quires to be under the seal of the Court in which the record <small>Robertson, J.</small>
is kept, and should be signed by the Clerk of the Peace,
in this case, or by the registrar of either of the Divisions
of the High Court in which it is entered as of record.

I quite concur in what has fallen from the learned Chancellor (a) in regard to what may arise in case the Clerk
of the Peace should decline to produce the original record,
at a future trial, or furnish a copy thereof. But I am
satisfied, that if either the original or a copy thereof is
produced and comes before the Court, although it may be
the duty of the officer charged with the custody of the
records, not to produce any record or give a copy of it,
but upon competent authority, yet if the officer notwithstanding gives a copy, or produces the original, the
evidence is unobjectionable, and the Court is in duty
bound to receive it. And in cases of misdemeanour, the
defendant is entitled to a copy as of right.

On the whole case I am of opinion the judgment dismissing the action must be set aside, and a new trial had.
Costs of the last trial, and of this motion, to be costs in
the cause to the plaintiff, should she ultimately succeed in
obtaining a verdict, but not otherwise.

BOYD, C. :—

Rex v. *Smith*, 8 B. & C. 341, merely decides that the
minute book of the Quarter Sessions cannot be received to
prove the finding of a bill of indictment, and it does not
affect the conclusion that the original record of acquittal
may not be proved by its production and verification :
The Queen v. *The Inhabitants of Yeoveley*, 8 A. & E. 806
and 817. The form of the record in case of speedy trial
by the county Judge is given by statute, and I am not
aware, nor was it suggested, that there is any other record

(a) The judgment of the learned Chancellor, though delivered before
that of Robertson, J., is printed after it on account of the full statement
of facts in the latter judgment.—REP.

of the proceedings before him: R. S. C. ch. 175, ss. 4, 7, and Form A.; 52 Vict. c. 47, ss. 4, 7, and Sched. A. (Dom).

The question always is, whether the document submitted is or amounts to a completed record ; if it falls short of that, it is rejected, but otherwise it is to be admitted whether it be the original record or an exemplification or otherwise, properly verified copy thereof: *Rex* v. *Bellamy*, R. & M. N. P. R. 174.

The trial Judge, in this case, rejected the evidence of the original record which was brought into Court by the Clerk of the Peace, on the ground that he had no business to have it away from his office, and that the only method of proof was to have the roll made up and exemplified. But the exemplification in this case would be of the document produced, which is the statutory record of the proceedings, and the question narrows itself to this, whether the original in the hands of the officer of the Court, and produced by him, was admissible. It was further said by the Judge at the trial that the proper evidence being an exemplification, it depended on the permission of the Attorney-General whether the plaintiff could procure such a copy. And it was suggested by counsel that the fiat had been applied for, and refused in this case. It is not necessary now to deal with this matter which may, however, arise, if the officer declines to produce the originals as he should do. But having taken upon himself to appear with them in Court, it does not appear to me according to the authorities to be competent for the Judge to decline to receive such evidence. I am dealing with, and my observations apply to a case of misdemeanour arising before the Criminal Code of 1892.

It has been questioned whether a person tried for felony and acquitted has a right to obtain a copy of the record of acquittal. This rests upon the efficacy or otherwise of the rule of the Judges passed 6 Car. 2, and referred to in *Browne* v. *Cumming*, 10 B. & C. 70. But in the note to that case it is said, at p. 74: " In cases of misdemeanour, it has been considered, that a party acquitted is entitled

to a copy of the record: *Morrison* v. *Kelly*, 1 W. Bl. 385 ;
Evans v. *Phillips*, Selw. N. P. 952. So also in cases of
summary conviction : *Rex* v. *Midlam*, 3 Burr. 1720. The
distinction between such cases and those of indictments
for felony seems to rest entirely on the order of the Judges,"
as already mentioned.

In *Morrison* v. *Kelly*, 1 W. Bl. 385, it was expressly
ruled by Lord Mansfield that no copy of acquittal need be
granted by the Court to found an action for malicious
prosecution, except in case of felony. In that case the
Clerk of the Peace attended with the original record of
acquittal, and it was received in evidence. This case is
referred to as settling the practice in the note to 1 Car. & P.
137, and is cited as shewing the existing practice in cases
of misdemeanour by Stephen on Malicious Prosecution, at
p. 101. Even in a case of felony where the officer attended
with the original record, though without authority, it was
said by Lord Ellenborough in *Legatt* v. *Tollervey*, 14 East
at p. 306, that he could not say that such evidence shall
not be received. The same rule was acted upon in *Lusty*
v. *Magrath*, 6 O. S. 340. See also *Caddy* v. *Barlow*, 1 M.
& R. 275 and note.

As to the admissibility of the original record, that is of
course the best evidence, but it is usual to prove by copy
because, as Starkie says, of the inconvenience to the public of removing such documents, which may be wanted in
ten places at the same time : Law of Evidence, 4th ed. at
p. 257. Other reasons suggest themselves, such as the
danger of loss or mutilation by their carriage from place
to place. Nevertheless, if the officer appears with the evidence, it is evidence to be accepted. At p. 388, *ib.*, Starkie
says that documents of record may be proved "either by
actual production from the proper repository, by an exemplification," etc. As to other cases in our own Courts :
Aston v. *Wright*, 13 C. P. 14, was based on *Rex* v. *Smith*,
8 B. & C. 341, already noted, in that the exemplification
produced was not evidence of a completed record (the caption being absent).

Judgment.

Boyd, C.

In *Regina* v. *Ivy*, 24 C. P. 78, the Court discussed the question as to the right to obtain a copy of the record in cases of felony only, and the case is not relevant to the present enquiry for this reason. *McCann* v. *Preneveau*, 10 O. R. 573, follows the ruling of *Rex* v. *Smith*, 8 B. & C. 341, and held that the original indictment endorsed " no bill," was not sufficient proof of the termination of the criminal proceedings. The point as to any distinction between felony and misdemeanour is not there touched upon, and though the head note states that " a record should have been regularly drawn up, and an examined copy produced," that does not conclude the question now before us as to what is sufficient proof of the termination of a misdemeanour disposed of under the Speedy Trials Act. Proper evidence being rejected this case must go back for trial.

If the officer on the next occasion declines to obey a subpœna, then the question will arise whether a copy of the record can be procured, and if this is objected to, the plaintiff will have to take such proceedings as will test the right of a person acquitted to a copy of the record of acquittal. This seems to have been considered as one of the rights of the subject in *Rex* v. *The Justices of Middlesex*, 5 B. & Ad. 1113, a case not cited in *Regina* v. *Ivy*, and which might have deepened the hesitation which marks the expression of judicial opinion in that case. See also the note of Mr. Greaves, at p. 350 of Russell on Crimes, 4th ed., vol. 3, p. 350.

There should be a new trial with costs to abide the event.

MEREDITH, J. :—

There must be a new trial.

The question was not whether the officer having the custody of the record had acted rightly or wrongly in producing it : the question was whether the plaintiff had been acquitted, and the record produced was the best evidence upon that question.

An examined copy of the record would have been sufficient evidence of the acquittal; that might have been made whilst the question of the admissibility of the original was under discussion, and might have been proved by anyone who had compared it with the original. Where such evidence is offered, it cannot be that there is to be a preliminary trial as to the means by which it has been obtained.

If these matters be the subject of enquiry, and need to be dealt with, I cannot think that the trial of an action such as this is the proper time for any such enquiry; they certainly cannot be then adequately dealt with.

I may add that C. S. U. C., ch. 110, which gave colour to the view that there was a restraint on actions for malicious prosecutions in this Province, under the Old Bailey order against giving a copy of any indictment for felony without special order, was repealed by 32-33 Vict. (D.), ch. 36. and does not appear to have been re-enacted.

A. H. F. L.

[CHANCERY DIVISION.]

THE QUEEN v. DOTY.

*Criminal Law—Conviction of Lesser Offence—Evidence of Greater Offence—
Seduction—Rape—R. S. C., ch. 157, sec. 3.*

A prisoner indicted and tried under section 3, clause (a), of the Act
respecting offences against public morals and public convenience, R.
S. C. ch. 157, with having seduced a girl under sixteen :—
Held, properly convicted of such offence, although the evidence given,
if believed in whole, would have supported a conviction for rape, an
indictment for which had been previously ignored by the grand jury.

Statement.   THIS was a case reserved by FALCONBRIDGE, J., at the
trial at Whitby Autumn Assizes, 1892, as follows :—

"The prisoner was tried before me at the last Fall
Assizes for the county of Ontario, upon an indictment
charging him under section 3, clause (a) of the Act
respecting offences against public morals and public convenience, R. S. C. ch. 157, with having on September 27th,
1891, unlawfully seduced and had illicit connection with
Margaret Louisa Caroline Dawson, a girl of previously
chaste character, the said Margaret Louisa Caroline Dawson being then above the age of fourteen years, and under
the age of sixteen years.

Margaret Louisa Caroline Dawson gave evidence which
would have been sufficient, if believed, to support a conviction for rape. An indictment for rape had been presented to the grand jury at the same assize, and had been
ignored. The counsel for the defence submitted that
taking the evidence of the prosecutrix, Margaret Louisa
Caroline Dawson, the crime was one of rape, and that the
grand jury having had a bill on a charge of rape against
the accused presented to them, and having ignored the bill,
the accused could not now be tried on a bill charging an
offence under the above Act. I decided to leave the case
to the jury and they convicted the prisoner.

The question reserved for the opinion of the Court is,
whether a conviction under section 3 of the Act respecting

offences against public morals and public convenience,
R. S. C. ch 157, could, under the above circumstances, be
supported."

The case was argued on March 1st, 1894, before BOYD,
C., and ROBERTSON and MEREDITH, JJ.

Du Vernet, for the prisoner. See Anderson's Dictionary of
Law, at p. 932, sub. v. Seduction. This shews "rape" and
"seduction" are entirely different offences. See also *The
Queen* v. *Nicholls,* 2 Cox C. C. 182; 1 East's P. C. 411;
Regina v. *Shott,* 3 C. & K. 206; *Regina* v. *Connolly,* 26
U. C. R. 317.

J. R. Cartwright, Q. C., for the Crown. Section 184 of
the Criminal Procedure Act, R. S. C. ch. 174, really covers
this case. This is a misdemeanour. The Judge saw fit to
let the case go on on the lesser charge, and the prisoner having been convicted, that is the end of the matter: *Wilkinson* v. *Dutton,* 3 B. & S. 821.

Du Vernet, in reply.

June 1st, 1894. BOYD, C.:—

Indictment for misdemeanour and carnally knowing
and abusing a girl under twelve: if it appears and the
jury find that the defendant effected his purpose by force
against the girl's will, this is no ground of acquittal, because it amounts to rape. The jury may still find the
defendant guilty of the misdemeanour. This was so ruled
by Rolfe, B., in *Regina* v. *Neale,* 1 C. & K. 591, and upon
a case reserved this result was affirmed by all the Judges
who considered it in *Neale's* case, 1 Den. C. C. 36 (1844).
This decision goes much beyond the question which is
involved in the present case reserved. A bill of indictment
for rape had been presented to the grand jury and ignored,
but they found a bill charging the defendant with having
seduced and had illicit connection with a girl under sixteen years of age (under section 3, clause (a) of R. S. C.
157). Upon trial the jury convicted, though the evidence

of the girl, if believed, would have supported a conviction for rape. The jury evidently while giving credit to her evidence in the main, did not accept her statement so far as related to violence—a course perfectly competent for them to take. It is sanctioned by what was said and by the decision in *Wilkinson* v. *Dutton*, 3 B. & S. 821, where the charge was of assault upon a female, and she deposed that the accused had connection with her despite her resistance. The justices disbelieving her in part, convicted the man of an assault. It was held they had jurisdiction to do so, though the evidence, if believed, disclosed a felony. The same point was much discussed in *Ex parte Thompson*, 6 Jur. N. S. 1247, and again in another application in the same matter, *In the matter of William Thompson*, 6 H. & N. 193, with divergence of opinion in the latter case, but on the whole, with a large preponderance in favour of the right to reject part of the complainant's evidence, and on the rest to convict of the minor offence. This conclusion is upon the present indictment quite irrespective of the effect of R. S. C. ch. 174, sec. 184.

I entertain no doubt that the conviction should be affirmed.

MEREDITH, J. :—

There is no room for doubt in this case. The ruling of the trial Judge must be confirmed.

It was his duty to determine whether there was any evidence to go to the jury upon which they might convict the prisoner of the offence charged ; he held that there was, and no question has been reserved upon that point, and the evidence is not before us.

We start, therefore, thus : there was evidence upon which the jury might rightly convict the prisoner, and they have convicted him, of the offence charged.

Had there been evidence of the other, and entirely different, offence only, the trial Judge would doubtless have directed an acquittal upon this indictment, and have made

an order under which another indictment for the offence
proved, would have been prepared.

That the witness upon whom the offence was committed, gave testimony upon which the jury might have convicted the prisoner of rape, if upon his trial for that crime,
is, in the circumstances of this case, no reason why the conviction upon this indictment for seduction should be now
interfered with. She also gave evidence upon which, with
the other evidence adduced at the trial, they might find,
and they did find, that only the offence charged was committed, a conclusion which the grand jury also reached,
as appears from their ignoring the one bill and finding the
other.

There could surely be no valid objection to a charge,
that if the jury found upon the whole evidence that the
graver offence was committed, they should find a verdict
of not guilty ; but if they found that the offence charged
only was committed—if they thought the evidence going
beyond that overdrawn and not to be credited—they should
find a verdict of guilty. It was a case of one or other or
neither crime, both could not have been committed. It can
not be that a prisoner is entitled to be acquitted of the
crime charged whenever some of the evidence for the Crown
discloses a different offence, if there be yet evidence sufficient to support a conviction of the crime charged.

The jury may credit or discredit a witness in part or
altogether. "The jurors are not bound to believe the evidence of any witness ; and they are not bound to believe
the whole of the evidence of any witness. They may believe that part of a witness's evidence which makes for
the party who calls him, and disbelieve that part of his
evidence which makes against the party who calls him,
unless there is an express or tacit admission that the whole
of his account is to be taken as accurate": *The Directors,
etc., of the Dublin R. W. Co.* v. *Slattery*, 3 App. Cas. 1155,
per Lord Blackburn, at p. 1201.

If authority be needed to support the conviction in this
case, the cases of *In re Thompson*, 6 H. & N. 193, and

Judgment.

Meredith, J.
Wilkinson v. *Dutton*, 3 B. & S. 821, are sufficient. Although in the former the Judges of the Court of Exchequer were equally divided in opinion on the question of the jurisdiction of the justices of the peace, those who were in favour of granting the writ of *habeas corpus*, based their opinions upon the fact, as they found it, that the offence charged was one in respect of which there was no jurisdiction; one of them using this very pertinent language : " When the evidence is examined, it is clear that it was evidence of a rape or nothing. There was no beating, no violence to the person beyond the violence in the attempt to commit the offence. What then was the duty of the magistrates ? I do not mean to say that if there is evidence of an offence over which the magistrates have no jurisdiction, the magistrates may not come to the conclusion that such an offence is not proved, and find that a less offence, over which they have jurisdiction, has been proved. If I could be satisfied that the magistrates had ignored the charge of rape, or attempt to commit a rape, and had *bonâ fide* come to the conclusion that all that took place was a common assault, I should be of opinion that the magistrates had acted rightly, and that there would have been no ground for this rule. But it is because I am satisfied that such was not the case, that I think the rule ought to be made absolute. The evidence clearly shewed that the charge was one of rape. Looking to the affidavit of the prosecutrix's attorney, we find an explanation of the anomaly of the prisoner having been convicted of a common assault, and then sentenced to six months' imprisonment. He says that when the facts were stated, the prisoner's advocate objected to his going into anything but a common assault, and after some argument between the attorneys and the justices, 'it was agreed that the case should be taken under the Aggravated Assaults Act.' I cannot, with that statement before me, shut my eyes to the fact that the charge being one of rape, the parties agreed to withdraw it from the proper jurisdiction and turn it into a charge of common assault of an aggravated description. I think

that the magistrates had no jurisdiction, and they could
not give themselves jurisdiction by the consent of the
prisoner to be tried on a charge of a different character
from that which was really before them. I cannot come
to the conclusion that the magistrates *bond fide* believed
that only a common assault had been committed."

Subsequently, the Court of Queen's Bench, in the other
case, unanimously held that the magistrates might rightly
convict of a common assault in such a case.

Substituting seduction for assault, each of those cases
is, in its facts, very like this case.

I would affirm the ruling of the trial Judge in refusing
to direct an acquittal and submitting the case to the jury.

I do not rely upon the case of *Regina* v. *Neale*, 1 C. &
K. 591, and 1 Den. C. C. 36. This case does not appear to
me to be one in which it can be said that upon the trial of
a person for a misdemeanour it appeared that the facts
given in evidence, while they included such misdemeanour,
amounted in law to a felony; but that case was one
coming quite within the words of such an enactment or
within such a principle : see R. S. C. 1886, ch. 174, sec. 184,
now sec. 712 of the Code, but considerably changed in
form. But the ruling and conviction in this case, do not
need the support of that case or of that enactment.

ROBERTSON, J., concurred.

                                        A. H. F. L.

SMITH v. BEAL.

Assignments and Preferences—Costs of Litigation in Respect to Disputed Claim—Right of Assignee to Charge same Against Estate—R. S. O., ch. 124.

An assignee for the benefit of creditors, on instructions of the inspectors, contested the plaintiff's claim, who then brought action, which was dismissed with costs, but, on appeal to the Divisional Court, this decision was reversed, with costs to be paid by the defendant, the assignee. The creditors after taking counsel's opinion, resolved to appeal to the Court of Appeal, but the appeal to that Court was dismissed with costs. The assignee charged against the estate the total sum he had to pay in respect of the costs of these proceedings :—
Held, that he was entitled so to do.
Decision of ROBERTSON, J., affirmed.

Statement. THIS was a motion before the Divisional Court by way of appeal from the following judgment of ROBERTSON, J., in which the circumstances of the case are fully set out.

January 15th, 1894. ROBERTSON, J. :—

The action was tried before me at last Stratford Sittings, and is brought by the plaintiff on his own behalf and on behalf of all other creditors of John Swift, who are in the same interest as the plaintiff. It appears that Swift carried on business in Stratford as a dealer in boots and shoes, on and prior to September 21st, 1891, on which day he made an assignment to the defendant Beal, for the benefit of all his creditors, under R. S. O. 1887, ch. 124. The plaintiff claimed to be a creditor of Swift to the amount of $600, for money lent. On September 28th, 1891, there was a meeting of creditors at which twelve creditors, including the plaintiff, representing $3,729.02 of claims amounting to $100 and upwards, were present. The total of claims for $100 and upwards, amounted to $6,260.10, held by twenty-two creditors, so that the creditors present represented a majority in number and amount of those who could vote on questions discussed at such meetings. These creditors appointed three inspectors, Messrs. Weston, Harvey, and McCrimmon. At this meeting the claim of the plaintiff was discussed, it being contended, that he was a partner of the insolvent, and could not, therefore, claim ; and he was asked if he was a partner. The evidence is, "He hesitated for a few moments, and then he acknowledged that he was a partner in the business." No resolution was proposed at that meeting in regard to this claim, but it was informally discussed. Afterwards, the plaintiff sent his claim in due form to the assignee under oath, in which he stated : "That the above named debtor John Swift, is justly and truly indebted to me in the sum of $632.44, on two promissory notes, etc., and five dollars for proving claim." When the claim came in, the assignee called the inspectors together, and asked for instructions in regard to it, when they unanimously decided to contest the same, and acting under these instructions, the assignee by his solicitors, sent the following notice to the plaintiff on October 15th, 1891 :—

[The learned Judge here set out the notice of contestation.]

Whereupon the plaintiff on October 26th, 1891, commenced an action in the Common Pleas Division, which came on for trial on January 8th, 1892, at London, before the Chief Justice of the Queen's Bench Division, and resulted in judgment, dismissing the action with costs. The plaintiff afterwards reheard the cause before the Divisional Court, which Court reversed the judgment of the learned trial Judge and ordered a verdict to be entered for the plaintiff, declaring that he was entitled to rank upon the estate for the amount of his claim, and that "the defendant do pay the plaintiff the costs of this action, including the costs of the trial and of this motion." This was on June 25th, 1892. Afterwards, at a meeting of creditors on September 22nd, 1892, it was resolved in writing that Mr. Meredith's opinion be taken as to the advisability of appealing from the judgment of the Common Pleas Divisional Court, and that the inspectors then act upon the

same. This opinion was obtained, and afterwards on October 24th, 1892, at a meeting of the inspectors, the assignee
being in the chair, it was resolved that the appeal in *Smith
v. Beal*, to the Court of Appeal, be proceeded with. Such
proceedings were thereupon had, that the appeal was in
due course heard before the Court of Appeal; and on
March 7th, 1893, was dismissed with costs to be paid by
the appellant to the respondent. Afterwards on June 5th,
1893, the assignee made up and prepared his statement of
the affairs of his estate, by which it appears that the
amount realized by him, was $4,891.66; disbursements
$1,803.06, of which $1,591.23, were for costs and disbursements in contesting claims of L. Smith, the plaintiff, and one
Quilter; and shewing that a first and final dividend of
thirty cents on the dollar amounting to $2,170.17, was in
hand to pay ordinary creditors, the plaintiff being among
them—the balance being absorbed in paying preferential
claims amounting to $653.36, and for printing, stationery,
inspector's fees, trustee's fees, etc.

The plaintiff now brings this action and charges *inter
alia* as follows:—

7. The defendant neglected and refused to carry out
the trusts contained in the said deed (the assignment for
benefit of creditors), and pay the creditors of the said
Swift ratably and proportionately without preference and
priority, but sought to prefer certain creditors contrary to
said trust and to exclude the plaintiff and other creditors
from receiving their share of the said estate until compelled so to do by the judgment of this Court establishing
their said claims as such creditors.

8. The defendant neglecting and refusing to perform
his duty under the said deed did not proceed with due
despatch to wind up the said estate and to distribute the proceeds thereof amongst the plaintiff and the other creditors
of the said John Swift, as it was his duty to have done,
but on the contrary, although more than one year has
elapsed prior to the commencement of this action, the
defendant did not wind up the said estate in the manner

aforesaid, nor did he render any sufficient or satisfactory Judgment.
account to the plaintiff or the other creditors of the said Robertson, J.
John Swift of his dealings therewith, but the defendant
has wasted and dissipated the said estate, and he now
claims that there is nothing left after the payment of
thirty cents on the dollar, paid by him to the creditors of
the said John Swift.

9. The plaintiff submits that he is entitled to an
account of the dealings of the said defendant with the
said estate, and to have the trusts of the said deed carried
out by this Court.

10. The defendant improperly seeks to charge the
estate of John Swift and to reduce the plaintiff's dividend
by the costs incurred by him in endeavouring to exclude
the plaintiff and one Quilter from their right to rank on
the said estate for the benefit of himself and others.

And he claims judgment, declaring the trusts of the said
deed, and to have the trusts therein carried out under the
judgment of the Court, an account of the dealings of
the defendant with the said estate : payment of such
additional sums as may be found due to him under said
judgment; and such further and other relief, etc., and the
costs of this action.

The defendant denies the allegations contained in the
7th, 8th and 10th paragraphs of the statement of claim,
and on the contrary, states that he well, truly, and faith-
fully, and with due expedition and under the direction of
the creditors and inspectors of the estate of the said John
Swift, carried out and executed the trusts contained in the
instrument set forth in the 4th paragraph of the statement
of claim ; and that he has at all times been and is now ready
and willing to render an account to the creditors of the said
estate of his dealings with the said estate ; and on or about
June 5th, 1893, caused a printed statement, containing a
detailed account of his dealings with the said estate and of
the disposition thereof, to be sent to the plaintiff and to
all the creditors of the said estate.

At the close of the case, I intimated that on the evi-

dence the defendant was entitled to have the issues joined
on the 7th, 8th, and 10th paragraphs of the statement of
claim found in his favour, but that I would reserve my
formal judgment in the matter for further consideration,
when I would also consider the claim for a reference. I
have now done so.

The matters in particular complained of, are : first, the
payment by the defendant out of the assets of the estate
of the large bills of costs incurred, and occasioned by two
actions brought by claimants on the estate, one being by
William Quilter, and the other by this plaintiff ; second,
the payment of preferred claims to a larger amount than
were due by the insolvent ; and, third, the amount realized
by the assignee. There was nothing else of any importance urged before me.

In regard to the first, the evidence was all one way, and
shewed clearly that the defendant, as such assignee, acted
not only under instructions, and by the advice of the inspectors, duly appointed at a large meeting of the creditors,
but by the direction and advice of the creditors in contesting the claims referred to ; and taking into account that
the learned Chief Justice who tried both cases, found in
favour of the assignee, and refused to declare that either
Quilter or this plaintiff should be allowed to prove against
the estate of the insolvent, and, also the fact, that after
the verdict against this plaintiff had been set aside, the
creditors instructed the inspectors to take the opinion of a
leading Queen's counsel, as to whether the decisions of the
Divisional Court reversing the trial Judge, should be carried to the Court of Appeal, and the fact that such counsel did so advise, and the fact that upon securing such
opinion, the defendant acted on the instructions of the
inspectors to proceed with such appeal, I have come to
the conclusion that the defendant acted in good faith, and
that he was justified in charging the estate with all the
costs incurred in consequence thereof.

[The learned Judge then proceeded to consider the evidence as to the second and third points above mentioned,
and concluded as follows :]

I find all the issues in favour of the defendant, and find Judgment.
nothing to warrant me in granting the reference, except Robertson, J.
on terms. If, therefore, the plaintiff will give security to
the satisfaction of the Master in Ordinary for the costs of
the reference, within one month from this date, such reference may go to the said Master, in which case I order
the plaintiff to pay to the defendant the costs of the
action, including the costs of the trial; and I reserve further directions and costs of the reference until after the
Master has reported. Should the plaintiff not furnish such
security within the time limited, the action will be dismissed with costs.

The plaintiff moved before the Divisional Court to
set aside this judgment, and the motion was argued on
February 23rd, 1894, before BOYD, C., and FERGUSON and
MEREDITH, JJ.

Aylesworth, Q. C., and *Harding*, for the plaintiff. If
the assignee has entered into litigation wrongfully, he may
be personally liable. He should not at any rate charge
the costs of the litigation against the estate. The judgments in *Smith* v. *Beal*, and *Quilter* v. *Beal*, were that
Beal pay the costs. This is a personal order against Beal.
The trusts on which the property came to the defendant
are of the same nature as in similar assignments before
R. S. O. ch. 124, and give the defendant no power to
do what he proposes to do.
[MEREDITH, J.—If he does only what the Act requires
him to do, can he not recoup himself ?]
When a quarrel arises among the *cestuis que trust* as to
whether one or the other is entitled to share, and the trustee in the interests of a majority enters on litigation, he
does so not in the general interest of the estate, and must
do so at his own peril. He should say to those who wish
to fight, if you want to do this, you must indemnify me.
An executor may find himself personally liable to pay costs
of litigation.

[MEREDITH, J.—But they might say we won't indemnify
you, go on and defend the action or we'll hold you responsible. He is between two fires.]

Practically, the assignor is being made liable to these
costs, because he remains under so much the greater liability, but the assignor never authorized the assignee to take
the course he took. This is not a case of a stranger attacking
the estate, but of an internecine strife between creditors.

[FERGUSON, J.—It seems hard on an assignee that he
should not be safe in acting on the direction of the inspectors in resisting a claim.]

I draw this distinction : If at the time a debtor assigns,
he is defending an action, then I can understand a trustee
should defend because it is an attack on the general fund,
and even if he fails, he should be indemnified. But to
resist the claim of a man who has proved his claim in a
regular way after assignment, is a different thing. Suppose a man accepted a trust to divide certain property
among children of a settlor or testator, and some one came
forward and said he was a child, and the question of legiti-
macy arose, the trustee could not litigate that at the expense of the fund. The fund is defined in amount, and
the litigation is not going to increase it or diminish it.

[MEREDITH, J.—Here is an assignee for unknown persons, and the statute imposes on him the duty of ascertaining who they are : see section 20, sub-sec. 5.]

If he litigates, he is doing it in the interests of those
who will have their private dividends increased and not
in the interests of the fund. No enquiry was made of the
assignor. If the assignee chooses to act without such
enquiry, relying on such information only as he had here,
surely he does it at his peril. Swift says he could have
prevented the whole litigation if he had been consulted, and
objects to his estate going to pay these costs. We are
at any rate entitled to object to so much of the costs as is
involved in the appeal to the Court of Appeal. The
assignee took the position of an actor in the litigation.

[FERGUSON, J.—If he was justified in resisting the litigation at first, was he not justified in fighting to the end ?]

After the judgment of the Divisional Court, at any rate
he could have insisted on indemnity.

[BOYD, C.—The first Court determined in Beal's favour.
It is hard to hold the action was a reckless action.]

Smith and Quilter at all events should not have to bear
·any part of the costs. Under the Creditors' Relief Act as
-amended, only those who bear the risk share the benefit.
Otherwise, those who were adverse to Smith and Quilter,
were by litigating, putting their adversaries in the position, whether they won or lost, of bearing the costs of the
litigation. We further complain that we have been ordered
to pay the costs of the action, and have been required to
give security before we can have the account we wish.

Snow, for the assignee. I refer to R. S. O. ch. 124, sec. 19,
which provides that all questions shall be decided at meetings of creditors by the majority of votes. The evidence
shews that the plaintiff had abundant grounds for suspect-
ing the validity of Smith's claim. The dividend sheet has
been prepared and no objection taken : Section 22.

There is no evidence of misconduct on the part of
the assignee, or unfair dealing on the part of the other
creditors; and it was on counsel's advice that the appeal was taken to the Court of Appeal. With every
trust deed there is by implication the right in the trustee
to deduct his costs : *Worrall* v. *Harford*, 8 Ves. 4. As to
our having to bear the costs of the litigation : See *In re
Silver Valley Mines*, 21 Ch. D. at p. 386.

Aylesworth, in reply. No such defence as is suggested
under section 22 is good. That is not a limitation upon
creditors that he shall object within eight days, but merely
directs that the dividends shall be paid after eight days.

[BOYD, C.—But if you allow the estate to be distributed
without objection, is not the assignee relieved ?]

But we did not do that here. The Creditors' Relief Act,
R. S. O. ch. 65, sec. 32, is very different. That gives the
sheriff a protection in case he acts after eight days have
elapsed without objection taken.

June 1st, 1894.   BOYD, C. :—

The scope of the Act (ch. 124) seems to be that a majority in number and value of creditors for $100 and upwards,
shall be able to direct proceedings : R. S. O. ch. 124, secs. 6,
(1), 11, 16, 17, 19.   The required number of creditors in
this case appointed inspectors, and thereby either directly
or mediately approved of and sanctioned the litigation
which arose in respect of the claims of Smith and Quilter
to rank as creditors on the estate.   The Act recognizes
the position of the assignee to be that of trustee (sec. 20,
sub-sec. 3), and in many respects the assets are subject
to the same rules as other trust funds.

The broad question is, whether the assignee must pay
personally the cost of litigation arising out of disputed
claims, in which he turns out to be ultimately unsuccessful—his action being at the instance of the majority
of the creditors and the inspectors.   The general rule is,
that a trustee in the absence of misconduct, shall be recouped his costs, charges, and expenses against the trust
estate even in the case of unsuccessful litigation : *Pitts*
v. *La Fontaine*, 6 App. Cas. 482 ; and even if the trustee
proceeds without the sanction of the Court (in a case
where he might have so protected himself), yet the costs
will be allowed out of the estate if it appears that the
defence or action would have been authorized had prior
application been made : *In re Beddoe, Downes* v. *Cottam,*
[1893] 1 Ch. at p. 557.   The only point about which I hesi-
tate is as to the costs incurred in the appeal from the
Divisional Court by the trustee, which was dismissed.   This
action was after taking counsel's opinion, and with the
express sanction of the creditors, and if they have control of the estate as the majority, I do not see how to draw
a distinction as to these costs, except it be by limiting the
right of the assignee to be recouped out of the share of the
funds applicable to the contesting creditors.   The English
and Irish cases are very strong against allowing a trustee to charge the costs of an unsuccessful appeal against

the fund : *Re Walters*, 34 Sol. J., 564, and *Dillon* v. *Arkins*,
17 L. R. Ir. 636.

The general rule as to costs is recognized in the New
York code covering the case of assignments for the benefit
of creditors, to the effect that costs incurred or paid
by the trustee, are chargeable upon and collectible out of
the estate, unless the Court directs them to be defrayed
personally from mismanagement or bad faith in the prosecution or defence of the action : Code Civil Procedure,
sec. 3246 ; Burrill on Assignments, 6th ed., sec. 360.

This is the only important matter ; the book debts are,
I judge, of little or no value, and the assignee is willing
to turn them over to the plaintiff. The plaintiff should
not be required to give security for costs before having an
account, but an account was offered by the pleadings and
there was no need for the contest which, at the best, could
only prevail as to the costs of appeal.

The best course will be to refuse relief on this appeal,
having regard to the costs that ought to be paid by the
plaintiff in his unsuccessful claims and the small relief
that would be obtained even as to the costs of appeal. I
would dismiss the appeal without costs, but if the plaintiff
still seeks an account, he should pay the costs of this appeal.

I agree in this view of my brother Ferguson, rather
than to make a more minute discrimination as to how
much of the costs he should pay.

FERGUSON, J. :—

As to whether or not the costs and expenses of the contestation of the claim of Smith and that of Quilter,
amounting together to a large sum, nearly $1,600 were
properly deducted from the moneys of the estate in the
hands of the defendant before paying dividends to the
creditors, I do not find any provision in the Act affording a
guide as to what should be the proper answer. It was not
said that the deed of assignment contained any provision

on the subject, and the Courts before which the trials were, did not make any specific direction as to the fund out of which, or the person or persons by whom such costs were to be paid. The orders made as to costs were of the general and ordinary character.

Sub-section 5 of section 20 of the Act, presupposes that there may be contestations of the claims of claimants upon the estate assigned, and provides that the assignee may give the notice of contestation, and that he is the person to do it, and if an assignee has information as to the claim of any claimant upon the estate in his hands, shewing that it is reasonably liable to contestation, that is, that there appear to be good and reasonable grounds for saying that such claim should not rank upon the estate or be paid out of the estate without contestation, one would say that it is his duty to advise with the inspectors and other creditors, and, if need be, to give the notice. And when this is done, if the claimant bring his action within the prescribed time, the assignee is involved in litigation on behalf of the estate in his hands, and in such a case he would be, no doubt, responsible for seeing that, in such litigation, the interest of the estate is properly protected.

I do not find any provision in the Act requiring the assignee to demand or obtain from those who desire that a claim should be contested security or indemnity against the costs of contestation of a claim before giving the notice.

In the present case the assignee had, one would say from a perusal of the papers and the evidence, sufficiently strong support from the inspectors and the creditors, if not before giving the notices, during the pendency of the proceedings, and throughout his conduct seems to have been reasonable and not in any degree rash or ill-advised, and the judgment of the Judge of first instance was in his favour, though final defeat came.

The Act being bald, as it is in some respects, it is not, I think, erroneous to consider the position of the assignee as in many respects analogous to that of the ordinary

trustee; and I cannot avoid thinking that in respect to
these costs that is his position, he having acted as he did
in respect to these claims with the approval of the inspectors; and, speaking in a general way, with the approval
of the creditors.

In an early case, *Worrall* v. *Harford*, 8 Vesey, at p. 7 (a),
Lord Eldon said: " It is in the nature of the office of a
trustee, whether expressed in the instrument or not, that
the trust property shall reimburse him all the charges and
expenses incurred in the execution of the trust. This is
implied in every such deed;" and, looking at the conduct
of this defendant from the beginning, and assuming that
this seemingly large sum was really expended in the litigation that arose upon his giving the notices, I think the
above statement of the law applies to his case. Probably
the assignee might with safety have stopped at the judgment of the Court against him, without proceeding to the
Court of Appeal in Smith's case, but he did not do this
rashly. He took the precaution to obtain the view of the
creditors, and they and he took the further precaution to
obtain the opinion of counsel of eminence before the step
was taken; and, besides, the costs occasioned by the appeal,
I would not suppose would be a large share of the whole
amount complained of.

It may be said that the Courts in which the litigation
was, might, or should have given directions that the costs
in question should be paid out of the estate in the hands
of the assignee, yet I do not see that their not having
done so, precludes this Court sitting here, from saying that
this should be done in deciding as to what is the right of
the defendant in this case.

In respect of this, which was the matter mainly argued,
I am of the opinion that the judgment should be affirmed.

Then as to the account spoken of. The rule seems to
be that the Court will not require from a trustee more
careful conduct than a prudent man would bestow in the
management of his own property, still it requires from
him full explanation of all his dealings, and the causes

which may have led to outstanding debts not having been
collected : *Chisholm* v. *Barnard*, 10 Gr. 479.

The evidence here shews a very considerable sum in
very small outstanding debts, and although it can be
readily seen that the collection of them would have been
very troublesome, and that possibly an effort to collect
more of them than was collected, might have turned out
to be fruitless, yet I cannot consider the evidence going
to shew the reason why a further effort was not made
full and satisfactory ; and I think it cannot be said on
principle that the plaintiff is not entitled to an account.
This, however, was offered by the pleading of the defendant, and the defendant there says that he was always
ready and willing to account. It is plain that an account
could have been had from the defendant without any
trouble, and little, if any costs.

On the whole case then, if the plaintiff is willing that
this appeal should be dismissed without costs, I think this
may be done.

If the plaintiff will not assent to this, and insists upon
having the account, then he should, I think, pay the costs
of this appeal; which, except as to such account, will be
dismissed, and for this an order may be framed in apt
words. The plaintiff should not, I think, be ordered to
give security for the costs of any reference as to the
account.

MEREDITH, J.:—

Care must always be taken to avoid anything like a
dissipation of trust property in needless litigation, needless expense of any kind, and especially so in case of a
trust of this character, where the controlling hand is often
the hand likely to be most substantially benefited by the
litigation. Inability to keep down such expense is often
charged with the death of the insolvent laws of the Dominion. Assignments for the benefit of creditors ought not
to be permitted to be turned into assignments for the

benefit of solicitors; this should be distinctly understood, Judgment.
for there must always otherwise be great danger of that Meredith, J.
result, where as is so often the case there is a close connection between the assignee or the assignees' appointment
and the solicitors.

I am not intimating that there is anything of that kind
in this case. There seems to have been in it a substantial
subject for litigation, though there also was beyond doubt
a very substantial amount of litigation over it.

So far as the assignee or those acting for him are
accountable for that, he had the approval and instructions
of the body of the creditors; as well as the judgment
of the trial Judge in his favour at the outset.

The assignment took effect under the Act, and its special
provisions, as well as the duties and rights of trustees
generally, must be borne in mind.

It was one of the assignee's duties to protect the estate
against unjust claims; the Act expressly provides the
mode in which this is to be done: see sec. 20, sub-sec. (5).

The assignee's position between allowing a claim which
may turn out to be an invalid one to go without contestation, or to incur the costs of a contestation, must often be
a difficult one; and where he in such a case acts upon the
instructions or authority of the inspectors, and the great
body of unquestioned creditors, there ought to be some
pretty strong evidence of misconduct to deprive him of
reimbursement out of the estate.

It may seem hard that a creditor whose claim to rank
on the estate has been unsuccessfully contested, should
have his dividends largely reduced by such contestation,
that the costs should not be at least first chargeable
against the dividends of the opposing creditors; but it is
to be borne in mind that his claim is not reduced; that
still remains, except in so far as reduced by the dividend,
recoverable just as it always was from the debtor; and
that in administration proceedings creditors formerly were
worse off, for here the creditor gets all his costs out of the
estate. The general rule for the general benefit of the

body of creditors prevails, though it may, or even must,
sometimes work hardly upon some particular one.

The general rule plainly is that trustees, who have not
been guilty of misconduct, are entitled to be recouped their
costs; they are entitled to full indemnity out of the trust
estate against costs, charges, and expenses not improperly
incurred; the rule is stated and the cases are collected in
such works as Robson's Laws of Bankruptcy, 7th ed. p.
597; Lewin on Trusts, 9th ed. pp. 716-7, 387-8; Godefroi
on Trusts, 2nd ed., pp. 812-6; Tudor's Law of Charitable
Trusts, 3rd ed., p. 347; Morgan on Costs, 2nd ed., p. 398-9;
Perry on Trusts, 4th ed., vol. 6, p. 545; Burrill on Assignments, 6th ed., p. 499; and see *Ex parte Brown*, 17 Q. B. D
488; and see also R. S. O. [1887] ch. 110, sec. 1.

I have no doubt the general rule covers this case down
to the costs of the appeal to the Court of Appeal, at all
events; but as to those costs the cases seem to throw
considerable doubt upon the assignee's right to them; to
shew that he should have been satisfied with the adverse
judgment, and to have, perhaps, taken indemnity from those
who desired to carry the case further: see *Tucker* v. *Herna-
man*, 4 DeG. M. & G. 395; *Ex parte Russell*, 19 Ch. D. 588;
Re Walters, 34 Sol. Jour. 564; *Dillon* v. *Arkins*, 17 L. R.
Ir. 636; *Bruce* v. *Presbytery of Deer*, L. R. 1 Sc. App. 96.
But in all those cases the judgment was in the first instance adverse to the trustee; here the judgment in the
first instance was in his favour; here there is greater free-
dom of and more opportunity for appeals; the costs are
less; the result before the end is reached perhaps considerably more uncertain. Whatever might have been my conclusion upon this question if it had come before me in the first
instance, I cannot say that the learned trial Judge erred
in this respect, and so must agree in affirming his judgment wholly upon this branch of the case.

The assignee's litigation was fruitless, but it cannot be
said that it was "idle," nor that the cost amounting to nearly
one quarter of a trust fund was "wasted with impunity,"
nor that the case one in which the assignor might by a sim-

ple application to the Court have avoided all risk as well as
all litigation: see *In re Beddoe, Downes* v. *Beddoe,* [1893]
1 Ch. 547 ; nor can it be said that his course was a " persistence in unnecessary proceedings ; " and indeed I cannot
say that the learned Judge was wrong in considering that
the assignee's course was a reasonable conduct of a properly
defended action.

Upon this, the main question then, the motion in my
opinion fails, and must be dismissed.

But it is said that the plaintiff is entitled to an account
of the defendant's dealings with the trust estate ; the usual
order of reference in cases of this character.

That he doubtless was entitled to : that he might have
had upon the pleadings without going down to trial at all
for the defendant plainly pleads his readiness and willingness to account. But the plaintiff chose rather to bring
his action on for trial, and, in an unusual manner, to go
into an investigation there of the several matters of complaint which would have been the subject of enquiry
before the Master if the usual and more convenient mode
of procedure had been followed, and has had a considered
judgment pronounced upon them by the learned trial
Judge, so that it becomes quite a different question now
whether he should have such a reference. Then, having
regard to the main question as well as the other minor
questions between the parties, an enquiry was his right,
afterward it was a matter of grace. He cannot of right
have his account twice taken : he cannot be permitted of
right to have his case heard piecemeal : failing at the trial,
to have practically a new trial. It would be the more
unfair if as it is said the costs of that trial cannot be
recovered because he has no exigible property.

Now should he have the reference as a matter of indulgence ? Having regard to the evidence upon the only
matters in respect of which it is sought—in respect of which
it is claimed that any advantage could be gained by him—
I would have been inclined to say no ; for it does seem to
me that the result of such a reference would be practically

Judgment.

Meredith, J.

"fruitless and idle," and a large increase of costs in litigation which has already gone far enough, if not too far;
and which the offer to assign to the plaintiff all the outstanding estate leaves absolutely without any excuse. We
need not trouble ourselves with any questionings of the
wisdom of the offer; the assignee has the legal power to
assign them, and if he have not the consent of all persons
concerned, he is perfectly good for any liability he may
incur to any one in so doing. But if the plaintiff really
have confidence in his claim, let him take it upon the terms
imposed by the trial Judge. We ought not to interfere
with the discretion of the trial Judge in the reasonable
terms he has imposed, as the price of an indulgence
granted.

I would be inclined to dismiss this motion with costs,
but do not object to the disposition of the case as proposed
by the Chancellor.

A. H. F. L.

[CHANCERY DIVISION.]

CARSON v. SIMPSON.

Fixtures — Execution — Mortgage of Fixtures as Chattels — Mortgage of Realty — Discharge of Chattel Mortgage.

The fact that fixtures affixed to the freehold in the usual way have sometimes been mortgaged as chattels, and on other occasions have passed
with a mortgage of the freehold does not render them exigible to an
execution against goods if at the time of the seizure the chattel mortgages are non-existent, and a mortgage of the freehold is in existence as
a first charge thereon.

THIS was an appeal from a judgment of ROBERTSON, J.,   Statement.
in an interpleader issue ordered in an action of *Simpson
v. Gardiner,* between Robert J. Carson, as claimant, and
Isaac Simpson, an execution creditor, as defendant, as to
the ownership of certain fixtures.

The issue was tried at Kingston, on 20th March, 1894,
before ROBERTSON, J.

Walkem, Q. C., appeared for Carson.
Macdonnell, Q. C., appeared for one Morrice, who had
become the assignee of Simpson's judgment.

It appeared that on August 13th, 1881, one Gardiner,
the then owner of a biscuit factory in the city of Kingston,
in which there were certain machinery fixtures at the
time, mortgaged the factory to the trustees of the Horsey
estate.   Two days afterwards (August 15th, 1881),
Gardiner, by chattel mortgage, mortgaged the machinery
then in the factory and some other machinery then in the
city of Guelph, which were about to be and were afterwards
removed to Kingston and erected as fixtures in the factory,
to one Forbes.   On November 3rd, 1881, Gardiner gave a
chattel mortgage on all the fixtures to the Horsey trustees,
and out of the proceeds of that mortgage the chattel mortgage to Forbes, was paid off.
On June 24th, 1884, Gardiner made another mortgage of

the factory in which the fixtures were, to one Harding, which was assigned to Morrice, on October 18th, 1886. Morrice had also become the assignee of a judgment recovered by Simpson against Gardiner on October 3rd, 1885, and he commenced an action on both the mortgage and the judgment. To that action, the claimant, Carson, was made a party, as he was entitled to redeem Morrice, being a tenant of the premises previous to the making of the mortgage to Harding, and Carson did redeem him, paying the amount found due and taking an assignment from Morrice of the Harding mortgage in November, 1887. On August 16th, 1888, the sheriff seized the fixtures as chattels, under an execution on the Simpson judgment. The Horsey chattel mortgage was kept in force until 1889, when it was allowed to expire.

In 1892, Carson also became the assignee of the mortgage of the factory to the Horsey trustees, and the question to be tried was whether the fixtures were part of the realty and passed under the Harding mortgage, or whether they were chattels, and as such, exigible under the execution.

April 17th, 1894. ROBERTSON, J. :—(After reviewing the facts.)

The chattel mortgages, therefore, must be treated as having ceased to be any charge on the goods and chattels therein mentioned at the date of the Harding mortgage, and it did not appear that any had been since that date granted.

At the time then of the granting of the Harding mortgage, these goods and chattels were all fixtures, and a part of the freehold, and Harding had the right to treat them as such, notwithstanding the prior action of his mortgagor; and as afterwards appears, his assignee, Morrice, so treated and claimed them against his assignee Carson.

Morrice claimed them as part of the freehold under the Harding mortgage, which was prior to the execution in *Simpson* v. *Gardiner*, and which became the property of

Carson, and in regard to which Morrice charged Carson
against his claim on the Harding mortgage an occupation
rent for the whole premises, including all the trade fixtures
therein, which the Master found to be at the rate of $350,
per year, and which I find should be made up by allowing
at the rate of $250 per year for the machinery or trade
fixtures, and $100 per year for the land and buildings.

In my judgment it would be most inequitable to allow
Mr. Morrice now to say : " True, it is, I made you account
to me as a subsequent incumbrancer, under a judgment in
which I held an execution against the goods and chattels
of the mortgagor, you having acquired from me, by right
of your equity of redemption, as prior mortgagee of the
lands and premises under which mortgage I claimed to
hold all the trade fixtures in the building on the lands as
part of the realty, and as part of my security.   Nevertheless, these very trade fixtures, which you so acquired, I
now claim the right to sell as the goods and chattels of
the mortgagor Gardiner, under my subsequent claim as
execution creditor against him.   And I do so because such
original owner, Gardiner, dealt with such trade fixtures at
one time as ordinary goods and chattels."

As between Gardiner, the mortgagor, and Harding, the
mortgagee, there was no such dealing in regard to the
trade fixtures.   The evidence shews that they were so
affixed to the freehold that they could not be removed
without destroying the character of the premises, as they
stood at the date of this mortgage, and *per se* passed under the said mortgage ; and there is no evidence of a contrary intention as between mortgagor and mortgagee, and
whatever may have been done by Gardiner previous to the
date of such mortgage, no subsequent chattel mortgage
could interfere with his, Harding's, security under the
mortgage in question.

The question, however, does not arise between two claimants, one being a real estate mortgagee and the other a
mortgagee of chattels fixed as " trade fixtures" to the
mortgaged real estate ; but between the former and one

who claims that these "trade fixtures" are liable to be sold under an execution against goods and chattels. In the one case I can see that the holder of the chattel mortgage might have rights, which do not attach to a mere execution creditor. If there had been no previous dealing by the owner of the trade fixtures as mere chattels, there would be no difficulty. The title acquired by Carson under the Harding mortgage would, in my judgment, be unassailable, and the mere fact that the owner had on a former or later occasion dealt with them temporarily as chattels, does not destroy the rights of Carson under the Harding mortgage; but I do not think it necessary to rest my judgment on that view of the case.

Carson now claims that when he became the assignee of the Harding mortgage from Morrice, and Morrice having treated that mortgage while it belonged to him as covering all these trade fixtures, and having compelled him, Carson, to account for an occupation rent of these fixtures, as well as having required him to account for the sale money received by him for the revolving oven, mentioned in the Master's Report, $300, all of which was deducted from the amount of the mortgage money, and sums paid by him, as set forth in the Master's report, he, Morrice, is now estopped and cannot, or should not, be allowed to take them as goods and chattels liable to be severed from the freehold, and sold under his execution.

I think this contention is right and proper under the circumstances presented to me, and I therefore find the issue in Carson's favour.

I have not considered the effect of the mortgage from James A. Gardiner to the trustees of the Horsey estate of date 13th August, 1881, assigned to Carson on the 5th of August, 1892, and put in by him at the trial, as it was objected to by Mr. Macdonnell, on the grounds that it was not referred to in Carson's original claim, on which the interpleader order was made, as it was not necessary for me to do so, in view of the grounds on which I have disposed of the issue.

I have referred to and considered the following cases: Judgment. *Keefer* v. *Merrill*, 6 A. R. at p. 126 ; *Dixon* v. *Hunter*, 29 Robertson, J. Gr. at p. 80 ; *Rogers* v. *The Ontario Bank*, 21 O. R. 416 ; *Rose* v. *Hope*, 22 C. P. 482 ; *Stevens* v. *Barfoot*, 13 A. R. at p. 371 ; *Joseph Hall Manufacturing Co.* v. *Hazlitt*, 11 A. R. at p. 752 ; *Dewar* v. *Mallory*, 26 Gr. at p. 623 ; *Gough* v. *Wood*, Weekly Notes, March 3rd. 1894, at p. 37 ; and several other cases referred to in the foregoing.

From this judgment the defendant appealed to the Divisional Court, and the appeal was argued on June 18th and 19th, 1894, before BOYD, C., and FERGUSON, J.

Langton, Q.C., for the appeal. The evidence shews that the fixtures were severed from the realty and so became personalty by virtue of the chattel mortgages made before the mortgage of the realty was made to Harding, and that as they did not pass under the Harding mortgage of the realty, Carson did not take them under the assignment of that mortgage to him. I refer to *Rose* v. *Hope*, 22 C. P. 482 ; *Joseph Hall Manufacturing Co.* v. *Hazlitt*, 11 A. R. at p. 752 ; *Stephens* v. *Barfoot*, 13 A. R. at p. 371.

Walkem, Q. C., contra. The evidence shews the machinery became fixtures, and consequently would pass under a mortgage of the realty. These fixtures did pass under the mortgage to Harding, subject of course, to whatever interests were secured by any previous chattel mortgages, and when these chattel mortgages became extinct, the fixtures became part of the realty. In *Rose* v. *Hope*, 22 C. P. 482, the point actually decided does not carry the doctrine any further than is necessary for the protection of the chattel mortgagee. It does not enure to the benefit of an execution creditor. I refer to *Whitmore* v. *Empson*, 23 Beav. 313 ; Amos and Ferrard's Law of Fixtures, 3rd ed., 312 ; *Ex p. Daglish*, 29 L. T. N. S. 168 ; *Ex p. Daglish*, *In re Wilde*, L. R. 8 Ch. at p. 1080. As to the rule that land includes fixtures, unless the contrary intention appears. See *Southport, etc. Banking Co.* v. *Thompson*, 58 L. T. N. S. at p. 148 ; *Stevens* v. *Barfoot*, 13 A. R. 366 ; *Gough* v. *Wood*, 70 L. T. N. S. 297.   The sheriff had no right to seize : *Rogers* v. *The Ontario Bank*, 21 O. R. at p. 420 ; *Gough* v. *Wood, supra,* at p. 300.

Langton, Q. C., in reply, referred to *Dewar* v. *Mallory*, 26 Gr. at p. 623; Amos and Ferrard's Law of Fixtures, 3rd ed., 393.

June 30th, 1894.   BOYD, C. :—

On 15th of August, 1881, Gardiner made a chattel mortgage to Forbes covering two kinds of property : (1) being machinery then in the biscuit factory, and (2) being articles then in Guelph and about to be removed to Kingston and erected as fixtures in the said factory.

The then existing fixtures would, however, be covered by a prior mortgage on the land given by the owner Gardiner to the trustees of the Horsey estate two days before on the 13th August, 1881, which, by assignment, has come to the hands of the interpleader plaintiff Carson (on 5th August, 1892).

The other contemplated fixtures would, however, be subject to the chattel mortgage, and after being affixed, they were again the subject of a chattel mortgage made by Gardiner to the said Horsey trustees on 3rd November, 1881.   These trustees so dealt with the prior Forbes mortgage as to have it released or discharged, so that the Horsey trustees became first and only mortgagees on both land and fixtures.

The next dealing was a mortgage of the lots by the biscuit manufacturer, Gardiner, to James Harding, on the 24th June, 1884, for value, and registered.   This instrument in terms mentions only the land, but did it not also become a second mortgage on the affixed chattels ?   That is the point in the case.

This Harding mortgage was assigned to Morrice, the present claimant, on 18th October, 1886.   He had obtained

a judgment against Gardiner for $1,553, and began an
action upon the mortgage and judgment in February,
1887.

Carson, the tenant of the biscuit factory, was made
a defendant as entitled to redeem, and after accounts duly
taken, he did redeem Morrice in November, 1887, and obtained a transfer of his interest as mortgagee under the
Harding mortgage. The plaintiff's claim in *Morrice* v.
Baily and Carson, sets up that on the lands stands a biscuit factory in which is a large amount of valuable plant
and machinery.

After this redemption of the Harding mortgage the
sheriff made a seizure of the said fixtures as personal
chattels under the Morrice judgment against Gardiner on
16th August, 1888, and the question is as to the title to
these things at that date as between Carson and the
execution creditor.

For the purposes of the Forbes and Horsey chattel mortgages there was a severance of the chattels. But at the
date of the seizure, the Forbes mortgage was at an end and
only the Horsey chattel mortgage existed. This expired
for want of renewal in the year 1889, so that it was in
force at the date of the seizure. But I think that the
whole place, land and fixtures, was mortgaged to Harding
by the mortgage of June, 1884, so as to indicate the intention of the owner Gardiner to reunite the property temporarily severed by the Horsey chattel mortgage, and
thereupon the whole became land, subject to the incum-
bency of that intermediate chattel mortgage. Then when
the Horsey mortgage became extinct, in 1889, the temporary character of personalty disappeared and the increased value went to feed the land owner's title, and was
not intercepted by the execution against goods.

Set aside the prior dealings and look at the case as when
the Harding mortgage was given, and that would attach
unquestionably upon the land and machinery as one concern, of which the character was realty. No place would
be left thereafter for an execution against goods to attach

upon the fixtures as against the mortgagee. The mortgagee, Morrice, as assignee of Harding, having passed this
title to Carson, cannot now claim as entitled to part of the
property as fixtures under cover of a subsequent execution
against goods. The mortgage of the freehold would of
itself carry all fixtures then annexed to the land. The advantage of having a separation between the land and the
fixtures by express provision to that effect is that the
mortgagee of trade machinery may be able to sell them
apart from the land property mortgaged: *In re Yates,
Batcheldor v. Yates*, 38 Ch. D., at pp. 126, 129, which otherwise would not be permitted by the Court.

I incline to think the true view to be that the chattel
mortgage is not to be operative to a greater extent than is
needful for the purpose of that mortgage. In this light
when the chattels, mortgaged to Forbes, were actually
annexed to the freehold premises covered by the Horsey
trustees mortgage, the property of the mortgagor in those
chattels which was an equity of redemption would form
part of the security of the pre-existing land mortgage. It
needed not, therefore, a distinct mortgage upon the chattels
afterwards to give them to the Horsey trustees subject to
that Forbes mortgage.

The question of the registry laws has not been dealt
with in the cases; but that ought not to be disregarded in considering the position of the Harding mortgage. At the time that was given, the premises were
a going factory with all the fixtures, now in question,
attached to the freehold, and why should not the operation
of the registry laws enable a mortgagee for value without
notice of the chattel mortgage (which is not registered
against the land) to prevail against that chattel mortgage?

The point does not here arise because of the disappear-
ance of the chattel mortgage for want of registration and
renewal. But the great weight of authority in the States
favours this result. Certainly if the doctrine is not to
prevail as against the prior chattel mortgage to the extent
necessary for its satisfaction, it should obtain to give the

Judgment.

Boyd, C.

mortgagee of the realty all that exists as physically annexed to the land, including the equity of redemption in the constructive chattels.

This position is not counter to the view held by Spragge, C., in *Dewar* v. *Mallory*, 26 Gr. at p. 623, for the giving of the mortgage on the land after the chattel mortgage (without excepting the fixtures) manifests sufficiently an intention that the character of personalty should no longer be retained. See *Campbell* v. *Roddy*, 44 N. J. Eq. 244, and cases collected in Jones on Chattel Mortgage, 4th ed., ss. 123-137; *Whitmore* v. *Empson*, 23 Beav. 313. The judgment should, in my opinion, be affirmed.

FERGUSON, J. :—

This was the trial of an interpleader issue, ordered in an action, of *Simpson* v. *Gardiner*, at the instance of the sheriff. In the issue, Robert J. Carson is the plaintiff and claimant, and Isaac Simpson is the defendant. The question is whether or not certain goods and chattels in the premises known as the Gardiner biscuit factory, in the city of Kingston, a list whereof is given by a schedule attached to the issue which were seized by the sheriff on the 16th day of August, 1888, under a writ of *fieri facias* in that action were, or some part of them was, at the time of such seizure, the property of Robert J. Carson, as against the execution creditor, Isaac Simpson.

At the trial it was admitted that the property in question and called chattel property was affixed to the freehold " in the usual way." It seems that it was and is machinery for the purpose of manufacturing biscuits, and before us, in the argument, it was admitted that it was and is affixed to the building in which it is in such a way that *primâ facie* it would be fixtures and part of the freehold.

James D. Morrice, the assignee of the defendant in the issue, represents as owner thereof, the rights that were of the execution creditor, and Robert J. Carson was, and is the owner of the freehold and all the interest in it at the

time of the seizure. The question seems to be whether or
not the property in dispute was at the time of the seizure
by the sheriff, fixtures, and hence part of the freehold. If
it was not, and was chattels, it seems that the defendant in
the issue, would be entitled to succeed, but if the property
were fixtures and part of the freehold, then Carson, the
plaintiff in the issue, should succeed.

The finding and decision of the learned Judge, before
whom the issue was tried, was in favour of Carson, the
plaintiff in the issue, and from this is the appeal.

On the 13th day of August, 1881, Gardiner, who was
then the owner of the land, executed a mortgage of the
land in favour of Horsey and others as trustees of the
Horsey estate, securing the sum of $1,600. This mortgage
simply describes the land referring to the numbers of the
lots as the property mortgaged. A part of the property in
dispute here was then in the factory and affixed to the
building.

On the 15th day of August, 1881, Gardiner executed a
chattel mortgage in favour of one Forbes, of the then town
of Guelph, to secure $950. This was upon certain
machinery and other property in the same factory, and
certain other machinery and property then in Guelph,
which was afterwards removed to Kingston and placed
and affixed in this factory by Gardiner. And on the 3rd
day of November, 1881, a chattel mortgage was made by
Gardiner in favour of the said trustees of the Horsey estate
to secure the sum of $1,500, upon all the machinery, etc., in
the same factory, and so far as can be seen, this embraced
all the machinery, etc., that had been brought from Guelph
as well as what was before in the factory. The $950
secured by the mortgage of the 15th of August, 1881, was
embraced in the $1,500 secured by this mortgage, and the
$950 mortgage to Forbes was satisfied in this transac-
tion. This $1,500 chattel mortgage was kept on foot as
a mortgage till after the time of the seizure by the sheriff,
but it has since been or become satisfied or permitted to
lapse.

On the 21st day of June, 1884, Gardiner executed a <u>Judgment.</u>
mortgage upon the land in favour of Harding. This <u>Ferguson, J.</u>
describes the land, and does not mention any machinery or
fixtures, by way of exception or otherwise. On the 18th
day of October, 1886, this mortgage was assigned by
Harding to Morrice. This assigns the mortgage debt and
the land, making no mention of machinery or fixtures.
And on the 7th day of November, 1887, Morrice assigned
the same mortgage to Carson, the plaintiff in the issue, and
in this assignment there is a reservation in favour of the
assignor Morrice of the lien or charge upon the land that
he had under and by virtue of the judgment and execution
in the action, *Simpson* v. *Gardiner*.

This assignment contains a recital in respect to proceedings that had been had upon the mortgage to which Carson
was a party by reason of his being a tenant of the premises, entitled to redeem the same, and that he had paid
the sum of $1,598.50 as the price of redemption, and that
in consideration of such payment, Carson was entitled to
an assignment of the mortgage.

The writ against goods in that action under which the
present claim is made, was tested the 3rd day of October,
1885, and from the renewals upon it, it appears to have
been delivered to the sheriff immediately thereafter,
although the seizure was not till the 16th day of August,
1888. I am unable to perceive how the reservation in the
assignment can affect the present issue.

On the 5th day of August, 1892, the trustees of the
Horsey estate assigned their mortgage of the 13th of
August, 1881, to Carson, for the expressed consideration
of $2,290 and some costs.

It appears that on the 5th day of November, 1885, one
Baily executed a chattel mortgage on this property in
favour of Carson, in some complicated transactions between
them, but this was allowed to drop, as being valueless.
As conceded on all hands and before stated, the property in question was and is affixed to the freehold
and *primâ facie* was part of the land. This was so at

the time of the making of the mortgage to Harding on the 21st of June, 1884, under which the proceedings had in respect of it and the assignment of it to him, Carson claims.   There was then upon the property in question the Horsey chattel mortgage, which had been made in November, 1881, and which was afterwards permitted to lapse. Gardiner made the mortgage to Harding, the land having these fixtures upon it, and so far as known, Harding had no notice or knowledge of the existence of the Horsey chattel mortgage.

When Morrice was the owner of the Harding mortgage, he must be taken to have considered that it embraced the property in question as part of the freehold, for he charged and recovered from Carson, occupation rent, for it : and this is found as a fact by the learned trial Judge, and in his statement of claim, in *Morrice* v. *Baily*, he refers to the factory, plant and machinery as part of the property embraced in the Harding mortgage on which he brought his action.

The mortgage of the 13th August, 1881, from Gardiner to the trustees of the Horsey estate, would, as it seems to me, cover and embrace the part of the property in question that was then upon and affixed to the land, for at that period, there had not been any mortgage of any part of this as chattels, nor, so far as seen, any act of the owner, the mortgagor, manifesting an intention to sever the land and fixtures. And the title to this mortgage came to Carson by purchase in August, 1892. The part of the machinery and fixtures now in dispute that came from Guelph and was placed and affixed in this factory, could not have been embraced in the chattel mortgage of the 3rd of November, 1881, in favour of the trustees of the Horsey estate at the time that mortgage was made, but the other part of the property in dispute was, I think, covered by this Horsey mortgage of the 13th of August, 1881, as being part of the freehold.

At the time of the making of the chattel mortgage of the 3rd of November, 1881, Gardiner was not, as I think, in a position to affect the character of the part of the ^{Judgment.} property now in dispute covered by the land mortgaged _{Ferguson, J.} to the trustees of the Horsey estate by any statement of intention respecting it and as against the rights under this mortgage of the land to these trustees, the chattel mortgage of the 3rd November, 1881, was good only in respect of the part of the property in dispute here that had been brought from Guelph and affixed in the factory after the making of that land mortgage.

By these two mortgages in favour of these trustees, they were mortgagees by virtue of the mortgage upon the land of the freehold and the part of the machinery and fixtures that were there at the time that mortgage was executed : and by virtue of the chattel mortgage, they were mortgagees of the remaining part of the machinery and fixtures that were there at the time of the execution of thé mortgage.   Matters seem to have stood in this way until the time of the mortgage on the land in favour of Harding on the 21st day of June, 1884.   It would of course make little, if any, difference to these trustees whether they held a part of these fixtures (the part that was there on the 13th of August, 1881), under their mortgage of the land, or under their chattel mortgage.

In the case *Rose* v. *Hope*, 22 C. P. 482, the chattel mortgage upon the fixtures was made before the mortgage on the freehold, and the holding was that it was good as against the subsequent mortgage on the freehold.

In the case *Dewar* v. *Mallory*, 26 Gr. 618, the mortgage upon the freehold and the mortgage upon the fixtures were made contemporaneously, and there was the plainest possible manifestation of the intention of the mortgagor that the fixtures and the freehold should be properties distinct one from the other.   In the present case it does not appear to me that there is that plain manifestation of intention on the part of Gardiner, but rather only the making of the chattel mortgage for a temporary purpose.   But be this as it may, while the property was in this condition with regard to the encumbrances upon it, Gardiner executed in

Judgment.

Ferguson, J.

favour of Harding the mortgage of the 24th June, 1884, describing in it the freehold to which all this machinery, etc., was most certainly affixed, it being, as the evidence shews, the most important and valuable part of the property, for the building was worth little without it. And in this mortgage no exception is made regarding the fixtures or any part of them. Even if what had been done before this time should be considered a manifestation by the owner of an intention that the fixtures and freehold should be and remain severed, and of different characters as property, I cannot but think · that the giving of this mortgage in these circumstances should be considered a manifestation of a counter intention, and that by the mortgage Harding became a mortgagee of the whole of the property, fixtures and freehold, subject only to the rights of prior mortgagees and encumbrancers upon it or part of it. And this is the view in which this Harding mortgage was treated by Morrice himself when he was the holder and owner of it, and compelled Carson to pay him an occupation rent for the fixtures as well as the freehold, and had the price of redemption to be paid, and paid by Carson, measured by the value of the fixtures as well as that of the freehold.

Carson claims or supports his claim under the Harding mortgage. Morrice makes no claim under any chattel mortgage, and can succeed only when it appears that the fixtures, the property in dispute, are chattels of the execution defendant, exigible under the writ at the time of the seizure on the 16th day of August, 1888, and this, I think, does not appear.

I am of the opinion that the judgment appealed from finding the issue in favour of Carson should be affirmed with costs.

G. A. B.

RE JENKINS AND THE CORPORATION OF THE TOWNSHIP OF ENNISKILLEN.

Municipal Corporations—Drainage—New Outlet—Municipal Act, 1892, secs. 569, 585—Petition—Township By-law—Adjoining Townships—Agreement as to Proportion of Cost—Report of Engineer—Description of Lands.

A township council finding that a government drain in the township did not carry off the water, by reason of the natural flow being in another direction, accepted a report made by their engineer and passed a by-law adopting a scheme for a new drain leading from the middle of the government drain into an adjoining township, where it was to find an outlet :—

Held, that the proposed drain properly came within the description of a new outlet, although not at the end of the government drain, and although the former outlet remained to serve to carry off a part of the water ; and, so long as the proposed drain was designed merely as an outlet for the water from the government drain, it might, under section 585 of the Municipal Act of 1892, be provided for without any petition under section 569, even although it should incidentally benefit the locality through which it ran, nothing being included in the plan beyond what was reasonably requisite for the purpose intended.

Although a township council is not powerless with regard to the drainage report of its engineer, it is contrary to the spirit and meaning of the Act that two adjoining councils should agree upon a drainage scheme, and upon the proportion of its cost to be borne by each, and that the engineer of one of them should be instructed to make a report for carrying out the scheme and charging each municipality with the sums agreed on ; for such a course would interfere with the independent judgment of the engineer, and pledge each township in advance not to appeal against the share of the cost imposed upon it, to the possible detriment of the property owners assessed for the portions of that share.

And where such a course was pursued, a by-law of one of the councils adopting the engineer's report was quashed.

In describing lands for assessment, "the north-east part," even with the addition of the acreage, is an ambiguous description ; and *quære* as to the effect upon the validity of a by-law.

APPLICATION to quash a by-law of the township of Statement. Enniskillen for levying a drainage assessment, under the following circumstances :

Upwards of twenty years ago a government drain, known as government drain No. 1, had been constructed from the 9th concession of Brooke, near the north end of that township, southerly through the township along the side road between lots 3 and 4 to the concession line between the 1st and 2nd concessions, where it turned to the east, and finally emptied into a creek leading into the river Sydenham. From the head of the drain to about the middle of the 5th concession, that is to say, for about half its length, the natural fall was steadily from the north to the south, but to the south of that point the ground rose in places, and there was much difficulty in making it carry off the water which came down from the north. The corporation of Brooke had spent $5,000 in endeavouring to remedy this defect, and to make the south part of the drain do the work for which it was constructed, but with little success; the water backed up in the drain so as to overflow the lands in the north part of the 5th concession of Brooke, west of the drain, and the adjoining portions of the township of Enniskillen, which lies immediately to the west of Brooke.

The township council of Brooke in 1892 instructed Mr. C. A. Jones, their engineer, to examine and report upon the best means of obtaining a proper outlet for the surplus water coming down the government drain from the north. He reported that the natural fall for the water was not along the portion of the government drain lying to the south of the fifth concession, but westerly into the township of Enniskillen to the head of a stream called Black creek, which had its source in the second lot of Enniskillen lying to the west of the town line of Brooke and Enniskillen. The engineer then completed a scheme for a new drain leading from the government drain, a little to the north of the centre of the 5th concession of Brooke, west to the town line, and thence to the head of Black creek. The total estimated cost of the work was $9,412, of which $2,524 was assessed against lands and roads in Enniskillen, and $6,888 upon lands and roads in Brooke.

The township council of Brooke then passed a by-law in March, 1893, for carrying this scheme into effect, and for raising their proportion of the cost, treating the scheme as one coming within the provisions of section 585 of the Municipal Act of 1892, and, therefore, as not requiring a petition of ratepayers for its foundation.

The corporation of the township of Enniskillen gave Statement.
notice of appeal against the assessment, contending, among
other things, that the amount charged against them was
too high, and that against the township of Brooke was too
low.

Conferences then took place between members of the
respective councils and their engineers ; the council of
Enniskillen insisted that if the new drain were made, the
course of Black creek should be straightened so as to give
more fall to the water, and to ensure its being carried off;
and in order further to prevent any detention of the water,
they wished the drain carried a few rods to the south of
the course mentioned in the by-law.

On 21st October, 1893, the following minute was made
in the minute-book of the township council of Brooke :
"Letter received from reeve of Enniskillen stating that
their council were willing to assume $500 of the extra cost
of constructing the new outlet drain according to their
request.   Moved by Mr. Sutherland, seconded by Mr. Mc-
Intyre, that the clerk instruct engineer to make out his
report and assessment for this drain, based on the offer of
Enniskillen council, and now accepted by this council.
Carried."   On 23rd October, 1893, the township clerk
wrote to Mr. Jones, the township engineer, as follows :—

" Dear Sir.—Brooke council is in receipt of a letter from
Mr. Ingram, who, on behalf of the council of Enniskillen,
states they are ' willing to assume $500 of the additional
cost of deepening and straightening' the No. 1 outlet drain
in and into Enniskillen.   Brooke council have accepted
this offer, and have directed me to request you to make
your report and assessment on this basis * * *.   Mr.
Ingram mentions or asks that you make the assessment on
lots in Enniskillen."

Upon receiving these instructions, the engineer prepared
a report upon the southerly course, leaving out some three
or four lots assessed for benefit in his former report.   The
estimated cost of the whole work under the new conditions was $11,660, being an increase of $2,248.   This increase he divided *pro rata* between the two townships,

upon the basis of the sums originally charged against
each township by his original report. The proportion
chargeable against Enniskillen upon this basis would have
been $3.126, but he fixed it at $3,100, being an increase of
$576 over the sum [charged to Enniskillen by the former
report. Having arrived at the sum chargeable to each
township in this way, he proceeded to alter the assessment
of the lots and roads affected. In Enniskillen he increased
the assessment on the township in respect of roads from
$550 to $760, and that on the lands apart from roads from
$1,974 to $2,340. The township council of Brooke, upon
receiving this report, repealed their former by-law and
passed a new one in accordance with the new report. The
township council of Enniskillen afterwards passed a by-
law for levying their proportion of the moneys required
for the work.

The present motion was by an owner of lands in Enniskillen assessed by the report of the engineer, to quash the
by-law of that township, upon the following, amongst
other, grounds :—

1st. That the township council of Brooke had no power
to pass the by-law in question without being called upon
to do so by a petition signed by the requisite proportion
of property owners interested, as prescribed by section
569.

2nd. That the report of the engineer, upon which the
by-law was passed, was not based upon the independent
judgment of the engineer, but upon the agreement of the
township council.

3rd. That a number of parcels intended to be assessed
were so insufficiently described in the report and by-law,
that the sums assessed against them could not be charged
against any lands.

The motion was argued on the 18th July, 1894, before
STREET, J., in Court.

Aylesworth, Q. C., and *Shaunessy*, for the motion.

McCarthy, Q. C., and *Moncrieff*, Q. C., for the corporation of the township of Enniskillen.

July 21, 1894. STREET, J. :—   Judgment.

                                                       Street, J.

I think that the township council of Brooke must be
held upon the evidence before me to have had the right
under section 585 of the Municipal Act of 1892 to undertake the works provided for by their by-law without the
petition required by section 569. Their object seems to
have been to relieve the neighbourhood of the 5th concession of the water brought down to that locality from
the north by the government drain, and retained there
because the southern portion of that drain was unable to
carry it further. They had tried at large expense to increase the capacity of that portion of the drain, and had
found that their money had produced no lasting result,
because the natural fall of the water was in another
direction. Under these circumstances, the drain recommended by their engineer and provided for by their by-law
properly comes within the description of a new outlet,
even though it be placed in the middle instead of at the
end of the drain, and although the former outlet remained
to serve to carry off the water which was left to run in
the southern portion of the drain. So long as the proposed
new outlet was designed merely as an outlet for the water
from the old drain, it might, under section 585, be provided for without any petition, even although, in carrying
out the object for which it was intended, it should incidentally benefit the locality through which it should run.
I cannot find upon the evidence here that anything has
been included in the plan of this outlet drain beyond
what was reasonably thought requisite for the purpose for
which it was intended.

The drain provided for in the first report of the engineer
was expected to bring a great deal of water from Brooke
into Black creek, and the Enniskillen council seem to have
feared that without some additional work upon Black
creek, the capacity of that stream would be too heavily
tried, and that the water would not be carried off fast
enough to avoid damage; they therefore suggested a

slightly different starting point, and the improvement of the course of Black creek, offering in the event of their proposal being accepted not only to abandon the appeal which they had begun from the assessment made against them under the scheme, but to consent to pay a further sum of $500 towards the increased cost of the drain proposed by them.

The Brooke council at once assented to this proposal and passed a resolution instructing their engineer to prepare a new report upon the basis proposed by Enniskillen, and he was so instructed by the township clerk. In his new report he clearly appears to have acted upon the agreement of the two councils, although he charged Enniskillen with $576, instead of $500, of the additional expense. He took the original amounts charged against the two townships in his first report and apportioned the additional cost between them in about the same proportion, instead of guiding himself entirely and absolutely by the amount of benefit derived by the different parcels of land in each township from the proposed drain.

The engineer acting under these sections is exercising functions of a judicial nature, and is bound to apportion the cost of the work amongst the different parcels of land receiving benefit from it, strictly according to the benefit derived, according to the best of his skill, judgment, and ability; each person and municipality charged with a portion of the cost is entitled to the advantage of his un-biassed judgment. The aggregate of the sums charged against the various lands benefited in each municipality form the sum total charged against that municipality. If the municipality is dissatisfied with the sum total of the assessment, it may appeal to the Drainage Referee to have it corrected, and when once finally settled, there remains only the task imposed on the Court of Revision of each township of settling disputes between the persons assessed, or who should have been assessed, as to the proportions in which the sum total charged against the township is to be borne *inter se*, for the aggregate cannot be changed.

Although, therefore, as pointed out in *Corporation of Raleigh* v. *Williams*, [1893] A. C. 540, a township council is not powerless with regard to the drainage report of its engineer, but may return it to him for alterations, it is clearly contrary to the spirit and meaning of the Act that two adjoining township councils should agree upon a drainage scheme and upon the proportions of its cost to be borne by each, and that then the engineer of one of them should be instructed to make a report for carrying out the scheme and charging each municipality with the sums agreed on. Such a course is calculated to interfere with the independent judgment which the engineer should be left free to bring to bear upon every detail of the scheme, and pledges each township in advance not to appeal against the share of the cost imposed on it, to the possible detriment of the property owners assessed for the portions of that share.

There is sufficient evidence here to shew that the engineer was not intended to exercise an unfettered judgment in making his assessment upon the lands in Enniskillen, and that he, in fact, acted substantially upon the lines laid down for him in the township clerk's letter of instructions. I refer particularly to his own evidence, from which I think it is evident that he felt himself required to distribute this sum of $600, or thereabouts, which was being added to the assessment of Enniskillen, amongst the lands and roads which were being benefited; he adds $210 to the assessment in respect of the roads in that township, and is unable to say that the added expenditure will have the effect of benefiting them to any appreciable extent; and he adds sums to the assessment of lots without being able to say that they will receive a correspondingly increased benefit from the straightening of the creek.

In other words, he appears to have reversed the proper mode of assessment; he started out with an arbitrary increase of $576 in the total assessment of Enniskillen, and then proceeded to distribute the increase as best he could amongst the lands affected, instead of in the first place

Judgment.

Street, J.

ascertaining the benefit derived by each parcel from the work and then charging it with a share of the whole cost in proportion to the benefit it derived. The Legislature did not intend that the sums to be assessed against the lands affected by drains constructed under these clauses should be governed by arrangements made between the councils of adjoining townships, but endeavoured to secure that they should be fixed in each case by a sworn professional man upon his own skill and judgment. In the present case the two councils have taken a course calculated to trammel and interfere with the judgment of the engineer, and therefore the by-law of the township of Enniskillen should not be allowed to stand, and must be quashed with costs.

It is unnecessary that I should deal with the other questions raised by the motion. I may say, however, that a number of the parcels intended to be assessed appear to be described in such a way as to leave in uncertainty the precise parcel meant. The north-east part or south-east part or centre part of a lot, even with the addition of the acreage, is generally, if not always, an ambiguous description, to say the least of it. What the effect of such descriptions upon the validity of the by-law might be, is a question which may be avoided by so framing them as to avoid any ambiguity.

By-law quashed with costs.

E. B. B.

[CHANCERY DIVISION.]

RE ONTARIO FORGE AND BOLT COMPANY (LIMITED).

Company—Winding-up—R. S. C. ch. 129, sec. 3—52 Vic. ch. 32, sec. 3 (D.)—Voluntary Winding-up — Compulsory Liquidation — "Doing Business in Canada."

There is no clashing between sec. 3 of the Winding-up Act, R. S. C. ch. 129, and sec. 3 of the Winding-up Amendment Act, 52 Vic. ch. 32; the latter Act provides for the voluntary winding-up of the companies falling within its provisions, and not for their compulsory liquidation, which is provided for by the former.

A company incorporated under an Act of the Province of Ontario, and carrying on business in Ontario, is "doing business in Canada" within the meaning of sec. 3 of the original Act.

PETITION by the Bank of British North America for an order for the winding-up of the company under R. S. C. ch. 129 and amending Acts. *Statement.*

The petition alleged, *inter alia,* that the company was a trading company, incorporated under the laws of the Province of Ontario, and carrying on business in the township of York and city of Toronto, in that Province; that the company was indebted to the petitioners in a sum exceeding $95,000, of which over $35,000 was then overdue and unpaid; that the company was insolvent, being unable to pay its debts as they became due; and that, at general meetings of the shareholders of the company, resolutions had been passed authorizing the winding-up of the company pursuant to the provisions of the Ontario Joint Stock Companies' Winding-up Act, and appointing James Worthington, the president of the company, liquidator.

The petition was verified by the affidavit of the manager of the petitioners' Toronto branch or agency.

An affidavit of James Worthington was filed in answer, in which he admitted that the company was in liquidation, and stated that he was attending as liquidator to its winding-up, and that if he was allowed to proceed therein, the assets would pay the liabilities.

The petition was argued before STREET, J., in Court, on the 11th September, 1894.

John Greer, for the petitioners. Upon the evidence the company is insolvent, within the meaning of R. S. C. ch 129, sec. 3, or at all events it is in liquidation and within sub-sec. (*b*). If the Act of 1889, 52 Vic. ch. 32 (D.), applies, the company have brought themselves within sec. 4, sub-sec. (*b*), and the evidence shews they are within sub-sec. (*d*) of that section. Even should the company not be within any of these provisions, the evidence adduced on the petition of the largest creditor, and with the approval of several other creditors, would justify the Court in making an order under sub-sec. (*e*) of sec. 4.

McCarthy, Q. C., (*W. B. Raymond* with him), for the company. This company, on the evidence, is not insolvent, and should not be ordered to be wound up. The amending Act, 52 Vic. ch. 32, by sec. 3 repeals sec. 3 of the original Act. The provisions of sec. 4 of the amending Act clearly were intended to be substituted for sec. 3 of the original Act, and if this is the case, then the Court has no jurisdiction to order the winding-up of this company, as it is incorporated under an Ontario Act, and the Dominion Winding-up Act does not apply to it. The company being in process of winding-up, and there being a liquidator under the Ontario Winding-up Act, R. S. O. ch. 183, there should be no interference by the Court, even if it has jurisdiction: *Wakefield Rattan Co.* v. *Hamilton Whip Co.*, 24 O. R. 107. The intention in passing the amending Act was clearly that in Ontario, where there is power to wind up, as provided by R. S. O. ch. 183, there should be no power to wind up under the Dominion Act.

Greer, in reply. The amending Act clearly does not repeal sec. 3 of the original Act by express words, and such being the case, it was not intended that it should be repealed. Sec. 3 of the amending Act does not apply to this company. Sec. 10 of the amending Act shews clearly that the original Act still remains, as applications under both Acts are

there referred to. If it was intended to substitute sec. 4
of the amending Act for 3 of the original Act, it would
have been done in so many words, as was done by secs. 18
and 20, where new sections were substituted for those in
the original Act. The number of companies incorporated
as the present one, which have been ordered to be wound
up under the Winding-up Act since the amending Act was
passed, would shew clearly that sec. 3 is still in force, and
applies to this company. As to liquidation being ordered
under this Act, this clearly should be done, as under the
Ontario Act creditors have no *locus standi*. The *Hamilton
Whip Company's Case* was one entirely different to this, as
there an assignment had been made, and creditors could,
under R. S. O. ch. 124, appoint an assignee, approved of by
them, in the place of the one to whom the assignment was
made, if they so desired, and in that case the majority of
the creditors supported the assignment and opposed the
winding-up, while in this case the majority object to the
winding-up proceedings under the Ontario Act.

September 14, 1894. STREET, J. :—

I have no doubt after comparing the provisions of the
Winding-up Act ch. 129, R. S. C., with those of the
Winding-up Amendment Act, 1889, 52 Vic. ch. 32 (D.),
that there is no clashing between sec. 3* of the former Act,
and sec. 3† of the later Act.

* R. S. C. ch. 129, sec. 3.—This Act applies to incorporated banks, savings banks, incorporated insurance companies, loan companies having
borrowing powers, building societies having a capital stock, and incorporated trading companies, doing business in Canada, wheresoever incorporated ; and—
  (a) Which are insolvent ; or—
  (b) Which are in liquidation or in process of being wound up, and on
petition by any of their shareholders or creditors, assignees or liquidators,
ask to be brought under the provisions of this Act ;
  2. This Act does not apply to railway or telegraph companies, or to
building societies which have not a capital stock.
  † 52 Vic. ch. 32, sec. 3.—This Act applies to all corporations incorporated by or under the authority of an Act of the Parliament of Canada
or by or under the authority of any Act of the late Province of Canada,

Judgment.   Creditors of a company have no rights under the amend-
Street, J.   ing Act; it gives certain rights to the companies falling
             within it, and to shareholders in those companies, but none
             to creditors.   In other words, it provides for the voluntary
             winding-up of the companies falling within its provisions,
             and not to their compulsory liquidation, which is provided
             for by the original Act.

             The present application is by creditors, and they are within
             their rights in asking for the compulsory winding-up of a
             company incorporated under an Act of the Province of
             Ontario, which was carrying on business in Canada, that is
             to say, in the Province of Ontario.   It is not denied that
             the company is in liquidation and in process of being
             wound up, and the present petitioners are large creditors
             who, by their petition, ask that the winding-up be brought
             under the provisions of the Winding-up Act.

                                                              E. B. B.

or of the Provinces of Nova Scotia, New Brunswick, Prince Edward
Island or British Columbia, and whose incorporation and the affairs
whereof are subject to the legislative authority of the Parliament of
Canada :
  2. This Act does not apply to railway or telegraph companies or to
building societies which have not a capital stock.

[QUEEN'S BENCH DIVISION.]

RE MARTIN AND COUNTY OF SIMCOE.

Public Schools—54 Vic. ch. 55, secs. 82, 96 (O.)—Boundaries of School Sec-
tions—Action of Township Council—Appeal—Time—County Council—
Jurisdiction—By-law—Appointment of Arbitrators—Award—Confir-
mation—Waiver—Evidence of.

In the absence of satisfactory evidence of waiver of the objection by all
persons interested, a county council has no jurisdiction under sub-sec.
3 of sec. 82 of the Public Schools Act, 54 Vic. ch. 55 (O.), to appoint
arbitrators to hear an appeal from the action or refusal to act of a township council and to determine or alter the boundaries of school sections,
unless a notice of appeal has been duly given within the time mentioned
in sub-sec. 1.

Where a by-law of the county council appointing arbitrators was passed
pursuant to a notice of appeal, in the form of a petition, filed with the
county clerk after such time had expired, and there was no waiver :—

Held, that the authority of the arbitrators to enter upon the inquiry being
affected by the want of jurisdiction of the council to pass the by-law,
their award could not be confirmed by sec. 96 of the Public Schools Act ;
and the by-law was quashed.

The application to quash was made by a ratepayer of the school section
whose boundaries were in question, acting at the request of the trustees
of the section, and the solicitors acting for him were also retained by
the trustees, whose secretary-treasurer appeared before the committee
of the county council, before the by-law was passed, and before the
arbitrators, and did not make objections to the jurisdiction of either
body :—

Held, that, in the absence of proof of the authority of the secretary-
treasurer to represent the trustees, it could not be said that they had
waived their right to object to the proceedings, nor that the rights of
the applicant were entirely gone and merged in those of the trustees.

THIS was originally an application to quash by-law No. Statement.
533 of the county of Simcoe, which was in the following
words :—

"By-law No. 533. For the appointment of arbitrators
re the petition of ratepayers of school section No. 4 in the
township of Medonte. Whereas it has been considered
advisable to appoint arbitrators to consider certain griev-
ances said to exist in school section No. 4 in the township
of Medonte :—

"Be it therefore enacted by the council of the corporation of the county of Simcoe, and it is hereby enacted by
the authority of the same, that His Honour Judge Ardagh,
Isaac Day, Esq., public school inspector, and Walter
Lawson, Esq., be and are hereby appointed such arbitrators.

"Council Hall, Barrie, June 15, 1893."

This was sealed with the corporate seal and signed by the warden and clerk.

This by-law was made in consequence of the receipt of a petition from some eighteen ratepayers of school section 4 of the township of Medonte, setting forth that they had applied to the council of that township to divide that school section, and that the council had fixed a date for considering the application, but had failed to appear; and praying that the county council would divide the section or would appoint arbitrators to settle the affair.

This petition was filed with the county clerk in June, 1893. It appeared from the affidavits that the township council had given notice that they would take the matter into consideration at a meeting to be held on 3rd April. 1893, and that the applicants had attended at the place of meeting on that day, but the council did not attend, and nothing was then done. It further appeared, however, that the township council had held a meeting at an earlier day, and had then decided to refuse the application to divide the section. The petition filed with the county clerk in June was the only notice of appeal from the neglect or refusal of the township council to consider the application made to them. The clerk of the county council, however, notified the secretary-treasurer of school section No. 4 of the receipt of the petition, and that it would be considered upon a day named by him, being the day following the giving of the notice, and the secretary-treasurer attended upon the day named before the education committee of the county council, and discussed the matter, but, so far as appeared, without the authority of the trustees.

The by-law moved against was passed in pursuance of a report of the education committee to the county council.

The arbitrators met, and, after notice to the trustees of the existing section No. 4 and the persons desiring to divide it, heard evidence without objection, and on 16th August, 1893, the majority of the three made their award adjudging that a new school section to be called

school section No. 15 should be formed, and fixing its
boundaries. The original award was deposited with the
county clerk during the same month, and a copy with
some clerical errors was served soon afterwards upon the
secretary-treasurer of school section No. 4. A perfect
copy of the award was produced by him as an exhibit to his
affidavit sworn in this matter on 29th March, 1894. The
ratepayers of the new school section met and appointed
trustees on 16th April, 1894, without any notice, so far as
appeared, that an application was to be made to test the
legality of the proceedings. Notice of this motion was
served on the warden of the county at Barrie on 14th
April, 1894. The applicant was a bailiff of a Division Court,
but a resolution of the trustees of school section No. 4 was
produced instructing the solicitors to take the present proceedings to quash the by-law, and the applicant appeared to
be acting on their behalf or with their concurrence in
making the application.

The grounds taken in the notice of motion were that
no notice of appeal under sec. 82, ch. 55, 54 Vic. (Ontario
Statutes of 1891), had been given ; that the county
council had no power to pass the by-law ; that the petition
upon which the council acted had been materially altered
after it had been signed by the petitioners ; and that it was
insufficient and indefinite ; and upon grounds disclosed in
the affidavits filed.

The motion was argued before STREET, J., in Court on
29th June, 1894.

C. E. Hewson, for the motion.

Pepler, Q. C., contra.

After argument the Court suggested that notice should
be given to the township council and to the school trustees
of the alleged new section, and that they should be made
parties to the motion ; and this having been done, the same
counsel appeared in Court on 12th September, 1894, when
the matter was further argued. Neither the township
council nor the school trustees appeared, although duly
notified.

September 14, 1894. STREET, J. :—

If the award made under this by-law be confirmed by the provisions of section 96 of the Public Schools Act of 1891,* it is plain, I think, that I should refuse to quash the by-law upon which it rests. The evidence shews, in my opinion, that a true copy of the award was in the possession of the secretary-treasurer of the school trustees of section 4 when he swore to an affidavit used upon this application, the date of the jurat being 29th March, 1894, and as it does not appear that notice to set aside the award has ever been filed in the office of the township clerk, the award seems to be established as against "any defect in substance or form or in the manner or time of * * making the same." No copy of the by-law has been shewn to have been served upon the secretary of the school trustees at any time, and section 96 cannot, therefore, apply directly in favour of the by-law. The objections here taken go, however, to the root of the matter; the authority of the arbitrators to enter upon the inquiry at all is questioned, and a defect of that nature does not appear to come within the intention of section 96. The question to be determined is, therefore, not incumbered by any consideration arising under that section, but is simply this: Whether the county council, not having received any notice of appeal within the twenty days prescribed by section 82,† had power to act after the

* 96. (1) Any by-law of a municipality for forming, altering or dissolving a school section or sections, and any award made by arbitrators appointed to consider an appeal from a township council with respect to any matter authorized by this Act shall be valid and binding, notwithstanding any defect in substance or form, or in the manner or time of passing or making the same, unless notice to quash such by-law or to set aside such award is filed in the office of the township clerk within one month of the publication of such by-law or award.

(2) Such by-law or award shall be deemed to be published when a copy thereof is served upon the secretary or secretary-treasurer of each board of trustees affected thereby.

(3) Any by-law or award confirmed, as in this section provided, shall be valid and binding for a period of five years.

† 82. (1) A majority of the trustees, or any five ratepayers of any one or more of the school sections concerned, may within twenty days, by notice filed in the office of the county clerk, appeal to the county council.

expiration of that time upon the petition filed with them some four or five weeks after the twenty days had elapsed.

I am of opinion that, in the absence of satisfactory evidence of waiver of the objection by all persons interested, the county council have no jurisdiction to act under sub-section 3 of section 82, unless a notice of appeal has been duly given within the time mentioned in the first subsection. The intention of the Legislature appears to be that the persons interested in supporting or opposing an alteration in the school section shall be in a position to know, when twenty days have elapsed from the action, or refusal to act, of the township council, whether their decision is confirmed or disputed. If not disputed within the period prescribed by the Act, their decision is absolutely confirmed ; the rights of the persons claiming under it become fixed and vested ; and no person or corporation has the right to disturb those rights or to enlarge the time for appealing. The Act carefully defines in sub-section 2 the period from which the time is to run, and by so doing emphasizes the importance intended to be attached to the time limit fixed by sub-section 1.

In the present case the township council fixed the 3rd April, 1893, as the day of their meeting to consider the application to divide the school section ; they did not meet at all on that day, but they had met on the 29th March, and decided to refuse the application ; they met again on the 22nd April, and took no action in the matter. The twenty days must be treated as running at latest from the 22nd April, and the petition, which is relied on as a notice of appeal,

of the county in which such section or sections are situated, against any by-law of the township council for the formation, division, union or alteration of their school section or school sections ; or against the neglect or refusal of the township council, on application being made to it by the trustees or any five ratepayers concerned, to alter the boundaries of a school section or school sections within the township.

(2) The time herein mentioned for appeal shall run from the date of the by-law complained of, or from the date of the meeting at which the council refused to pass such by-law, or from the first meeting after which

was not handed in to the county clerk until after the 1st June, long after the twenty days had expired.

The present application is made by a ratepayer in the school section, who is apparently acting at the request of the trustees of the section, and the solicitors acting in the matter are also retained by the trustees, a resolution of theirs for the purpose being in evidence. Their secretary-treasurer appeared before the committee of the county council before the by-law was passed, and again before the arbitrators upon the proceedings before them, and did not make objections to the jurisdiction of either body to deal with the matter. In the absence of any proof of authority on his part to represent the school trustees, I could hardly say that they have waived their right to object to the proceedings because he did not do so, nor I think could I properly hold that the rights of the present applicant are entirely gone and merged in those of the school trustees, because he is acting with their consent, and because his solicitor is also retained by them.

Upon these facts I must deal with the case as one of a by-law which the county council had no right to pass under the circumstances, and which has not been confirmed in any way, and there must be an order quashing it with costs.

notice was received from the clerk of the application of the trustees or ratepayers asking for such by-law to be passed, as the case may be.

(3) The county council may, if it thinks fit, appoint as arbitrators not more than five, or less than three competent persons, two of whom shall be the County Judge, or some person named by him, and the county inspector, and a majority of whom shall form a quorum to hear such appeal and to revise, determine or alter the boundaries of the school section or school sections, so far as to settle the matters complained of ; but the alterations or determination of the said matters shall not take effect before the 25th day of December in the year in which the arbitrators so decide, and shall thence continue in full force for the period of five years at least, and until lawfully changed by the township council.

(4) No person shall be competent to act as arbitrator, who is a member of the township council, or who was a member at the time at which the council passed, or refused or neglected to pass the by-law or resolution ;

(5) Due notice of the alterations or the determination of the said matters made by the arbitrators shall be given by the inspector to the clerk of the township, and to the trustees of the school sections concerned.

It is unnecessary that I should consider whether the
award made by the arbitrators has any foundation in the
terms of the by-law conferring their only authority upon
them, nor whether that award could be attacked upon a
motion of this nature.   It has at all events no other
foundation than the by-law, and cannot stand when
deprived of that foundation.

E. B. B.

[COMMON PLEAS DIVISION.]

MIDDLETON v. FLANAGAN.

Contract—Horses—" Plant "—Meaning of.

By one of the clauses of a railway contract for excavation, "all
machinery and other plant, materials and things whatsoever," provided
by the contractor were until the completion of the work to be the property of the company, when such as had not been used and converted
into the works and remained undisposed of were to be delivered over
to the contractor, but in other clauses the words " teams and horses '
were respectively used as well as the word "plant" :—
Held, under the contract, that horses were not included in the word
"plant ;" and that expert evidence was not admissible to explain its
meaning.

THIS was an action tried before FALCONBRIDGE, J., without a jury, at the Port Arthur Assizes on the 16th June,
1893.

The action was in replevin for eight teams of horses and
harness and their attachments.

The learned trial Judge decided that the horses were
included in the term "plant" mentioned in the contract
referred to in the judgment, and that the plaintiffs were
entitled to judgment.

The defendant moved on notice to set aside the judgment entered for the plaintiffs, and to have the judgment
entered in his favour.

Argument. In Easter Sittings, May 21, 1894, before a Divisional
Court composed of ROSE and MACMAHON, JJ., *Aylesworth,*
Q. C., supported the motion. Under the terms of the agreement horses are not included in the word " plant." Under
clause 6 plant is limited to the material which might be
built into and form part of the work itself, and therefore
clearly could not refer to horses : while in clauses 9 and
10 a clear distinction is pointed out. In clause 9 the word
" teams" is used as well as " plant," and in clause 10 the word
" horses." The case of *Yarmouth* v. *France,* 19 Q. B. D.
647, which the learned trial Judge seemed to think
governed this case is quite distinguishable. That case was
decided under the Workmen's Compensation for Injuries
Act, where the word " plant " has a more extensive meaning
than under the contract here. The next point is that the
horses never belonged to Earls, but were the property of
Flanagan. This is expressly provided for by clause 2 of
the agreement.

Osler, Q. C., contra. The horses are clearly " plant "
within the meaning of the agreement. The case of *Yarmouth* v. *France,* 19 Q. B. D. 647, is conclusive on the
point. There it was held that horses came within the
term " plant." It was pointed out that " plant " in its
ordinary sense includes whatever apparatus is used in the
business, and that there were many businesses where horses
and carts formed the most material part of the plant.
That was the case here. The case is not decided on any
particular use of the word in the statute, but on the general
meaning of the word. See also *Blake* v. *Shaw,* 8 W. R.
410 ; *Ashfield* v. *Edgell,* 21 O. R. 195, 198 ; *Joseph Hall
Manufacturing Co.* v. *Hazlett,* 8 O. R. 465 ; 11 A. R. 749.
There is nothing in the contract to exclude the general
meaning of the word. Under clause 6 they are clearly
included, while clauses 9 and 10 do not intend to limit
the meaning of the word. The words " teams and horses "
are used for greater particularity. In old contracts before
the introduction of machine excavators, horses, carts, and
scrapers, would include the whole plant. Then as to the

horses belonging to Flanagan alone. They formed part of the partnership property : *Ashfield* v. *Edgell,* 21 O. R. 195.

June 23rd, 1894. MacMahon, J. :—

On the 10th of April, 1891, William Earls, trading under the name of William Earls & Co., entered into an agreement (in which he is therein called "the contractor") with Middleton and Conmee (therein called "the company") to perform certain work, consisting of rock and other excavation, on the line of "The Port Arthur, Duluth & Western Railway," at certain schedule prices, which work was to be completed by the 1st of August, 1891.

Earls commenced the work, and had been for a few weeks prosecuting the same under his contract, when on the 10th of May, 1891, a partnership was entered into between himself and the defendant Flanagan, for the purpose of completing the work "as specified in the contract signed by William Earls & Co. on the 10th of April, 1891."

The terms of the partnership necessary to be considered are :—"(2) That in consideration of the said James Flanagan placing eight teams of horses, with harness, etc., on the work (which shall be the property of James Flanagan), he, and the said Earls are to share alike in the profits, and to have equal privileges in every respect, and both can at any time sign the partnership name, viz., W. Earls & Co., whenever the circumstances of the business require it," etc.

Flanagan sent the eight teams of horses, with the necessary harness, to the railway works shortly after the partnership agreement was executed. On his second visit to the works, during the latter part of the month of June, 1891, the labourers on the work not having been paid their wages, had stopped working, and Flanagan directed that his horses be taken to a place called Murillo, a distance of between forty and forty-five miles from the railway. The plaintiffs there replevied the horses, harness, etc., claiming their right so to do as forming a part of the "plant" under the contract between Earls and the plaintiffs.

Clause 5 of the contract provides: "During the entire
continuance of the work included under this contract, all
material which the engineer shall determine to be unsuit-
able for use in the execution of the work, shall be removed
by the contractor at his own expense to such a distance as
the engineer may direct," etc.

The 6th clause reads: " All machinery and other plant,
materials, and things whatsoever, provided by the contractor for the work hereby contracted for, and not rejected
under the provisions of the last preceding clause, from
the time of their being so provided, become, and until the
final completion of the said works, shall be the property
of the company for the purpose of the said works, and the
same shall on no account be taken away, or used, or disposed of, except for the purposes of the said works, without
the consent in writing of the engineer; * * provided
always that upon the completion of the works and upon
payment by the contractor of all such moneys, if any,
as shall be due from him to the company, such of the said
machinery and other plant, material, and things as shall
not have been used and converted in the works, and shall
remain undisposed of, shall upon demand be delivered up
to the contractor."

These two clauses must be read together, and that was
evidently the intention of the draftsman. The "plant"
referred to in the 6th clause had reference to such plant
as might possibly be converted in the work. This is apparent from the whole scope and tenor of the clause itself,
although in the execution of the contract for this particular work there would have been little of the "plant" required for the work of excavation which could possibly be
so converted.

The first part of the 6th clause, where it mentions
"other plant, materials, and things whatsoever," refers to
what might be rejected by the engineer as unfit to be incorporated in the work, and being an addition to the word
"materials" in the 5th clause.

Then the latter part of the 6th clause was evidently

framed from a contract providing for the execution of
work of a wholly different character to that which Earls
was contracting to do, as it provides that "all machinery,
and other plant, material and things as shall not have been
used and converted in the works and shall remain undisposed of, shall upon demand be delivered up to the contractor." Thus unquestionably referring to a class of
"plant" which might be built into and form part of the
works. And that at least part of what is designated
"plant" in a contract is sometimes built into or connected
in the works, is shewn by a reference to Hudson on Building Contracts, p. 630, where it is said, "In large works the
following definition of plant may be inserted :—The word
'plant' shall be held to mean every temporary and acces-
sory means necessary or required by the engineer to complete the works, * * and all temporary materials built
into the works, which cannot (in the opinion of the engineer) be removed without any injury to the works * *
including * * all tramways fixed and moveable,
machinery, engines, vehicles, carts, stages, scaffolding,
* * pumps, dams, coffer-dams, * * timbers, planks,
* * and all special or other appliances of every sort,
kind and description whatsoever."

In Ogilvie's Scientific Dictionary, "plant" is defined as
"the fixtures, tools, apparatus, etc., necessary to carry on
any trade or mechanical business. The locomotive carriages,
vans, trucks, etc., constitute the plant of a railway."
And the Imperial Act 38 & 39 Vic. ch. 31, defines what
the "plant" of a railway company is, which cannot be
taken in execution, viz., the engines, carriages, etc., constituting the rolling stock and plant of a railway company :
Hodge on Railways, vol. 1, p. 131.

The 9th clause of the contract between Earls and the
company also shews that horses were not included or
intended to be included in the word "plant" under the
contract. For that clause provides if the company is of
opinion that the contractor is not prosecuting the work
with due diligence, "the company may employ additional

workmen, teams, plant, and other things necessary, and
may go on and take charge of and perform the said work,"
etc.

A "team" is two or more horses, oxen, or other beasts,
harnessed together to the same vehicle for drawing: Imperial Dictionary. This clause shews that "teams" of
horses or oxen or mules were regarded in the contract as
distinctive from "plant."

The whole contract as framed shews to my mind that
the plaintiffs themselves did not intend to include horses
as part of the "plant." The expert evidence of contractors shewing that horses would be included in the term
"plant," was therefore under the terms of the contract
not properly receivable.

The learned trial Judge, however, without considering
the expert testimony, found, that under the contract,
"horses" formed part of the contractors' plant.

As pointed out by Lord Esher in *Yarmouth* v. *France*,
19 Q. B. D. 647, at p. 655, there are many businesses where
horses and carts form the most material part of the plant,
as the employer must use them for carrying on his business. And in the same case, Lindley, L. J., at p. 658, says,
that "plant" in its ordinary sense, "includes whatever
apparatus is used by a business man in carrying on his
business, * * all goods and chattels fixed or moveable,
live or dead, which he keeps for permanent employment
in his business." He refers to *Blake* v. *Shaw*, Johns. 732,
8 W. R. 410. See also *In re Nutley and Finn*,W. N. 1894,
p. 64, as to what constitutes "fixed plant."

Horses would likely be a necessary part of the contractor's plant in connection with earth excavation, for
hauling short distances, or to use with scrapers, unless the
cutting was deep, when a steam excavator would be used,
and an engine would be employed to haul the trucks, if
the dump or fill was at a distance from the cut. But
horses would, during the night and on wet days, be off
the works in the owner's stable and under his control,
and it may be for that reason they were by the very

terms of the contract, as already pointed out, excluded _{Judgment.} from the operation of the sixth clause of the contract, _{MacMahon,} which includes "machinery, plant, and other things." _{J.}

Even could it be held as between Earls and the plaintiffs that horses formed part of the "plant" within the meaning of the contract, I still think the defendant is entitled to succeed.

The contract being between Earls and the plaintiffs, there is no privity between the plaintiffs and the defendant. Earls was to have no interest whatsoever in the horses furnished by Flanagan—the second clause of the agreement between Earls and Flanagan putting that beyond the realm of controversy. What the company had authority to prevent being removed from the work was "the machinery and other plant, etc., provided by the contractor."

These horses were not provided by the contractor, and the company could have no more right to detain them than if Earls had agreed with the owner of a dozen teams to work on the contract, and these teams were on the works when the company took possession. And if the contractor purchased a piece of machinery under the usual lien contract, providing that the property should not pass to the purchaser until paid for, and brought the same on the works, the company could not have retained it against the owner, the lienholder.

The company would have no higher rights than Earls as to such machinery. And this defendant does not occupy a less favourable position than a lien holder in the case put.

The motion must be absolute, setting aside the judgment for the plaintiffs, and to enter judgment for the defendant for the return of the horses and harness with costs.

ROSE, J. :—

There seems to be no doubt that horses may sometimes be included under the term "plant" : *Yarmouth* v. *France*, 19 Q. B. D. 647. The question remains, does this contract by any fair interpretation include horses under the terms "All machinery, and other plant, materials, and things whatsoever," as found in clause 6 ?

The first and natural reading of the clause would not, I think, suggest to the mind that horses used on the works were intended to be included.

The reference to clause 5, while not certainly excluding horses, would ordinarily lead the mind to conclude that the "material" was at all events something that might be used in, on, and enter into the construction of the works subject to acceptance or rejection—and this view is somewhat strengthened by the words "used and converted in the works and shall remain undisposed of." It is not used *or* converted, but used *and* converted. "Undisposed of," would imply a right to sell or otherwise dispose of the material. If it can reasonably be contended that the company had under the contract, the right to sell the horses, then this does not present a difficulty, but if not, how otherwise could horses be disposed of ? It may be said that a consideration of the word "machinery," might lead to similar difficulties and perhaps that would be so.

But apart from the difficulty arising from construing clause 6 to refer to and include horses within its provisions, I find a consideration of clauses 9 and 10 leading to a reasonably clear conclusion that horses are not included within the word "plant," for in clause 9 we have "teams, plant," etc., and in clause 10, "horses and plant." Reading clauses 5, 6, 9 and 10 together, I am on the whole, of the opinion that on a proper construction of the whole contract, horses are not included within the provisions of clause 6.

It is, therefore, unnecessary to consider how it would have been, had the clause applied to horses, but in view of such cases as *Walker* v. *Hyman*, 1 A. R. 345, and similar authorities, I do not at present see how the plaintiffs could take Flanagan's horses to secure the performance of Earls' contract.

I do not see my way clear to finding, as contended by

the plaintiffs' counsel, that the signature by Earls of Judgment.
"William Earls & Co.," was by the authority of Flanagan Rose, J.
and included Flanagan as a member of such firm of Earls
& Co. I, however, have not given this branch of the
argument such consideration as enables me to pronounce
more positively any opinion on the point.

The motion must succeed, and the judgment be entered
for the defendant with costs.

G. F. H.

[COMMON PLEAS DIVISION.]

CHRISTIE V. THE CORPORATION OF THE CITY OF TORONTO.

*Assessment and Taxes—Assessment Act—55 Vic. ch. 48, sec. 124 (O.)—
Goods Subject to Distress—Occupancy.*

Section 124 of the Consolidated Assessment Act, 55 Vic. ch. 48 (O.), does
not authorize a distress for non-payment of taxes of the goods of strangers
on the premises, unless such goods are in the possession of the person
who ought to pay the taxes or of a legal occupant of the property.

THIS was an action tried before MACMAHON, J., without Statement.
a jury, at Toronto, on the 9th and 10th of February, 1894.

The action was commenced against the city by the plaintiff for a declaration that his lands were freed from certain
taxes.

At the instance of the city one Charles Farquhar was
made a third party defendant.

The facts of the case appear in the judgment.

Hall, for the plaintiff.
Chisholm, for the corporation of the city of Toronto.
W. R. Smyth, for Farquhar.

July 5th, 1894. MACMAHON, J.:—

The property in question was assessed for the year 1892,
to Ernest Walker, who is assessed therefor as "owner," and
in the collector's warrant issued on the 19th of November,

1892, the bailiff, is directed to distrain the goods and chattels of Ernest Walker, to satisfy the taxes for 1892, amounting to $92.21.

The assessment for 1892 would be made during the
autumn of 1891, and confirmed by by-law early in 1892.

In December, 1891, Christopher Dempsey appears to
have been the owner of the land, as on the 2nd of that
month he entered into an agreement to sell to John and
James Sturdy, who covenanted to pay off a mortgage
then existing on the property, and to erect and complete certain buildings thereon by the 1st of September,
1892.

Dempsey covenanted to pay the taxes and interest on
the mortgage up to the 1st of December, 1891. The
taxes and the interest on the mortgage after that date,
the Sturdys covenanted with Dempsey to pay.

On the 21st of April, 1892, Dempsey conveyed to the
plaintiff Christie, subject to the agreement for sale to the
Sturdys ; and on the 13th of September, 1892, the Sturdys
quit-claimed their interest to Christie. The quit-claim,
although bearing date the 10th of September, was in fact
not executed until the 12th of October.

At the time of the conveyance by Dempsey to Christie in April, 1892, the Sturdys were in possession of the
land, and had thereon a large quantity of lumber purchased from Farquhar and W. F. Donaldson, and placed
there by the Sturdys, to be used in erecting the buildings
on the land under their agreement with Dempsey.

To secure the payment of the purchase money for this
lumber, Donaldson had taken from the Sturdys a chattel
mortgage thereon, dated the 7th of March, 1892, which
was duly filed on the following day. The Sturdys were,
through their tenants, in possession, and collected the rents
from the tenants of the dwelling-houses until the summer,
when they gave the tenants notice to quit. After the
tenants had vacated the premises, the Sturdys commenced
pulling down the dwellings.

The chattel mortgage given to Donaldson, matured in

July, and the Sturdys having informed Farquhar in September that they did not intend building, and that Farquhar was to take the lumber away, which he and Donaldson did as fast as they could secure purchasers. But hearing in November that one of the Sturdys was about leaving Canada, Farquhar obtained from them a written authority to Donaldson to take possession of the lumber under his chattel mortgage and remove the same. And when the lumber was seized under the tax warrant on the 21st of November, 1892, Farquhar and Donaldson were removing the lumber under such authority, and as being covered by the chattel mortgage.

On the 22nd of November, Farquhar gave to the tax collector an order on the city treasurer authorizing the latter to retain in his hands any moneys payable by the city to him (Farquhar) to satisfy the taxes distrained for. Upon receiving this order, the collector withdrew his bailiff from possession. On the 26th of May, 1893, Farquhar wrote the city treasurer directing him not to apply any moneys in his hands to the payment of these taxes. And on the 3rd of June, 1893, Farquhar gave to the city and John Kidd, the tax collector, a bond indemnifying them against all claims, demands, and actions by any person claiming to be the owner of the said premises, etc.

The deputy-treasurer said that the order given by Farquhar to the collector (Kidd) was not accepted by the city, but in the margin of the collector's return, opposite the name of Ernest Walker, the following reason is given for nonpayment of the taxes: "Mr. Kimber holds an order from Ewart Farquhar to take the amount out of any account the city owes him. There are some bailiff's costs to be paid and are included in the order."

The roll is indorsed as having been returned on the 14th of April, 1893, and I assume the return was made as indorsed, as on the 16th of March the collector was notified by the treasurer that the roll must be returned by the 15th of April. The return, however, was not sworn to until the 18th of October, 1893. In December, 1892,

the plaintiff Christie, sold the land to one McLaughlin,
who, to indemnify himself in the event of his having to
pay the taxes, retained with Christie's consent, the sum
of $100 out of the purchase money to pay the same.

Christie took the place of his vendor Dempsey, in April,
1892, and when on the 12th of October, he obtained the
quit-claim from the Sturdys, he became the owner of the
land from that date, although from the fences being removed and the dwellings partly torn down, there was no
one in actual " occupation."

By section 124 of the Consolidated Assessment Act, 55
Vic. ch. 48 (O.), the collector, after having complied with certain preliminaries therein provided, may, if the taxes are
not paid, " levy the same with costs, by distress of the
goods and chattels of the person who ought to pay the
same, or of any goods and chattels in his possession,
wherever the same may be found within the county in
which the local municipality lies, or of any goods or chattels found on the premises, the property of, or in the possession of, any other occupant of the premises."

The person who " ought to pay," is Ernest Walker, and
his goods might have been followed to any place within
the county of York. The lumber was not the property
of the Sturdys, for they had redelivered it to Farquhar and
Donaldson who had removed a considerable portion prior
to the 21st of November, when the distress was made.
The Sturdys were not " occupants" of the premises when
the distress was made. They had conveyed all their
interest in the land to Christie, who had become the
owner ; the gate and fences had been removed ; and the
dwellings were partially destroyed. In fact there was
no " occupant" of the premises at that time. Mr. Christie
said he considered the Sturdys were in occupation by
reason of the lumber being piled on the land. But, as
already pointed out, the lumber had ceased to be theirs,
and Farquhar and Donaldson had taken possession of and
were selling it as their own lumber from September
(about the time that the quit-claim to Christie is dated),

so that the lumber was Farquhar and Donaldson's and in their possession when seized, although they were not " occupants" of the land. See *Great Western R. W. Co.* v. *Rogers*, 29 U. C. R. 245, at p. 254, which is nearly this case, the difference being that in the *Great Western R. W.* case, the cars seized were not on that portion of the Erie and Niagara Railway Company's premises, for which the taxes were payable.

Frazer v. *Page*, 18 U. C. R. 327, was decided in 1859, and the Consolidation of the Statutes of Upper Canada, took place the same year when the 16 Vic. ch. 182, sec. 42, was amended in the consolidation by leaving out that part of the 42nd section which provided that no claim, lien, or privilege on the goods distrained, should avail to prevent the sale or payment of the taxes. See C. S. U. C. ch. 55, sec. 96.

In the absence of any goods of Walker's, it was only goods found on the premises, " the property of or in the possession of any other occupant," which could be levied upon and so made available for the payment of the taxes ; and as this lumber was the goods and chattels of Farquhar and Donaldson, and as they were not the " occupants" of the premises, it was not property which could lawfully have been levied upon to satisfy the taxes due on the land. And I conceive it was the deliberate intention of the framers of the Act to confine the right to levy on goods which the occupant was possessed of.

An illustration of what was intended by the statute in confining the right to levy upon goods the property of or in possession of an occupant is, where a builder, without the consent of the owner, puts building materials for a temporary purpose on vacant land: although he thus becomes a trespasser, his materials could not be distrained for taxes which had theretofore accrued upon the land as he was not an " occupant." So if a person turns his horses in on a vacant lot for the purpose of grazing there, the collector of taxes could not lawfully levy on the horses for taxes on the land, the owner of the horses not being an

Judgment.

MacMahon,
J.

"occupant." See as to general and special occupants : Co.
Litt. ch. 6, sec. 56 (41 *b*). And see Stroud's Judicial
Dictionary under " Occupier" and " Occupation."

The lumber was not, I consider, distrainable for these
taxes; but had Farquhar, with full knowledge of the facts,
paid the amount of the taxes, the sum so paid could not
have been recovered back by him from the corporation
unless it could be considered as under a wrongful seizure,
and was paid to prevent the goods from being sold as in
Valpy v. *Manley*, 1 C. B. 594. Then has he by giving
to the collector the order already referred to on the city
treasurer, paid the taxes to the corporation so as to entitle
this plaintiff to say that the land should be freed therefrom ? I think not. Supposing, instead of giving the
order, Farquhar had given a cheque on his bankers, and before its presentation, he had stopped payment of the cheque,
and set up that the levy was illegal ; that he gave the
cheque to prevent his property from being sold, and in an
action brought by the collector on the cheque, Farquhar had
succeeded, the city would not have been paid the taxes,
and the plaintiff would not have been in any better position than when he commenced this suit. The order was
not accepted ; the city has not been paid the taxes,
and Farquhar has done nothing which estopped him as
against the city from setting up that his goods levied upon
were not liable for the payment of those taxes due on
Walker's land now owned by the plaintiff.

As against the corporation, this plaintiff cannot claim to
have his land freed from the taxes of a former owner, unless he can shew that the taxes have been paid, or that the
goods seized were liable therefor.

This case is not like *Goldie* v. *Johns*, 16 A. R. 129, where
the person in occupation had possession of, and in fact had
title to the goods distrained, subject to the plaintiff's lien
thereon.

There will, therefore, be judgment for the defendants
the corporation, dismissing the plaintiff's action with
costs.

And as to the issue between the corporation and Farquhar,
I direct that judgment be entered in favour of the said
third party Farquhar, and that the city do pay to him the
costs of and incident to making him a third party defendant, and of the said issue which the corporation are to
add to their costs as against the plaintiff, and recover the
same as part of their costs.

G. F. H.

[COMMON PLEAS DIVISION.]

REGINA v. FRAWLEY.

*Criminal Law—Conspiracy—Failure to Complete Fraud—Indictment of
One of Two Conspirators.*

A conspiracy to defraud is indictable, even though the conspirators are
  unsuccessful in carrying out the fraud.
One of two conspirators can be tried on an indictment against him alone
  charging him with conspiring with another to defraud, the other conspirator being known in the country.

THIS was a case reserved by Michael Houston, Esq., police
magistrate for the town of Chatham, for the consideration
of the Justices of this Division :—

The defendant, Thomas Frawley, of the town of Chatham, in the county of Kent, was, on the 31st day of
January, in the year of our Lord 1894, charged before me
the undersigned, Michael Houston, police magistrate in
and for the town of Chatham, in the county of Kent, for
that he did on or about the 24th day of December, 1892,
at the town of Chatham, in the said county, unlawfully
conspire with one William Irwin by deceit and falsehood
to defraud one James Percy Moore, receiver of the estate of
the said Frawley, of the sum of $200 then due to him to
defeat the action then brought by the said Moore against
the said Irwin, by pretending and alleging that the said
Irwin had paid the said money to the said Frawley and

by the said Frawley giving the said Irwin a receipt therefor, dated the 6th day of December, 1892.

Upon the hearing of the said complaint, to wit, upon the 7th day of February, 1894, the defendant by his counsel consented to the said charge being summarily tried before me, the undersigned, and thereupon pleaded "not guilty" to the said charge, and after hearing the evidence and the argument of counsel I found the prisoner guilty.

The questions for the opinion of the Court are : (1) Is the intent to defraud in this case, although unsuccessful in carrying out the fraud intended, an indictable offence ? (2) Can Frawley be tried alone, the other conspirator being known in the county ?

In Easter Sittings, June 8th, 1894, before ROSE and MACMAHON, JJ., *McBrady* appeared for the defendant. The offence here was never perfected. There was merely an intent to defraud, which was never carried out. Then as to the second point, one person cannot be indicted and tried alone for conspiracy. A conspiracy must be by two persons at least, and two or more must be indicted. One cannot be convicted of conspiracy unless he has been indicted with persons to the jury unknown or since dead : Archbold's Criminal Pleading and Evidence, 21st ed., 1104-1106 ; Taschereau's Criminal Code, p. 429 ; *Rex* v. *Turner*, 13 East 228 ; Broom's Common Law, 8th ed., 983, note (c) ; *Regina* v. *Steinburg*, 8 Legal News 122 ; *Mulcahy* v. *The Queen*, L. R. 3 H. L. 306 ; Wright's Criminal Conspiracies and American Cases, Black. ed., pp. 55, 129 ; Russell on Crimes, 5th ed., vol. 3, p. 125.

J. R. Cartwright, Q. C., for the Crown. The offence here was clearly an indictable offence. The gist of the offence is the conspiring together, and not the actual commission of the fraud which was the subject of the conspiracy : Russell on Crimes, 5th ed., vol. 3, p. 127 ; *Regina* v. *Mulcahy*, L. R. 3 H. L. 306, at p. 317. The Criminal Code, sec. 64, is clear on the point. It is there laid down that everyone who having an intent to commit an offence does or omits an act for the purpose of accomplishing his object is guilty of an attempt to commit the offence intended whether under the circumstances it was possible to commit such offence or not. The result of the authorities is that one may be indicted and committed for conspiracy so long as the indictment charges that he conspired with another or others. The section 394 of the Code is : " Every one who conspires, etc., not where two or more conspire " : *Regina* v. *Manning*, 12 Q. B. D. 241 ; *Rex* v. *Cooke*, 5 B. & C. 538 ; *Regina* v. *Ahearne*, 6 Cox C. C. 6 ; Russell on Crimes, vol. 3, p. 128, note ; *People* v. *Olcott*, 2 Johns. Cas. N. Y. 300 ; 2 Bishop's Criminal Law, 8th ed., vol. 2, sec. 188.

McBrady, in reply. The only exception to one person being indicted is where the other person to the conspiracy is unknown or dead. Here it is admitted that he was known and was alive. Then as to the other point section 64 does not apply, as the alleged offence was before the passing of the Code.

June 23rd, 1894. ROSE, J. :—

I read the first question reserved for our opinion as if stated thus : " Is a conspiracy to defraud indictable where the conspirators have been unsuccessful in carrying out the fraud ? " Stating the question thus, it answers itself— for a conspiracy is beyond question an indictable offence.

The law is collected in Archbold's Criminal Pleading and Evidence, 21st ed., 1087, 1106, *et seq.* ; and Taschereau's Canada Criminal Acts p. 636. See also *Regina* v. *Connolly*, 25 O. R. 151.

The case was argued on the supposition that this was what the question meant, and I so deal with it.

The second question I would answer also in the affirmative.

If A. and B. conspire together, each is guilty of an offence, and I see no reason in principle why each may not be indicted separately, tried alone and convicted, although both be living and within the country and county at the time of the indictment, trial and conviction.

Judgment.

Ross, J.

And I venture to think that there is no decision to the contrary. The text writers have, I think, been a little careless in their statement of the law, and so have been misleading.

In the Principles of Criminal Law by Harris, 6th ed., at p. 128, it is thus stated : " The gist of the offence is the combination. Of this offence a single person cannot be convicted, unless indeed, he is indicted with others, who are dead or unknown to the jurors ": citing 1 Hawk. P. C. ch. 27, sec. 8, p. 448. But what is there said is, " It plainly appears from the words of the statute that one person alone cannot be guilty of a conspiracy within the purport of it, from whence it follows, that if all the defendants who are prosecuted for such a conspiracy be acquitted but one, the acquittal of the rest is the acquittal of that one also."

In Archbold's Criminal Pleading and Evidence, 21st ed., 1106, it is said, " But one person alone may be tried for a conspiracy, provided that the indictment charged him with conspiring with others who have not appeared: *Rex* v. *Kinnersley*, 1 Str. 193, or who are since dead: *Rex* v. *Niccolls*, 2 Str. 1227." The latter case is better reported in 13 East, p. 412—in a footnote to *Rex* v. *Inhabitants of Oxford.*

In *Rex* v. *Kinnersley*, two were indicted for conspiracy together, namely, Kinnersley and Moore. Kinnersley only appeared and pleaded to the indictment and was found guilty. The Court, as is found in the headnote, there being no full report of the judgments, held that " if one be convicted, judgment shall be given against him before the trial of the other." Counsel for the Crown in argument said, " Yet as the matter now stands, Moore, himself, is found guilty, for the conspiracy is found as it is laid, and therefore judgment may be given against one before the trial of the other."

This language, I venture to say, affords the test, viz.: Does the indictment set out the conspiracy in accordance with the fact, so that charging A. with conspiring with B. the jury may, on the evidence, find A. guilty of con-

spiracy as it is laid ? If so, it is good pleading, and the
verdict finding the fact as laid in the indictment the
conviction will be good.   Whether A. be indicted alone or
with B., it will of course be necessary to aver and prove
that A. and B. did conspire together; and if that be
not averred, the pleading would, of course, be bad, and if
it be not proven there could be no conviction of A. if
indicted alone, or of either if indicted together.

In *Rex* v. *Nichols*, 13 East 412 note, it is thus stated :
"The defendant was indicted for a conspiracy at Hick's
Hall.   The jury found him guilty of a conspiracy with one
Bygrave.   They likewise found that Bygrave died before
this indictment was found."   Lee, C.J., said, at p. 413 : " It is
certain that in all conspiracies there must be two at least, or
no indictment will lie ; and therefore if one be acquitted,
the other cannot be guilty.   But that case differs ; because
one being acquitted on record, the conviction of his companion on the same record must be directly repugnant and
contradictory to the other.   But there can be no contradiction in the present case, any more than where one of
the conspirators refuses to come in ; yet judgment may be
given against him."

The text in the 5th ed. of Russell on Crimes, at p. 127,
is more accurate, and does not suggest that one may not
be indicted alone if it be averred that he conspired with
another not found in the indictment.

I do not see how the argument is advanced by considering an indictment where the conspiracy is stated to have
been between A. and B. and many other persons, or
between A. B. and persons to the jurors unknown, because
with such pleadings the conspiracy must be proved as
laid.   See *Regina* v. *Thompson*, 5 Cox C. C. 168; and
Regina v. *Manning*, 12 Q. B. D. 241.

In *Regina* v. *Thompson*, A., B. and C. were charged with
conspiring together, and with divers other persons to the
jurors unknown.   No evidence was offered affecting any
other persons than A., B. and C.   The jury found A.
guilty, but acquitted B. and C., being of opinion that

either B. or C. was guilty, but not being able to determine which of the two. *Held*, Erle, J., dissenting, that the verdict was inconsistent, and that A. was entitled to an acquittal.

That case shews that the conspiracy charged must be proved. 2. That to charge a conspiracy between one or more and others unknown will not assist unless evidence be given that the conspiracy was with persons unknown.

These cases are certainly no authority for saying that it aids the indictment to charge a conspiracy with persons unknown unless that be in accordance with the fact.

If, therefore, two conspiring together, each be guilty of an offence, and one alone may be tried and convicted on an indictment charging both, though the other does not appear and plead, and one alone may be tried and convicted on an indictment against him alone, the other being dead, I see no reason why one may not be indicted, tried and convicted alone as long as the indictment sets out a conspiracy in which he was a conspirator, whether such conspiracy be between him and one other or others known or unknown, and whether the other conspirators be or be not alive, or within or not within the county and country.

I have answered this question as if it had been: " Can Frawley be tried alone on an indictment against him only charging him with conspiracy with another to defraud, etc., the other conspirator being known in the country?" *Regina* v. *Connolly*, 25 O. R. 151, may be referred to also as to the form of pleading.

There must be judgment for the Crown.

MacMahon, J. :—

What constitutes the crime of conspiracy is clearly and concisely stated in the opinion delivered by the Judges through Lord Chief Justice Tindal to the House of Lords in *O'Connell* v. *The Queen*, 11 Cl. & F. 155, at p. 233, taking the law from two very old cases of *Regina* v. *Best*, 1 Salk. 174, and *Rex* v. *Edwards*, 8 Mod. 320, as follows :—

Judgment.

MacMahon, J.

" The crime of conspiracy is complete if two, or more than two, should agree to do an illegal thing; that is, to effect something in itself unlawful, or to effect, by unlawful means, something in itself which may be indifferent or even lawful. That it was an offence known to the common law, and not first created by the 33 Edward I., is manifest. That statute speaks of conspiracy as a term at that time well-known to the law, and professes only to be ' a definition of conspirators.' It has accordingly been always held to be the law that the gist of the offence of conspiracy is the bare engagement and association to break the law, whether any act be done in pursuance thereof by the conspirators or not." And in Chitty's Criminal Law, vol. 3, p. 1140, it is said: " In every case that can be adduced of conspiracy, the offence depends on the unlawful agreement, and not on the act which follows it; the latter is but evidence of the former." Citing *Rex* v. *Rispal*, 3 Burr. at p. 1321. And Mr. Justice Willes in answering the question submitted to the Judges by the House of Lords in *Mulcahy* v. *The Queen*, L. R. 3 H. L. 306, at p. 317, thus defined the offence : " A conspiracy consists not merely in the intention of two or more, but in the agreement of two or more to do an unlawful act, or to do a lawful act by unlawful means."

The magistrate states he convicted the defendant of the offence charged against him, which was for " unlawfully conspiring with one William Irwin by deceit and falsehood to defraud one James Percy Moore." He (the magistrate) sends with the reserved case the evidence taken before him, but there being no reservation as to the sufficiency of the evidence upon which the conviction took place, we are not concerned with it further than to know that evidence was given to shew that the defendant, Frawley, and William Irwin had agreed to defraud Moore, and in order to prove the agreement or conspiracy to defraud, certain overt acts were given in evidence. The " attempt" to carry out the agreement to defraud Moore failed, and we are only concerned with

it to the extent stated because of the use of the word
"intent" in the first question submitted in place of the
word "attempt," as otherwise we might have considered
it necessary to return the reserved case for amendment.
Besides which the question itself indicates that an unsuccessful "attempt" had been made to carry out the fraud.

The first question must be answered in the affirmative.

As to the second question reserved.

"A conspiracy must be by two persons at least; one
cannot be convicted of it unless he have been indicted
for conspiracy with persons to the jurors unknown" : Archbold's Criminal Pleading and Evidence, 21st ed., 1106. And
Warburton's Criminal Cases, at p. 85, thus states the law :
"One person alone may be tried for conspiracy provided the
indictment charges him with conspiracy with others who
have not appeared, or who are since dead : *Rex* v. *Kinnersley*, 1 Str. 193 ; and *Rex* v. *Niccolls*, 2 Str. 1227 ;
and one of several prisoners indicted for conspiracy may
be tried separately, and upon conviction, judgment may be
passed on him, although the others who have appeared
and pleaded have not been tried."

The law is laid down in like terms in Wharton's Criminal Law, 9th ed., vol. 2, sec. 1388 : and in Chitty's Criminal
Law, vol. 3, he says, at p. 1141 : "And it is holden, that
if all the defendants mentioned in the indictment, except
one, are acquitted, and it is not stated as a conspiracy
with certain persons unknown, the conviction of the
single defendant will be invalid, and no judgment can be
passed upon him."

Reading the text of these authorities on criminal law,
and even from an examination of some of the cases upon
which the text is founded, the impression conveyed was that
unless two were charged in the indictment the indictment
would be bad. However, after a perusal of the case of *Rex*
v. *Nichols*, as reported in a note in 13 East, at p. 412, I
regard it as properly interpreting the law on the question
raised. The defendant was indicted for a conspiracy, and

the jury found him guilty of a conspiracy with one Bygrave. Judgment.
They likewise found that Bygrave died before the indict- MacMahon,
ment was found. The indictment was removed into the   J.
Court of King's Bench by *certiorari*, and Lee, C. J., said, at
p. 415, note: "As to the point of law, it is clear from the
cases that have been cited, that the Court will be well
warranted in giving judgment against the defendant."
See also the judgment of Holroyd, J., in *Regina* v. *Cooke*,
5 B. & C. 538, at p. 545, cited by Mr. Cartwright.

The answer to the second question must be in the affirmative. The Crown is therefore entitled to judgment.

G. F. H.

[QUEEN'S BENCH DIVISION.]

Re Wilson and the Corporation of the Town
of Ingersoll.

*Intoxicating Liquors—By-law to Fix Number of Licenses—Passed without
Required Two-thirds' Vote—Read a Third Time only at Subsequent
Meeting on Two-thirds' Vote—Validity.*

A by-law to regulate the proceedings of a town council required that
every by-law should receive three readings, and that no by-law for
raising money, or which had a tendency to increase the burdens of the
people should be finally passed on the day on which it was introduced,
except by a two-thirds' vote of the whole council.

A by-law to fix the number of tavern licenses, and which, therefore,
required such two-thirds' vote, was read three times on the same day,
and was declared passed. It did not, however, receive the required
two-thirds' vote. A special meeting of council was then called for the
following evening, when the by-law was merely read a third time,
receiving the required two-thirds' vote:—

Held, that the by-law was bad, for having been defeated when first
introduced by reason of not having received a two-thirds' vote, it was
not validated by merely reading it a third time at the subsequent
meeting.

The by-law did not shew, as required by the Liquor License Act the year
to which it was to be applicable:—

Held, that it was bad for this reason also.

This was an application for an order to quash by-law No. Statement.
393, of the municipal corporation of the town of Ingersoll,
entituled a by-law for regulating the number of tavern and

Statement. shop licenses to be granted within the town of Ingersoll, and for fixing the sum to be paid for said licenses, etc., on the grounds :—

1. That it was introduced and passed through its first, second, and third readings, on Tuesday, the 27th day of February, 1894, and declared by the Mayor as finally passed, and that it was not passed by a vote of two-thirds of the whole council, contrary to section 36 of by-law No. 360.

2. That it was not open to the municipal council to take any proceedings; which they did, on Wednesday, the 28th day of February, 1894, but that the same were invalid and void.

3. That the resolution to fix the number of tavern licenses at six, and which was passed, was not a resolution that could have been passed in committee of the whole on the 27th day of February, 1894, being in contravention of sections 29 and 39 of by-law No. 360, as a motion of a like character fixing the number at six had just been disposed of and declared lost, and the said resolution was illegal and void.

4. The special meeting held on Wednesday, the 28th day of February, 1894, was illegal and void as regards this by-law, and no sufficient notice was given of holding the same.

5. The said by-law did not state any time when the same was to come into force.

April 5th, 1894. *Osler*, Q. C., and *Jackson*, for the applicants.

Fullerton, Q. C., contra.

April 6th, 1894. ROBERTSON, J. :—

It appears that the council of this municipality has a by-law No. 360, which was revised and adopted by the council on the 3rd October, 1892, to regulate the proceedings in council, etc., and by section 36 it is enacted :—

36. That every by-law shall receive three several readings previous to its being passed: but no by-law for raising
money, or which in its operation shall have a tendency to
increase the burdens of the people shall be finally passed
on the day on which it is introduced, except by a two-
thirds' vote of the whole council.

It was admitted that the by-law in question came within
the provisions of this section in regard to a two-third vote.
The minutes of council shew that on the 27th February,
1894, at a full meeting of the council it was moved and
seconded, in due form, and " Resolved, that the mover have
leave to introduce a by-law for the issuing of tavern and
shop licenses, and that the by-law be now read a first time."

"The by-law read a first time"—whereupon it was moved
and seconded, and " Resolved, that the by-law for the
granting of licenses be now read a second time."

· " By-law read a second time"—whereupon it was moved
and seconded, and " Resolved, that the council does now
go into committee of the whole on the by-law granting
licenses."

" Carried in committee of the whole, Dr. Williams remaining in the chair." After being discussed and passed
in committee of the whole, it was "Resolved, that committee do now rise and report the by-law as passed in
committee of the whole, with blanks filled up."

" Council resumed, Mayor in the chair," whereupon it
was " Resolved, that the council concur in the finding of
the committee of the whole on Liquor License by-law."

Whereupon it was " Moved by T. Shelden, seconded by
William Motterworth, and resolved, that the by-law for
granting tavern and shop licenses, be now read a third
time, and signed, sealed, and numbered 393."—Carried.
By-law read a third time and declared passed.

The yeas and nays on being taken, were as follows :—
Yeas : Motterworth, Macaulay, Noxon, Butler, Archibald
Thompson, Williams, and Sheldon—8. Nays : Jones,
Christopher, Ruddick, Berry, and Alderson—5.

The result was the by-law was defeated on the third

reading, under the two-third vote provision before referred to.   On the next evening, however, a special
meeting of the council was called, and councillors Motterworth, Macaulay, Noxon, Butler, Archibald Thompson,
and Sheldon, with the Mayor in the chair, were present,
and on motion the minutes of the last meeting were read
and adopted; and the next matter proceeded with was a
motion by Mr. Motterworth, seconded by Mr. Macaulay,
" that the by-law *Re* the issue of tavern and shop licenses
be now read a third time, passed, signed, sealed and numbered 393."

It is contended that this proceeding was irregular and
void; and it was contended that the by-law had been
regularly voted upon and passed through all its proper
stages, at the previous meeting of the council, until the
motion for its third reading was put, when, according to
section 36 of the by-law regulating the proceedings in
council, it was defeated, which put an end to that by-law
as introduced.

I am of opinion this contention must prevail. It was
competent, however, for the council at its subsequent meeting to have introduced and read a new by-law, in exactly
the same terms, if they were so disposed; but the new by-
law required to be introduced *de novo*, read a first and
second time, referred to a committee, and could then be
read a third time, but to pick up an old defeated by-law,
and re-read it a third time is contrary, not only to the
rules of this council, but to the rules of all deliberative
assemblies for the enacting of laws.

The by-law, on the face of it, shews that it was read a
first, second, and third time on the 27th February, 1894,
and again read a third time on the 28th February, 1894.
This is wrong, because it was not read a third time on the
27th; the motion was put to read it a third time on that
date, but inasmuch as it required a vote of two-thirds of
the whole council, the motion was defeated and the by-law
was defeated; in other words all the previous proceedings
taken on the by-law had been rendered nugatory by reason

of the third reading being defeated. The proceedings in
council are regulated by by-law of their own passing—the
rules there declared to be in force cannot be set aside,
unless by unanimous consent.

I think the by-law is defective on another ground taken
by the applicant. The Liquor License Act, R. S. O. ch. 194,
sec. 20, declares that the council of every city, town, village,
or township, may, by by-law to be passed before the 1st
March in any year, limit the number of tavern licenses to
be issued therein *for the then ensuingl icense year*, beginning on the 1st May, or *for any future license year*, etc.
Now this by-law is silent as to the year it is applicable—
for all that appears it may be applicable to the year 1895
or 1896, it does not state when it is to come in force, nor
whether it is to be applicable to this current year or not.
The power to pass these license by-laws are of statutory
creation and they must be strictly in accordance with
that power.

On the whole facts before me I must quash this by-law,
and I think with costs.

                                              G. F. H.

JONES v. GODSON.

Arbitration and Award—Excessive Charge for Arbitrator's Fees—Penalty
—R. S. O. ch. 53, sec. 29—Demand—Liability.

The liability imposed on arbitrators by section 29 of R. S. O. ch. 53 in
case of an overcharge of fees, to pay treble the amount of the fees
charged or paid, is penal in its nature, and does not arise where a person entitled to take up the award has voluntarily paid the charges
without any previous demand of the award by such person, followed by
a refusal or delay to make, execute, or deliver the same by the arbitrator until payment of the excessive charges.
Taxation of the fees is not a condition precedent to maintaining an action
for the penalty.

Statement.   THIS was an action to recover damages against two of
three arbitrators who had signed an award, and was tried
before STREET, J., without a jury, at the Toronto Assizes
on January 17th, 1894.   The claim was that the two arbitrators had charged a larger sum for fees than they were
entitled to, and the plaintiffs were therefore, entitled, under
section 29 of R. S. O. ch. 53, to recover treble the amount
charged.

The award was made on the 15th of February, 1894, and
on its being made by the two arbitrators, the third arbitrator having refused to join in it, it was placed in an
envelope addressed to the Imperial Bank, Toronto, and
left there with an indorsement on the back of the envelope
of the figures $526.30. On the same day that the award
was made, the two arbitrators signed a letter addressed to
the parties to the reference, stating that they had made an
award and that their fees were $526.30, and that the award
was at the Imperial Bank, Toronto, and on payment of
the said amount, the award would be delivered over. The
solicitor for the plaintiff, one of the parties to the reference,
took a marked cheque to the bank and delivered it to the
manager of the bank, who took the cheque and handed
over the award ; and on the following day the writ in this
action was issued and came to the defendants' knowledge.

The defendants refused to receive the cheque, on the

ground that the manager of the bank had no authority to
receive a cheque, but only the payment of the amount in
cash. The manager thereupon returned the cheque to the
solicitor, but he sent it back again to the bank where it
remained, both the plaintiff and defendants refusing to
receive it.

At the conclusion of the case, the learned Judge delivered the following judgment:—

STREET, J. :—

I need not, I think, delay this matter, as it is not a
matter of law, it appears to me, but a question of fact.
The arbitrators, the defendants, are sued for what I think
must be treated as being penalties under the 29th section
of R. S. O. ch. 53. They are made liable by that statute in
treble the amount of the fees they claim provided they have
received a larger sum for fees than the statute authorizes
them to charge.

The facts here are these: They wrote to the parties
stating that the award was with the Imperial Bank and
that their charges amounted to $526.30, which is admitted
to have been more than the sum that they could lawfully
charge The solicitor for the plaintiff in the present action,
upon receiving the letter, took a marked cheque for that
amount and left it with the Imperial Bank and received the
award. There is no evidence whatever that the Imperial
Bank was entitled to receive a marked cheque for the
amount. There is no evidence that the Imperial Bank was
ever authorized to receive payment in that way. In fact I
do not know that there is any evidence that the Imperial
Bank was authorized to receive the money at all excepting
inferentially from this letter. The next day after receiving
this cheque from the Imperial Bank the writ in the present
action was issued and came to the knowledge of the defendants. Very likely for that reason—at any rate for
some reason or other—they refused to receive the cheque
and therefore, as I look at the facts, they have never re-

ceived the amount of their fees. The cheque remains in the hands of the Imperial Bank, the defendants refusing to receive it; and the plaintiff has refused to receive it back, as I think it is stated. At all events the amount of it has never come to the hands of the defendants, and the Imperial Bank never was authorized to receive a cheque for the amount by the defendants. So that neither actually nor as a matter of law can they be treated in an action of this kind as having received the money. In other words, I think that under the circumstances of this case until the money actually came to their hands there was a *locus peni-tentiæ* for them.

I think the action must fail upon that ground and that it should be dismissed with costs.

The plaintiff moved on notice to set aside the judgment entered for the defendants and to have the judgment entered in his favour.

In Easter Sittings, May 23rd, 1894, before a Divisional Court composed of ROSE and MACMAHON, JJ., *W. R. Smyth* supported the motion. There was a clear overcharge. Sec. 29 of R. S. O. ch. 53, provides that where arbitrators have charged and received a larger sum than is by the Act allowed, the arbitrators making the overcharge shall be liable in treble the amount of the whole sum so overcharged. There was clearly an overcharge here, and the defendants are liable. The delivery of the marked cheque and its acceptance by the manager of the bank, who was the agent of the defendants to receive payment and who received payment without objection, constitutes a good payment. It was paid to the person directed to receive payment and received by him as payment, and it was only when the defendants ascertained that the writ had been issued that they refused to receive the cheque as payment. It was then too late to set up that the payment by cheque was not a good payment, and that the payment should have been in money: *Shipton* v. *Casson*, 5 B. & C. 378;

Hodgson v. *Anderson*, 3 B. & C. 842, 854 ; *Hough* v. *May*, 4 A. & E. 954 ; *Bridges* v. *Garrett*, L. R. 5 C. P. 451 ; *Pearson* v. *Scott*, 9 Ch. D. 198 ; *Pape* v. *Westacott*, [1894] 1 Q. B. 272.

Wallace Nesbitt and *A. Monro Grier*, contra. The action is a penal one, and the plaintiff is put to the strictest proof. The statute requires a demand to be made and a refusal or delay after such demand. There was no such refusal or delay here. The object is to give the arbitrators an opportunity to rectify the overcharge especially where, as here, it is made in good faith. The plaintiff must, at least shew *mens rea* : *Dickenson* v. *Fletcher*, L. R. 9 C. P. 1, 5 ; *Ambergate Local Board* v. *Hammett*, L. R. 10 Q. B. 162. Then there was no payment of the fees. The payment means payment in money. The marked cheque was not sufficient. The fees also should have been taxed before action brought.

W. R. Smyth, in reply. This is not a penal action, but to enforce a statutory right. It is not intended as a punishment of the arbitrators, but as a compensation to one who is unable to get the award without first paying the fees charged. The amount fixed by the statute is given as liquidated damages. What took place here amounted to a demand and refusal. Taxation of the fees was not required. Section 24 only refers to a taxation of the whole costs of the arbitration in which the costs payable by the arbitrators are an incident ; while the words used in section 29, " may be taxed," does not make taxation a condition precedent. It is permissive merely and not compulsory. The taxation may take place at any time, even after the action has been brought : *Chilton* v. *London and Croydon R. W. Co.*, 16 M. & W. 212 ; *Adams* v. *Battley*, 18 Q. B. D. 628 ; *Bradlaugh* v. *Clarke*, 8 App. Cas. 354.

June 23rd, 1894. ROSE, J. :—

The decision in this case turns largely on the construction of section 29 of R. S. O. 1887, ch. 53.

The section is involved, and some of its provisions are
capable of at least two interpretations. It is penal in its
nature, and care must be taken to so construe it if possible
as not to make an arbitrator liable to pay a penalty for an
act done in good faith and without any wrong intent.
The penalty provided is for refusal or delay to make, execute, and deliver an award, after the expiration of the
time named for the purpose of extorting a larger sum for
fees than is by the Act permitted, and may be taxed, and
this penalty is given to any one entitled to obtain the
award who has demanded it, and recovery may be
had if an excessive sum has been paid. If no payment
has been made the penalty will be treble the amount
demanded by the arbitrator, and if payment has been
made then treble the sum actually paid. The person paying the fees must be a person entitled to obtain the award
and must have demanded the award before payment.

The person entitled, having demanded the award, and
refusal or delay having ensued, may then sue or may pay
the amount demanded, or such other sum as the arbitrator
may accept, and, if excessive, may then bring his action.
The penalty is only for refusal or delay—" he shall for
every such refusal or delay," and it is for *every* refusal or
delay, and hence a previous demand is clearly necessary
else there could not be more than one continuing refusal
or delay.

I cannot bring my mind to interpret the clause to mean
that where there has been a payment without protest of
an excessive amount without any previous refusal or delay,
an action at once lies, because such a construction would
be, in the first place, ungrammatical, and in the second
place, unjust.

The refusal or delay is until an excessive sum is paid,
and, as I have said, the action lies either during the time
of such refusal or delay, or after it has ceased by reason
of the payment of an excessive sum whether it be the sum
first demanded or some other sum which the arbitrator
has consented to receive, and has received.

I do not say what else may be necessary to entitle a

plaintiff to succeed, but at least he must be a person entitled to obtain the award, and must have demanded it,
and such demand must be followed by a refusal or delay,
and then either with or without payment an action lies if
all other conditions have been fulfilled, all other things
have happened, and all times have elapsed.

I do not think a plaintiff must, prior to demand or
action, have had the fees taxed. I read the words "by
this Act permitted and may be taxed," as meaning that
the arbitrator is not subject to a penalty for demanding a
sum in excess of what may thereafter be taxed if such
demand do not exceed the amount which may be taxed,
i. e., the outside sum the tariff provides for, otherwise an
arbitrator honestly charging what he thought fair—being
it may be the outside figure permitted by the Act, might
be liable to a penalty because a taxing officer differed from
him as to the propriety of such charge.

It is clear that here there was no demand of the award
at all, and hence no refusal or delay within the section.

I do not find it necessary in view of what I have said
to consider carefully whether there was, prior to action,
a payment to the arbitrators. As far as I have formed an
opinion I am not inclined to dissent from the view of my
learned brother Street.

The plaintiff here having neither remonstrated with the
defendants, nor pointed out their error or overcharge, nor
in anywise notified them of any objection to the charge,
but having issued the writ of summons with much haste
after payment, his conduct is open to the observation that
his action was for the purpose of making money rather
than to enforce the law for his own protection or the punishment of wrong-doers.

In my opinion the motion fails and must be dismissed
with costs.

MacMahon, J., concurred.

G. F. H.

SCOTT v. REBURN.

Malicious Arrest—Constable—Notice of Action—Requisites of.

Where in an action against a constable for false arrest it is found by the
jury that the defendant acted in the honest belief that he was discharging his duty as a constable, and was not actuated by any improper
motive, he is entitled to notice of action, and such notice must state
not only the time of the commission of the act complained of, but that
it was done maliciously.

Statement.   THIS was an action for false arrest, tried before ROSE, J.,
and a jury, at Toronto, at the Spring Assizes of 1894.

The action was brought by the plaintiffs against the defendant who was a police constable of the city of Toronto.

The charge was that the plaintiffs were passengers on the
steamer "Cibola," and that "upon the arrival of the said
steamer at Toronto, and upon the said plaintiffs landing
from said steamer upon the wharf whereat the said steamer
landed, and upon Esplanade street and streets adjacent
thereto, and in a building close to said Esplanade street in
the city of Toronto, the said defendant falsely, vexatiously,
maliciously, and without reasonable or probable cause
assaulted, unlawfully detained, arrested, and imprisoned,
and took into custody the said plaintiffs for a considerable
period of time, namely, until about one hour after the
arrival of the said steamer."

To this the defendant pleaded not guilty by statute
R. S. O. ch. 73, secs. 1, 13, 14, 15, 20.

A notice of action was put in by the plaintiffs, which
was as follows:—

TORONTO, 27th July, 1894.

W. G. REBURN,
    69 Huron street,
        Toronto.

DEAR SIR,—   *Re* SCOTT.

We are instructed with Mr. G. A. Stevenson, Barrister,
Manning Arcade, by the Misses Ida May, Bertha and
Harriet Scott, by their next friend Alexander Scott, to

bring an action against you in the High Court of Justice
for without reasonable and probable cause assaulting and
falsely arresting and imprisoning them in the Custom
House at the wharf where the Niagara Navigation Company's boats land. The young women are residing at
present in Lewiston, N. Y. We are also instructed to take
proceedings against the Niagara Navigation Company and
purser Chapman. Kindly call and see us about it. Our
offices are at 53 King street west, Toronto.

This was signed by Armstrong & Elliott, solicitors, practising in the city of Toronto.

The plaintiffs were passengers from Lewiston to Toronto,
on the steamer "Cibola." On the way over they went to
the toilet-room. A Mrs. Telfer also was there at the same
time. The plaintiffs shortly afterwards left the room and
went into the cabin where they remained for some time
and then went on deck, when Mrs. Telfer came up to one
of the plaintiffs and said she had lost her purse and asked
her if she knew anything about it, to which the plaintiffs
replied they did not. Nothing further took place until
the boat arrived at Toronto, when, as the plaintiffs were
coming down the stairs, with the view of landing, they
were told by the purser to remain on board for the purpose
of being searched, as he said everybody was going to be
searched. They accordingly remained until nearly all the
passengers had left the boat when they got up and walked
on to the wharf, where they were met by the defendant, a
police officer, who came up to them, laid his hand on the
shoulder of one of them and told them to come with him,
and they were taken to the Custom House office on the
wharf. The defendant then closed the door and turning
to the plaintiffs said : "Come now, give up the purse and
have no more trouble over it." The plaintiffs said that
they did not know anything about it. The defendant
then said, "You had better give it up." One of the plaintiffs said, "How are we going to give up something we
have not got ?" He then asked the plaintiffs if they were
willing to be searched, to which the plaintiffs replied that

they were, and the defendant then spoke about sending for the matron of the steamer. Mrs. Telfer then came in, and one of the plaintiffs asked her if she said that they had taken her purse, and she replied no. She then asked her if she suspected them, and she said no. The defendant spoke of sending for the patrol waggon and taking the plaintiffs off in it; but the defendant apparently decided to take no further action in the matter, and after the plaintiffs had been detained in the room for about an hour, they were allowed to go.

It appeared that Mrs. Telfer had informed the purser of the steamer of the loss of her purse, and of her suspicions against the plaintiffs, and he had reported the matter to the defendant, telling him that Mrs. Telfer suspected the plaintiffs of having taken her purse, and requesting him to detain them.

On the part of the defence it was objected that no case was made out; that the defendant was a police officer acting in the honest belief that he was discharging his duty, and without any improper motive.

It was also objected that the notice of action was not sufficient to entitle the plaintiffs to maintain the action, because the time of the commission of the alleged arrest was not stated in the notice, nor that the act complained of was done maliciously; and also that the evidence as to service was insufficient.

The learned Judge declined to give effect to the objections but said he would reserve his decision until the evidence was in, and the opinion of the jury taken.

Questions were submitted to the jury, which, with the answers thereto, were as follows:—

1. Did the purser fairly state to Reburn the facts as narrated to him by Mrs. Telfer? A. No.

2. Were the facts as stated such as to a reasonable man would make it seem probable that a theft had been committed? A. No.

3. If so, would it also seem probable that the theft had been committed by the plaintiffs, or one of them? A. No.

4. Did Reburn act in the honest belief that he was discharging his duty? A. Yes. Or was he actuated by some improper motive? A. No.

5. Was notice of action left for Reburn at his usual place of abode? A. Yes.

The learned Judge subsequently delivered the following judgment:—

May 10, 1894. ROSE, J. :—

Were the question open for decision freed from the trammels of authority, I should, I think, be of opinion that the notice of action herein gave the defendant full information of the cause of action and the Court in which it was intended to be brought. But, as pointed out by the learned Chief Justice of Ontario in *Bond* v. *Conmee*, 16 A. R. 398, at p. 404, the earlier decisions proceeded upon the special demurrer system that once prevailed as to pleading, and in the course of such decisions it has been held necessary in the notice to state that the act was done maliciously as well as without reasonable and probable cause. See *Howell* v. *Armour*, 7 O. R. 363, at pp. 375-6. And also that time and place must both be set out. In *Langford* v. *Kirkpatrick*, 2 A. R. 513, at p. 518, the late Chief Justice Moss stated the rule to be that the time and place of the act complained of must be set forth.

The notice of action in that case as well as in *Bond* v. *Conmee*, 16 A. R. 398, did state the time although not the very day, and the decisions in *Parkyn* v. *Staples*, 19 C. P. 240, 243; *Sprung* v. *Anderson*, 23 C. P. 152, were not dissented from.

I have no doubt the defendant had all the notice he required to enable him to make amends, and was as fully informed of the cause of complaint as if a formal statement of claim had been served upon him.

If, as stated in *Martins* v. *Upcher*, 3 Q. B. 662, the plaintiff will not always be strictly bound to prove the time and place named in his notice ; and, as said by Alderson, B., in *Jucklin* v. *Fytche*, 14 M. & W. 381, the proper test of sufficiency is whether the notice gives all reasonable information, if as held by Moss, C. J. O., in *Langford* v. *Kirkpatrick*, a test of the sufficiency of the statement of time and place is whether the defendant could have been misled ; and as observed by Hagarty, C. J. O., in *Bond* v. *Conmee*, at p. 404, the course of modern decisions has been to construe the notice of action not on the special demurrer system that once prevailed as to pleading, but on a more liberal and common sense interpretation of the true requirements of the statute, then I think the notice should be held sufficient. Yet as in neither of the above cases in the Court of Appeal were the cases I have referred to in the Court of Common Pleas dissented from, I think I should, as Judge of first instance, follow them and hold the notice not sufficient in that no time is stated when the offence complained of was committed.

The jury found that the defendant acted in the honest belief that he was discharging his duty, and that he was not actuated by any improper motive. He was, therefore, entitled to notice of action : *Bond* v. *Conmee*, 16 A. R. 398, at p. 411 ; *Sinden* v. *Brown*, 17 A. R. 173, at pp. 187-8.

There must be judgment for the defendant dismissing the plaintiffs' action with costs.

The plaintiffs moved on notice to set aside the judgment entered for the defendant and to have the judgment entered in their favour.

In Easter Sittings, June 5th, 1894, before a Divisional Court composed of GALT, C.J., and MACMAHON, J., *Fullerton*, Q. C., supported the motion. There was no ground shewn for taking the plaintiffs into custody. No charge was laid against the plaintiffs, and the defendant did not act on the belief that the plaintiffs had committed any offence. To justify an arrest, there must be a charge laid and a reasonable belief that a crime has been committed. The defendant, therefore, acted without reasonable and probable cause, and there was no necessity to prove malice: *Lister v. Perryman*, L. R. 4 H. L. 521 ; Addison on Torts, 7th ed., 781. The notice of action was sufficient. It is not necessary that the time the offence was committed should be alleged in the notice, nor that the defendant acted maliciously. All that section 14 of R. S. O. ch. 73, requires is, that the cause of action and the name of the Court in which the action is intended to be brought, should be stated. The notice gives the cause of action and the name of the Court. It thus gives the defendant full information of everything required by the statute: *Bond v. Conmee*, 16 A. R. at p. 403. The notice was also duly served. The defendant, however, was not entitled to a notice of action, as he acted without any jurisdiction: *Agnew v. Jobson*, 13 Cox C. C. 625 ; *Ibbottson v. Henry*, 8 O. R. 625 ; *Chamberlain v. King*, L. R. 6 C. P. 474 ; *Smith & Co. v. Derry West Local Board*, 3 C. P. D. 529 ; *Cox v. Hamilton Sewer Pipe Co.*, 14 O. R. 300 ; *Whitman v. Pearson*, L. R. 3 C. P. 422 ; *O'Dea v. Hickman*, 18 Ir. C. L. (1887), 233 ; *Friel v. Ferguson*, 15 C. P. 384.

J. B. Clarke, Q. C., contra. The defendant acted with reasonable and probable cause and without malice. There were no facts in dispute on which the jury should have passed, and therefore the learned Judge should have ruled on the question himself, and should have entered a nonsuit : *McLaren v. Archibald*, 21 S. C. R. 588 ; *Lister v. Perryman*, L. R. 4 H. L. 521. The defendant is also entitled to succeed on the ground of the insufficiency of the notice of action, because neither the time of the commission of the offence is stated therein ; nor that the act was done maliciously ; and further, that no due service of the notice was proved. Section 1 of R. S. O. ch. 73, expressly enacts that it must be alleged and proved that the defendant acted maliciously : *Bond v. Conmee*, 16 A. R. 398 ; *Booth v. Clive*, 10 C. B. 827 ; *Howell v. Armour*, 7 O. R. 363 ; *Cox v. Reid*, 13 Q. B. 558 ; *City of St. John v. Christie*, 21 S. C. R. 1. The findings of the jury to the fourth question dispose of the whole case, for they expressly find that the defendant acted *bonâ fide*, in the execution of his duty and without malice. The defendant was entitled to notice of action. He believed he was acting in the discharge of his duty. *Bonâ fides* is the test of the necessity for notice, even though it may be found that the trespass is not justifiable.

June 23, 1894. GALT, C. J.:—

At the conclusion of the plaintiffs' case a motion was made to dismiss the action on the ground that the defendant was entitled to a notice of action, and that no sufficient notice had been given.

The learned Judge declined to give effect, to this objection but waived his decision until after the evidence was in and the opinion of the jury taken. Certain questions, amongst others, were submitted to the jury, viz. :—

4. Did Reburn act in the honest belief that he was discharging his duty ? A. Yes. Or was he actuated by some improper motive ? A. No.

Upon these answers of the jury apart from any question of want of notice, in my opinion the defendant was entitled to judgment under section 1 of the Act.

By section 14, notice of action must be given "in which notice the cause of action and the Court in which the same is intended to be brought, shall be clearly and explicitly elected."

The notice served, was as follows [setting it out] :—

It is plain from the foregoing that no time is stated at which the arrest took place, and there is no allegation that the act complained of was done *maliciously*. By section 14 the notice must contain a statement of the cause of action and the Court in which the same is intended to be brought, and the cause of action shall be clearly and explicitly stated. By section 1 it is enacted that it shall be expressly alleged in the statement of claim that the act was done " maliciously," and without reasonable and prob-

able cause, and if at the trial of the action the plaintiff Judgment.
fails to prove such allegation judgment shall be given for Galt, C.J.
the defendant.

It appears to me manifest from this express provision
that in the notice of action it must be alleged that the act
complained of was done maliciously.

The judgment of my brother Rose is in accordance with
the decision of this Division in *Sprung* v. *Anderson*, 23
C. P. 152, at p. 160 : " However, the notice served in respect
of this cause of action states no time whatever when what
is complained of herein is contended to have been done, and
is therefore defective."

There is no reference in any of the cases cited by my
learned brother to the absence of an allegation of malice,
because in all of them such allegation was made, and, as I
have already said apart altogether from the question of
time, in my opinion the notice in this case was defective
for that reason.

The motion must be dismissed with costs.

MacMahon, J. :—

As to the defect in the notice of action. The answer to
the fourth question is a finding by the jury that the defendant when he arrested the plaintiffs acted in the honest
belief that he was discharging his duty as a constable, and
that he was not actuated by any improper motive. The
defendant was therefore entitled to notice of action as
provided by sec. 14 of R. S. O. ch. 73.

If we are not to reverse the decisions going back nearly
half a century, the notice in this case is bad on two
grounds : First, because it should have alleged both
time and place ; and second, because it does not allege
that the act charged was done " maliciously and without
reasonable and probable cause."

As to the first defect. *Martins* v. *Upcher*, 3 Q. B. 662
(decided in 1842), has been followed in our own Courts in
Parkyn v. *Staples*, 19 C. P. 240 ; *Sprung* v. *Anderson*,

23 C. P. 152, and *Langford* v. *Kirkpatrick*, 2 A. R. 513, where the cases above referred to of *Parkyn* v. *Staples*, *Sprung* v. *Anderson*, and also the case of *Selmes* v. *Judge*, L. R. 6 Q. B. 724, are reviewed in the judgment of Moss, C. J. A., at pp. 517-519, and he says: "That while the rule is that the time and place of the act complained of must be set forth, the disposition of the Courts is to exact no more than reasonable certainty."

There is no time whatever mentioned in the notice of action served in this case. The place mentioned in the notice would likely in view of the decision in the *Langford* case, be regarded as reasonably certain.

As to the second defect in the notice in not alleging that the defendant acted "maliciously" as well as "without reasonable and probable cause," the authorities are equally clear that without such statement in the notice it is bad. The last decided case on the point is *Howell* v. *Armour*, 7 O. R. 363, at p. 376, where the Queen's Bench Division held that notice was defective by reason of the want of the allegation that the defendants acted maliciously.

The plaintiffs have failed to prove that the defendant acted "maliciously." The jury have negatived the allegation of malice in the statement of claim, and there must not only be allegation but the finding of malice, without which the plaintiffs cannot recover.

I agree that the motion fails and must be dismissed with costs.

G. F. H.

[COMMON PLEAS DIVISION.]

REGINA V. WETTMAN.

Gaming—Keeping a Common Gaming House—Offence in United States.

In a betting game called "policy," the actual betting and payment of
   the money, if won, took place in the United States ; all that was done
   in Canada being the happening of the chance, on which the bet was
   staked, by means of implements operated in the house of the defendant :—

Held, there was no offence under sec. 198 of the Criminal Code of 1892 of
   keeping a common gaming house within that section.

THIS was a case reserved by the chairman of the General Statement.
Sessions of the Peace for the county of Welland.

The reserved case as amended was as follows :

The defendant was indicted under section 198 of the
Criminal Code, 1892, for keeping on the 18th day of
November, A. D. 1893, at Fort Erie, in the county of
Welland, a disorderly house to wit a common gaming
house, as defined by sub-sections (*b*), (*ii*) of section 196,
and was convicted at the December Sessions, 1893.

A second count charged him with keeping said house on
the 20th, and a third count on the 22nd day of said
month.

The evidence adduced by the Crown and relied on to
sustain the conviction shewed :

1. That the defendant was, under sub-section 2, of section
198, the person appearing to have the care, government
or management of the house.

2. That the game which the defendant was charged
with carrying on was the game of "policy," the implements
used being a wheel, a quantity of numbers on printed
slips from one to seventy-eight, both inclusive, and a
board with the same numbers painted thereon.

3. That the manner of playing the game, as carried on
by the defendant, was as follows :

A number of agencies were scattered through Buffalo, in
New York State, where persons desirous of playing the

game went, and there made a selection of numbers (usually of three) between the numbers one and seventy-eight. Having chosen his numbers, the player put them down on two slips, one of which he gave to the agent, the other he retained, and at the same time he paid whatever sum (it was shewn that five or ten cents was the ordinary amount staked) he desired to stake on the game. The agent delivered these slips and the money so staked to the head office of the defendant (also in Buffalo). In Fort Erie, in the county of Welland, the other part of the game, viz., determining the winning or losing numbers was carried on, and the operation was as follows:

The operator went to the room where the wheel before referred to was kept, each day at twelve and five o'clock.

He had the individual numbers from one to seventy-eight, before mentioned, in small individual boxes—one in each box. These he opened to shew any one present that there was one number in each box. Having done this, he deposited all the boxes in the wheel before mentioned, which was a hollow wheel resembling a cheese box with glass sides.

He then revolved the wheel so as to effectually shuffle the boxes. He then opened the wheel, and out of the seventy-eight boxes, withdrew twelve, opened them singly and called out the numbers contained therein. He then returned the numbers to the boxes, closed the boxes, deposited them in the wheel, and went through the same operation of revolving the wheel, shuffling the boxes and withdrawing twelve, the numbers in which he also read out. Having done this, he telegraphed these numbers, which were the winning numbers, over to the head office in Buffalo where printed slips were issued and delivered to the different agencies. If a player had chosen three numbers which appeared on these slips, he had won and got two dollars for each cent he had so staked. He must have chosen all three to win. And the odds were in favour of the banker or other person by whom the game is managed.

4. The only thing done in this country was the revolving of the wheel and the determining of the winning numbers. The money was staked, and if won, paid in Buffalo.

5. The implements used in the game were instruments of gaming, as shewn in section 702.

6. It was also proved in evidence :

1. That on the 23rd day of November, 1893, the house where the implements aforesaid were kept and used was entered under section 702 of the Criminal Code, 1892, by the constable (who made the arrest of the defendant) under a search warrant properly issued under the Criminal Code ; that the defendant was there in the same room where the implements aforesaid were, and that these implements were seized at that time by the constable and retained in his custody and produced by him at the trial.

2. No evidence was given on behalf of the defendant that there was no gaming going on in the house to meet the *primâ fucie* case established under section 702.

At the request of the defendant's counsel and under the authority of the Criminal Code, the following question arising upon the evidence was reserved by me for the opinion of the Justices of the Common Pleas Division of the High Court of Justice.

Was the defendant properly convicted of the offence charged upon the foregoing statement of facts ?

On May 30th, 1894, the case was argued.

Osler, Q. C., for the defendant.
Cartwright, Q. C., for the Crown.
The arguments and cases referred to sufficiently appear in the judgment.

June 23rd, 1894. ROSE, J. :—

The statute is aimed at gaming. The object is to save the unwary from hurtful temptation ; to protect the residents of this Dominion from the injury which results not only to them, but to society at large from the waste of their substance in gaming. It is not to be supposed that the legislation is for the protection of the residents in a foreign State. Such persons make laws for themselves.

The facts here shew that the betting or gaming in this case took place not in Canada but in Buffalo. The persons betting, the money paid and received, the tickets obtained, all these were in Buffalo. The happening of the chance upon which the money was risked took place in Canada, but nothing more. The players under the statute mean the persons playing the game in which the chances happened.

I do not see how on any fair construction of the language of the statute, it can be said that the defendant was keeping " a house, room, or place, kept or used for playing therein any game of chance, or any mixed game of chance or skill, in which any game is played, the chances of which are not alike favourable to all the players, including among the players, the banker or other person by whom the game is managed, or against whom the game is managed, or against whom the other players stake, play, or bet."

A reference to the Imperial statute from which this section was drawn, viz., 8 & 9 Vic. ch. 109, sec. 2, and the preamble to the Act, will make it plain that such a case as the one before us was never contemplated by the framers of the provision, and was not provided against.

The plain duty of the Court is to construe existing legislation according to its true meaning as far as it is made to appear, and not to add by judicial legislation new provisions to an Act of Parliament to cover cases not thought of, and therefore not intended to be covered when the Act was passed.

There must be judgment for the defendant declaring that he was not properly convicted of the offence charged, viz., keeping a disorderly house, to wit, a common gaming house as defined by sub-sections (b), (ii) of sec. 196 of the Criminal Code.

MacMahon, J. :—

By section 196 of the Code 55 & 56 Vic. ch. 29 (D.) : "A common gaming house is :—

"(b) A house, room or place kept or used for playing therein at any game of chance, or any mixed game of chance and skill, in which—

*　　*　　*　　*　　*

"(ii) In which any game is played, the chances of which are not alike favourable to all the players, including among the players the banker or other person by whom the game is managed, or against whom the game is managed, or against whom the other players stake, play or bet."

The case reserved, states that the defendant was, under sub-section 2 of section 198, the person appearing to have the management of the house. And the case also gives the effect of the evidence adduced by the Crown, describing the instruments made use of in carrying on the game of "policy," as it is called, as well as the *modus operandi* in conducting the game.

This was the use of a gaming instrument in this country, for deciding who were the winners of moneys staked, and if won, paid in a foreign country. This is not gaming here. In order to constitute gaming, there must be a stake of some kind. There being no stake in this country, there could be no violation of the law against gaming here.

In *Jenks* v. *Turpin*, 13 Q. B. D. 505, Mr. Justice Hawkins, in his judgment, refers to all the Imperial enactments respecting gaming and gaming-houses, as well as citing from text writers on criminal law, dealing with the question. And in addition, numerous decisions on the law relating to gaming are referred to. The judgment, therefore, contains in a small compass a mine of information on the subject.

It is not necessary I should draw from this, except when referring to section 702 of the Code, which I now do.

It was urged by Mr. Cartwright, that no effect is given to section 702 if the instruments of gaming found in the

house, which the case states was in the care and management of the defendant, is not sufficient to convict him of
keeping a common gaming-house. But the answer to
that is, that under section 702, the instruments found
must be "instruments of gaming used in playing any
unlawful game," and the case reserved shews that where
the instruments were used there were no stakes placed
here on the result, and if no stakes, there was no gaming;
and if no gaming, then there could be no common gaming-
house.

Section 702, although not following section 2 of 8 &
9 Vic. ch. 109, is framed from it, and in *Jenks* v. *Turpin*,
13 Q. B. D., at p. 522, Hawkins, J., gives the section in
full, and by it it is provided that: " in default of other evidence proving any house or place to be a common gaming-
house, * * it shall be sufficient in support of the allegation in any indictment or information that any house or
place is a common gaming-house, to prove that such house
or place is kept or used for playing therein at any unlawful
game, and that a bank is kept there by one or more of the
players exclusively of the others, or that the chances of
any game played therein are not alike favourable to all
the players, including among the players the banker or
other person by whom the game is managed, or against
whom the players stake, play, or bet; and every such house
or place shall be deemed a common gaming-house, such as
is contrary to law and forbidden to be kept by 33 Henry
VIII."

This shews that in the absence or default of other evidence proving the house or place to be a common gaming-
house, evidence shewing that unlawful games are played,
that there is a bank, and that the chances are not alike
favourable to all the players, etc., will be sufficient to
convict of keeping a common gaming-house. So under
section 702, in the absence of other evidence, proof that
an instrument found in the house " used in playing any
unlawful game," etc., "shall be *primâ facie* evidence on
the trial of a prosecution, under section 198, that such

house * * is used as a common gaming-house." But Judgment.
as already pointed out, there was not only no evidence MacMahon,
that the instruments were used for unlawful gaming, but
the case reserved shews there was no gaming carried on
in the house—there being no stakes put up.

The statute does not reach such a case as we are now
considering, and there must therefore be judgment for the
defendant quashing the conviction.

G. F. H.

[COMMON PLEAS DIVISION.]

THE CANADIAN PACIFIC RAILWAY COMPANY v. THE CORPORATION OF THE TOWNSHIP OF CHATHAM.

Municipal Corporations—Contract—Drainage—Ultra Vires—Liability— By-law—Necessity for—R. S. O. ch. 184, secs. 569, 583, 585.

Under a by-law passed under the provisions of sections 569 and 576 of the Municipal Act R. S. O. ch. 184, a drain was built in the defendant's township, which benefited lands in an adjoining township, and which, therefore, had been assessed for a portion of the cost. After the drain was built, it was found that an opening through the plaintiffs' embankment which, when the by-law was passed, was deemed sufficient to carry off the water brought down by the drain, was insufficient therefor, whereby the adjoining lands were flooded, and actions were threatened against the defendants. To prevent such actions and to enable the water to be carried off, an agreement was entered into between the plaintiffs and defendants under their respective corporate seals, whereby the plaintiffs were to build, and defendants to pay for a culvert through the embankment sufficient to carry off the water. The culvert was built by plaintiffs at a cost of over $200.00, and on its completion was accepted and used by defendants, who, however, refused to pay for it on the ground that the agreement for its construction was *ultra vires*. No by-law had been passed authorizing the construction of the culvert, nor were any of the proceedings required by sections 569-582 of the Municipal Act, taken :—

Held, by STREET, J., and affirmed by the Divisional Court, ROSE, J. dissenting, that the work in question was new work, and, therefore, did not come within sec. 573; but came within sub-secs. 1 and 3 of sec. 583; and inasmuch as the cost exceeded $200.00 no liability could arise until the proceedings pointed out by sec. 585 had been complied with, namely, the proceedings required by secs. 569-582 ; and as these had not been taken, the agreement was invalid and could not be enforced.

Per ROSE, J., there being an executed contract for the performance of work within the purposes for which the corporation was created, and

the defendants having adopted and received the benefit thereof, were
liable.

The case of *Bernardin* v. *Corporation of North Dufferin*, 19 S. C. R. 581,
considered on the question of absence of a by-law where there is an
executed contract.

Statement. THIS was an action tried before STREET, J., without a
jury, at the London Assizes, on 9th and 10th May, 1893.

It was brought to recover the balance alleged to be due
by the defendants on a contract for the construction of a
culvert through an embankment of the plaintiffs' railway.

Moss, Q. C., and *A. MacMurchy* for the plaintiffs.

Matthew Wilson, Q. C., and *Pegley*, Q. C., for the defendants.

The learned Judge reserved his decision, and subsequently delivered the following judgment, in which the
facts are fully stated.

June 15th, 1893.   STREET, J. :—

The construction of the Big Creek outlet drain was
provided for by by-law No. 169 of the township of Chatham. The money required, according to the estimates of
the engineer, for the making of the drain was duly assessed
by that by-law upon the lands to be benefited, was raised
and was expended with the exception of some $90, when
application was made by the defendants to the plaintiffs
to build a culvert through their embankment which crossed
the drain. A small cattle pass existed at the point where
the culvert was required, and it appears to have been
originally supposed that this would be sufficient for the
purposes of the drain, at all events no allowance was made
in the engineer's estimate for the cost of a culvert through
the railway embankment. As soon, however, as the water
got into the drain above, that is, on the north side of the
railway, having no way of passing through the embankment, it backed upon the adjoining lands, the proprietors
of which made claims against the defendants for their

damages. The defendants then pressed the plaintiffs very
urgently to build a culvert to let the water through, and
after much negotiation the plaintiffs agreed to do so at the
expense of the defendants. Thereupon two agreements
were made : the first, dated 30th November, 1891, by
which the owners of the right to the cattle pass released
the plaintiffs and defendants from certain claims to
damages, owing to the cattle pass having been taken for a
drain, and gave up their right to it in consideration of
$200 paid them by the defendants ; the second, dated 12th
December, 1891, by which the plaintiffs agreed to build
the culvert required by the defendants according to certain
specifications attached to the agreement, and the defendants agreed to repay them for their outlay in building it.
The cost was approximately stated at a certain sum, but
the agreement expressly provided that the defendants
should not be limited to this sum, but should be entitled
to be repaid the actual cost, whatever it might be. These
agreements were both under the corporate seals of the
plaintiffs and defendants, and on behalf of the defendants
were signed by the reeve and clerk of the township.

The correspondence leading up to the agreements on the
part of the defendants was entirely conducted by the
township solicitor, Mr. Pegley.

In answer to enquiries on the part of the plaintiffs as to
whether the defendants would be in funds to make the
payments they were about to agree to pay the plaintiffs
for the construction of the culvert, he repeatedly assured
the plaintiffs that if the funds provided by the original
by-law should be insufficient, the defendants would amend
the original by-law under section 573 of the Municipal
Act, and thus obtain the additional sum required.

No by-law was passed by the defendants for the construction of the culvert, nor for the execution of the agreements above referred to ; but it is impossible to read the
minutes of their proceedings without being satisfied that
what was done was done with the sanction of the council.
The plans and specifications were submitted to Mr. W. G.

McGeorge, the township engineer, who, moreover, was specially named in a resolution of 9th March, 1891, as the
person to be consulted by the commissioner for the drain.

These plans were adopted by the council by resolution
of June 25th, 1891 ; and by the same resolution the reeve
and two deputy reeves were authorized to settle with the
railway company to the best advantage.

An entry on September 7th, 1891, shews that the council
were aware of the correspondence between Mr. Pegley,
their solicitor, and the plaintiffs upon the subject of the
payment of the cost of the culvert.

On October 5th, 1891, after the terms had been finally
agreed to, there is a note that " The reeve reported in connection with the Big Creek outlet under the C. P. R.
Report adopted."

On the 28th October, 1891, a resolution authorizing the
reeve to settle with the owners of the right to the cattle
pass under the railway was adopted. On April 20th, 1892,
the existence of the agreement with the plaintiffs appears
on the face of the minutes.

On the 21st September, 1892, the council passed a resolution dealing with certain material which had been used
and charged to the defendants by the plaintiffs in the construction of the culvert, and which, being no longer
required, was the defendants' property. The plaintiffs
discovered during the progress of the work that, owing, as
they alleged, to difficulties in the work which had not been
foreseen, the cost would be largely increased. This was at
once reported to the defendants, who, on 20th April, 1892,
referred the communication to Mr. Pegley, their solicitor.
At his request the work was proceeded with, and upon its
completion on 10th May, 1892, he wrote that the defendants would pay the amount of the additional cost.

The drain was opened through the culvert upon its completion, and has ever since been serving the purpose for
which it was intended, without any protest or objection
on the part of the defendants, by whose servants the water
was let into it.

Before the commencement or during the progress of the work the defendants paid to the plaintiffs a sum of upwards of $2,000, being the amount of the original estimated cost of the work, and the present action is brought to recover the balance.

If the only objection to the plaintiffs' right to recover were the absence of a by-law authorizing the work and the execution of the agreement sued on, I should have no hesitation, upon the authority of *Bernardin* v. *Corporation of North Dufferin*, 19 S. C. R. 581, in holding that the defendants were liable, because they had in the first place as a council agreed that the work should be done, had promised to pay for it, had accepted and used it when it was completed, and had only then disputed their liability and refused to pay for it. But unfortunately there appears to be no clause in the Municipal Act which makes them liable or enables them to contract under the circumstances here existing. Their powers under that Act, so far as the drainage of land is concerned, are circumscribed most carefully so as to throw the cost of drainage works upon the persons benefited by them and not upon the township at large.

The case does not appear to me to come under section 573 for two reasons, first, because I think the funds provided by the by-law were sufficient for the completion of the work contemplated by the engineer's report, the defect being that the part of the drain which passed through the company's embankment was too narrow to allow the escape of the water ; second, because the section does not appear to me to apply to cases like the present, where land in two townships is assessed for the work.

It will be seen, I think, that the Act affords no means to the township doing the work and amending its by-law under section 573 to recover from the other township the amount which may be added to the assessment by the amendment to the by-law. The defect is one which comes under section 583, sub-sections (1) and (3), and as the cost is more than $200, the council can proceed only under section 585, and they had, therefore, no power to bind the municipality at large by summarily entering into a contract for the completion of the necessary work without the preliminary inquiries and assessments pointed out by that section.

Nor would it be possible, I think, to grant a mandamus compelling the defendants to proceed under that section and the sections to which it refers, after the whole of the work has been done, for the engineer might report an entirely different scheme for getting rid of the obstacles, and could not be compelled to report according to the scheme which has been carried out.

For these reasons I am compelled to the conclusion that the plaintiffs have no remedy, and that their action must be dismissed, but under the circumstances I give the defendants no costs.

The plaintiffs moved on notice to set aside the judgment and to enter the judgment in their favour, on the following grounds:

1. That the judgment is contrary to law and evidence, and the weight of evidence.

2. That the learned Judge erred in holding that the defendants were not empowered under the provisions of the Municipal Act, R. S. O. ch. 184, to pass a by-law amending the original by-law, No. 169, in order to provide sufficient funds for the completion of the work contemplated or intended thereby.

In Michaelmas Sittings, December 2nd and 3rd, 1893, before a Divisional Court composed of GALT, C. J., ROSE and MACMAHON, JJ., *Moss*, Q.C., and *A. MacMurchy*, supported the motion. The case properly comes within section 573. The learned Judge at the trial was of the opinion that section did not apply, on the ground that this was new work not authorized by the original by-law, and also that the section does not apply to cases where the land in two townships is assessed for the work. The building of the

CANADIAN PACIFIC R. W. CO. V. TP. OF CHATHAM.

culvert was not new work, but was work properly coming Argument. within the work contemplated by the by-law as originally passed, and it was only after it was found that the outlet was insufficient for the purposes contemplated it became necessary to build the culvert and incur the expense which is the subject of this action. The terms of the section are general that when there are not sufficient means provided for the completion of the work, then the council are authorized from time to time to amend the by-law in order to fully carry out the original intention by providing the funds necessary for the purpose. The section is not limited to the case of the particular township in which the work was done, but applies to the case of where, as here, two townships are assessed for the work. The amount may be recovered against the township generally, leaving it to work out its rights under the statute. The corporation having brought down the water which the outlet was insufficient to carry off, would be liable to damages therefor, and to escape such liability the contract was made, and judgment would have been recovered against them generally, without regard to how they would have to raise the money for the building of the culvert, and therefore the cost is a charge against the corporation generally : *Corporation of Sombra v. Corporation of Chatham*, 18 A. R. 252; 21 S. C. R. 305. In *Re Suskey and Corporation of Romney*, 22 O. R. 664, it is laid down that where sufficient funds have not been furnished by the original by-law to complete the work so as to make it effective, the amount can be raised under section 573. In that case, which was the construction of a drain, it was found that stone portals were needed for the work, and that the outlet to a lake had to be deepened and certain other work and necessities were recommended by the engineer, it was held that the by-law providing for them was an amending by-law under this section and the township council had power to pass it. Section 583, sub-sections 1 and 3, do not apply. These sub-sections only apply where the work is wholly completed and the work in question is new work not within the contemplation of the original by-law. Neither does section 585 apply, for that only applies to new work. It was not essential that there should be a by-law, the work having been done under a contract executed by the defendants under the corporate seal, and of which the defendants have received the benefit; this has been expressly held by the Supreme Court in *Bernardin* v. *Corporation of North Dufferin,* 19 S. C. R. 581. It is contended that case does not apply, because there is a distinction between the Manitoba statute under which that case was decided and our statute; but when the statutes are carefully considered, it will be found that there is in substance no distinction.

M. Wilson, Q.C., and *Pegley,* Q.C., contra. In dealing with this matter we have to look at the case in the light of the decisions on the liability of municipal corporations, and from them it is found that no liability exists against a municipal corporation unless the terms of the statutes governing such corporations have been complied with, and it is the duty of the person entering into a contract with a municipal corporation to see that the corporation has the power to enter into the contract: *Cowley* v. *Newmarket Local Board,* [1892] A. C. 345; *Municipality of Pictou* v. *Geldert,* [1893] A. C. 524; *Hiles* v. *Corporation of Ellice,* 20 A. R. 225, 233, 240; *Stephen* v. *Corporation of McGillivray,* 18 A. R. 516; *Smart* v. *Guardians of West Ham,* 10 Ex. 867; *Frend* v. *Dennett,* 4 C. B. N. S. 576; *Quaintance* v. *Corporation of Howard,* 18 O. R. 95, 99; *Dillon* v. *Corporation of Raleigh,* 13 A. R. 53, 64; Dillon on Municipal Corporations, 4th ed., sec. 459, p. 534; *Scott* v. *Corporation of Peterborough,* 19 U. C. R. 469-475; *Cross* v. *Corporation of Ottawa,* 23 U. C. R. 288; *Waterous Engine Co.* v. *Corporation of Palmerston,* 20 O. R. 420; 19 A. R. 47; 21 S. C. R. 556; *Young* v. *Mayor, etc., of Leamington,* 8 App. Cas. 517, 519; *Hunt* v. *Wimbledon Local Board,* 4 C. P. D. 48, 53, 59. The learned Judge found correctly on the evidence that the work, as originally contemplated, was completed, and that this culvert was not provided for in the original by-law, but was new work.

Section 573, therefore, does not apply. The case comes
within sub-sections 1 and 3 of section 583, under which,
where the amount required exceeds $200, no liability is to
arise until the proceedings pointed out by section 585 have
been taken, namely, the proceedings required by sections
569 to 582 inclusive, except as regards the petition
required by section 569. No report was made by the
engineer of the cost of the new work, or the amount
of the assessment required to be imposed on the lands to
be benefited, nor was any notice served on the head of the
municipality of the proposed assessment, nor in fact were
any of the requirements of these sections complied with.
The statute points out a particular mode in which the
work can be done and the money raised to pay for it, and
unless the terms of the statute are complied with there can
be no liability. There is the further objection that no
by-law has been passed authorizing the work, or providing
for the raising of the money to pay for it. There was
never an acceptance of the work so as to bring the case
within the principles laid down in *Bernardin* v. *Corporation of North Dufferin*, 19 S. C. R. 581; but even if there
were an acceptance of the work, that case would not apply
here. It was decided under a section of the Manitoba
Act which is not in our Act. There are no means whereby
the defendants can raise the money. They certainly cannot compel the township of Camden to pay the portion
which would be chargeable against them, and therefore
neither an action nor a mandamus could lie.

Moss, Q.C., in reply. A mandamus would clearly lie to
compel the township of Camden to pay their share:
Corporation of Elderslie v. *Corporation of Paisley*, 8 O. R.
270; *Regina* v. *Mayor, etc., of Maidenhead*, 9 Q. B. D.
494; *Regina* v. *Mayor, etc., of Wigan*, L. R. 5 Q. B. 267;
White v. *Corporation of Gosfield*, 2 O. R. 287; 10 A. R.
555; *Grand Junction R. W. Co.* v. *Corporation of Peterborough*, 6 A. R. 339; 8 S. C. R. 76.

June 23rd, 1894. GALT, C. J. :—

This action is brought to recover the balance alleged to
be due by the defendants on a contract for the construction
of a culvert through the railway embankment of the
plaintiffs.

The origin of the transaction may be stated as follows:

There is a large drain called "Big Creek Drain," which
runs through the townships of Camden and Chatham. This
drain discharges into the Thames in the township of Chatham, some distance westerly from the culvert. In consequence of the quantity of water in this drain, which
injuriously affected some lands in the townships of Camden
and Chatham, a petition was presented to the council of
Chatham in accordance with provision of section 569 of
the Municipal Act (I may mention that all the work
intended was to be done in Chatham, although some of
the lands to be benefited were in Camden), and a by-law
was passed by which the lands to be benefited were
assessed for the cost, and an outlet from the Big Creek
Drain was to be made. What subsequently took place is
very clearly stated by the learned Judge. It is as follows:—[The learned Judge then read the judgment of the
trial Judge, and proceeded.]

There is no question as to the evidence. The judgment
as respects the facts is correct. The by-law 169 was
passed under the provision of section 569 and section 576.
The lots which were assessed in Chatham were in number
about twenty-five, situate in the 3rd, 4th and 5th concessions, and in the township of Camden about sixteen, in
the 1st, 2nd and 3rd concessions. By sub-section 2 of section 569 the council is empowered to pass a by-law for
borrowing on the credit of the municipality the funds
necessary for the work, although the sewer extends beyond
the limits of the municipality, etc. By section 571, before
such by-law shall be passed it shall be published for four
weeks, or a copy may, at the option of the council, be
served on each of the owners, so that they may have an

opportunity of objecting to it. By section 573 power is
given to the council to amend the by-law when no sufficient means are provided for completion of the work.
Such amended by-law need not be published.

In the present case the work as originally contemplated
was completed.

The provisions of the statute up to this section have
reference to works done within the municipality, except
as regards the sub-section 2 of section 569, which authorizes the council to include in the money borrowed sufficient to complete the work, although it extends beyond
the limits of the municipality.

By section 575 the work may be extended beyond the
limits of any municipality; but this clause has no application to the present case, as the work done was within the .
township of Chatham.

By section 576, where the works do not extend beyond
the limits of the municipality, but in the opinion of the
engineer or surveyor benefit lands in an adjoining municipality, the engineer is empowered to charge the lands so
benefited.

It was under this section the by-law was passed. By
section 579 the council of the municipality in which the
deepening or drainage is to be commenced shall serve the
head of the municipality whose lands are to be benefited
with a copy of the report and estimates, etc., and unless
the same is appealed from it shall be binding.

By sub-section 3 of section 583, "the deepening, extending or widening of a drain in order to enable it to carry
off the water it was originally designed to carry off, shall
be deemed a work of preservation, maintenance, or keeping
in repair within the meaning of this section; provided the
cost of such extension does not exceed the sum of $200,
and in every case when it exceeds that amount, proceedings shall be taken under the provisions of section 585."

There can be no question as to the facts in the present
case—the cost of deepening and widening the drain was
upwards of $4,000.

Section 585 is as follows:—" In any case wherein the better to maintain any drain," etc., " it shall be deemed expedient to change the course of such drain, or make a new outlet, or otherwise improve, extend or alter the drain, the council of the municipality, or any of the municipalities whose duty it is to preserve and maintain the said drain, may, on the report of an engineer appointed by them to examine and report on such drain, undertake and complete the alterations and improvements or extension specified in the report, under the provisions of sections 569 to 582 inclusive, without the petition required by section 569."

It is to be observed that section 583 is obligatory on municipalities, " It shall be the duty of each municipality," etc., to maintain the work in a proper state of repair ; and, if the cost does not exceed $200 the deepening or widening a drain shall be considered as a part of that duty, but if it exceeds that sum proceedings shall be taken under section 585.

By that section it is optional with the municipality—they may undertake, etc.—but if they do they must proceed under the sections 569 to 582, with the single exception as regards the original petition.

The case now before us is one in which two municipalities are concerned, the township of Camden, which had already been assessed for nearly $2,000, would have been assessed for nearly a similar amount in the event of their being liable for a proportionate share of the cost of the culvert, and without having received any notice.

Section 579 is imperative: " The municipal council in which the deepening or drainage is to be commenced, shall serve the head of the council of the municipality ∗ ∗ whose lands or roads are to be benefited with a copy of the report, plans, specifications, assessment, and estimates of the engineer," etc. This was not done, nor was any one of the sections 569 to 582 complied with.

Bearing in mind this express provision, it appears to me the agreement set forth in the statement of claim was *ultra vires.* It is in effect: "That if the said sum of $2,327.50 shall prove to be insufficient, the corporation shall thereupon forthwith raise by by-law and pay to the company such further sum as may be necessary to meet the extra cost," etc. It is to meet this extra cost this action is brought.

By section 340 by-laws must be passed in order to create debts. In the present case there was no by-law; and by section 341: "If the by-law is for a work payable by local assessment, it shall recite: (a) The amount of the debt," etc. By the agreement sued on there was no ascertained amount.

This is a hard case on the plaintiffs; but, on the other hand, this being a work payable under local assessment, the interest of the ratepayers must be considered, and I cannot believe the ratepayers in the townships of Camden or Chatham would have consented to a by-law taxing them to the extent of a large sum of money for a work which in reality was more for the interest of the plaintiffs than of the ratepayers of either Chatham or Camden.

The case of *Young* v. *Mayor, etc., of Leamington*, 8 App. Cas. 517, was a much harder case on the plaintiffs than that now before us.

It is unnecessary to refer to the report of the case in 8 Q. B. D. 579, as the judgments of the learned Judges in the Court of Appeal are fully set out in the judgment of Lord Blackburn. In quoting the judgment of Lindley, L. J., the following statement appears: "The Act draws a line between contracts for more than £50 and contracts for £50 and under. Contracts for not more than £50 need not be sealed, and can be enforced whether executed or not, and without reference to the question whether they could be enforced at common law by reason of their trivial nature. But contracts for more than £50 are positively required to be under seal; and in a case like that before us, if we were to hold the defendants liable to pay for what has been done under the contract, we should in effect be repealing the Act of Parliament and depriving the ratepayers of that protection which Parliament intended to secure for them."

These words are peculiarly applicable to the present case. On referring to the original assessment under by-law 169 it will be found that some of the lots are rated at very considerable sums, varying from $200 to $400.

The appeal must be dismissed. No costs.

ROSE, J. :—

I am not quite sure but that there was a slight misapprehension of the facts at the trial on a point that may be material, and I shall, therefore, briefly state the facts as I understand them.

The defendant corporation on the 7th October, 1890, passed a by-law for the purpose of making a new and additional outlet to certain drains known as the "Louisville Tap" and "Big Creek Drains." This by-law was based upon the report of Messrs. McGeorge and Flatter, the corporation engineers, which report embodied a plan or profile shewing the excavation down to the river Thames, through and under the railway embankment, upon which the tracks were laid. The estimate in the report of the cost of the work was for such excavation. It was known to the engineers that the work could not be completed—that is to say, that there could be no excavation under the railway embankment—without the building of a culvert; but they made no provision for a culvert, and without any provision for such purpose the report went before the council, the by-law was passed, and the work entered upon and carried on as far as was practicable, the engineers relying upon an opening through a small existing culvert to carry off any water that might be brought down by the new or extended drain.

The engineer McGeorge, on his examination at the trial, in answer to the learned Judge, gave the following evidence :—

"Q. Did that outlet go down to the river? A. To the river Thames. Q. How could an estimate be made of such a work without estimating for getting through the railway? A. Well, I supposed that would be a matter that would have to be arranged for afterwards. I could not tell what kind of culvert the railway would want. If I put in a small estimate of a few hundred dollars they might want something else. Q. And it was, however, an absolute necessity before that work could be completed? A. They must have something there to get through. * * * Q. Then do I understand that that expenditure was all useless until this culvert was put in? A. No; it would be about useless until this culvert was put in. Q. So that the culvert was an actual and necessary part of that Big Creek Drain? A. Oh, yes, the opening was absolutely necessary.

"Mr. Wilson (Q.) An opening was necessary? A. Yes.

"Q. I see your report merely recommended a drain through the present existing opening? A. There was a small drain there, and there was a cattle pass that was used as a drain and for the passage through of cattle. Q. And you were running through the same opening? A. Yes, but it was not nearly deep enough. Q. And that opening was a wooden structure? A. Yes. Q. Then your profile carried the work right through as if that were deepened, making no provision for a culvert at all? A. Yes. I didn't know what to provide for a culvert there."

Looking at the profile and the report, I think any one not an engineer, and not realizing the necessity for a superstructure to carry the earth, in order that an excavation in accordance with the profile might be made, would have come to the conclusion that the profile drawing with the report provided for a drain of a proper depth and proper levels to give a sufficient fall to the river. And it is manifest from the above evidence that the engineer did not call the attention of the council, by his report or his profile drawing, to the fact that a culvert was necessary. Whatever other information they may have had I do not now stop to enquire. It is further manifest that without a culvert it was impossible to have the drain of the depth provided for by the report and the drawing. The natural

Judgment.

Rose, J.

result followed. When the drain was deepened and extended, the water was brought down, and the existing opening was not sufficient to carry it away.

The municipality, having brought this water down upon these lands, was liable to actions for damages; and, according to the decision in *Corporation of Sombra* v. *Corporation of Chatham*, 21 S. C. R. p. 305, judgment could have been obtained against the corporation generally without regard to the mode in which the money was to be raised under the Municipal Act. That being the state of affairs, it became necessary for the municipal corporation to obtain the permission of the railway company to pass under the embankment in order to save itself from many actions for damages which might be brought from time to time, and on the 12th December an agreement was entered into between the plaintiff and the defendant corporation providing for the construction of a culvert. The approximate cost was the sum of $2,327.50, the corporation covenanting, however, to pay whatever sum would be sufficient to meet the extra cost of construction. The work was carried out pursuant to the contract, a portion of the amount was paid, but when the balance, some $2,004.85, was asked for, the defendant corporation refused to pay, raising the defence of *ultra vires*.

The contract was under seal, but no by-law had been passed authorizing the council to enter into it.

My learned brother has found that the council agreed that the work should be done, promised to pay for it, accepted and used it when completed, and not until after completion disputed the liability to pay, and refused payment; and further said that he should have no hesitation on the facts, upon the authority of *Bernardin* v. *Corporation of North Dufferin*, 19 S. C. R. 581, in holding the defendant liable as on an executed work, but for the fact that there appeared to him to be no clause in the Municipal Act making the defendant corporation liable or enabling it to contract under the circumstances here existing.

It is manifest that this is a case in which the defendant

corporation ought to pay, unless there is some valid reason in law for it not being ordered to pay. I agree to what my learned brother has said that the facts of this case shew an executed work, accepted by the defendant corporation, and bring the case within the decision in *Bernardin* v. *Corporation of North Dufferin*, unless the distinction in enactment to which attention is called by Mr. Justice Patterson, at p. 631, between the provisions of our Municipal Act and that in force in Manitoba, makes a difference, and I have arrived at the conclusion that it does not.

As I understand the judgment in the *Bernardin* case, it proceeds upon the liability of a corporation generally for work done within the scope of its powers, of which it accepted the benefit, and for payment of the cost of which it would have been liable had it been a person instead of a corporation, and for which, therefore, it should be liable as a corporation, unless there was something in the charter or statute giving it existence, which freed it from liability. The legislation in Manitoba was permissive as to the passing of by-laws, and such permissive legislation was not considered by the majority of the Supreme Court to prevent the attaching of liability. The Municipal Act for this Province provides that a corporation shall exercise its powers through its council, and that its council shall exercise its powers by by-law. But our Courts have never held that such form of legislation prevented a liability attaching to a municipal corporation for executed contracts.

The case of *Pim* v. *Corporation of Ontario*, 9 C. P. 104, which is so much referred to in the *Bernardin* case, was decided in the 22nd Vict., and in the same year, as far as I can make out, the provision of the statute requiring a council to exercise its powers by by-law, was passed. But I find that six years after, the Court in *Perry* v. *Corporation of Ottawa*, 23 U. C. R. 391, followed the case of *Pim* v. *Corporation of Ontario*, saying that it was bound by the decision, without referring at all to the change in the statute law, or in any way indicating that it made any difference.

I need not refer to the subsequent cases until we come
to the case of *Robins* v. *Corporation of Brockton*, 7 O. R.
481, where the law was again discussed in the light of
the cases in this Province, and of *Young* v. *Mayor, etc., of
Leamington*, 8 App. Cas. 517, which case is also considered by the Supreme Court in the *Bernardin* case.

The result of the decisions appears to me to be as follows:
—By the case of *Waterous Engine Co.* v. *Corporation of
Palmerston*, 21 S. C. R. 566, it was decided that an
executory contract under seal, but unauthorized by by-
law, does not bind a municipal corporation.   There the
contract was under seal, but there was no by-law.   The
Bernardin case determined that on an executed contract,
without either by-law or contract under seal, a municipality might be liable, and unless there is some distinction
between the effect of the legislation in Manitoba and
Ontario, that case would govern the present if the facts
bring it within the decision ; and the case of *Robins* v.
Corporation of Brockton, following the line of decisions
in our own Courts, shews that there is no distinction to be
drawn between the legislation in Manitoba and in Ontario
as affecting the question of liability.

Further, the decisions in the Supreme Court in the
Bernardin case, and in our own Court in *Robins* v. *Corporation of Brockton*, shew that notwithstanding the
decision in *Young* v. *Mayor, etc., of Leamington*, and
Hunt v. *Wimbledon Local Board*, 4 C. P. D. 48, the
law as laid down and followed by our Courts since *Pim*
v. *Corporation of Ontario* is to govern.

The facts necessary to render a municipal corporation
liable are, an executed contract for the performance of the
work within the purposes for which the corporation was
created, and the adoption of such work of which it had
received the benefit.   And I think that the decision in *Corporation of Sombra* v. *Corporation of Chatham* shews that
the defendant here may be liable without reference to
whether or not there is a provision in the Municipal Act
under which this work might have been carried on.

In *Corporation of Sombra* v. *Corporation of Chatham*, the plaintiff Murphy, sustained damage by the overflow of water on his lands. It was argued and held by some of the Judges in the Courts through which the case proceeded, that there could be no liability except such as rested upon the area benefited by the work, and that the recovery of damages must be confined to such limited area ; and proceeding upon such theory the provisions of the Act were carefully scanned to ascertain whether or not there was any clause which enabled the municipality to charge damages upon the limited area. But in the Supreme Court recovery was had generally against the corporation, leaving it to work out any provisions which might exist to enable it to raise the money.

It seems to me that, following the principle of that decision, what the plaintiff corporation may well say, in answer to the municipal corporation setting up that there is no provision in the statute enabling it to charge the money claimed in this action against the limited area benefited : " We are not concerned as to that. We have performed the work for you. You have had the benefit of it. You have adopted it. You as a corporation are liable to us. If your Act of incorporation or statute governing you enables you to charge the money when paid upon a limited area, either within your own municipality or partly within and partly without, then it is for you to take such steps as may be necessary to raise the money in that manner. But if there is no such provision that is no reason why you should not pay us the money, and raise it as you would raise any other money that it might become necessary for you to raise for any purpose which it was incumbent upon you to provide for. If we had not done this work for you, you would have been liable to actions for damages, and such damages would have been assessed against you generally, and you would have had to provide for their payment, and out of the same fund from which you would have procured money to pay such damages you should now pay the cost of the work which we have executed to save you from damages."

I therefore do not enquire whether the sections referred
to in the judgments of my learned brother Street and the
learned Chief Justice avail to enable the defendant corporation to raise the money required by charging it upon
the limited area. If they do, let the defendant corporation
take advantage of the provisions. If they do not, then it
must be paid out of the general funds of the municipality
in the same way as in *Corporation of Sombra* v. *Corporation of Chatham*, the damages were directed to be paid.

In my opinion the appeal must be allowed with costs,
and judgment entered for the sum claimed, with interest
and costs.

MacMAHON, J. :—

The tendency in this case would naturally be to carefully scan the sections of the Act giving municipalities
power to contract in respect to drainage works, to see if
by any possibility the township could not be held liable
under its contract entered into with the railway company.
For the work under the contract has been completed, and
the township is now enjoying the benefits resulting therefrom.

The initial step to enable any municipality to pass a
by-law for the drainage of lands, is a petition to the council
by a majority in number of the persons shewn to be the
owners of lands in any part of a municipality to be benefited, and the legislature has, therefore, for manifest reasons
carefully circumscribed the powers of municipal councils
in dealing with drainage matters. It is necessary, therefore, to consider the position of the work on this drain
when the contract was entered into between the township
and the railway company.

For the work as contemplated by the engineer—which
was to make a new and additional outlet for the Louisville Tap and Big Creek Drains—he, from the report and
plans, assumed that a then existing small drain and
cattle pass under the railway would be sufficient to carry

the water to its final outlet at the river Thames.   For the
report recommends " the construction of a drain through
the present existing opening in the Canadian Pacific Railway on lot 23, in Chatham township, and continuing the
present existing drain on said lot."   The township by-
law provided ample means for the completion of the work
thus contemplated, and left a small surplus.   Through
some error or miscalculation of the engineer as to the
volume of water that would be brought down by the
drain, it was found that the outlet provided was inadequate.   Upon this discovery being made the township
entered into the contract with the railway company out
of which the present litigation has arisen.

It may, from the evidence of Mr. McGeorge, the township engineer, now be assumed, that the outlet originally
provided rendered the rest of the drainage works wholly
ineffective and almost valueless.   It therefore became
necessary, if the former expenditure was not to be totally
thrown away, that an improvement should be made by
means of a new outlet under the railway.

How, then, does the legislature direct that such improvement when required shall be provided for ?   Two municipalities were interested in the drainage works in question ;
the township of Chatham, in which the drainage works
were commenced, and the township of Camden, the lands
in which were to be benefited without the work being
carried within its limits.   The work undertaken under the
by-law passed by the township of Chatham upon the
report of its engineer, and of which the township of
Camden had notice, and for which the lands of those
benefited thereby had been duly assessed, was fully completed.

The railway company's contention is that the work
performed by it under the contract was done under the
authority which the corporation of Chatham possessed by
virtue of section 573 ; and that the corporation through
its officers and authorized agents had agreed, under the
power conferred by such section of the Act, to amend by-

Judgment.

MacMahon,
J.
law No. 169 so as to provide for the raising of sufficient
funds with which to complete the work. But by-law No.
169 provided sufficient means to carry out the intention
of the by-law, and of the petition on which it was founded,
for the work petitioned for, and provided for in the by-
law had been completed, and there was an unexpended
surplus. Moreover, section 573 does not apply where there
are two or more municipalities interested in carrying out
drainage works. This is made abundantly clear by referring to subsequent sections of the Act, commencing with
section 575.

The statute, according to my view, duly authorized the
municipal corporation to carry out this work, either as an
"alteration and improvement" to the drain under section
585, or as a deepening and widening of the drain to enable
it to carry off the water it was originally designed to carry
off, and so coming within section 583, sub-sections 1 and 3.
In either case (as the cost under section 583 would
exceed $200) all the requirements of the statute in con-
nection with the passing of a drainage by-law, with the
exception only of the petition from the owners of the
property to be benefited, would have to be complied with,
including the examination and report of an engineer; the
assessing and levying of a special rate for the payment of
the principal and interest of the debentures to be issued to
meet the outlay for the works; service on the head of the
municipality of Camden of a copy of the report, plans,
specifications, assessments, etc., for such improvements, in
order that such township might have an opportunity to
appeal.

The contract entered into was between the township of
Chatham and the railway company, in respect to a fresh
outlet for a drain already completed, in so far as it could
be under the plans and specifications of the engineer. It
was contemplated that an expenditure of at least $2,327.50
would be required to build this stone culvert under the
railway, and such expenditure might be much increased
and was increased to over $4,440, and the only manner in

which the township of Chatham could contract was by
passing a by-law after complying with the formalities
prescribed by the Act.

This is not the ordinary case of a municipal council
entering into a contract, the expenditure in connection
with which must be borne by the general taxes levied
from the whole of the ratepayers.   Had the contract
between the township of Chatham and the railway company been one of that character, *Bernardin* v. *Corporation
of North Dufferin*, 19 S. C. R. 581, might possibly have been
followed, although no by-law had been passed authorizing
the contract, as the work had been performed under the contract, and the township had accepted the benefit. But under
the Act the municipal council has no authority to pass a by-
law authorizing a contract, except for the benefit of those
interested in the drainage works, and such by-law is only
valid when it provides for assessing and levying a special
rate on the property to be benefited, for the payment of
the debentures issued for the works. In fact what the
municipality does by passing the by-law is simply to guarantee the payment of the debentures issued at the instance
of the persons who are to be benefited by the construction
of the drainage works. The authority of municipal corporations is well stated in such cases as the present in
Dillon, 4th ed., sec. 459: "So where the corporation
orders local street improvements to be made, for which the
abutters are the parties ultimately liable, and which by
the charter must be made in a prescribed mode, if made
without any contract or a valid one, the doctrine of implied
liability does not apply in favour of the contractor, unless,
indeed, the corporation has collected the amount from the
adjoining owners and has it in its treasury."

Where, as in *Corporation of Sombra* v. *Corporation of
Chatham*, 21 S. C. R. 305, and *Corporation of Raleigh* v.
Williams, [1893] A. C. 540, an action has been brought
against a municipality in which drainage works are situated for damages for injury to lands caused by neglect
of the municipality to perform the statutory duty imposed

Judgment.

MacMahon,
J.

of keeping such drainage works in repair, and judgment
is recovered against the corporation, such judgment is
against the corporation generally, and the corporation
must pay the amount thereof out of the general funds
of the township. But in such cases section 592 of the
Municipal Act provides a special means by which the corporation is to recoup itself for the amount of the judgment
so paid, which is "to charge the amount *pro rata* upon
the lands and roads liable to assessment for such drainage
works." Could a judgment be recovered against the township in the present case, there would be no authority to
charge the amount against the lands of those liable to
assessment for drainage works, because it would not be a
judgment for damages caused by such drainage works, and
section 592 would therefore not apply. And if the amount
could not be charged back upon the lands benefited, then
the corporation—which means the whole of the ratepayers
in the township—would be paying for works from which
only a few derived any benefit, and in respect of which
the council had no authority to contract so as to make the
corporation liable. A judgment would therefore be an
indirect means of effecting that which the corporation was
not legally empowered to do.

Much as one may regret at having to dismiss this motion,
that result is inevitable according to my view of the law.

I think the conduct of the defendant corporation has
been such as disentitles it to the costs of this motion. The
motion will therefore be dismissed without costs.

G. F. H.

[CHANCERY DIVISION.]

EDWARDS V. FINDLAY.

Will—Codicil—Revocation of Bequest.

A testatrix by the third clause of her will bequeathed to S., the interest
on the sum of $3,000 for life, and after his death directed the $3,000 to
be divided among his children, and by a subsequent clause she directed
her executors to deduct out of the $3,000 all payments made to S. after
the date of the will. By a codicil she directed that the bequest number three, bequeathing to S. the interest on $3,000 be revoked, and in
lieu thereof the sum of $500 be paid to him, or his heirs, and that the
direction as to payments made after the date of the will should apply
thereto :—

Held, that the effect of the codicil was to revoke the whole of the third
clause.

THIS was an action brought for the construction of certain   Statement.
doubtful clauses in the will of Mary Atkinson, dated 14th
August, 1884, and of the codicil to it, dated 10th April,
1885. A motion for judgment upon the pleadings came
on before STREET, J., in Court on 3rd May, 1894.

Clarke, Q.C., for plaintiffs, the executors.

S. H. Blake, Q. C., and *Canniff*, for certain residuary
legatees.

Dr. Hoskin, Q. C., for the infants and certain adults in
the same interest.

Hoyles, Q. C., for the Synod of Toronto and Mary
Nighswander.

May 8th, 1894. STREET, J. :—

The portions of the will in question material to be considered are the following clauses :—

" Third. I bequeath to Richard R. Simmonds, son of
James Simmonds, the interest of the sum of $3,000, which
$3,000 is to be raised out of the interests to which the
hereinbefore recited declaration of trust would have applied, and no other source, during the term of his natural
life, and on his decease direct that the said $3,000 be

divided equally among his then surviving children and
the survivors thereof in equal portions, to be invested and
paid them with any profits that may accrue as they attain
the age of 21 years; and in case the said Richard R. Simmonds die without children surviving him, I then direct
that the said $3,000 be divided among the legatees herein-
after mentioned in the proportion of their legacies."

Then follow clauses numbered "fourth" to "fifteenth,"
respectively, by which legacies are given to various persons therein named. The sixteenth and seventeenth
clauses are as follows :—"Sixteenth. I direct and hereby
instruct my executors to deduct from the $3,000 men-
tioned in the bequest to Richard R. Simmonds any sum or
sums that I may advance the said Richard R. Simmonds
subsequent to the date of this my last will, or that my
estate may have to pay on account of any bonds or securities I may have given on his behalf."

"Seventeenth. I bequeath to May Simmonds, daughter
of James Simmonds, the sum of $500, to be paid out of
the residue after payment of all prior bequests; and should
there be any further residue I direct that it be divided
among the legatees hereinbefore mentioned in the bequests
numbered four to fourteen inclusive, in the proportion of
their legacies."

The codicil is as follows: "I do hereby direct that the
bequest numbered three, bequeathing to Richard Simmonds, son of James Simmonds, the interest on the sum of
$3,000 be revoked and annulled, and in lieu thereof I
bequeath to the said Richard Simmonds, son of James
Simmonds, the sum of $500, to be paid to him or his heirs
in cash by my executors as soon as convenient after my
decease. I further direct that the conditions mentioned in
number sixteen shall apply to this bequest."

It is contended on the one hand that the whole of the
third clause of the will is revoked by the codicil; on the
other hand, that only the portion of the third clause referred to in the codicil in express terms, viz., the bequest to
Richard Simmonds of the interest on the $3,000, is re-
voked.

The rule is well settled that a legacy once given is not to be held to be revoked unless the intention to revoke it is clear, and that a revocation by codicil shall not be allowed to interfere with the provisions of the will to any greater extent than the terms of the codicil require. These, however, are, mere amplifications of the rule that the intention of the testator as gathered from the language he has used is to be carried out.

I find little help towards the construction of this will from either rules or cases, and am driven to consider the ambiguous phrases used without other light than that shed upon them by the remainder of the will itself.

The grammatical construction of the codicil is in favour of the revocation of the whole of the third clause of the will, but the misrecital of the contents of the third clause leaves the construction to be placed upon the codicil open to be determined either way according to the context.

I think the key to the solution of the difficulty is to be found in the sixteenth clause of the will and in the references to it. In that clause the testatrix directs in effect that the $3,000 mentioned in the third clause is to be reduced by any sums that she or her estate may have to pay on account of Richard R. Simmonds. So that in case she had to pay for him $3,000, neither he nor his children would take anything under the will.

It is plain from this clause that she had felt called upon for some reason which does not appear to lay aside a sum of $3,000 for the benefit of Richard R. Simmonds and his children, but that she had in view the possibility that it might in effect be *adeemed* by payments made to him or on his account during her lifetime, or after her death upon liabilities assumed by her on his account, and that to the extent of such payments, her intended benefits in favour of him and his children were to be taken as satisfied : in other words, there was no independent intention to benefit his children as distinguished from himself, and the gift in the codicil therefore fulfils the whole intention.

The same intention is very plainly expressed in the

codicil; the $500 is directed to be paid to him or to his heirs, but it is coupled with the provision that the sixteenth paragraph of the will shall be applied to the substituted as it was to the original gift. A difficulty which appears to me to be decisive is raised in the way of the construction of the codicil contended for by the children of Richard R. Simmonds by the application of the sixteenth paragraph to the gift substituted by the codicil. Suppose the testatrix to have advanced to Richard R. Simmonds after the date of the codicil a sum of $500, is that sum to be deducted from the $3,000 mentioned in the third paragraph or is it to be applied to wipe out altogether the substituted gift? She must have intended that it should be deducted from only one of the gifts, and that gift must have been the gift of the $500.

The conclusion I come to is that between the date of the will and that of the codicil the testatrix, for some reason or other which does not appear, had determined to cut down her gift to Richard R. Simmonds and his family from $3,000 to $500; that she intended to revoke the third clause of her will absolutely; that she has used language sufficient for the purpose of carrying out her intention, and that the gift in the codicil is substituted for all the gifts in the third clause of the will. The language used in the codicil relied on as restricting the revocation to the life interest given to Richard R. Simmonds must be read as merely an inaccurate recital or description of the purport of the third clause of the will and not as limiting the revocation to the portion of the third clause specially mentioned. The $3,000 will not be raised, but the benefit of it will go under the residuary clause to all the legatees who would have taken it in default of children of Richard R. Simmonds, excepting only the Synod of the Diocese of Toronto and Mary Nighswander.

The difficulty in the construction of the will rendered this action necessary, and the costs of all parties must come out of the estate—those of the plaintiffs to be taxed as between solicitor and client.

G. F. H.

[COMMON PLEAS DIVISION.]

DISHER v. CLARRIS.

*Principal and Agent—Undue Influence—Excessive Payment for Services
Procured by—Right to Recover Back.*

Where, by reason of the confidential relationship existing between plaintiff and defendant and the influence he was able to exert over her by
asserting knowledge of matters which he alleged could be used to her
prejudice, and which at the trial he admitted had no existence, he was
enabled to procure from plaintiff an excessive amount for services performed, and which was paid by her even after she had obtained independent advice, the plaintiff was held entitled to recover the same back,
less a reasonable amount for the services performed.

THIS was an action tried before MEREDITH, J., without a Statement.
jury at St. Thomas on the 7th of May, 1894.

The action was to recover the sum of $2,000, which the
plaintiff claimed that the defendant had induced her to
pay him for alleged services rendered to her in obtaining
payment of certain insurance moneys. The plaintiff's husband had died leaving some $27,500 insurance on his life,
payable to his wife, the plaintiff. The defendant who had
been a warm personal friend of the husband during his
lifetime, and also of the plaintiff, tendered his services to the
plaintiff to assist her in securing the payment of the
insurance moneys. There were rumours of the husband
having committed suicide, which came to the knowledge
of the insurance companies, who employed detectives to
investigate the matter, and the defendant claimed that
in consequence of these rumours it required great skill
to procure the payment of the moneys without litigation, with possible loss. The defendant had conducted
negotiations with the companies for payment and had
taken a trip to Galesburg, U. S., in reference to one of
the policies. On the claim being made the plaintiff at first
refused to entertain it, and after consultation with her solicitor, offered the defendant $300, but subsequently on threats
being made by the defendant that he had knowledge of
facts which might prevent the insurance moneys being
paid, presumably relating to the alleged suicide, the plain-

tiff was at last induced to pay the $2,000, but immediately afterwards she repented having done so and brought this action to recover back the amount. Evidence was given to shew that one per cent. on the amount of the fund was a reasonable sum to be paid for the services performed by the defendant.

The learned Judge allowed the defendant $300, and directed that judgment should be entered for the plaintiff for the balance, $1,700.

The defendant moved on notice to set aside the judgment and to have judgment entered in his favour.

In Easter Sittings, May 28th, 1894, before a Divisional Court, composed of ROSE, and MACMAHON, JJ., *Wallace Nesbitt*, supported the motion. The plaintiff here claimed that the $2,000 was exorbitant, and that the circumstances under which it was obtained, amounted to fraud and coercion. Fraud and coercion were disproved at the trial. The learned Judge seemed to think that because the defendant refused at the trial to refer the matter to a referee, it constituted evidence against him; but the defendant having been charged with fraud and coercion insisted on having the action gone on with. The law laid down in *Sheard* v. *Laird*, 15 A. R. 339, governs this case. There it was held that undue influence cannot be presumed; it must be proved; and where a party has had ample time to take advice, and does take advice, that removes it from the ground of undue influence. In this case the plaintiff had ample opportunity to decide whether she would pay the defendant $2,000 or not; and after consulting her solicitor, she decided of her own free will to do so. What took place amounted to a settlement entered into with a full knowledge of all the facts, and, therefore, the plaintiff is bound by it. It is a difficult matter to value skill at so much an hour. Men occupying high positions, as leading counsel, physicians, and engineers, charge what to some might seem very exorbitant fees, but if people wish to procure their services they must pay them what they charge.

and having done so they cannot afterwards repudiate the
payment and recover back the amount paid on the ground
that it is too large. In this case the defendant was specially
employed because the plaintiff thought he could carry on
negotiations of the most delicate character, and where less
skill might have resulted in failure to obtain the payment
of insurance moneys without litigation, which would have
been long and tedious, causing her great worry and expense
with the possible result of her claim being disallowed. The
plaintiff considered all this and decided to pay the defendant
the $2,000, and having paid it, she cannot now recover it
back.   He referred to *Hunter* v. *Atkins*, 3 My. & K. 113 ;
Harrison v. *Guest*, 8 H. L. 481.

McCarthy, Q. C., contra. At the trial the defendant
based his right to retain the $2,000 not only on the ground
that it had been paid under a settlement, but also that
such sum was a fair remuneration for his services. The
learned Judge then remarked that if he based his right on
the latter ground that it had better be referred to a referee
to ascertain what would be a proper sum to be paid. The
defendant refused to assent to this, and this raised the inference that the defendant was not willing to take what
his services were worth, but was endeavouring to stand on
the settlement, whether fair or not. The evidence in this
case shewed that, the defendant tendered his services to
the plaintiff more in the character of a friend than as a
professional agent, and acting in that capacity he would
have no legal claim for any services he performed. But
even assuming that he was acting in the capacity of an
agent, he could only recover what his services were actually
worth. It is shewn that the trouble and time expended
in recovering this money, was very trifling, the insurance
moneys being paid upon receipt of the proof papers. Evidence was given to shew that $300 would be a fair sum to
pay for an agent's services in such a case as this. The
defendant might just as well have charged $5,000 as $2,000.
The evidence also shews that the plaintiff's feelings were
worked upon so that she really was not a free agent in

Argument. giving the cheque. The real reason for giving it was a threat that defendant would divulge something which, if divulged, would prevent the recovery of the money. This is a very different case from *Sheard* v. *Laird.* Here the claim, if maintainable at all, must be on the ground of a fiduciary relationship. He also referred to *Waters* v. *Donnelly,* 9 O. R. 391; *Broun* v. *Kennedy,* 33 Beav. 133, 4 D. G. J. & S. 217, 223; Evans on Principal and Agent, 294-305; *Kennedy* v. *Broun,* 13 C. B. N. S. 677; *Cooke* v. *Lamotte,* 15 Beav. 234; *Huguenin* v. *Baseley,* 2 W. & T. L. C., 6th ed., 607; *Watson* v. *Rodwell,* 11 Ch. D. 150; *Mitchell* v. *Homfray,* 8 Q. B. D. 587; *Harvey* v. *Mount,* 8 Beav. 439; *Tate* v. *Williamson,* L. R. 2 Ch. 55, 61; *Hunter* v. *Atkins,* 3 My. & K. 113; *Billage* v. *Southee,* 9 Hare 534.

Wallace Nesbitt, in reply. There was no such fiduciary relationship then existing as would prevent the arrangement being entered into. The plaintiff was not relying on the defendant at the time the matter was settled for she consulted with her lawyer, and was acting under his advice when the settlement was effected : *McEwan* v. *Milne,* 5 O. R. 100.

June 23rd, 1894. ROSE, J. :—

It, to my mind, simplifies this case to state upon what the defendant based his claim to be remunerated, and what grounds he by his counsel at the trial repudiated taking.

He was not in any sense supplying such service as would be required from a solicitor—for Mr. McCrimmon was retained and paid most handsomely for his services. He was acting as an agent simply—tendering his services under the guise of friendship.

According to the plaintiff, what took place when the policies were handed to the defendant, was as follows :—

" He (Mr. Clarris) said : ' Have you given the policies to any person, Mrs. Disher ? No, said I. Well, you had better hand them over to me, I will do well by you ?' Mrs.

Clarris says, 'Yes, Mrs. Disher, my husband will do well
by you as he would by his own sister, he will do what is
honest and straight.'"

Mrs. Disher would reasonably expect services to be
rendered for which remuneration would be sought, and
that the defendant would continue to be a friend to whom
she might resort whenever she needed the comfort that
comes from counsel with a friend.

For such services of friendship, of course no recompense
could be claimed; but it seems to me they have been relied
upon as shewing greater value in the services rendered as
an agent, and care must be exercised lest confusion should
arise.

The defendant, by his counsel, stated that his claim was
for the value of his services as rendered ; that he had
earned all he received from Mrs. Disher.

Further, the defendant's counsel stated in effect that the
claims under the policies were just and legal claims which
the plaintiff could have enforced, and against which no
just defence could have been urged.

The defendant was, therefore, not aware of any defence
on the ground that Mr. Disher had committed suicide, and
did not, at the trial, claim remuneration on the ground
that he had succeeded in obtaining the moneys from the
companies by concealing any such fact, or by inducing
any company to waive any defence it might have on such
ground, or leading any company to suppose that such fact
would not afford a ground of defence to a claim on the
policy.   There was, therefore, no finesse required to obtain
payment.

It follows, therefore, that—apart from any trouble and
loss of time occasioned by the plaintiff, a nervous woman
in trouble, going often to one whom she had been invited
to regard as a friend, and to whom she had committed her
affairs—the only services the defendant rendered were in
presenting claim papers and obtaining payment—steps involving loss of time and some trouble for which the defendant was clearly entitled to be paid.

The fact as to the alleged suicide was brought to the notice of the companies ; detectives were employed to investigate, and after full enquiry the claims were paid.

It is clear that the ground upon which the defendant based his claim for handsome remuneration, was that the suspicion of suicide having been raised, it required the most delicate management on his part to obtain settlements with the company, and that had he not exercised great skill and caution, and manifested great diplomatic powers, litigation might have resulted with delay, anxiety and possible loss as the result. Assume all this. Apart from such a consideration, the services rendered might have been performed by any solicitor's clerk, and a few dollars would have covered the work actually done. There is no doubt the plaintiff required the services of a man of business with tact and skill, and for such services she must pay a fair sum. True, the defendant went to Galesburg, but so did Mr. McCrimmon go to New York.

The business judgment which was needed in one case, was, no doubt, required in the other.

If a solicitor without the assistance of an agent had transacted all the business, obtained all the money, made all the trips, and had all the interviews, and had charged a lump sum of $2,000 in addition to his disbursements, I should unhesitatingly say his conduct should pass in review before the discipline committee of the Law Society.

The fact is, that the plaintiff has paid to Mr. McCrimmon..................................... $600 00
To the defendant, travelling expenses........   101 00
  "   " 2,000 00
And for her husband's debt allowed him to
  retain, say, out of $589.................   250 00

Total $2,951 00
There may be other sums I have not noted.

My own judgment of what the defendant should be entitled to for everything he did is, that the one per cent. named by Mr. Plummer would be fair and full remuner-

ation. Such a sum would well pay for getting in a just Judgment.
and legal claim, to which there was no defence, and should Rose, J.
insure business activity, skill and judgment. But assume
that greater liberality might be expected, and allow two
per cent., for which there is, on the record of evidence, in
my opinion, no warrant, the amount paid to the defendant is still so excessive as to compel one to look for a
reason why it was paid.

That reason is not far to find. Assuming that the plaintiff was a shrewd woman with some force of character—
she was still a woman with a woman's weaknesses, in
her case aggravated by sorrow, trouble, anxiety, and physical ailments, unaccustomed to business and acted upon by
a man of business experience, who apparently was not
unwilling in her presence to exhibit violence of manner,
and use words and expressions such as suggested, if they
did not actually express, threats, that from his stores of
knowledge obtained by his intimacy with her husband and
her, he could bring out one fact, at least, so potent, that
the moneys, although in hand. might be recovered by the
companies which had paid them in ignorance of such
knowledge as he possessed, and thus, indeed, by fraud.

This threat sends her home from his house in tears and
causes her to spend a sleepless night; drives her to seek
him to ask him to keep silence on the subject, and eventually, when to its force is added that of a threat to sue, so
pleasing a thing to a solicitor, and amusing sometimes to
a plaintiff, but often so terrifying to the one threatened,
leads her to sign a cheque under a pressure so active as
to be open to observation, which cheque she instantly tries
to recall, crying out against the injustice of the claim.

Had he knowledge of a fact which invalidated the
claims, and had he assisted her to commit a fraud on the
companies? He says "No." Then he had no knowledge
of any fact, the revelation of which would have placed
her in peril; and the threat was idle and based on a false
suggestion.

The cases I cited in *Sheard* v. *Laird*, 15 O. R. 533, bear

with great force upon this view of the case, and although
the Court of Appeal thought that as between debtor and
creditor the decision could not be supported, I venture
to repeat the argument in this case, and to rely on the
authorities as between an agent and his principal.

I cannot think that the plaintiff freely and willingly
made the defendant so excessive a payment; and I conclude that it was in consequence of their relation to each
other, and the influence he had over her by reason of
such relation, and the assertion of knowledge of facts
which he might use to her prejudice that he was enabled
to make an attack which she failed to successfully resist,
and the spoils obtained by the defendant, I think he
cannot be allowed to retain. That the plaintiff had advice and opportunity of consultation, does not make the
payment unattackable as a settlement. That only goes
to shew the vigour of the attack and the potency of the
influence. Nor would it have sufficed to have shewn a
consultation with Mr. Macdougall—even if on the material before us, we would be warranted in opening up the
case for further evidence and argument—unless much more
could be shewn than is even suggested. But in face of
the positive denial by the plaintiff, we do not think on
the facts of this case the defendant should have further
consideration. The order made at the trial was quite as
generous to the defendant as the facts warranted.

The motion must be dismissed with costs, to which will
be added the costs of the motion by the defendant to put
in further evidence.

In addition to the cases cited in my judgment in *Sheard*
v. *Laird*, 15 O. R. 533, I refer to *Miller* v. *Cook*, L. R. 10
Eq. 641 ; Evans on Principal and Agent pp. 343-350 ; *Brown*
v. *Kennedy*, 33 Beav. 133 ; *Cooke* v. *Lamotte*, 15 Beav.
234; White and Tudor's L. C., 6th ed., vol. 2, p. 607.

MacMahon, J.:—

What strikes one at the threshold, in the consideration of this case is, that out of the total amount of insurance on the life of the plaintiff's husband, viz., $27,500, no less a sum than $22,500, had been paid by the companies within two months from the death of the insured without any difficulty being experienced, and without any inclination being manifested to contest the plaintiff's right to recover.   Indeed, even as to the policy for the largest sum, $15,000, in the Mutual Life, the defendant admitted it was all "plain sailing."   That was paid by the last of February—$7,500, having been paid by other companies previous to that date.

At the trial, the defendant admitted that he was not aware of any fact disentitling the plaintiff to recover on the policies, nor was he cognizant of any fraudulent claim being made upon the insurance companies.

If he was not possessed of information which he asserted was known to himself, and of which the plaintiff and Mr. McCrimmon were not aware, why did he make the statement to Mrs. Disher ?   If the statement made by the defendant was false, then why was an untruth uttered ? Was there an object to be gained by the agent making a statement to his principal that a fact existed within the agent's knowledge, which, if disclosed, would affect his principal's interests—which statement the agent afterwards had to admit was utterly foundationless ?   It is only upon the hypothesis that the agent had an ulterior object in view looking to his own benefit, that the making of an untrue statement can be accounted for, particularly where a fiduciary relationship existed and the utmost good faith was demanded at the agent's hands.

Was it not this professed knowledge that he was using to influence Mrs. Disher, and was it not the belief that the defendant was possessed of a secret, and the fear that it might be used to her detriment, that influenced the plaintiff to give Mr. Robinson the cheque when the demand for $2,000 was made upon her ?

That is the natural conclusion that one would come to from a perusal of the evidence.

Mrs. Disher offered the defendant $300, as being in her opinion a fair remuneration for his services, and this offer was made after consultation with her solicitor. It then must have been for a reason other than that she thought he had earned it, that the cheque for $2,000 was given, which had no sooner passed from her hands than she desired to recall it.

The defendant sought to get a benefit resulting from alleged knowledge of facts connected with the cause of the death of the insured, and that it was through the diplomacy he exercised that settlements were effected with the insurance companies without their acquiring a knowledge of such facts. Hence his demand for the $2,000.

As said by Jessel, M. R., in *Redgrave* v. *Hurd*, 20 Ch. D. 1: "A man is not allowed to get a benefit from a statement which he now admits to be false."

The statement being false, it was a fraud by this agent to make it, as it ultimately resulted in his securing for himself an advantage over his principal. But it would not be necessary to characterize what was accomplished by means of the untrue statement as a "fraud." All that it is necessary to do is bring it within the category of cases referred to by Lord Selborne in *Earl of Aylesford* v. *Morris* L. R. 8 Ch. 484, at pp. 490-1. See also *Slator* v. *Nolan*, Ir. R. 11 Eq. 367, 386, referred to in the judgment of the Chancellor in *Waters* v. *Donnelly*, 9 O. R. at p. 401.

In Story's Equity of Jurisprudence, 12th ed., sec. 315, that high authority refers to the influence often possessed by an agent over his principal. He says: "In all cases of this sort, the principal contracts for the aid and benefit of the skill and judgment of the agent; and the habitual confidence reposed in the latter, makes all his acts and statements possess a commanding influence over the former. Indeed, in such cases the agent too often so entirely misleads the judgment of his principal, that, while he is seeking his own peculiar advantage, he seems but consulting the advantage and interest of his principal."

Here there was not only the influence occasioned by the confidential relationship, but there was the fear engendered by the alleged possession of a secret, the divulging of which might result disastrously to Mrs. Disher, and it cannot be said there was that total severance of the relationship which had existed, and the opportunity for that independent advice, without which the money procured, should not, under the name of a settlement, be allowed to be retained by the defendant. And I refer again to the language of Sir Edward Sullivan in the case of *Slator* v. *Nolan*, already cited.

I entirely concur in the result as indicated in the judgment of my learned brother.

G. F. H.

[CHANCERY DIVISION.]

The Molsons Bank v. Heilig.

Principal and Surety—Security held by Creditor—Release of Same without Consent of Surety—Rights of Surety—Judgment.

The plaintiffs sued the defendant as endorser of a promissory note made by a customer, of which they held a number, endorsed by various parties, and also a mortgage from the customer on certain lands to secure his general indebtedness. Before this action the plaintiffs had released and discharged certain of the lands comprised in the mortgage, without the consent of the defendant, but, in consideration of such discharge, had received the full value of the lands, and had applied the proceeds in reduction of the general indebtedness of the customer :—

Held, that the defendant as a surety was entitled to have credited in reduction of his liability upon the note a *pro rata* share of the amount realized by the plaintiffs on the mortgage, and also a *pro rata* share of the value of the security still in their hands.

THIS was an action against the endorser of a promissory note who claimed to be released from liability on account of the dealings of the plaintiffs with securities under circumstances which are set out in the judgment.

Statement.   The action was tried before ROBERTSON, J., at Hamilton, on May 9th and 12th, 1894.

Crerar, Q.C., and *P. D. Crerar*, for the plaintiffs, cited *Duncan Fox & Co.* v. *North and South Wales Bank*, 6 App. Cas. 1, at p. 18 : DeColyar's Law of Guarantee, 2nd ed., p. 392.

J. W. Nesbitt, Q. C., and *Gauld* for the defendant, cited *Polak* v. *Everett*, 1 Q. B. D. 669 ; *Pearl* v. *Deacon*, 24 Beav. 186 ; *Forbes* v. *Jackson*, 19 Ch. D., at p. 622.

June 1st, 1894. ROBERTSON, J. :—

Action on a promissory note made by Patterson Brothers on the 5th February, 1894, payable to the order of Thomas Patterson, twenty-one days after date, at the plaintiffs' bank, for $7,685.04. Thomas Patterson endorsed the same ; and thereafter the defendant Heilig, endorsed the same. Note was protested, etc.

The defendant admits the endorsement, dishonour and notice thereof. There are other paragraphs in the defendant's statement of defence, all of which are withdrawn from, and the defendant relies on the second, eighth, ninth, tenth, and eleventh paragraphs, which allege, in substance, that the discounting of the note in question was merely in renewal of certain indebtedness of Patterson Brothers to the plaintiffs created in or about the months of April, May, and June, 1888, as security for which Patterson Brothers deposited with the plaintiffs certain other promissory notes purporting to bear the signature of the defendant; that the plaintiffs on or about June 30th, 1888, took from Patterson Brothers a mortgage on certain lands in Hamilton, as a security for the amount of their indebtedness, which is still represented by the note now in question ; and on the 26th of December, 1893, the plaintiffs, without the consent of the defendant, released and discharged the property comprised in the said mortgage, or a large portion thereof, etc., whereby the defendant was relieved from his liability

as a surety for Patterson's indebtedness. The defendant
also says that on November 14th, 1888, the plaintiffs took
a further security from Patterson Brothers on real estate
in Hamilton, and on the 26th of December, 1893, and without the consent of the defendant, released and discharged
a large portion of the property comprised in the said mortgage, whereby the defendant was relieved from his liability
as a surety for the said indebtedness; and the defendant
further says that the plaintiffs by the said securities gave
time to Patterson Brothers for payment of the said indebtedness without the consent of the defendant; and that the defendant did not become aware of the foregoing facts until
the 2nd of April, 1894.   The plaintiffs in answer or reply to
this defence say that the two mortgages mentioned constituted but one security, the instrument of the later date
having been executed to take the place of the mortgage of
former date, and both covered the same lands and were
intended to secure the general indebtedness of Patterson
Brothers to the plaintiffs, amounting to over $40,000; and
the portions of lands released from the said mortgages were
so released in consideration of a payment to the plaintiffs
of over $5,000, being the full amount of the purchase money
of the said lands so released, and the most that could be
obtained for the same, after payment of prior incumbrances
on the same, and the said moneys were applied by the
plaintiffs in reduction of the general indebtedness of the
said Patterson Brothers to the plaintiffs. The plaintiffs also
say they were under no obligation in law to get the defendant's consent to their dealing with the said securities, and
such dealings do not in law affect the defendant's liability
on the note in question.

The facts are admitted as stated in the pleadings, and
the question is one of law, raised by the allegation that
the plaintiffs were under no obligation in law to get the
defendant's consent to their dealings with the said securities, etc.

In my judgment the principles laid down by Lord
Chancellor Selborne in *Duncan Fox & Co.* v. *North and*

South Wales Bank, 6 App. Cas. 1, govern in the case now under consideration. At pp. 10-11, he says : "In examining the
principles and authorities applicable to this question, it
seems to me to be important to distinguish between three
kinds of cases: (1) Those in which there is an agreement
to constitute, for a particular purpose, the relation of
principal and surety, to which agreement the creditor
thereby secured is a party ; (2) Those in which there is a
similar agreement between the principal and the surety
only, to which the creditor is a stranger ; and (3) Those
in which, without any such contract of suretyship, there is
a primary and secondary liability of two persons for one
and the same debt, the debt being, as between the two,
that of one of them only, and not equally of both, so that
the other, if he should be compelled to pay it, would be
entitled to reimbursement from the person by whom (as
between the two) it ought to have been paid."

The case before me comes within the third class of the
cases above mentioned, and it is upon such principles that
it must be disposed of.

Now here Patterson Bros. are primarily liable, and, if the
defendant be compelled to pay, he would be entitled to
reimbursement from Patterson Bros. by whom (as between
them and the defendant) the note in question ought to
have been paid. In such a case, in my judgment, the
equity is direct in favour of the defendant, who is the
surety debtor, against the principal debtors Patterson Bros.,
but this affects the creditor (in this case the plaintiffs)
towards whom they are both principals only as a man who
has notice of the obligations of one of his own debtors
towards the other. As between Patterson Bros. and the
defendant, they being the two debtors, the "established
principles of a court of equity are fully applicable.
Natural justice requires that the surety shall not have
the whole thrown upon him by the choice of the creditor,
not to resort to remedies in his power ": *Craythorne* v.
Swinburne, 14 Ves. at p. 162. A surety's equity rests
upon the same principles as that of marshalling, when one

creditor of the same debtor is able to resort to either of
two funds, and another creditor to only one. " It is not,"
says Lord Eldon, " by force of the contract; but that equity,
upon which it is considered against conscience that the
holder of the securities should use them to the prejudice
of the surety ; and, therefore, there is nothing hard in the
act of 'the court, placing the surety exactly in the situation
of the creditor" : *Aldrich* v. *Cooper*, 8 Vesey 382, at page
388.

Now, taking the rights of the defendant here as not
arising by contract, there is no doubt he has an equitable
right to say to the creditor who holds security, " that security enures to my benefit; I am entitled to be protected
to the extent that such security will protect me, you
should, therefore, realize all you can out of the principal
debtor, for whom I am only a surety, or out of the securities which he has placed in your hands, and I am entitled
to be protected *pro rata*, share and share alike, with other
sureties ; in other words, realize on your securities, apply
the proceeds *pro rata* on all the indebtedness covered by
such, and should there not be sufficient to pay all in full,
then you can call upon me to pay whatever balance may
be due to you on the note on which I am endorser, but it
would be most inequitable for you to compel me to pay
the full amount of the note, on which I am endorser, and
for you to apply the whole of the proceeds of the securities
which you hold in payment of the other indebtedness of
your debtors, on which I am not liable."   But the defendant goes further than that; he says, " I am entitled to
all the securities placed in your hands by the principal
debtor; you have parted with some of these; it is no
matter whether they are the most valuable or not ; you
acted in the matter without consulting me ; you gave me
no opportunity to say whether it would be to my advantage
or not, that the lands released by you for certain consideration should be released for such consideration or not, and
by your so doing in equity I am released from all liability
on the note in question." I cannot subscribe to this latter

contention, in the circumstances of the present case. The
defendant is one of several sureties, and the security taken
by the plaintiffs is as much for the benefit of other sureties
as for his benefit; he is only entitled to a *pro rata* share
of what those securities are worth, and, therefore, he is
entitled, if he thinks it worth while, to an account, not
only to have the amount already realized, but what still
remains to be realized upon, to be valued, and a *pro rata*
share of the total applied in reduction of the amount due
on the note in question.

I therefore find that the plaintiffs are entitled to judgment for whatever sum may be found to be due on the
promissory note in question, after it is ascertained how
much of the securities realized upon, and yet on hand,
should be applied by the plaintiffs in reduction thereof;
and for that purpose I direct judgment to be entered, referring it to the Master at Hamilton, to take an account of
the amount due by this defendant to the plaintiffs on the
promissory note in the pleadings mentioned, after deducting
therefrom a *pro rata* share of the amount already realized
on the collateral securities held by the plaintiffs for the
indebtedness of Patterson Brothers to them, and also a *pro
rata* share of the value of such securities still in their
hands to be ascertained by the said Master, and directing
payment by the defendant to the plaintiffs of the balance
which shall be found due on the taking of such account,
together with the plaintiffs' costs of this action, and of the
reference to be taxed.

Should the plaintiffs and the defendant agree on the
proper amount to be allowed to the defendant in the reduction of the promissory note, without a reference, then
the Master may enter judgment for that amount with
full costs to be taxed.[*]

A. H. F. L.

---

[*] See *Wright* v. *Simpson*, 6 Ves. Jun. 714, 734.—Rep.

[QUEEN'S BENCH DIVISION.]

JOURNAL PRINTING COMPANY OF OTTAWA v. MACLEAN.

*Defamation—Libel—Incorporated Newspaper Company—Charge of
Corruption—Injury to Business—Special Damage.*

A company incorporated for the purpose of publishing a newspaper can
maintain an action of libel in respect of a charge of corruption in the
conduct of their paper, without alleging special damage.
Metropolitan Saloon Omnibus Co. v. *Hawkins,* 4 H. & N. 87, commented
on and distinguished.
South Hetton Coal Co. v. *North-Eastern News Association,* [1894] 1 Q. B.
133, followed.
Non-suit by FALCONBRIDGE, J., set aside.

THE statement of claim alleged: (1) That the plaintiffs   Statement.
were a body corporate carrying on business as printers and
publishers at the city of Ottawa, and the proprietors and
publishers of the *Evening Journal,* a newspaper published
there. (3) That on or about the 6th January, 1894, the
defendant wrote and caused to be printed and published
in the *Daily Citizen,* a newspaper published at the city of
Ottawa, an address entitled " To the electors of Victoria
ward," in the course of which he falsely and maliciously
wrote and caused to be printed and published of and concerning the plaintiffs, and in relation to their trade and
business as publishers of the said *Evening Journal,* the
words following (as set out in the judgment) ; that the
defendant meant thereby and imputed that the plaintiffs
in the conduct of their trade and business as publishers of
a newspaper habitually misrepresented facts in the columns
of such newspaper, for unlawful gain, hire, or reward, with
intent thereby to defraud and deceive the public, and were
guilty of fraudulent and dishonest practices. (4) That in
the course of such address the defendant further falsely
and maliciously wrote, etc., the words following (as set out
in the judgment) ; that the defendant meant thereby and
imputed that the conduct by the plaintiffs of their trade
and business as publishers of a newspaper was characterized by ignorance and prejudice, and that the plaintiffs

conducted their business in a fraudulent, dishonest, depraved, and perverted manner, from unlawful and improper motives, and were therefore unworthy of public confidence. (5) That in the course of such address the defendant further falsely and maliciously wrote, etc., the words following (as set out in the judgment); that the defendant thereby meant and imputed that the plaintiffs in the conduct of their trade and business as publishers of a newspaper habitually applied themselves to base and infamous purposes, and devoted their newspaper to unworthy, low, and indiscriminate uses, unlawfully, improperly, and for hire, gain, or reward, and were unworthy of public esteem and confidence. (6) That by reason of the publication by the defendant of such libellous statements the plaintiffs had been and were greatly prejudiced and injured in credit and reputation in the conduct of their business as aforesaid, and had been otherwise damnified. And the plaintiffs claimed $10,000 damages and an injunction and costs.

The defendants delivered a statement of defence, upon which issue was joined.

The action was tried before FALCONBRIDGE, J., and a jury, at Ottawa, in March, 1894.

At the close of the plaintiffs' evidence the trial Judge withdrew the case from the jury and dismissed the action, on the ground that an action of libel at the suit of a corporation cannot be based upon a charge of corruption.

At the Easter Sittings of the Divisional Court, 1894, the plaintiffs moved to set aside the judgment of non-suit and for a new trial, and the motion was argued before ARMOUR, C. J., and STREET, J., on the 28th May, 1894.

Shepley, Q. C., for the plaintiffs. The charge was that the plaintiffs' newspaper was corrupt, and the non-suit was on the ground that libel would not lie for such a charge against a corporation. The libel, however, was one affecting property, and the action lies. The trial Judge gave too narrow an interpretation to *Metropolitan Saloon Omnibus Co.* v. *Hawkins*, 4 H. & N. 87, and *The Mayor*,

Aldermen, and Citizens of Manchester v. *Williams,* [1891]
1 Q. B. 94. I rely on *South Hetton Coal Co.* v. *North-Eastern News Association,* [1894] 1 Q. B. 133 ; *Owen Sound Building Society* v. *Meir,* 24 O. R. 109.

McCarthy, Q. C. (with him *Stuart Henderson*), for the defendant. I do not contend that it was necessary for the plaintiffs to allege special damage. To say of a corporation that it has been guilty of corruption is not actionable *per se.* It is not enough that loss of business may be inferred. A corporation, *quâ* corporation, cannot be guilty of corruption ; a corporation cannot sue for defamation of character. I rely on the cases mentioned by counsel for the plaintiffs.

Shepley, Q. C., in reply. The effect of this charge was to diminish profits. It is no matter what word is used, if it involves a charge that affects the business of the plaintiffs. I refer to *Abrath* v. *North-Eastern R. W. Co.,* 11 App. Cas. 247.

June 8, 1894. The judgment of the Court was delivered by

ARMOUR, C. J. :—

I do not think that this case ought to have been withdrawn from the jury.

The plaintiffs were duly incorporated for the purposes and objects following : (*a*) to publish a newspaper or newspapers and to carry on a general newspaper, lithographing, printing, bookbinding, and job printing business ; and (*b*) to acquire by purchase or otherwise any newspaper or newspapers, and any printing, lithographing, publishing, bookbinding, or job printing business or plant under the name the Journal Printing Company of Ottawa (Limited).

At the time of the publication of the alleged libel the plaintiffs were and had been for some time carrying on their business at Ottawa and publishing a newspaper there, called the *Journal,* and the defendant had been a success-

ful candidate for the office of alderman for Victoria ward
of Ottawa for the then previous municipal election, and in
an address to the electors of Victoria ward, thanking them
for the honour they had conferred upon him, which he
caused to be published in the *Daily Citizen*, another newspaper published in Ottawa, the defendant made use of the
following words, which were charged to be a libel upon
the plaintiffs: "I have had the distinction and gratifica-
tion of being for weeks past the object of abuse from the
grand army of cranks, led by a journal that, on the confes-
sion of its moving spirit, reports favourably or adversely at
ten cents a line, that comes to the front with every dis-
carded economic fallacy that it finds lying around, and
that has ridden to exhaustion every crude and vicious
hobby from equal rights down to sawdust in the river."
And the following words, which were also charged to be
a libel upon the plaintiffs: "The verdict of the electors of
Victoria ward is for me sufficient assurance that an intelli-
gent people may be successfully appealed to against the
declamation of the cranks, and the calumnies of an ignorant,
prejudiced, and corrupt press. From the latter source I
will (*sic*) probably be answered, as on former occasions, with
false assumptions and conclusions or with childish prattle
that it mistakes for what since the literary era of Artemus
Ward has been called 'sarkasm.'" And the following words,
which were also charged to be a libel upon the plaintiffs:
"The *Journal's* position. The election of Monday last
affords a lesson to a prostitute press. The candidates, from
those from the mayoralty down, whom the *Journal* took
especially under its patronage were summarily rejected, and
those whom it went especially out of its way to prejudice
were accepted as with a certificate of good character by
the electors."

Evidence was given to shew that the plaintiffs' newspaper, the *Journal*, was aimed at in the above quoted
words.

The allegations contained in these words that the plaintiffs' newspaper reported favourably or adversely at ten

cents a line, that it was corrupt and prostitute, might well
be held by a jury to import the charge that the plaintiffs
were in the habit of selling the advocacy of their newspaper, and it might well be held by a jury that such a
charge tended to bring the plaintiffs into contempt, and to
injure their business, and was therefore a libel.

It was contended that such a charge made against the
plaintiffs could not be a libel, because the plaintiffs were a
corporation and could not as such be guilty of such a
charge.

In *Metropolitan Saloon Omnibus Co.* v. *Hawkins*, 4
H. & N. 87, Pollock, C. B., said (p. 90) that a corporation
could not sue "in respect of a charge of corruption, for a
corporation cannot be guilty of corruption, although the
individuals composing it may ;" but he said this by way
of illustration, and although no doubt true as to some corporations, it is too wide as to all corporations, and although
applicable to a municipal corporation, it cannot be held
applicable to a corporation such as the plaintiffs.

Could a charge such as this, if made against the corporation, if such it is, that publishes the London *Times*, that
it was in the habit of selling the advocacy of the *Times*, be
said not to be a charge tending to bring that corporation
into contempt, and not to be a charge tending to injure the
business of that corporation, and not to be a libel ? The
test of the tendency of such a charge would be, what
would be its effect on the business of that corporation if it
were proved to be true, and could it be said that such
effect would not be injurious ?

I think that the tendency of such a charge against that
corporation could not fail to be injurious to its business,
and I think that the charge here made might well be held
to be injurious to the business of the plaintiffs.

The charge made in this case was clearly a charge in
relation to the conduct of the plaintiffs of their business,
and was a reflection upon such conduct, and was a libel
upon the plaintiffs in the view taken of the law by Lord
Esher in *South Hetton Coal Co.* v. *North-Eastern News*

Association, [1894] 1 Q. B. 133; and what is said by
Lopes, L. J., in that case is quite applicable to this case :—
"With regard to the first point (will the action lie by the
plaintiffs, who are a corporation ?) I am of opinion that,
although a corporation cannot maintain an action for libel
in respect of anything reflecting upon them personally, yet
they can maintain an action for a libel reflecting on the
management of their trade or business, and this without
alleging or proving special damage."

The injury likely to arise from such a charge as is here
made would be a loss of subscribers for and of purchasers
of the plaintiffs' newspaper, and a consequent loss of profits
in their business.

In my opinion, there must be a new trial, and the costs
of the last trial and of this motion will be costs in the
cause to the plaintiffs in any event of the suit.

I refer to *Heriot* v. *Stuart*, 1 Esp. 437; *Trenton Mutual
Life and Fire Ins. Co.* v. *Perrine*, 3 Zab. 402; *Shoe and
Leather Bank* v. *Thompson*, 23 How. Pr. R. 253; *Knicker-
bocker Life Ins. Co.* v. *Ecclesine*, 42 How. Pr. R. 201; *The
Mayor, Aldermen, and Citizens of Manchester* v. *Williams*,
[1891] 1 Q. B. 94.

E. B. B.

[QUEEN'S BENCH DIVISION.]

FINDLEY v. THE FIRE INSURANCE COMPANY OF NORTH AMERICA.

Insurance—Fire Insurance—Policy—Statutory Conditions—Other Conditions—Variations—55 Vict. ch. 39, sec. 33 (O.)—Representations in Application—R. S. O. ch. 167, sec. 114, Condition 1—Moral Risk—Apprehension of Incendiarism.

Where a fire insurance policy does not contain the statutory conditions, but contains other conditions not printed as variations, it must be read as containing the statutory conditions and no others.
Citizens' Insurance Co. v. *Parsons*, 7 App. Cas. 96, followed.
And the law in this respect has not been altered by 55 Vict. ch. 39, sec. 33 (O.)
Where the policy is based upon an application containing statements or representations relating to matters as to which the insurers have required information, the first of the statutory conditions in sec. 114 of R. S. O. ch. 167 must be taken to refer to such statements and representations, whether the risk they relate to is physical or moral.
Reddick v. *Saugeen Mutual Fire Insurance Co.*, 15 A. R. 363, followed.
And where in the application the insured was asked whether any incendiary danger to the property was threatened or apprehended, and untruly answered "no":—
Held, that the policy was avoided.

ACTION upon a policy of insurance against fire issued by the defendants, tried before STREET, J., at the Chatham Spring Assizes, 1894, without a jury, and in whose judgment the defence relied on is stated. Statement.

J. S. Fraser, for the plaintiff.
Wallace Nesbitt and *Ryckman*, for the defendants.

May 3, 1894. STREET, J. :—

The insurance policy does not contain the statutory conditions ; a number of conditions are incorporated in it, but they are not printed as variations from the statutory conditions, and they must, therefore, be disregarded. I must treat the policy as subject to the statutory conditions and to no other conditions : *Citizens Ins. Co.* v. *Parsons*, 7 App. Cas. 96.

In the application for insurance the applicant is asked : " Is there any incendiary danger to the property threatened

Judgment.

Street, J.

or apprehended ?" to which she replied, "no." As a matter of fact an attempt had been made a short time before the application to burn the building in question, and the applicant's husband, who was also her agent for the purpose of managing the property and applying for the insurance, had watched the building at night after the attempt at setting it on fire until the insurance had been effected.

This was a circumstance material to be made known to the company in order to enable it to judge of the risk it was undertaking, within the meaning of the first statutory condition* ; instead of being made known to the company, its existence was denied, and I must hold that the insurance was of no force.

Other defences were relied on by the company which it is not necessary to dispose of.

The action must be dismissed with costs.

The plaintiff appealed from this decision, and his appeal was argued before the Divisional Court (ARMOUR, C. J., and FALCONBRIDGE, J.) on the 1st June, 1894.

Masten, for the plaintiff. The policy being without conditions, the trial Judge held that the statutory conditions (R. S. O. ch. 167, sec. 114) were applicable, following *Citizens Ins. Co.* v. *Parsons*, 7 App. Cas. 96. But the whole effect of that case is taken away by 55 Vict. ch. 39, sec. 33, (O.) The result is that if the statutory conditions are to apply, they must be printed on the policy. In the next place, this case is not within the first statutory condition, even if applicable. The risk, if any, was not a physical but a moral risk. In the third place, the defendants' agent had notice of the attempt to burn the building, or he should have had; it was a matter of general knowledge in the

* R. S. O. ch. 167, sec. 114.—1. If any person or persons insures his or their buildings or goods, and causes the same to be described otherwise than as they really are, to the prejudice of the company, or misrepresents or omits to communicate any circumstance which is material to be made known to the company, in order to enable it to judge of the risk it undertakes, such insurance shall be of no force in respect to the property in regard to which the misrepresentation or omission is made.

town. On this point see *People's Ins. Co.* v. *Spencer*, 53 Pa. St. 353.

Ryckman, for the defendants. We are entitled to the benefit of the statutory conditions as well as our own conditions, and the recent Act has made no difference. The danger here is within the meaning of the first condition : *Reddick* v. *Saugeen Mutual Fire Ins. Co.*, 15 A. R. 363 ; *Campbell* v. *Victoria Mutual Fire Ins. Co.*, 45 U. C. R. 412. The evidence does not shew that the danger was known to the agent, but if it was, it did not absolve the plaintiff from the obligation to communicate it : *Greet* v. *Citizens Ins. Co.*, 27 Gr. 121 ; May on Insurance, 3rd ed., sec. 208. We are entitled also to rely on other grounds of misdescription, etc., shewn by the application and the evidence.

Masten, in reply.

June 21, 1894. The judgment of the Court was delivered by

ARMOUR, C. J. :—

In *Reddick* v. *Saugeen Mutual Fire Ins. Co.*, 15 A. R. 363, Osler, J. A., in discussing the question referred to in the first statutory condition as to whether it was to be confined to the physical risk or whether it also included the moral risk, said : " I agree that the condition may, to some extent, be limited to the former, where there is no express stipulation or representation in the application, but speaking generally, where the policy is, as in this case, based upon an application containing statements or representations relating to matters as to which the company have thought proper to require information, the condition must be taken to refer to such statements and representations, whether the risk they relate to is the physical risk or the moral risk."

This statement of the construction to be placed upon the first statutory condition appears to have been concurred in

Judgment. by the other members of the Court, and is decisive of this
Armour, C.J. case.

The policy in this case is to be read as containing this
condition : *Citizens Ins. Co.* v. *Parsons*, 7 App. Cas. 96.

And I do not think that the Act 55 Vict.ch. 39, sec. 33 (O.),
has altered the law in this respect, for it provides that
nothing therein contained shall be deemed to impair the
effect of the provisions contained in sections 114 to 118,
inclusive, of the Ontario Insurance Act.

In the application the plaintiff was asked : " Incendiarism.
Is there any incendiary danger to the property threatened
or apprehended ?" to which she answered " no," and the
learned Judge having found that this answer was untrue,
the policy was avoided.

In my opinion, the motion must be dismissed with costs.

E. B. B.

[QUEEN'S BENCH DIVISION.]

REGINA v. ALWARD.

Justice of the Peace—Indian Act—Sale of Intoxicating Liquors—Information—Several Offences—Objection Taken at Hearing—Summary Conviction.

When an information laid against the defendant under the Indian Act charged that he sold intoxicating liquor to two persons on the 5th July and to two persons on the 8th July, and the justices, notwithstanding that the defendant's counsel objected to the information on this ground, proceeded and heard evidence in respect of all the offences so charged, then amended the information by substituting the 8th August for the 8th July, proceeded and heard evidence in respect of the substituted charge and dismissed it, and convicted the defendants for selling to two persons on the 5th July, the conviction was quashed.

Regina v. *Hazen*, 20 A. R. 633, distinguished.

Per STREET, J.—It was the duty of the justices when the objection was taken to have amended the information by striking out one or other of the charges, and to have heard the evidence applicable to the remaining charge only.

AN information upon oath was on the 21st day of September, 1893, laid by one John Jackson before S. W. Howard, one of Her Majesty's justices of the peace for the county of Haldimand, "that Leonard Alward did, at Hagersville, on the 5th day of July, 1893, sell to Elijah Wasson and John Jackson, Indians, intoxicating liquor, contrary to the Indian Act of Canada, and did also unlawfully sell intoxicating liquor on the 8th day of July, at Hagersville, to the said John Jackson and John VanEvery, contrary to the provisions of the said Indian Act."

Upon this information the defendant was brought before the said S. W. Howard and one Hugh Stewart, two of Her Majesty's justices of the peace for the said county on the 22nd day of September, 1893, and evidence was given of a sale by the defendant of intoxicating liquor to John Jackson on the 5th day of July, 1893. The evidence failed as to a sale on the 8th day of July, 1893, and that charge was abandoned, and the information was amended by substituting the 8th day of "August" for the 8th day of "July" therein "in the presence of the defendant and his counsel, and not expressing any dissent but disclaiming

Statement. any assent to the information as amended;" and evidence
was given of a sale by the defendant of intoxicating liquor
to John Jackson on the 8th day of August, 1893. Evidence was also given on the defendant's behalf.

"The charge for the offence of the 8th of August was
dismissed, and the charge for selling liquor to John Jackson
and Elijah Wasson was held to be proven on July 5th.
Defendant was fined $50 and costs $7.15."

It appeared that the defendant's counsel objected to the
information because it disclosed two distinct offences.

A *certiorari* having been obtained, the following conviction was returned :—

"Be it remembered that on the twenty-second day of
September in the year of our Lord 1893, at Hagersville,
in the said county of Haldimand, Leonard Alward is convicted before the undersigned Samuel W. Howard and
Hugh Stewart, justices of the peace in and for the county
of Haldimand, for that he, the said Leonard Alward, at
Hagersville, on the fifth day of July, 1893, did sell to John
Jackson and Elijah Wasson intoxicating liquor, contrary
to the Indian Act of Canada, and we adjudge the said
Leonard Alward for his said offence to forfeit and pay the
sum of fifty dollars, to be paid and applied according to
law, and also to pay the said John Jackson the sum of
seven dollars and fifteen cents for his costs in this behalf,
and if the several sums be not paid forthwith, we order
that the same be levied by distress and sale of the goods
and chattels of the said Leonard Alward, and in default of
sufficient distress, we adjudge the said Leonard Alward to
be imprisoned in the common gaol of the said county of
Cayuga, in the said county of Haldimand, for the space of
thirty days, unless the said several sums and all costs and
charges of the said distress and of the commitment and
conveying of the said Leonard Alward to the said goal
shall be sooner paid.

"Given under our hands and seals the day and year first
above mentioned, at Hagersville, in the county aforesaid.

HUGH STEWART, J.P."   [L.S.]
S. W. HOWARD, J.P."   [L.S.]

At the Hilary Sittings, 1894, the defendant obtained a rule *nisi* to quash the said conviction upon the following, among other, grounds :—

1. That the complaint on which the said conviction proceeded was for more than one matter of complaint, and the defendant was, notwithstanding the objection of his counsel thereto, tried at the same time before the said justices upon two separate and distinct matters of complaint.

2. That the said justices illegally and improperly heard the full evidence for the prosecution upon each of the said charges before adjudicating upon either.

4. That the conviction itself charged two offences, a sale to Jackson and another sale to Wasson ; it did not allege that the said Jackson and Wasson were, or that either of them was, an Indian, or that the alleged sale of liquor was unlawful.

May 30, 1894. *Aylesworth*, Q. C., for the defendant, moved the rule absolute. The conviction discloses no offence; it does not say that the two men named were Indians ; but that appears in the evidence. The information charged and the defendant was tried for two offences at the same time, viz., selling on two occasions. This is not like *Regina* v. *Hazen*, 23 O. R. 387 ; 20 A. R. 633. Here there were two quite distinct charges. The prisoner protested, taking the objection at the outset, before plea, but the magistrate refused to amend. See the Criminal Code, sec. 845, sub-sec. 3. In the next place, the offence was not established by any other evidence than that of the informant : see 51 Vict. ch. 22, sec. 4 (D.), amending the Indian Act.

T. W. Howard, for the magistrate and informant, shewed cause. The real charge is selling liquor to Indians. The proof of one offence did not strengthen the other. I rely on *Regina* v. *Hazen*, 20 A. R. 633. Under sec. 883 of the Code the Court has jurisdiction to amend or make the proper order.

Judgment.   June 21, 1894. ARMOUR, C. J. :—

Armour, C.J.

This conviction must, in my opinion, be quashed for the reasons given by me in quashing the conviction in *Regina* v. *Hazen*, 23 O. R. 387.

It is true that the decision of *Regina* v. *Hazen* was reversed by the Court of Appeal in 20 A. R. 633, but not, as I understand the decision, on the ground that the principle of law applied by me to that case was wrong, but on the ground that the facts of that case, as viewed by the Court of Appeal, did not warrant the application of the principle.

The facts of this case, however they may be viewed, present the same features as the facts in *Regina* v. *Hazen*, as I viewed them.

In this case there can be no doubt that more offences than one were charged in the information ; that the justices, notwithstanding that the defendant's counsel objected to the information on this ground, proceeded and heard evidence in respect of all the offences originally charged in the information ; that they then amended the information by substituting the 8th day of August for the 8th day of July therein, and thereupon proceeded and heard evidence in respect of the substituted charge, and thereupon dismissed that charge and made the conviction returned to this Court.

I think, therefore, that the principle of law I applied to the facts, as I viewed them, in *Regina* v. *Hazen*, is entirely applicable to the facts in this case, however they may be viewed, and that the conviction must be quashed.

FALCONBRIDGE, J., concurred.

STREET, J. :—

It has been decided in *Regina* v. *Hazen*, 20 A. R. 633, that to charge two offences in one information is a defect in substance in the information within the meaning of sub-sec. 1 of sec. 847 of the Criminal Code, and that therefore

no objection founded merely upon the form of the information could be sustained. In that case it was further
held that where an information disclosed two offences, and
evidence had been taken upon both without objection
before judgment had been given upon either, the conviction should stand.

In the present case it appears that before the defendant
was called on to plead his counsel objected that two offences were charged in the information, but the objection was
evidently overruled. Again, at the time the amendment
was allowed to the information during the progress of the
trial the objection was again mentioned. I think it appears
plainly enough from the proceedings that the magistrates
proceeded to take evidence upon both charges in spite of
the objection of the defendant's counsel previously made
to this course.

The case, therefore, is not within the decision of *Regina
v. Hazen*, 20 A. R. 633. It was, I think, the duty of the
magistrates when the objection was taken to have amended
the information by striking out one or other of the charges,
and to have heard the evidence applicable to the remaining
charge only: *Rodgers v. Richards*, [1892] 1 Q. B. 555;
Regina v. Hazen, 20 A. R. 633, judgment of Osler, J. A.;
Hamilton v. Walker, [1892] 2 Q. B. 25.

I agree, therefore, that the conviction should be quashed.

E. B. B.

[QUEEN'S BENCH DIVISION.]

CRAM v. RYAN ET AL.

Negligence — Fire — Liability for Acts of Another — Control — Navigable Waters — Access to Shore and Navigation Rights — Public Rights — Private Rights.

Held, affirming the decision of STREET, J., 24 O. R. 500, that the defendants were liable for the negligence of the owner of the tug hired by them in so placing it as to communicate fire to the plaintiff's scow, as in doing so he was obeying the orders of the defendants' foreman, and was under his direct and personal control.

Bartonshill Coal Co. v. *Reid*, 3 Macq. Sc. App. Cas. 266, followed :—

Held, however, reversing the decision of STREET, J., that the plaintiff in mooring his scow where he did was not a trespasser, at all events as against the defendants, who were mere licensees "to take sand from in front of " the land granted by the Crown.

The grant to the shore of the river, reserving free access to the shore for all vessels, boats, and persons, carried the land to the water's edge, and not to the middle of the stream.

The effect of the removal of the shore line back from its natural line was to make the water so let in as much *publici juris* as any other part of the water of the river, and such removal did not take away the right of free access to the shore so removed.

Statement.

AN appeal by the defendants from the judgment of STREET, J., (24 O. R. 500) in favour of the plaintiff.

The action was for damages for the destruction of the plaintiff's scow by fire caused by sparks from a tug hired by the defendants under the circumstances set forth in the former report.

The appeal was on the following, among other, grounds :—

(1) That the direction to enter judgment was against law and evidence and the weight of evidence.

(2) That the plaintiff's scow was not set on fire by the tug *Hattie Vinton*, and if it was, that the defendants were not liable therefor, as they were not the owners of, nor were they responsible for, the tug in any way, nor had they any control over it.

(3) That the plaintiff's scow was illegally in the bay when burned, and the defendants were not, in any view of the facts, responsible for its destruction.

(4) That there was no evidence to support the finding of negligence on the defendants' part, there being no duty on their part towards the plaintiff as respects his scow.

The appeal was argued on the 28th May, 1894, before the Divisional Court (ARMOUR, C. J., and FALCONBRIDGE, J.).

McCarthy, Q. C., for the defendants. I find fault with the proposition that the defendants were bound to omit no reasonable precaution to avoid the chance of injuring the plaintiff's property. The defendants could not deliberately set fire to the plaintiff's scow, but there was no duty owing by them to him: *Le Lievre* v. *Gould*, [1893] 1 Q. B. 491, in which case *Heaven* v. *Pender*, 11 Q. B. D. 503, is distinguished. As against a trespasser, the owner of property is liable only for injury arising from a concealed danger, such as a spring gun, and here the defendants warned the plaintiff off the bay. Under the circumstances of this case there can be no liability for negligence : Beven on Negligence, pp. 1097, 1102, 1114; *Jordin* v. *Crump*, 8 M. & W. 782; *Woodley* v. *Metropolitan District R. W. Co.*, 2 Ex. D. 384; *Degg* v. *Midland R. W. Co.*, 1 H. & N. 773; *Bolch* v. *Smith*, 7 H. & N. 736 ; *Griffiths* v. *London and North-Western R. W. Co.*, 14 L. T. N. S. 797. In the next place, the defendants were not the owners or controllers of the tug. The master of the tug was not their servant. The alleged negligence was not in placing the tug where it was, but in applying a violent draught, a matter over which the defendants had no control. *Respondeat superior* does not apply. In the third place, the plaintiff was there *volens*, with his eyes open, taking his chances. In *Smith* v. *Baker*, [1891] A. C. 325, the doctrine of *volens* is said to be applicable to cases other than between master and servant. Lastly, the defendants by excavating have not irrevocably given away their property. They may fill it up again, if they have shewn no intention to dedicate it.

Watson, Q. C., for the plaintiff. The defendants are liable because they did a reckless act, knowing it might result in the destruction of property. I refer to *Davies* v. *Mann*, 10 M. & W. 546; *Clark* v. *Chambers*, 3 Q. B. D. 327 ; *Roe* v. *Village of Lucknow*, 21 A. R. 1. The recent case of *Thompson* v. *Fowler*, 23 O. R. 644, was one of the

Argument. hiring of a tug, but here there was a general employment, which serves to distinguish it.

Masten, on the same side. The plaintiff was not a trespasser. The owners of the land took away sand, and the water fell to the Crown. It is the converse of the case where artificial accretions of land go to the riparian proprietor: Hunt on Boundaries, 3rd ed., p. 33. Artificial accretions do not differ from natural, if gradual: Gould on Waters, 2nd ed., p. 314. Under the rule there laid down, where owners have withdrawn soil from the bank, either on the basis of dedication or abandonment, a right of navigation at once arises. There was nothing to indicate to the plaintiff that he was a trespasser. A trespasser is not in the position of one who is guilty of contributory negligence: Shearman and Redfield on Negligence, 4th ed., secs. 97, 98. A trespasser is not precluded by law from recovering: *Barnes* v. *Ward*, 9 C. B. at p. 420 Beven on Negligence, p. 1090.

McCarthy, in reply. *Davies* v. *Mann*, 10 M. & W. 546, is not applicable, for it was a case of a highway. In *Simkin* v. *London and North-Western R. W. Co.*, 21 Q. B. D. 453, it was held that the defendants were not liable to passers by for not screening their railway from the adjacent road. The principle of that case applies to this.

June 21, 1894. The judgment of the Court was delivered by

ARMOUR, C. J. :—

Two contentions were chiefly insisted on before us, namely, first, that the defendants were not answerable for the negligence by which the plaintiff was injured, but that the master and owner of the tug was alone answerable for it ; second, that the plaintiff was a trespasser in mooring his scow where it was moored, and could not, therefore, recover for the injury which he sustained.

I do not think that it can be properly said that the

injury which the plaintiff sustained was caused by the
negligence of the owner of the tug alone, for in placing
the tug where he did, and using it when so placed as he
did, he was obeying the orders of Sullivan, the defendants'
foreman, and was under his direct and personal control.

In *Bartonshill Coal Company* v. *Reid*, 3 Macq. Sc. App.
Cas. 266, Lord Cranworth said (p. 282) : "Where an injury is
occasioned to any one by the negligence of another, if the
person injured seeks to charge with its consequences any
person other than him who actually caused the damage, it
lies on the person injured to shew that the circumstances
were such as to make some other person responsible. In
general it is sufficient for this purpose to shew that the
person whose neglect caused the injury was at the time
when it was occasioned acting, not on his own account, but
in the course of his employment as a servant in the business of a master, and that the damage resulted from the
servant so employed not having conducted his master's
business with due care. In such a case the maxim *respondeat superior* prevails, and the master is responsible."

Applying the principle here laid down to the facts found
by my brother Street, it is plain that the defendants were
responsible for the negligence which caused the injury to
the plaintiff. See also *Stephen* v. *Police Commissioners of
Thurso*, 3 Ct. of Sess. Cas., 4th series, at p. 542.

I do not agree with my brother Street that the plaintiff
in mooring his scow where he did was a trespasser, although,
assuming that he was a trespasser, I do not dissent from
the conclusion at which my learned brother has arrived as
to the liability of the defendants.

The grant from the Crown to Beatty carried the land
granted to the water's edge, and not to the middle of the
river, and it reserved free access to the shore of the lands
thereby granted for all vessels, boats, and persons : *Scotten
v. Barthel.**

The defendants were mere licensees under Fitzsimmons

* A case decided by this Court on the 3rd March, 1894, and not reported.
It has since been carried to the Court of Appeal.

and Moran, who were Beatty's successors in title to the lands so granted, and the license to the defendants was "to take sand from in front of" the land so granted.

It is unnecessary to discuss the question whether the removal of the shore line back from its natural line, by the license of Fitzsimmons and Moran, had the effect of removing the boundary of their land back to the new shore line, and of making the land covered with water, by reason of such removal, the property of the Crown.

But it is plain, I think, that the effect of such removal was that the water so let in was as much *publici juris* as any other part of the water of the river, and the removal of the shore line back from its natural line did not take away the free access to the shore so removed for all vessels, boats, and persons.

I think, therefore, that the plaintiff's scow was lawfully moored where it was moored, and the plaintiff was not in respect thereof a trespasser, and was certainly not so as regarded the defendants, who were mere licensees as above: Gould on Waters, 2nd ed., sec. 155, note 4 at p. 314, and cases there cited.

In my opinion, the judgment of my learned brother should be affirmed, and the appeal dismissed with costs.

E. B. B.

[QUEEN'S BENCH DIVISION.]

MORTON v. COWAN ET AL.

Company—Shares—Sale under Execution—Validity of Assignment not
Entered in Books—R. S. O. ch. 157, sec. 52—Equity of Redemption—
R. S. O. ch. 64, sec. 16.

A *bonâ fide* assignment or pledge for value of shares in the capital stock
of a company incorporated under R. S. O. ch. 157 is valid between the
assignor and the assignee, notwithstanding that no entry of the assignment or transfer is made in the books of the company ; and, as only
the debtor's interest in property seized can be sold under execution, the
rights of a *bonâ fide* assignee cannot be cut out by the seizure and sale
of the shares, under execution against the assignor, after the assignment.

R. S. O. ch. 157, sec. 52, considered and construed.

Semble, that nothing passes by such a sale under execution ; for the words
"goods and chattels" in sec. 16 of the Execution Act, R. S. O. ch. 64,
do not include shares in an incorporated company so as to authorize the
sale of the equity of redemption in such shares.

THIS was an action brought by Robert Morton against Statement.
John Cowan and the Ontario Malleable Iron Company
(Limited).

The statement of claim alleged that on and after the
4th November, 1893, the plaintiff was possessed absolutely
and as owner of seven shares of the capital stock of the
defendant company, and on that day he caused notice of
his acquisition of the shares to be given to the defendants ; that on the 11th November, 1893, the defendant
Cowan, who was the president of the defendant company,
well knowing that the shares were the property of the
plaintiff, caused them to be seized in execution under a
writ of *fi. fa.* issued in an action in the High Court of
Justice for Ontario, wherein the defendant Cowan was the
plaintiff, and one Henry F. White was the defendant, and
under the direction of the defendant Cowan the shares
were on the 24th November, 1893, sold under the writ to
himself, and transferred to him by the defendant company
upon their books ; that the shares were each of the par
value of $100, and of the actual value of $125 ; and that by
reason of the premises the plaintiff had been unlawfully

deprived of his property and endamaged in $875 ; for which sum he claimed judgment.

The defendant Cowan by his statement of defence alleged that the shares in question belonged to Henry F. White, against whom he had recovered judgment and issued execution, and that the sheriff sold them for $350 to one Jones, who subsequently transferred them to him, Cowan; that the sale to Jones and the transfer to the defendant were duly entered in the books of the company ; that no transfer of the shares by White had been entered in the books of the company ; that no notice of any claim by the plaintiff to any shares in the company was ever given to the defendant Cowan or to the company until after the sale by the sheriff, and no transfer of any shares to the plaintiff had ever been entered in the company's books. The defendant submitted that it was the duty of the plaintiff, if he had acquired any shares, to have the transfer entered in the company's books, and that under sec. 52 of R. S. O. ch. 157 any alleged transfer had no effect except as set out in the section ; and he also alleged that the stock had not the value ascribed to it by the plaintiff.

The defendant company by their statement of defence alleged that they were a joint stock company incorporated under R. S. O. ch. 157, and set up substantially the same facts as were contained in the statement of their co-defendant, with the addition that they had no notice of any claim to any of their shares by the plaintiff, nor had any application been made to them to make entry in their books of any transfer to him ; and they submitted that the statement of claim shewed no right of action against them and claimed the same benefit as if they had demurred.

The action was tried before BOYD, C., at the Sandwich Spring Sittings, on the 14th March, 1894.

Evidence was given of an assignment of the shares in question by Henry F. White to the plaintiff, before the date of the seizure, in consideration of advances made by the plaintiff to White. The assignment was by indorse- ment of the stock certificate; and a power of attorney was given by White to J. W. Hanna to transfer the shares to the plaintiff. No transfer was ever entered on the books of the company, and there was a dispute on the evidence as to whether Hanna had notified the officers of the company of the assignment. The facts as to the seizure and sale of the stock were as set up in the statements of defence.

M. K. Cowan, for the plaintiff.
Wallace Nesbitt and *Cleary*, for the defendants.

April 4, 1894. BOYD, C.:—

The stock of incorporated companies is declared to be and is personal property, and by the statute is saleable under execution " in like manner as other personal property:" R. S. O. ch. 64, sec. 9. Now the rule as to sales by the act of the law is that the measure of what is sold is the extent of the debtor's interest in the property sold, and not the exact specific property itself—whether it be real or personal. That was the principle adopted by James, V.-C., in *DeWolf* v. *Pitcairn*, 17 W. R. 914 (1869), and explicitly laid down by the Privy Council in *Wickham* v. *New Brunswick R. W. Co.*, L. R. 1 P. C. 64 (1865). I see nothing in the statute under which this company was incorporated to derogate from that broad rule of justice. What was relied on was the provision found in R. S. O. ch. 157, sec. 52, which was said to be specially framed to meet such a case as this and render the execution operative as to the share itself, notwithstanding intervening equities and rights as between the shareholder and a *bond fide* assignee or pledgee. But I do not so read the section, which indeed is but a reproduction of the same language found in an earlier Dominion statute : 32 & 33 Vict. ch. 12, sec. 25 (now R. S. C. ch. 118, sec. 25).*

*R. S. O. ch. 157, sec. 52.—No transfer of stock, unless made by sale under execution, or under the order or judgment of some competent

This very section admits, recognizes, or declares that a transfer may be valid as exhibiting the rights of the parties thereto towards each other, and that concedes all that has to be ascertained in this case.

Whatever the company might do in such a case in the way of disposing of stock against defaulting holders, the provision is not pointed at dealings between the holder and others, pending which an execution comes in. The sale, which is the act of the law, is not permitted to have a tortious effect so as to cut out the rights of a *bonâ fide* assignee or pledgee, which is the present case. Therefore, I think, irrespective of the question of notice to the company, that there was a valid dealing with these shares as between the plaintiff and the judgment debtor, which has not been extinguished or affected by the sale of the shares under execution.

The plaintiff is, in my opinion, entitled to judgment with costs. I hold this with more willingness both because the shares were paid in full, and therefore property over which the owner had practically unfettered right of disposition, and also because the purchase was made in the interests of one of the officers of the company.

At the Easter Sittings of the Divisional Court, 1894, the defendants moved to set aside the judgment of the trial Judge, or to vary it by declaring that the defendant Cowan was entitled to redeem the shares on payment of the actual money disbursed by the plaintiff, and for which the assignment of the shares was taken as security, upon the following, among other, grounds :—

1. That the trial Judge should have held that the plaintiff was debarred by sec. 52 of R. S. O. ch. 157.

2. That he should have held, in any event, that the

Court in that behalf, shall be valid for any purpose whatever, save only as exhibiting the rights of the parties thereto towards each other, and as rendering the transferee liable, *ad interim*, jointly and severally with the transferor, to the company and its creditors, until entry thereof has been duly made in the books of the company.

plaintiff was a mortgagee of the shares, and that the defen- Statement. dant Cowan was entitled to redeem.

3. That the action should have been dismissed with costs as against the defendant company.

The motion was argued before ARMOUR, C. J., and FALCONBRIDGE and STREET, JJ., on the 29th and 30th May, 1894.

Wallace Nesbitt and *Monro Grier*, for the defendants, referred to R. S. O. ch. 157, sec. 52; *Dodds* v. *Hills,* 2 H. &. M. 424; *Skowhegan Bank* v. *Cutler,* 49 Me. 315; *Oxford Turnpike Company* v. *Bunnel,* 6 Conn. 552; secs. 9 and 16 of the Execution Act, R. S. O. ch. 64; *Brown* v. *Nelson,* 10 P. R. 421.

W. R. Riddell, for the plaintiff, cited *McMurrich* v. *Bond Head Harbour Co.,* 9 U. C. R. 333; *Woodruff* v. *Harris,* 11 U. C. R. 490; *Smith* v. *Bank of Nova Scotia,* 8 S. C. R. 558.

June 21, 1894. The judgment of the Court was delivered by

ARMOUR, C. J. :—

I am of the opinion that the judgment of the learned Chancellor was right and should be affirmed for the reasons given by him, and I refer, in addition to the cases cited by him, to the cases of *Rex* v. *Gade,* 2 Leach C. C. 732; *Foster* v. *Bank of England,* 8 Q. B. 689; *Woodruff* v. *Harris,* 11 U. C. R. 490; *Dodds* v. *Hills,* 2 H. & M. 424.

It was contended, however, that the equity of redemption of White in the shares in question passed by the sheriff's sale to Jones, and was transferred by him to the defendant Cowan, and that we ought to make a decree in favour of the defendant Cowan for redemption.

No case for redemption is made by the pleadings, and I do not think that we ought to make such a decree upon the record as constituted and upon the evidence before us,

but leave the defendant Cowan to seek such remedy, if he
has it, by a suit for that purpose.

I do not think, however, that the law authorizes the
sale of an equity of redemption in the shares of an incorporated company, and that, therefore, nothing passed
by the sheriff's sale to Jones.

Shares in incorporated companies were first made saleable under execution in this Province by 2 Will. IV. ch. 6,
which provided " that the stock held by any person in any
bank, or in any corporation or company in this Province
having a joint transferable stock, shall be liable to be taken
and sold in execution, in the same manner as other personal
property of the debtor."

Afterwards the Act 12 Vict. ch. 23 was passed, which
provided " that all shares and dividends of stockholders
in incorporated companies shall be held, considered, and
adjudged to be personal property, and shall be liable as
such to *bond fide* creditors for debts, and may be attached,
seized, and sold under writs of execution issued out of any
of Her Majesty's Courts in this Province, in like manner
as other personal property may be sold under execution."

It was not until after this that the Chattel Mortgage
Act, 20 Vict. ch. 3, was passed, which provided (sec. 11) that
" on any writ, precept, or warrant of execution against goods
and chattels, it shall be lawful for the sheriff or other
officer to whom such writ, warrant, or precept may be
directed, to seize and sell the interest or equity of redemption in any goods or chattels of the party or parties against
whom such writ may issue ; and such sale shall be held to
convey whatever interest the mortgagor had in such goods
and chattels at the time of such seizure."

This provision appears in R. S. O. ch. 64 as sec. 16 ; and
the provisions of 12 Vict. ch. 23 appear in R. S. O. ch. 64
as secs. 8 to 15, inclusive.

I do not think that the words " goods and chattels" in
sec. 16 include shares in incorporated companies so as
to authorize the sale of the equity of redemption in such
shares, for special provisions are made in secs. 8 to 15,

inclusive, for the sale of such shares, and these provisions exclude the notion that an equity of redemption in them is made saleable. Provision is made for the sale of such shares, but no provision is made for the sale of an equity of redemption in them.

The purchaser of the shares shall thereafter be the holder, and shall have the same rights, and be under the same obligations as if he had duly purchased the shares from the proprietor thereof ; and the proper officer of the company shall enter such sale as a transfer in the manner by law provided : sec. 13. But no provision whatever is made for the seizing or selling of an equity of redemption in the shares, nor for the transfer thereof by the sheriff, nor by any officer of the company, nor declaring what shall be the rights and obligations of the purchaser.

In my opinion the motion must be dismissed with costs.

E. B. B.

[QUEEN'S BENCH DIVISION.]

WILLIAMS v. THOMAS.

*Landlord and Tenant—Distress—Action for Conversion—Double Value—
Pleading—Chattel Mortgage—Jus Tertii—Assessment of Damages—
Recovery of Amount Received from Sale of Goods—Claim and Counter-
claim—Set-off.*

In an action for wrongful distress for rent before it was due, there was
no allegation in the statement of claim that the action was brought
upon 2 W. & M., sess. 1, ch. 5, sec. 5, nor that the goods distrained
were " sold," but merely an allegation that the defendant " sold and
carried away the same and converted and disposed thereof to his own
use ;" nor was a claim made for double the value of the goods distrained and sold, within the terms of the statute :—

Held, reversing the decision of FERGUSON, J., that the action was the
ordinary action for conversion, and that the value, and not the double
value, of the goods distrained was recoverable :—

Held, also, reversing the decision of FERGUSON, J., that a wrong-doer
taking goods out of the possession of another, cannot set up the *jus
tertii*, but the person out of whose possession the goods are taken, may
shew it, and in such case the wrong-doer may take advantage of it ; and
the plaintiff, having shewn a chattel mortgage subsisting upon a portion of the goods distrained, could not be allowed to recover the value
of such portion without protecting the defendant against another action
at the suit of the mortgagee :—

Held, also, *per* FERGUSON, J., that the plaintiff was not entitled to recover from the defendant the amount received by him from the sale of
the plaintiff's goods in addition to the value thereof ; nor was the
defendant obliged to deduct the amount so received by him from the
rent which afterwards fell due.

Hoare v. *Lee*, 5 C. B. 754, followed.

Judgment being given in favour of the plaintiff upon his claim, and in
favour of the defendant upon his counterclaim :—

Held, reversing the decision of FERGUSON, J., that the amounts should
be set off.

Statement.   THIS was an action tried before FERGUSON, J., without
a jury, at St. Thomas, in the Spring of 1894. The facts
are stated in his judgment.

April 23, 1894.   FERGUSON, J.:—

The action is by a tenant against his landlord for an
alleged wrongful distress for rent when, as alleged, no rent
was due.

The plaintiff also makes a claim upon what may be
called the common counts.

At the close of the trial I delivered judgment in favour

of the plaintiff in respect of the alleged wrongful distress,
and, on the conflicting evidence as to value, I fixed the
value of the goods distrained at the sum of $246, and found
that at the time the distress was made no rent whatever
was due from the tenant to the landlord.

The goods distrained were, as I thought, in a large
measure sacrificed by the sales made by the defendant, the
landlord. He, however, received for them the sum of $93.

I held this to be a case in which the plaintiff is entitled
as damages to "double value" under the statute, which
double value would be $492. The plaintiff contended that
he was also entitled to recover as well the above mentioned
sum of $93.

I think the case of *Hoare* v. *Lee*, 5 C. B. 754, is against
this contention, shewing, as I think it does, that there was
but the one trespass, the damages in respect of which are
measured by the statute, namely, the "double value." In
that case the Court refused to allow a second count for
entering and taking goods to be pleaded with a count for
a distress for rent falsely pretended to be due, and a perusal
of the judgment shews one that the ground of the decision
was that there had been but the one trespass by the defendant, and that the damages were measured as above stated.

I expressed the opinion that the plaintiff did not prove
any substantial amount against the defendant on the common counts or the equivalent of these counts in the statement of claim, and I am still of the same opinion.

There was a chattel mortgage in favour of Mr. McConnell
upon part of the goods, securing originally the sum of $80.
This mortgage contained what has been called (perhaps a
little loosely called) the re-demise clause. Only the sum
of $55 remained unpaid upon the mortgage, and this amount
had not fallen due, nor did it fall due for some months after
the time of the distress. The defendant contended that,
owing to the existence of this mortgage, the plaintiff could
not as to the goods embraced in it sustain the action, on
the ground that he, the plaintiff, was not in law the owner
of these goods. The plaintiff was in possession of all the

goods distrained; this was undisputed, and there was no
pretence whatever that the defendant claimed under or had
any authority or any title under the mortgage, and, so far
as I can perceive, the contention, or rather the matter of
it, falls under the common and well-known rule thus
stated: "As possession in fact is evidence of the right of
possession, it is sufficient to maintain an action against a
wrong-doer who cannot shew a better title in himself or
authority under a better title:" *Elliott* v. *Kemp*, 7 M. &
W. 312; *Northam* v. *Bowden*, 11 Ex. 70; and *Armory* v.
Delamirie, 1 Sm. L. C., 8th ed., p. 374, and notes.

In a case where the plaintiff is not in possession at the
time of the alleged wrongful act by the defendant, the
plaintiff must shew title to the goods, and the defendant is
at liberty to rebut the plaintiff's title by shewing a *jus
tertii*: *Gadsden* v. *Barrow*, 9 Ex. 514; *Leake* v. *Loveday*,
4 M. & G. 972. This, however, the defendant cannot do
where he has disturbed the actual possession of the plaintiff
(as in the present case) unless he can justify under the
authority of the third party: *Jeffries* v. *Great Western R.
W. Co.*, 5 E. & B. 802; *White* v. *Mullett*, 6 Ex. 713.

As already stated, the plaintiff was, in fact, in possession
of the goods when they were wrongly distrained by the
defendant, and there was no pretence of any authority or
title from the mortgagee.

It seems to me entirely plain that this contention of the
defendant must fail.

The plaintiff is, as I think, entitled to judgment against
the defendant for the sum of $492 with his costs of the
action.

· The rent that was accruing due, but which did not fall
due for some months after the distress, was the sum of
$125. This was a yearly rent. The defendant pleaded a
counterclaim in which he claimed, amongst many other
items, the sum of $50 as the balance of the year's rent
after deducting the $93 for which he sold the plaintiff's
goods, less the costs of the distress, which, he said, reduced
this $93 to $75. This claim was, no doubt, made in this

way by the defendant, he believing when making it that
he would be able to sustain the position he had taken
respecting the distress, in which case he would desire to
be paid the balance of his rent.

All the other items of the counterclaim were disposed
of at the close of the trial against the defendant, excepting
an item of $25, which had relation to what was alleged as
a default of the plaintiff as tenant in not properly clearing
and ploughing certain land, called wood land, on the demised premises. The claim in this respect on the record is
$100, but defendant's counsel on the argument voluntarily
reduced it to $25. I am now of the opinion that I then
entertained, but did not express, namely, that nothing
should be, in respect of this, allowed to the defendant; so
that, apart from any claim in respect of rent, nothing will
be allowed to the defendant upon his counterclaim.

The writ in the action was issued the 15th November,
1893. The year's rent fell due according to the letting the
5th December, 1893. The counterclaim was pleaded on
the 16th December, 1893. The defendant's counsel did not,
I think, formally move for an amendment of the counter-
claim in respect of the rent, but did suggest that in a
certain event there should be an amendment by which he
would be enabled to claim as rent the whole $125. The
event has, I think, taken place, and I do not perceive any
good reason why the defendant should not be allowed so
to amend his counterclaim, and that amendment is now
allowed.

As the record now stands with such an amendment, the
defendant by his counterclaim claims his year's rent, $125.
Though the distress that I have held illegal, for the reasons
assigned, was made during the currency of the year, the
tenant was not ousted by his landlord, nor, so far as the
possession of the land had concern, was he disturbed, though
the effect of the distress was to, I may say, entirely break
up his business, which was that of a market gardener.

The defendant has (as already stated) received by a
wrongful seizure and sale of the plaintiff's goods the $93,

less his expenses of the distress, and the question arises as to whether or not this sum received, putting it (after deducting expenses) at $75, should be reckoned against him on his claim for rent.

According to the case *Hoare* v. *Lee,* above referred to, this is money that the plaintiff could not recover from the defendant in addition to recovering the double value of the goods distrained. The defendant did deduct this money from the amount of the year's rent, but the rent was not due at all when he received this money, and I have allowed an amendment in this respect.

Though the plaintiff was sorely injured in his business by the wrongful, and, as I think, reckless, conduct of the defendant in making and in the manner of carrying out the distress, I do not perceive a valid legal reason why the rent should not be paid; and the money received by the defendant on the sale of the goods being money that the plaintiff could not recover in addition to the double value that I think he is entitled to recover, and which he does recover, I am unable to see how this money can be deducted from the amount of the year's rent. I think the defendant should recover upon his amended counterclaim $125, the amount of the year's rent, without interest and without costs.

There will then be judgment for the plaintiff against the defendant for the sum of $492, with his costs of the action; and there will be judgment for the defendant for the sum of $125 upon his counterclaim, but without interest or any costs.

Shortly. Judgment for plaintiff for $492 with costs, and judgment for defendant for $125 without costs.

I do not make any set-off of these sums or any part of them, as the interests of solicitors might possibly be affected by such a course.

Order accordingly.

The defendant appealed from this judgment to the Divisional Court, and his appeal was argued before ARMOUR,

C. J., and FALCONBRIDGE and STREET, JJ., on the 30th
May, 1894.

N. McDonald, for the defendant. There is no right to
double damages except where the goods are actually sold ;
only a portion of the goods was sold, and a large part of
the remainder was covered by a chattel mortgage to a third
person. Double damages are allowed only to the owner
by the statute 2 W. & M., sess. 1; ch. 5, sec. 5. Upon the
evidence the trial Judge should have found that the rent
was due. There should be a new trial.

Tremeear, on the same side. The proper plaintiff as to
the goods covered by the chattel mortgage is the mortgagee,
who may still sue. The value of the goods is the measure
of damages : *Swire* v. *Leach,* 18 C. B. N. S. 479 ; Jones on
Chattel Mortgages, sec. 444. The plaintiff cannot recover
double value because he has not claimed it in his pleading :
Roscoe's N. P., 16th ed., p. 899 ; Sutherland on Damages,
2nd ed., vol. 1, sec. 464. The claim for double damages is
not favoured by the Courts : *Brown* v. *Blackwell,* 35 U. C.
R. at p. 246. The defendant is at any rate entitled to a
stay of proceedings until the proper parties are all before
the Court : *McKenzie* v. *McDonnel,* 15 Gr. 442. The
defendant can set up the *jus tertii* : *Leake* v. *Loveday,* 4
M. & G. at p. 983 ; *VanGelder* v. *Sowerby Bridge Society,*
44 Ch. D. 374 ; *Wilbraham* v. *Snow,* 2 Wms. Saund. 96, *n.*
The rent should be set off in any event.

R. H. McConnell, for the plaintiff. Nothing was due
upon the chattel mortgage until after the rent came due.
The judgment of the trial Judge should not be interfered
with upon the evidence. I rely on the cases cited in the
judgment.

McDonald, in reply.

June 21, 1894. The judgment of the Court was
delivered by

ARMOUR, C. J. :—

The learned Judge found that the rent distrained for
was not due on the 1st October, 1893, as the defendant

claimed it was, and was not due until the 4th December,
1893, and consequently that the distress complained of,
which was made on the 3rd October, 1893, was illegal.

The only direct evidence that the rent was due on the
1st October, 1893, was that of the defendant and his wife,
and their evidence was strongly corroborated by the fact
that in the previous years of his tenancy the plaintiff had
always paid his rent before the 4th December, and never
later than in November of each year.

The learned Judge, however, found that the defendant
and his wife were not worthy of belief, and it is impossible for us, who had not the opportunity of seeing them,
as the learned Judge had, to find that they were worthy
of belief, and to reverse his finding that the rent distrained
for was not due at the time of the distress.

There was no allegation in the statement of claim that
the action was brought upon the statute 2 W. & M.,
sess. 1, ch. 5, sec. 5 ; nor was there any allegation that the
goods distrained were "sold," but an allegation that the
defendant "sold and carried away the same and converted
and disposed thereof to his own use ;" nor was any claim
made in the statement of claim to recover double of the
value of the goods distrained and sold, within the terms of
that statute.

We think that the action set forth in the statement of
claim must be held to be the ordinary action for conversion, and that the value, and not the double value, of the
goods distrained should be recovered.

The learned Judge made a liberal assessment of the
damages at $246, and properly made it liberal according to
his finding that no rent was due at the time of the distress, and we see no reason to alter it.

A wrong-doer taking goods out of the possession of another is not at liberty to set up the *jus tertii*, but the
person out of whose possession the goods are taken may
shew the *jus tertii*, and in such case the wrong-doer may
take advantage of its being so shewn, and in this case the
plaintiff, having shewn a chattel mortgage subsisting upon

a portion of the goods distrained, cannot be allowed to
recover the value of the mortgaged goods from the defendant and to leave the defendant liable to another action at
the suit of the mortgagee for the value of the mortgaged
goods.

The judgment in favour of the plaintiff on his statement
of claim will be reduced to the sum of $246, with full
costs of suit, and the judgment will be for the defendant
on his counter-claim for $125 without costs; and the
amount of the judgment on the counter-claim will be set
off against the plaintiff's judgment on his claim; and no
judgment will be entered or execution issued unless and
until the plaintiff shall procure a release to the defendant
from the mortgagee of any action he may have against the
defendant for the conversion of the mortgaged goods.

The defendant will have the costs of the motion, which
will be set off against the plaintiff's judgment and costs.

E. B. B.

[QUEEN'S BENCH DIVISION.]

STEWART v. SCULTHORP.

Bailment—Delivery of Seed on Contract to Plant—Damages to Land from Impurity of Seed—Remoteness—Estoppel—Slander—Privilege—Actual Malice.

Where seed is delivered by one person to another without any warranty, honestly believing it to be clean, to be grown on the land of the latter, the produce thereof to be returned and paid for at a fixed price per bushel, the transaction is a bailment and not a sale ; and damages arising from other innocuous seed having been mixed therewith, and on harvesting having become scattered on the ground and coming up the following year on the land, are too remote, and not within the rule laid down in *Hadley* v. *Baxendale*, 9 Ex. 341, and *Cory* v. *Thames Ironworks Co.*, L. R. 3 Q. B. 181.

McMullen v. *Free*, 13 O. R. 57, and *Smith* v. *Green*, 1 C. P. D. 92, distinguished.

The plaintiff, having received seed from the defendant to be grown under the circumstances and conditions above mentioned, became aware while it was growing that vetches were coming up with it, but did not inform the defendant of the fact, and permitted them to grow, and delivered the produce mixed to the defendant, and was paid for it :—

Held, that he could not recover damages for an injury which his own conduct was responsible for.

McCollum v. *Davis*, 8 U. C. R. 150, specially referred to.

The plaintiff claimed damages for slander in respect of words spoken to him by the defendant, in the presence of others, to the effect that he had sold the seed given him. The jury found that the words were not spoken in good faith in the usual course of business affairs for the protection of his own interests :—

Held, that there was no evidence to sustain such a finding ; that the evidence shewed that the defendant honestly and justifiably believed that the plaintiff had defrauded him ; that the occasion was privileged and the plaintiff had failed to shew actual malice ; and therefore he could not recover.

Statement.   THE plaintiff alleged by his statement of claim (2) that he made a special business of growing seed peas on his farm ; (3) that in the Spring of 1892, in pursuance of an arrangement then made, the defendant delivered to him a bag of seed, which he represented was a special and valuable quality of sweet peas, and requested the plaintiff to plant the same on his farm, the arrangement being that the seed and the produce thereof were to remain the property of the defendant, and the plaintiff was to plant, cultivate, harvest, thresh, and deliver the produce to the defendant in Port Hope, by the end of the season, and the defendant was thereupon to pay to the plaintiff as and for

ground rent of the land and for his time and trouble, $2
per bushel of the produce delivered over and above
the quantity of seed furnished; (4) that the plaintiff
entered into the arrangement in good faith, relying upon
the representations of the defendant and on the full performance by him of his part, and accepted delivery of the
seed and planted it on his farm and attended to the culti-
vation, harvesting, and threshing of it; (5) that the seed
produced twenty-eight bushels of grain, which the plaintiff, in the Autumn of 1892, delivered to the defendant at
Port Hope, who paid him therefor at the rate agreed
upon; (6) that in September, 1893, the defendant falsely
and maliciously spoke and published of the plaintiff to one
David Crowley, in the hearing of others, the words
following: "He" (meaning the plaintiff) "sold the peas he
growed for me to another man, and brought me this stuff
and got his pay for the good seed, representing it was the
produce of the seed I delivered to him," meaning thereby
that the plaintiff had obtained money from the defendant
by false pretences; (7) or meaning that the plaintiff had
wrongfully taken and appropriated the goods and property
of the defendant and was guilty of larceny; (8) or that the
plaintiff had wrongfully and wilfully appropriated to his own
use the property and goods of the defendant and was guilty
of fraud in connection therewith; (9) or that the plaintiff was
a cheat and a fraud, and had in the course of his business
with the defendant cheated and defrauded him, and was
guilty of cheating and fraudulent practices in business;
(10) that on or about the 5th October, 1893, the defendant
in the presence and hearing of the plaintiff and James
Stewart and George Stewart, falsely and maliciously spoke
to and of the plaintiff the words following: "You sold the
peas you grew for me to another man, and I know him,
and you brought me this stuff, representing it to be the
produce of the seed I delivered to you, and demanded from
me and received pay for the good seed," meaning thereby,
etc. (repeating the three first innuendoes as above);
(13) that the seed delivered by the defendant to the plain-

tiff was not as represented by him, but was a certain kind
of vetch, or having in it a noxious weed; (14) that the
plaintiff by planting the seed on his farm had suffered
very serious loss and damage, because in the planting,
growing, and harvesting it it had become scattered upon the
farm, and the plaintiff had been unable to exterminate it,
and the plaintiff's business of growing and dealing in seed
and grain had thereby also been seriously injured; (15)
and the plaintiff claimed for the wrongs set out $2,000
damages.

The defendant by his statement of defence denied the
allegations made by the plaintiff, and alleged : (5) that the
plaintiff in the Autumn of 1892 delivered to the defendant twenty-six bushels and twenty-five pounds of seed,
alleging it to be the produce of the two bushels of variegated sweet peas supplied to the plaintiff under the agreement; (6) that the plaintiff did not deliver the pea seed
grown by him for the defendant under the contract, but
fraudulently delivered the seed of a certain coarse plant or
noxious weed known as vetches ; (7) that the defendant
sold and shipped the grain delivered to him as the product
of his seed, as variegated sweet peas, to customers and others,
and to farmers to grow seed for him in 1893, and, in consequence of the false representation made by the plaintiff,
the defendant had suffered great loss and damage, and his
business as a seedsman had been greatly injured ; (8) that
if the defendant spoke to Crowley the words alleged, which
he denied, he spoke them solely for the purpose of obtaining information through Crowley as his agent in reference
to the growing of the crop, the plaintiff having stated that
Crowley had threshed the crop, and spoke them *bond fide*
and without malice, and in the honest belief that they
were true, and the occasion was privileged; (9) that if the
defendant spoke to the plaintiff the words alleged, which
he denied, he spoke them at the invitation of the plaintiff
and to him alone and *bond fide*, without malice, and honestly
believing them to be true, and the occasion was privileged ;
(10) as to both of the alleged slanders that, if spoken at

all, they were, without the alleged meanings and according to their natural and ordinary signification, true in substance and in fact ; (11) and by way of counter-claim the
defendant claimed $2,000 damages for the wrongs set out
in the 5th, 6th, and 7th paragraphs, and for the injury
done to his business.

Issue.

The action was tried at the Spring Sittings, 1894, at
Peterborough, before ROSE, J., with a jury.

It appeared that the plaintiff was a farmer residing in
the township of Otonabee, and the defendant was a seed
merchant residing and carrying on business in the town of
Port Hope. That the defendant was in the habit of making
contracts with farmers for growing seed in the following
form :—

"PORT HOPE,   , 189 .

" It is agreed between Henry Sculthorp and
parties signing this agreement as follows : Said Sculthorp
agrees to furnish said   ,   bushels of peas to be
planted by him as hereinafter mentioned, for seed the
coming season, which seed and the crop growing therefrom
and the produce of such crop shall at all times be the property of the said Henry Sculthorp, and shall be delivered
to him at Port Hope on or about the middle of October,
189   , at such place in the said town as he may direct.
Said Sculthorp agrees for the use of the land on which
such seed may be planted, and the labour attending the
growing, cultivating, harvesting, and delivering the crop
from therefrom, to pay to the said   such sum as
shall equal the sum of   per bushel of such crop grown
therefrom and delivered as aforesaid, after being screened
as hereinafter mentioned. The quantity of seed so furnished to be returned free of charge to the said Sculthorp
at the above date. Said party above named agrees to
plant such seed in proper soil, properly cultivated, and
when growing to pull runners and all foreign varieties of
pea plants generally not belonging to variety sown. It is

also understood and agreed between said parties to this agreement, that in case the crop to be raised from the said seed shall be unmerchantable or unfit for garden seed peas by reason of the same being buggy or injured in the growing or harvesting of the same, the price to be paid by the said Sculthorp shall be regulated by and be the average market price per bushel of common peas for shipment and not the above specified sum. And it is also agreed that the said party above mentioned shall free such grain from thistle heads and pods before delivery, otherwise a charge equal to ten cents per bushel will be made for · cleaning them properly. Peas to be screened at the expense of the first party. Screenings to be paid for at the price of common peas.

"Lot   , con.   , Tp."

In the years 1890 and 1891 the defendant had made a contract in this form with the plaintiff, and in the year 1892 a contract was made for variegated sweet peas, but no contract was signed by the defendant as to it.

The plaintiff gave evidence to the effect that in the Spring of 1892 the defendant came to him and said he had some variegated sweet peas which he wished the plaintiff would take and grow; the plaintiff took them, sowed, cultivated, harvested them, and delivered to the plaintiff the product of the bag; the defendant said he would guarantee to give the plaintiff two dollars a bushel for growing them.

The plaintiff's counsel then said : " We agree upon the contract; it was that the peas should remain the property of Mr. Sculthorp, and Mr. Stewart was to get so much for growing them."

On cross-examination the plaintiff said that the bargain was made with the defendant's son when he came out to his (the plaintiff's) house; that in 1893 he had a written contract with the defendant; in 1892 he had not, but the verbal contract was the same in substance ; the defendant said they were all clean seed, but he specified that if weeds grew the plaintiff was to weed them out so as to keep the

seed clean, and that was so expressed in the written contract in the following year.

In answer to his own counsel, the plaintiff then said
that that applied to weeds that were to spring up; that he
(the plaintiff) was not to pull any of what the defendant
gave him.

Then to the defendant's counsel he said that that was in
the written contract, in these words: "The said party
above named agrees to plant said seed in proper soil, properly cultivated, and when growing to pull runners and
all foreign varieties of pea plants generally not belonging
to variety sown." The plaintiff then said that there was
no such contract as that in the verbal arrangement.

In March, 1892, the defendant received from Carter,
Dennet, & Beale, extensive dealers in seeds in London, England, four bushels of variegated sweet peas in two bags of
two bushels each, and it was admitted that these bags when
sent from England contained no vetches. They were sealed
when they arrived as when they were sent, and had no
appearance of having been tampered with.

After they arrived the defendant sent one bag to his farm,
where its contents were sowed and produced nothing but
variegated sweet peas; the other bag the defendant opened
and it remained in his warehouse for about a month, but
no one had access to the warehouse but the defendant and
his son: out of this bag he gave a handful to one Helm,
to one Andros, and to one Bennett, who each sowed them,
and they produced nothing but variegated sweet peas; the
defendant sent the residue, in the bag in which they came,
to the plaintiff, by railway, who received them and sowed
them; the defendant and a Mr. Gould, an expert in plants
and seeds, went to the plaintiff's farm in the month of
July, and saw the peas growing and then in flower, and
examined them carefully, and testified that there were no
vetches at all among them. On the other hand, W. B.
Stewart, a brother of the plaintiff, testified that he was
through the peas once when they were growing, and that
they were about half vetches; and one Johnston, who had

hoed the peas for the plaintiff, and had seen vetches in
Ireland, testified that they were about half vetches, and
that he told the plaintiff of it. The plaintiff admitted
that he was told this before the defendant and Gould came
out to look at the peas in July, and that, although he saw
them on that occasion and they had dinner with him, he
never mentioned to them that he had been told that there
were vetches in them, nor did he ever tell the defendant of
it. In the Autumn he delivered the produce of these peas,
as he testified, to the defendant in Port Hope, and was paid
for them. It was sworn by the defendant and not denied
by the plaintiff, that David Crowley had threshed the peas,
and this turned out to be untrue. The defendant did not
know vetch seed when he saw it, but he said that one bag
received from the plaintiff was better looking than the
other bag, and that he kept it separate, and it along with
a large portion of the other bags was sent to Carter, Dennet, & Beale, and this bag, according to their report, which
was admitted to be true, turned out to be sweet peas of a
uniform purple colour, and the other bags nearly all
vetches.

In 1893 the plaintiff entered into a contract in writing
with the defendant, in the form above set out, for the planting of twenty-seven bushels of Alaska peas, and he afterwards received the report of Carter, Dennet, & Beale of
the quality of the peas sent by him to them as the product
of the peas sowed by the plaintiff.

Some time afterwards the defendant went to see David
Crowley, who had a farm near the plaintiff's. With respect
to that interview David Crowley testified that the defendant said he was in quite a scrape about peas that John
Stewart grew for him, and that if witness could get any
track of them doing anything with them, to let him (defendant) know, and say nothing about it. The defendant
gave witness to understand that the plaintiff did not return the peas that he was growing for him; that was
about the height of what he said; he said that he thought
Stewart had changed the peas, and if witness could get

any track of his doing so, to let him (defendant) know ; he did not give him back the same seed that he had given him to grow; or at least witness took it that way.

In October, 1893, the plaintiff delivered the produce of the Alaska peas sowed by him that year under the last mentioned contract; and coming to the defendant's office for his pay, the defendant called him aside, and, according to the plaintiff's account, took some sweet peas out of a paper and asked plaintiff if he knew what they were; plaintiff said, no ; defendant said, " this is what grew from some of the damned trash that you grew me last year; you sold the peas, and I know where you sold the peas, and know who you sold them to, and know all about it." The plaintiff asked the defendant if he was not going to pay him for the peas, and the defendant said he would not pay him a damned cent.

George Stewart, who was a brother of the plaintiff, gave the following account : " He called John over and he took out a paper bag with some peas in, and he asked John if he knew these, and he said, no; and there was some blossoms, and he asked John if he knew them, and he said, no ; and, says Sculthorp, ' I know them and I know where you got them; I know the man you got them from, and I know who you got the stuff from that you brought me.' I don't know what you call it. He called it damned trash, or something like that, 'and,' he says, ' I can prove it.' "

James Stewart, who was a cousin of the plaintiff, testified that he heard Mr. Sculthorp say he knew the man Mr. Stewart sold the peas to, and knew all about them ; that was all he heard.

Evidence was given of vetches being on the plaintiff's farm in the summer of 1893, in the field in which the peas had been sown the previous year, and in some other parts.

The plaintiff had never complained to the defendant of the vetches being on his farm.

Statement. The trial Judge left the following questions to the jury, who answered them as follows :—

1. Was the seed delivered by Sculthorp to Stewart mixed with vetch seed at the time of delivery ? A. Yes.

2. If it was, then what damage has Stewart suffered by his land being planted with vetch seed ? A. $250.

3. If it was not, then what damage has Sculthorp suffered by reason of Stewart delivering to him seed mixed with vetch seed ? No answer.

4. Did Sculthorp charge Stewart with theft either in the warehouse or in his conversation with Crowley ? Distinguish the occasions in your answer. A. Yes, in the wareroom.

5. If he did not, then you need not consider the remaining questions.

6. If he did, was such charge true ? A. No.

7. Were the words spoken by Sculthorp to Stewart in the warehouse spoken in good faith, in the usual course of business affairs, for the protection of his own interests ? A. No.

8. If the charge made in the warehouse was untrue and made in bad faith, what damages do you allow for such words so spoken ? A. $150.

9. Were the statements made by Sculthorp to Crowley made in good faith, with an honest belief in their truth, for the purpose of procuring the assistance of Crowley to ascertain to whom Stewart had sold or disposed of the sweet pea seed ? No answer.

10. If the statements made to Crowley charged theft and were untrue and made in bad faith, what damages do you allow for so speaking them to Crowley ? No answer.

The Judge thereupon entered judgment for the plaintiff for $400 damages with full costs of suit.

At the Easter Sittings of the Divisional Court, 1894, the defendant moved to set aside the judgment and to enter judgment for him or for a new trial, on the grounds

that the verdict was against law and evidence and the
weight of evidence, and, as to the judgment on the plaintiff's claim for slander, that the occasion of speaking the
words complained of was privileged, and that the jury
should have been so directed.

At the same sittings the plaintiff made a cross-motion :—
1. That in case of a new trial of the action or of the slander counts being ordered, it might still be open to the
plaintiff to proceed for damages for the slander claimed as
having been published to Crowley, notwithstanding that
no answers were given by the jury to the 9th and 10th
questions submitted.

2. That in case the defendant should be successful in his
motion upon the slander counts, either by obtaining an
order for a new trial or by an order to enter judgment for
him, then that judgment might be ordered to be entered
for the plaintiff or for a new trial upon the claims for slander based upon the statements made by the defendant to
Crowley, and for an assessment of damages either by the
Court or by another jury.

Both motions were argued before ARMOUR, C. J., and
FALCONBRIDGE and STREET, JJ., on the 29th May, 1894.

Aylesworth, Q. C. (with him *Gunther*), for the defendant.
The plaintiff was to weed, and he did not do so ; he knew
of the vetches and said nothing to the defendant about
them ; he, therefore, cannot succeed in establishing the
defendant's liability for damage to the farm.   This is not
like *McMullen* v. *Free*, 13 O. R. 57, where there was an
express guaranty.   The words spoken to the plaintiff were
not actionable without proof of special damage.   The
charge was not of any criminal offence, but merely of conversion.   Then the occasion was one of qualified privilege,
and no malice was shewn : *Somerville* v. *Hawkins*, 10 C. B.
583 ; *Toogood* v. *Spyring*, 1 C. M. & R. 181 ; *Wells* v. *Lin-
dop*, 13 O. R. 434 ; *Gorst* v. *Barr, ib.* 644 ; *Ross* v. *Bucke*,
21 O. R. 692; *Hargreaves* v. *Sinclair*, 1 O. R. 260 ; *Blagden*
v. *Bennett*, 9 O. R. 593.   The privilege is not destroyed by

the presence of another person who overheard; the defendant spoke to the plaintiff as quietly as possible: *Jones* v. *Thomas*, 34 W. R. 104; *Tompson* v. *Dashwood*, 11 Q. B. D. 43. The cross-motion is in respect of the other slander, and the jury has found in the defendant's favour in regard to it.

W. R. Riddell (with him *E. B. Stone*), for the plaintiff. If an article is supplied for a definite purpose, it carries with it an implied warranty: *Randall* v. *Raper*, E. B. & E. 84; *Randall* v. *Newson*, 2 Q. B. D. 102; *Wagtsaff* v. *Clinton*, 1 Cab. & El. 45. The charge made by the defendant was theft: Criminal Code, sec. 305. The jury have found that the occasion was not privileged. Under the circumstances here there can be no privilege: *Fryer* v. *Kinnersley*, 15 C. B. N. S. 422; *Palmer* v. *Hummerston*, 1 Cab. & El. 36; *Senior* v. *Medland*, 4 Jur. N. S. 1039; *Royal Aquarium Society* v. *Parkinson*, [1892] 1 Q. B. 431; *Oddy* v. *Paulet*, 4 F. & F. 1009; Odgers, 2nd ed., p. 286. There was malice here; the defendant has justified.

Aylesworth, in reply. Pleading justification is no evidence of malice: *Corridan* v. *Wilkinson*, 20 A. R. 184.

June 21, 1894. The judgment of the Court was delivered by

ARMOUR, C. J. :—

The transaction between the plaintiff and the defendant may be thus fairly stated. The giving by the defendant to the plaintiff, to be by him planted and the produce thereof to be cultivated, harvested, threshed, and delivered to the defendant, of two bushels of variegated sweet peas for the reward to the plaintiff of $2 per bushel for the produce so to be delivered.

And the transaction so stated is the transaction as stated in the statement of claim, and is the transaction in respect of which, the peas not turning out to have been variegated sweet peas, but partly variegated sweet peas and partly vetches, the action is brought to recover damages for the Judgment. injury sustained by the plaintiff by reason of the peas Armour, C.J. turning out to be partly vetches.

In answer to the question on his cross-examination, "You were to cultivate the peas and keep down any weeds?" the plaintiff said, "Well, he said those were all clean seed;" and it was argued before us that this was a representation that the peas were free from any other seed, but this, the plaintiff stated, was said by the defendant; but it could not have been said by him with respect to these peas, for it was the defendant's son and not the defendant who arranged with the plaintiff to give him these peas to plant, and the statement of claim is not framed upon any such representation, nor did the plaintiff launch his case upon it, and we may, therefore, dismiss the further consideration of it.

There is no doubt that the defendant delivered the seeds to the plaintiff as and for variegated sweet peas, honestly believing them to be such, and the plaintiff received them as and for variegated sweet peas, and that neither the defendant nor the plaintiff knew that there were any vetch seeds among them, nor did either of them at that time know vetch seeds from variegated sweet peas.

If the transaction had been a sale of the peas, it would have been a condition of the transaction that the seeds delivered should have been variegated sweet peas, and if they were not, the plaintiff would have been at liberty to reject them.

In *Chanter* v. *Hopkins*, 4 M. & W. 399, Lord Abinger, C. B, said (p. 404): "A good deal of confusion has arisen in many of the cases on this subject, from the unfortunate use made of the word 'warranty.' Two things have been confounded together. A warranty is an express or implied statement of something which the party undertakes, shall be part of a contract; and though part of the contract, yet collateral to the express object of it. But in many of the cases, some of which have been referred to, the circumstance of a party selling a particular thing by its proper description, has been called a warranty; and the breach of such contract, a breach of warranty; but it would be better to distinguish such cases as a non-compliance with a contract which a party has engaged to fulfil; as, if a man offers to buy *peas* of another, and he sends him *beans*, he does not perform his contract; but that is not a warranty; there is no warranty that he should sell him peas; the contract is to sell peas, and if he sends him anything else in their stead, it is a non-performance of it. So if a man were to order copper for sheathing ships—that is a particular copper, prepared in a particular manner; if the seller sends him a different sort, in that case he does not comply with the contract: and though this may have been considered a warranty, and may have been ranged under the class of cases relating to warranties, yet it is not properly so."

If, however, instead of rejecting the peas sold, the plaintiff had accepted them, the condition would have become an implied warranty, for the breach of which the plaintiff would have been entitled to compensation: *Behn* v. *Burness*, 3 B. & S. 751.

. The transaction in question, was, however, not a sale, for the property did not pass, but was merely a bailment of the fifth sort enumerated by Holt, C. J., in the well known case of *Coggs* v. *Bernard*, 1 Sm. L. C., 9th ed., at pp. 207, 208.

Assuming that the principles above stated as applicable to a sale are equally applicable to a bailment such as this, about which there may be much to be said, what damages could the plaintiff recover for the breach of the implied warranty that the seeds delivered to him to plant were variegated sweet peas?

According to the rule laid down in *Hadley* v. *Baxendale*, 9 Ex. 341, and in *Cory* v. *Thames Ironworks Co.*, L. R. 3 Q. B. 181, " Where two parties have made a contract, which one of them has broken, the damages which the other party ought to receive in respect of such breach of contract should be such as may fairly and reasonably be considered either arising naturally, *i. e.*, according to the usual course of things, from such breach of contract itself, or such as may reasonably be supposed to have been in the contemplation of both parties at the time they made the contract, as the probable result of the breach of it."

If the planting, cultivating, harvesting, threshing, and delivering variegated sweet peas mixed with vetches, had cost more than the planting, cultivating, harvesting, and delivering variegated sweet peas alone, or if the produce of variegated sweet peas and vetches mixed had been less than the produce of variegated sweet peas alone, or if the plaintiff had informed the defendant that vetches were growing with the variegated sweet peas as the produce of the seeds delivered, and the defendant had caused them to be destroyed, the loss which the plaintiff would have sustained in such cases might have been recoverable by him as damages arising naturally from such breach of contract.

But the damages which the plaintiff seeks to recover by reason of some of the seeds of the vetches dropping upon the ground when harvested, in like manner as the seeds of the variegated sweet pea and of other plants do, and coming up in the following year on his farm, are not, in my opinion, within the rule, and are too remote.

In *McMullen* v. *Free*, 13 O. R. 57, there was an express warranty that the seed was clean; and in *Smith* v. *Green*, 1 C. P. D. 92, there was an express warranty that the cow was free from foot and mouth disease; these cases, therefore, cannot be said to govern the present case.

The vetch, the seeds of which were mixed with the seeds of the variegated sweet pea, and delivered to the plaintiff to plant, was not the wild vetch, nor was it a noxious seed, nor a weed, but a plant cultivated in husbandry, and if the plaintiff had strictly performed his contract and had delivered to the defendant the entire produce of the seed delivered to him, he could not have been damnified.

Even if, however, the damages sought to be recovered were within the rule, and were properly recoverable for the breach of the said implied warranty, the plaintiff has, in my opinion, disentitled himself to recover them.

For he admitted that he knew at and before the time when the defendant and Mr. Gould went to his farm to look at the peas, that there were vetches growing with the peas from the seed which the defendant had delivered to him to plant as variegated sweet peas, and he did not inform the defendant of it.

But, notwithstanding this knowledge on his part, he permitted and suffered the vetches to continue to grow with the peas, and harvested, threshed, and delivered them to the defendant and received his pay for them without ever mentioning the fact to the defendant.

Under these circumstances it would be unjust that he should be allowed to recover damages against the defendant for an injury which his own conduct was responsible for, and I do not think that the law would permit it: *McCollum* v. *Davis*, 8 U. C. R. 150.

As to the words spoken by the defendant to Crowley, the jury found that the defendant did not in them charge the plaintiff with a crime, and that put an end to any claim of the plaintiff against the defendant in respect of these words. As to the defamatory words spoken by the defendant to the plaintiff, I am of the opinion that the occasion was privileged, and that there was no evidence whatever of actual malice.

The occasion being privileged, it was for the plaintiff to shew actual malice, and in this he, in my opinion, failed.

It is true that the jury found that the words were not spoken in good faith, in the usual course of business affairs, for the protection of his own interests ; but there was, in my opinion, no evidence whatever to go to the jury in support of such a finding.

It is impossible for any one reading the evidence to come to any other conclusion than that the defendant honestly believed that the plaintiff had defrauded him, and that the circumstances known to the defendant at the time of the speaking the words justified such belief :

Clark v. *Molyneux*, **3** Q. B. D. 237; *Blagden* v. *Bennett*, Judgment.
9 O. R. 593.   Armour, C.J.

In my opinion, the action should be dismissed with costs,
and the counter-claim dismissed without costs.

                                                        E. B. B.

[QUEEN'S BENCH DIVISION.]

WESTBROOK ET UX. V. WHEELER ET UX.

WHEELER ET UX. V. WESTBROOK.

*Partnership—Assignment of Interest of Partner—Termination of Partner-
ship—Possession of Partnership Premises—Notice to Quit—Tavern
License—Transfer of—R. S. O. ch. 194. sec. 37.*

A partnership for a definite term, which has not expired, can be put an
end to by the voluntary assignment by one of the partners of his interest in the business, at his own instance or at the instance of his assignee, against the will of the other partner.
And where a partnership was so put an end to, the assignor being the
lessee of the premises on which the business was carried on, and assigning the term to the assignee, the latter was held entitled to recover
possession of the premises against the other partner without notice to
quit or demand of possession.
Where the holder of a tavern license enters into partnership with
another person, to whom he assigns an interest in his tavern business,
such assignment is not an assignment of his business within the meaning of section 37 of the Liquor License Act, R. S. O. ch. 194, and
does not require a transfer of the license.
Upon the construction of the partnership agreement in this case, the
new partner did not take an undivided one-half interest in the license.
Judgment of ROBERTSON, J., varied.

THE first action was brought by Frederick Westwood   Statement.
and Mattie F. Westbrook, his wife, against Edward
Wheeler and Josephine Wheeler, his wife, to recover possession of the premises known as the Brunswick Hotel, in
the city of Brantford, and for mesne profits from the 14th
March, 1894.

The second action was brought by Edward Wheeler and
wife against Frederick Westbrook for damages for expell-

71—VOL. XXV. O.R.

ing the plaintiffs from the bar-room and other portions of the hotel premises, and depriving them of the enjoyment thereof; for a declaration that the plaintiff Josephine Wheeler was entitled to an undivided half interest in a lease of the hotel premises made by one Andrew McMeans to one Dale, and in the license to sell intoxicating liquors therein, and in the chattels in the hotel; to compel the defendant to assign to the plaintiff Josephine Wheeler an undivided one-half interest in the license; for damages for conversion; and for other relief.

The actions were tried together before ROBERTSON, J., without a jury, at Brantford, in the Spring of 1894.

The facts in evidence, so far as material to the present report, were as follows:

Andrew McMeans, being the owner in fee of the premises in question, on the 3rd March, 1892, by an indenture made in pursuance of the Act respecting Short Forms of Leases, demised and leased the premises to William A. Dale for one year, to be computed from the 1st March, 1892; proviso, that the lessee should have the right to extend the term for a further period of two years by giving two months' previous notice in writing. The rent reserved was $1,100, to be paid monthly in advance. The indenture contained a covenant by the lessee not to assign or sublet without leave.

The lessee, Dale, took possession and obtained a tavern license for the year 1892-93, and on the 6th October, 1892, entered into an agreement in writing with Josephine Wheeler, by which he agreed that she should occupy the whole of the premises except the bar-room, a cellar, and a small room, for one year from the date of the agreement, and that she should have the use of all the goods and furniture on the premises, with certain specified exceptions, in return for which she was to perform certain services.

Dale continued in possession and paid the rent under the lease, and procured his license to be renewed for the year 1893-94.

On the 6th October, 1893, another agreement in writing

Statement.

(not under seal) was entered into between the same parties
by which it was agreed that, in consideration of the payment of $500, Dale sold and assigned to Josephine Wheeler
an undivided one-half interest in the hotel business, and
the same interest in all the goods and household furniture,
etc., in the hotel, the property of Dale. By this agreement,
Josephine Wheeler, in addition to paying $500, was to
assume and satisfy one-half of the amount due upon two
chattel mortgages made by Dale, and to pay one-half of
another debt. And the parties also agreed to form a
partnership in the hotel business and to carry it on until
the 1st March, 1895; the profits to be equally divided,
except as provided. There was a provision that either
party might buy out the other, upon giving one month's
notice, whereupon the partnership was to become dissolved.
The parties were to become jointly liable for the rent, taxes,
and other expenses of the business, on, from, and after the
morning of the 7th October, 1893, " at which time said
partnership shall begin."

There had been no renewal or extension of the term
under the lease, but the lessor received the rent, and in
that way it was continued.

On the 13th December, 1893, McMeans conveyed the
hotel premises to the plaintiff Mattie F. Westbrook, in fee,
subject to the term mentioned in the lease, in consideration of $15,000; and the rent for January and February,
1894, was paid to her.

On the 14th March, 1894, Dale, by indenture, conveyed
and set over to the plaintiff Frederick Westbrook the remainder of the term which would expire on the 1st
March, 1895, subject to the payment of the rent and the
performance of the lessee's covenants and agreements contained in the lease. And on the same day Dale also conveyed to Frederick Westbrook all the goods and chattels
on the premises belonging to him (Dale), and not covered
by the two chattel mortgages.

On the 17th March, 1894, Dale having then left the country, the mortgagees seized all the goods covered by their

respective mortgages, which were in default, and sold and conveyed the same to Frederick Westbrook, in consideration of $500.

On or about the 14th March, 1894, the license was also transferred by Dale to Frederick Westbrook, with the consent and approbation of the license inspector and commissioners, in due form, which transfer was written on the original license and hung up, as required by law, in the bar-room, where Wheeler was in charge.

On the 17th March, 1894, the bailiff of the chattel mortgagees being in possession, Frederick Westbrook went to the hotel to take possession, when he was resisted by the defendants Josephine and Edward Wheeler, who claimed possession.

J. W. Nesbitt, Q. C., and *W. D. Jones*, for the Westbrooks.

Brewster and *L. F. Heyd*, for the Wheelers.

[The judgment of the trial Judge set out the facts and dealt fully with the numerous questions involved. As only two of the questions are of importance, except to the parties, large portions of the judgment are omitted.]

April 24, 1894. ROBERTSON, J.:—

I find as a fact that the agreements of the 6th October, 1892, and 6th October, 1893, were all along kept latent, and were secret arrangements entered into by the parties, one object being to defraud the revenue, and that no other person, except the solicitor who drew the agreements, had notice thereof * *. The evidence is conclusive that both Dale and Wheeler denied point blank to the inspector of licenses, who had the right to know, and who made, in discharge of his duty, particular inquiry in January last, that there was any change in the business from the time that the license was issued to Dale for 1893-94. This denial had the effect of defrauding the revenue of $25, transfer fee payable on the license. * *

In my judgment, Mrs. Wheeler could not set up title to Judgment.
the possession of the premises against the owner in fee, or Robertson, J.
the assignee of the term. The owner would have the
right to take possession, whenever the tenant, Dale, abscon-
·ded, and he having assigned the residue of the term to
Westbrook, it was open to the owner to adopt him, Westbrook, as his tenant, and neither Wheeler nor Mrs.Wheeler
·could properly object.   *   *

[Judgment for the plaintiffs in the first action for the
·recovery of the premises with costs. Judgment dismissing
the second action with costs.]

The Wheelers appealed to the Divisional Court from the
judgments in both actions, and their appeal was argued
before ARMOUR, C. J., and FALCONBRIDGE and STREET, JJ.,
·on the 1st June, 1894.

Brewster and *L. F. Heyd,* for the appellants.

Wallace Nesbitt, for the respondents, the Westbrooks.

June 21, 1894. The judgment of the Court was de-
·livered by

ARMOUR, C. J.—(who, after dealing with some of the
·questions in the action not necessary to be referred to in
·this report, proceeded) :—

The partnership created by the agreement of 6th October, 1893, between Dale and the female defendant (Josephine Wheeler) was, in my opinion, put an end to by the
·assignment by Dale to the male plaintiff (Frederick Westbrook), of the said lease, of the license for the hotel, and
of the goods in the hotel not covered by the chattel mortgages, and by the seizure of the goods in the chattel
mortgages by the mortgagees, and the sale of them by the
·mortgagees to the male plaintiff.

There is no authority to be found in England for holding
that a partnership for a definite term, which has not ex-
·pired, can be put an end to by the voluntary assignment

by one of the partners of his interest in the business, and at
his instance or at the instance of his assignee, against the
will of the other partner : Lindley on Partnership, 6th ed.,
p. 575.

But authority for so holding is not wanting in the United
States : Story on Partnership, 7th ed., sec. 308 ; *Marquand*
v. *New York Manufacturing Co.*, 17 Johns. 525.

The partnership having been put an end to, the male
plaintiff was entitled to recover possession of the land in
question without notice to quit or demand of possession :
Doe Colnaghi v. *Bluck,* 8 C. & P. 464 ; *Benham* v. *Gray.*
5 C. B. 138.

Judgment must, therefore, be for the male plaintiff to
recover possession of the land in question with costs. • •

I do not think that the partnership created by the agreement of the 6th October, 1893, operated as an assignment
of his business by Dale within the meaning of R. S. O. ch.
194 (the Liquor License Act), sec. 37, for it was only an
assignment of an one-half interest in his business, and did
not call for any notification thereof to the license inspector,
nor require a transfer of the license, nor the consent of the
license commissioners, nor the payment of any fee, and
there was, therefore, no defrauding of the revenue by notice
thereof not having been given to the license inspector.

And the agreement of the 6th October, 1893, did not, in
my opinion, give, as claimed, to the female plaintiff
(Josephine Wheeler) an undivided half interest in the
license : *Regina ex rel. Brine* v. *Booth,* 3 O. R. 144.

I think, therefore, that the action (the second), except the
claim for conversion, must be dismissed with costs. • •

E. B. B.

[COMMON PLEAS DIVISION.]

HEROD v. FERGUSON.

Contract—Remuneration for Services—Collateral Contract—Judgment on— Novation.

Where services have been performed by one person for the benefit and at the request of another, and which have been charged to the latter, the fact that a third person has subsequently agreed to pay for such services, and has had judgment recovered against him, therefor, by the person rendering them, will not prevent the latter recovering in an action against the person liable in the first instance, unless the subsequent agreement amounts to a novation.

THIS was an appeal by the defendant from the finding Statement. of the referee to whom the plaintiff's claim against the defendant had been referred at the hearing by consent under the 102nd section of the Judicature Act, and who had found for $250 in favour of the plaintiff.

The action was upon an account for surgical and medical services rendered by the plaintiff to the defendant. The defence was that although these services had been rendered to the defendant he had not, but his son J. D. Ferguson had, promised to pay for them, and that the plaintiff had recovered judgment against the son for the amount. It was shewn that the plaintiff had throughout charged the defendant in his books; that after all the services had been rendered and charged to the defendant, the son had asked the plaintiff to send the account to him; that the plaintiff had done so, making out the account in the son's name; and that the son had promised to pay. The plaintiff recovered judgment by default against the son for the amount, but, finding him to be worthless, had not issued execution against him, and had then brought the present action.

The appeal was argued before STREET, J., in Court on the 12th September, 1894.

F. Fitzgerald, for the defendant, referred to Pollock on Contracts, 5th Eng. ed., pp. 11, 448; *Boston Ice Co.* v. *Potter*, 123 Mass. 28.

Moss, Q. C., and *Guthrie,* Q. C., for the plaintiff, referred
to R. S. O. ch. 148, sec. 39 ; *Wegg Prosser v. Evans.* [1894]
2 Q. B. 101 ; *Garrey* v. *Stadler,* 30 N. W. Repr. 787 ; 1
Parsons on Contracts, 8th ed., p. 11 ; *Ex p. Ford,* 16 Q. B.
D. 305 ; *Robinson v. Read,* 9 B. & C. 449 ; *Nichols v.
King.* 5 U. C. R. 324.

September 22, 1894.   STREET, J. :—

Upon the evidence I find, as the learned referee has found,
that the contract of the plaintiff was made with the defendant, and not with J. D. Ferguson, the son of the defendant.
The services rendered were such as the defendant must
have known the plaintiff would charge for ; the plaintiff
did charge the defendant, and the defendant only, for these
services in his books, and he had no notice of any understanding between the defendant and his son, if any such
existed, that the son and not the defendant was to be his
debtor.   Then after all the services had been performed
the son asked the plaintiff to send him his bill, and the
plaintiff did so, making out the bill in the son's name ; the
son promised to pay the amount, but did not do so, and the
plaintiff sued him and obtained judgment by default for
the amount.   This judgment has never been satisfied, and
it appears that the judgment debtor is and has long been
in insolvent circumstances.   Then the plaintiff brought
the present action against his original debtor, the father,
to whom the plaintiff's services were actually rendered.
The defendant sets up the judgment against the son as a
bar to the action.

I do not see any ground for the contention of the defendant that the plaintiff had an election to sue either the son
as agent, or the father as principal, and that, having elected
to sue the agent, he cannot afterwards turn round and sue
the principal.   Treating the contract here as one made by
the son as agent for the father, the plaintiff knew the
principal throughout and charged him and gave credit to
him and to him only.   The agent did not contract in his

own name, as I should find upon the evidence, but for a known principal, viz., his father, to whom credit was given, and was, therefore, not liable to the plaintiff at all. The plaintiff, having charged the father, could not say that he gave credit to the son. The doctrine sought to be invoked by the defendant does not apply to such a case but to the case of an agent contracting for an undisclosed principal : *Priestly* v. *Fernie*, 3 H. & C. 977 ; *Kendall* v. *Hamilton*, 4 App. Cas. 504.

The son became liable to the plaintiff, if at all, upon a subsequent promise made by him, which was not a satisfaction of the original cause of action, but was collateral to it. There is no evidence of any novation by which the plaintiff agreed to accept the son as his debtor, and to release the father, who was the original debtor.

Under these circumstances, the recovery by the plaintiff of the judgment upon the collateral contract of the son does not affect the liability of the father upon the original contract : *Drake* v. *Mitchell*, 3 East 251 ; *Wegg Prosser* v. *Evans*, [1894] 2 Q. B. 101.

To put the matter shortly, the only question in the case is whether the contract was made with the father or with the son. The referee has found, and I agree with him, that it was with the father. The plaintiff then had a cause of action against the father, which still exists, because there has been no novation of it, no payment or release of it, and no judgment has been recovered upon it.

The appeal of the defendant must, therefore, be dismissed with costs.

E. B. B.

Judgment.

Street, J.

[QUEEN'S BENCH DIVISION.]

RE O'CONNOR AND FIELDER.

Arbitration—Award by Two out of Three Arbitrators.

Where a submission to arbitration provides that the award thereunder shall be made by three arbitrators, the award to be valid must be made by the three unanimously.

Statement. SUMMARY application by Patrick O'Connor to set aside an award made by two of the three arbitrators appointed under a reference to fix the renewal rent to be paid under a lease dated 28th August, 1884, of certain hotel premises in the city of Toronto. The applicant was the landlord, and Robert J. Fielder, the other party to the arbitration, was the tenant. The third arbitrator dissented from the award of the two.

The submission was in the lease, and did not contain a clause to the effect that the award of a majority of the arbitrators should be binding upon the parties.

The motion was argued before BOYD, C., in Court, on the 11th October, 1894.

N. F. Davidson, for O'Connor. The award is invalid and should be set aside; it is not the award of the three arbitrators, but only of the two who sign: Russell on Awards, 7th ed., p. 216.

Haverson, for Fielder. The meaning of the submission is that in case of disagreement, the opinion of two of the three should prevail: *Little* v. *Newton,* 2 M. & G. 351; *Grindley* v. *Barker,* 1 B. & P. 229.

October 13, 1894. BOYD, C. :—

It is a general rule applicable to all cases of private authority, trust or reference, to be exercised by several persons, that unless the constituent instrument permits action or decision by a majority, then the office is regarded as joint and all must act collectively. Thus as to trusts it is said by Lewin : " When the administration of the trust is vested in co-trustees, they all form as it were but one collective trustee, and therefore must execute the duties of the office in their joint capacity :" Lewin on Trusts, 8th ed., p. 258. The same is said as to arbitrators by Russell: " On a reference to several arbitrators together, when there is no clause providing for an award made by less than all being valid, each of them must act personally in performance of the duties of his office, as if he were sole arbitrator ; for, as the office is joint, if one refuse or omit to act, the others can make no valid award :" Russell on Awards, 7th ed., p. 216.   So in case of the execution of powers or the like : see *Sykes* v. *Sheard*, 9 Jur. N. S. 886, affirmed 3 N. R. 144.

Different considerations arise when the duties are of a public nature, but in transactions between individuals they make their own bargain, and so become a law unto themselves.

Here the contract set forth in the lease provides that the award shall be made by three arbitrators ; an award by two of them—the other dissenting—does not satisfy the terms of the reference, and the application to set aside cannot be answered.

I vacate the award, therefore, but without costs.

E. B. B.

[CHANCERY DIVISION.]

DODDS ET AL. v. THE ANCIENT ORDER OF UNITED WORKMEN ET AL.

Insurance—Life Insurance—Infants—Payment to Executors—Security—Discharge—R. S. O. ch. 136, secs. 11, 12.

Moneys payable to infants under a policy of life insurance may, where no trustee or guardian is appointed under secs. 11 and 12 of R. S. O. ch. 136, be paid to the executors of the will of the insured, as provided by sec. 12, without security being given by them, and payment to them is a good discharge to the insurers.

Statement.   SPECIAL case stated for the opinion of the Court in an action brought by the executors of the will of Henry Carson, deceased, against the above-named Order and the four infant children of the testator.

The case stated that the testator died on the 6th March, 1894, leaving him surviving the infant defendants ; that the deceased was at the time of his death a workman degree member in good standing of the Order, a paternal and benevolent society incorporated on the 11th August, 1879, under R. S. O. 1877 ch. 167, and was the holder of a beneficiary certificate issued by the Grand Lodge of Ontario of the Order, dated 10th February, 1892, wherein the sum of $2,000 was declared to be payable at his death out of the beneficiary fund of the Order to his four youngest children, the infant defendants ; that the certificate was issued in pursuance of section 1 of article 7 of the constitution of the Order, providing that " upon the death of a workman degree member in good standing, such person or persons as the said member may have named while living shall be entitled to receive of the beneficiary fund the sum of $2,000 ;" that on the 3rd July, 1894, the testator made his will, whereby he appointed the plaintiffs executors; that the executors had proved the will and taken upon themselves the burden of the trusts contained in it; that by the third paragraph of his will the testator bequeathed to the four infant defendants the sum of $500 each, to be paid out of the policy or certificate of the Order, and to be paid over to each child when he or she should reach the age of twenty years, and each of them to receive all interest and benefits accruing from the said sums after they should have reached the age of fourteen ; that by his will the testator also directed that his executors should have power after each child should have arrived at the age of fourteen years to grant to any child any sum or sums that they should think necessary and for the interest of the children in educating them ; that the plaintiffs, the executors, contended that they were entitled to receive from the Order the sum of $2,000 for the purposes of the trusts of the will, while the infant defendants contended that the executors were not the proper persons to receive it ; and that the defendant society were ready and willing to pay over that sum to such persons as the Court should direct.

The questions submitted are set out in the judgment, *infra.*

The Act to secure to wives and children the benefit of life insurance, R. S. O. ch. 136, contains the following provisions :—

Section 11.—The insured may, by the policy or by his will or by any writing under his hand, appoint a trustee or trustees of the money payable under the policy. * * Payment made to such trustee or trustees shall discharge the company.

Section 12.—If no trustee is named in the policy, or appointed as mentioned in section 11, to receive the shares to which infants are entitled, their shares may be paid to the executors of the last will and testament of the insured, or to a guardian of the infants duly appointed by one of the Surrogate Courts of this Province or by the High Court, or to a trustee appointed by the last named Court, upon the application of the wife, or of the infants or their guardian ; and such payment shall be a good discharge to the insurance company.

Section 14.—A guardian appointed under section 12 shall give security to the satisfaction of the Court or Judge for the faithful performance of his duty as guardian, and for the proper application of the money which he may receive.

The case was argued before BOYD, C., in Court, on the 11th October, 1894.

Totten, Q. C., for the plaintiffs and the defendant society. The society are merely stakeholders and wish to pay over the money and obtain a proper discharge. This society has for years paid moneys to executors under like circumstances. The money should in this case be paid to the plaintiffs, no other trustee being appointed. The statute does not require security from executors. I refer to *Re Cameron*, 21 O. R. 634.

A. J. Boyd, for the official guardian, representing the infant defendants. The executors do not receive these moneys in their capacity as executors, but as persons named in the statute. They should give security, or the money should be paid into Court for the infants. See section 14 of the Act and *Campbell* v. *Dunn*, 22 O. R. 98.

October 13, 1894. BOYD, C. :—

Special case as to payment of insurance moneys by the defendants under R. S. O. ch. 136, sec. 12. No trustee is named by the testator who effected the insurance for the benefit of his children (infants), and his will recognizes that the executors are to handle the money. Even without that the statute is framed to permit of the payment of such money to the executors—there being no trustee or guardian—and declares that such a payment is a good discharge to the company. The executors are those appointed by the testator, and according to the practice are not called on to give security—nor are they required to give special security in order to become the proper recipients of these insurance moneys. The matter thus rests, not on the course of the Court, which calls for security to be given by the custodians of infants' money, but upon the express

enactment of the legislature, which, being plain and une- Judgment.
quivocable, has simply to be followed.   Boyd, C.

The questions submitted are answered thus:

1. Can payment be made lawfully to the executors named in the last will of the testator? Under the statute, yes.

2. Can the executors give a lawful discharge to the society defendants? Under the statute, yes.

3. Are the executors in all cases bound to give proper security before receiving the funds; if so, whose duty is it to determine the sufficiency thereof? I do not speak as to "all cases," but in this case no security is needed.

4. Whether or not the money should be paid into Court? It is optional with the society to pay into Court or to pay the executors.

E. B. B.

Re Reid v. Graham Brothers.

Prohibition—Division Court—Judgment Summons—Examination—Refusal of Evidence—Partnership—Judgment Against Firm—Parties—Members of Firm—Commitment.

The refusal of evidence is not ground for prohibition.

An order having been made in a Division Court upon judgment summons committing a defendant under sec. 240, sub-sec. 4 (c), of R. S. O. ch. 51, for having made away with his property, it is not a ground for prohibition that the Judge has refused to allow the defendant under examination to make explanations as to his dealing with money lent by and repaid to him after judgment.

The members of a firm sued in the firm name are parties to the litigation; and when judgment is obtained in a Division Court against a firm as such, though execution can go only against the goods of the firm and against the individual goods of one who is sued as and found to be a partner, yet a judgment summons may be issued against another member of the firm not served with first process, if only to get discovery of goods of the firm available for execution, and if he makes wilful default in attendance, he is liable to be committed as for contempt of Court.

MOTION by the defendants for prohibition to the third Statement. Division Court in the county of Perth. The facts are stated in the judgment.

The motion was argued before BOYD, C., in Chambers, on the 12th October, 1894.

R. S. Neville, for the defendants.

D. Armour, for the plaintiff.

Ex p. Dakins, 16 C. B. 77 ; *Re Young* v. *Parker*, 12 P. R. 646 ; *Ex p. Young*, 19 Ch. D. 124 ; and Bicknell and Seager's Division Courts Act, p. 145, were referred to.

October 13, 1894. BOYD, C. :—

On judgment summons in the Division Court the Judge has ordered the defendant John Graham to be committed for ten days under section 240, sub-section 4 (c), for having made away with his property.   It is now objected that the further action of the Court should be prohibited on that order, because the Judge refused to allow the defendant under examination to make explanations as to his dealing with a sum of money lent by and repaid to him after judgment.   The evidence on affidavit is contradictory, and the Judge has not certified, but this is not to my mind a case for prohibition.   The Judge had jurisdiction in the premises, and the manner of his exercising that (in whatever way it may be subject to review) is not to be dealt with by way of prohibition.   It is for the Judge to gauge the value of the answers and to draw his conclusions as to whether the witness is veracious or prevaricating.   This discretion is not to be cut short by the absolute method of prohibition, especially when the examination is not brought before me. The refusal of evidence is not a ground for prohibition : *Re Dunford*, 12 Jur. 361, where Parke, B., says : " The use of the writ is to prevent inferior tribunals acting without authority, and not to remedy improper decisions to which they may come."

The Judge also directed the committal of another defendant, Robert S. Graham, because he made default in appearing upon the return of a judgment summons.   It was made to appear that he was personally served with the summons, that he was at home, in good health, and in his brother's opinion there was nothing to prevent him from appearing.

The point raised is want of jurisdiction, because the
judgment summons is in the nature of an execution, and
that no execution can issue against the individual member
of a firm, sued as a firm, who has not been personally
served with first process. The firm of Graham Brothers
here is sued, and this defendant was not served. He is
identified in the plaintiff's affidavit as being, in fact, one
of the defendants (*i. e.*, as a member of the firm), and this is
not denied. Now, in my opinion, when judgment is obtained
against a firm as such, though execution can go only against
the goods of the partners and against the individual goods
of one who is sued as and proved to be a partner—yet as
to another member of the firm, a judgment summons may
be issued. One purpose of this summons is to get discovery
of goods available for execution, *i. e.*, in the case supposed,
partnership goods of which the partner not individually
sued may have valuable knowledge to which the plaintiff
is entitled. If he makes default in attendance (that is,
wilful default) he is liable to be committed as for contempt
of Court. A sufficient affidavit was made under section 235
to justify the issue of the summons. The summons was
directed to R. S. Graham, and notified him that if he did
not appear in obedience to it, he was liable to be committed to the common gaol of the county. Sections 240
and 241 direct the procedure which was observed in the
case, and they also protect a defendant who attends, if he
can shew the Judge that he ought not to have been sum-
moned. In this case the defendant could have objected to
make answer as to any personal property of his own,
though he might be interrogated and would have to have
disclosed as to partnership goods and property.

The only question that suggests itself as raising a doubt
about this course is whether the members of a firm sued in
the firm name can be regarded as parties to the litigation.
This, I think, must be so, for the firm itself has not
individual or corporate existence; though it has a jural
entity for the purposes of litigation, yet the constituents
of the firm are the parties defendant in the eye of the law;

Judgment. though the individual goods may not be liable in execu-
Boyd, C. tion unless the particular partner is sued as and adjudged
to be a member of the firm.

The opinion is expressed by a much experienced County
Court Judge that upon a judgment against a firm any
member of the firm is subject to a judgment summons:
Sinclair's Division Courts Act, 1888, p. 148, note, and this
opinion is, in my judgment, well founded on common sense
and common law.

The clauses in the Division Courts Act as to execution
against partners are in *pari materiâ* with the like provisions in the Con. Rules of the High Court 317 and 876.
The practice in both Courts is linked by section 304 of the
Division Courts Act, R. S. O. ch. 51; and it is to be noted
that in the meaning attributed to "party" in the Judicature Act, it includes every person served with notice of or
attending any proceeding, although not named on the
record: Rule 2 (8).

Both applications for prohibition should be refused and
with costs.

E. B. B.

[QUEEN'S BENCH DIVISION.]

REGINA v. MINES.

Criminal Law—Summary Conviction—" Procuring " a Weapon with Intent —Criminal Code, sec. 108—Amended Conviction—Information for Shooting with Intent—Justices of the Peace—Substituting New Charge Imprisonment—Habeas Corpus—Discharge.

The defendant was brought before justices of the peace on an information charging him with the indictable offence of shooting with intent to murder, and they, not finding sufficient evidence to warrant them in committing for trial, of their own motion, at the close of the case, summarily convicted the defendant for that he did "procure a revolver with intent therewith unlawfully to do injury to one J. S." It appeared by the evidence that the weapon was bought and carried and used by the defendant personally.

By the Criminal Code, sec. 108, it is matter of summary conviction if one has on his person a pistol with intent therewith unlawfully to do any injury to any other person.

The return to a writ of *habeas corpus* shewed the detention of the defendant under a warrant of commitment based upon the above conviction ; and upon a motion for his discharge :—

Held, that the detention was for an offence unknown to the law ; and, although the evidence and the finding shewed an offence against sec. 108, the motion should not be enlarged to allow the magistrates to substitute a proper conviction, for it was unwarrantable to convict on a charge not formulated, as to which the evidence was not addressed, upon which the defendant was not called to make his defence, and as to which no complaint was laid ; and the prisoner should, therefore, be discharged.

MOTION, on the return of a writ of *habeas corpus*, for an   Statement. order discharging the defendant from custody, under the circumstances set forth in the judgment.

On the 8th October, 1894, the motion was made before BOYD, C., in Chambers.

A. H. Marsh, Q. C., for the defendant. The conviction returned shews no offence known to the law, and the defendant should be discharged forthwith.

No one appeared for the Crown.

October 15, 1894. BOYD, C. :—

The return to the *habeas corpus* shews detention on a warrant of commitment on a charge that the prisoner did "procure a revolver with intent therewith unlawfully

Judgment.

Boyd, C.

to do injury to one J. S." It purports to be based on a conviction under the Code, sec. 108, which makes it matter of summary conviction if one has on his person a pistol with intent therewith unlawfully to do injury to any other person. But the term used in the commitment, "procure," does not mean, or may not mean, *personal* use and handling of the weapon; had it said that "he did procure and have in his hand (or upon his person)," then the offence would be well defined. Now a copy of the evidence is before me, and it appears that the weapon was bought and carried and used by the defendant personally, and the magistrates have found the unlawful intent connected therewith. Should I on this information discharge the prisoner? The better course, seeing that the evidence would justify an amended form of conviction, would be to enlarge the matter to give an opportunity to the magistrates, if so advised, to substitute a more accurate conviction according to the facts as proved before them and found by them. This would be permissible according to *Regina* v. *Lavin*, 12 P. R. 642, inasmuch as there has been no formal return upon a *certiorari* and the form of conviction now before me is not a finality.

But I am induced not to take this course for this reason: it appears that the magistrates' jurisdiction was founded upon an information charging the defendant with shooting with intent to murder—that is an indictable offence, and they were charged with the duty of investigating that, and committing for trial if they found it proved *prima facie*; but, not finding sufficient evidence to warrant this course, they adopted the expedient of seeking to punish the defendant in a short way, under sec. 108 of the Code, for an offence punishable on summary conviction. The jurisdiction invoked was to commit for trial; they, of their own motion, changed this at the close of the case into jurisdiction to convict. That is an unwarrantable course: to convict on a charge not formulated, as to which the evidence was not addressed, upon which the defendant was not called to make his defence, and as to which no complaint was laid before them.

Therefore, I think it is my duty to act merely on the Judgment.
invalid return to the *habeas corpus*, which shews detention Boyd, C.
for an offence unknown to the law : *Re Timson*, L. R. 5
Ex. 257 ; and so order the prisoner's discharge.

E. B. B.

[COMMON PLEAS DIVISION.]

IN THE MATTER OF ETHEL DAVIS AN INFANT.

*Infant—Custody of—British Subjects Married in this Province—Removal
to the United States—Husband Naturalized—Divorce Obtained by Wife.*

The parents of a child seven years old, British subjects and married in
this Province, where the child was born, removed to the United States,
where the husband took out naturalization papers. In consequence of
the husband's alleged intemperance and adultery the wife left him, and
on the ground of such adultery, she applied to the Court there and
obtained a decree granting her a divorce, and the custody of the child.
Shortly before the decree was pronounced, and with the object of escaping its effect, the husband returned to this Province, bringing the child
with him.

On an application by the wife for the custody of the child an order was
made granting her such custody.

A writ of *habeas corpus* was issued upon the application Statement.
of Maria Davis, the mother of the infant, commanding
John W. Davis, the father of the infant, to produce her
before the Court. Upon a return to the writ and upon
the production of the infant in Court on the 5th May,
1894, the question as to the right to her custody was
argued upon the affidavits and evidence then read and
heard, the effect of which is set out in the judgment.

May 5th, 1894.   *L. M. McCarthy*, for the applicant.
W. H. Blake, for the father.

May 13th, 1894.   STREET, J. :—

The parents of the child were married at Dunnville, Ont.,
on the 4th June, 1883, and the child in question, the only
surviving child of the marriage, was born on the 13th

January, 1886. In April, 1890, they moved to Buffalo,. N. Y., where the husband went into business; and on the 12th August, 1891, he filed in the office of the county clerk at Buffalo, a sworn declaration as follows:—

"The declaration of John W. Davis, of Erie County, late of Canada. I, John W. Davis, do solemnly swear that it is *bond fide* my intention to become a citizen of the United States of America, and renounce for ever all allegiance to any foreign Prince, Potentate, State. or Sovereignty whatsoever, particularly the Queen of Great Britain and Ireland to whom I now owe allegiance.

"(Signed)   JOHN W. DAVIS.

"Sworn before me August 12, 1891.

" C. A. ORR, *Clerk.*"

In February, 1892, his wife left him taking with her the child in question, and another younger child, since deceased. She gives as her reason for leaving him his habits of drunkenness, his neglect to provide for her and his children, by reason of which she alleges that she was obliged to support him as well as her children and herself: and his accusations against her of adultery with a boarder. She lived apart from him and supported the children until July, 1893, when he took away the children during her absence and placed them, without her knowledge, in the German Roman Catholic Orphanage in Buffalo, where the youngest child died shortly afterwards.

In September, 1893, the wife instituted proceedings against her husband in the Superior Court at Buffalo for a divorce from him upon the ground of his adultery: he was served with notice of the proceedings and appeared by his attorneys but offered no evidence in his defence. Evidence was given on the part of the wife, and the Court found all the material facts charged in the complaint to be true and granted the divorce, awarding also to the wife the custody of Ethel Davis the infant here in question: the Court further ordered that the wife should be at liberty to marry again, but that the husband should not be at liberty to marry during the lifetime of the wife.

This judgment was pronounced on the 15th December,
1893.

Shortly before it was pronounced the husband left
Buffalo, taking the infant with him and went to Smith-
ville, in the county of Lincoln in this Province, where he
now resides with his mother.

In his answer to the application, the husband denies
having been guilty of adultery, and while admitting having
been occasionally guilty of excess in the use of intoxicating
liquors, denies having indulged in them to the extent
charged, or to an extent justifying his wife in leaving him,
and asserts that although he still continues to use them in
moderation, he never now uses them to excess. He appears
to have led a proper life since his return to Canada ; he
and his child live with his mother, who is a most respect-
able woman of seventy-five years of age : and he has a
married sister living in the neighbourhood who assists in
the care of the child. He repeats in his affidavits his
charges of adultery against his wife and asserts his belief
from having seen her last June that she was at that time
in the family way by reason of some adulterous intercourse.

The applicant is a professional nurse, and lives in Buffalo
with a sister there who is married ; she earns seven dollars
a week with a prospect of increasing her earnings to ten
dollars a week.

The conclusion I must draw from the evidence, I think,
is that the husband was in the habit of drinking to excess,
and that he repeatedly accused his wife of infidelity, and
by his conduct in these respects justified her in leaving
him : that he has entirely failed to support his accusations
against her of improper or immoral conduct either during
their cohabitation or since their separation, but that since
the separation he has himself committed adultery with
the woman named in the affidavits.

Then upon the question of the divorce proceedings, I can
come to no other conclusion than that he went to Buffalo
with the intention of permanently residing there. He
went into business there and filed a formal sworn

declaration of his intention to renounce his allegiance to
the Queen and to become a citizen of the United States.
It is true, that he now swears quite as strenuously, that
he never had any such intention, and that he only made
the declaration because he could not get a government
contract except by doing so. I think the facts lead to the
conclusion, that at the time he made the declaration his
intention was as set forth in it; his evidence upon the
other matters involved in the present application is
certainly not assisted by his explanation of his motives for
making this declaration.

He was, therefore, domiciled in Buffalo, when the proceedings for divorce were instituted, and he continued his
actual residence there until a very short time before the
decree was made. The Court there, finding the adultery
proved, gave to Mrs. Davis the custody of the child. It
undoubtedly had jurisdiction over all the parties at the
time the proceedings were instituted, and I can find no
authority for the position that their jurisdiction was taken
away by the departure of the defendant from the country
with the apparent object of escaping the consequences of
the impending judgment.

The foreign guardian has no absolute rights as such
under this judgment in this country, but the fact of her
appointment by the Court in Buffalo is entitled to great
weight in determining the proper custody here: *Johnstone
v. Beattie*, 10 Cl. & F. 42; *Hope* v. *Hope*, 4 DeG. M. &. G.
328.

In addition to the weight to be attached to the appointment of Mrs. Davis by the Court in Buffalo, the
weight of the other circumstances is, I think, strongly in
her favour. The separation of the husband and wife
seems to have been principally, if not entirely, due to his
misconduct; she seems at least as likely to be able to
support the child in comfort as he does; he has been found
guilty of adultery, and has confessed to occasional intoxica-
tion, and to continued use of liquor, though, he says, only
in moderation. If all these events had happened in this

Province, and not in the United States, I think I should
not have hesitated to say, that the wife, and not the
husband, ought to have the child, and I do not think I
should refuse to give the custody to her because she will
take it to Buffalo.   I think, therefore, that an order must
be made, giving to the applicant, Maria Davis, the custody
of the child, until or unless some further order shall be
made, and she should have the costs of the application.

G. F. H.

[COMMON PLEAS DIVISION.]

HELLEMS v. THE CORPORATION OF THE CITY OF ST. CATHARINES.

Municipal Corporations—Officer of—Tenure of Office—Removal of Officer.

The effect of section 279 of the Consolidated Municipal Act, **55** Vict.
ch. 42 (O.), which enacts that officers appointed by a municipal council
shall hold office until removed by the council, is that all such officers
hold office during the pleasure of the council, and may be removed at
any time without notice or cause shewn therefor, and without the
council incurring any liability thereby.

THIS was an action for wrongful dismissal, tried before
ROSE, J., without a jury, at St. Catharines, at the Spring
Assizes of 1894.

The facts are set out in the judgment of GALT, C. J.

The learned trial Judge entered judgment for the defendants.

The plaintiff moved on notice to set aside the judgment
and to have judgment entered in his favour.

In Easter Sittings, May 29th, 1894, before a Divisional
Court composed of GALT, C. J., and MACMAHON, J.,
G. H. Watson, Q. C., and *Lancaster*, supported the motion.

The learned trial Judge dismissed the action under a mis-
conception of the effect of *Vernon* v. *Corporation of Smith's.
Falls*, 21 O. R. 331. In that case, the appointment was of
a chief constable, which is made under section 445. That
section expressly provides that the persons appointed
thereunder shall hold office during the pleasure of the
council. The appointment here was made under section 279, under which the persons appointed are to hold
office until removed by the council. This merely means
that there is the right of removal, and it is implied that
the removal can only be made on good cause being shewn,
and subject to the usual right to compensation for wrongful dismissal. The case of *Wilson* v. *Corporation of York,*
46 U. C. R. 289, is quite distinguishable. The plaintiff
there was appointed in the year 1866, by the council of
that year, and held office until 1880, when he was dismissed at the first meeting of the council elected for that
year, and before they had in any way recognized his
appointment. This was, therefore, merely following the
decision of *Hickey* v. *Corporation of Renfrew*, 20 C. P.
429, 431. There the officer was appointed under section
177 of the Act of 1866, which is similar to the present
section 279. The Court were of the opinion, that the appointment was a yearly one, and that there could be no
dismissal within the year by the council appointing him,
but at the same time they held that on the election of a
new council, that council, before they had done anything to
recognize the appointment, could dismiss, without incurring
any liability. Thus, while holding that the council appointing him could not dismiss, that their successors
could. The case of *Broughton* v. *Corporation of Brantford*, 19 C. P. 434, 437, referred to in the last case, is
expressly in point here. It was also decided under section
177 of the Act of 1866. It is there expressly laid down,
that the appointment must be deemed an annual one, and
the dismissal of the officer before the expiration of the
year by the council appointing him was wrongful, and

that he was entitled to recover damages for his wrongful Argument.
dismissal.

Aylesworth, Q. C., and *Ronald Macdonald*, contra. No
time was fixed by the resolution for the duration of the
appointment and therefore, he merely held during pleasure.
No doubt, under section 279, the officer appointed holds
office until removed by the council, but there is no limit
fixed to the time of removal. It may, therefore, be at any
time and so at pleasure. In *Wilson* v. *Corporation of
York*, 46 U. C. R. 289, it is expressly laid down, that until
removed by the council means during the pleasure of the
council, and nothing turned on the fact, that the dismissal
was by a succeeding council. Sections 279 and 445 are
therefore in substance the same. The case of *Vernon* v.
Corporation of Smith's Falls, 21 O. R. 331, in which the
previous cases are considered, does not turn in the special
use of the words " during pleasure," nor that the officer was
the chief constable, but on the general principle embodied
in the statute, that all officers appointed by the council are
to hold office during pleasure. The by-laws of the defendants relating to the appointment to office expressly provide
that all appointments are only to be during pleasure, of
which the plaintiff was aware, and they asked leave to
put such by-law in.

G. H. Watson, Q. C., in reply. The appointment was
for a year. The resolution appointing the plaintiff was at
$600 a year, which clearly means at one year at least.

June 23rd, 1894. GALT, C. J. :—

The defendants are the municipal corporation of the
city of St. Catharines. On the 2nd of February, 1893, the
plaintiff applied for the position of street superintendent
which was then vacant. On the 13th of March, a resolution of the council was passed appointing him street superintendent. On the 27th of March, a resolution of the
council was passed rescinding the former resolution. In
accordance with this last resolution the plaintiff was not

employed as street superintendent, and this action was brought.

The learned Judge at the trial held that under the provisions of the Consolidated Municipal Act, 55 Vict. ch. 42, sec. 279, the corporation had the right at any time to dismiss any officer appointed by a council. The words of the section are : " All officers appointed by a council shall hold office until removed by the council." I quite concur in the opinion expressed by my brother Rose.

The case of *Wilson* v. *Corporation of York*, 46 U. C. R. 289, is in accordance with this view. At p. 299, Armour, J., in delivering the judgment of the Court, states as follows :—

" The Municipal Act expressly provides that 'all officers appointed by the council shall hold office until removed by the council.' The effect of this is, that all such officers hold their offices during the pleasure of the council, and may be removed by the council at any time without any notice of such intended removal, and without any cause being shewn for such removal, and without the council thereof incurring any liability to such officers for such removal. There is no hardship in this, for such officers accept their offices upon these terms ; and were it otherwise, councils might be greatly embarrassed in the transaction of their public duties by the frowardness of any officer whom they would have no means of immediately removing without subjecting themselves to the liability of an action."

The motion must be dismissed with costs.

MACMAHON, J., concurred.

G. F. H.

[CHANCERY DIVISION.]

IN RE THE ONTARIO EXPRESS AND TRANSPORTATION
COMPANY.

THE DIRECTORS' CASE.

Company—Appointment of Directors to Salaried Offices—Right to Remuneration—Winding-up.

Where an Act of Incorporation provides that no by-law for the payment of the president or any director, shall be valid or acted on until the same has been confirmed at a general meeting of the shareholders, this applies only to payment for the services of a director *qua* director, and for the services of the president as presiding officer of the board.
Where a company appoints the directors to various salaried offices without a by-law fixing the amount of the salaries as required by the Act of Incorporation, and such appointments are afterwards confirmed by legislation, they are entitled to prove in the winding-up for a *quantum meruit* for services rendered.

THIS was an appeal from the decision of the Master in Statement. Ordinary in reference to certain claims for salary, as officers of the company, made by the directors of the above company in winding-up proceedings under the Dominion Winding-up Act, R. S. C. ch. 129.

The company was incorporated by 41 Vict. ch. 43 (D.), which amongst other things provided (s. 12) that "No by-law for the payment of the president or any director shall be valid or acted upon until the same has been confirmed at a general meeting."

On January 29th, 1891, certain shareholders of the company met in Toronto and constituted themselves a meeting of the company and proceeded to elect certain of their number as directors, and then adjourned to Montreal, when those so elected as directors met, and appointed themselves to all the various offices necessary, president, vice-president, general manager, secretary and auditor, treasurer, and general superintendent. They also provided by by-law that each director should be paid $500 per annum, and the president in addition $2,000, and also framed a resolution fixing the salary of the treasurer, secretary and auditor, general superintendent, and general manager at varying amounts.

The by-law aforesaid was confirmed at a meeting of shareholders at Montreal on the same day which purported to be specially called by the president to confirm the by-laws.

The Master allowed the claim of the president because it had the sanction of a by-law confirmed at a meeting of shareholders validated by the Act of 1891, 54-55 Vict. ch. 110, referred to in the judgment of ROSE, J., but disallowed the claims of the others on the ground that there was no by-law confirmed at a general meeting appropriating salaries to them as required by the Act of incorporation, and he referred to *Re Bolt and Iron Co., Livingstone's Case*, 14 O. R. 211.

The latter claimants now appealed on the ground that the provision in the Act of incorporation above cited, did not apply to the claims made as officers and servants of the company, but had only reference to the remuneration of directors as such.

The appeal was argued on September 25th, 1894, before ROSE, J.

F. A. Hilton and *W. R. Smyth*, for the claimants, referred to *In re Dale and Plant*, 43 Ch. D. 255; *Regina* v. *Stuart*, 10 R., April, 246; *Harte* v. *Ontario Express Co.*, 24 O. R. 216.

Hoyles, Q. C., for the liquidators, referred to *Re Bolt and Iron Co.*, 14 O. R. 211; *Ex parte Cannon*, 30 Ch. D. 629; *Fellows* v. *Albert Mining Co.*, 3 Pugs. 203; *Mallory* v. *Mallory Wheeler Co.*, 23 Atl. R. 708.

September 28th, 1894.   ROSE, J. :—

It is manifest that the appointment of the officers in question was not in accordance with the provisions of section 12 of 43 Vict. ch. 41 (D.), being an Act respecting the Ontario Express and Transportation Company, which provided that the directors should have power to make by-laws to regulate the appointment, functions, duties and

removal of all agents, officers, and servants of the company, the security to be given by them to the company,
their remuneration, and that (if any), to the directors, and
further providing that every such by-law, unless in the
meantime confirmed at a general meeting of the company
duly called for that purpose, should only have force until
the next annual meeting of the company. These officers
were not appointed by by-law at all, and therefore they
had no contract with the company upon which they could
recover remuneration. By chap. 110, 54-55 Vict. (D.), it
was declared that the company, as then organized, was
capable of doing business. Having regard to the interpretation of such statute in the matter of this company by
the learned Chancellor in 24 O. R. p. 216, I think it must
be held that the appointment of the officers was valid, and
that after the passing of that Act, the various officers who
had been informally and irregularly appointed, and who
were *de facto* officers of the company, became officers *de
jure*, such appointment being part of the reorganization
of the company, and necessary for the purpose of transacting the business of the company.

But I do not think that such last mentioned Act affected
at all the resolution fixing the salaries of the officers,
namely, treasurer, secretary and auditor, general superintendent and general manager. There is nothing in the
language of the statute, either in the preamble or in the
enacting clauses which necessarily refers to such a matter,
and I think that it would be legislating if I held that a
resolution, not permitted by law, could be practically
turned into a by-law and given effect to by such statute.

The judgment of the learned Master must be affirmed
to the extent of disallowing the salaries which were ordered
to be paid by the resolution referred to in his judgment.

I have not been able to come to the conclusion that such
salaries would be within the proviso of section 12 enacting
that no by-law "for the payment of the president or any
director," should be valid or acted upon until the same had
been confirmed at a general meeting, for I am not of the

opinion that where a director is appointed an officer of the company, he holds such appointment as director. It seems to me that the words referred to apply to the payment of money for the services of a director *qua* director, and of the services of the president as presiding officer of the board of directors, and that if a company chooses to appoint a director to any salaried office, he holds such office, not as director or by virtue of his office as director, but by virtue of his appointment by the board or the company as the charter or by-laws may provide. This view, I think, is in direct accord with the decision of the Court for Crown Cases Reserved in *Regina* v. *Stuart*, reported in the Reports by Mr. Mews, 10 R., April, p. 246, and is not in conflict with the decision of the learned Chancellor in *Re Bolt & Iron Co.*, 14 O. R. at p. 216. The decision of the learned Chancellor in that case must be read in reference to the point to be decided, which may be found in the following sentence: " The rules as to hiring and notice between master and servant, are, therefore, not applicable, and the measure of the rights of a salaried managing director is to be settled by what is provided in that behalf by the charter and by-laws of the company."

Finding, as I do, that the appointment of the officers named was confirmed by the statute of September, 1891, namely, ch. 110 of 54 & 55 Vict., I think that they are entitled to recover *quantum meruit* for services rendered to the company during the time they discharged the duties of their respective offices, and if the parties desire it there will be a reference back to ascertain the value of such services.

It was mentioned at the close of the argument that one of the officers had to perform duties for the liquidator during the process of liquidation. I do not think that is a matter to be dealt with upon this appeal. I do not find anything in the order of the learned Master in Ordinary on the question.

There will be no costs of this appeal to any party.

A. H. F. L.

[CHANCERY DIVISION.]

RE FERGUSON, BENNETT V. COATSWORTH.

*Will—Construction—" Right Heirs "—Period of Ascertainment—Distribu-
tion of Estate—" Equally "—Per Capita and not per Stirpes.*

Upon appeal from the Master's report on a reference for the administration of the estate of the testator whose will was construed in *Coatsworth
v. Carson,* 24 O. R. 185 :—

Held, having regard to the judgment in that case, that the "right heirs"
were to be ascertained at the date of the death of the testator's daughter, and among them the whole of the estate was to be divided equally,
share and share alike.

The expression " *per stirpes* " in the former judgment was improvidently
used, due weight not having been given to the word "equally."

A SUMMARY order having been made on the 3rd May, *Statement.*
1893, for the administration of the estate of Edward
Ferguson, upon the application of Mary Ann Bennett, as
plaintiff, against the trustees of the will of the deceased
and another, as defendants, a question arose in the administration proceedings before the Master in Ordinary as to
who were entitled to share in the estate under the words
in the will "my own right heirs," and the action *Coatsworth* v. *Carson,* 24 O. R. 185, was brought to construe
these words. After judgment had been given in that
action, the Master in Ordinary reported that, upon the
reference directed to him by such order, he was attended by the solicitors for the plaintiff and defendants
and for some of the descendants of Eliza Purdy and Jane
Ball, sisters of the testator, and having taken evidence as
to the persons entitled to share in the estate under the
will, directed an advertisement to be published, and having
considered the evidence and the affidavits of claim filed,
he found, 1st, that the testator died on the 9th January,
1874; 2nd, that the persons entitled to share in the estate,
having regard to the judgment in *Coatsworth* v. *Carson,*
dated 12th October, 1893, as amended by an order of the
22nd January, 1894, were the descendants of the sisters of
the testator, Jane Ball and Eliza Purdy, as being the

"right heirs" of the testator mentioned in the said will and judgment and order ; 3rd, that the descendants of Jane Ball, who died on the 27th November, 1878, were entitled to one-half of the estate, and the descendants of Eliza Purdy, who predeceased the testator, but left children her surviving who were living at the testator's death, to the other half of the estate.

Emily Barnes and William Charles Ball, grandniece and grandnephew of the testator, appealed from the 3rd paragraph of the report of the Master, on the ground that the Master erred in finding that the descendants of Jane Ball were entitled to only one-half of the estate, and the descendants of Eliza Purdy to the other half, and in finding that the period of distribution dated back to the death of the testator, and that he should have found that the period of distribution was at the time of the death of the testator's wife.

The testator died on the 9th January, 1874, leaving a widow and only daughter, and both real and personal estate, and by his will, after giving a house and premises to the daughter, devised and bequeathed all his other real and personal property to his executors to hold the same for the use of his wife and daughter jointly as long as they both survived and the wife remained unmarried; and, in case the wife did not marry and survived the daughter, for her use for life; and in case the daughter survived her mother, for the use of the daughter as her separate estate with power to dispose of the same by will in case she married ; and then proceeded : " I direct that in case my daughter shall have died without leaving issue and without having made a will as aforesaid, that my trustees shall (after the death of my wife, if she survive my said daughter) sell all my estate, real and personal, and divide the same equally amongst my own right heirs who may prove to the satisfaction of my said trustees their relationship within six months from the death of my said wife or daughter, whichever may last take place."

The daughter died unmarried on the 1st January, 1892,

in the lifetime of the mother, and the wife died on the
1st February, 1893, without having married again.

The testator had two sisters, Jane Ball, who was alive
at his death, and died in 1878, and Eliza Purdy, who predeceased him. Jane Ball had nine children, three of whom
were alive at the death of the testator's daughter, 1st January, 1892. The others were all dead before the 1st January,
1892, and each left a number of children alive on 1st
January, 1892. Eliza Purdy had two children, William
Purdy and Jane Eggleston. William Purdy was still alive
at the date of these proceedings. Jane Eggleston was alive
at the testator's death, but died before the 1st January,
1892, leaving three children named Eggleston, who were
all alive at the date of these proceedings.

The collateral relatives of the testator alive at the time
of his daughter's decease were, therefore, on the Ball side,
Samuel Ball, his nephew, Mary Ann Bennett and M. J.
Carson, his nieces, and a large number of persons (about
forty), some of whom were infants, his grandnephews and
grandnieces ; and on the Purdy side, William Purdy, his
nephew, and the three Egglestons, his grandnephews and
grandnieces.

In *Coatsworth* v. *Carson*, 24 O. R. 185, BOYD, C., held
that the words "my own right heirs" signified those who
would take real estate upon an intestacy, and that children
of any deceased heir-at-law were entitled to share *per*
stirpes.

The present appeal from the Master's report was argued
before BOYD, C., in Court, on the 11th October, 1894.

Starr, for the appellants. The Master held that the
division should be made as at the death of the testator.
I contend it should be as at the death of the daughter.
The distribution should be made equally among the "right
heirs" alive at the death of the daughter. The Master
has disregarded the word "equally." To give effect to that
word the estate must be divided equally among all the
descendants of the two sisters. The descendants of Eliza

Purdy should, therefore, not get half of the estate, but each of them a distributive share. I refer to *Coatsworth* v. *Carson*, 24 O. R. 185 ; *Tiffin* v. *Longman*, 15 Beav. 275 ; *Doe King* v. *Frost*, 3 B. & Ald. 546.

A. J. Boyd, for the infant grandnephews and grand-nieces on the Ball side, supported the appeal.

W. M. Clark, Q. C., for the nephew and nieces on the Ball side, also supported the appeal.

Macklem, for William Purdy and the Egglestons, opposed the appeal. We have to go to the date of the death of the testator to find out his " right heirs." One sister was then alive, and half the estate goes to her, and the other half to the descendants of the other sister. The Master was bound by and has followed *Coatsworth* v. *Carson*, 24 O. R. 185. All the parties to this action were parties to the action of *Coatsworth* v. *Carson*, and that action was brought to construe this clause of the will, and the parties are bound by the judgment ; the rights of the parties under the will are merged in the judgment ; the reference proceeded under that judgment ; and the Master's report based upon it is correct. I refer to R. S. O. ch. 108, secs. 29, 38 ; R. S. O. ch. 109, sec. 31 ; *Tylee* v. *Deal*, 19 Gr. 601 ; *Mays* v. *Carroll*, 14 O. R. 699 ; *Totten* v. *Totten*, 20 O. R. 505 ; *Re Bowey*, 21 O. R. 361.

F. E. Hodgins, for the trustees.

Starr, in reply.

October 15, 1894. BOYD, C. :—

Having regard to my former judgment, the " right heirs" of the testator are to be ascertained at the time of his daughter's death, though the distribution is not to be made among them till the period fixed by the will after death of daughter and wife.

The daughter was his " right heir " till she died ; then the estate was to go to those who should then be his right heirs, though the division was suspended till the death of his widow.

I think the Master is to find who were "the right heirs" Judgment.
on 1st January, 1892, when the daughter died without Boyd, C.
issue and intestate, and then among these right heirs the
whole of the blended fund is to be divided equally, share and
share alike. This particular aspect of the case was not
before me upon the former argument, and I think the expression then used, "*per stirpes*," was improvidently used,
as my attention was not called to the word "equally," nor
was it necessary to the then decision.

E. B. B.

[QUEEN'S BENCH DIVISION.]

Ross et al. v. Orr et al.

Gaming—Bicycle Race—Protest—Award of Trophy—Private Tribunal—
Decision of—Refusal of Court to Interfere—Injunction.

Where a challenge cup, to be won in a bicycle race between competing
clubs, was held by trustees under an instrument of trust by which all
arrangements pertaining to the course, race, protests, and matters
"connected with the welfare of the cup" were to be decided by the
trustees according to certain rules, the Court, upon the mere allegation
of fraud, and before any decision of the trustees, refused to exercise
jurisdiction restraining the trustees from parting with the cup to an
alleged winner under protest, upon the ground that one of the winning
riders did not go round the course, that being a matter of fact for the
decision of the trustees.
Brown v. *Overbury*, 11 Ex. 715 ; *Ellis* v. *Hopper*, 3 H. & N. 768 ; and
Newcomen v. *Lynch*, Ir. R. 9 C. L. 1 ; Ir. R. 10 C. L. 248, followed.

THIS was an action brought by Frederick H. Ross and Statement.
the Royal Canadian Bicycle Club, plaintiffs, against G. H.
Orr, R. Garland, A. T. Johnston, Fred. Bryers, Thomas B.
McCarthy, and the Athenæum Cycling Club, defendants.

Upon the *ex parte* application of the plaintiffs, on the
3rd October, 1894, an injunction order was granted by
Rose, J., restraining the defendants Orr, Garland, Johnston, and Bryers, from parting with the possession of the
" Dunlop Challenge Cup" or " Trophy," or delivering it to

the other defendants or to any person or club other than the plaintiffs, and restraining the other defendants from receiving such cup or trophy.

The cup was of about the value of $1,000, and was presented for competition among Canadian bicycle clubs, and held by the defendants Orr, Garland, Johnston, and Bryers, as trustees.

The competition for 1894 took place at Toronto on the 29th September, the plaintiff and defendant clubs and three other clubs competing. Ten riders were entered from each club, making fifty in all, but only forty-seven started, and thirty-four finished the race.

The course was four times round the Woodbine race track, four miles, then down the Kingston road seven and a-half miles to a barrel, around which the riders were to turn, and then return to the Woodbine track, and run once around, in all twenty miles.

The result of the race was to be decided according to a computation of " points" scored by each competing club.

Upon the *ex parte* application the plaintiffs shewed these facts by affidavits, which also stated that the trophy had been awarded to the defendants the Athenæum Cycling Club, who claimed it, but the plaintiffs the Royal Canadian Bicycle Club disputed their right to it, upon the ground that the defendant McCarthy, who was one of the riders entered from the Athenæum Club, did not ride round the barrel at the turn. Several affidavits testified to his not having done so, and the plaintiff Ross swore that unless the defendants the trustees should be immediately restrained from handing over the cup to the Athenæum Club, it would be so handed over. It was shewn that a protest had been entered against McCarthy's conduct.

The agreement upon which the defendants the trustees accepted the trust, was exhibited. By it the trustees agreed to promote, arrange, and advertize all details of the contests in accordance with the instructions of the donors of the cup, which was to remain in their possession until it permanently became the property of a club, which should be the winner at two successive competitions, or at three, if not consecutive. The dates of the contests and all arrangements pertaining to the course and race, protests, and matters concerning the welfare of the cup, were to be decided by the trustees, who agreed to act according to rules subscribed, etc.

The plaintiffs gave notice of motion for an order continuing the injunction till the trial, and affidavits were thereupon filed by the defendants, including one from the defendant McCarthy himself, asserting that he had properly made the turn round the barrel, and fairly ridden the whole twenty miles, coming in second.

The defendant Orr made an affidavit stating that the decision of the trustees had not yet been given, and that they were going to submit the matters in question to the judgment of the referee of the race.

The motion to continue the injunction was argued before BOYD, C., in Court, on the 10th October, 1894.

W. R. Riddell, for the plaintiffs. We ask the interference of the Court on the ground of fraud.

[BOYD, C.—If there is jurisdiction, it will be better to continue the injunction and leave the cup in the hands of the trustees till the action has been tried. I cannot decide the question of fact here. I will hear the defendants on the question of jurisdiction.]

Du Vernet (C. B. Jackes with him), for the defendants McCarthy and the Athenæum Cycling Club. By the terms of the trust this matter is for the decision of the trustees. A protest has been made against McCarthy. It is for the trustees to pass upon it. They are the proper forum. Where internal provisions are made for settling disputed matters, there can be no resort to a Court of law till these are exhausted: *Essery* v. *Court Pride,* 2 O. R. 596; *Ellis* v. *Hopper,* 3 H. & N. 766. The trustees alone can consider and decide, and there is no appeal: *Dines* v. *Wolfe,* L. R. 2 P. C. 280. The plaintiffs have no right of property to assert, and an injunction will not be granted: *Baird* v. *Wells,* 44 Ch. D. 661; *Forbes* v. *Eden,* L. R. 1 Sc. App. 568.

Ryckman, for the defendants the trustees.

Riddell, in answer. The Court has jurisdiction, fraud being alleged, to inquire into the matter, and should in the meantime stay the hands of the trustees. The cases cited say that the decision of the private tribunal is to be final, but it appears here that the decision of the trustees is not final ; they leave the whole matter to a referee. Have the rules of the contest been observed ? That is what is to be inquired into.

Du Vernet, in reply, referred to *Guinane* v. *Sunnyside Boating Co.,* 21 A. R. at p. 54 ; *Corrigan* v. *Coney Island Jockey Club,* 48 N. Y. St. Repr. 582 ; 51 N. Y. St. Repr. 592.

October 11, 1894. BOYD, C. :—

The bicycle race was entered upon subject to the conditions expressed in the declaration of trust made by the trustees of the challenge cup. By that it is provided that " all arrangements pertaining to the course and race, protests, and matters connected with the welfare of the cup, will be decided by the trustees, who will act according to the rules hereunder subscribed." This is broad enough to cover all details, and especially as to the decision of who is the winning club. There has been no decision as yet, and the Court cannot in such a case undertake to decide. In *Brown* v. *Overbury,* 11 Ex. 715, it is said by Alderson, B., " that in order to ascertain who is to have the stakes, it must first be determined who is the winner, not in the opinion of a jury, but of the persons appointed to decide it, viz., the judge or the stewards." And Martin, B., said: " The judgment of the stewards in the case of a horse-race must necessarily be conclusive ; they are appointed expressly to decide the matter, and there is no appeal from them :" p. 717, (1856). The same principle of decision was declared by Pollock, C. B., two years later in *Ellis* v. *Hopper,* 3 H. & N. at p. 768, where he laid it down (respecting a race): " This is a reference according to certain rules, one of which was that the stewards should decide all disputes : the object being to prevent the necessity of resorting to litigation or arbitration."

The later cases are all referred to and their effect discussed in an Irish case *Newcomen* v. *Lynch*, Ir. R. 9 C. L. 1, and Ir. R. 10 C. L. 248, in which the Exchequer Chamber held, reversing the Court below, that the decision of stewards in a race cover all questions whether of fact or law— and as to the interpretation and application of the rules under which the race is run, and their decision *bonâ fide* given, though it may be unsound, or not such as would be given by a court of law, must, nevertheless, prevail—for such is the expressed condition of the contest, that the stewards, or in this case the trustees, are to decide all questions.

The complaint here, so far as developed on the affidavits, is one as to a matter of fact, whether one of the riders turned the goal or shot inside of it ; as a matter of fact, upon due protest, that is peculiarly a case for the consideration of the trustees, and it does not require that they should have to take evidence on oath in order to be able to dispose of it satisfactorily and as the donors of the cup intended : *Benbow* v. *Jones*, 14 M. & W. 193.

It appears to me, therefore, that this *ex parte* injunction was issued improvidently ; I have no difficulty in vacating it, as the learned Judge who granted it would himself have done, if, upon cause being shewn, he was satisfied that the jurisdiction of the Court ought not to be exercised in such a case.

The injunction will be discharged with costs.

E. B. B.

[QUEEN'S BENCH DIVISION.]

RE STEPHENS ET AL. AND TOWNSHIP OF MOORE.

Municipal Corporations—Drain Constructed out of General Funds—Maintenance and Repair—Assessment of Lands Benefited—By-law—Petition—55 Vict. ch. 42, secs. 569, 586—Complaints as to Assessment—Court of Revision—Notice—Service—Section 571 (2)—Irregularities—Lands "to be Benefited"—Policy of Drainage Legislation—Interference by Court.

A township council has power under section 586 (2) of the Consolidated Municipal Act, 55 Vict. ch. 42, to maintain and repair a beneficial drain, originally constructed out of general funds, at the expense of the local territory benefited, by passing a by-law to that effect, without a petition therefor. And although such a by-law refers to lots "to be benefited," it does not bring the work within the category of drains to be constructed under section 569 of the Act.

Application to quash the by-law in question being made by several persons, who among them owned one of the lots assessed, alleging that they were not benefited by the original drain and could not be by its continuance and repair, and that the amount charged against their lot was not duly apportioned among them :—

Held, that they should have applied to the Court of Revision for relief ; and not having done so, and the work having all been done and the benefit of it enjoyed, this Court would not interfere to declare the by-law invalid :—

Held, also, having regard to section 571 (2), that the applicants had sufficient notice of the by-law, service having been effected upon a grown-up person at the house where they all lived as members of one family :—

Held, also, that upon this application the Court would not inquire what other persons were not served who were not seeking relief, nor consider irregularities or errors in the assessment of such others.

It appeared on the face of the by-law that the drain in question was an old one, constructed out of general funds, and out of repair ; and although the assessment was referred to as on the property "to be benefited," yet the same clause spoke of it as "upon the property benefited :"—

Held, that the by-law was not bad on its face.

In drainage matters the policy of the legislature is to leave the management largely in the hands of the localities, and the Court should refrain from interference, unless there has been a manifest and indisputable excess of jurisdiction, or an undoubted disregard of personal rights.

Statement. A SUMMARY application by D. T. Stephens, Hattie Stephens, and Emma Stephens for an order quashing a by-law of the corporation of the township of Moore passed on the 14th October, 1893, entitled, "Drainage By-law No. 23 of 1893, a by-law to provide for draining a portion of the township of Moore by the repairing of the Dodds outlet drain on lot No. 4 in the 2nd concession of the township of Moore, and for levying on the lands and

roads to be benefited the sum of $47 for completing the
same."

The by-law recited that notices had been served on the
township council that the Dodds drain, which was originally constructed out of the general funds of the municipality, was out of repair, and application had been made
in writing to the council to have it repaired ; that the
council had procured an examination to be made by William M. Manigault, O. L. S., of the locality proposed to be
drained and benefited, and plans, estimates, and an assessment to be made by him (setting out his report) ; and that
the council were of opinion that the drainage of the locality described by the repairing of the outlet was desirable.
The by-law then enacted: " 1st. That the said report,
plans, and estimates be adopted, and the said drain
be repaired in accordance therewith, at the expense of the
parties immediately interested, and whose lands are to be
benefited, and the municipality for the roads, and that
the amount mentioned be assessed and levied upon the
property benefited as set forth in the said assessment,
against each lot, or portion of lot and road, to pay the
expense of said outlet."

By the report of the engineer $15 was assessed against
lot 5 in the 3rd concession, owned by the applicants.

The motion to quash was made on the following among
other grounds :—

1. No petition was presented to the council for the work
proposed to be done.

2. The original drain being constructed out of the general funds of the township, the only lands liable to be
assessed for repairs were those benefited by the original
drain and lying in the 2nd concession ; and lot 5 in the 3rd
concession, not being so benefited, was not liable.

6. The engineer's report assessed the whole of lot 5, 200
acres, as though it were owned by the same person, while
195 acres were owned by D. T. Stephens, Byron Stephens,
Frank Stephens, and Louis Stephens, and the remaining
five acres were owned by and assessed to Hettie Stephens,
Emma Stephens, and Mrs. Walter Firman.

7. There was no publication of the by-law, nor was any copy served upon Hettie Stephens, Emma Stephens, or Mrs. Walter Firman.

11. The drainage of lot 5 was naturally into the drain on the north side of the 2nd and 3rd concession roads, and thence to the Parr and McGill drains as outlets, and for the construction of all three drains lot 5 had been heavily assessed.

October 9, 1894. The motion was argued before BOYD, C., in Court.

M. Wilson, Q. C., for the applicants.

Lister, Q. C., for the township corporation.

Re Clark and Township of Howard, 14 O. R. at pp. 604, 605; 16 A. R. at p. 85; *Smith* v. *Township of Raleigh*, 3 O. R. at p. 412; *Township of Thurlow* v. *Township of Sidney*, 1 O. R. at pp. 257-9; *Re White and Township of Sandwich East, ib.* 530; *Re County of Essex and Township of Rochester*, 42 U. C. R. 523; *Rose* v. *Township of West Wawinosh*, 19 O. R. 294; *Re Robertson and Township of North Easthope*, 16 A. R. 214; and *Begg* v. *Township of Southwold*, 6 O. R. 184, were referred to.

October 13, 1894. BOYD, C.:—

This application to quash a drainage by-law, as to the real merits, appears to be narrowed to this alternative: whether the township had the right to repair and maintain the Dodds ditch and charge the expense on the lots benefited, or whether that expense must come out of the general funds? It is conceded by the applicants that the municipality could do the work in question, but it is argued that the municipality could not make them contribute to the expense by the mere passing of a by-law therefor. It is urged that the case does not fall within sub-sec. 2 of sec. 586 of the Municipal Act of 1892, because the by-law, etc., speaks of the lots to be benefited, and so contemplates prospective advantages, and, in such a case, that a petition of those interested is an indispensable pre-requisite. But I do not think this application should suc-ceed upon literalities of construction which might prosper in the days of special demurrer. The sub-section men-tioned has to do with drains actually constructed by the outlay of general funds; and if it is the fact that these benefit certain lots and roads, then the scope of the legis-lation is to enable the council to keep their drains open and efficient at the local expense of the lots and roads benefited. They have been benefited in the past, *ex hypothesi*, and they will, therefore, be benefited in the future. Though the by-law to maintain at local cost in such a case may speak of the lands as "to be benefited," that does not negative the fact that there has been prior and concurrent benefit even before the work of repair is undertaken or completed. In other words, the mere phraseology of the draftsman as found in the by-law does not place such an existing drain (constructed originally out of general funds) in the category of drains to be constructed under sec. 569. Given a beneficial drain, con-structed out of general funds, the council has power to keep this drain on foot, or bettered by repairs, at the expense of the local territory benefited, by passing a by-law to that effect. So I read the section, and such I take to be the meaning of the legislature. This meaning is, I think, sufficiently expressed by the language of the by-law in question, when viewed in the light of local history. Upon the prime question of merits, therefore, I think the corporation had jurisdiction to enact this by-law.

The old drain of 1872 (Parr drain), for which the appli-cant was assessed, gave him, I suppose, some measure of benefit. That was followed by the Dodds drain in 1882, which as a fact drew off water from the concession line in front of the applicants' lot 5. There is recognition of this in the fact that the applicant by his son in 1892 assisted in the putting in of the culvert in this road which connected the Dodds ditch with the north side of the concession road

Judgment.

Boyd, C.

abutting on the applicants' land and so made a better
off-take for the drainage therefrom.

Now, if the applicant was not benefited by this old
drain and could not be benefited by its continuance and
repair, it was open for him to appeal and so be relieved
from the assessment—but though he went before the Court
of Revision, it was not for this purpose. And again, if
the applicants or any of them were aggrieved because the
small amount charged on lot 5 was not apportioned
among them according to their alleged several interests,
that was also a matter to be adjusted upon appeal, and I
do not feel disposed (now that the work is all done and
the actual benefits of it enjoyed by the applicants and
others) to interfere by declaring the by-law invalid on this
ground.

It is said also that the applicants were not properly
served with notice of it. Upon this there is a dispute of
facts: service upon all is sworn to, and as a matter of
common sense one must believe all had sufficient notice,
when it was served upon a grown-up person at the house
on the place where all the applicants lived as members of
one family. Such a course is sanctioned by sec. 571, sub-
sec. (2). On this application I am not going to inquire
what other persons were not served who are not seeking
relief, and who do not, therefore, complain Nor am I
going to enter upon the consideration of irregularities or,
it may be, errors as to the assessment of others, or the
readjustment of assessments which were not moved against
by those directly interested, and which, for all I know, are
assented to by those who have to pay.

I do not read the by-law as bad on its face: it appears
on the by-law that the Dodds drain was an old drain constructed out of general funds, and that it was out of
repair; and although it is said that the assessment is on
the property "to be benefited," yet the same enacting
clause of the by-law speaks of the assessment as being
"upon the property benefited," as set forth in the assessment. The whole scope of the by-law shews that the

work to be done is the repair of an old drain at a small cost, which is charged upon the property benefited.

In matters of drainage and other business of local concern the policy of the legislature is to leave the management largely in the hands of the localities, and the Court should be careful to refrain from interference—the meaning of which is always a large outlay for costs—unless there has been a manifest and indisputable excess of jurisdiction or an undoubted disregard of personal rights. Here the entire of the evidence induces me to believe that the natural course of the drainage is by way of Dodds gulley to Plum creek, and that the work now finished for about a year, at a trifling cost, has already demonstrated its usefulness.

I discharge the application with costs.

E. B. B.

[QUEEN'S BENCH DIVISION.]

CHRISTIE v. CITY OF TORONTO.

Assessment and Taxes—55 Vict. ch. 48, sec. 124 (O.)—Goods Subject to Distress—Occupancy.

Statement.   THE plaintiff appealed to the Divisional Court of the Common Peas Division from the judgment of MACMAHON, J., the trial Judge, reported *ante* p. 425.

The appeal was by order transferred for hearing to the Divisional Court of the Queen's Bench Division, and was heard on the 29th November, 1894, before ARMOUR, C. J., and FALCONBRIDGE and STREET, JJ.

Kilmer, for the plaintiff.

W. C. Chisholm, for the defendants, and

W. R. Smyth, for Farquhar, a third party, were not called on.

THE COURT dismissed the appeal with costs, agreeing with the judgment of the trial Judge.

E. B. B.

[QUEEN'S BENCH DIVISION.]

RE CUMMINGS AND COUNTY OF CARLETON ET AL.

Prohibition—Arbitration and Award—Lands Injuriously Affected—Joint Work by City and County—Remedy—Appointment of Arbitrator—Powers of County Judge—One Arbitrator for Two Municipalities—Municipal Act, 55 Vict. ch. 42, secs. 391, 483, 487—Interpretation Act, R. S. O. ch. 1, sec. 8 (24).

An order of prohibition is an extreme measure, to be granted summarily only in a very plain case of excessive jurisdiction on the part of a subordinate tribunal.

A land-owner alleged that by the building of a bridge over a river forming the boundary between a county and city, a joint work undertaken by the two municipalities, his land in the county had been injuriously affected, for which he sought damages from both municipalities:—

Held, having regard to sec. 483 of the Municipal Act, 55 Vict. ch. 42, that he had no remedy except by arbitration under the Act.

Pratt v. City of Stratford, 14 O. R. 260, 16 A. R. 5, followed :—

Held, also, that the case was covered by sec. 391 of the Act; the expression "a municipal corporation," by force of the Interpretation Act, R. S. O. ch. 1, sec. 8 (24), being capable of being read as a plural :—

Held, also, that it was competent for the County Judge to appoint the same arbitrator for both corporations, upon their making default in naming an arbitrator, and that he could proceed to do so *ex parte* :—

Held, lastly, that sec. 487 did not apply to the case of a joint claim against city and county.

Prohibition to the arbitrators refused.

MOTION by the municipal corporation of the city of **Statement.** Ottawa for an order prohibiting William Whillans, John Deacon, and James Reeves, and each of them, and Robert Cummings, from proceeding with an alleged arbitration between Robert Cummings and the corporation of the county of Carleton and the applicants.

Robert Cummings, alleging that certain of his lands in the township of Gloucester had been injuriously affected by the two corporations in the exercise of the powers belonging to them, by raising the grades of the road upon which the parcels of land abutted, in order to form the approach to a bridge over the Rideau river, erected by the two corporations jointly, served upon each of the corporations a notice claiming compensation for the alleged injury, naming William Whillans as his arbitrator to fix such compensation, and requiring each of the corporations within seven days to name an arbitrator on their behalf. The corporations failing to name an arbitrator within the time limited, Robert Cummings applied *ex parte* to the Judge of the County Court of Carleton, who, upon such application, appointed John Deacon as arbitrator on behalf of the two corporations. The two arbitrators so appointed met and appointed James Reeves as third arbitrator; he accepted the appointment; and the three arbitrators thereupon appointed the 9th October, 1894, to proceed with the arbitration.

Notice of this appointment having been served on the corporation of the city of Ottawa, they moved for the order of prohibition, upon the following, among other, grounds :—

1. That Robert Cummings had no claim for compensation which ought to be settled by three arbitrators under the Municipal Act, and proceedings under that Act did not apply.

2. That the notice of the alleged claim and of the appointment of an arbitrator by Cummings was void under the Act.

3. That there was no disagreement between Cummings and the corporation which ought to be settled by arbitrators.

4. That if Cummings ever had any such claim, the corporation was released therefrom by deed of Cummings dated 31st August, 1892.

5. That William Whillans was not duly appointed arbitrator by Cummings.

6. That John Deacon was not legally appointed arbitrator on behalf of the corporation, and the County Judge had no jurisdiction to make an *ex parte* order for his appointment, or to appoint him for both corporations.

7. That James Reeves was not legally appointed third arbitrator.

8. That the corporation of the city of Ottawa had no notice of the application to appoint the arbitrators, or of the appointment of any of them.

The motion was argued before BOYD, C., in Chambers, on the 8th October, 1894.

Moss, Q. C., for the corporation of the city of Ottawa. There was no jurisdiction in the County Judge to appoint an arbitrator for the municipalities on the *ex parte* application of the land-owner ; nor could he make any appointment unless and until it appeared that the claim was for more than $1,000 damages : section 487 of the Consolidated Municipal Act, 55 Vict. ch. 42 (O.). At all events, he had no power to appoint one arbitrator for the two corporations, because the notice served called on each to name an arbitrator. The sections of the statute dealing with arbitrations of this kind are 385 and 483-488. This case does not seem to be provided for at all. The lands are said to be injuriously affected, and they are not in the city. No by-law was passed by the city. This was a case of building a new bridge under the joint jurisdiction of the city and county : sections 530, 532, 533 (*b*), 535 (1). The land-owner makes no claim of a given sum of money, as is contemplated by section 487, and the municipalities could make no tender under section 488, and so the Act does not apply.

H. M. Mowat, for the corporation of the county of Carleton. If section 487 applies, we should have the benefit. There was no material before the County Judge to shew a failure to agree upon the compensation. On the contrary, the land-owner had agreed to take $250 for his claim. I refer to *Re Anderdon and Colchester,* 21 O. R. 476.

W. M. Douglas, for Robert Cummings. Prohibition does not lie, even if the proceedings are irregular. The $1,000 limit applies only where a city alone is concerned. The notice need not specify the amount claimed. The case is within *Pratt* v. *City of Stratford,* 16 A. R. 5. No by-law was necessary ; the two municipalities acted conjointly ; the land-owner has no right of action, and his remedy is by arbitration alone. Notice was given to each ; they refused to appoint an arbitrator ; and the Judge appointed one for both, as he had the right to do under section 394. The agreement spoken of by counsel for the county does not include the three lots in question. There is no right to prohibition; the County Judge here is not a judicial officer, but *persona designata*, exercising a statutory jurisdiction : *Re Godson*, 16 A. R. 452 ; *North London R. W. Co.* v. *Great Northern R. W. Co.*, 11 Q. B. D. 30 ; Shortt on Informations, etc., p. 436 ; *London and Blackwall R. W. Co.* v. *Cross*, 31 Ch. D. 354. If the proceedings are invalid, an action upon the award cannot be sustained.

Moss, in reply. The right to prohibition is affirmed by *Re Anderdon and Colchester*, 21 O. R. 476, under the drainage sections of the Act. I refer also to *The Queen* v. *The Local Government Board*, 10 Q. B. D. 309 ; *Farrar* v. *Cooper*, 44 Ch. D. 323 ; *Re Colquhoun and Berlin*, 44 U. C. R. 631. The proceedings to enforce the award would be summary; no action on it would be necessary. The statute does not apply to this case of joint liability, if section 487 does not. I refer to *Hammond* v. *Bendyshe*, 13 Q. B. 869 ; *Painter* v. *Liverpool Gas Co.*, 3 A. & E. 433 ; *Gibbs* v. *Stead*, 8 B. & C. 528.

Mowat, in reply. If the proceedings are void as to the city, the arbitration should not be allowed to go on as against the county ; we should be allowed now to choose our own arbitrator.

Douglas asked leave to refer to *Re Smith and Plympton*, 12 O. R. 20 ; *Briton Medical Association* v. *Asher*, 35 Sol. J. 262 ; *Ex p. Simons*, 4 Times L. R. 754.

October 9, 1894. BOYD, C. :—

This is the case of a bridge over a river (Rideau) forming a boundary line between the county of Carleton and the city of Ottawa, which, according to the Municipal Act, 1892, sec. 535 (1), is to be erected and maintained by the councils of county and city. It is a joint work, to be paid for by the two municipalities as they may agree, or as the expense may be apportioned by arbitration.

Judgment.

Boyd, C.

In the work of erecting this bridge, the proprietor
Cummings alleges that his land in the county of Carleton
has been injuriously affected, and he seeks damages therefor from both municipalities. He seems to be shut down
to proceeding by way of arbitration, having regard to section 483 of the Act of 1892, and *Pratt* v. *City of Stratford*,
14 O. R. 260 and 16 A. R. 5. This being a case of joint
action by two corporations, I am disposed to read section
391 as covering the case, though it reads in case of arbitration between "a municipal corporation" and the owners ; for the operation of the Interpretation Act turns the
singular into a plural : R. S. O. ch. 1, sec. 8 (24). The
literal reading was avoided in *Pratt* v. *City of Stratford*,
because it would work injustice. If the claimant in this
case has no relief by way of arbitration, he seems to have
no right of action, and I lean against holding the case to
be one of omission from the Municipal Act. These corporations have at present no distinct interests as against the
proprietor—they have a common interest in keeping down
his claim, though, after it is ascertained, then they may
contest as between themselves respecting the division of
the burden.

It appears to me to be competent for the Judge to appoint an arbitrator for both, or the same arbitrator for
each—upon their making default in naming an arbitrator,
and that he could proceed *ex parte* : *Re Smith and Plympton*, 12 O. R. at p. 36.

I do not read section 487 as compelling me to prohibit
for want of jurisdiction; the section does not apply to the
case of a joint claim against city and county, and I do not
see that I can sever the claim so as to introduce that section.

Altogether, without giving a decision upon the ultimate
legality of the award, I do not feel so pressed by the plain
and manifest usurpation of power on the part of the
County Judge or of the board as now constituted as to
direct that a writ or order of prohibition should issue.
That appears to be an extreme measure to be exercised

78—VOL. XXV. O.R.

summarily only in a very plain case of excessive jurisdiction on the part of a subordinate tribunal.

I give no costs, as the statutes are of difficulty in any
view of the application.

[An appeal from this decision was argued before a
Divisional Court of the Queen's Bench Division on the
21st November, 1894. Judgment was reserved.]

E. B. B.

[CHANCERY DIVISION.]

BROUN v. BUSHEY ET AL.

*Way—Highway—Closing of—Adjoining Lands—Rights of Mortgagee of—
"Owner"—Con. Mun. Act, 1892, sec. 550, sub-sec. 9.*

A mortgagee of land adjoining a highway is one of the persons in whom
the ownership of it is vested for the purposes of sub-sec. 9 of sec. 550
of the "Consolidated Municipal Act, 1892," and as such is entitled to
pre-emption thereunder, subject to the right of the mortgagor to redeem
it along with the mortgage, or to have it sold to the mortgagor subject
to the mortgage, if the mortgagor so prefer.

Statement. ACTION by Lady Elizabeth Broun against Alice Bushey,
Francis Bushey and Ellen McIver, to reform a mortgage
made by the two first named defendants.

The following facts are taken from the judgment :

On the 3rd December, 1890, the defendant Alice Bushey,
was the owner in fee of lot 505, in the ordnance survey of
the Herchmer Farm, in the city of Kingston, and on that
day she and her husband, Francis Bushey, conveyed the
lot, describing it merely by its number and not by metes
and bounds, to the plaintiff by way of mortgage to secure
a loan of $1,500 and interest.

On the 25th August, 1893, the same mortgagors made a
further mortgage with the same description to the defen-

dant Ellen McIver, to secure $327 previously advanced by Statement. her to them.

Lot 505 had been laid out upon the original government plan in 1873, as follows, according to the black lines :

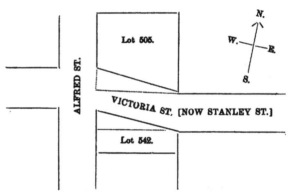

but it had been laid down upon the published maps of the city as a rectangular lot as shewn by the dotted line, and for eight or ten years it had been fenced in and occupied as a rectangular lot: the city had built a sidewalk along the south side of the fence upon the dotted line, and Stanley or Victoria street had been travelled as if it had continued straight to Alfred street without any turn such as is shewn above.

The Busheys had built three houses upon the property lying within the fences before they mortgaged to the plaintiff: one of these houses was wholly upon the lot as laid out by the government; the other two were almost entirely built upon the land shewn upon the government plan as Victoria street. The Busheys, at the time they built these houses and mortgaged them to the plaintiff, believed they were all built upon their own land, and that their lot was a rectangular lot, and they so represented the matter to the plaintiff's solicitor before the advance was made. Before they made the mortgage to Mrs. McIver they had been made aware, or had heard, as also had she, that part of the houses was upon the street.

Francis Bushey, early in 1894, acting for his wife and himself, then applied to the streets committee of the city council to pass a by-law for the purpose of continuing Stanley street in a straight line, and conveying to him the portion shewn within the dotted line; and they recommended the council that the application should be granted upon his procuring a conveyance to the city of the portion of lot 542 which would be required for the purpose of producing the street.

About the same time that this recommendation was made, Mrs. McIver entered into an agreement with the owners of lot 542 for the purchase of the portion of that lot required by the city. At the time Mrs. McIver entered into this agreement she had received from Alice and Francis Bushey a quit claim deed of the triangular piece of land shewn within the dotted lines: the consideration mentioned in this deed is $800, but the grantee, within three or four days, gave back a declaration of trust whereby she agreed to hold the property, after payment of her mortgage of $327 and interest, in trust for a son of Mr. and Mrs. Bushey.

On the 5th April, 1894, the plaintiff's solicitor became aware of the steps being taken by the Busheys and Mrs. McIver, and he wrote to the city notifying them of the plaintiff's rights, and asking that the city should not convey the street to the plaintiff's prejudice.

Finally, by consent of all parties, the owners of lot 542 conveyed to the city the portion of that lot required for the straightening of Stanley street, and the city conveyed to Mr. McIntyre, Q.C., the triangular piece of land enclosed in the dotted lines upon trust to convey it to that one of the two adverse claimants, the plaintiff herein and Mrs. McIver, as should establish a right to it in the pending litigation. The purchase money of the part of lot 542 which was conveyed to the city was paid by the plaintiff to the owners, with the understanding that she should have a lien for it in any event upon the property now in dispute, but should not acquire any other right by the fact of her having paid it.

On 9th July, 1894, the city council passed a by-law under the authority of which the conveyance to Mr. McIntyre, above referred to, was made. This by-law provides for the closing up of the original part of the street, as marked above in dotted lines, and for the sale and conveyance of it in exchange for the land required for the straightening of Stanley street, and closes with this provision: "Provided that if all the parties interested and claiming to be interested agree, the conveyance of the said part of Stanley street in exchange, as aforesaid, may be made to such person and in such terms as they may desire."

The object of the present action is to have the plaintiff's mortgage reformed, so as to make it cover the part enclosed in dotted lines, and to declare it a first charge as against the mortgagors and Ellen McIver and those claiming under her.

The action was tried at Kingston, on September 25, 1894, before STREET, J., without a jury.

G. M. Macdonnell, Q. C., for the plaintiff. The evidence shews that the whole rectangular parcel, as built upon, was known as lot 505. The corporation of the city had even built a sidewalk on the outside limit of the part in dispute: *McNish* v. *Munro,* 25 C. P. 290; *Winfield* v. *Fowlie,* 14 O. R. 102. The plaintiff has a right to prevent the closing up of a highway on which her property is situate. The defendant is in possession of the road allowance, and, as against other private parties, he is the owner: R. S. O. ch. 184, sec. 552.

Dr. Smythe, Q.C. There was no highway travelled in lieu of the original allowance for highway. I refer to Story's Equity Jurisprudence, 2nd Eng. ed., sec. 165; Taylor's Equity, sec. 133; Snell's Principles of Equity, 10th ed., p. 354.

Macdonnell, Q.C., in reply.

September 28, 1894. STREET, J. :—

The by-law of the Kingston city council under which a
part of the original street has been altered and sold by
them, was passed under sub-sec. 9 of sec. 550, Con. Mun.
Act 1892, which gives the council of every city, etc., power
to pass by-laws "for selling the original road allowance, to
the parties next adjoining whose lands the same is situated,
when a public road has been opened in lieu of the original
road allowance, and for the site or line of which compensation has been paid, and for selling, in like manner, to the
owners of any adjoining land, any road legally stopped up
or altered by the council; and in case such parties respectively refuse to become the purchasers at such price as the
council thinks reasonable, then for the sale thereof to any
other person for the same or a greater price."

The persons entitled to pre-emption under this sub-section
are "the parties next adjoining whose lands" the original
allowance is situated, and "the owners" of any land
adjoining a road which has been stopped up and is being
sold.

There is no precise legal meaning attached to the
word "owner," nor to the other phrase used in the section,
both being manifestly intended to convey the same idea,
which is that the persons to whom the adjoining land
belongs should have the first right to acquire and add to
that land the accretion formed by the closing up of the
highway.

I think it is plain that a mortgagee of land adjoining
a highway must be treated as one of the persons at least
in whom the ownership of it is vested for the purposes of this sub-section. His interest in the land is not
unfrequently the only valuable interest belonging to any
one. Even where the equity of redemption of the mortgagor is a valuable one, he might seriously impair the
security of the mortgagee if allowed to become the owner,
as against him, of a highway upon which the property originally had a front, and to close this front against him.

On the other hand, any such accretion acquired by the mortgagee would necessarily be redeemable by the mortgagor as part of the mortgaged premises.

The result of the sub-section as applied to this case is, then, that the plaintiff, as the owner of the legal estate under her mortgage, was entitled to insist upon a right to have the highway sold to her as mortgagee subject to the rights of the mortgagors to redeem it along with her mortgage, or to have it sold to the mortgagors subject to her mortgage, if the mortgagors preferred having the matter in that shape.

The plaintiff's contention upon this point was notified to the council before they had passed any by-law for closing or selling the highway, and has not been waived in any way.

The defendant Mrs. McIver, insists that by her superior diligence in acquiring the contract to purchase the part of lot 542 which was necessary to the arrangement with the city, she has obtained a right to the conveyance from the city over the head of the plaintiff, but plainly, I think that is not the case. By her purchase of that part of lot 542 which was necessary to the arrangement with the city, she held in her hands the right to say, for the time at all events, that the street should not be altered except upon her own terms; but she never took this position; she simply conveyed to the city the portion of lot 542 which they required, and agreed that the title conveyed by the city in the highway to the trustee, Mr. McIntyre, should be conveyed by him to the person legally entitled to it.

Nor has the quit claim deed made by the Busheys to Mrs. McIver, in any manner, improved her position. The grantors, at the date of its execution, 5th February, 1894, had no title to the portion of the highway described in it. The value of the highway as a highway was not increased, but was rather lessened by the buildings put upon it by Bushey under his mistake as to the title, and he could not, I think, have enforced any lien against the corporation based upon the value of his improvements.

If it be a material circumstance to be mentioned here, I may say that it is clear that no new consideration passed from Mrs. McIver to the Busheys at the time the quit claim was made : it was intended simply as a voluntary addition to the mortgage security which she held upon the original lot 505, and had the further object of benefiting the son of the grantors at the expense of the plaintiff. At most, therefore, that which passed by the quit claim deed to Mrs. McIver was the qualified and partial right of pre-emption of the property conveyed, which, as I have pointed out, could not be exercised to the prejudice of the plaintiff without her consent.

It was expressly agreed by counsel that under any cir-cumstances the plaintiff should have a lien upon the por-tion of the highway conveyed to her for the $250, which she paid to the owners of lot 542. She cannot have that portion of the highway, to which she is entitled, taken away from her, except upon payment of her mortgage money.

There should, therefore, be a declaration that as against the defendants, she is entitled to a conveyance from Mr. McIntyre, the trustee of the land in question, and to hold that land along with the original lot 505 as security for her mortgage debt, interest and costs, as well as for the $250 and interest on it, and to an order for the payment by the defendants of the costs of the action, and the usual order for foreclosure or sale, in default of payment.

G. A. B.

[CHANCERY DIVISION.]

RE THE DOMINION PROVIDENT BENEVOLENT AND ENDOWMENT ASSOCIATION.

Constitutional Law—Local Legislature—Powers of—Company—Insurance Act of Ontario—Powers of Master—Creditors' Schedules—Contributories' Schedules.

The Ontario Legislature has power to confer upon the Master the powers given by " The Insurance Corporations Act of 1892."

The Master has power under that Act to settle schedules of creditors, which implies power to adjudicate upon the claims of officials of a company for services to ascertain whether they shall appear as creditors in the schedules ; but he cannot adjudicate upon the question whether they have been guilty of such conduct as deprives them of their right to claim as creditors.

He has also power to settle schedules of contributories, but cannot adjudicate upon the question whether officials of the company have been guilty of such a breach of duty as to make them liable for any loss by reason thereof. Such matters can only be determined by action.

THIS was an appeal from a report of a local Master made under section 56 of the Insurance Corporations Act of 1892. *Statement.*

In answer to the usual advertisement for creditors, certain officials of the association, namely, directors, trustees, auditors, manager and secretary, sent in claims for directors' fees, and for alleged services rendered to the association, which the Master adjudicated upon and disallowed, as well as a gratuity of one hundred dollars granted to one of the directors (the president) by resolution ; such disallowance being based upon alleged neglect of various duties by said officials to the association.

The Master also found several of these officials indebted in various sums to the association for non-payment of dues and overdrawn accounts, and reported in favour of their being ordered to pay the amounts into Court, and found them guilty of misfeasance in their respective offices, and other matters.

From this report the officials reported against appealed, and the appeal was argued on April 17th, 1894, before ARMOUR, C. J.

W. D. McPherson, for Hessin, the President. The Master derives whatever authority he has under 55 Vict. ch. 39 (O.). The Ontario Legislature, while it may have power to deal with insurance companies, cannot make the Master a Judge. Even if the Act is *intra vires* he has assumed greater authority than the Act gives him.

[ARMOUR, C. J.—That has already been decided against the appellants' contention in *quo warranto* matters before the Master in Chambers : *Regina ex rel. McGuire* v. *Birkett*, 21 O. R. 162 ; and by the Queen's Bench Division, that the Local Legislature has power to appoint Division Court Judges : *In re Wilson* v. *McGuire*, 2 O. R. 118.]

The Dominion Government appoints the Judges in the High Court, who alone have jurisdiction in amounts involving more than $400.00 ; here our claim was over $16,000.00.

[ARMOUR, C. J.—If the Local Legislature has power to incorporate the association it has power to say what are the rights of the parties under the incorporation.]

The Local Legislature only has power to appoint the Judges when it has power over the jurisdiction : *In re Wilson* v. *McGuire*, 2 O. R. 118. *In re County Courts of British Columbia*, 21 S. C. R. 446, is distinguishable. In *Wilson* v. *McGuire* jurisdiction was given to properly appointed persons, here jurisdiction is taken from the Court and given to the appointee of the Lieutenant-Governor, and he is thus made a Superior Court Judge. The Provincial Legislature cannot do indirectly what it has no power to do directly. I refer also to *Gibson* v. *McDonald*, 7 O. R., at p. 419 ; *The Attorney-General for Quebec* v. *Queen Ins. Co.*, 1 Cart., at p. 151 ; *Leprohon* v. *The Corporation of the City of Ottawa*, 2 A. R. at p. 526 ; *Regina ex rel McGuire* v. *Birkett*, 21 O. R. 162, and to the report of the Minister of Justice for Canada on the 13th February, 1889, disallowing the "District Magistrates Bill," and the reasons therein referred to.

[ARMOUR, C. J.—I think there is nothing in the objection on the constitutional question that the Local Legisla-

ture has exceeded its authority in passing the Insurance
Corporations Act of 1892. The logical conclusion from the
judgments already given is that that is decided. If that
Legislature has power to incorporate, it has power to deal
with rights acquired under the incorporation.]

The Master has dealt here with rights not acquired under
the incorporation. Again, the Act provides (sec. 9, sub-
sec. 4), that a notice of the granting of the certificate of
the registrar of friendly societies shall be filed with the
Master. The report here sets out that a copy of the certificate was filed. Nothing signed by the registrar has
been filed. The Act has not been complied with ; the proceedings are not properly instituted.

[ARMOUR, C. J.—I think a certificate is a notice.]

What was filed here is not a certificate, but a copy.
Then section 56 of the Act particularizes the Master's
duties and jurisdiction which he has exceeded. He should
not have disallowed the directors' fees and the bonus voted
to the president, and had no right to direct payment into
Court of the amounts found due. Hessin was not notified
to defend himself on a charge of misfeasance, and there is
no evidence of dereliction of duty.

[ARMOUR, C. J.—Does an appeal lie from the report of
the Master in this matter ?]

Yes, by sec. 56, sub-secs. 5 and 6. See also Con. Rules
848-850 ; *Chennell* v. *Martin*, 4 Sim., at p. 344, *per* Chad-
dell, V. C.; and *Ford* v. *Mason*, 16 P. R. 25. The Act gives
the Master extraordinary powers and authority, and should
be strictly construed.

E. Sydney Smith, Q.C., for Barnsdale, the manager, and
Robertson, the treasurer. The Master can settle the
schedules of contributories, but he has gone beyond that.
He has found the directors guilty of misfeasance in office,
and that without calling on them to answer such a charge.
Actions must be brought to decide what he has decided.
I refer to *In re Royal Hotel Company of Great Yar-
mouth*, L. R. 4. Eq. 244 ; *In re East of England Bank*, L.
R. 1 Eq. 219 ; *Overend Gurney & Co.* v. *Gurney*, 4 Ch.

701; *In re Imperial Land Company of Marseilles*, L. R. 10 Eq. 298.

J. M. Clark, for Baker, a director, referred to *In re The Ontario Express and Transportation Co.*, 24 O. R. 216; *Painter* v. *Liverpool Oil Gas Light Co.*, 3 Ad. & E. 433; *The Bewdley Case*, 1 O. M. & H. 174, at p. 176; *In re Hoylake R. W. Co.*, 9 Ch. 257; and, as to the necessity of bringing an action, to: *In re The Central Bank of Canada, York's Case*, 15 O. R. 625; *In re Hoylake R. W. Co., Ex p. Littledale*, L. R. 9 Ch. 257; *Bickford* v. *The Grand Junction R. W. Co.*, 1 S. C. R. 696; *McDougall* v. *Lindsay Paper Mill Co.*, 10 P. R. 247; Holmested & Langton, p. 158.

T. H. Loscombe for other members of the executive council.

J. P. Mabee for the certificate holders.

G. G. McPherson for M. C. Moderwell and J. A. McFadden, appointed receivers, supported the report.

Idington, Q.C., for the infants. No one had authority to release the infants' rights.

Smith, Q.C., in reply. There is an adjudication upon the liability in the report, and so an unauthorized assumption of jurisdiction which must be appealed against.

August 29th, 1894. ARMOUR, C. J.:

The question raised upon the appeal in this matter of the power of the Local Legislature to confer upon the Master the powers conferred upon him by the Insurance Corporations Act, 1892, was disposed of by me upon the argument against the appellants' contention.

The principal other question raised by the appeal involved the question of the jurisdiction of the Master under the powers so conferred to adjudicate as he did in his report made herein.

And as to this question, I am of the opinion that the Master exceeded his jurisdiction.

The Master had power to " settle schedules of creditors," and this implied the power to adjudicate upon the claims of creditors in order to ascertain whether they ought to appear as creditors in the schedules so settled, but I do not think he was empowered to adjudicate upon the question whether the directors had been guilty of such neglect of duty as deprived them of their right to claim as creditors, nor do I think that he was empowered to adjudicate upon the right of Hessin to the grant made to him of $100.

The Master had also power to "settle the schedules of contributories," but I do not think that the persons adjudicated by the Master to be liable to pay were "contributories" in the sense of that term as used in the statute : *In re The Central Bank of Canada, Yorke's Case*, 15 O. R. 625.

But whether they could be held to come within that term or not, I do not think that the Master was empowered to adjudicate upon the question whether they had been guilty of such a breach of duty as made them liable for any loss by reason of their breach of duty.

I do not think that he had power to adjudicate upon any matter which involved the determination of the question whether the appellants, as officers of the corporation, had been guilty of a breach of their duty as such officers.

I think that all such matters could only be determined in an action brought in respect of such matters.

Nor do I think that he had the power to adjudicate upon the question of the indebtedness of the officers of the corporation to the corporation under the circumstances under which it is alleged that such indebtedness arose, nor as to the liability of any such officers for any such alleged indebtedness as was held to have arisen under the circumstances appearing in the evidence.

In the result, my judgment is that clauses 19, 20 and 21 of the report cannot be interfered with, but that all other clauses of the report imposing any liability upon the appellants, or any of them, by reason of any neglect or breach of duty, of them, or any of them, or holding them liable for any alleged indebtedness were beyond the powers

of the Master, and that such liability and indebtedness
could only be established in an action brought for that
purpose.

Such an action the Master has power to direct the
bringing of under the power conferred upon him to " direct
the realization of assets."

I refer as to the limitation of the powers of the Master
to *Bickford* v. *The Grand Junction R. W. Co.*, 1 S. C. R.
696; *McDougall* v. *Lindsay Paper Mill Co.*, 10 P. R.
247.

The proper course for me, therefore, will be to stay all
proceedings upon the report except upon clauses 19, 20 and
21, as if the motion had been for prohibition.

The Master was within his powers in taking the examination of the witnesses in order to ascertain the assets of
the corporation, and only exceeded his powers when he
came to adjudicate upon the evidence.

No objection was taken before the Master as to his
jurisdiction to adjudicate as he did, and was first taken in
the notice of appeal.

The appellants will have no costs; but the infants,
members and certificate holders will have their costs out of
the estate.

G. A. B.

[CHANCERY DIVISION.]

RE MOBERLY V. THE CORPORATION OF THE TOWN OF COLLINGWOOD.

Prohibition—Division Court—Jurisdiction—Rent—Incorporeal Heredita-
ment—Title to.

The bare assertion of the defendant in a Division Court action that the
right or title to any corporeal or incorporeal hereditament comes in
question under R. S. O. ch. 51, sec. 69, sub-sec. 4, is not sufficient to
oust the jurisdiction of that Court. The Judge has authority to enquire
into so much of the case as is necessary to satisfy himself on the point,
and if there are disputed facts or a question as to the proper inference
from undisputed facts that is enough to raise the question of title. If
the facts can lead to only one conclusion, and that against the defendant, then there is no such *bond fide* dispute as to title as will oust the
jurisdiction of the Court.
In an action in a Division Court for rent on a covenant in a lease, in
which it was contended that the lease had been surrendered, prohibition
was refused (MEREDITH, J., dissenting, on the ground that a *bond
fide* defence against the plaintiff's right to any rent due under the lease
was raised).
Decision of ARMOUR, C. J., affirmed.

APPEAL by the defendants from an order of ARMOUR, Statement.
C. J., refusing prohibition to a Division Court Judge, in an
action in which Moberly and Gamon were plaintiffs, and the
corporation of the town of Collingwood were defendants.

The plaintiffs were suing for rent on a covenant in a
lease, and the defendants set up, under R. S. O. ch. 51, sec.
69, sub-sec. 4, that the title to an incorporeal hereditament
came in question; they contending that the lease had
been, in effect, surrendered : and that the plaintiffs had sold
portions of the reversion.

The appeal was argued on June 12, 1894, before the
Divisional Court, composed of BOYD, C., FERGUSON and
MEREDITH, JJ.

W. H. P. Clement, for the appeal. The question in dispute is the title to the rent, an incorporeal hereditament.
The learned Chief Justice so thought, but considered he
was bound by *Talbot* v. *Poole,* 15 P. R. 99. That the

Argument. defendants are setting up the defence in question in good faith is not questioned. The Division Court has no jurisdiction, and that question being raised cannot be tried there: R. S. O. ch. 51, sec. 69, sub-sec. 4; *Mountnoy* v. *Collier*, 1 E. & B. 631; *Adey* v. *The Deputy Masters of Trinity House*, 22 L. J. Q. B. 3; Bicknell and Seager's D. C. Act, vol. 1, p. 68.

Bicknell, contra. Rent may be an incorporeal hereditament, but it is not so in this case. The plaintiffs are suing for a certain sum of money on a covenant to pay it. Even if it is an incorporeal hereditament, the right or title to it cannot be disputed when the only question is, was the lease surrendered: *In re English* v. *Mulholland*, 9 P. R. 145. The plaintiffs would willingly accept a surrender, and not having got that, must be entitled to the rent. I refer to Woodfall's Landlord and Tenant, 14th ed., 322; *Re Crawford* v. *Seney*, 17 O. R. 74; *The Colonial Bank of Australasia* v. *Willan*, L. R. 5 P. C. 417; *Re Whitling* v. *Sharples*, 9 C. L. T. Occ. N. 141.

Clement, in reply.

October 13, 1894. BOYD, C.:—

The affidavit on which this motion is based has two passages interlined which state, (1) that the plaintiffs had parted with the reversion in the land, and (2) that Moberly and Gamon had sold portions of the said land since the lease from them to the corporation of Collingwood.

In answer, it is said that the defendants have never parted with the said lease, and, although a small portion of the land has been sold, the lease has not in any way been assigned or parted with, nor have the purchasers in any way attempted to claim the rent.

The first assertion, that the plaintiffs had parted with the reversion, is not proved, nor does it mean more, I suppose, than what is secondly stated, that by selling part of the land leased the reversion has been severed.

But the evidence does not shew more than a sale, which
may or may not have been carried out by a conveyance, and
as to which, till there is a conveyance, there is no severance
of the reversion and no apportionment of the rent. It is
only when the lessor grants away part of his reversion,
that an apportionment of the rent follows, as incident to
the part granted : Foa's Law of Landlord and Tenant, pp.
105, 335.

On the other question raised, that title is in question
because of certain dealings whereby the lease was to be
surrendered, I see no objection to the judgment now in
appeal. The question of surrender or no surrender did not
turn on disputed facts; the lease still exists and has not
been surrendered, because the defendants have not been
able to procure the assent to the surrender of sub-lessees
to whom they demised the premises.

The word "title" in the County Court Acts (the original
of our clause excluding the jurisdiction of Division Courts
where the right or title to any hereditament comes in
question) has been interpreted to include not only the right
to what exists, but also the question of its existence :
The Queen v. *Everett*, 1 E. & B. 273. In that case Wightman,
J., said : "The question involves the very existence of one
of the tolls claimed, and so involves the title of the trustees
to that toll," p. 279.

Here the rent is said to be non-existent because of the
dealings, which amount to a surrender of the term. That
would be enough to raise the question of title, if there are
disputed facts or a question as to the proper inference
from undisputed facts; but if the facts can lead to only
one conclusion, and if the inference can be only in one
way, and that against the defendants, then it does not
appear that there is such a *bonâ fide* dispute respecting
title as will oust the jurisdiction of the lower Court.

When the Judge is satisfied that the question of title is
bonâ fide raised, he should stop the cause and go no further :
Mountnoy v. *Collier*, 1 E. & B. at p. 638. The question of
title must be really and *bonâ fide* in question : *Latham* v.

Judgment.
Boyd, C.

Spedding, 17 Q. B. at p. 444. And the evidence must be
such as would be proper to submit to a jury: see *per*
Williams, J., in *Emery* v. *Barnett,* 4 C. B. N. S. at p. 430.
To warrant prohibition it must be shewn that the Judge
below disposed of a question of title, and not merely that
a claim of title was made before him: *per* Willes, J., *ib.,*
at p. 432.

If the facts are all one way, the better view appears to
be that the Division Court should not be interfered with,
though there is a case intimating that jurisdiction ceases if
there is a real dispute, even if the Judge is satisfied that
the defendants' evidence is insufficient, or not *bonâ fide:*
In re Marsh v. *Dewes,* 17 Jur. 558.

Here the defendants' own act in assigning the leasehold
to the dock company, and so putting it out of their power
to re-assign or to comply with the judgment of the Court,
is against their setting up that the title of the landlord has
ended by surrender. In brief, there was no evidence
before the Judge below to establish that there had been a
surrender, and so there was no dispute of title.

In this case in the Division Court there are no pleadings, and the undisputed facts brought before the Judge
are set forth in the affidavit of Mr. Birnie. That does not
touch on the matter of possession, and we cannot import
into the appeal what may appear in the pleadings of the
action in the Chancery Division.

I am content to leave the matter upon the grounds so
fully and clearly stated by Wightman, J., in *Lilley* v. *Harvey,* 5 D. & L. 648, in cases where, as here, there are no
pleadings or the pleadings do not raise the issue of title.
He goes through all the facts and says, "It appeared upon
these facts clear that the defendant had no ground for
bringing the title into question, and that it was not really
in question in the case": p. 653. He says again: "The
Judge must be satisfied that it is in question; and for that
purpose must have authority to inquire into so much of
the case as is necessary to satisfy him upon that point":
p. 653.

The Court also, I think, should not be solicitous to
reduce the jurisdiction of the lower Courts in reference to
the collection of small sums of money.

There is no ground for prohibition, because the question
as to this liability also arises in an action pending in the
High Court. That might be a reason for staying proceedings, or for an application in the Court above.

The application fails, and the appeal should be dismissed
and with costs.

FERGUSON, J. :—

This is an appeal from an order made by the Chief
Justice of the Queen's Bench, refusing an application for a
writ of prohibition.

The action in the Division Court is upon a covenant for
the payment of rent contained in an indenture of lease,
the amount claimed by the plaintiffs being in the neighbourhood of $20.

The contention of the appellants is that in the Division
Court the title to land came in question; and that by
reason of the provisions of sub-section 4, of section 69, of
chapter 51, R. S. O., that Court had no jurisdiction.

The defendants in the Division Court, as it appears,
sought to say that there had been a surrender of the lease
containing the covenant sued on, and that thus a matter
of right or title to a hereditament came in question.

The evidence does not, as I think, disclose anything to
make the question different from the plain and simple
question as to whether or not a lease of land, produced in
Court, had been surrendered.

It was contended that this alone brought the title to
land into question. In a certain sense this may be so ; but
the further question necessarily arises here, which is this :
Should the Judge presiding in the Division Court decline
to proceed with the case before him, on the ground that he
has not jurisdiction, because the defendant has asserted that
a certain lease of land has been surrendered, and that for

Judgment.
─────
Ferguson, J. this reason title to land is in question in the case ?   If such is the course that the Judge is bound to adopt, it is, as I think, plain, that there are many cases in which the jurisdiction of the Court would be ousted by the bare assertion of the defendant.   Such is not, I think, the course to be adopted by the Judge.

Where, as in this case, there are no special pleadings raising a question of title, the Judge must be satisfied that the title to corporeal or incorporeal hereditaments is in question, and, as said by Wightman, J., in *Lilley* v. *Harvey*, 5 D. & L., at p. 653, for that purpose has authority to inquire into so much of the case as is necessary to satisfy him upon that point.

Assuming this to be so, then, in the present case, it is difficult, as I think, to see that the learned Judge in the Division Court was wrong, or acting in excess of his jurisdiction or without jurisdiction, in entertaining the inquiry as to whether or not the lease had been surrendered, as asserted by the defendants.   He must, as it appears to me, either do this, or act upon the assertion of the defendants alone.   It seems not to differ the case where the assertion is made upon oath.   Then if, entertaining the inquiry, the Judge finds that the lease has not been surrendered, he properly proceeds, so far as this objection has concern, with the trial of the case.

It was also asserted by the defendants in the Division Court that there had been a severance of the reversion, so that there was, as a matter of law, an apportionment of rent, or, at least, the right to an apportionment thereof, and that, for this reason, the plaintiff was not entitled to recover the whole, if any, of the rent sued for, and that the title to land, or at least to an incorporeal hereditament, came in question, and the Court had not jurisdiction.

I think I need not here state the manner in which a severance of a reversion takes place, or the rights that arise upon a severance of a reversion.   See however, Woodfall's Landlord and Tenant, 13th ed., 255; R. S. O. ch. 143, secs. 2 to 8 inclusive; Foa's Law of Landlord and Tenant, pp. 105, 335.

As to the contention based upon this assertion, I may
apply also the language of Wightman, J., referred to above,
which seems supported by the words of Sir John Coleridge,
in 1 E. & B. at p. 638.   The learned Judge was called
upon to satisfy himself that the title to the incorporeal
hereditament did come in question (was in question before
him), and for that purpose had authority to inquire into
so much of the case as was necessary to satisfy him upon
that point, otherwise he would be driven to act upon the
bare assertion of the defendants.

The learned Judge sitting in the Division Court had, as
I think, authority and jurisdiction to entertain the inquiry
as to whether or not there had been a severance of the
reversion, in order to ascertain whether or not title to the
incorporeal hereditament (the rent) was really in question
before him.   The result indicates that he must have found
and determined that it was not, and, assuming that it was
not, he was, so far as this assertion and contention have
concern, justified in proceeding with the case.

I have perused the pleadings in the action in the High
Court (which were put in and used upon this application),
as well as all the evidence.   It may not be necessary or
proper here to attempt to review the findings of the learned
Judge upon the inquiry entertained by him in order to
ascertain whether or not a matter of title, such as the ones
mentioned in the statute, really came in question before
him; but, assuming such a review to be proper here, then
I think it plain that no surrender of the lease containing
the covenant sued on was shewn.

It may well be that the plaintiffs in the Division Court
were entitled, as between them and the defendants, to
have such a surrender or a release; but, as shewn, these
defendants had, by assigning the unexpired term of the
lease, placed it out of their power to grant such a surrender,
and their assignee refused to grant one.

As to the alleged severance of the reversion, I am
of the opinion that such a severance has not been shewn
as would entitle a purchaser of part of the reversion

to claim and recover a part of the rent.   There has been
no legal apportionment of the rent, and it does not appear
that there has been any deed of transfer of any part of the
land; besides, the ninth clause of Mr. Moberly's affidavit
indicates that such bargains or sales of small portions as
may have been made, were subject to the rights of the
plaintiffs to claim and recover the rents from the defendants, notwithstanding such bargains or sales, and that no
one of such purchasers has ever made claim to any part of
the rents.

On the whole case, I am of the opinion that the learned
Chief Justice was right in refusing the order, and that this
appeal should be dismissed with costs.

MEREDITH, J.:—

The lease, under which the plaintiffs in the Division
Court suit claimed the rent, provides that, in certain
events, a portion of the property shall be " re-assigned " to
the lessors, and that the rent for the rest shall be $1 a
year only.

The defence there was that, under that provision and
otherwise, the plaintiffs had lost all right to any rent;
that the events provided for had substantially arisen; and
that the plaintiffs had taken possession of the portion
which was to be " re-assigned," and had sold part of it to
persons who had gone into possession; and that some new
agreement had been come to under which the plaintiffs
had conveyed absolutely, to the defendants' assignee of the
term, all their right and title to the rest of the demised
property.

Whatever one may think of the merits of the defence—
whatever one may, on the meagre evidence before us,
think of the defendants' chances of succeeding upon it—
there is no doubt that a *bond fide* defence against the
plaintiffs' right to any rent due, or to become due, under
the lease was raised—the pending action in the High Court
shews that—and that is enough to oust the jurisdiction of

the Division Court if that defence raises or involves the Judgment.
trial of "the right or title to any corporeal or incorporeal Meredith, J.
hereditament": The Division Courts Act, sec. 69, sub-sec.
4, R. S. O. ch. 51.

Even though we should think the learned Division
Court Judge clearly right in law and as to the facts upon
the merits of the case, yet we ought to prohibit, if the case
be one in which he had not jurisdiction; but, having
regard to the alleged taking of possession of one part, and
the alleged absolute conveyance of the other part, of the
demised property, I would be far from thinking that the
defendants cannot have a good defence, if that were a
material question here.

That the rent reserved in this lease is an incorporeal
hereditament is not disputed: *Hopkins* v. *Hopkins*, 3
O. R. 223. If the defendants succeed in their defence,
they must succeed because the plaintiffs' right to that rent
is gone; if they fail, the plaintiffs will succeed because of
a determination that the right to the rent has not been
ended or lost, but yet exists. It seems to me, therefore,
that the case is one in which the jurisdiction of the Division
Court is expressly excluded.

In re English v. *Mulholland*, 9 P. R. 145, was quite
a different case, and rather makes for than against
the appellants here. There, the right to the rent was
admitted, the defence was that the amount claimed had
been paid. By proving payment of rent the right and
title are admitted; a successful defence merely avoids payment a second time. It is only when the right or title to
the hereditament is involved that jurisdiction is ousted.
In this case it is the very right and title and nothing else—
the very existence of the term—that is in question; and
so there was no jurisdiction, and prohibition should have
gone.

Cases in which the existence of the right is not denied,
or in which by estoppel or otherwise, as a matter of law,
the defendant is absolutely precluded from denying the
right, the jurisdiction is not ousted: where the right can

be, and in good faith is, brought in question, there is no
jurisdiction, and it is not for us to consider the case upon
its merits; though it is right to bear in mind that the whole
rent reserved is involved; that though this suit is for a
paltry amount, the same question applies equally to all the
rest of the rent reserved, so that the judgment in this suit
would estop the parties upon this question in any suit for
subsequent rent: *In re South American and Mexican
Company—Ex p. Bank of England*, W. N. [1894] p. 147.*

In re Whitling v. *Sharples*, of which a note appears in
9 C. L. T. Occ. N. at p. 141, seems to me, like *In re
Mulholland* v. *English*, to have been rightly decided,
and on the same ground: *In re Crawford* v. *Seney*, 17
O. R. 74, is a case in which it was considered that by reason of estoppel no question of title could be raised, and in
which it was also considered that the question was not
raised in good faith; whilst *The Queen* v. *Everett* 1 E. &
B. 273, affords a good illustration of a case in which the
right or title does come in question, and in which, therefore,
jurisdiction is ousted. Bearing in mind the differences
which I have endeavoured to point out in the cases before
mentioned, all the cases to which we were referred, and
which I have been able to find, may, I think, be understood and reconciled.

But all parties against whom the order is sought have
not been served with notice of this motion; no order
should now go against them, but the motion should stand
over until the first day of the next sittings of this Court,
and meanwhile they should be served with such notice,
returnable then, so that they may have opportunity for
shewing cause against the order sought; if no cause be then
shewn, the order should go without costs; if cause be shewn,
the whole matter can be dealt with upon the further argument: there is no need for any order removing the action
into the High Court—if the recent legislation, 57 Vict.,
ch. 23, sec. 16 (O.), be wide enough to include this case—
for the whole matter can better be dealt with in the action
now pending there.

* Affirmed on appeal, *ib.* p. 184.

I have read the pleadings in the High Court action as part Judgment. of the evidence before us; they were so put in and appear Meredith, J. with the papers in the case, and were referred to in argument.

Leave to appeal was applied for and granted.—REP.

G. A. B.

[CHANCERY DIVISION.]

CRAWFORD ET AL. V. BRODDY ET AL.

Will—Devise—Conditional Fee—Executory Devise.

A testator by his will devised as follows:—"I give and bequeath to my son F. * * lot No. * * at the age of twenty-one years, giving the executors power to lift the rent and to rent, said executors paying F. all former rents due after my decease up to his attaining the age of twenty-one years.

*   *   *   *   *

At the death of any one of my sons or daughters having no issue their property to be divided equally among the survivors."
F. attained twenty-one and died unmarried and without issue:—
Held, a conditional fee, with an executory devise over.
Decision of FERGUSON, J., reversed.
Little v. *Billings,* 27 G. R. 353, distinguished.

APPEAL from a judgment of FERGUSON, J., in an action Statement. brought by Adeline Crawford and Margaret Harkley, two sisters of one Francis Nixon against Alexander Broddy and others, executors of one Adam Nixon, a deceased brother, to set aside a deed made by the said Francis Nixon in his lifetime, to the said Adam Nixon.

The action was tried at Walkerton on April 4th, 1894, before FERGUSON, J., without a jury.

T. Dixon, for the plaintiffs.
W. H. McFadden, for the defendants, Broddy and Ellis.
T. Blain, for the defendant Francis Nixon.

81—VOL. XXV. O.R.

Francis Nixon was devisee of the lands in question under the will of his father, and had made a conveyance to his brother, Adam Nixon.

The material parts of the will under which he claimed were as follows :

"Third. I give and bequeath to my son, Francis Nixon, lot   *   *   at the age of twenty-one years, giving the executors power to lift the rents and to rent, said executors paying Francis all former rents due after my decease up to his attaining the age of twenty-one years.

"Fourth.   *   *   .

"At the death of any one of my sons or daughters, having no issue, their property to be divided equally among the survivors."

The devisee, Francis, attained twenty-one years and died unmarried and without issue, leaving no brothers or sisters except the two plaintiffs.

They also sought to set aside the deed from Francis Nixon, on grounds of undue influence, improvidence, etc.

At the close of the case the following judgment was given :

FERGUSON, J. :—

Usually one has to reserve judgment in a case for the construction of a will for the reason that the law is sometimes very difficult to get at, and it is not easy to find one will so much like another that there is any guide afforded by any particular case as to the true construction of the will in hand.

I do not, however, think I am called upon to reserve this case for consideration, for if there was nothing before me but the will and my own knowledge and opinions of the laws of construction, I should entertain the view that an estate tail is given by this will : that is an estate tail is given to Francis Nixon in the land that is said to be only a half of the lot; although the whole lot is mentioned the will would only operate on the half. I would think, on

the face of the will, there is an estate tail by implication,
on the general law of construction, but further than that
the case does not appear to me to be distinguishable from
Little v. *Billings*, 27 Gr. 353.

I have seldom found, in endeavouring to construe a will,
a case so nearly in point as *Little* v. *Billings* is to this
case. It seems to me almost impossible to distinguish the
one from the other, and I am prepared to hold, and take
the responsibility of holding, that the meaning of the will
is in this respect, that Francis Nixon took an estate tail.

He then would be, so far as I can see, the tenant in tail
in possession ; that is, there would be no tenant between
him and the estate, and if a tenant in tail in possession
executes a conveyance of the land, it operates, as I understand the cases, as a disentailing assurance without the
intervention of the protector of any settlement.

If a tenant in tail who is not in possession should execute an ordinary conveyance of the land, it would not
operate as a disentailing assurance perhaps any further
than to create a base fee.   But here the tenant in tail was
in possession, and he made a conveyance of his estate, and
that disentailed and gave the title in fee to his transferee.
So, a transferee from Francis owns this land for such title
as the testator had—that is assuming that the deed made
by Francis to Adam is a good deed, but its validity is now
questioned.   If the testator had the title in fee, the transferee from Francis took the same, if the deed is good.   I
do not think I could get at it any more clearly by going
through the cases.

In *Little* v. *Billings, supra,* Mr. Justice Proudfoot seems
to have gone through a vast number of cases, and a very
excellent lawyer he was on such a subject as that.   My
own opinion, as it occurred to me, when the will was first
read, is that there is an estate tail by implication, and that
is fortified by that case.   I, therefore, decide that upon
the true construction of the will, Francis Nixon took an
estate tail by implication.

From this judgment the plaintiffs appealed to the Divisional Court, and the appeal was argued on June 8th, 1894, before BOYD, C., and MEREDITH, J.

J. C. Hamilton and *T. Dixon* for the appeal. The learned trial Judge was wrong in holding that Francis Nixon took an estate tail under the will. Francis Nixon died without issue and had no further interest after his decease. Under the terms of the will, the property was then to be divided among his brothers and sisters living at the time of his death without issue. The devise to Francis, with the gift over on his death without issue, was a gift of the fee with an executory devise over in the event of his death without issue: Hawkins on Wills, 2nd Am. ed., 211 : citing *Greenwood* v. *Verdon*, 1 K. & J. 74. There are no words to qualify the word "survivors." The time of the division is fixed, *viz.* : at the death of Francis. We refer also to *Re Chisholm*, 17 Gr. 403, reported as *Chisholm* v. *Emory* in 18 Gr. 467; *Coltsman* v. *Coltsman*, L. R. 3 H. L. 121; *Gray* v. *Richford*, 2 S. C. R. 431, at p. 466 ; 2 Jarman on Wills, 3rd ed. 80, 492, 679 ; *Doe d. King* v. *Frost*, 3 B. & Ald., 546 ; *Ashbridge* v. *Ashbridge*, 22 O. R. 146 ; *Travers* v. *Gustin*, 20 Gr. 106, *per* V. C. Strong, at p. 110. There are bequests of personalty to some legatees, of realty to others, and realty and personalty to others. The will does not shew two intentions, so the intention as to personalty will govern as to the realty. The words " at the death " shew whole intention. The class of persons to take is ascertained.

W. H. McFadden contra. This is not the case of a grant of an estate in fee with an executory devise over. It is a fee without a devise over: *Farrell* v. *Farrell*, 26 U. C. R. 652. The intention of the will as to dying without having issue applied before the devisee became twenty-one. When he became twenty-one the property vested : *Gould* v. *Stokes*, 26 Gr. 122 ; *Griffith* v. *Griffith*, 29 Gr. 145. If it did not vest as a fee simple it did as a fee tail, and this case is the same as *Little* v. *Billings*, 27 Gr. 353. If it was an estate

tail the deed is valid. The rule is, where real estate is
devised by way of executed trust for a person and his
issue, the word " issue " will be construed a word of limitation and confer an estate tail: *Gray* v. *Richford*, 2 S. C.
R. at p. 446. The law that it is an estate in fee simple
with a devise over, decided in *Ashbridge* v. *Ashbridge*, 22
O. R. 146, was dissented from by STREET, J., in *Nason* v.
Armstrong, 22 O. R. 542.

T. J. Blain, on same side. The intention is shewn in
the form of the will. The clause under which Francis
takes, is nearly identical with the absolute devise to his
brother Adam. When Francis became twenty-one the
estate vested: *Cook* v. *Noble*, 5 O. R. 43. Only one con-
tingency happened: *Griffith* v. *Griffith*, 29 Gr. 145. A certain devise in a will cannot be cut down by a subsequent
uncertain clause: *Meyers* v. *The Hamilton Provident &
Loan Co.*, 19 O. R. at p. 365.

October 13, 1894. BOYD, C. :—

This will does not contain the phrase " die without issue,"
which, in early wills before the Act, has, standing alone,
a technical meaning indicating an indefinite failure of issue.
Here I read a restriction in time to the date of the death
of the first taker at which point, if he has or leaves no
issue, the estate goes over.

These are the words : " At the death of any one or more
of my sons or daughters, having no issue, their property to
be divided equally among the survivors."

The division among the survivors is to take place at the
death of any of the sons or daughters (having no issue).
If no issue at the death, then division : and the term " survivors " means, I think, a personal benefit contemplated to
those sons or daughters who outlive the one dying without
issue living at his death.

In *Little* v. *Billings*, 27 Gr. 353, the survivors were those
living at the testator's death—here it is those who are alive
at the death of the childless devisee : and in that case the
failure of issue was not limited to a particular time by the

Judgment.

Boyd, C.

context, as in this case, by the words "at the death," etc. :
Doe d. King v. *Frost,* 3 B. & Ald. 546 ; Jarman, 5th ed., p.
1332.

The better construction I take to be a conditional fee with
executory devise of the fee to the survivors upon the death
of Francis, the devisee, issueless.   Nothing, therefore,
passed by the conveyance of Francis except this estate
which terminated at his death.

Judgment should be reversed and entered in favour of
the plaintiffs with a reference as to defendants' improvements as under mistake of title.

MEREDITH, J. :—

The words in question are " at the death of any one or
more of my sons or daughters having no issue, their property to be divided equally among the survivors."

There are bequests of pecuniary legacies only, to the
daughters and to one son ; devises in fee to the other two
sons ; the words quoted must refer to both the bequests
and the devises.

And they, in my opinion, point with sufficient clearness
to a division, " at the death " of the legatee or devisee,
among the then surviving brothers and sisters, to warrant,
in reason and upon authority, the taking of the case out of
the old rule that words referring to the death of a person
without issue must be construed as importing *primâ facie*
an indefinite failure of issue : see *Coltsman* v. *Coltsman,*
L. R. 3 H. L. 121, and cases there referred to, and *Greenwood*
v. *Verdon,* 1 K. & J. 74.

And I am also of opinion that sufficient was shewn in
the plaintiffs' case at the trial, of the improvidence of the
impeached transaction, to throw the onus of supporting it
upon the defendants.

But upon the question of construction of the will the
plaintiffs succeed, and there is no need for recourse to the
other branch of the case.

                                                    G. A. B.

[CHANCERY DIVISION.]

HENDERSON v. THE BANK OF HAMILTON.

*Banks and Banking—Special Deposit—Wrongful Refusal to Pay Out—
Action—Damages—Costs.*

The damages recoverable by a non-trading depositor in the savings bank
department of a bank who has made his deposit subject to special
terms, on the wrongful refusal of the bank to pay it to him personally,
are limited to the interest on the money.
Marzetti v. *Williams*, 1 B. & Ad. 415; and *Rolin* v. *Steward*, 14 C. B.
594, distinguished.
A bank having received a deposit subject to certain notice of withdrawal,
if required, cannot set up as a defence to an action for the deposit the
absence of such notice, unless the refusal to pay was based on that
ground.
The defendants having paid into Court twenty cents less than the correct
amount due by them, the plaintiff was held entitled to full costs.

THIS was an action against the defendants to recover Statement.
money on deposit, and for damages under the circumstances
set out in the judgment.

The action was tried before STREET, J., without a jury,
at Stratford, on October 2nd, 1894.

Mabee, for the plaintiff, referred to Byles on Bills, 15th
ed., pp. 19-20; *Kymer* v. *Laurie,* 18 L. J. Q. B. 218; *Rolin*
v. *Steward,* 14 C. B. 595; *Robinson* v. *Marchant,* 7 Q. B.
918; *Martin* v. *Rocke Eyton & Co.,* 34 W. R. 253.

Idington, Q. C., for the defendants, referred as to costs
to *Tobin* v. *McGillis,* 12 P. R. at p. 60, note.

October 25th, 1894.   STREET, J. :—

This action was tried before me without a jury at the
Stratford Autumn Assizes on October 2nd, 1894.

The plaintiff is a clergyman living at Atwood; the defendants are a chartered bank having a branch office at
Listowel, at which they received deposits in what was
termed their saving's bank department, as well as ordinary
deposits. On December 20th, 1893, the plaintiff had at his
credit in respect of deposits in the saving's bank depart-

ment of the defendants the sum of $657.34, all of which was subject to certain special terms, amongst which were the following : " The bank will receive on deposit sums from one dollar and upwards, and pay interest thereon from date of deposit to date of withdrawal. All withdrawals must be made personally, or by order in writing, duly authenticated when the signature is not known to the bank, and must be accompanied by the bank book."

" The bank reserves the right to require fifteen days' notice when all or any portion of a deposit is withdrawn."

On December 20th, 1893, the plaintiff personally applied to the defendants' manager to withdraw $100 of the moneys at his credit. The manager refused, upon instructions from the head office, to allow any part of the money to be withdrawn, claiming a lien upon it for some costs of a litigation then in progress between the plaintiff and the bank in connection with another matter. The plaintiff required the $100 in order that he might lend it to a third person, and he so informed the manager at the time. Failing to get it from the manager he took a train to a brother of his living at Blyth, and paid $1.10 railway fare, and procured the amount. He made a further demand on the bank for the $100 on December 27th, when it was paid to him. The plaintiff on January 4th, 1894, demanded the remainder of his money, and was refused, the bank claiming to be entitled to hold it as security for the costs above mentioned, and this action was brought on January 8th, 1894, to recover it. In it the plaintiff claims his money and damages for the trouble, loss and disgrace to which he alleges he has been put by the defendants' refusal to pay him his money. After the commencement of the action, namely, on February 3rd, 1894, the plaintiff gave the defendants an order on his account for $236.96, being the amount at which certain costs payable to them by him had been taxed, and on the same day he gave security for $235.54, the amount of certain other costs which had been taxed against him on January 9th, 1894, pending an appeal by him to the Court of Appeal.

On February 12th, 1894, the defendants filed their statement of defence, setting up the terms of the deposit, and brought into Court $322.21 as being the balance of the deposit account, with interest to date, and $3.66 for other damages, and offered to pay the plaintiff's costs. The plaintiff joined issue, and replied that the defendants never put their refusal to pay the money upon the ground that they were entitled to notice, nor did they notify the plaintiff that they would require the notice, and that in any event more than fifteen days had elapsed between the first demand and the issuing of the writ.

The plaintiff in this action is a clergyman, and not a trader; his account was not the ordinary current account with the bank, but was founded upon deposits made upon the special terms that the plaintiff should receive interest upon them, and should not be entitled to withdraw them upon demand, but only upon fifteen days' notice, if the bank should require such notice; and the withdrawals were to be either in person or by written order, accompanied by the bank book; and finally, the plaintiff made his demand for the money in person, and not by a written order to some other person. All these circumstances distinguish the present case from the cases of *Marzetti* v. *Williams*, 1 B. & Ad. 415, and *Rolin* v. *Steward*, 14 C. B. 594, and withdraw it from the principles acted upon in the latter case.

A trader who gives a cheque to his creditor upon a bank at which he has funds, is almost necessarily injured in his credit by the dishonour of the cheque, for it is a slur upon it of a similar character to that which is caused by the utterance of a slander throwing doubt upon his solvency. In both cases he is allowed to recover substantial damages without proving any special damage. But a clergyman or other non-trader who has opened a savings bank account with a bank, and who goes to withdraw a part of it, is put, by the refusal of the banker, to no greater or other loss than is experienced by any ordinary creditor of any ordinary debtor when the debtor answers the creditor's

demand by saying that he cannot or he will not pay. The
damages in the one case as in the other must be limited to
the interest on the money: *Fletcher* v. *Tayleur*, 17 C. B.
21 ; *Mennie* v. *Leitch*, 8 O. R. 397.

The defendants, however, admittedly had in their hands
on January 4th, 1894, when the plaintiff demanded it,
a sum of $320.38 beyond the $236.96 at which the defendant's costs of appeal in the other action had been taxed.
It is true that they had judgment against the plaintiff for
a further sum for costs in the Divisional Court which had
not at that time been taxed, but they had no right at the
time to set off these costs against the plaintiff's demand,
because the amount had not then been ascertained, and
they had no right at the time of the trial to set them off
because payment of them had after taxation been suspended by the giving of security in the Court of Appeal for
their payment. The plaintiff then when he made his
demand, when he issued his writ, and when the action
came on for trial, was entitled to payment of this $320.38,
with interest from the time of his demand on January 4th,
1894. The defendants might, upon his making his demand,
have required fifteen days' notice, but they did not do so—
their refusal to pay was put upon other grounds, and as
they have only reserved in their conditions a right to
require it, which they have not exercised, they are in the
same position as if they had reserved no such right. At
the date when the defendants paid into Court $322.21,
namely, on February 12th, 1894, as being in full satisfaction of the plaintiff's deposit and interest, he was entitled
to $320.38, with interest from January 4th, 1894, at 6 per
cent., that is thirty-nine days, and the interest would
amount to $2.05, making the plaintiff's proper claim
$322.43, or 22c. more than the amount paid in. The
plaintiff did not take out the amount, but went on with
his action. Both parties are standing on their strict rights,
and the defendants cannot complain if the plaintiff has
refused to take an offer which is a tittle less than he was
entitled to recover.

I think the plaintiff should recover $320.38, with interest from January 4th, 1894, and his costs of an action to recover that sum, and that the claim to unliquidated damages should be dismissed with costs, which are to be set off. Money in Court to be applied *pro tanto* in payment of plaintiff's claim.

Judgment.

Street, J.

A. H. F. L.

[COMMON PLEAS DIVISION.]

REGINA V. DEFRIES.

REGINA V. TAMBLYN.

Habeas Corpus — Warrant Issued in Quebec—Conspiracy — Locality of Offence—Affidavit Evidence—R. S. O. ch. 70, secs. 4 and 5—Criminal Code secs. 394 and 752.

A Judge cannot upon the return to a *habeas corpus*, where a warrant shews jurisdiction, try on affidavit evidence the question where the alleged offence was committed.

Sections 4 and 5, R. S. O. ch. 70 are not intended to apply to criminal cases where no preliminary examination has taken place.

Section 752 of the Criminal Code, 55-56 Vict. ch. 29 (D.), only applies where the Court or Judge making the direction as to further proceedings and enquiries mentioned therein has power to enforce it, and a Court or Judge in Ontario has no power over a Judge or Justice in Quebec to compel him to "take any proceedings or hear such evidence," etc.

It is a crime under section 394 of the Code to conspire by any fraudulent means to defraud any person, and so a conspiracy to permit persons to travel free on a railroad as alleged in these cases would be a conspiracy against the railway company.

THIS was a motion to discharge two prisoners in the above cases on the returns to writs of *habeas corpus* or for a direction for enquiries under R. S. O. ch. 70, sec. 4, or section 752 of the Criminal Code under the circumstances set out in the judgment.

Statement.

The motion was argued in Court on October 2nd, 1894, before MACMAHON, J.

Argument.] *E. B. F. Johnston*, Q.C., for the motion. An enquiry should be directed under section 752 of the Criminal Code to ascertain the jurisdiction. The return does not shew where the offence was committed. [*McCarthy*, Q.C., who appeared for the Crown. That is merely a clerical error; the return should be amended as the warrant correctly shews it.] The warrant may, on its face, state that the offence was committed in Montreal, but that is only *primâ facie* evidence that such allegation is true, and it is not irrebuttable, and it may be shewn to be not true by evidence outside the proceedings appearing on record. The prisoners are entitled to go behind the warrant under R. S. O. ch. 70, sec. 4, and section 752 of the Code, otherwise those sections would be useless. To displace the warrant the prisoners shew by affidavits they have not been in Montreal, or had any communication with that place for a long time, and cannot be connected with any conspiracy in that city. That fact warrants an enquiry being directed under the statutes. It is more than a question of mere jurisdiction. It involves the question whether on the mere production of Quebec warrants, Ontario residents in such a case can be sent to Quebec for trial without testing the legality of the proceedings. There was no offence committed there by the defendants on the facts as they appear, even admitting there was an offence committed at all. Even if there was communication, the conspiracy, if any, was not in Montreal, but must have taken place in Kingston. The affidavits displace the warrants. The real question is, can the Court, on a return to a writ of *habeas corpus*, enquire into the legality of the warrant on the point of jurisdiction as to the offence alleged? It is submitted this may be done, otherwise there is no redress for persons arrested on false warrants, or warrants issued wholly without jurisdiction.

W. Mortimer Clark, Q.C., with him. The warrants shew no offence within the Code. Permitting persons to pass free on a railroad is not an indictable offence.

McCarthy, Q.C., contra. The return should be amended:

Re Leonard Watson, 9 A. & E. 731. [MacMahon, J.—I ^{Argument.} think I must allow the returns to be amended to conform to the warrants.]

McCarthy. The prisoners were arrested on warrants of competent authority properly backed, which shew on their face criminal offences. There is an offence here: Code, section 394. The only possible enquiry would be, is the information properly recited in the warrant? Section 554, sub-sec. (*b*) of the Code gives the magistrate jurisdiction. The offence is a conspiracy to defraud the Grand Trunk Railway Company. If the magistrate had no power to try the offence proved he would send the prisoner before a tribunal which had. Any one may lay the information. Section 558 provides for the information. Section 559 provides for the warrant. Section 562 for a summons before the proper magistrate. This is not a question of jurisdiction. It is merely a question of whether there is an information disclosing an indictable offence. There is no jurisdiction here to try that. The English Act 56 Geo. 3, ch. 100, referred to in Short & Mellor's Crown Practice at p. 359, is not applicable to criminal offences. The truth of a return in a criminal case cannot be questioned: 2 Burn's Justices, 945. The affidavits filed should not be read: Short & Mellor, 361. The Ontario statute R. S. O. ch. 70, does not apply to criminal matters.

Johnston, Q.C. After the amendment allowed, the Court cannot, of course, be asked to discharge the prisoners, but should direct the enquiry.

October 3, 1894. MacMahon, J.:—

In the above cases writs of *habeas corpus* had issued directed to Adolphe Bissonnette, high constable in and for the district of Montreal, and Eugene P. Flynn, special constable for the Province of Quebec, commanding them to bring up the bodies of Frederick Tamblyn and Samuel Henry Defries, detained in their custody.

On the 2nd day of October the said constables made the

following return in the case of the said Samuel Henry
Defries " We, Adolphe Bissonnette, high constable in and
for the district of Montreal, in the Province of Quebec, and
Eugene P. Flynn, special constable for the Province of
Quebec, in obedience to the writ herewith, do certify and
return that before the said writ came to us, that is to say,
on Monday, the 1st day of October, 1894, Samuel Henry
Defries, in the said writ named, was taken, and in the
police station for the city of Toronto, and under our custody is detained by virtue of a warrant issued under the
hand and seal of Mathias C. Desnoyers, Esquire, one of the
Judges of the Sessions of the Peace for the city of Montreal, in the Province of Quebec, having jurisdiction as a
magistrate or justice of the peace in and for the said Province of Quebec. Whereby we, as and being constables
and peace officers in the district of Montreal aforesaid,
were commanded in Her Majesty's name forthwith to
apprehend the said Samuel Henry Defries and others, and
to bring them before the said Mathias C. Desnoyers, or
some of Her Majesty's justices of the peace in and for the
said district, to answer a certain charge which had on the
28th day of September, in the year of Our Lord one thousand eight hundred and ninety-four, been made upon oath
before the said Mathias C. Desnoyers, Esquire, Judge of
the Sessions of the Peace, acting in and for the district of
Montreal, to wit : that the said Samuel Defries and one
John Mulligan, one John Stone, one William Lewis and
one Frederick Tamblyn did, on or about the 9th day of
August, 1894, at the city of Montreal, conspire, combine,
confederate and agree together to defraud and injure the
Grand Trunk Railway Company of Canada by allowing
certain persons to ride upon some parts of the railroads of
said company without paying their fares against the form
of the statute in such case made and provided, and the said
warrant was indorsed by Hugh Miller, a justice of the
peace in and for the city of Toronto, in the county of York
and Province of Ontario, as follows :

" Canada, Province of Ontario, city of Toronto—To wit :
Whereas, proof upon oath has this day been made before

me, one of Her Majesty's justices of the peace in and for the
said city, that the name of M. C. Desnoyers to the within
warrant subscribed is of the handwriting of the justice of
the peace within mentioned, I do, therefore, authorize
Adolphe Bissonnette, who bringeth me this warrant, and
all other persons to whom this warrant was originally
directed, or by whom the same may be lawfully executed,
and also all constables and other peace officers in the said
city to execute the same within the said city.

"Given under my hand this 1st day of October, in the
year of Our Lord one thousand eight hundred and ninety-
four.

(Sgd.)   " HUGH MILLER, J.P."

A similar return was made to the writ obtained in Frederick Tamblyn's case.

Upon the return being filed, counsel for the respective
prisoners moved for their discharge.

I permitted the return to be amended so as to correctly
recite the warrant, which alleged that the conspiracy took
place in the city of Montreal.

Counsel admitted that the warrant on its face shewed
jurisdiction, but contended that they were entitled to traverse the allegation in the warrant that an offence had
been committed by the prisoners in Montreal. Upon the
motion to discharge the prisoners, the only mode by which
such traverse could be made would be by affidavits, or by a
direction under section 752 of the Criminal Code, which
Mr. Johnston urged should be resorted to in these cases.

A Judge could not, upon a return to a *habeas corpus*,
where the warrant of arrest on its face shews jurisdiction
in the magistrate issuing it, try on affidavit evidence the
question as to where the alleged offence was committed,
and so as it were, get behind the warrant for the purpose
of controverting the return. This may be done where the
person is confined otherwise than for some criminal or supposed criminal offence : Short's Crown Office Practice, p.
359; *In re Charles Smith*, 3 H. & N. 227.

If the criminal proceeding provided by R. S. O. ch. 70,

sec. 4, is not *ultra vires*, and the proceedings have been instituted in Ontario, the Judge before whom the writ of *habeas corpus* is returnable may proceed under that section to examine into the truth of the facts set forth in the return, by affidavit, or other evidence. And under section 5 a *certiorari* may issue requiring the evidence, depositions and conviction, and all proceedings, to be returned into Court.

I am quite satisfied that what a Judge may do under secs. 4 and 5 of the Ontario Act was not intended to apply to cases like these now before me, where no preliminary examination has taken place.

Then as to section 752 of the Criminal Code, it provides that wherever any person in custody, charged with an indictable offence, has taken proceedings before a Judge or criminal court having jurisdiction in the premises by way of *certiorari, habeas corpus*, or otherwise, to have the legality of his imprisonment inquired into, such Judge or Court may, without determining the question, make an order for the further detention of the person accused, and direct the Judge or justice under whose warrant he is in custody, or any other Judge or justice, to take any proceedings, hear such evidence, or do such further act as in the opinion of the Court or Judge may best further the ends of justice.

This section only applies to cases where the *habeas corpus* has issued from a Court of the same Province in which the magistrate's warrant of arrest or commitment has issued. A Court or a Judge in Ontario would have no jurisdiction over a justice or a Judge in the Province of Quebec, whereby the latter could or would be required or compelled " to take any proceedings, hear such evidence," etc. This can only apply where the Court or Judge making the direction has power to enforce the carrying out of the order or direction made. A direction or order from a Court or Judge here would be unavailing, as it could not be enforced.

The other point urged was that the warrant disclosed no criminal offence ; that it is not a crime for a conductor to

permit a person to travel on the cars of the railway com- Judgment.
pany without collecting the fare.   MacMahon,
                                            J.

The charge against these prisoners is that they conspired
with others named, " to defraud and injure the Grand
Trunk Railway Company, by allowing certain persons to
ride upon some parts of the railroads of the said company
without paying their fares."

Section 394 of the Code enacts that " every one is guilty
of an indictable offence, and is liable to seven years
imprisonment who conspires with any other person, by
deceit or falsehood, or other fraudulent means, to defraud
the public or any person," etc. The offence is complete
when the unlawful agreement is entered into between
the parties, for the conspiring is the essence of the
charge, and it is not necessary that any act should be done
in pursuance of the unlawful agreement. Even if section
394 was not in existence, and if, as urged by Mr. Clark,
there was only a civil wrong done to the railway company
by permitting persons to ride on the railway cars free,
yet, as said by Lord Cockburn, C.J., in *The Queen* v. *James
Warburton*, L. R. 1 C. C. R. 274, " A civil wrong was therefore intended to Lister. The facts of this case fall within
the rule that when two fraudulently combine, the agreement may be criminal, although if the agreement were
carried out no crime would be committed, but a civil
wrong only would be inflicted on a third party. In this
case the object of the agreement was, perhaps, not criminal.
It is not necessary to decide whether or not it was criminal;
it was, however, a conspiracy, as the object was to commit
a civil wrong by fraud and false pretences," p. 276.

Section 394 of the Code makes it a crime to conspire by
any fraudulent means to defraud any person. If there
was a conspiracy to permit persons to travel free on the
railway from whom the conductors should collect fares, it
would be a conspiracy to defraud the railway company.

On all the grounds urged the application fails, and the
prisoners must be remanded to the custody of the officers.

                                            G. A. B.

[CHANCERY DIVISION.]

THOMPSON ET AL. V. SMITH.

Will—Devise—" My Lawful Heirs"—Time when Heirs Ascertained.

A testator by his will after a gift to his daughter and her mother for
their joint lives, and to the survivor of them, directed that, " at the
decease of both, the residue of my real and personal property shall be
enjoyed by, and go to the benefit of my lawful heirs." Both survived
the testator and died, the daughter surviving the mother. At the
death of the testator his daughter was his only heir :—

Held, that the testator had himself excluded his daughter from being
treated as one of his heirs, and by the expression "my lawful heirs"
meant the persons who at the time of the death of the last survivor of
his wife and daughter should then be his heirs-at-law.

Jones v. *Colbeck*, 8 Ves. 38, approved and specially referred to.

Statement.   ACTION by the nephews and nieces of a testator for the
construction of his will.

Charles Palmer Thompson by his will provided that "the
profits of the interest in any the residue of the property
or estate, real or personal, that I may be possessed of at
the time of my decease shall be enjoyed solely by my beloved wife, Lissy Thompson, and my beloved daughter,
Mary Anna Thompson, the profits and interest thereof and
therein to be equally divided share and share alike between
my said beloved wife and daughter during their natural
lives," and then proceeded as follows :—

" I do further will and desire that at the decease of both
the said Lissy Thompson and Mary Anna Thompson the
said residue of my real and personal property shall be
enjoyed and go to the benefit of my lawful heirs, and in
order to carry out my desires and for the accomplishment
of this my last will and testament I hereby constitute and
appoint " (naming his executors.)

Both his wife and daughter survived him. The wife
then died, leaving the daughter her surviving. The daughter married the defendant, Joseph Smith, and died, having
made her will, by which she devised all her real and
personal estate to her husband, who, under the will of

his wife, entered into possession of the property devised
by Charles Palmer Thompson, and this action was brought
by the plaintiffs for its recovery and the construction of
his will.

The action was tried at Ottawa on the 15th of October,
1894, before BOYD, C.

Wyld, for the plaintiffs. The mother and daughter only
took life estates.

O'Gara, Q. C., and *MacTavish*, Q. C., for defendant. The
daughter Mary Anna, the lawful heir at the time of the
testator's death, took an absolute estate, subject to a life
interest to the widow in a moiety during their joint lives.
Except where there is a manifest intention to the contrary,
a remainder after a life estate vests at the death of the
testator. When a devisee of real estate is described under
a general name, as " heir," or " lawful heir," etc., the meaning
of the general words is to be ascertained on the death of
the testator. The life estate to the daughter and widow,
and to the survivor of them, is not inconsistent with the
lawful heir being ascertained at the testator's death; 1 Jarman on Wills, 3rd ed., 758, 766 ; 2 Jarman on Wills, 3rd
ed., 55, 77 ; *Tylee* v. *Deal*, 19 Gr. 601 ; *Baldwin* v. *Kingston*, 18 A. R., at p. 73. The word "survivor" was inserted to protect the widow, after the death of the daughter,
in the whole during her life. This case is the same as
Wrightson v. *Macauley*, 14 M. & W. 214. There, there
was a life interest given to the heir by name, yet he
was held to take the remainder devised generally to the
heir, as he answered that description at the death of
the testator. The defendant as devisee of Mary Anna is
entitled. Should defendant fail as to the construction of
the will, he is entitled to a reference as to permanent
improvements.

Wyld, in reply. The terms of the will shew that the
testator did not contemplate that his daughter was his
heir or one of his heirs. The heir must be ascertained at

the decease of both widow and daughter : *Brennen* v. *Munro*, 6 O. S. 92 ; *Doe d. Keeler* v. *Collins*, 7 U. C. R. 519 ; *Clow* v. *Clow*, 4 O. R. 355.

October 23rd, 1894.   BOYD, C. :—

This case appears to me to be governed by *Doe d. King* v. *Frost*, 3 B. and Ald. 546, the important words are (after a gift to his daughter and her mother for their joint lives and to the survivor of them) : "*At the decease* of both the said Lissy Thompson (his wife) and Mary Anna Thompson (his daughter) the residue of my real and personal property shall be enjoyed and go to the benefit of my lawful heirs." At the decease of the daughter (who survived the mother) the will gives the blended residue to the testator's lawful heirs. Adopting the words of Holroyd, J., in the case cited. " By the expression ' my lawful heirs,' is meant the persons who at the time of the decease of Mary Anna Thompson should be then the heirs-at-law of the testator," p. 556.

The testator himself, as I read the will, excludes his daughter, his only heir at his death, from being treated as one of the heirs ; he may, when the will was drawn, have thought she would marry and have children, and these would then be his heirs and they would as such enjoy the property after the death of their mother ; but upon her death without issue the estate vested in the then lawful heirs of the testator, who are admitted to be the plaintiffs. The rule is that the intention of the testator as expressed in the will, fairly construed, is to govern, and here he declares that upon the determination of the life estates given to his wife and daughter, the remainder (contingent as to those who should take) was to vest in those who should be at that time his heirs.

I acted upon this rule of construction the other day in *Coatsworth* v. *Carson*, 24 O. R. 185, and *Bennett* v. *Coatsworth*, 25 O. R. 591, where there was a demonstrative context. See also *Locke* v. *Southwood*, 1 M. & Cr. 411.

Upon the point that his daughter was his sole heir and that he does not refer to her in speaking of "my lawful heirs" at her death, see the language of Grant, M. R., in *Jones* v. *Colbeck*, 8 Ves. 38, and *Miller* v. *Eaton*, G. Coop. 272.

Jones v. *Colbeck* has been adversely criticized by a much inferior Judge in *Re Trust of Barber's Will*, 1 Sm. & Giff., at p. 122, but I prefer to follow the precedent of the Master of Rolls, which is certainly in accord with the modern method of giving the greatest weight to the manifest intention and plain meaning of the testator, *per* Lord Halsbury, in *Leader* v. *Duffey*, 13 App. Cas., at pp. 301, 302.

With a more just appreciation of the value of *Jones* v. *Colbeck*, it is reproduced in Sir F. Pollock's Rev. Rep., vol. 6, p. 207; see also the reasoning of the V. C. Wigram in *Say* v. *Creed*, 5 Ha., at p. 587, and *Clark* v. *Hayne*, 42 Ch. D. 529. I notice also that the case of *Jones* v. *Colbeck* seems to be completely re-established by what is said by the Judges in appeal in *Lees* v. *Massey*, 3 D. F. & J., pp. 122 & 124. This fact should have been noted, but is omitted in both 2 Jarman on Wills, 984 (*n*), 5th ed., and Watson's Compendium of Equity, 2nd ed., p. 1405.

Putting one's self in the position of the testator and remembering that the will speaks from the death, I cannot hold but that he meant to give no more to his daughter than a life estate. He knew she was his sole heir-at-law and next of kin, and the class to take at her death he did not know and so calls them "his lawful heirs." See *Lees* v. *Massey*, 3 D. F. & J., at p. 121.

The judgment will be framed accordingly.

G. A. B.

[QUEEN'S BENCH DIVISION.]

REGINA v. PLOWMAN.

Constitutional Law—Criminal Code, sec. 275—Bigamy—Offence Committed in Foreign Country—Intent—Ultra Vires.

Conviction for bigamy quashed where the second marriage took place in
. a foreign country, and there was evidence that the defendant, who was
a British subject, resident in Canada, left there with the intent to
commit the offence.

The provisions of sec. 275 of the Criminal Code making such a marriage
an offence are *ultra vires* of the Parliament of Canada.

Macleod v. *Attorney-General for New South Wales*, [1891] A. C. 455,
followed.

Statement.   CROWN case reserved by the chairman of the General
Sessions of the Peace for the county of York upon an
indictment and conviction of the defendant for bigamy.

The indictment charged that the second marriage took
place on the 24th May, 1893, at the city of Detroit, in the
State of Michigan, one of the United States of America;
and further, that the defendant "was prior to the date of
the said (second) marriage a British subject, resident in
Canada, and he then left Canada (being at the time of his
leaving Canada a British subject) with intent to commit
the said last mentioned marriage in the United States of
America."

. It was shewn that the defendant was a British subject,
resident in Canada, and there was evidence to go to the
jury of the defendant's intention of entering into or going
through the form or ceremony of a second marriage at the
time he left Ontario for the city of Detroit.

The question reserved was whether the Court had jurisdiction to try the prisoner for the offence as charged, the
second and bigamous marriage having taken place in a
foreign country, outside the Dominion of Canada, under
the circumstances referred to.

Section 275 of the Criminal Code, 1892, enacts as follows:
"Bigamy is—(a) the act of a person who, being married,
goes through a form of marriage with any other person in
any part of the world.   *   *   4. No person shall be liable

to be convicted of bigamy in respect of having gone through a form of marriage in a place not in Canada, unless such person, being a British subject resident in Canada, leaves Canada with intent to go through such form of marriage."

The case was argued before ARMOUR, C. J., and FALCON-BRIDGE, J., on the 19th November, 1894.

DuVernet, for the defendant. I rely on *Macleod* v. *Attorney-General for New South Wales*, [1891] A. C. 455. (Stopped by the Court.)

J. R. Cartwright, Q. C., for the Crown. The statute was different in that case. Under our statute the intention is the criminal offence. Intent may be a crime. There may be a difficulty in getting at an intent; but if you can prove it, you can punish it. If the legislature chooses to make an intent a crime, it can do so. We must take the two together, the intent and the ceremony, and neither without the other constitutes an offence. This is exactly in line with *Regina* v. *Jones*, 4 F. & F. 25. See also *Regina* v. *Pierce*, 13 O. R. 226; *Regina* v. *Brierly*, 14 O. R. 525.

DuVernet not called on again.

ARMOUR, C. J. :—

The Imperial Parliament could enact that it should be a crime for a British subject to go through a form or ceremony of marriage abroad, but it has not done so. The Dominion Parliament, being a subordinate legislature, has no such power; and that is the effect of the case of *Macleod* v. *Attorney-General for New South Wales*, [1891] A. C. 455, which covers this case. The second marriage is the offence, and the Dominion Parliament has no power to legislate about such an offence committed in a foreign country.

FALCONBRIDGE, J. :—

I agree.

Conviction quashed.

E. B. B.

[QUEEN'S BENCH DIVISION.]

FITZGERALD v. CITY OF OTTAWA.

*Municipal Corporations—Drainage—New Territory—Old Drain—
Liability.*

Where one municipality acquires territory from another, the property in
a drain for the purpose of carrying off the surface water constructed in
the highway by the land-owners before such acquisition becomes vested
in the transferees, and they are liable to the land-owners for injury
caused by subsequent neglect to keep it in repair.

Statement.   ACTION for damages for flooding the plaintiff's lands,
tried before BOYD, C., without a jury, at Ottawa, on the
16th October, 1894.   The facts are stated in the judgment.

Wyld, for the plaintiff.
O'Gara, Q. C., for the defendants.

October 23, 1894.   BOYD, C. :—

The plaintiff's land has been damaged by the overflow
of water which would have been carried off had the drain
along the highway to the north of his land been kept in
proper repair.   While the territory was a part of the
township of Nepean, the frontagers on the south side of
the street in question (now called Pine street), for their own
convenience and comfort, constructed a box drain to carry
away surface water which collected on the western end of
that street.   This water was thereby carried down to an
outlet on Preston street.   The drain was covered over
with earth to a depth of about two feet to make easy
entrance to the yards and houses of the frontagers.   In
course of time the wood-work of the drain collapsed or
caved in, so as to obstruct the flow of the water, and the
earth covering of the drain was thus converted into a sort
of dam, which penned back the water and caused its overflow upon the plaintiff's lots and houses.   After the construction of the drain and before its collapse, the locality
had become part of city of Ottawa, and the street was

thereupon vested in the municipality, and was subject to the urban authorities. The attention of the city engineer and officials was called by the plaintiff to the state of this drain and to the injury which he was suffering from its unsound and inefficient state, and the city engineer made an inspection of the place. The plaintiff says that he offered to repair the drain if the city would grant the necessary permit, but this was refused, because it was said that the engineer did not approve of box drains. Then a temporary remedy was applied by means of a cut angling across the road to the north side of the street, and the construction of an open channel along that side in order to discharge the water into Preston street. This served the purpose and protected the plaintiff's property for one season, but after this it also ceased to do its work, because the cut across leading to it became trodden down or filled up, so that the water again began to overflow to the plaintiff's damage. The corporation were again notified, but did not remedy the matter till substantial injury had been done to the plaintiff's property.

The question of legal liability arises on this state of facts.

It is said in Wood on Nuisances that when a municipal corporation has ample power to remove a nuisance which is injurious to the health, endangers the safety, or impairs the convenience of its citizens, it is liable for all the injuries that result from a failure on its part to properly exercise the power preserved by it : sec. 749. The rule is very much the same as in the case of individuals who permit the existence of anything on their land which injures their neighbour. Thus in *Broder* v. *Saillard*, 2 Ch. D. 692, it was held that the occupier of a house is liable for allowing the continuance on his premises of any artificial work which causes a nuisance to a neighbour, even though it has been put there before he took possession. And in *Hurdman* v. *North Eastern Railway Co.*, 3 C. P. D. at p. 173, it was laid down that if anyone by artificial erection on his own land causes water, even though arising from natural rainfall only, to pass into his neighbour's land, and thus sub-

stantially to interfere with his enjoyment, he will be liable
to an action at the suit of him who is so injured. The
principles of these decisions apply to and cover the question of liability upon the present state of facts.

I think the city is liable: because their predecessors in
title having allowed the people to make their own drain in
a clumsy make-shift way, it was transferred to the city in
that condition; the property in the highway and drain
vested in the city; and they alone had power to deal with
it or to make those attend to it and keep it in repair who
had put it down; the plaintiff could not go on the highway
and redress himself, but called the attention of the officers
of the city to what was wrong, and they then undertook
to divert the water into another channel, and so assumed
the responsibility of draining that locality; the duty of
the city was either to keep in a state of efficiency the new
channel to the north, or to see that the old drain was
properly repaired so as to carry off the water which was
accumulated by the two feet of earth which covered it.

The plaintiff should get substantial damages, but I do
not think he suffered so long or to so great an extent as is
claimed in his evidence. I assess the damages at $400, and
give him the costs of the action.

E. B. B.

[QUEEN'S BENCH DIVISION.]

TALLMAN v. SMART.

Chattel Mortgage—Validity of Renewal—Right of Assignee for Creditors to Question—R. S. O. ch. 125, secs. 4, 11—55 Vict. ch. 26, sec. 2 (O.)

Sec. 2 of 55 Vict. ch. 26 (O.) does not enable an assignee for the general benefit of creditors to question the validity of the renewal of a chattel mortgage.

ACTION tried before ROSE, J., without a jury, at Perth, Statement. on the 9th October, 1894. The facts are stated in the judgment.

Moss, Q. C., and *Lavell,* for the plaintiff.

Evertts, for the defendant.

October 16, 1894. ROSE, J. :—

The plaintiff brought this action against the defendant, as assignee for creditors, to have it declared that he, the plaintiff, as mortgagee of certain chattels, had a preferential lien or charge upon such chattels in the assignee's hands, and claimed also the amount of an account not included in the chattel mortgage. The defendant did not attack the *bona fides* of the transaction, and his counsel admitted at the trial that there was an open account not covered by the mortgage, but asked to have the amount of such account ascertained by a reference. The defendant, however, set up that the mortgage had ceased to be valid by reason of non-compliance with the provisions of the statute requiring the renewal of a mortgage in the manner provided by sec. 11 of R. S. O. ch. 125, the objection being that the statement required by that section did not properly shew all payments made on account of the principal and interest secured by the mortgage. It was not charged that this was by any want of *bona fides* on the part of the plaintiff. If the statement was inaccurate, it was by error and omission.

The plaintiff contended that the assignee could not raise such a question. It was admitted that he could not unless sec. 2 of 55 Vict. ch. 26 (O.) applied. By such section the words "void as against creditors" are declared to extend to any assignee for the general benefit of creditors, within the meaning of the Act respecting assignments and preferences by insolvent persons and amendments thereto.

Adapting the language of the learned Chancellor in *Re Gilchrist and Island*, 11 O. R. at p. 539, the words in section 2 "void as against creditors" are but symbolical words, for the meaning of which reference is to be had to the exponential words. And again, "resort cannot be had to the exponential clause unless there is first found in the instrument the symbolical clause of which the former is the parliamentary equivalent."

The words "void as against creditors" are found in section 4 of R.'S. O. ch. 125, where it is provided that "in case such mortgage or conveyance and affidavits are not registered as hereinbefore provided, the mortgage or conveyance shall be absolutely null and void as against creditors," etc. We, therefore, understand by sec. 2 of ch. 26 that the provisions of sec. 4 extend to assignees. But we find no such words as "void as against creditors" in sec. 11. The words there are, "every mortgage, or copy thereof, filed in pursuance of this Act, shall *cease to be valid*, as against the creditors of the persons making the same," etc. By sec. 4 the mortgage is declared to be void. It, therefore, not having complied with the statute, was void from the beginning. Sec. 11 presupposes a valid mortgage which, by reason of the non-observance of the requirements as to renewal, ceases to be valid. The conditions are not the same; the words are not the same; and I, therefore, am unable to find in sec. 2 of ch. 26 any exponential words applying to any language in sec. 11.

The defendant's counsel having admitted that without the aid of chapter 26 he could not contend that the assignee had any right to raise the question here raised, I must declare the right of the plaintiff to rank upon the estate

Judgment.

Rose, J.

as a preferential creditor to the extent of the balance due upon his mortgage, and also to rank upon the estate as an ordinary creditor for the amount of his unsecured account.

The minutes may be spoken to providing for a reference, as was suggested at the trial.

The plaintiff must have his costs up to and including the trial. Further directions and costs are reserved until after the report is made upon the reference.

E. B. B.

———

[CHANCERY DIVISION.]

The Corporation of the Township of Burford
v.
Chambers et al.

Arbitration—Injunction Restraining Arbitrator Acting—Jurisdiction of High Court—Arbitrator Solicitor for Parties.

The High Court has power to prevent a non-indifferent arbitrator from acting without waiting until the award is made, though perhaps the better course is to apply for leave to revoke the submission if another arbitrator be not substituted.

Malmesbury R. W. Co. v. *Budd*, 2 Ch. D. 113, and *Beddow* v. *Beddow*, 9 Ch. D. 89, followed.

A barrister and solicitor who had acted as counsel for the husband on an indictment and trial for obstructing an alleged highway claimed by his wife to be her property, and who had written a letter concerning the matter as solicitor for both husband and wife was restrained from acting as arbitrator in an arbitration between the wife and the municipal corporation in which the highway was situate.

Vineburg v. *The Guardian Fire and Life Association Co.*, 19 A. R. 293, followed.

Statement.

THIS was a motion for an injunction to restrain an arbitrator from acting, on the ground of unfitness for the position from possible bias.

The arbitration was between the corporation of the township of Burford and one Margaret Chambers in respect of a piece of property which the corporation claimed was a highway, and Mrs. Chambers claimed was part of her farm.

Mrs. Chambers and her husband, had been previously
indicted and tried for an alleged obstruction of the highway ; and the proposed arbitrator, one Bowlby, who was
a barrister and solicitor, had defended the husband at the
trial.

He had subsequently written a letter, as solicitor for both
the husband and the wife, to the Reeve of the township
of Burford, in which he alleged a breach of faith on the
part of the predecessors in office of the plaintiff corporation,
which letter is fully set out in the judgment of the learned
Judge.¹

The motion * was argued in Court on October 30th, 1894,
before MEREDITH, J.

Herbert Mowat, for the plaintiff.   The proposed arbitrator is disqualified from acting in that capacity.   His relation as counsel for the husband at the trial and solicitor
for the husband and wife, as stated in his letter disqualify
him as he could not be an unbiased arbitrator.   The evidence shews that he has already expressed himself against
the corporation.   These circumstances have the tendency
to produce a bias.   I refer to *Walker* v. *Frobisher*, 6 Ves.
70 ; *Conmee* v. *Canadian Pacific R. W. Co.*, 16 O. R. 639 ;
Dobson v. *Groves*, 6 Q. B. 637 (cited in the Conmee case
at p. 649) ; Russell on Arbitration, 7th ed. pp. 112, 116 ;
Race v. *Anderson*, 14 A. R. 213 ; *Vineburg* v. *The Guardian
Fire and Life Ass'ce. Co.*, 19 A. R. 293 ; *Eckersley* v. *The
Mersey Docks and Harbour Board*, [1894] 2 Q. B. 667.
The parties should be satisfied that the tribunal is an
impartial one: *Re Clout & The Metropolitan & District
R. W. Co.*, 46 L. T. N. S. 141.

S. A. Jones, contra.   The High Court here has no jurisdiction to enjoin the arbitrator from acting.   There was
no original jurisdiction in the Court of Chancery to enjoin
in such a case: *Pickering* v. *Cape Town R. W. Co.*, L. R.

---

* During the argument, the motion for injunction was turned into a
motion for judgment, with the concurrence of both counsel.—REP.

XXV.] TOWNSHIP OF BURFORD V. CHAMBERS. 665

1 Eq. 84. There is no power to enjoin given by the Judicature Act, where no such power existed in the Court
before: *The North London R. W. Co.* v. *The Great Northern
R. W. Co.*, 11 Q. B. D. 30; *Jackson* v. *Barry R. W. Co.*,
[1893] 1 Ch. 238. The arbitrator may have defended
the husband, but he was not counsel for the wife for whom
another counsel acted. Even if he was solicitor for the
wife, such position merely would not disqualify him, as the
evidence does not shew any such bias as would disqualify:
Re Christie and Town of Toronto Junction, 24 O. R.
443.

Mowat, in reply. There is no doubt the Court has the
jurisdiction: *Malmesbury R. W. Co.* v. *Budd*, 2 Ch. D.
113; *Beddow* v. *Beddow*, 9 Ch. D. 89.

November 28th, 1894. MEREDITH, J.:—

In the present state of the authorities, I must hold that
in a case of this kind the Court has power to grant the relief
sought in this action. The cases of *Malmesbury R. W. Co.*
v. *Budd*, 2 Ch. D. 113, and *Beddow* v. *Beddow*, 9 Ch. D. 89,
are directly in point and expressly decide the question in
favour of that power; and in such cases it is obviously the
better course, for the parties concerned, to prevent an
incompetent arbitrator acting, than, after all the delay,
expense and trouble of a reference and award, to set aside
the award, rendering all the proceedings nugatory, because
of the same incompetence: though, perhaps, the best course,
in cases where such a course can be taken, is to apply for
leave to revoke the submission, if another arbitrator be not
substituted.

Those cases have not been overruled, nor, so far as I have
been able to find, found fault with. In the cases in which
the power to enjoin has been denied, they have been distinguished and generally spoken of approvingly: see *The
North London R. W. Co.* v. *The Great Northern R. W. Co.*, 11
Q. B. D. 30; *London & Blackwall R. W. Co.* v. *Cross*, 31
Ch. D. 355: *Farrar* v. *Cooper*, 44 Ch. D. 323; and *Jackson*
v. *Barry R. W. Co.*, [1893] 1 Ch. 238.

So that I find no difficulty, upon the cases as they now
stand, in reaching the conclusion that I am bound, without
considering the principle involved, to hold that this Court
has the jurisdiction which the plaintiffs invokes, and ought
to exercise it if the plaintiffs' contention respecting the
arbitrator's unfitness be sustained ; there being here no
power of revocation.

The authorities, upon the latter question, are more perplexing to me. That question is : " Have the plaintiffs
shewn that the arbitrator is unfit to perform the duties of
his office ? "

I am quite unable to reconcile all the cases upon the subject ; for instance, I am unable to understand how the
case *Re Arbitration between Hopper, Barningham and
Wrightson*, L. R. 2 Q. B. 367, can have been well decided
if the case *Conmee* v. *Canadian Pacific R. W. Co.*, 16 O. R.
639, were ; or how the case *Re Christie and Town of Toronto
Junction*, 24 O. R. 443, can well be supported if the case
Vineburg v. *The Guardian Fire and Life Ass'ce. Co.*,
19 A. R. 293, correctly expounds the law upon the subject.

However, I am clearly bound by the last named case,
the latest decision of the Court of Appeal for this Province
upon the subject.

In that case the arbitrator had been a " canvasser
for insurance risks," some of which he placed in the defendant company, he getting a share of the commission allowed
to the company's agent for the new business. He was not
bound to place them in that company, but might place
them where his customers could do best or preferred, and,
in point of fact, did place them in that company to so small
an extent that the sum total received by him from the
company's agent seems to have been too insignificant to be
named in the report of the case; he had had nothing, in
even the most remote way, to do with the risks in question ; and one might have thought that if he had any bias
in a matter in which he had been in no way concerned,
that bias would rather be generally in favour of than
against the insured, from whom alone he sought anything—

Judgment.

Meredith, J.

who were his customers, if one may so term them—and
not the company which was rather favoured than favour-
ing when risks were placed with them instead of any of
the many other keenly competing companies. But even in
that case, it was held by Rose, J., that the arbitrator was
so unfit that the award made by him and another could
not stand, and that holding was sustained by Ferguson, J.,
in the Divisional Court and unanimously affirmed in the
Court of Appeal, because, as the Chief Justice of Ontario,
in delivering the judgment of the Court, finally put it,
" certainly those relations would naturally suggest—perhaps unjustly—a presumption of ' non-indifference,' " at p.
298. And this too, though the arbitrator's duties consisted
merely of a valuation of the loss.

The rule adopted here appears to be that an arbitrator
is unfit to act in any case in which he might be suspected
of a bias in favour of or against one of the parties; unless,
indeed, the parties have, by their agreement, otherwise
indicated, as they often do, for instance, in building agreements: see *Eckersley* v. *The Mersey Docks & Harbour
Board*, [1894] 2 Q. B. 667; and as the Parliament of Canada
and the Legislative Assembly of this Province have each,
in one case at least, otherwise provided: see "The Railways Act," sec. 159, and " The Railway Act of Ontario,"
sec. 22, sub-sec. 17.

The rule, in the extreme limit to which, in this Province, it has been carried, seems to be founded, in a
measure at all events, upon sentiment rather than practical
utility. One's eyes cannot be shut against the fact that in
many, very many cases, the arbitrator for each party is
expected to be, and is, an active advocate of the party by
whom he was appointed, however much Courts may insist
upon impartiality and deprecate such conduct; nor against
the fact that an honest and able arbitrator may, because
of a suspicion of bias, of quite unconscious bias, be removed
only to make place for another who will act the part of
advocate instead of arbitrator, but in such a manner as to
leave the Court powerless to interfere.

But such is the rule and such the extent to which it has been carried here, and I am obliged to give effect to it.

Now, in this case, I must accept the arbitrator's letter of 16th February, 1893, rather than his memory, as the safe guide to the actual state of facts. From his affidavit, I would gather that he would himself depend more upon it than upon his memory. He states that he had quite forgotten having written such a letter until his attention was called to it in reading an affidavit filed in support of this motion; nor can he object to my acceptance of the statements made in that letter as true.

The letter is in these words :

"Brantford, 16th February, 1893.

"*To the Reeve*

Of the township of Burford,

New Durham, Ont.

"DEAR SIR :—I have been instructed by Mr. Anson Chambers, and I have also been instructed by his wife, Margaret Chambers, to proceed against the township of Burford, on account of their being forced to give bail before Magistrate Cox in the road case, and being illegally detained, also for illegal prosecution.

"I have advised them to a moderate course. They are out of pocket largely by the council's course. The council's course was a breach of faith on the agreement of their predecessors in office. With other losses they have suffered the following :

Time of team of Mr. and Mrs. Chambers before J.P.	$ 3 00
Ditch made last fall which has to be refilled, say..	10 00
Witness fees of T. H. Jones at $4 per day	8 00
David Huffman for two days and mileage	4 00
T. Costin " " "	4 00
T. Lloyd Jones " " "	3 00
Margaret Chambers...........................	3 50
Anson Chambers............................	4 50
Counsel fee of J. W. Bowlby, and for his previous advice, attendings and taking copies..........	40 00
Counsel fee of L. F. Heyd	25 00
	$105 00

"This takes no account of their injured feelings, their
pain and anxiety.

"Your Mr. Metcalf was given unlimited powers as your
books shew.   What are you going to do about it ?   A
prompt answer will oblige.   This letter is without prejudice.

"Yours, etc.,

"(Sgd.)   J. W. BOWLBY."

So that as late as the 16th February, 1893, he was acting as solicitor for his co-defendant and for her husband
in the very matter mainly involved in this arbitration—
that is, whether the land in question is part of the public
highway, or part of his co-defendant's farm ; and claimed
damage for them because the plaintiffs had, by way of
complaint and indictment for obstruction of the highway,
sought to establish their claim that the place in question
is a public highway, and charged the plaintiffs with a
breach of faith towards his co-defendant and her husband
in taking such proceedings ; and stated that he had advised
his clients to a moderate course ; that moderate course
being a claim for damages amounting to $105, made up of
the items set out in the letter, including a counsel fee to
himself, and for his previous advice and taking copies, etc.,
$40 ; foregoing any claim in respect of the injured feelings,
pain and anxiety of his clients.

Before that, in December, 1892, he had defended the
husband on his trial upon the indictment against him
before referred to, and after that, in the month of June,
1894, he met the plaintiffs' Reeve and spoke to him about
his co-defendant's claim for compensation for the land in
question, of which the plaintiffs had meanwhile taken
possession, and, according to the Reeve's testimony, asked
why the plaintiffs' council did not settle the case, as "he
was satisfied that the Chamberses had a good claim against
the township," and as the Reeve thinks, stated further,
"that the Chamberses had a good case for arbitration" : but,
according to his own testimony, only suggested that the
township and the Chamberses had better settle the matter
without any further trouble about it.

Judgment.

Meredith, J.

In these circumstances, I feel bound by the *Vineburg* case, to hold that the arbitrator is not competent to act, because open to the suspicion of bias in favour of his co-defendant by whom he was appointed, notwithstanding the plaintiff's earnest objection, if not because it might also fairly be said that he has prejudged the most substantial question between the parties in the arbitration: in view of that case, I feel bound to say, at least, that "certainly those relations would naturally suggest—perhaps unjustly—a presumption of 'non-indifference,'" which is enough to render him incompetent.

The parties desired that the case should not go down to trial, and their counsel urged me to give final judgment in the action now : I, therefore, allow the motion, and grant the injunction sought, and make it perpetual, with costs of the action, including, of course, this motion.

During the argument I suggested that whatever the strict rights of the parties might be, it might be wiser for the arbitrator to retire, all imputations against him being withdrawn ; the case seeming to me to be a proper one for the adoption of such a course, the plaintiffs, undoubtedly, being sincere in their objection, and, undoubtedly, taking these proceedings in good faith without any desire to prejudice or hamper the defendant Chambers in her choice of a good arbitrator, a course somewhat similar to that which I have since seen was taken in the case *Malmesbury R. W. Co.* v. *Budd, supra ;* but the arbitrator declined to act upon the suggestion, and required that the case be dealt with according to the strict rights of the parties, and so dealing with it, the plaintiffs having succeeded, are entitled, against both defendants, to their costs of the action.

I am not concerned with any question whether an arbitration, under the provisions of the Municipal Act, or an action for trespass to lands, is the proper mode of enforcing the claims of the defendant Chambers, against the plaintiffs in this action. The parties are proceeding by way of arbitration, and the only questions raised in this action

are whether the defendant Bowlby is disqualified, and if ^Judgment.^
so, whether the plaintiffs can have relief by way of injunc- ^Meredith, J.^
tion.   But I may add that, according to the view of the
majority of the Judges of the Court of Appeal for this Province, the question depends on the form of the by-law:
see *Connor* v. *Middagh* and *Hill* v. *Middagh*, 16 A.
R. 356; cases which were settled between the parties while
standing for judgment in the Supreme Court of Canada.

G. A. B.

[CHANCERY DIVISION.]

PIERCE V. CANADA PERMANENT LOAN AND SAVINGS COMPANY. (a.)

*Mortgage—Building Loan—Further Advances—Priority of Subsequently
Registered Mortgage—Registry Act—Notice—R. S. O. ch. 114, sec. 80.*

After purchasing land under an agreement which provided that $2,000 of
the purchase money was to be secured by mortgage subsequent to a
building loan not exceeding $12,000, the purchaser executed a building
mortgage to a loan company for $11,500, which was at once registered,
but only part of that sum was then advanced.   The plaintiff, who had
succeeded to the rights of the vendor under the above agreement, then
registered her mortgage for $2,000, and claimed priority over subse-
quent advances made by the loan company under their mortgage, but
without actual notice of the plaintiff's mortgage, or of the terms of the
agreement for the sale of the land :—

Held (ROBERTSON, J., dissenting), that the plaintiff was not entitled to
the priority claimed by her.

Decision of FERGUSON, J., 24 O. R. 426, reversed.

Per BOYD, C.—The further advances were made upon a mortgage providing for such advances, and to secure which the legal estate had been
conveyed, and equity as well as law protected the first mortgage so
advantageously placed, as against the subsequent mortgage, even
though registered, where notice had not as a fact been communicated
to the first mortgagee respecting the subsequent instrument and the
Registry Act did not apply.

THIS was a motion by the defendants before the Divi- ^Statement.^
sional Court, by way of appeal from the decision of
FERGUSON, J., reported 24 O. R. 426, in whose judgment
the material facts are set out.

(a) See now 57 Vict., ch. 34, (O.).

The motion was argued on March 1st, 1894, before
BOYD, C., and ROBERTSON and MEREDITH, JJ.

S. H. Blake, Q.C., and *Beverley Jones*, for the Canada
Permanent Loan and Savings Company. This was a building loan to Wilson, and we advanced the money towards
the putting up of the building. This takes the case out
of *Hopkinson* v. *Rolt*, 9 H. L. C. 514. The plaintiff contracted that our mortgage was to stand prior to her's to
the extent of $12,000, and if we had notice of her mortgage
we had notice of all equities connected with it: *Menzies*
v. *Lightfoot*, L. R. 11 Eq. 459. This arrangement controls.
Can the plaintiff, by the mere registration of her mortgage,
commit a fraud by claiming priority ? FERGUSON, J., treats
the case as though there was an advance of money actually
made by the plaintiff. The plaintiff has no equity. It is
a fraud on her part to endeavour to take advantage of the
registry law, so as to commit a wrong, not prevent a
wrong. On the faith of the building mortgage the money
was advanced and the building put up. The whole agreement and arrangement takes it out of *Hopkinson* v. *Rolt*,
where, and in other such cases, there was actual notice.
The Court is struggling more and more against that
constructive notice, which so often works a wrong. Suppose, at a critical point of the building, such a mortgage as the plaintiff's had been put on for a pre-existing debt, the loan company's hands would have been
tied. Cases following *Hopkinson* v. *Rolt* are: *Boucher*
v. *Smith*, 9 Gr. 347, 353, and *Trust and Loan Co.* v. *Shaw*,
16 Gr. 446. The loan company were not acquiring land ;
it was carrying out an arrangement by which they had
acquired the land : *Beck* v. *Moffatt*, 17 Gr. 601 ; *Brown*
v. *McLean*, 18 O. R. 533 ; *Richards* v. *Chamberlain*,
25 Gr. 402 ; *Douglas* v. *Chamberlain*, 25 Gr. 288 ;
Hutson v. *Valliers*, 19 A. R. 154 ; *London and County
Banking Co.* v. *Ratcliffe*, 6 App. Cas. 722 ; *Union Bank
of Scotland* v. *National Bank of Scotland*, 12 App. Cas.
53 ; *Shaw* v. *Foster*, L. R. 5 H. L. 321 ; *Abell* v. *Morrison*,

Argument.

19 O. R. 669. The registry law does not apply : R. S. O. ch. 114, secs. 76, 80. As to section 76, the plaintiff was not a subsequent mortgagee, she was a prior mortgagee so far as time was concerned. Her mortgage was dated October, 1890. Then she had actual notice of our mortgage, and agreed it should have priority. As to section 80, it cannot be said the loan company claimed an interest in the land subsequent to the registration. Everything which affected the land was given by this mortgage. By that they got their title, and made subsequent advances by virtue of that title. The agreement is incorporated in our mortgage : Jones on Mortgages, 4th ed., sec. 368, referring to *Truscott* v. *King*, 2 Seld. (6 N. Y.) 147 ; *Nelson* v. *Iowa Eastern R. W. Co.*, 8 Am. R. R. Rep. 82; *McDaniels* v. *Colvin*, 16 Verm. 300; *Platt* v. *Griffith*, 27 N. J. Eq. 207.

Beverley Jones, on same side, referred to Dart on Vendors and Purchasers, 6th ed., p. 528.

G. Bell, for the plaintiff. The plaintiff denies that she ever agreed to what is in the paper, and there is no finding that the writing truly sets out the agreement between the plaintiff and Wilson, who is not a party to the action. There is no privity of agreement between the plaintiff and the company, who were not even aware of the agreement between the plaintiff and Wilson, and did not advance their money on the faith of it : *The Frontenac Loan and Investment Society* v. *Hysop*, 21 O. R. 577. The company's mortgage was one for future advance, a building loan. It might be different if the company had bound themselves to advance the whole of the balance of the $12,000, or if the mortgagor had covenanted to accept for them the balance. The agreement in the company's mortgage was not registered, and the mere reference to it in the mortgage was not notice to the plaintiff of its terms under the Registry Act. At all events it does not alter the position of matters, it does not make it obligatory on the company to advance the balance of the money. The cases on the Registry Act are cited in the judgment, and I may refer to *Hynes* v. *Smith*, 27 Gr. 150 ; *Cook* v. *Belshaw*, 23 O. R. 545. Every

Argument. advance made by the company after the registration of the
plaintiff's mortgage was of the nature of a new advance
upon a new security. As to the advances made by the
company there is no evidence to shew that they were used
for the building.

Blake, in reply. The money was advanced to Wilson in
the way suggested. We cannot be in a worse position if
Wilson cheated us in the matter, but there is no evidence
that he did so. The question of privity has nothing to do
with finding the fact whether there was or was not the
alleged agreement, and whether the plaintiff acceded to it,
and the judge finds in the affirmative. At what time was
the plaintiff to be at liberty to alter her position? When
she wished to do so, it was her duty to give notice to all
parties.

October 13th, 1894. BOYD, C. :—

The security of a first mortgage providing for future
advances is not impaired unless notice of a second mortgage
comes to the mortgagee, and after knowledge of this he
makes subsequent advances. The whole question in this
case is whether the registration of the second mortgage
operates as notice thereof to the first mortgagee in respect
of subsequent advances,—for other notice there is none.

In *Hopkinson* v. *Rolt,* 9 H. L. C. 514, Lord Cranworth's
opinion was that the subsequent advances when made
attach themselves to the mortgage so as to put them in the
same position as if they had all been made when the mortgage was originally created.

In *Bradford Banking Co.* v. *Briggs,* 12 App. Cas. at p.
36, Lord Blackburn says : "The first mortgagee is entitled
to act on the supposition that the pledgor who was owner
of the whole property when he executed the first mortgage
continued so, and that there has been no second mortgage
or pledge until he has notice of something to shew him
that there has been such a second mortgage, but as soon as
he is aware that the property on which he is entitled to

rely has ceased so far to belong to the debtor, he cannot make a new advance in priority to that of which he has notice." And he adds in explanation of the principle of *Hopkinson* v. *Rolt*: " It seems to me to depend entirely on what I cannot but think a principle of justice, that a mortgagee who is entitled, but not bound, to give credit on the security of property belonging to the debtor, cannot give that credit after he has notice that the property has so far been parted with by the debtor :" p. 37.

He further remarks : " The second pledgee, for his own sake, must take care to give notice of his security to the first pledgee," p. 37 ; and he puts it on p. 38, that there was such knowledge that the pledgor " had ceased to be owner, as would have made it unjust to allow.him credit on the faith of that property which had once been his."

And in *Union Bank of Scotland* v. *National Bank of Scotland*, 12 App. Cas., at p. 95, Lord Halsbury puts the decision in *Hopkinson* v. *Rolt* on the broadest grounds of natural justice, and that it would be contrary to good faith to give priority to advances made by the first mortgagee after notice of the creation of a second mortgage.

I have made these extracts in order to shew the broad ground of decision. I do not find that it is put on the footing of the subsequent advances amounting to the acquisition of a new interest in the land, and so to bring it within the provisions of the Registry Act.

This is the aspect of the case advanced by Mr. Justice Maclennan in *Hutson* v. *Valliers*, 19 A. R. 154, 161, on which my brother Ferguson acted in the judgment now in appeal. Treated practically, it cannot be regarded as such a dealing with the land as requires to be registered—or such as necessitates a search before making the advance. The instrument securing all the advances past and prospective has been registered,—the function of the Registry Act has been satisfied by this initial transaction, and the scope of the Act contemplates no further registration and consequently no further search in order to justify the payment of the further advances, as called for by the mortgagor.

The *onus* is not on the first mortgagee who has registered
to do something more to complete his claim upon the land
for all that is specified in the mortgage: the *onus* is on the
one subsequently acquiring an interest in the land by conveyance from the mortgagor to give express notice of that
to the first mortgagee in order to intercept payments or
advances thereafter made pursuant to the first mortgage.

In the absence of notice, (*i. e.*, notice which gives him
real and actual knowledge, and so affects his conscience),
the mortgagee is entitled to assume and act on the assumption that the state of the title has not changed That
protection is given to him by virtue of the Registry Act,
as well as by the doctrine enunciated in *Hopkinson* v. *Rolt*,
until he is made aware of a change, not by the hypothetical
operation of an instrument registered subsequent to his,
but by a reasonable communication of the fact by the one
who comes in under the subsequent instrument.

Otherwise, consider the consequences. Before making
any subsequent advance the first mortgagee would need to
have telegraphic or other electrical advice as to the state
of registration on the land each time he paid, for if, before
the payment, some transfer from the mortgagor intervened
his advance would be postponed to the claim of the new
comer.

Apart from these considerations, when the legal estate
is held by the first mortgagee, as is the fact in the case
now in hand, the true principle of decision is to be sought
in the rules which obtained when tacking was in vogue.
Though that is not now permitted in Ontario, so as to
prevail against the Registry Act, R. S. O. ch. 114, sec. 83,
the reasons for it apply *mutatis mutandis*.

In *Brace* v. *Duchess of Marlborough*, 2 P. Wms. 491, in the
fourth holding, it is said: "If a first mortgagee lends a
further sum to the mortgagor on a statute or judgment,
he shall retain against a *mesne* mortgagee, till both the
mortgage and statute or judgment be paid, because it is
to be presumed that he lent his money upon the statute
or judgment, as knowing he had hold of the land by the

XXV.]   PIERCE V. CAN. PERMANENT LOAN CO.   677

mortgage, and in confidence ventured a further sum on a Judgment.
security which, though it passed no present interest in the Boyd, C.
land, yet must be admitted to be lien thereon."

In *Atherley* v. *Brunell*, 33 W. R. 780, Pearson, J., said:
"The old doctrine has been laid down from time immemorial
that, if there is a first mortgage to A. and a second mortgage to B., who is, therefore, equitable mortgagee, and
there is a third mortgage to C., who is also equitable mortgagee, and who has advanced his money without notice of
B.'s mortgage, and C. takes a transfer of the first mortgage,
so as to obtain the legal estate, he gets priority over B."

So in *Carlisle Banking Co.* v. *Thompson*, 28 Ch. D. at
p. 401, North, J., dealt with a like case. Land was mortgaged to a friendly society, and by way of second mortgage
to a bank. Another society (building) agreed to pay off
the first mortgage and to make a further advance, having
no notice of the second mortgage. Accordingly, by deed endorsed on the first mortgage, the first mortgagees reconveyed
to the mortgagor, and he conveyed to the building society
to secure repayment of the sum paid to the first mortgagees
and the further advance. North, J., held, as both sums
.were advanced on the security of the legal estate conveyed
by the mortgagor to the building society mortgagees, without any notice, express or otherwise, of the existence of the
bank's prior equitable mortgage, it was clear that the building society had priority over the bank. See also, *Hosk-
ing* v. *Smith*, 13 App. Cas. 582.

These cases turn on the value attached to the possession
of the legal estate whereby subsequent advances are
attracted thereto if there is no notice of an intervening
incumbrance. Our registry law would interfere in such a
case, because the subsequent advance would be a thing
independent of the first mortgage, but where the further
advance is in pursuance of the terms of the first and registered mortgage, there is no room left for the operation of
a subsequent registered incumbrance, which, to my mind,
possesses no more efficacy as between the mortgagor and
the first mortgagee, and as respects the legal estate already

vested in the first mortgagee than if it had remained unre-
gistered. In other words, the further advances were made
upon a mortgage providing for such advances, and to
secure which the legal estate has been conveyed, and equity
as well as law protects the first mortgagee so advantageously placed, as against a subsequent mortgagee, even
though registered, if notice has not, as a fact, been communicated to the first mortgagee respecting the subsequent
instrument. The difference between statutable and actual
notice is aptly expressed by Lord Redesdale in *Underwood*
v. *Lord Courtown*, 2 Sch. & Lef. 41 : " Actual notice might
bind the conscience of the parties ; the operation of the
Registry Act may bind their title, but not their conscience."
Now, as to the case in hand, the title is not bound by the
registration of the second mortgage, so as to detract from
the operation of the first mortgage, and the conscience of
the first mortgagee is not affected by the subsequent act
of merely registering the second mortgage. So that the
grounds of broad natural justice on which *Hopkinson* v.
Rolt depends are non-existent. I find also an old case
which appears strongly confirmatory of the views I have
endeavoured to express. It was decided at the Rolls in
1737, before Sir Joseph Jekyll, of whom Lord Cottenham
spoke as a " high authority," and Lord St. Leonards as a
" very high authority." I give the case, *Wrightson* v.
Hudson, as reported in 2 Eq. Ca. Abr. 609. Wrightson
advanced £800 on a mortgage in Yorkshire, and registered
his mortgage, and afterwards Hudson lent a sum of money
and took a judgment for it, which was registered ; and
then Wrightson advanced £270 more, but without any express notice of Hudson's judgment. Though it was argued
on a bill brought by Wrightson to foreclose, that Hudson
ought to redeem on paying the first mortgage ; for that
where such registers prevail, every incumbrancer should be
satisfied according to the priority of his registry, and that
the registering Hudson's judgment was constructive notice
to Wrightson, sufficient to deprive him of the common
benefit of a Court of Equity, whereby a first mortgagee,

without notice, is to hold till all subsequent incumbrances are discharged, yet it was resolved, that these statutes avoid only prior charges not registered, but did not give subsequent conveyances any further force against prior ones registered than they had before ; that to have affected Mr. Wrightson, Hudson ought to have given him notice when he advanced his money ; and that though Wrightson might have searched the register, yet he was not bound to do it, and, therefore, it was decreed that Hudson and the mortgagor should be foreclosed, unless they paid off both plaintiff's securities.

Another case by King, L.C.,in the same volume, p. 615, of *Bedford* v. *Backhouse*, is also noteworthy. "A. lent money on mortgage of lands in Middlesex, and the mortgage was duly registered ; afterwards B. lent money on the same security, and his mortgage was registered. Then A. advanced a further sum on the same lands, without notice of the second mortgage." It was held that the registering of the second mortgage was not constructive notice to the first mortgagee before his second advance, for though the statute avoids deeds not registered as against purchasers, yet it gives no greater efficacy to deeds that are registered than they had before ; and the constant rule of equity is that if a first mortgagee lends a further sum of money without notice of a second mortgage, his whole money shall be paid in the first place. These cases were followed in *Morecock* v. *Dickins*, Ambl. 678, so as to protect the holder of the legal estate against a prior equitable mortgage, of which he had no actual notice, though it was registered.

Looking at the Ontario Registry Act, R. S. O. ch. 114, sec. 80, the provision is, "that the registration of any instrument under the Act shall constitute notice of the instrument to all persons claiming any interest in the lands subsequent to such registration." That does not hit the present case. The company claims interest in the lands under a prior mortgage carrying the legal estate, and the fact that advances were made on this first mortgage subsequent to the registration of a second mortgage is not contemplated or covered by the statute.

The importance of the case as regards the operation of building societies has induced me to give, at greater length than usual, the reasons why I cannot support the judgment in appeal.

This is, besides, a case in which there should be no compunction in postponing the plaintiff's mortgage, for her contract was to have a second mortgage, which was to be postponed to the building mortgage for $12,000, and in consideration of this her rate of interest was increased to seven per cent. This is not a contract of which the company can directly take advantage, as there is no privity, nor was there communication of it to the company; but it is most significant as going to indicate where the locality of natural justice is to be sought in this controversy.

ROBERTSON, J.:—[After referring to the facts as stated in the pleadings.]

The action was tried before my brother Ferguson, and he found in favour of the plaintiff against the defendant company, declaring that the mortgage of the plaintiff is a prior charge to the mortgage of the defendant company to the extent of the advances made by the company after the date of the registration of the plaintiff's mortgage, and referred it to the Master, etc. From this decision the defendant company now appeals.

My learned brother, in his judgment, says, as to the facts: " Wilson, as was contemplated at the time of his purchase from the plaintiff and her then co-owner, made a mortgage upon the property for a sum less than the $12,000, namely, $11,500. This was called, and I think it the kind of mortgage known as a 'building mortgage.' The defendants, the Canada Permanent Loan and Savings Company, were the mortgagees. This mortgage was duly registered, and then, or very soon thereafter, large sums advanced upon it by the mortgagees, a large part of these sums being employed in paying off prior incumbrances on the land. A few days after the registration of this mortgage, and

after such large advances made by the mortgagees, the
mortgage in favour of the plaintiff was registered. There
remained, however, a large proportion of the $11,500 that
had not then been advanced to the mortgagor. The
defendants, the Canada Permanent Society, had no knowledge or actual notice of the existence or the registration
of the plaintiff's mortgage, and they went on with their
contract and advanced to their mortgagor large sums after
the registration of the plaintiff's mortgage and before
gaining any actual notice of its existence or registration.
They advanced all that they did advance in perfect ignorance in fact of the plaintiff's mortgage. Nor had they any
knowledge or notice of, or any concern with, the terms of
the agreement of purchase and sale between the plaintiff
and her then co-owner and Wilson. They simply saw that
the title was clear or made clear of prior encumbrances,
had their mortgage registered, and proceeded with their
transaction as contemplated between them and Wilson,
their mortgagor. This mortgage contained a clause to the
effect, that neither the execution, nor the registration of
it, nor the advance of part of the money should bind the
mortgagees to advance any unadvanced portion of it. It
also contained a reference to an agreement relating to the
buildings in the course of erection on the property, which
last has, I think, no bearing on the contentions here.

" The contention of the plaintiff is that her mortgage was
not and should not be postponed to the advances made to
Wilson, their mortgagor, by the company after the registration of her mortgage, and if the company when making
such advances had had notice, that is actual notice of the
plaintiff's mortgage, the authorities shew, I think, that
this contention should succeed: *Hopkinson* v. *Rolt*, 9 H.
L. C. 514; *Union Bank of Scotland* v. *National Bank of
Scotland*, 12 App. Cas. 53; *Blackley* v. *Kenny*, 16 A. R.
522. I need not pursue this further, for at the bar this
was not disputed.

"The case is to be treated, I think, in regard to the
matter in dispute, in the same manner as if the plaintiff

had lent and advanced to Wilson the sum of $2,000 at the
time of the registration of her mortgage, for, as before
stated, the company had no notice of the terms of the contract by which the sale of the lands to Wilson took place,
or that any part of the purchase money was unpaid by him.
For the plaintiff it was contended that the company had
by reason of the registration of her mortgage notice of it,
and that any advances made to their mortgagor after such
registration are postponed to her mortgage, that is to say,
that the company was called upon when making such
advances, or any of them, to search the registry as to any
encumbrances or conveyances after their mortgage, otherwise the advances would be made at the peril of being
postponed to whatever claims on or in respect of the lands
were registered after the registration of the company's
mortgage."

After much consideration, and taking into account the
fact that the learned Chancellor and my learned brother
Meredith have come to a different conclusion, I cannot say
that I am free from doubt; but, with great respect for
their opinions, I cannot see how my learned brother
Ferguson can be said to be wrong. The defendant company
did not set up any agreement entered into between the
plaintiff and Thomas W. Wilson, in fact they disclaim any
knowledge of it whatever, and treat the transaction as one in
which there was no such agreement. This being the case,
how can it be said that they have suffered any wrong by
the judgment appealed against? It is clear from the
authorities relied upon by the learned trial Judge, if there
were no such agreement the defendant company could
only rank for the advances made up to the date of the
registration of the mortgage to the plaintiff. In *Union
Bank of Scotland* v. *National Bank of Scotland*, 12
App. Cas., at p. 95, the Lord Chancellor says : " If
I am right as to the true nature of the contract between
the parties," (in this case it would be the contract between the defendant company and Thomas W. Wilson),
" each fresh advance must have been the subject of a fresh

agreement, in this sense, that the bank must have consent- Judgment.
ed to advance it, and upon that consent Mrs. McArthur's Robertson, J.
previous contract would make such fresh advances a charge
upon her interest in the reversionary right." Now, here
Wilson had charged his reversionary right, looking at the
matter from the date of registration of the mortgage to the
plaintiff, with the amount of the mortgage to the plaintiff.
And the defendant company is bound by the registration,—it was their duty, before they made a fresh advance,
to search the registry, and if they had done so, they would
have found the plaintiff's mortgage; they had then the
right to hold their hand; they could not have been required,
according to the very terms of their mortgage, to advance
another dollar, for the reason that Wilson had for a valuable consideration already assigned to the plaintiff. Then
the Lord Chancellor goes on to say: "It seems to me
that such a proceeding," (*i. e.*, obtaining further advances
upon the security of an interest which had been already
assigned for a valuable consideration to another person),
"is contrary to good faith, and the decision of your Lord-
ships' House, in *Hopkinson* v. *Rolt*, 9 H. L. C. 514, establishes the principle and establishes it upon the broadest
grounds of natural justice."

I do not think it necessary to pursue the matter further
than to say, for the reasons given by my learned brother
Ferguson, I think his judgment is correct, and the appeal
should be disallowed with costs.

MEREDITH, J.:—

The learned trial Judge has given priority to the plaintiff's mortgage over the greater part of the amount of the
mortgage of the defendants, the loan company, although
he has found, without hesitation, that by a clear agreement
in writing between the mortgagor and the plaintiff, her
mortgage was to be subsequent to the whole amount of
the other mortgage. That is, that which, in truth, is but
a second mortgage is made a first mortgage upon the pro-

perty in question. Surely the registry laws cannot have
such an effect.

That which the plaintiff was to get, and which, in equity,
she did take, was the land in question as security for the
$2,000 due to her from the mortgagor, but subject to the
mortgage of the defendants the loan company for such
sums as there had been and might thereafter properly be
advanced upon the security of it, not exceeding in the
whole the $12,000.

It is said that because there was no privity of contract
between the plaintiff and the defendants, the loan company, as against them, the real transaction can be enlarged
into the unreal one appearing on the face of the registered mortgage; that the mortgage can be severed from
the accompanying agreement in writing for the purpose of
giving the plaintiff rights she in truth never acquired,
enabling her to take that which she expressly agreed in
writing she should not have.

Upon what principle can the right which the plaintiff
contracted to take in the lands be so enlarged? If on the
face of the registered mortgage the whole agreement had
been set out, could it be contended that yet the plaintiff
took that priority which she agreed—and so expressed in
the agreement—she should not have?

Can it be that in the face of her agreement the plaintiff
might, at her whim, bring the whole building scheme to
naught at any stage of the work, causing, may be, the
total loss of all that may then have been done, by even giving actual notice of her mortgage to the loan company and
expressly claiming priority over subsequent advances by
them; unless the mortgagor chose to interpose, and by
litigation in his own interest prevent it?

Put the defendants, the loan company, in the most dis-
advantageous position possible, namely :—that, in respect
of advances made subsequent to the registration of the
plaintiff's mortgage, they were subsequent mortgagees, with
notice of it under the registry laws. Well, what then?
Are they to be charged with notice of the real transaction

or of an unreal one? Surely they can be in no worse
position than if the registry laws were out of the question
and they had actual notice of the real—the whole—transaction; and having notice that the mortgage is to be subject to such future advances to be made by them, how can
the whole thing be reversed, in this court of equity as well
as of law, and they be told that instead of it being subject
to such advances, the advances are to be subject to it?

But it is said that the trial Judge was constrained by
the cases to hold as he did upon this question of law; and
that we are bound by the like authority to affirm his
judgment. Is that so? What case is even an authority
in the plaintiff's favour, having regard to the facts upon
which this judgment is based? None was cited; and I
have found none. Are not rather such cases as the *Union
Bank of Scotland* v. *National Bank of Scotland*, 12 App.
Cas. 53, and *Menzies* v. *Lightfoot*, L. R. 11 Eq. 459, authorities against the plaintiff—quite opposed to her claim?
Are we here bound to give effect to the mere *ex facie* title
as registered, of the plaintiff; or may we regard the real,
the true, nature of the security the plaintiff was to have
upon this land? Looking upon the defendants, the loan
company, as subsequent purchasers for value in respect of
their subsequent advances, are they to take, as their mortgage provides, "all the estate, right, title, interest, inheritance, use, trust, property, profit, possession, claim and
demand whatsoever of the grantor of, in, to, out of or upon
the lands": R. S. O. ch. 107, sec. 4: and "all and all manner
of right, title, interest, claim and demand whatsoever of,
unto and out of the said lands," or only such right as the
mortgagor upon the face of the registered instruments
appeared to have? And is not the agreement between
the plaintiff and her mortgagor just such a provision as
the Master of the Rolls, in the latter case, suggested for
the saving of the first mortgagee's priority for subsequent
advances?

The case of *Hopkinson* v. *Rolt*, 9 H. L. C. 514, is not at
all in point. Whether the doctrine there established would

Judgment.

Meredith, J.

be applicable if the plaintiff had not bargained for a security subsequent to the whole amount advanced and to be advanced upon the mortgage of the defendants, the loan company; whether it would be applicable to the simple case of a building loan where a certain sum is to be advanced, if advanced at all, within a certain time and for the sole purpose of increasing the value of the mortgaged lands, and which loan is intended to be and can be really secured only if the lender obtain the full benefit of such increased value; whether the doctrine can be invoked in a case where it might be capriciously, or for spite, made applicable to the destruction of the purposes of the loan, the abandonment of buildings, partially constructed, to ruin, and to the loss of all persons interested in the property, it is not needful to consider; and, therefore, I shall say only that upon first impression it would seem to me to be a thing to be regretted if we were obliged to apply a doctrine so just in the one case to so unjust a use in the other.   Regard must be had to the reasons upon which that doctrine was in that case established: it certainly was not to give some other person a first charge upon the fruits of the money of the lender in the shape of buildings or other improvements upon the land made with his money, lent upon the faith of having a first charge upon them as well as the land of which they become a part.

Is not such a loan in substance like a mechanic's lien, which may be registered before or during the progress of the work, or within thirty days after its completion, and, when registered, making, it has been said, the lienholder a mortgagee of the land: *Hutson* v. *Valliers*, 19 A. R. 154, at p. 161: and, if so, may such a loan be prejudiced, perhaps rendered worthless, or at least reduced to a claim upon the increased selling value of the land by reason of the work subsequently done, by the intervention of a mortgage taking priority from the time of registration, or actual notice to the lien holder of it.

I would allow the motion, and dismiss the action, with costs.   A. H. F. L.

A DIGEST

OF

ALL THE CASES REPORTED IN THIS VOLUME

BEING DECISIONS IN THE

QUEEN'S BENCH, COMMON PLEAS, AND CHANCERY DIVISIONS

OF THE

HIGH COURT OF JUSTICE FOR ONTARIO.

ABSCONDING DEBTOR.

See MALICIOUS ARREST AND PROSECUTION.

ACCIDENT.

See MASTER AND SERVANT—MUNICIPAL CORPORATIONS, 1 — NEGLIGENCE—RAILWAYS.

ACQUIESCENCE.

See MORTGAGE, 1.

ACTION.

Cause of.]—See WATER AND WATERCOURSES.

Notice of — Requisites of.]—See MALICIOUS ARREST AND PROSECUTION, 5—MUNICIPAL CORPORATIONS, 1.

Release of—Cause of—Settlement of.]—See RAILWAYS.

ADMINISTRATORS.

See EXECUTORS AND ADMINISTRATORS.

AFFIDAVIT.

See BILLS OF SALE AND CHATTEL MORTGAGES, 1—HABEAS CORPUS—MALICIOUS ARREST AND PROSECUTION, 1.

AGENT.

See PRINCIPAL AND AGENT.

AMENDMENT.

Of Pleadings.]—See SALE OF GOODS.

APPEAL.

To Divisional Court.]—*See* IN-SURANCE, 2.

See DISTRICT COURTS — PUBLIC SCHOOLS.

ARBITRATION AND AWARD.

1. *Excessive Charge for Arbitrator's Fees—Penalty—R. S. O. ch. 53, sec. 29—Demand—Liability.*]—The liability imposed on arbitrators by section 29 of R. S. O. ch. 53 in case of an overcharge of fees, to pay treble the amount of the fees charged or paid, is penal in its nature, and does not arise where a person entitled to take up the award has voluntarily paid the charges without any previous demand of the award by such person, followed by a refusal or delay to make, execute, or deliver the same by the arbitrator until payment of the excessive charges.

Taxation of the fees is not a condition precedent to maintaining an action for the penalty. *Jones* v. *Godson*, 444.

2. *Award by Two out of Three Arbitrators.*]—Where a submission to arbitration provides that the award thereunder shall be made by three arbitrators, the award to be valid must be made by the three unanimously. *Re O'Connor and Fielder*, 568.

3. *Injunction Restraining Arbitrator Acting—Jurisdiction of High Court—Arbitrator Solicitor for Parties.*]—The High Court has power to prevent a non-indifferent arbitrator from acting without waiting until the award is made, though perhaps the better course is to apply for leave to revoke the submission if another arbitrator be not substituted.

Malmesbury R. W. Co. v. *Budd*, 2 Ch. D. 113, and *Beddow* v. *Beddow*, 9 Ch. D. 89, followed.

A barrister and solicitor who had acted as counsel for the husband on an indictment and trial for obstructing an alleged highway claimed by his wife to be her property, and who had written a letter concerning the matter as solicitor for both husband and wife, was restrained from acting as arbitrator in an arbitration between the wife and the municipal corporation in which the highway was situate.

Vineburg v. *Guardian Fire and Life Association Co.*, 19 A. R. 293, followed. *Corporation of Burford* v. *Chambers et al.*, 663.

Lands Injuriously Affected—Appointment of Arbitrator.]—*See* PROHIBITION.

See PUBLIC SCHOOLS — WATER AND WATERCOURSES.

ARREST.

See MALICIOUS ARREST AND PROSECUTION.

ASSESSMENT AND TAXES.

Assessment Act—55 Vict. ch. 48, sec. 124 (O.)—Goods Subject to Distress—Occupancy.]—Section 124 of the Consolidated Assessment Act, 55 Vict. ch. 48 (O.), does not authorize a distress for non-payment of taxes of the goods of strangers on the premises, unless such goods are in the possession of the person who ought to pay the taxes or of a legal occupant of the property. *Christie* v. *Corporation of Toronto*, 425.

On appeal to the Divisional Court, the judgment was affirmed, 606.

See MUNICIPAL CORPORATIONS, 9.

ASSIGNMENT.

For Benefit of Creditors.]—*See* BANKRUPTCY AND INSOLVENCY.

Of Mortgage.]—*See* MORTGAGE, 2.

Of Tavern License.]—*See* PARTNERSHIP.

AUCTIONEER.

·*License to—Power of Corporation to refuse.*]—*See* MUNICIPAL CORPORATIONS, 3.

AWARD.

See ARBITRATION AND AWARD.

BAILMENT.

Delivery of Seed on Contract to Plant—Damages to Land from Impurity of Seed—Remoteness—Estoppel — Slander — Privilege —Actual Malice.]—Where seed is delivered by one person to another without any warranty, honestly believing it to be clean, to be grown on the land of the latter, the produce thereof to be returned and paid for at a fixed price per bushel, the transaction is a bailment and not a sale; and damages arising from other innocuous seed having been mixed therewith, and on harvesting having become scattered on the ground and coming up the following year on the land, are too remote, and not within the rule laid down in *Hadley* v. *Baxendale*, 9 Ex. 341, and *Cory* v. *Thames Ironworks Co.*, L. R. 3 Q. B. 181.

McMullen v. *Free*, 13 O. R. 57, and *Smith* v. *Green*, 1 C. P. D. 92, distinguished.

The plaintiff, having received seed from the defendant to be grown under the circumstances and conditions above mentioned, became aware while it was growing that vetches were coming up with it, but did not inform the defendant of the fact, and permitted them to grow, and delivered the produce mixed to the defendant, and was paid for it:—

Held, that he could not recover damages for an injury which his own conduct was responsible for.

McCollum v. *Davis*, 8 U. C. R. 150, specially referred to.

The plaintiff claimed damages for slander in respect of words spoken to him by the defendant, in the presence of others, to the effect that he had sold the seed given him. The jury found that the words were not spoken in good faith in the usual course of business affairs for the protection of his own interests:—

Held, that there was no evidence to sustain such a finding; that the evidence shewed that the defendant honestly and justifiably believed that the plaintiff had defrauded him; that the occasion was privileged, and the plaintiff had failed to shew actual malice; and therefore he could not recover. *Stewart* v. *Sculthorp*, 544.

BANKRUPTCY AND INSOLVENCY.

1. *Assignments and Preferences— R. S. O. ch. 124, sec. 4—Assignment for Benefit of Creditors—Several Pro-*

perty of Partners—Covenant of Indemnity — Creditors —Execution of Assignment by.]—An assignment under R. S. O. ch. 124, for the general benefit of creditors, made by the members of a trading partnership, in the words mentioned in section 4, vests in the assignee all the properties of each of the partners, several as well as joint, including a covenant to indemnify one of the partners against a mortgage, which covenant vests under the term "property."

Where such an assignment has been acted upon by the creditors, it is not open to the objection, even if made by an execution creditor, that no creditor executed it.

Cooper v. *Dixon*, 10 A. R. 50, distinguished.

Judgment of ROBERTSON, J., varied. *Ball et al.* v. *Tennant*, 50.

Reversed by the Court of Appeal.

2. *Fraudulent Preference — Voluntary Transfer—Subsequent Sale to Innocent Purchaser—Following Proceeds Thereof.*]—An insolvent debtor, for the purpose of defeating the plaintiffs' claim against him, by voluntary deed conveyed the equity of redemption in certain lands to another creditor who, as previously arranged with the grantor, sold the property to an innocent purchaser and applied the proceeds in payment of all encumbrances on the property and all his own debts and those of certain other creditors of the grantor, and of a commission to himself in respect to the sale, and paid over the final balance to the grantor :—

Held, that the plaintiffs had no right of action against the fraudulent grantee to recover any part of the purchase money.

Masuret v. *Stewart*, 22 O. R. 290, and *Cornish* v. *Clark*, L. R. 14 Eq.

184, distinguished. *Tennant & Co.* v. *Gallow*, 56.

3. *Assignments and Preferences— Costs of Litigation in Respect to Disputed Claim—Right of Assignee to Charge same Against Estate— R. S. O. ch. 124.*]—An assignee for the benefit of creditors, on instructions of the inspectors, contested the plaintiff's claim, who then brought an action, which was dismissed with costs, but, on appeal to the Divisional Court, this decision was reversed, with costs to be paid by the defendant, the assignee. The creditors, after taking counsel's opinion, resolved to appeal to the Court of Appeal, but the appeal to that Court was dismissed with costs. The assignee charged against the estate the total sum he had to pay in respect of the costs of these proceedings :—

Held, that he was entitled so to do.

Decision of ROBERTSON, J., affirmed. *Smith* v. *Beal*, 368.

Rights of Assignee.]—*See* BILLS OF SALE AND CHATTEL MORTGAGES.

BANKS AND BANKING.

Special Deposit — Wrongful Refusal to Pay Out—Action—Damages —Costs.]—The damages recoverable by a non-trading depositor in the savings bank department of a bank who has made his deposit subject to special terms, on the wrongful refusal of the bank to pay it to him personally, are limited to the interest on the money.

Marzetti v. *Williams*, 1 B. & Ad. 415 ; and *Rolin* v. *Steward*, 14 C. B. 594, distinguished.

A bank having received a deposit subject to certain notice of withdrawal, if required, cannot set up as a defence to an action for the deposit the absence of such notice, unless the refusal to pay was based on that ground.

The defendants having paid into Court twenty cents less than the correct amount due by them, the plaintiff was held entitled to full costs. *Henderson* v. *Bank of Hamilton*, 641.

BIGAMY.

Offence Committed in Foreign Country.] — *See* CONSTITUTIONAL LAW, 2.

BILLS OF SALE AND CHATTEL MORTGAGES.

1. *Affidavit of Bona Fides—Incorporated Company—Officer of—Agent—Authority—R. S. O. ch. 125, sec. 1.*]—Where the affidavit of *bona fides* of a chattel mortgage to an incorporated trading company was made by the secretary-treasurer, who was also a shareholder in the company and had an important share in the management of its affairs, there being, however, a president and vice-president :—

Held, that the affiant was to be regarded not as one of the mortgagees, but as an agent, and, as no written authority to him was registered, as required by R. S. O. ch. 125, sec. 1, the mortgage was invalid as against creditors.

Bank of Toronto v. *McDougall*, 15 C. P. 475, distinguished.

Freehold Loan Co. v. *Bank of Commerce*, 44 U. C. R. 284, followed. *Greene & Sons Co. (Limited)* v. *Castleman et al.*, 113.

2. *Chattel Mortgage—Validity of Renewal — Right of Assignee for Creditors to Question—R. S. O. ch. 125, secs. 4, 11—55 Vict. ch. 26, sec. 2 (O.).*]—Section 2 of 55 Vict. ch. 26 (O.) does not enable an assignee for the general benefit of creditors to question the validity of the renewal of a chattel mortgage. *Tallman* v. *Smart*, 661.

See LANDLORD AND TENANT.

BY-LAW.

Necessity of Two-thirds Vote on.]— *See* INTOXICATING LIQUORS.

Invalid Debentures Issued under.] —*See* MUNICIPAL CORPORATIONS, 2.

Affecting Highways.]—*See* MUNICIPAL CORPORATIONS, 4.

Drainage.]—*See* MUNICIPAL CORPORATIONS, 6, 7, 9.

Prohibiting Swearing in public place.] — *See* PUBLIC MORALS AND CONVENIENCE.

Appointment of Arbitrators.]—*See* PROHIBITION—PUBLIC SCHOOLS.

CASES.

Abell v. *Morrison*, 19 O. R. 669, distinguished.]—*See* MORTGAGE, 1.

Alexander v. *Township of Howard*, 14 O. R. 22, followed.]—*See* MUNICIPAL CORPORATIONS, 2.

Allen v. *Furness*, 20 A. R. 34, distinguished.]—*See* EXECUTION.

Bailey v. *Neal*, 5 Times L. R. 20, commented on and distinguished.]— *See* NEGLIGENCE, 1.

Bank of Toronto v. *McDougall*, 15 C. P. 475, distinguished.]—*See* BILLS OF SALE AND CHATTEL MORTGAGES, 1.

Batchelor v. *Fortescue*, 11 Q. B. D. 474, distinguished.]—*See* NEGLIGENCE, 2.

Bartonshill Coal Co. v. *Reid*, 3 Macq. Sc. App. Cas. 266, followed.]—*See* NEGLIGENCE, 3.

Beer v. *Stroud*, 19 O. R. 10, referred to.]—*See* WATER AND WATERCOURSES.

Beddow v. *Beddow*, 9 Ch. D. 89, followed.]—*See* ARBITRATION, 3.

Bernardin v. *Corporation of North Dufferin*, 19 S. C. R. 581, considered.]—*See* MUNICIPAL CORPORATIONS, 7.

Brown v. *McLean*, 18 O. R. 533, distinguished.]—*See* MORTGAGE, 1.

Brown v. *Overbury*, 11 Ex. 715, followed.]—*See* GAMING, 2.

Cameron v. *Nystrom*, [1893] A. C. 308, followed.]—*See* NEGLIGENCE, 2.

Citizens Ins. Co. v. *Parsons*, 7 App. Cas. 96, followed.]—*See* INSURANCE, 3.

Clark v. *Township of Howard, Re*, 16 A. R. 72, followed.]—*See* MUNICIPAL CORPORATIONS, 2.

Cooper v. *Dixon*, 10 A. R. 50, distinguished.] — *See* BANKRUPTCY AND INSOLVENCY, 1.

Cornish v. *Clark*, L. R. 14 Eq. 184, distinguished.] — *See* BANKRUPTCY AND INSOLVENCY, 2.

Cory v. *Thames Iron Works Co.*, L. R. 3 Q. B. 181, referred to.]—*See* BAILMENT.

Ellis v. *Hopper*, 3 H. & N. 768, followed.]—*See* GAMING, 2.

Emeris v. *Woodward*, 43 Ch. D. 185, distinguished.]—*See* RAILWAYS.

Erickson v. *Brand*, 14 A. R. 614, distinguished.]—*See* MALICIOUS ARREST AND PROSECUTION, 1.

Freehold Loan Co. v. *Bank of Commerce*, 44 U. C. R. 284, followed.]—*See* BILLS OF SALE AND CHATTEL MORTGAGES, 1.

Gardner v. *Grace*, 1 F. & F. 359, approved of.]—*See* NEGLIGENCE, 1.

Gordon v. *O'Brien, Re*, 11 P. R. 287, not followed.]—*See* DIVISION COURTS, 1.

Griffin v. *Kingston and Pembroke R. W. Co.*, 17 O. R. 665, dissented from.]—*See* COPYRIGHT.

Harvey v. *Murray*, 136 Mass. 377, approved.]—*See* HIRE OF GOODS.

Hadley v. *Baxendale*, 9 Ex. 341, referred to.]—*See* BAILMENT.

Hoare v. *Lee*, 5 C. B. 754, followed.]—*See* LANDLORD AND TENANT.

Hughes v. *Macfie*, 2 H. & C. 744, commented on and distinguished.]—*See* NEGLIGENCE, 1.

Johnstone v. *Sutton*, 1 T. R. 547, considered and distinguished.]—*See* MALICIOUS ARREST AND PROSECUTION, 3.

Jones v. *Colbeck*, 8 Ves. 38, approved and specially referred to.]—*See* WILL, 7.

Kinnaird v. *Trollope*, 39 Ch. D. 636, followed.]—*See* MORTGAGE, 2.

Little v. *Billings*, 27 Gr. 353, distinguished.]—*See* WILL, 6.

Malmesbury R. W. Co. v. *Budd*, 2 Ch. D. 113, followed.]—*See* ARBITRATION AND AWARD, 3.

Mangan v. *Atherton*, 4 H. & C. 388, commented on and distinguished.]—*See* NEGLIGENCE, 1.

Marsh v. *Fulton County*, 10 Wall. U. S. R. 676, specially referred to.] *See* MUNICIPAL CORPORATIONS, 2.

Marzetti v. *Williams*, 1 B. & Ad. 415, distinguished.]—*See* BANKS AND BANKING.

Masuret v. *Stewart*, 22 O. R. 290, distinguished.] — *See* BANKRUPTCY AND INSOLVENCY, 2.

Metropolitan Saloon Omnibus Co. v. *Hawkins*, 4 H. & N. 87, commented on and distinguished.]—*See* DEFAMATION.

Mulcahy v. *The Queen*, Ir. R. 1, C. L. 12, followed.]—*See* CRIMINAL LAW, 1.

McCollum v. *Davis*, 8 U. C. R. 150, specially referred to.] — *See* BAILMENT.

McGillivray v. *Great Western R. W. Co.*, 25 U. C. R. 69, distinguished.]—*See* WATER AND WATERCOURSES.

Macleod v. *Attorney-General for New South Wales*, [1891] A. C. 455, followed.] — *See* CONSTITUTIONAL LAW, 2.

McMullen v. *Free*, 13 O. R. 57, distinguished.]—*See* BAILMENT.

Newcomen v. *Lynch*, Ir. R. 9 C. L. 1, Ir. R. 10 C. L. 248, followed.]— *See* GAMING, 2.

Pratt v. *City of Stratford*, 14 O. R. 260, 16 A. R. 5, followed.]—*See* PROHIBITION.

Reddick v. *Saugeen Mutual Fire Ins. Co.*, 15 A. R. 363, followed.]— *See* INSURANCE, 3.

Reed v. *Taylor*, 4 Taunt. 616, followed.] — *See* MALICIOUS ARREST AND PROSECUTION, 3.

Regina v. *Hazen*, 20 A. R. 633, distinguished.]—*See* JUSTICE OF THE PEACE.

Robertson v. *Coulton*, 9 P. R. 16, approved and followed.]—*See* MALICIOUS ARREST AND PROSECUTION, 2.

Rolin v. *Steward*, 14 C. B. 594, distinguished.] — *See* BANKS AND BANKING.

Scane v. *Coffee*, 15 P. R. 112, referred to.]—*See* MALICIOUS ARREST AND PROSECUTION, 1.

Smith v. *Baker*, [1891] A. C. 325, applied and followed.]—*See* NEGLIGENCE, 2.

Smith v. *Green*, 1 C. P. D. 92, distinguished.]—*See* BAILMENT.

South Hetton Coal Co. v. *North Eastern News Association*, [1894] 1 Q. B. 133, followed.]—*See* DEFAMATION.

Toothe v. *Frederick*, 14 P. R. 287, commented on and not followed.]— *See* MALICIOUS ARREST AND PROSECUTION, 2.

Taylor v. *Caldwell*, 3 B. & S. 826, followed.]—*See* HIRE OF GOODS.

Teevan v. *Smith* 20 Ch. D. 724, distinguished.]—*See* MORTGAGE, 2.

Vineburg v. *Guardian Fire and Life Ass. Co.*, 19 A. R. 293, followed.] — *See* ARBITRATION AND AWARD, 3.

Webb v. *Commissioners of Herne Bay*, L. R. 5 Q. B. 642, distinguished.]—*See* MUNICIPAL CORPORATIONS, 2.

CHARITABLE BEQUEST.

See WILL, 3.

CHATTEL MORTGAGES.

See BILLS OF SALE AND CHATTEL MORTGAGES.

COMPANY.

1. *Winding-up Act—Master in Ordinary — Jurisdiction — Fraudulent Transfer—R. S. C., ch. 129—52 Vict. ch. 32 (D.).*]—The Master in Ordinary, or other officer of the Court, to whom its powers may be delegated is not a competent tribunal to decide questions of fraudulent transfer arising in the course of a reference in winding-up proceedings, under the Dominion Winding-up Act and amending Acts. *Harte* v. *Ontario Express and Transportation Co., Molson's Bank Claim*, 247.

2. *Mining Company — Acquisition of Land—Mortgage to Secure Purchase Money—Execution of Contract — Presumption.*] — Where a company has power to acquire land for the purposes of its incorporation, it has the power to give a mortgage for and to bind itself by covenant to pay the purchase money.

Where the power to contract exists, a person contracting with the company need not enquire whether the proper formalities of execution by the company have been complied with in a contract under its corporate seal. *Sheppard* v. *Bonanza Nickel Mining Co. of Sudbury*, 305.

3. *Contract to Transfer all Shares—Winding-up Order before Completion—Specific Performance.*]— The shareholders of a company sold and transferred part of their property, and also contracted that they would, within a year, transfer their charter by assigning all their stock to the purchaser's nominee. Part of the purchase money was paid at once, but the purchaser did not nominate a person to whom the shares should be transferred. After an order for the winding-up of the company had been made, the liquidators brought this action for the balance of the purchase money :—

Held, that they were entitled to recover.

Decision of MACMAHON, J., affirmed. *Redfern et al.* v. *Polson et al.*, 321.

4. *Winding-up—R. S. C. ch. 129, sec. 3—52 Vict. ch. 32, sec. 3 (D.)— Voluntary Winding-up — Compulsory Liquidation—" Doing Business in Canada."*]—There is no clashing between sec. 3 of the Winding-up Act, R. S. C. ch. 129, and sec. 3 of the Winding-up Amendment Act, 52 Vict. ch. 32 ; the latter Act provides for the voluntary winding-up of the companies falling within its provisions, and not for their compulsory liquidation, which is provided for by the former.

A company incorporated under an Act of the Province of Ontario, and carrying on business in Ontario, is " doing business in Canada " within the meaning of sec. 3 of the original

Act. *Re Ontario Forge and Bolt Co. (Limited)*, 407.

5. *Shares—Sale under Execution —Validity of Assignment not Entered in Books—R. S. O. ch. 157, sec. 52—Equity of Redemption—R. S. O. ch. 64, sec. 16.*]—A *bond fide* assignment or pledge for value of shares in the capital stock of a company incorporated under R. S. O. ch. 157 is valid between the assignor and the assignee, notwithstanding that no entry of the assignment or transfer is made in the books of the company ; and, as only the debtor's interest in property seized can be sold under execution, the rights of a *bonâ fide* assignee cannot be cut out by the seizure and sale of the shares, under execution against the assignor, after the assignment.

R. S. O. ch. 157, sec. 52, considered and construed.

Semble, that nothing passes by such a sale under execution ; for the words " goods and chattels " in sec. 16 of the Execution Act, R. S. O. ch. 64, do not include shares in an incorporated company so as to authorize the sale of the equity of redemption in such shares. *Morton v. Cowan et al.*, 529.

6. *Appointment of Directors to Salaried Offices—Rights to Remuneration—Winding-up.*]—Where an Act of Incorporation provides that no by-law for the payment of the president or any director, shall be valid or acted on until the same has been confirmed at a general meeting of the shareholders, this applies only to payment for the services of a director *qua* director, and for the services of the president as presiding officer of the board.

Where a company appoints the directors to various salaried offices

without a by-law fixing the amount of the salaries as required by the Act of Incorporation, and such appointments are afterwards confirmed by legislation, they are entitled to prove in the winding-up for a *quantum meruit* for services rendered. *Re Ontario Express and Transportation Co., The Directors' Case*, 587.

See BILLS OF SALE AND CHATTEL MORTGAGES, 1 — CONSTITUTIONAL LAW, 1.

COMPENSATION.

Diversion of Watercourse.]—*See* WATER AND WATERCOURSES.

CONDITIONAL FEE.

See WILL, 6.

CONSTABLE.

Notice of Action.]—*See* MALICIOUS ARREST AND PROSECUTION, 5.

CONSPIRACY.

See HABEAS CORPUS.

CONSTITUTIONAL LAW.

1. *Local Legislature—Powers of—Company—Insurance Act of Ontario — Powers of Master — Creditors' Schedules — Contributories' Schedules.*]—The Ontario Legislature has power to confer upon the Master the powers given by " The Insurance Corporation Act of 1892."

The Master has power under that Act to settle schedules of creditors, which implies power to adjudicate upon the claims of officials of a company for services to ascertain whether they shall appear as creditors in the schedules ; but he cannot adjudicate upon the question whether they have been guilty of such conduct as deprives them of their right to claim as creditors.

He has also power to settle schedules of contributories, but cannot adjudicate upon the question whether officials of the company have been guilty of such a breach of duty as to make them liable for any loss by reason thereof. Such matters can only be determined by action. *Re Dominion Provident Benevolent and Endowment Association*, 619.

2. *Criminal Code, sec. 275—Bigamy—Offence Committed in Foreign Country—Intent—Ultra Vires.*]— Conviction for bigamy quashed where the second marriage took place in a foreign country, and there was evidence that the defendant, who was a British subject, resident in Canada, left there with the intent to commit the offence.

The provisions of sec. 275 of the Criminal Code making such a marriage an offence are *ultra vires* of the Parliament of Canada.

Macleod v. *Attorney-General for New South Wales*, [1891] A. C. 455, followed. *Regina* v. *Plowman*, 656.

CONTRACT.

1. *Restraint of Trade — Partial Covenant—Limited Time—Reasonableness—Public Policy.*]—On the purchase of a manufacturing business by the plaintiff from the defendants, the latter entered into a covenant with the plaintiff which was part of the terms of sale, that they would not engage directly or indirectly in the manufacture or sale of "bamboo ware and fancy furniture, either as principal, agent or employee at any place in the Dominion of Canada for the term of ten years from the date hereof. This clause does not prevent" (defendants) " from engaging in the retail business of furniture and bamboo ware selling. It covers wholesale or jobbing business " :—

Held, that as the restraint of trade was partial only, being confined to manufacturing certain articles and to selling them by wholesale or by jobbing and for a limited time, and as there was no evidence on which it could be held to be unreasonable, and the interests of the public were not interfered with, the agreement was not contrary to public policy. *Cook* v. *Shaw et al.*, 124.

2. *Horses —" Plant "— Meaning of.*]—By one of the clauses of a railway contract for excavation, "all machinery and other plant, materials and things whatsoever," provided by the contractor were until the completion of the work to be the property of the company, when such as had not been used and converted into the works and remained undisposed of were to be delivered over to the contractor, but in other clauses the words "teams and horses" were respectively used as well as the word " plant " :—

Held, under the contract, that horses were not included in the word " plant ; " and that expert evidence was not admissible to explain its meaning. *Middleton* v. *Flanagan*, 417.

3. *Remuneration for Services— Collateral Contract—Judgment on— Novation.*]—Where services have

been performed by one person for the benefit and at the request of another, and which have been charged to the latter, the fact that a third person has subsequently agreed to pay for such services, and has had judgment recovered against him therefor, by the person rendering them, will not prevent the latter recovering in an action against the person liable in the first instance, unless the subsequent agreement amounts to a novation. *Herod* v. *Ferguson*, 565.

See BAILMENT—CRIMINAL LAW, 1 —HIRE OF GOODS—MUNICIPAL CORPORATIONS, 7—PRINCIPAL AND AGENT—SALE OF GOODS—STATUTE OF FRAUDS.

CONVICTION.

See JUSTICE OF THE PEACE.

CONTRIBUTORY NEGLIGENCE.

See NEGLIGENCE.

CONSPIRACY.

See CRIMINAL LAW, 1, 3.

CONVERSION.

See LANDLORD AND TENANT.

COPYRIGHT.

Circulars—Forms—" Books and Literary Compositions"—R. S. C. ch. 62, and Amendment.] — The purely commercial or business character of a composition or compilation does not oust the right to protection of copyright, if time, labour, and experience have been devoted to its production.

The plaintiff, the proprietor of a school for the cure of stammering, had obtained copyright for publications consisting of : (1) "Applicant's Blank," a series of questions to be answered by entrants to the school ; (2) "Information for Stammerers," an advertisement circular ; (3) "Entrance Memorandum," an agreement to be signed by entrants, and (4) "Entrance Agreement," similar to No. 3, but more formal :—

Held, that the plaintiff had copyright in the publications, and was entitled to an injunction restraining infringement thereof.

Griffin v. *Kingston and Pembroke R. W. Co.*, 17 O. R. at p. 665, dissented from. *Church* v. *Linton*, 131.

CORPORATIONS.

See COMPANY—MUNICIPAL CORPORATIONS.

COSTS.

Of Disputed Claim.]—*See* BANKRUPTCY AND INSOLVENCY, 3.

See BANKS AND BANKING—INSURANCE, 2.

COUNTY JUDGE.

Powers of, Appointment of Arbitrator.]—*See* PROHIBITION.

COURTS.

Jurisdiction of.]—*See* DIVISION COURTS, 4.

698   DIGEST OF CASES.   [VOL.

CRIMINAL CODE.

See CONSTITUTIONAL LAW, 2 —
CRIMINAL LAW, 4 — GAMING, 1—
HABEAS CORPUS.

CRIMINAL LAW.

1. *Conspiracy – Agreement – Overt
Acts—Acts of Co-conspirators—Acts
before Date Alleged in Indictment
— Engineer's Report — Entries in
Books — Secondary Evidence — Examination in Civil Action—Present to Official—Fictitious Tenders—
Deceit— "Unlawful" — Right of
Reply.*]—L. C. & Co., a firm of contractors in Quebec, tendered to harbour commissioners for certain work
to be done with the approval of the
Government, sending in three tenders, one in their own name, and
two in the names of others, with a
common mistake as to price of a
portion of the work in all three.
The defendant McG., whose brother
had been admitted to the firm as a
partner without the payment of any
capital, was both a member of Parliament and of the harbour commission. The three tenders with others
were received and opened by the
commissioners, the defendant McG.
being present, and were then forwarded to the Government at Ottawa, Ontario. The defendant McG.
went to Ottawa and succeeded in
obtaining from the government
engineer particulars of the calculations and results of all the tenders
sent in, of which he advised his
brother by letters. When the mistake in the price was notified by the
government engineer to the three
tenderers, one tender was withdrawn, one was varied, so as to make
it higher than others, and the firm's
was allowed to remain as it was

with the manifest error, and so became the lowest tender, and was
thus accepted. One government engineer was given a situation on the
harbour commission, and the chief
engineer of the Public Works Department received a valuable present
from the firm. As soon as the contract was executed, promissory notes
to an amount of many thousand
dollars were signed by the firm and
given to the defendant McG., and
he also received money from his
brother, whose only means of paying
were his profits as a partner. On
an indictment for conspiracy against
McG. and C., a member of the
firm :—

Held, that there is no unvarying
rule that the agreement to conspire
must first be established before the
particular acts of the individuals
implicated are admissible in evidence, and that the letters written
by the defendant McG. at Ottawa
were overt acts there in furtherance
of the common design, and admissible in evidence against all privy to
the conspiracy for which they might
be prosecuted in this Province, and
as the defendant C. was, by his own
admission, privy to the large payment after it was made, it was a
matter for the jury to say whether
he was not throughout a participator
in the proceedings : *Mulcahy v. The
Queen*, I. R. 1 C. L. 12, followed :—

(2) The transactions, conversations, and written communications
between R. H., McG. (the partner),
and his brother, the defendant McG.,
and the other members of the firm,
were receivable in evidence in the
circumstances of this case. If at
first not available against both defendants they became so when the
proof had so far advanced and cumulated as to indicate the existence of
a common design :—

(3) Evidence as to the manner in which other contracts were obtained by the firm previous to the date mentioned in the indictment was properly received as introductory to the transaction in question :—

(4) Letters written by a member of the firm in the name of an employee, and purporting to be signed by him, were also properly in evidence :—

(5) The report of the government engineer recommending the acceptance of the firm's tender, was also properly in evidence as the object of all that was done was to obtain a report in favour of the firm :—

(6) Entries in the books of the firm were evidence against the defendant C., and statements prepared therefrom by an accountant were good secondary evidence in the absence of the books withheld by the defendants :—

Query.—How far they were evidence against the defendant McG. who was not a member of the firm.

(7) The examination of the defendant C. in a civil action arising out of these matters, he not having claimed privilege therein, could be used against him on this trial :—

(8) The evidence of an expert in calculating results on *data* supplied and proper for an engineer to work upon, was admissible :—

(9) Evidence of a present being made to an engineer in charge of the work with the knowledge of one of the defendants was proper to be considered by the jury as casting light on the relations between the firm and that officer :—

(10) The use of fictitious tenders was a *deceit,* and if done to evade the results of fair competition for the contracts it was " unlawful " :—

(11) Although evidence was called by only one of the defendants it might have enured to the benefit of both, so the right to a general reply was with the counsel for the Crown. *Regina* v. *Connolly and McGreevy,* 151.

2. *Conviction of Lesser Offence— Evidence of Greater Offence—Seduction—Rape— R. S. C. ch. 157, sec. 3.*]—A prisoner indicted and tried under section 3, clause (*a*), of the Act respecting offences against public morals and public convenience, R. S. C. ch. 157, with having seduced a girl under sixteen :—

Held, properly convicted of such offence, although the evidence given, if believed in whole, would have supported a conviction for rape, an indictment for which had been previously ignored by the grand jury. *The Queen* v. *Doty,* 362.

3. *Conspiracy—Failure to Complete Fraud—Indictment of One of Two Conspirators.*]—A conspiracy to defraud is indictable, even though the conspirators are unsuccessful in carrying out the fraud.

One of two conspirators can be tried on an indictment against him alone charging him with conspiring with another to defraud, the other conspirator being known in the country. *Regina* v. *Frawley,* 431.

4. *Summary Conviction—" Procuring " a Weapon with Intent— Criminal Code, sec. 108—Amended Conviction—Information for Shooting with Intent—Justices of the Peace—Substituting New Charge— Imprisonment —Habeas Corpus — Discharge.*] — The defendant was brought before justices of the peace on an information charging him with the indictable offence of shooting with intent to murder, and they, not finding sufficient evidence to

warrant them in committing for trial, of their own motion, at the close of the case, summarily convicted the defendant for that he did "procure a revolver with intent therewith unlawfully to do injury to one J. S." It appeared by the evidence that the weapon was bought and carried and used by the defendant personally.

By the Criminal Code, sec. 108, it is matter of summary conviction if one has on his person a pistol with intent therewith unlawfully to do any injury to any other person.

The return to a writ of *habeas corpus* shewed the detention of the defendant under a warrant of commitment based upon the above conviction ; and upon a motion for his discharge :—

Held, that the detention was for an offence unknown to the law ; and, although the evidence and the finding shewed an offence against sec. 108, the motion should not be enlarged to allow the magistrates to substitute a proper conviction, for it was unwarrantable to convict on a charge not formulated, as to which the evidence was not addressed, upon which the defendant was not called to make his defence, and as to which no complaint was laid ; and the prisoner should, therefore, be discharged. *Regina* v. *Mines*, 577.

Bigamy — Criminal Code, sec. 275.]—*See* CONSTITUTIONAL LAW, 2.

Foreign Country.]—*See* GAMING, 1—HABEAS CORPUS.

DAMAGES.

Inadequacy of—Negligence—New Trial.]—Although it is unusual to interfere with a verdict of a jury in an action of tort on the ground of inadequacy of the damages found, still such verdicts are subject to the supervision of the Court, and if the amount awarded be so small that it is evident the jury must have overlooked some material element of damage in the plaintiff's case, a new trial will be granted.

A practising physician having been badly if not permanently injured through the negligence of the defendants, it appearing also that his professional business had suffered to a considerable extent, was awarded $700 by the jury :—

Held, that there must be a new trial on the ground of inadequacy of the damages. *Church* v. *Corporation of Ottawa*, 298.

Remoteness.]—*See* BAILMENT.

Special Injury to Business.]—*See* DEFAMATION.

Unforeseen Accident.]—*See* HIRE OF GOODS.

See BANKS AND BANKING—LANDLORD AND TENANT — MALICIOUS ARREST AND PROSECUTION, 3 — WATER AND WATERCOURSES.

DEBENTURES.

Issued under Void By-law.]—*See* MUNICIPAL CORPORATIONS, 2.

DEFAMATION.

Libel — Incorporated Newspaper Company—Charge of Corruption—Injury to Business—Special Damage.]—A company incorporated for the purpose of publishing a newspaper can maintain an action of libel

in respect of a charge of corruption
in the conduct of their paper, without alleging special damage.

Metropolitan Saloon Omnibus Co.
v. *Hawkins*, 4 H. & N. 87, commented on and distinguished.

South Hetton Coal Co. v. *North-Eastern News Association*, [1894] 1
Q. B. 133, followed.

Nonsuit by FALCONBRIDGE, J., set
aside. *Journal Printing Company
of Ottawa* v. *MacLean*, 509.

Slander — Privilege — Malice.]—
See BAILMENT.

DEMAND.

See ARBITRATION AND AWARD, 1.

DESCRIPTION.

Of Lands.]—*See* MUNICIPAL COR-
PORATIONS, 4, 6.

DEVISE.

See WILL.

DEVOLUTION OF ESTATES ACT.

See DOWER—EXECUTORS AND AD-
MINISTRATORS.

DIRECTORS.

Appointment to Salaried Offices.]
—*See* COMPANY, 6.

DISCHARGE.

Of Mortgage.]—*See* MORTGAGE, 1.

DISTRESS.

See ASSESSMENT AND TAXES—
LANDLORD AND TENANT.

DISTRICT COURTS.

*Order of Master for Trial of Action
Therein—Subsequent Judgment of
High Court Judge—Jurisdiction of
Master — Appeal.*] — In an action
brought for damages to the plaintiff's
house situated in a provisional judicial district, an order was made by
the Master in Chambers, assuming
to act under the Unorganized Territory Act, R. S. O. ch. 91, directing
that the issues of fact be referred to
the District Judge, reserving further
directions and questions of law arising at the trial for the disposal of a
Judge in single Court. Notice of
trial was given for the District
Court, and the case was heard by
the District Judge, who made certain findings of fact, assessed the
damages, and directed judgment to
be entered for the plaintiff. The
plaintiff moved for judgment on such
findings before a Judge in single
Court, the defendant at the same
time appealing from the judgment or
report, whereupon the Judge disposed of both motions, directing
judgment to be entered for the plaintiff for the amount found by the
District Judge.

On appeal to the Divisional
Court:—

Held, that, apart from the question of the jurisdiction of the Master
to make the order, as the parties had
treated it as valid, and the subsequent order of the Judge in single
Court remained unreversed and not
appealed from the Court would not
interfere; that if the question of
the jurisdiction of the Master were

involved the appeal should have been to the Court of Appeal. *Fraser v. Buchannan*, 1.

DIVISION COURTS.

1. *Prohibition — Money Payable by Instalments with Interest—Splitting Demand—Division Court Act, sec. 77.*]—Where, under an agreement for the sale of land, the balance of the purchase money was payable by instalments with interest at a named rate half-yearly, and three of the instalments, amounting to $240, as well as the interest, amounting to $70, and three years' taxes were overdue ; and an action was commenced in the Division Court for the arrears of interest and two years' taxes, amounting to $95.30 :—

Held, that the action did not come within section 77 of the Division Court Act, whereby the splitting of causes of action is forbidden, and prohibition was refused. *Re Gordon* v. *O'Brien*, 11 P. R. 287, not followed. *Re Clark* v. *Barber*, 253.

Reversed by Q. B. Divisional Court.

2. *Prohibition—Claim for $200 on Contract signed by Defendant—Evidence of Performance of Conditions on Plaintiff's Part.*]—A Division Court has no jurisdiction to entertain a claim for $200 on a contract signed by defendant where to entitle plaintiff to recover evidence *ultra* must be given to shew that conditions of the contract on the plaintiff's part have been complied with. *Re Shepherd and Cooper*, 274.

3. *Prohibition — Judgment Summons — Examination — Refusal of Evidence—Partnership — Judgment Against Firm—Parties—Members of Firm—Commitment.*]—The refusal of evidence is not ground for prohibition.

An order having been made in a Division Court upon judgment summons committing a defendant under sec. 240, sub-sec. 4 (c), of R. S. O. ch. 51, for having made away with his property, it is not a ground for prohibition that the Judge has refused to allow the defendant under examination to make explanations as to his dealing with money lent by and repaid to him after judgment.

The members of a firm sued in the firm name are parties to the litigation ; and when judgment is obtained in a Division Court against a firm as such, though execution can go only against the goods of the firm and against the individual goods of one who is sued as and found to be a partner, yet a judgment summons may be issued against another member of the firm not served with first process, if only to get discovery of goods of the firm available for execution, and if he makes wilful default in attendance, he is liable to be committed as for contempt of Court. *Re Reid* v. *Graham Brothers*, 573.

Reversed by the C. P. Divisional Court.

4. *Prohibition — Jurisdiction — Rent—Incorporeal Hereditament—Title to.*]—The bare assertion of the defendant in a Division Court action that the right or title to any corporeal or incorporeal hereditament comes in question under R. S. O. ch. 51, sec. 69, sub-sec. 4, is not sufficient to oust the jurisdiction of that Court. The Judge has authority to enquire into so much of the case as is necessary to satisfy himself on the point, and if there are disputed facts or a question as to the proper inference from undisputed facts that is

enough to raise the question of title. If the facts can lead to only one conclusion, and that against the defendant, then there is no such *bonâ fide* dispute as to title as will oust the jurisdiction of the Court.

In an action in a Division Court for rent on a covenant in a lease, in which it was contended that the lease had been surrendered, prohibition was refused (MEREDITH, J., dissenting, on the ground that a *bonâ fide* defence against the plaintiff's right to any rent due under the lease was raised).

Decision of ARMOUR, C. J., affirmed. *Re Moberly v. Corporation of Collingwood*, 625.

DIVISIONAL COURT.

Appeal to.]—*See* INSURANCE, 2.

DIVORCE.

See INFANT, 3.

DOWER.

Release by Marriage Settlement— Devolution of Estates Act—Right of Election.]—Section 4 of the Devolution of Estates Act, R. S. O. ch. 108, which gives the widow a right of election between her dower and a distributive share in her deceased husband's lands, does not apply where by marriage settlement she has accepted an equivalent in lieu of dower. In such case she has no right to any share in the lands. *Toronto General Trusts Co. v. Quin*, 250.

DRAINAGE.

See MUNICIPAL CORPORATIONS, 1, 2, 5, 6, 7, 9, 10—WATER AND WATER-COURSES.

ELECTION.

See DOWER.

EQUITABLE EXECUTION.

See EXECUTION.

EQUITY OF REDEMPTION.

In Shares.]—*See* COMPANY, 5.

ESTOPPEL.

See BAILMENT—MUNICIPAL CORPORATIONS, 2—WILL, 1.

EVIDENCE.

Proof of Acquittal—Production of Original Record.]—*See* MALICIOUS ARREST AND PROSECUTION, 4.

Secondary.]—*See* CRIMINAL LAW, 1.

See CRIMINAL LAW, 2—NEGLIGENCE, 2.

EXECUTION.

Equitable Execution—Receiver— Will—Devise—Right to "a Home" —Interest in Land.]—A testator devised land to one in trust, first, to permit his nephew and his wife and children to use it for a home, and, second, to convey it to such child of the nephew as the latter should nominate in his will. The nephew and his family were living upon the land at the time of the making of the will and at the death of the testator, when there were two dwelling-houses thereon. Afterwards the trustee and the nephew's father-in-law, at their expense, improved and altered the property so that the number of houses was increased to seven. The nephew lived with his family in one and received the rents of the others.

In an action by judgment creditors of the nephew and his wife seeking the appointment of a receiver to receive the rents in satisfaction of the judgment :—

Held, that the judgment debtors took no estate in the land under the will, and nothing more than the right to call upon the trustee to permit them to use the land for "a home," which expression, however, meant more than simply a house to live in ; that they were entitled to the advantage of the increased value of the land ; and that their right to the use of the land for a home could not be reached through a receiver so as to make it available for the satisfaction of the plaintiffs' claim.

Allen v. *Furness*, 20 A. R. 34, distinguished. *Cameron et al.* v. *Adams et al.*, 229.

Sale of Shares Under.] — *See* COMPANY, 5.

See FIXTURES.

EXECUTORS AND ADMINIS-TRATORS.

Will—Power of Sale—Surviving Executors — Devolution of Estates Act, R. S. O. ch. 108 and Amendments.]—Where executors are given express power to sell lands, whether coupled with an interest or not, such power can be exercised by a surviving executor.

The Devolution of Estates Act and amendments do not interfere with an express power of sale given by a will to executors extending beyond the periods of vesting prescribed by those Acts. *In re Koch and Wideman*, 262.

Insurance Moneys of Infants.]—*See* INSURANCE, 4.

See WILL, 2.

EXECUTORY DEVISE

See WILL, 6.

FACTORIES ACT.

See MASTER AND SERVANT, 1.

FEES.

Excessive.]—*See* ARBITRATION AND AWARD, 1.

FIRE INSURANCE.

See INSURANCE.

FIXTURES.

Execution—Mortgage of Fixtures as Chattels—Mortgage of Realty—Discharge of Chattel Mortgage.]—The fact that fixtures affixed to the freehold in the usual way have sometimes been mortgaged as chattels, and on other occasions have passed with a mortgage of the freehold does not render them exigible to an execution against goods if at the time of the seizure the chattel mortgages are non-existent, and a mortgage of the freehold is in existence as a first charge thereon. *Carson* v. *Simpson*, 385.

FRAUDS.

Statute of.] — *See* STATUTE OF FRAUDS.

GAMING.

1. *Keeping a Common Gaming House—Offence in United States.*]—In a betting game called "policy," the actual betting and payment of the money, if won, took place in the United States; all that was done in Canada being the happening of the chance, on which the bet was staked, by means of implements operated in the house of the defendant :—

Held, there was no offence under sec. 198 of the Criminal Code of 1892 of keeping a common gaming house within that section. *Regina* v. *Wettman*, 459.

2. *Bicycle Race—Protest—Award of Trophy—Private Tribunal—Decision of—Refusal of Court to Interfere—Injunction.*]—Where a challenge cup, to be won in a bicycle race between competing clubs, was held by trustees under an instrument of trust by which all arrangements pertaining to the course, race, protests, and matters "connected with the welfare of the cup" were to be decided by the trustees according to certain rules, the Court, upon the mere allegation of fraud, and before any decision of the trustees, refused to exercise jurisdiction restraining the trustees from parting with the cup to an alleged winner under protest, upon the ground that one of the winning riders did not go round the course, that being a matter of fact for the decision of the trustees.

Brown v. *Overbury*, 11 Ex. 715; *Ellis* v. *Hopper*, 3 H. & N. 768; and *Newcomen* v. *Lynch*, Ir. R. 9 C. L. 1; Ir. R. 10 C. L. 248, followed. *Ross et al.* v. *Orr et al.*, 595.

GOODS.

Hire of.]—*See* HIRE OF GOODS.

Sale of.]—*See* SALE OF GOODS.

GUARDIAN.

Religious Faith of.]—*See* INFANT.

HABEAS CORPUS.

Warrant Issued in Quebec—Conspiracy—Locality of Offence—Affidavit Evidence—R. S. O. ch. 70, secs. 4 and 5—Criminal Code secs. 394 and 752.]—A Judge cannot upon the return to a *habeas corpus*, where a warrant shews jurisdiction, try on affidavit evidence the question where the alleged offence was committed.

Sections 4 and 5, R. S. O. ch. 70, are not intended to apply to criminal cases where no preliminary examination has taken place.

Section 752 of the Criminal Code, 55-56 Vict. ch. 29 (D.), only applies where the Court or Judge making the direction as to further proceedings and enquiries mentioned therein has power to enforce it, and a Court or Judge in Ontario has no power over a Judge or Justice in Quebec to compel him to "take any proceedings or hear such evidence," etc.

It is a crime under section 394 of the Code to conspire by any fraudulent means to defraud any person, and so a conspiracy to permit persons to travel free on a railroad as alleged in these cases would be a conspiracy against the railway company. *Regina* v. *Defries, Regina* v. *Tamblyn,* 645.

See CRIMINAL LAW, 4.

HIGH COURT.

Jurisdiction to Restrain Arbitrator from Acting.]—*See* ARBITRATION AND AWARD, 3.

HIGHWAY.

See WAY.

HIRE OF GOODS.

Agreement to Return — Contract —Damage Occasioned by Unforeseen Accident—Liability.]—Where there is a positive contract to do a thing not in itself unlawful, the contractor must perform it or pay damages for non-performance, although in consequence of unforeseen causes the performance has become unexpectedly burdensome or even impossible.

The defendants hired the plaintiff's scow and pile driver, at a named price per day, they to be responsible for damage thereto, except to the engine, and ordinary wear and tear, until returned to the plaintiff. While in the defendants' custody, by reason of a storm of unusual force, the scow and pile driver

were driven from their moorings and damaged :—

Held, that the defendants were liable for the damages thus sustained, and for the rent during the period of repair.

Taylor v. *Caldwell,* 3 B. & S. 826. followed.

Harvey v. *Murray,* 136 Mass. 377, approved. *Grant* v. *Armour et al.,* 7.

HORSES.

Plant.]—*See* CONTRACT, 2.

HUSBAND AND WIFE.

Married Woman—Separate Estate —Contract Respecting—R. S. O. ch. 132.]—A married woman having been informed by a relative that he had made his will in her favour, signed a promissory note three days after his death, before she had seen the will, and some weeks before it was proved. The will gave her a vested interest in the property bequeathed. She also owned a promissory note of her husband :—

Held, that she was possessed of separate estate and had contracted with respect to it.

Decision of STREET, J., 24 O. R. 441, affirmed. *Mulcahy* v. *Collins,* 241.

Custody of Infant.]—*See* INFANT, 3.

INFANT.

1. *Action in Name of, Without Next Friend—Motion to Set Aside Proceedings After Coming of Age— Laches.*]—An infant was a part owner of a patent right and engaged in business transactions with respect

to it. Along with other part owners he signed a retainer to solicitors to take proceedings to stop the infringement of the patent, and the solicitors, not knowing that he was an infant, brought an action for that purpose, using his name as a plaintiff, without a next friend. The action was prosecuted for a time with the result that the infringement ceased but it was subsequently dismissed with costs against the plaintiffs for want of prosecution. More than a year after he came of age, he moved to set aside all proceedings in the action :—

Held, that, under the circumstances mentioned, he was not entitled to relief on the ground of infancy. *Millson et al. v. Smale*, 144.

2. *Custody of—Religious Faith of Father—Testamentary Guardian.*]— Orphan children having been clandestinely taken from the custody of their uncle, the testamentary guardian under the will of their father, who had predeceased his wife, by their aunt, a Roman Catholic, claiming guardianship under an invalid instrument in her favour, signed by the mother of the children, and it appearing that their father, a Protestant, had desired the children to be brought up in his own faith, an order was made for their delivery to the custody of their uncle as testamentary guardian. *Re Chillman Infants*, 268.

3. *Custody of—British Subjects Married in this Province—Removal to the United States—Husband Naturalized—Divorce Obtained by Wife.*] —The parents of a child seven years old, British subjects and married in this Province, where the child was born, removed to the United States,

where the husband took out naturalization papers. In consequence of the husband's alleged intemperance and adultery the wife left him, and on the ground of such adultery, she applied to the Court there and obtained a decree granting her a divorce, and the custody of the child. Shortly before the decree was pronounced, and with the object of escaping its effect, the husband returned to this Province, bringing the child with him.

On an application by the wife for the custody of the child an order was made granting her such custody. *Re Ethel Davis an Infant*, 579.

See INSURANCE, 4—NEGLIGENCE, 1.

INFORMATION.

See JUSTICE OF THE PEACE — MALICIOUS ARREST AND PROSECUTION, 2.

INJUNCTION.

High Court—Jurisdiction to Restrain Arbitrator Acting.]—*See* ARBITRATION AND AWARD, 3.

Disputed Race.]—*See* GAMING, 2.

INSURANCE.

1. *Fire Insurance—Interim Contract—Termination of—Notice—R. S. O. ch. 167, sec. 114, Condition 19.*] —The plaintiff's testator applied to the defendants in writing for an insurance against loss by fire, and undertook in writing to hold himself liable to pay to the defendants such amounts as might be required, not to exceed $46.50, and signed a promissory note, in favour of the

defendants, for $15.25. The defendants' agent gave him a written provisional receipt for his undertaking for $46.50, "being the premium for an insurance," etc.

The receipt contained a condition to the effect that unless the insured received a policy within fifty days, with or without a written notice of cancellation, the insurance and all liability of the defendants should absolutely be determined. No policy was sent within the time limited, nor was any notice of cancellation given within that time, nor until, by letter, two days before a fire occurred on the insured premises :—

Held, that the application, undertaking, note, and receipt constituted a contract of fire insurance within the provisions of R. S. O. ch. 167, which could be terminated only in the manner prescribed by the 19th of the conditions set forth in section 114, that is, when by post, by giving seven days' notice, and thus the contract was still subsisting at the time of the fire. *Barnes* v. *Dominion Grange Mutual Fire Ins. Association*, 100.

2. *Fire Insurance—Statutory Condition 9—Divided Risk—Proportion of Loss—Costs — Appeal to Divisional Court.*]—Statutory condition 9 of the Ontario Insurance Act, provides that in the event of there being other insurances on the property, the company shall only be liable for the payment of a ratable proportion of the loss or damage.

Plaintiff had insured his building against fire in two different companies in separate amounts for the front and rear portions, and the whole building, without division, in a third company. A fire took place damaging both front and rear, nearly all the injury being done to the rear :—

Held, by ROSE, J., that the proper method of ascertaining the relative amounts payable by the different companies, was to add the amount of all the policies together without reference to the division of the risks, and that each company was liable for its relative proportion to the whole amount insured.

An appeal lies to a Divisional Court from the order of a trial Judge who has awarded costs on a wrong principle. *McCausland* v. *Quebec Fire Ins. Co. et al.*, 330.

3. *Fire Insurance— Policy—Statutory Conditions—Other Conditions —Variations—55 Vict. ch. 39, sec. 33 (O.)—Representations in Application—R. S. O. ch. 167, sec. 114, Condition 1—Moral Risk—Apprehension of Incendiarism.*]—Where a fire insurance policy does not contain the statutory conditions, but contains other conditions not printed as variations, it must be read as containing the statutory conditions and no others.

Citizens' Insurance Co. v. *Parsons*, 7 App. Cas. 96, followed.

And the law in this respect has not been altered by 55 Vict. ch. 39, sec. 33 (O.).

Where the policy is based upon an application containing statements or representations relating to matters as to which the insurers have required information, the first of the statutory conditions in sec. 114 of R. S. O. ch. 167 must be taken to refer to such statements and representations, whether the risk they relate to is physical or moral.

Reddick v. *Saugeen Mutual Fire Insurance Co.*, 15 A. R. 363, followed.

And where in the application the

insured was asked whether any incendiary danger to the property was threatened or apprehended, and untruly answered " no " :—

Held, that the policy was avoided. *Findley* v. *Fire Insurance Company of North America*, 515.

4. *Life Insurance—Infants—Payment to Executors—Security—Discharge—R. S. O. ch. 136, secs. 11, 12.*]—Moneys payable to infants under a policy of life insurance may, where no trustee or guardian is appointed under secs. 11 and 12 of R. S. O. ch. 136, be paid to the executors of the will of the insured, as provided by sec. 12, without security being given by them, and payment to them is a good discharge to the insurers. *Dodds et al.* v. *Ancient Order of United Workmen et al.*, 570.

See CONSTITUTIONAL LAW, 1.

***

INTOXICATING LIQUORS.

By-law to Fix Number of Licenses —Passed without Required Two-thirds' Vote—Read a Third Time only at Subsequent Meeting on Two-thirds' Vote—Validity.]—A by-law to regulate the proceedings of a town council required that every by-law should receive three readings, and that no by-law for raising money, or which had a tendency to increase the burdens of the people should be finally passed on the day on which it was introduced, except by a two-thirds' vote of the whole council.

A by-law to fix the number of tavern licenses, and which, therefore, required such two-thirds' vote, was read three times on the same day, and was declared passed. It did not, however, receive the required two-thirds' vote. A special meeting of

council was then called for the following evening, when the by-law was merely read a third time, receiving the required two-thirds' vote :—

Held, that the by-law was bad, for having been defeated when first introduced by reason of not having received a two-thirds' vote, it was not validated by merely reading it a third time at the subsequent meeting.

The by-law did not shew, as required by the Liquor License Act the year to which it was to be applicable :—

Held, that it was bad for this reason also. *Re Wilson and the Corporation of Ingersoll*, 439.

See JUSTICE OF THE PEACE—PARTNERSHIP.

***

INVENTION.

See PATENT FOR INVENTION.

***

JUDGE.

County—Powers of—Appointment of Arbitrator.]—*See* PROHIBITION.

***

JURY.

Findings of.]—*See* MASTER AND SERVANT, 2—RAILWAYS.

***

JUDGMENT.

See PRINCIPAL AND SURETY.

***

JURISDICTION.

Of Division Courts.]—*See* DIVISION COURTS, 4.

Of County Council—Appointment of Arbitrators to hear Appeal.]—See PUBLIC SCHOOLS.

JUSTICE OF THE PEACE.

Indian Act—Sale of Intoxicating Liquors—Information—Several Offences—Objection Taken at Hearing —Summary Conviction.]—When an information laid against the defendant under the Indian Act charged that he sold intoxicating liquor to two persons on the 5th July and to two persons on the 8th July, and the justices, notwithstanding that the defendant's counsel objected to the information on this ground, proceeded and heard evidence in respect of all the offences so charged, then amended the information by substituting the 8th August for the 8th July, proceeded and heard evidence in respect of the substituted charge and dismissed it, and convicted the defendants for selling to two persons on the 5th July, the conviction was quashed.

Regina v. *Hazen,* 20 A. R. 633, distinguished.

Per STREET, J.—It was the duty of the justices when the objection was taken to have amended the information by striking out one or other of the charges, and to have heard the evidence applicable to the remaining charge only. *Regina* v. *Alward,* 519.

See CRIMINAL LAW, 4—HABEAS CORPUS — MALICIOUS ARREST AND PROSECUTION, 2.

LACHES.

See INFANT, 1.

LAND.

Interest in.]—*See* EXECUTION.

Description of.]—*See* MUNICIPAL CORPORATIONS, 4, 6.

Injuriously Affected—Arbitration — Appointment of Arbitrator.]— *See* PROHIBITION.

Title to.]—*See* WILL, 1.

LANDLORD AND TENANT.

Distress—Action for Conversion —Double Value— Pleading—Chattel Mortgage—Jus Tertii—Assessment of Damages — Recovery of Amount Received from Sale of Goods —Claim and Counterclaim—Set-off.] —In an action for wrongful distress for rent before it was due, there was no allegation in the statement of claim that the action was brought upon 2 W. & M., sess. 1, ch. 5, sec. 5, nor that the goods distrained were "sold," but merely an allegation that the defendant "sold and carried away the same and converted and disposed thereof to his own use;" nor was a claim made for double the value of the goods distrained and sold, within the terms of the statute :—

Held, reversing the decision of FERGUSON, J., that the action was the ordinary action for conversion, and that the value, and not the double value, of the goods distrained was recoverable :—

Held, also, reversing the decision of FERGUSON, J., that a wrong-doer taking goods out of the possession of another, cannot set up the *jus tertii,* but the person out of whose possession the goods are taken, may shew it, and in such case the wrong-doer may take advantage of it ; and the plaintiff, having shewn a chattel mortgage subsisting upon a portion of the goods distrained, could not be allowed to recover the value of such portion without protecting the defendant against another action at the suit of the mortgagee :—

Held, also, *per* FERGUSON, J., that the plaintiff was not entitled to re-cover from the defendant the amount received by him from the sale of the plaintiff's goods in addition to the value thereof ; nor was the de-fendant obliged to deduct the amount so received by him from the rent which afterwards fell due.

Hoare v. *Lee*, 5 C. B. 754, fol-lowed.

Judgment being given in favour of the plaintiff upon his claim, and in favour of the defendant upon his counterclaim :—

Held, reversing the decision of FERGUSON, J., that the amounts should be set off. *Williams* v. *Thomas*, 536.

Action for Rent—Title to Land in Question.]—*See* DIVISION COURTS, 4.

LIBEL.

See DEFAMATION.

LICENSE.

Auctioneer.]—*See* MUNICIPAL COR-PORATIONS, 3.

Tavern.]—*See* PARTNERSHIP.

To Cut Timber.]—*See* TIMBER.

91—VOL. XXV. O.R.

LIEN.

Artisan's Lien—Manufacture of Bricks on Property of Another Per-son—Possession.]—The plaintiff was employed to manufacture bricks for another in a brickyard belonging to the latter, of which, however, the plaintiff held possession for the pur-pose of his contract, and remained and was in possession of the bricks at the time of their seizure by the sheriff under an execution against the owner of the brickyard, who, immediately after such seizure, made an assignment for the benefit of creditors :—

Held, that the plaintiff was en-titled to a lien upon the bricks in priority to the execution and assign-ment for the benefit of creditors, and also in priority to the claim of a chattel mortgagee, though his mort-gage covered brick in course of manu-facture during its continuance. *Rob-erts* v. *Bank of Toronto et al.*, 194.

LIQUORS.

See INTOXICATING LIQUORS.

LOCAL LEGISLATURE.

See CONSTITUTIONAL LAW, 1.

MAGISTRATE.

See JUSTICE OF THE PEACE.

MALICIOUS ARREST AND PROSECUTION.

1. *Arrest—Order for—Discharge from Custody under—Order not Set Aside—Action for Malicious Arrest —Reasonable and Probable Cause—*

Departure from Ontario—Inference of Intent to Defraud—Action for Imposing on Judge by False Affidavit—Material Facts—Burden of Proof—"Absconded," Meaning of— Misdirection.]—In an action for damages for arrest under an order made in a former action the plaintiff recovered a verdict for $1,000. Upon motion to set it aside, made before a Divisional Court composed of ARMOUR, C. J., and FALCONBRIDGE, J. :—

Held, per ARMOUR, C. J., that so long as the order for arrest stood, an action for maliciously and without reasonable and probable cause arresting the plaintiff could not be maintained.

Erickson v. *Brand,* 14 A. R. 614, distinguished.

2. Where a creditor, by affidavit, satisfies the Judge that there is good and probable cause for believing that his debtor, unless he be forthwith apprehended, is about to quit Ontario, the inference is raised that he is about to do so with intent to defraud ; for he is removing his body, which is subject to the jurisdiction of the Courts of Ontario, and liable to be taken in execution, beyond the jurisdiction of such Courts.

Toothe v. *Frederick,* 14 P. R. 287, commented on and not followed.

Robertson v. *Coulton,* 9 P. R. 16, approved and followed.

3. The fact that the plaintiff, being a resident of Ontario, and having numerous creditors therein, including the defendant, left the Province without paying them, and went to reside permanently in the United States, whether he left openly or secretly, and whether he announced his departure and intentions beforehand or concealed them, and that he came back to Ontario for a temporary purpose, intending to return to the United States, afforded reasonable and probable cause for and justified his arrest.

4. Considering the action as one for imposing upon the Judge by some false statement in the affidavit to hold to bail, and thereby inducing him to grant the order for arrest, the fact falsely suggested or suppressed must be a material one for the Judge to consider in granting the order, and the burden is upon the plaintiff of shewing that the Judge was imposed upon.

5. The word "absconded" truly described the going away of the plaintiff, whether he went away secretly or openly, and he was properly described as an absconding debtor.

FALCONBRIDGE, J., adhering to the views expressed in *Scane* v. *Coffey,* 15 P. R. 112, was of opinion that the plaintiff had a cause of action, but thought there should be a new trial on the grounds of excessive damages and misdirection ; and concurred *pro forma* in the decision of ARMOUR, C. J. *Coffey* v. *Scane,* 22.

2. *Arrest—Trespass to Person— Malicious Prosecution—Information —Uttering Forged Note—Disclosing Offence—Warrant—Jurisdiction of Justice of the Peace.*]—The defendant laid an information charging that the plaintiff "came to my house and sold me a promissory note for the amount of ninety dollars, purporting to be made against J. M. in favour of T. A.. and I find out the said note to be a forgery." Upon this a warrant was issued reciting the offence in the same words, and the plaintiff was under it apprehended and brought before the justice of the peace who issued it, and by him committed for trial by a warrant

reciting the offence in like terms. The plaintiff was tried for forging and uttering the note, and was acquitted :—

Held, that the information sufficiently imported that the plaintiff had uttered the forged note, knowing it to be forged, to give the magistrate jurisdiction, and therefore the warrant was not void, and an action of trespass was not maintainable against the defendant, even upon evidence of his interference with the arrest.

Semble, that if the offence were not sufficiently laid in the information to give the magistrate jurisdiction, and the warrant were void, an action for malicious prosecution would nevertheless lie. *Anderson* v. *Wilson*, 91.

3. *Malicious Prosecution—Charge of Stealing Several Articles—Reasonable and Probable Cause for Part of Charge—Damages.*]—In an action for malicious prosecution of a charge of theft of several articles, the trial Judge held that there was no reasonable and probable cause for charging the theft of some of the articles, and withdrew the case as to them from the jury, but held otherwise as to the other articles, and directed the jury that the fact that there was reasonable and probable cause to charge the theft of some of the articles only bore upon the question of damages, and the jury found a verdict for the plaintiff :—

Held, that there was no misdirection.

Per MEREDITH, J., dissenting : that if the ruling of the trial Judge were right, the damages were excessive, and apparently assessed under a misunderstanding of the effect of such ruling ; that the trial Judge could not in any case rightly have ruled as he did without first having

findings of the jury upon certain material facts ; that there had been a mistrial, and that there ought to be a new trial.

Johnstone v. *Sutton*, 1 T. R. 547, considered and distinguished ; *Reed* v. *Taylor*, 4 Taunt. 616, followed. *Wilson* v. *Tennant*, 339.

4. *Evidence—Action for Malicious Prosecution—Proof of Acquittal —Production of Original Record by Clerk—Certified Copy.*]—In an action for malicious prosecution, the plaintiff sought but was not permitted to prove his acquittal before the County Judge's Criminal Court of a charge of misdemeanour, by means of the production of the original record signed by the County Judge under the Speedy Trials Act, R.S.C. ch. 175, and produced and verified by the Clerk of the Peace in whose custody it was, or else by being allowed to put in a copy thereof, certified by that officer :—

Held, that the evidence should have been admitted in either of the above two forms, and judgment dismissing the action was set aside and a new trial ordered.

Decision of MacMahon, J., at the trial reversed. *O'Hara* v. *Dougherty*, 347.

5. *Malicious Arrest—Constable—Notice of Action—Requisites of.*]—Where in an action against a constable for false arrest it is found by the jury that the defendant acted in the honest belief that he was discharging his duty as a constable, and was not actuated by any improper motive, he is entitled to notice of action, and such notice must state not only the time of the commission of the act complained of, but that it was done maliciously. *Scott* v. *Reburn*, 450.

MARRIAGE SETTLEMENT.

See DOWER.

MASTER.

Jurisdiction of.]—*See* COMPANY, 1.

Power of.]—*See* CONSTITUTIONAL LAW, 1.

Order for Trial of Action.]—*See* DISTRICT COURTS.

MASTER AND SERVANT.

1. *Negligence — Dangerous Machinery—Absence of Guard—Common Law Liability — Workmen's Compensation for Injuries Act—Factories Act.*]—A drilling machine manufactured by a well-known maker and similar to those generally in use was put up for the defendants in their factory. The plaintiff a workman acting under the orders of the defendants' foreman for the purpose of oiling the shafting on the arm in which the drill worked tried to push a portion of it up and down the arm, and in order to do so, knowing that the machine was in motion, pressed his body against the revolving drill, which was not in motion when the order was given to him, and his clothes catching in an unguarded set-screw on the spindle, he was seriously injured. No other accident had occurred on the machine, which was quite new and in good order, and which according to the evidence was sometimes made with the set-screw sunk in the spindle.

In an action for damages the jury found that the accident was caused by the defendants' negligence, and

without any negligence on the part of the plaintiff.

On appeal the Divisional Court was equally divided.

Per GALT, C. J.—There was no evidence of negligence to submit to the jury either at common law or under the Workmen's Compensation for Injuries Act, nor any liability under the Factories Act.

Per ROSE, J.—There was evidence of negligence both at common law and under the Workmen's Compensation for Injuries Act ; the want of a guard to the set-screw as required by the Factories Act constituted such negligence at common law ; and the absence of such guard being also a defect in the condition or arrangement of the machinery within the Workmen's Compensation for Injuries Act. *O'Connor* v. *Hamilton Bridge Co.*, 12.

Affirmed by the Court of Appeal.

2. *Workmen's Compensation Act —56 Vict. ch. 26 (O.)—"Servant in Husbandry" — Knowledge of Danger — Questions for Jury — General Verdict — Non-Direction — New Trial.*]—In an action under the Workmen's Compensation Act and at common law for damages for injuries sustained by the plaintiff while engaged in digging a drain upon the defendant's farm, it did not appear that the plaintiff engaged with the defendant to do any particular work, but that he was first put by the defendant at mason work and then at digging the drain :—

Held, that it was a question for the jury whether the hiring of the plaintiff was as a servant in husbandry within the meaning of 56 Vict. ch. 26 (O.), and whether the work he was engaged in was in the usual course of his employment as such, and also whether the danger was known to the defendant and unknown to the plaintiff or the converse.

The jury were asked certain questions, one being whether the hiring was as a servant in husbandry, but they were told that they might give a general verdict, and they gave one for the plaintiff, answering none of the questions. The trial Judge in his charge gave them no instruction on this point and no direction as to what the law was :—

Held, that they were not competent to find a general verdict, and there should be a new trial. *Reid v. Barnes,* 223.

Liability of Servants of Corporation.] — *See* MUNICIPAL CORPORATIONS, 1.

See NEGLIGENCE, 2.

MECHANICS' LIEN.

See LIEN.

MISDIRECTION.

See MALICIOUS ARREST AND PROSECUTION, 1—MASTER AND SERVANT, 2—WATER AND WATERCOURSES.

MONEY HAD AND RECEIVED.

Right to Recover Money Paid.]— *See* MUNICIPAL CORPORATIONS, 2— PRINCIPAL AND AGENT, 2.

MORALS.

See PUBLIC MORALS AND CONVENIENCE.

MORTGAGE.

1. *Payment and Discharge of first Mortgage—Ignorance of Subsequent Incumbrance—Right to Priority— Acquiescence.*]—The plaintiff paid off a first mortgage on certain lands, and procured its discharge, taking a new mortgage to himself for the amount of the advance in ignorance of the fact of the existence of a second mortgage. Shortly afterwards on ascertaining this fact he notified the defendant, the holder, that he would pay it off, and defendant relying thereon, took no steps to enforce his security. Subsequently, on the property becoming depreciated and the mortgagor insolvent, the plaintiff brought an action to have it declared that he was entitled to stand in the position of first mortgagee :—

Held, that the plaintiff by his acts and conduct had precluded himself from asserting such right.

Brown v. *McLean,* 18 O. R. 533, and *Abell* v. *Morrison,* 19 O. R. 669, distinguished. *McLeod* v. *Wadland,* 118.

2. *Payment Off—Demand of Assignment to Nominee of Mortgagor— Subsequent Encumbrancers—R.S.O. ch. 102, sec. 2.*]—Where a mortgagor of land subsequently conveyed his equity of redemption to several grantees, one of whom agreed to pay off the mortgage, and some of whom also executed further mortgages upon the land, and the first mortgagee proceeding to foreclose and to sue the mortgagor upon his covenant, the latter requested him to assign his mortgage to a third party who had advanced the money and paid off the mortgage :—

Held, that the first mortgagee was bound under R. S. O. ch. 102, sec. 2, to execute the assignment as asked, notwithstanding the subsequent encumbrances.

Teevan v. *Smith*, 20 Ch. D. 724, distinguished ; *Kinnaird* v. *Trollope*, 39 Ch. D. 636, followed.

Decision of ARMOUR, C. J., followed.

Per BOYD, C.—Even if the redemption money had been that of the mortgagor himself, it would have made no difference. *Queen's College* v. *Claxton*, 282.

3. *Building Loan—Further Advances — Priority of Subsequently Registered Mortgage—Registry Act —Notice—R. S. O. ch. 114, sec. 80.*] —After purchasing land under an agreement which provided that $2,000 of the purchase money was to be secured by mortgage subsequent to a building loan not exceeding $12,000, the purchaser executed a building mortgage to a loan company for $11,500, which was at once registered, but only part of that sum was then advanced. The plaintiff, who had succeeded to the rights of the vendor under the above agreement, then registered her mortgage for $2,000, and claimed priority over subsequent advances made by the loan company under their mortgage, but without actual notice of the plaintiff's mortgage, or of the terms of the agreement for the sale of the land :—

Held (ROBERTSON, J., dissenting), that the plaintiff was not entitled to the priority claimed by her.

Decision of FERGUSON, J., 24 O. R. 426, reversed.

Per BOYD, C.—The further advances were made upon a mortgage providing for such advances, and to secure which the legal estate had been conveyed, and equity as well as law protected the first mortgage so advantageously placed, as against the subsequent mortgage, even though registered, where notice had not as a fact been communicated to the first mortgagee respecting the subsequent instrument and the Registry Act did not apply. *Pierce* v. *Canada Permanent Loan and Savings Co.*, 671.

Company—Right to Acquire Land —Mortgage for Purchase Money.]— *See* COMPANY, 2.

See BANKRUPTCY AND INSOLVENCY, 1—BILLS OF SALE AND CHATTEL MORTGAGES—FIXTURES—WAY.

MUNICIPAL CORPORATIONS.

1. *Rebuilding of Culvert — Obstructions in Highway—Negligence —Accident—Liability of Servants of Corporation—Municipal Councillors —Officers Fulfilling Public Duty— R. S. O. ch. 73—Notice of Action— Pathmaster.*] — Two of the defendants, members of a township council, were appointed by resolution of the council a committee to rebuild a culvert, and they personally superintended the work, and were paid for doing it, but there was no by-law authorizing their appointment or payment. The other defendants were employed by them, and did the work. The plaintiff met with an accident on the highway near the culvert, owing, as she alleged, to the negligence of the defendants in obstructing the road with their building materials, and brought this action for damages for her injuries:—

Held, that the defendants were not fulfilling a public duty, and were not entitled to notice of action under R. S. O. ch. 73 :—

Held, also, that that statute is applicable only to officers and persons fulfilling a public duty for anything done by them in the performance of it, when it may be properly averred that the act was done maliciously and without reasonable and probable cause, and therefore not to actions for negligence in the doing of the act :—

Held, lastly, that one of the defendants, who was pathmaster for the beat in which the culvert was situated, did not come within the protection of the statute as pathmaster, because he was not employed as such in doing this work, but as a day labourer. *McDonald* v. *Dickenson et al.*, 45.

2. *Drainage--Void By-law—Debenture Issued Under—Action on—Estoppel — Money Had and Received.*] — Action to recover the amount of a debenture, one of a series issued by the defendants pursuant to their by-law passed for the levying of a special rate upon a particular locality for the purpose of cleaning out and repairing a drain:—

Held, following *Alexander* v. *Township of Howard*, 14 O. R. 22, and *Re Clark and Township of Howard*, 16 A. R. 72, that the by-law was void, the defendants having no power to pass it for such a purpose.

The debenture was silent as to the purposes for which it was issued, but referred to the by-law, which disclosed such purposes. There was no representation by the defendants that it was good :—

Held, that, although the plaintiffs were innocent holders and had paid the full value of the debenture, they could not recover upon it, because the defendants had no power to make the contract professedly made by it.

Webb v. *Commissioners of Herne Bay*, L. R. 5 Q. B. 642, distinguished.

Marsh v. *Fulton County*, 10 Wallace U. S. R. 676, specially referred to.

Held, however, that as the defendants were bound to keep the drain in repair and to pay for repairs out of their general funds, and as they had received the price of the debenture directly from the plaintiffs and had the full benefit of it, without giving any consideration, the plaintiffs were entitled to recover for money received by the defendants. *Confederation Life Association* v. *Township of Howard*, 197.

3. *Auctioneer—Right to Issue License therefor—Power to Prohibit— R. S. O. ch. 184, sec. 495, sub-sec. 2.*] —Section 495, sub-sec. 2 of the Municipal Act, R. S. O. ch. 184, which empowers any city, etc., to pass by-laws for the " licensing, regulating and governing of auctioneers," etc., is only for the purpose of raising a revenue and does not confer any right of prohibition so long as the applicant is willing to pay the sum fixed for the license. Where, therefore, a city refused to license the plaintiff as an auctioneer on the ground that he was a person of a notoriously bad character and ill-repute, a mandamus was granted, compelling the issue of the license to him. *Merritt* v. *City of Toronto*, 256.

4. *Way—Highway By-law—Description of Land—Clerical Error— Publication — Semi-monthly Newspaper.*]—A municipal by-law establishing a public highway is not void for uncertainty when the boundaries of the land so declared are described in the by-law with sufficient precision to enable them to be traced upon the ground, and if so properly described, it is not necessary when

private ground has been taken to distinguish it as such.

The fact that one of two parallel courses in a description has by obvious clerical error been incorrectly given in the published notice is not a valid objection to such a by-law.

Where there is no paper published in the township weekly or oftener, it is not obligatory to publish the required statutory notice of the by-law in a paper issued therein semi-monthly. *Re Chambers and the Corporation of Burford*, 276.

5. *Construction of Sewer—General Plan—Subsequent Erection of Houses—Insufficient Fall — Negligence.*]—A municipal corporation having properly constructed a sewer in a street in the municipality according to a general plan of drainage adopted by them is not liable to the owner of houses subsequently erected on the street, because the sewer has not been constructed sufficiently deep to allow a proper fall to the drains from the houses.

Decision of STREET, J., at the trial affirmed. *Johnston v. Corporation of Toronto*, 312.

6. *Drainage—New Outlet—Municipal Act, 1892, secs. 569, 585— Petition--Township By-law—Adjoining Townships — Agreement as to Proportion of Cost—Report of Engineer — Description of Lands.*]—A township council finding that a government drain in the township did not carry off the water, by reason of the natural flow being in another direction, accepted a report made by their engineer and passed a by-law adopting a scheme for a new drain leading from the middle of the government drain into an adjoining township, where it was to find an outlet :—

Held, that the proposed drain properly came within the description of a new outlet, although not at the end of the government drain, and although the former outlet remained to serve to carry off a part of the water ; and, so long as the proposed drain was designed merely as an outlet for the water from the government drain, it might, under section 585 of the Municipal Act of 1892, be provided for without any petition under section 569, even although it should incidentally benefit the locality through which it ran, nothing being included in the plan beyond what was reasonably requisite for the purpose intended.

Although a township council is not powerless with regard to the drainage report of its engineer, it is contrary to the spirit and meaning of the Act that two adjoining councils should agree upon a drainage scheme, and upon the proportion of its cost to be borne by each, and that the engineer of one of them should be instructed to make a report for carrying out the scheme and charging each municipality with the sums agreed on ; for such a course would interfere with the independent judgment of the engineer, and pledge each township in advance not to appeal against the share of the cost imposed upon it, to the possible detriment of the property owners assessed for the portions of that share.

And where such a course was pursued, a by-law of one of the councils adopting the engineer's report was quashed.

In describing lands for assessment, "the north-east part," even with the addition of the acreage, is an ambiguous description ; and *quære* as to the effect upon the validity of a by-law. *Re Jenkins and the Corporation of Enniskillen*, 399.

7. *Contract — Drainage — Ultra Vires—Liability — By-law — Necessity for—R. S. O. ch. 184, secs. 569, 583, 585.*]—Under a by-law passed under the provisions of sections 569 and 576 of the Municipal Act R. S. O. ch. 184, a drain was built in the defendant's township, which benefited lands in an adjoining township, and which, therefore, had been assessed for a portion of the cost. After the drain was built, it was found that an opening through the plaintiffs' embankment which, when the by-law was passed, was deemed sufficient to carry off the water brought down by the drain, was insufficient therefor, whereby the adjoining lands were flooded, and actions were threatened against the defendants. To prevent such actions and to enable the water to be carried off, an agreement was entered into between the plaintiffs and defendants under their respective corporate seals, whereby the plaintiffs were to build, and defendants to pay for a culvert through the embankment sufficient to carry off the water. The culvert was built by plaintiffs at a cost of over $200.00, and on its completion was accepted and used by defendants, who, however, refused to pay for it on the ground that the agreement for its construction was *ultra vires.* No by-law had been passed authorizing the construction of the culvert, nor were any of the proceedings required by sections 569-582 of the Municipal Act, taken :—

Held, by STREET, J., and affirmed by the Divisional Court, ROSE, J., dissenting, that the work in question was new work, and, therefore, did not come within section 573 ; but came within sub-sections 1 and 3 of section 583 ; and inasmuch as the cost exceeded $200.00 no liability could arise until the proceedings pointed out by section 585 had been complied with, namely, the proceedings required by sections 569-582 ; and as these had not been taken, the agreement was invalid and could not be enforced.

Per ROSE, J., there being an executed contract for the performance of work within the purposes for which the corporation was created, and the defendants having adopted and received the benefit thereof, were liable.

The case of *Bernardin* v. *Corporation of North Dufferin,* 19 S. C. R. 581, considered on the question of absence of a by-law where there is an executed contract. *Canadian Pacific R. W. Co.* v. *Corporation of Chatham,* 465.

8. *Officer of—Tenure of Office— Removal of Officer.*]—The effect of section 279 of the Consolidated Municipal Act, 55 Vict. ch. 42 (O.), which enacts that officers appointed by a municipal council shall hold office until removed by the council, is that all such officers hold office during the pleasure of the council, and may be removed at any time without notice or cause shewn therefor, and without the council incurring any liability thereby. *Hellems* v. *Corporation of St. Catharines,* 583.

9. *Drain Constructed out of General Funds—Maintenance and Repair—Assessment of Lands Benefited —By-law—Petition—55 Vict. ch. 42, secs. 569, 586—Complaints as to Assessment— Court of Revision— Notice—Service—Section 571 (2)— Irregularities—Lands "to be Benefited"—Policy of Drainage Legislation — Interference by Court.*]—A township council has power under

section 586 (2) of the Consolidated Municipal Act, 55 Vict. ch. 42, to maintain and repair a beneficial drain, originally constructed out of general funds, at the expense of the local territory benefited, by passing a by-law to that effect, without a petition therefor. And although such a by-law refers to lots " to be benefited," it does not bring the work within the category of drains to be constructed under section 569 of the Act.

Application to quash the by-law in question being made by several persons, who among them owned one of the lots assessed, alleging that they were not benefited by the original drain and could not be by its continuance and repair, and that the amount charged against their lot was not duly apportioned among them :—

Held, that they should have applied to the Court of Revision for relief ; and not having done so, and the work having all been done and the benefit of it enjoyed, this Court would not interfere to declare the by-law invalid :—

Held, also, having regard to section 571 (2), that the applicants had sufficient notice of the by-law, service having been effected upon a grown-up person at the house where they all lived as members of one family :—

Held, also, that upon this application the Court would not inquire what other persons were not served who were not seeking relief, nor consider irregularities or errors in the assessment of such others.

It appeared on the face of the by-law that the drain in question was an old one, constructed out of general funds, and out of repair ; and although the assessment was referred to as on the property " to be benefited," yet the same clause spoke of it as " upon the property benefited : "—

Held, that the by-law was not bad on its face.

In drainage matters the policy of the Legislature is to leave the management largely in the hands of the localities, and the Court should refrain from interference, unless there has been a manifest and indisputable excess of jurisdiction, or an undoubted disregard of personal right. *Re Stephens et al. and Township Moore*, 600.

10. *Drainage—New Territory—Old Drain—Liability.*]—Where a municipality acquires territory from another, the property in a drain for the purpose of carrying off the surface water constructed in the highway by the land-owners before such acquisition becomes vested in the transferees, and they are liable to the land-owners for injury caused by subsequent neglect to keep it in repair. *Fitzgerald* v. *City of Ottawa*, 658.

Lands Injuriously Affected.]—See PROHIBITION.

See INTOXICATING LIQUORS—PUBLIC SCHOOLS—WAY.

NEGLIGENCE.

1. *Injury to Buyer in Shop—Invitation—Child of Tender Years—Accident—Active Interference—Contributory Negligence.*]—A woman went with her child two and a-half years old to the defendants' shop to buy clothing for both. While there a mirror fixed to the wall, and in front of which the child was, fell and injured him :—

Held, that it was a question for the jury whether the mirror fell without any active interference on the child's part ; if so, that in itself was evidence of negligence ; but if not, the question for the jury would be whether the defendants were negligent in having the mirror so insecurely placed that it could be overturned by a child ; and if that question were answered in the affirmative, the child, having come upon the defendants' premises by their invitation and for their benefit, would not be debarred from recovering by reason of his having directly brought the injury upon himself.

Hughes v. *Macfie*, 2 H. & C. 744 ; *Mangan* v. *Atherton*, 4 H. & C. 388 ; and *Bailey* v. *Neal*, 5 Times L. R. 20, commented on and distinguished.

Semble, that the doctrine of contributory negligence is not applicable to a child of tender years.

Gardner v. *Grace*, 1 F. & F. 359, approved of.

Semble, also, that if the mother was not taking reasonably proper care of the child at the time of the accident, her negligence in this respect would not prevent the recovery by the child. *Sangster et al.* v. *The T. Eaton Co. (Limited)*, 78.

2. *Railways—Licensee—Volenti non Fit Injuria—Loan of Engine and Crew—Evidence of.*]—In an action under Lord Campbell's Act for damages arising from the death of a servant of a lumber company, who was engaged in counting lumber in a car of the defendants in the lumber company's yard, caused by his being squeezed between two piles of lumber, owing, as the jury found, to the negligence of the defendants' servants in charge of an engine in giving the car too strong a push :—

Held, that, assuming knowledge on the part of the crew of the engine of the position of the deceased in the car, it would be a negligent act to propel the car so rapidly against another as to be likely to injure him ; and, there being a conflict of evidence as to the rate of speed, the case could not have been withdrawn from the jury.

(2) That the knowledge of the crew that the deceased was in the car and of the probable consequences to him of the work in which they were engaged, if done without due care, imposed upon them a duty, whether he was there as a mere licensee or otherwise, to use the care necessary to avoid causing that injury.

Batchelor v. *Fortescue*, 11 Q. B. D. 474, distinguished.

(3) The finding of the jury that the deceased voluntarily accepted the risks of shunting, did not entitle the defendants to judgment ; he voluntarily accepted the risks of shunting, but did not give the defendants leave to run the risk of killing him by doing their shunting negligently.

Smith v. *Baker*, [1891] A. C. 325, applied and followed.

(4) Upon the evidence, there was no loan to the lumber company by the defendants of the engine and its crew ; and the fact that the latter were acting under the direction of the servants of the lumber company in moving such cars as they were told to move did not make them the servants of the lumber company.

Cameron v. *Nystrom*, [1893] A. C. 308, followed. *Hurdman* v. *Canada Atlantic R. W. Co.*, 209.

3. *Fire—Liability for Acts of Another—Control—Navigable Waters—Access to Shore and Navigation Rights—Public Rights—Private Rights.*]—*Held*, affirming the decision of STREET, J., 24 O. R. 500, that the

defendants were liable for the negligence of the owner of the tug hired by them in so placing it as to communicate fire to the plaintiff's scow, as in doing so he was obeying the orders of the defendants' foreman, and was under his direct and personal control.

Bartonshill Coal Co. v. *Reid,* 3 Macq. Sc. App. Cas. 266, followed:—

Held, however, reversing the decision of STREET, J., that the plaintiff in mooring his scow where he did was not a trespasser, at all events as against the defendants, who were mere licensees " to take sand from in front of " the land granted by the Crown.

The grant to the shore of the river, reserving free access to the shore for all vessels, boats, and persons, carried the land to the water's edge, and not to the middle of the stream.

The effect of the removal of the shore line back from its natural line was to make the water so let in as much *publici juris* as any other part of the water of the river, and such removal did not take away the right of free access to the shore so removed. *Cram* v. *Ryan et al.,* 524.

See DAMAGES—MASTER AND SERVANT—MUNICIPAL CORPORATIONS, 1, 5—RAILWAYS.

NEWSPAPER.

Publication of By-law.]—See MUNICIPAL CORPORATIONS, 4.

NEW TRIAL.

See DAMAGES—MALICIOUS ARREST AND PROSECUTION, 3—MASTER AND SERVANT, 2—WATER AND WATERCOURSES.

NOTICE.

See INSURANCE, 1—MORTGAGE, 2—MUNICIPAL CORPORATIONS, 9.

NOTICE OF ACTION.

See MALICIOUS ARREST AND PROSECUTION, 5 — MUNICIPAL CORPORATIONS, 1.

NOTICE TO QUIT.

See PARTNERSHIP.

NOVATION.

See CONTRACT, 3.

OCCUPANT.

See ASSESSMENT AND TAXES.

PARTNERSHIP.

Assignment of Interest of Partner—Termination of Partnership—Possession of Partnership Premises—Notice to Quit—Tavern License—Transfer of—R. S. O. ch. 194, sec. 37.]—A partnership for a definite term, which has not expired, can be put an end to by the voluntary assignment by one of the partners of his interest in the business, at his own instance or at the instance of his assignee, against the will of the other partner.

And where a partnership was so put an end to, the assignor being the lessee of the premises on which the business was carried on, and assigning the term to the assignee, the latter was held entitled to recover possession of the premises against the other partner without notice to quit or demand of possession.

Where the holder of a tavern license enters into partnership with another person, to whom he assigns an interest in his tavern business, such assignment is not an assignment of his business within the meaning of section 37 of the Liquor License Act, R. S. O. ch. 194, and does not require a transfer of the license.

Upon the construction of the partnership agreement in this case, the new partner did not take an undivided one-half interest in the license.

Judgment of ROBERTSON, J., varied. *Westbrook et ux.* v. *Wheeler et ux.*, *Wheeler et ux.* v. *Westbrook*, 559.

See BANKRUPTCY AND INSOLVENCY, 1—DIVISION COURTS, 3.

PATENT FOR INVENTION.

R. S. C. ch. 61, sec. 46—Rights of Prior Manufacturer.]—Section 46 of the Patent Act, R. S. C. ch. 61, does not authorize one who has, with the full consent of the patentee, manufactured and sold a patented article for less than a year before the issue of the patent, to continue the manufacture after the issue thereof, but merely permits him to use and sell the articles manufactured by him prior thereto. *Fowell* v. *Chown*, 71.

PATHMASTERS.

Notice of Action.]—*See* MUNICIPAL CORPORATIONS, 1.

PENALTY.

Excessive Charge for Fees.]—*See* ARBITRATION AND AWARD, 1.

PETITION.

Necessity for.]—*See* MUNICIPAL CORPORATIONS, 6.

PLAN.

See WATER AND WATERCOURSES.

PLANT.

See CONTRACT, 2.

PLEADING.

See LANDLORD AND TENANT.

PRINCIPAL AND AGENT.

1. *Contract—Commission on Sales—Time—Absence of Express Contract to Manufacture.*]—In a written contract of agency the principal agreed to pay to the agent a fixed commission on all sales of goods manufactured by the former effected by or through the latter. The contract was made terminable at the end of a year on a month's notice by either party; but it contained no express agreement by the principal to employ for any period or to manufacture any goods :—

Held, that these terms could not be imported into the contract by implication. *Morris* v. *Dinnick et al.*, 291.

2. *Undue Influence — Excessive Payment for Services Procured by —Right to Recover Back.*]—Where, by reason of the confidential relationship existing between plaintiff and defendant and the influence he was able to exert over her by assert-

ing knowledge of matters which he alleged could be used to her prejudice, and which at the trial he admitted had no existence, he was enabled to procure from plaintiff an excessive amount for services performed, and which was paid by her even after she had obtained independent advice, the plaintiff was held entitled to recover the same back, less a reasonable amount for the services performed. *Disher* v. *Clarris*, 493.

Authority of Agent.]—See BILLS OF SALE AND CHATTEL MORTGAGES, 1.

See NEGLIGENCE, 2.

PRINCIPAL AND SURETY.

Security held by Creditor—Release of Same without Consent of Surety—Rights of Surety—Judgment.]—The plaintiffs sued the defendant as endorser of a promissory note made by a customer, of which they held a number, endorsed by various parties, and also a mortgage from the customer on certain lands to secure his general indebtedness. Before this action the plaintiffs had released and discharged certain of the lands comprised in the mortgage, without the consent of the defendant, but, in consideration of such discharge, had received the full value of the lands, and had applied the proceeds in reduction of the general indebtedness of the customer :—

Held, that the defendant as a surety was entitled to have credited in reduction of his liability upon the note a *pro rata* share of the amount realized by the plaintiffs on the mortgage, and also a *pro rata* share of the value of the security still in their hands. *Molsons Bank* v. *Heilig*, 503.

PRIORITY.

See MORTGAGE, 1, 3.

PROHIBITION.

Arbitration and Award—Lands Injuriously Affected — Joint Work by City and County—Remedy—Appointment of Arbitrator—Powers of County Judge—One Arbitrator for Two Municipalities — Municipal Act, 55 Vict. ch. 42, secs. 391, 483, 487—Interpretation Act, R. S. O. ch. 1, sec. 8 (24).]—An order of prohibition is an extreme measure, to be granted summarily only in a very plain case of excessive jurisdiction on the part of a subordinate tribunal.

A land-owner alleged that by the building of a bridge over a river forming the boundary between a county and city, a joint work undertaken by the two municipalities, his land in the county had been injuriously affected, for which he sought damages from both municipalities :—

Held, having regard to sec. 483 of the Municipal Act, 55 Vict. ch. 42 (O.), that he had no remedy except by arbitration under the Act.

Pratt v. *City of Stratford*, 14 O. R. 260 ; 16 A. R. 5, followed :—

Held, also, that the case was covered by section 391 of the Act ; the expression " a municipal corporation," by force of the Interpretation Act, R. S. O. ch. 1, sec. 8 (24), being capable of being read as a plural :—

Held, also, that it was competent for the County Judge to appoint the same arbitrator for both corporations, upon their making default in naming an arbitrator, and that he could proceed to do so *ex parte* :—

Held, lastly, that section 487 did not apply to the case of a joint claim against city and county.

Prohibition to the arbitrators refused. *Re Cummings and County of Carleton et al.*, 607.

See DIVISION COURTS.

PUBLIC MORALS AND CONVENIENCE.

Public Morals—By-law against Swearing in Street or Public Place —Private Office in Custom House.] —A city by-law enacted that no person should make use of any profane swearing, obscene, blasphemous or grossly insulting language, or be guilty of any other immorality or indecency in any street or public place :—

Held, that the object of the by-law was to prevent an injury to public morals, and applied to a street or a public place *ejusdem generis* with a street, and not to a private office in the custom house. *Regina* v. *Bell*, 272.

See CRIMINAL LAW, 2.

PUBLIC SCHOOLS.

54 Vict. ch. 55, secs. 82, 96 (O.) —*Boundaries of School Sections— Action of Township Council—Appeal —Time —County Council —Jurisdiction — By-law — Appointment of Arbitrators—Award —Confirmation —Waiver—Evidence of.*]—In the absence of satisfactory evidence of waiver of the objection by all persons interested, a county council has no jurisdiction under sub-sec. 3 of sec. 82 of the Public Schools Act, 54 Vict. ch. 55 (O.), to appoint arbitrators to hear an appeal from the action or refusal to act of a township council and to determine or alter the boundaries of school sections, unless a notice of appeal has been duly given within the time mentioned in sub-sec. 1.

Where a by-law of the county council appointing arbitrators was passed pursuant to a notice of appeal, in the form of a petition, filed with the county clerk after such time had expired, and there was no waiver :—

Held, that the authority of the arbitrators to enter upon the inquiry being affected by the want of jurisdiction of the council to pass the by-law, their award could not be confirmed by sec. 96 of the Public Schools Act; and the by-law was quashed.

The application to quash was made by a ratepayer of the school section whose boundaries were in question, acting at the request of the trustees of the section, and the solicitors acting for him were also retained by the trustees, whose secretary-treasurer appeared before the committee of the county council, before the by-law was passed, and before the arbitrators, and did not make objections to the jurisdiction of either body :—

Held, that, in the absence of proof of the authority of the secretary-treasurer to represent the trustees, it could not be said that they had waived their right to object to the proceedings, nor that the rights of the applicant were entirely gone and merged in those of the trustees. *Re Martin and County of Simcoe*, 411.

PUBLIC POLICY.

See CONTRACT, 1.

RACE.

Dispute as to Result—Right of Court to Interfere by Injunction.]— *See* GAMING, 2.

RAILWAYS.

Accident at Crossing—Negligence — Findings of Jury — Release of Cause of Action—Settlement Pending Action—Validity of—Trial of Issue as to.]—In an action to recover damages for the death of the plaintiff's husband, who was killed at a railway crossing by a train of the defendants, the jury found that the engine bell was not rung on approaching the highway nor kept ringing until the engine crossed it ; that the deceased did not see the train approaching in time to avoid it ; and that he had no warning of its approach ; and assessed damages at $1,000 :—

Held, that the plaintiff was entitled to judgment upon these findings, notwithstanding that the jury, to a question whether the deceased, if he saw the train approaching, used proper care to avoid it, answered " we don't know."

After the action was at issue an agreement was made between the defendants and the plaintiff, the latter an ignorant person and without the advice of her solicitor or other competent advice, and misled by statements made on behalf of the defendants, whereunder she received $500 from the defendants and executed a release under seal of the cause of action. She afterwards re-pudiated the agreement and paid back the $500. At the trial the defendants set up the release :—

Held, upon the evidence, that the release was ineffectual :—

Held, also, that it was not necessary that a separate action should be brought to try the validity of the release.

Emeris v. *Woodward,* 43 Ch. D. 185, distinguished. *Johnson* v. *Grand Trunk R. W. Co.,* 64.

Affirmed by the Court of Appeal.

See NEGLIGENCE, 2—WATER AND WATERCOURSES.

RAPE.

See CRIMINAL LAW, 2.

REASONABLE AND PROBABLE CAUSE.

See MALICIOUS ARREST AND PROSECUTION, 1.

RECEIVER.

See EXECUTION.

REGISTRY LAWS.

See MORTGAGE, 3.

RELEASE.

Cause of Action.]—*See* RAILWAYS.

See DOWER—PRINCIPAL AND SURETY—WILL, 1.

RESTRAINT OF TRADE.

See CONTRACT, 1.

SALE OF GOODS.

Contract — Payment of Price — Property — Possession — Trespass — Trover — Amendment — Account.]— The defendant agreed to get out wood for the mortgagors of the plaintiffs, whose mortgage covered certain wood then piled, as also future acquired wood brought on the premises, and to place it upon the premises at a specified price, and the mortgagors agreed to pay part of the price as the wood was got out, and the balance in cash upon and according to a measurement to be made by them. Subsequent to the date of the mortgage, wood was got out, placed on the premises, and measured in the presence of all parties, and the quantity agreed upon, and marked with plaintiffs' mark :—

Held, that the property in the wood became at once vested in the mortgagors, and through them in the plaintiffs ; but such vesting did not transfer the right of possession without payment of the price; and therefore, the plaintiffs could not maintain trespass or trover for wood taken away by the defendant after appropriation and before payment of the full price; but were entitled, upon amendment of the pleadings, to a declaration of their right to the property, and to possession upon payment of the amount due, and to an account of the wood not received by them. *Rogers et al.* v. *Devitt,* 84.

See BAILMENT—LANDLORD AND TENANT—PRINCIPAL AND AGENT, 1.

93—VOL. XXV. O.R.

SALE OF LAND.

Standing Timber.]—*See* TIMBER.

SCHOOLS.

See PUBLIC SCHOOLS.

SEDUCTION.

Evidence of Rape.]—*See* CRIMINAL LAW, 2.

SEPARATE ESTATE.

See HUSBAND AND WIFE.

SERVANT.

See MASTER AND SERVANT.

SET-OFF.

See LANDLORD AND TENANT.

SEWERS.

Improper Construction of.]—*See* MUNICIPAL CORPORATIONS, 5.

SLANDER.

See DEFAMATION.

SOLICITOR.

Acting as Arbitrator.]—*See* ARBITRATION AND AWARD, 3.

SPECIFIC PERFORMANCE.

See COMPANY, 3.

STATUTE OF FRAUDS.

Statute of Frauds—" Giving of Sheep to Double "—Contract not to be Performed within a Year—Executed Contract.]—The Statute of Frauds does not apply to a contract which has been entirely executed on one side within the year from the making so as to prevent an action being brought for the non-performance on the other side.

And, therefore, where the plaintiff delivered sheep to the defendant within a year from the making of a verbal contract with the defendant under which the latter was to deliver double the number to the plaintiff at the expiration of three years :—

Held, that the contract was not within the statute. *Trimble* v. *Lanktree,* 109.

Sale of Standing Timber.]—*See* TIMBER.

STATUTE OF LIMITATIONS.

See WILL, 1.

STATUTES.

2 W. & M. sess. 1, ch. 5, sec. 57.]—*See* LANDLORD AND TENANT.

R. S. C. ch. 61, sec. 46.]—*See* PATENT FOR INVENTION.

R. S. C. ch. 62.]—*See* COPYRIGHT, 1.

R. S. C. ch. 129.]—*See* COMPANY, 1, 4.

R. S. C. ch. 157.]—*See* CRIMINAL LAW, 2.

R. S. C. ch 175.]—*See* MALICIOUS ARREST AND PROSECUTION, 4.

R. S. O. ch. 1, sec. 8 (24).]—*See* PROHIBITION.

R. S. O. ch. 51, secs. 69, 77, 240, sub-sec. 4 (c).]—*See* DIVISION COURTS, 1, 3, 4.

R. S. O. ch. 53, sec. 29.]—*See* ARBITRATION AND AWARD, 1.

R. S. O. ch. 64, sec. 16.]—*See* COMPANY, 5.

R. S. O. ch. 70, secs. 4, 5.]—*See* HABEAS CORPUS.

R. S. O. ch. 73.]—*See* MUNICIPAL CORPORATIONS, 1.

R. S. O. ch. 91.]—*See* DISTRICT COURTS.

R. S. O. ch. 102, sec. 2.]—*See* MORTGAGE, 2.

R. S. O. ch. 108.]—*See* DOWER—EXECUTORS AND ADMINISTRATORS.

R. S. O. ch. 114, sec. 80.]—*See* MORTGAGE, 3.

R. S. O. ch. 124, sec. 4.]—*See* BANKRUPTCY AND INSOLVENCY, 1, 3.

R. S. O. ch. 125, secs. 1, 4, 11.]—*See* BILLS OF SALE AND CHATTEL MORTGAGES, 1, 2.

R. S. O. ch. 132.]—*See* HUSBAND AND WIFE.

R. S. O. ch. 136, secs. 11, 12.]—*See* INSURANCE, 4.

R. S. O. ch. 157, sec. 52.]—*See* COMPANY, 5.

R. S. O. ch. 167.]—*See* INSURANCE, 1, 3.

R. S. O. ch. 184, secs. 495, sub-sec. 2, 569, 583, 585.]—*See* MUNICIPAL CORPORATIONS, 3, 7.

R. S. O. ch. 194, sec. 37.]—*See* PARTNERSHIP.

51 Vict. ch. 29, secs. 90 (h), 123, 144, 145, 146, 147 (D.).]—*See* WATER AND WATERCOURSES.

52 Vict. ch. 32 (D.).]—*See* COMPANY, 1.

52 Vict. ch. 32, sec. 3 (D.).]—*See* COM-PANY, 4.

54 Vict. ch. 55, secs. 82, 96 (O.).]—*See* PUBLIC SCHOOLS.

55 Vict. ch. 6 (O.).]—*See* WILL, 2.

55 Vict. ch. 26, sec. 2 (O.).]—*See* BANK-RUPTCY AND INSOLVENCY, 2.

55 Vict. ch. 39, sec. 33 (O.).]—*See* IN-SURANCE, 3.

55 Vict. ch. 42, secs. 568 (2), 279, 391, 483, 487, 550, sub-sec. 9, 569, 571 (2), 585, 586.]—*See* MUNICIPAL CORPORATIONS, 6, 8, 9—PROHIBITION—WAY.

55 Vict. ch. 48, sec. 124 (O.).]—*See* ASSESSMENT AND TAXES.

55 and 56 Vict. ch 29, secs. 108, 198, 275, 394, 752 (D.), Criminal Code.]—*See* CONSTITUTIONAL LAW, 2—CRIMINAL LAW, 4—GAMING, 1—HABEAS CORPUS.

56 Vict. ch. 26 (O.).]—*See* MASTER AND SERVANT, 2.

STREET.

See WAY.

SUCCESSION DUTY.

See WILL, 2.

SUMMARY CONVICTION.

See CRIMINAL LAW, 4—JUSTICE OF THE PEACE.

SURETY.

See PRINCIPAL AND SURETY.

TAVERNS.

See INTOXICATING LIQUORS.

TAXES.

See ASSESSMENT AND TAXES.

TENANT.

See LANDLORD AND TENANT.

TIMBER.

Standing Timber—Parol Sale of —License to Cut—Revocation of—Statute of Frauds—Trespass—Justification.] — As a general rule a contract for the sale of standing timber which is not to be severed immediately is a sale of an interest in land.

Upon a parol sale of timber for valuable consideration, with a parol license to enter upon the land during such time as should be necessary for the purpose of cutting and removing the timber, the defendant during the period allowed by the contract continued to cut and remove, notwithstanding he was notified not to do so :—

Held, in an action of trespass and for damages for timber cut after the notice, that he was at liberty to shew the existence of the parol agreement in justification of what he had done, and under which no right of revocation existed, and to shew the part performance as an answer to the objection founded on the Statute of Frauds. *Handy* v. *Carruthers et al.*, 279.

TIME.

Appointment of Arbitrators to Hear Appeal.]—*See* PUBLIC SCHOOLS.

TITLE TO LAND.

Jurisdiction of Division Courts.]
—*See* DIVISION COURTS, 4.

TRESPASS.

See MALICIOUS ARREST AND PROSE-
CUTION, 2—NEGLIGENCE, 3—SALE
OF GOODS—TIMBER.

TROVER.

See SALE OF GOODS.

UNDUE INFLUENCE.

See PRINCIPAL AND AGENT, 2.

ULTRA VIRES.

See CONSTITUTIONAL LAW, 2—
MUNICIPAL CORPORATIONS, 7.

VERDICT.

General.]—*See* MASTER AND SER-
VANT, 2.

WAIVER.

See PUBLIC SCHOOLS.

WARRANT.

See MALICIOUS ARREST AND PRO-
SECUTION, 2.

WATER AND WATERCOURSES.

*Diversion of Watercourse by Rail-
way Company—Remedy—Compensation—Arbitration Clauses of Railway Act, 51 Vict. ch. 29 (D.)—Plan
—Riparian Proprietors—Infringement of Rights—Cause of Action—
Damages—Permanent Injury—Definition of Watercourse—Permanent
Source—Surface Water—Misdirection—New Trial.*]—By sec. 90 (*h*)
of the Railway Act of Canada, 51
Vict. ch. 29, a railway company
have power to divert any watercourse, subject to the provisions of
the Act; but in order to entitle
themselves to insist upon the arbitration clauses of the Act, they must,
having regard to secs. 123, 144, 145,
146, and 147, shew upon their registered plans their intention to divert.

The defendants built an embankment which entirely cut off the
plaintiff's access to the water of a
stream by diverting it from his
farm :—

Held, that the diversion, not the
damage sustained therefrom, gave
him his cause of action ; and the
proper mode of estimating the damages was to treat the diversion as
permanent and to consider its effect
upon the value of the farm.

McGillivray v. *Great Western R.
W. Co.*, 25 U. C. R. 69, distinguished.

The alleged watercourse was a
gully or depression created by the
action of the water. The defendants
disputed that any water ran along
it, except melted snow and rain
water flowing over the surface merely. The plaintiff contended that
there was a constant stream of water,
only, if ever, ceasing in the very dry
summer weather :—

Held, per STREET, J., that without
a permanent source, which, however,
need not necessarily be absolutely
never failing, there cannot be a
watercourse ; and that, as the attention of the jury was not expressly
called to the difference in effect
between the occasional flow of sur-

face water and the steady flow from a source, and as a passage read to the jury from the judgment in *Beer v. Stroud*, 19 O. R. 10, divorced from its context, might have misled the jury, there should be a new trial.

Per ARMOUR, C. J., that what the Judge told the jury could not be held to be a misdirection without reversing the decision in *Beer* v. *Stroud ;* and the objection to the charge was too vague and indefinite. *Arthur* v. *Grand Trunk R. W. Co.*, 37.

Affirmed by the Court of Appeal.

See MUNICIPAL CORPORATIONS, 2 —NEGLIGENCE, 3.

WAY.

Highway—Closing of—Adjoining Lands—Rights of Mortgagee of— "Owner"—Con. Mun. Act, 1892, sec. 550, sub-sec. 9.]—A mortgagee of land adjoining a highway is one of the persons in whom the ownership of it is vested for the purposes of sub-sec. 9 of sec. 550 of the "Consolidated Municipal Act, 1892," and as such is entitled to pre-emption thereunder, subject to the right of the mortgagor to redeem it along with the mortgage, or to have it sold to the mortgagor subject to the mortgage, if the mortgagor so prefer. *Brown* v. *Bushey et al.*, 612.

Public Place, Swearing in.]—*See* PUBLIC MORALS AND CONVENIENCE.

See MUNICIPAL CORPORATIONS, 1, 4.

WIFE.

See HUSBAND AND WIFE.

WILL.

1. *Devise — Falsa Demonstratio —Deed of Release—Recital—Estoppel — Title to Land—Statute of Limitations.*]—A testator by his will devised to his son G. "the property I may die possessed of in the village of M., also lot 28 in the 10th concession of B." In the early part of the will he had used the words "wishing to dispose of my worldly property." The testator did not own lot 28, and the only land he did own in the 10th concession of B. was a part of lot 29. The will contained no residuary devise.

Upon a petition under the Vendor and Purchaser Act :—

Held, that the part of lot 29 owned by the testator did not pass by the will to the son.

After the death of the testator, all his children executed a deed of release to the executors of his will, containing a recital that the part of lot 29 owned by the testator was devised to the son G., and that he was then in possession :—

Held, that there was no estoppel as among the members of the family, who together constituted one party to the deed :—

Held, however, upon the evidence, that G. had acquired a good title to the lands in question by virtue of the Statute of Limitations. *Re Bain and Leslie*, 136.

2. *Executors and Administrators —Succession Duty—55 Vict. ch. 6 (O.)—Residue—Pro Rata, Meaning of.*]—A testator devised and bequeathed all his real and personal estate to his executors and trustees for the purpose of paying a number of pecuniary legacies, some to personal legatees, and others to charitable associations, and provided that

the residue of his estate should be divided *pro rata* among the legatees :—

Held, that it was the duty of the executors to deduct the succession duty payable in respect of the pecuniary legacies, before paying the amounts over to the legatees, and they had no right to pay such succession duty out of the residue left after paying the legacies in full.

Where the residue of an estate is directed to be divided *pro rata* among prior legatees they take such residue in proportion to the amount of their prior legacies. *Kennedy et al.* v. *Protestant Orphans' Home et al.*, 235.

3. *Devise—Charitable Bequest—Indefiniteness—Scheme.*]— A testator by his will devised to certain named persons who were appointed the executors and trustees thereof, the remainder of his estate to be used to further " the cause of our Lord Jesus Christ " :—

Held, that the legacy was not void for indefiniteness, and discretion having been given to the executors and trustees, it was not necessary that a scheme should be directed. *Phelps* v. *Lord et al.*, 259.

4. *Codicil—Revocation of Bequest.*]—A testatrix by the third clause of her will bequeathed to S., the interest on the sum of $3,000 for life, and after his death directed the $3,000 to be divided among his children, and by a subsequent clause she directed her executors to deduct out of the $3,000 all payments made to S. after the date of the will. By a codicil she directed that the bequest number three, bequeathing to S. the interest on $3,000 be revoked, and in lieu thereof the sum of $500 be paid to him, or his heirs, and that

the direction as to payments made after the date of the will should apply thereto :—

Held, that the effect of the codicil was to revoke the whole of the third clause. *Edwards* v. *Findlay*, 489.

5. *Construction—" Right Heirs " —Period of Ascertainment—Distribution of Estate—" Equally "—Per Capita and not per Stirpes.*]—Upon appeal from the Master's report on a reference for the administration of the estate of the testator whose will was construed in *Coatsworth* v. *Carson*, 24 O. R. 185 :—

Held, having regard to the judgment in that case, that the " right heirs " were to be ascertained at the date of the death of the testator's daughter, and among them the whole of the estate was to be divided equally, share and share alike.

The expression *" per stirpes "* in the former judgment was improvidently used, due weight not having been given to the word " equally." *Re Ferguson, Bennett* v. *Coatsworth*, 591.

6. *Devise — Conditional Fee — Executory Devise.*]—A testator by his will devised as follows :—" I give and bequeath to my son F. * * lot No. * * at the age of twenty-one years, giving the executors power to lift the rent and to rent, said executors paying F. all former rents due after my decease. up to his attaining the age of twenty-one years.

* * * * *

" At the death of any one of my sons or daughters having no issue their property to be divided equally among the survivors."

F. attained twenty-one and died unmarried and without issue :—

Held, a conditional fee, with an executory devise over.

Decision of FERGUSON, J., reversed.

Little v. *Billings,* 27 Gr. 353, distinguished. *Crawford et al.* v. *Broddy et al.,* 635.

7. *Devise*—"*My Lawful Heirs*" —*Time when Heirs Ascertained.*]— A testator by his will after a gift to his daughter and her mother for their joint lives, and to the survivor of them, directed that, "at the decease of both, the residue of my real and personal property shall be enjoyed by, and go to the benefit of my lawful heirs." Both survived the testator and died, the daughter surviving the mother. At the death of the testator, his daughter was his only heir :—

Held, that the testator had himself excluded his daughter from being treated as one of his heirs, and by the expression "my lawful heirs" meant the persons who at the time of the death of the last survivor of his wife and daughter should then be his heirs-at-law.

Jones v. *Colbeck,* 8 Ves. 38, approved and specially referred to. *Thompson et al.* v. *Smith,* 652.

Testamentary Guardian—Religious Faith.]—*See* INFANT, 3.

See EXECUTION—EXECUTORS AND ADMINISTRATORS.

WINDING-UP.

See COMPANY, 1, 3, 4, 6.

WORDS AND PHRASES.

"*Absconded.*"] — *See* MALICIOUS ARREST AND PROSECUTION, 1.

"*A Home.*"]—*See* EXECUTION.

"*Books and Literary Compositions.*"]—*See* COPYRIGHT.

"*Doing Business in Canada.*"]— *See* COMPANY, 4.

"*Equally.*"]—*See* WILL, 5.

"*Giving of Sheep to Double.*"]— *See* STATUTE OF FRAUDS.

"*My Lawful Heirs.*"]—*See* WILL, 7

"*Owner.*"]—*See* WAY.

"*Per Stirpes.*"]—*See* WILL, 5.

"*Plant.*"]—*See* CONTRACT, 2.

"*Procuring.*"] — *See* CRIMINAL LAW, 4.

"*Pro rata.*"]—*See* WILL, 2.

"*Public Place.*"] — *See* PUBLIC MORALS AND CONVENIENCE.

"*Right Heirs.*"]—*See* WILL, 5.

"*Servant in Husbandry.*"]—*See* MASTER AND SERVANT, 2.

"*To be Benefited.*"]—*See* MUNICIPAL CORPORATIONS, 9.

"*Unlawful.*"] — *See* CRIMINAL LAW, 1.

WORKMEN'S COMPENSATION FOR INJURIES ACT.

See MASTER AND SERVANT.

Ex. J. M.

In Trinity Term, 1894, the under-mentioned gentlemen were called to the Bar :—

WILLIAM NORMAN TILLEY (*with Honours and Gold Medal*), WALTER GOW (*with Honours and Silver Medal*), BENJAMIN MORTON JONES (*with Honours*) ; also, WILLIAM HERBERT CAWTHRA, WILLIAM ARTHUR FRASER CAMPBELL, JOHN LYNDEN CRAWFORD, ARTHUR BREDIN CUNNINGHAM, SAMUEL JAMES COOLEY, JOHN CRAWFORD, HAMPDEN ZANE CHURCHILL COCKBURN, THOMAS WESLEY EVANS, ALEXANDER EDWARD GARRETT, NORMAN ST. CLAIR GURD, FRANCIS WILLIAM HALL, ALFRED ERSKINE HOSKIN, JOHN GILMOUR HAY, WILLIAM ALEXANDER LEWIS, JOHN THOMAS LOFTUS, WILLISTON LENT, AUGUSTIN NOVERRE MIDDLETON, ARCHIBALD JOHN MACKINNON, JAMES KENNETH MACLENNAN, JOHN SUTHERLAND MCKAY, GEORGE HAMILTON PETTIT, WILLIAM JOHN PORTE, ROBERT RUDDY, DAVID IRVING SICKLESTEEL, DANIEL THOMAS SMITH, WILLIAM HENRY BUCHAN SPOTTON, JOSEPH WESLEY ST. JOHN, WILLIAM PATTISON TELFORD, JAMES GRAHAM VANSITTART, URIAH MORLEY WILSON, CHARLES ROBERT WEBSTER.

In the same Term the under-mentioned gentlemen were admitted and sworn in as Solicitors :—

T. K. ALLAN, J. G. BURNHAM, A. B. CUNNINGHAM, S. J. COOLEY, J. L. CRAWFORD, H. Z. C. COCKBURN, W. FARNHAM, F. B. FETHERSTONHAUGH, A. E. GARRETT, N. S. GURD, W. GOW, W. A. D. GRANT, J. G. HAY, W. LENT, W. A. LEWIS, J. T. LOFTUS, A. N. MIDDLETON, J. S. MCKAY, G. H. PETTIT, D. I. SICKLESTEEL, D. T. SMITH, W. H. B. SPOTTON, J. F. SMELLIE, W. P. TELFORD, C. R. WEBSTER, U. M. WILSON.

Lightning Source UK Ltd.
Milton Keynes UK
UKHW020726191218
334233UK00007B/669/P